Insurance Administration

Third Edition

LOMA (Life Office Management Association, Inc.) is an international association founded in 1924. LOMA is committed to a business partnership with its worldwide members in the insurance and financial services industry to improve their management and operations through quality employee development, research, information sharing, and related products and services. Among LOMA's activities is the sponsorship of several self-study education programs leading to professional designations. These programs include the Fellow, Life Management Institute (FLMI) program and the Fellow, Financial Services Institute (FFSI) program. For more information on all of LOMA's education programs, please visit www.loma.org.

Statement of Purpose: LOMA Educational Programs Testing and Designations. Examinations described in the *LOMA Education and Training Catalog* are designed solely to measure whether students have successfully completed the relevant assigned curriculum, and the attainment of the FLMI and other LOMA designations indicates only that all examinations in the given curriculum have been successfully completed. In no way shall a student's completion of a given LOMA course or attainment of the FLMI or other LOMA designation be construed to mean that LOMA in any way certifies that student's competence, training, or ability to perform any given task. LOMA's examinations are to be used solely for general educational purposes, and no other use of the examinations or programs is authorized or intended by LOMA. Furthermore, it is in no way the intention of the LOMA Curriculum and Examinations staff to describe the standard of appropriate conduct in any field of the insurance and financial services industry, and LOMA expressly repudiates any attempt to so use the curriculum and examinations. Any such assessment of student competence or industry standards of conduct should instead be based on independent professional inquiry and the advice of competent professional counsel.

Insurance Administration

Third Edition

Mary C. Bickley, J.D., FLMI, FFSI, CLU, AIRC, ACS, AIAA, PAHM, AAPA, ARA
Jane Lightcap Brown, Ph.D., FLMI, ACS, ALHC
Kristen L. Falk, FLMI, AAPA, ACS, AIAA, AIRC, ARA
Miriam A. Orsina, FLMI, PCS, AAPA, ARA, PAHM
Dorinda Paige, ACS

LOMA Education and Training
Atlanta, Georgia
www.loma.org

Information in this text may have been changed or updated since its publication date. For current updates visit www.loma.org

PROJECT TEAM:

Authors:	Mary C. Bickley, J.D., FLMI, FFSI, CLU, AIRC, ACS, AIAA, PAHM, AAPA, ARA Jane Lightcap Brown, Ph.D., FLMI, ACS, ALHC Kristen L. Falk, FLMI, AAPA, ACS, AIAA, AIRC, ARA Miriam A. Orsina, FLMI, PCS, AAPA, ARA, PAHM Dorinda Paige, ACS
Manuscript Editors:	Mary C. Bickley, J.D., FLMI, FFSI, CLU, AIRC, ACS, AIAA, PAHM, AAPA, ARA Miriam Orsina, FLMI, PCS, AAPA, ARA, PAHM
Examinations Editor:	Vivian Heeden, FLMI, CLU, FLHC, AIRC, AAPA, ARA, PCS
Project Manager:	Mark Adel, FLMI, FFSI, PCS, AAPA, AIRC, PAHM
Copyeditor:	Eastman Communications
Indexer:	Amy Souwan
Production Manager:	Stephen J. Bollinger, ACS
Typesetter/ Production Coordinator:	Amy Souwan
Product Sourcing Manager:	Carol Wiessner
Printing Coordinator:	Natalie Cape Sanders
Administrative Support:	Mamunah Carter
Cover Design:	Amy Souwan

16 15 14 13 12 11 10 09 08 10 9 8 7 6 5 4 3 2 1

While a great deal of care has been taken to provide accurate, current, and authoritative information in regard to the subject matter covered in this book, the ideas, suggestions, general principles, conclusions, and any other information presented here are for general educational purposes only. This text is sold with the understanding that it is neither designed nor intended to provide the reader with legal, accounting, investment, marketing, or any other types of professional business management advice. If legal advice or other expert assistance is required, the services of a competent professional should be sought.

Library of Congress Control Number: 2007936895

ISBN 13: 978-1-57974-312-3
ISBN 10: 1-57974-312-9
Printed in the United States of America

Contents

Preface xv

Acknowledgements xvi
Introduction xxiii

Part 1: Introduction to Insurance Administration 1

Chapter 1: Overview of Insurance Administration 2

Insurers' Ethical Duties to Customers **4**
Equity in Risk Acceptance 4
Prompt and Equitable Claim Handling 5
Honest, Objective, and Fair Customer Service 5
Privacy and Confidentiality of Customer Information 5
Adequate Financial Resources 6
Insurance Administration Functions **6**
Underwriting 7
Reinsurance 7
Claim Administration 8
Customer Service 8
Other Insurance Functions **8**
Marketing 8
Actuarial 9
Accounting and Treasury 9
Legal and Compliance 10
Human Resources 10
Information Technology 10
Staffing **11**
Administration Systems **12**
Technology Components 12
Technologies that Enhance Insurance Administration Processes 15
Systems Integration 21
Security 22
Quality Control **22**
Quantitative Performance Measurement 24
Qualitative Performance Measurement 25

Part 2: Underwriting 27

Chapter 2: Overview of the New Business Process and Underwriting 28

New Business Process 29
Field Underwriting 29
Teleunderwriting 35
Data Entry and Review 35
Underwriting... 36
Policy Issue 37
New Business/Underwriting Quality Control 38
Underwriting Principles... 40
Risk Assessment 41
Risk Classification 42
Underwriting Philosophy and Underwriting Guidelines 44
Underwriting Organization 48
Job Positions 48
Authority Levels 49
Organizational Systems 51

Chapter 3: Legal Aspects of Underwriting 56

Valid Contract Requirements 57
Mutual Assent 58
Legally Adequate Consideration 58
Contractual Capacity 59
Lawful Purpose 62
Regulatory Compliance Issues Affecting Individual Insurance Underwriting 63
Privacy Protection 64
Nondiscrimination 70
Medical Testing 71
Replacements 73
Money Laundering and Financing Terrorists............................... 74
Regulatory Compliance Issues Affecting Group Insurance Underwriting ... 76
U.S. State Regulatory Requirements 76
U.S. Federal Regulatory Requirements 79
Canadian Regulatory Requirements 82
Underwriting Standards... 83
Reviewing Applications for Proper Completion 83
Processing Applications Promptly 85
Documenting Underwriting 85

Chapter 4: Underwriting Individual Life Insurance: Assessing Mortality Risk 90

Medical Risk Factors **91**
Sources of Medical Information 91
Assessing Medical Factors 106
Personal Risk Factors **108**
Sources of Personal Information 109
Assessing Personal Factors 114

Chapter 5: Underwriting Individual Life Insurance: Financial Underwriting and Risk Classification 124

Financial Underwriting **125**
Risks Deterred by Financial Underwriting 125
Sources of Financial Information 127
Assessing Life Insurance Needs and Financial Factors 131
Tools to Determine the Appropriate Amount of Insurance 135
Risk Classification **136**
Numerical Rating System 137
Charging for Substandard Risks 139

Chapter 6: Underwriting Individual Life Insurance: Niche Policies, Business Life Insurance, Replacements, and Supplemental Benefits 144

Underwriting Niche Policies **145**
Multi-Life Policies 145
Juvenile Insurance Policies 146
Monthly Debit Ordinary Policies 147
Direct Response Policies 148
Underwriting Business Life Insurance **149**
Financial Assessment of a Business 151
Underwriting Considerations for Various Types of Business Life Insurance 157
Underwriting Policy Replacements **163**
Underwriting Supplemental Benefits **164**
Waiver of Premium for Disability Benefit 165
Accidental Death Benefit 166
Family Benefit 166
Guaranteed Insurability Benefit 167
Accelerated Death Benefit 168

Chapter 7: Underwriting Individual Health Insurance 170

Information Sources for Individual Health Underwriting 172
Risk Factors for Individual Health Underwriting 173
Age 175
Health History 175
Family History 176
Occupation 176
Avocation 176
Driving History 177
Alcohol and Drug Abuse 177
International Residence or Travel 178
Foreign Citizenship 178
Finances 178
Existing Health Coverage 178
Underwriting Substandard Health Risks 179
Premium Rating Methods 180
Policy Modifications 182
Underwriting Individual Disability Income Insurance 184
Antiselection 185
Health History 186
Occupation 186
Finances 187
Underwriting Individual Critical Illness Insurance 190
Underwriting Individual Long-Term Care Insurance 191
Field Underwriting 193
Sources of LTC Underwriting Information 194
Risk Factors 197

Chapter 8: Underwriting Group Life and Health Insurance 200

Group Underwriting Process 201
Information Sources for Group Underwriting 204
Request for Proposal 204
Producer's Letter 205
ERISA Documents 206
The Master Application 206
Risk Factors for Group Underwriting 207
The Group Prospect 209
The Proposed Coverage 215
Rating Methods for Group Cases 217
Manual Rating 219
Experience Rating 219
Blended Rating 220

Rating Approaches for Small Groups 221
Post-Issue Underwriting for Group Insurance 222
Underwriting of Late Enrollees 222
Renewal Underwriting 223

Part 3: Reinsurance 227

Chapter 9: Overview of Reinsurance 228

Roles of Insurance Companies in Reinsurance Arrangements 229
Types of Reinsurance Providers 230
Reciprocal Arrangements 231
Reinsurance Pools 233
Assumption and Indemnity Reinsurance 233
Assumption Reinsurance 234
Indemnity Reinsurance 234
Basic Financial Aspects of Indemnity Reinsurance 236
Purposes of Indemnity Reinsurance for the Direct Writer 237
Managing Capacity 237
Easing Surplus Strain 238
Reducing Fluctuations in Claim Payments 238
Obtaining Information and Expertise 238
Documentation of Reinsurance Arrangements 239
Cession Arrangements in Reinsurance 239
Automatic Reinsurance 240
Facultative Reinsurance 240
Facultative-Obligatory Reinsurance 242
Comparison of Cession Bases 242
Reinsurance Activities 243
Reinsurance Staffing 244
Reinsurance Analysts 244
Other Staff Involved in Reinsurance Activitie 244
Reinsurance Information Systems 248
Regulation of Reinsurance 249
Licensing 249
Monitoring Financial Condition 252
Reserves 253

Chapter 10: Types of Reinsurance and Reinsurance Agreements ... 256

Nonproportional and Proportional Reinsurance 257
Nonproportional Reinsurance 257
Proportional Reinsurance 260

The Cession Amount in Proportional Reinsurance **261**
Excess-of-Retention Arrangements 262
Quota Share Arrangements 263
Plans of Reinsurance **265**
Coinsurance 265
Modified Coinsurance 266
Yearly Renewable Term Reinsurance 267
Reinsurance Agreements **268**
Defining the Reinsurance Coverage 272
Reinsurance Administration Procedures 277
Financial Arrangements 285

Chapter 11: Reinsurance Administration 288

Administering New Business **289**
Preplacement of Reinsurance 290
Placement of Reinsurance 297
Administering In-Force Business **298**
Reporting on In-Force Business 298
Processing Changes in Reinsurance Coverage 302
Processing Billing Statements 303
Recording Policy Reserves 305
Administering Terminations of Reinsurance **305**
Administering Claims under Reinsured Policies **306**
Establishing the Claim File 307
Verifying Claim-Related Information 308
Approving the Claim Liability 311
Settling the Claim Liability 311
Notifying Retrocessionaires of a Claim Liability 311
Auditing Reinsurance Operations **312**
Internal Audits 312
External Audits by the Reinsurer 313

Part 4: Claim Administration 317

Chapter 12: Overview of Claim Administration 318

Claim Philosophy and Practices **319**
Claim Evaluation Process **321**
Claim Staffing and Organization **323**
Staffing 323
Authority Levels 323
Organizational Systems 324

Relationships with Other Insurer Functions **325**
Legal Issues Affecting Claim Administration **326**
Unfair Claims Settlement Practices 327
Privacy 328
Financing Terrorists 329
Fraud 330
Technology **333**
Claim Administration Quality Control **333**

Chapter 13: Administering Life Insurance Claims 336

Evaluating Life Insurance Claims **337**
Verifying the Coverage Was in Force 340
Verifying that the Deceased Is Covered 341
Verifying the Death Occurred 341
Determining Whether the Policy Is Contestable 343
Determining Whether the Death Is Covered 344
Calculating the Amount of the Policy Proceeds and How They Are Payable 346
Determining Who Is Entitled to Receive the Policy Proceeds 349
Handling Supplemental Benefits **356**
Waiver of Premium for Disability Benefit 356
Accidental Death Benefit 357
Family Benefit 358
Accelerated Death Benefit 358

Chapter 14: Administering Medical Expense, Critical Illness, and Long-Term Care Insurance Claims 360

Processing Medical Expense Insurance Claims **361**
Verifying the Coverage Was in Force 363
Verifying the Claimant Is Covered 363
Verifying Medical Expenses 363
Determining Whether the Policy Is Contestable 366
Determining Whether a Medical Expense Is Covered 366
Calculating Policy Benefits Payable 370
Determining Who Is Entitled to Receive the Benefits 373
Processing Critical Illness Insurance Claims **374**
Processing Long-Term Care Insurance Claims **375**
Long-Term Care Benefits 376
Verifying the Coverage Was in Force 377
Verifying the Claimant Is Covered 378
Verifying the Insured Needs Long-Term Care 378

Determining Whether the Policy Is Contestable 381
Determining Whether Long-Term Care Is Covered 381
Calculating Policy Benefits Payable 383
Determining Who Is Entitled to Receive the Benefits 386

Chapter 15: Administering Disability Income Insurance Claims ... 388

Sources of DI Insurance Claim Information 389
Claim Form 389
Medical Information 390
Personal Information 395
Financial Information 395
Employment Information 396
Processing DI Insurance Claims 396
Verifying the Coverage Was in Force 396
Verifying the Claimant Is Covered 399
Verifying a Disability Has Been Incurred 400
Determining Whether the Policy Is Contestable 402
Determining Whether the Disability Is Covered 402
Calculating Policy Benefits Payable 405
Administering Continuing DI Insurance Claims 406
DI Insurance Supplemental Benefits 409
Waiver of Premium for Disability Benefit 409
Cost-of-Living Adjustment Benefit 409
Rehabilitation Benefit 409
Transplant Donor Benefit 412
Future Increase Option Benefit 412
Terminating DI Insurance Benefits 412
End of Benefit Period 413
End of Disability 413
End of Eligibility for a Group Member or a Group 413
Settling DI Insurance Claims 414
Disputed Claims 415
Undisputed Claims 415

Part 5: Customer Service 417

Chapter 16: Organization of Customer Service 418

Qualities of Effective Customer Service 420
Benefits of Providing Effective Customer Service 421

Customer Service Organization **421**
Staffing 422
Levels of Authority 423
Organization 423
Customer Service Activities **426**
Service for Individual Policyowners, Insureds, and Beneficiaries 427
Service for Group Policyholders and Group Insureds 427
Service for Producers 428
Legal Issues Affecting Customer Service **428**
Delivering Effective Customer Service **429**
Determining Strategies for Effective Customer Service 430
Automating and Simplifying Customer Service Delivery 430
Ensuring Excellent Telephone Communication 433
Documenting Customer Service Guidelines and Procedures 433
Customer Service and Conservation **434**
Conservation Through Communication with Policyowners 436
Conservation of Orphan Policyowners 436
Conservation Through Superior Claim Service 437
Conservation Through Customer Feedback 437
Conservation Through Producers 438
Customer Service Quality Control **439**
Quantitative Performance Measurement 440
Qualitative Performance Measurement 440

Chapter 17: Customer Service Practices 444

Basic Customer Service Practices for Life and Health Insurance **445**
Providing Information and Answering Questions 447
Changing Names and Addresses 448
Administering Policy Changes 449
Handling Premium Payments 455
Handling Returned Mail 457
Handling Complaints 458
Fulfilling Other Customer Needs 459
Customer Service Practices Specific to Life Insurance **464**
Changing a Beneficiary 464
Assigning Policy Ownership 467
Administering Loans and Dividends 467
Handling Variable Life Insurance Products 471

Glossary 473

Index 521

Preface

Insurance Administration, Third Edition, describes the principles and practices of individual and group life and health insurance administration. The text begins with an introductory chapter and then is divided into four parts:

- **Part 1: Introduction to Insurance Administration (Chapter 1)**
- **Part 2: Underwriting (Chapters 2–8)**
- **Part 3: Reinsurance (Chapters 9–11)**
- **Part 4: Claim Administration (Chapters 12–15)**
- **Part 5: Customer Service (Chapters 16–17)**

Although the text focuses primarily on the United States and Canada, the principles and practices described in this text are instructive of the principles and practices found worldwide.

Acknowledgements

LOMA's texts always are the result of a joint effort between industry experts and LOMA's own staff. Both groups make invaluable contributions to the success of LOMA's texts, and *Insurance Administration*, Third Edition, is no exception.

Textbook Review Panel

Industry experts reviewed all editions of this text prior to publication. These individuals made many substantive comments on the outline and chapters, provided suggestions for content, submitted relevant research materials, and answered numerous questions from the authors during the course of the text's development. Writing this text would not have been possible without the efforts of the reviewers, who care enough about the educational needs of current and future industry employees to volunteer their time and expertise to this project. They improved the accuracy and clarity of the text, although the authors claim responsibility for any errors.

This text required more than the typical number of reviewers because of the diversity of the subject matter. The following individuals devoted countless hours to the third edition's review, for which we are most grateful:

All Sections

- Tim Kuraszek, FLMI, ACS, AIRC, HIA, AHLC, Independent Reviewer

- Julio E. Payés O., FLMI, ACS, Reinsurance Manager, HSBC Seguros Salvadoreño, S.A.
- Patricia E. Stevenson, FLMI, ACS, AIAA, AIRC, AAPA, ARA, Compliance and Tax Specialist, The Baltimore Life Insurance Company
- Sandi Weinberg, FLMI, ACS, AIAA, AIRC, HIA, Administrative Assistant, Physicians Mutual Insurance Company

Underwriting

- David K. Anderson, FALU, CLU, FLMI, Corporate Vice President, Atlanta Underwriting Center, New York Life Insurance Company
- Carole Bellm, HIA, FLMI, GBA, Director, Group Underwriting, RGA Life Reinsurance Company of Canada
- Nazir Damji, FLMI, FALU, Vice President and Chief Underwriter, Max New York Life Insurance Co. LTD
- Dean Franzen, RHU, HIA, MHP, DIA, DHP, HCSA, LTCP, EHBA, Senior Underwriting Consultant, Wisconsin Underwriting Associates
- Nicolle G. Galipeau, J.D., FLMI, LTCP, HCAFA, Associate Counsel, Transamerica Life Insurance Company
- Pamela F. Hilton, FLMI, ACS, AIRC, Senior Underwriter, Munich American Reassurance Company
- David Kanney, AALU, CLU, FLMI, Officer, Life Underwriting, Nationwide Financial
- Carol G. King, FLMI, ACS, AIAA, AIRC, FLHC, HIA, MHP, Supervisor, Group Life Underwriting, HCC Life Insurance Company
- Paula L. Mango, CIPP, CLU, FLMI, ALHC, ACS, Assistant Vice President, AML and Privacy Officer, Lincoln Financial Group
- David M. Rose, ChFC, FLMI/M, ACS, ARP, Assistant Vice President—Information Technology, Lincoln Financial Group
- Sharon B. Smith, FALU, FLMI, ALHC, ACS, President, Amalfi Consulting, Inc.
- Gerry T. Stewart, ASA, MAAA, FFSI, FLMI, AIRC, ARA, AAPA, AIAA, ACS, Assistant Vice President and Assistant Actuary, Protective Life Insurance Company

- Nancy L. Sulkers, FLMI, FALU, RHU, Director Living Benefits Administration, Great-West Life/Canada Life
- Laurie Szabo, CEBS, ACS, ARA, Chief Underwriter, Hartford Life

Reinsurance

- Suzanne L. Bathke, ARA, ACS, AIRC, CPIW, Vice President, Business Administration, Hannover Life Reassurance Company of America
- Glenn Beuschel, ACS, Director, Treaties, Optimum Reassurance Inc.
- Shaun Downey, FLMI, ARA, ACS, AVP–Market and Project Research, Manulife Reinsurance
- Jill Y. Dupuis, ARA, ACS, Manager, Operations Analysis, Reinsurance Division, Manulife Financial
- Dean Franzen, RHU, HIA, MHP, DIA, DHP, HCSA, LTCP, EHBA, Senior Underwriting Consultant, Wisconsin Underwriting Associates
- Pamela F. Hilton, FLMI, ACS, AIRC, Senior Underwriter, Munich American Reassurance Company
- Josée Malboeuf, FLMI, ALHC, Vice President, Underwriting & Claims, RGA Life Reinsurance Company of Canada
- Nina Rhines, FLMI, AFSI, ACS, ARA, Investment Accountant, Securian Financial Group
- Carol A. Rubsam, ALHC, HIA, Six Sigma Green Belt, Life Reinsurance Claims Audit Director, Employers Reassurance Corporation
- Maureen Shippy, FLMI, ARA, ACS, Vice President, Global Technical Accounting & Services, Swiss Re Life and Health America, Inc.
- Sharon B. Smith, FALU, FLMI, ALHC, ACS, President, Amalfi Consulting, Inc.
- Gerry T. Stewart, ASA, MAAA, FFSI, FLMI, AIRC, ARA, AAPA, AIAA, ACS, Assistant Vice President and Assistant Actuary, Protective Life Insurance Company
- Nancy L. Sulkers, FLMI, FALU, RHU, Director Living Benefits Administration, Great-West Life/Canada Life
- Laurie Szabo, CEBS, ACS, HIAA, Chief Underwriter, The Hartford

Claims

- Linda J. Brissette, ALHC, Lead Disability Benefits Specialist, Unum Group
- Susan C. Fletcher, FLMI, FLHC, ACS, AIAA, AIRC, Retired Vice President of Compliance, Harleysville Life Insurance Company
- Nicolle G. Galipeau, J.D., FLMI, LTCP, HCAFA, Associate Counsel, Transamerica Life Insurance Company
- Kevin C. Glasgow, ACS, FLMI, FLHC, Senior Vice President, Claims and Liability Management, Swiss Re Life and Health America, Inc.
- Jerry A. Kapitz, FLHC, CLU, ChFC, AIRC, AALU, ACS, FLMI/M, Manager: Policyowner Services, Northwestern Mutual
- Anthony O'Neale Mayers, FLMI, FLHC, AIAA, ACS, Chief Claims Consultant, North American Company for Life and Health Insurance
- Jon P. McElhaney, FLHC, ACS, Manager, Specialty Support Unit, Claims Operations, FSO, Thrivent Financial for Lutherans
- Carol A. Rubsam, ALHC, HIA, Six Sigma Green Belt, Life Reinsurance Claims Audit Director, Employers Reassurance Corporation
- Sharon B. Smith, FALU, FLMI, ALHC, ACS, President, Amalfi Consulting, Inc.
- Laurie Szabo, CEBS, ACS, HIAA, Chief Underwriter, The Hartford
- Deborah Taylor, Director of Life and Disability Claims, HCC Life Insurance Company
- William W. Wade, Jr., FLMI, ACS, FLHC, HIA, Director, Insurance Services Division, Combined Insurance Company
- Cynthia K. Weurdig, ACS, ALHC, Manager, Claims Consumer Affairs, Transamerica Life Insurance Company

Customer Service

- Dean Franzen, RHU, HIA, MHP, DIA, DHP, HCSA, LTCP, EHBA, Senior Underwriting Consultant, Wisconsin Underwriting Associates
- Nicolle G. Galipeau, J.D., FLMI, LTCP, HCAFA, Associate Counsel, Transamerica Life Insurance Company

- Sue Jacobson, ACS, FLMI, Contact Center Manager, CUNA Mutual Group

- Paula L. Mango, CIPP, CLU, FLMI, ALHC, ACS, Assistant Vice President, AML and Privacy Officer, Lincoln Financial Group

- Jon P. McElhaney, FLHC, ACS, Manager, Specialty Support Unit, Claims Operations, FSO, Thrivent Financial for Lutherans

- Nina Rhines, FLMI, AFSI, ACS, ARA, Investment Accountant, Securian Financial Group

- David M. Rose, ChFC, FLMI/M, ACS, ARP, Assistant Vice President—Information Technology, Lincoln Financial Group

- Michele D. Smith, FLMI, PCS, AIAA, AVP, Customer Service, The Baltimore Life Companies

- Nancy L. Sulkers, FLMI, FALU, RHU, Director Living Benefits Administration, Great-West Life/Canada Life

- Laurie Szabo, CEBS, ACS, HIAA, Chief Underwriter, The Hartford

- Cynthia K. Weurdig, ACS, ALHC, Manager, Claims Consumer Affairs, Transamerica Life Insurance Company

We also wish to thank the following individuals who reviewed portions of the text:

- Brian Eichhold, ACS, Assistant Vice President and Director, New Business, Western & Southern Financial Group

- Robert Frank, CLU, FLMI, ACS, Chief Underwriter, AXA–Equitable

- James B. Hiers, III, FLMI, ALHC, HIA, ACS, Assistant Vice President, Munich American Reassurance Company

- Irene Klatt, CFP, Vice President, Health Insurance, Canadian Life and Health Insurance Association Inc.

- Luke C. McLaren, J.D., FFSI, FLMI, AAPA, ACS, AIAA, AIRC, ARA, Associate General Counsel, Genworth Financial

- Jonathan Sager, J.D., FLMI, Vice President and General Counsel, MIB Group, Inc.

- Frank Zinatelli, LL.B., FLMI, Vice President and Associate General Counsel, Canadian Life and Health Insurance Association Inc.

LOMA Staff

LOMA has many talented staff members who contribute in a myriad of ways to the success of LOMA's products. Deserving of special thanks are Jane Lightcap Brown, Ph.D., FLMI, ACS, ALHC, Senior Associate, who wrote the first edition of this text and Kristen Falk, FLMI, AAPA, ACS, AIAA, AIRC, ARA, Senior Associate, who wrote the second edition and provided valuable input on this third edition. Thanks also go to Mark Adel, FLMI, FFSI, PCS, AAPA, AIRC, PAHM, Assistant Vice President, Education and Training Products (E&T), who served as Project Manager and provided excellent guidance throughout the project and to Susan Conant, FLMI, CEBS, HIA, Senior Associate, who lent her technical expertise to the project. Also to be thanked are Mamunah Carter, Administrative Assistant III, and Carol Wiessner, Product Sourcing Manager.

Individuals in LOMA's Examinations Department who contributed to the text include Vivian Heeden, FLMI, CLU, FLHC, AIRC, AAPA, ARA, PCS, Senior Associate, who made many valuable contributions to the chapters as they were being developed in her capacity as Exams Editor and who is co-developer of the Test Preparation Guide accompanying this text along with Melanie Green, FLMI, ACS, AIAA, Senior Associate; Sean Schaeffer Gilley, FLMI, ACS, HIA, CEBS, AIAA, MHP, AIRC, AAPA, ARA, FLHC, PAHM, Senior Associate; and Maggie Mills-Turner, FLMI, Senior Associate. Also to be thanked is Robert H. Hartley, FLMI, FFSI, ACS, ALHC, CLU, ChFC, RHU, Assistant Vice President, Examinations, who oversaw the project from an exams perspective.

In LOMA's Production Department, thanks go to Stephen J. Bollinger, ACS, Manager of Graphics and Production, who oversaw production of this text, and Amy Souwan, Production Coordinator II/Scheduling Coordinator, who coordinated production of and typeset the text. Also to be thanked are Eastman Communications for copyediting the manuscript; and Iris F. Hartley, FLMI, ALHC, a LOMA consultant, who secured the necessary permissions.

A special thanks goes to Lawrence M. Scott, FLMI, ACS, Second Vice President–Information Systems, Office of the Secretary/Treasurer, who reviewed portions of the manuscript and patiently answered questions about technology.

Also deserving of thanks are the individuals in LOMA's Information Center who provided valuable research services: Jean C. Gora, ACS, Manager of Research and the Information Center; Olivia Blakemore, ACS, Technical Administrator; and Mallory Eldridge, Research Analyst.

Special thanks go to Katherine C. Milligan, FLMI, ACS, ALHC, Vice President, Education and Training, who provided guidance, support, and encouragement for this project.

Mary C. Bickley, J.D., FLMI, FFSI, CLU, AIRC, ACS, AIAA, PAHM, AAPA, ARA
Miriam A. Orsina, FLMI, PCS, AAPA, ARA, PAHM
Dorinda Paige, ACS
Atlanta, Georgia
2007

Introduction

This text is designed for students who are preparing to take the examination for LOMA 301—Insurance Administration—which is part of the Fellow, Life Management Institute (FLMI) program. Each chapter in the text includes features designed to help you organize your studies, reinforce your understanding of the materials, and prepare for the examination. As we describe each of these features, we give you suggestions for studying the material.

- **Learning Objectives.** The first page of each chapter contains a list of learning objectives to help you focus your studies. Before reading each chapter, review these learning objectives. Then, as you read the chapter, look for material that will help you meet the learning objectives.
- **Chapter Outline**. The first page of each chapter contains an outline of the chapter. Review this outline to gain an overview of the major topics that will be covered; then scan through the chapter to familiarize yourself with the presentation of the information. Looking at the headings and figures will give you a preview of how the various subjects relate to each other.
- **Key Terms.** This text reviews the key terms associated with life and health insurance administration. Important terminology is highlighted with bold italic type when the term is defined, and a list of these key terms appears at the end of each chapter. All key terms also appear in a comprehensive glossary at the end of the book. As you read each chapter, pay special attention to the key terms.
- **Figures and Insights.** Figures and insights that appear throughout the text illustrate and amplify the text's discussions of selected important topics. Note that information contained in figures and insights may be tested on the examination for the course.
- **Glossary.** A comprehensive glossary containing definitions of all key terms appears at the end of the book. Following each glossary entry is a number in brackets that indicates the chapter in which the key term is defined. The glossary includes references to important equivalent terms, acronyms, and contrasting terms.

The text and study aids for LOMA courses may be revised periodically. To ensure that you are studying from the correct materials, check the current LOMA *Education and Training Catalog* for a description of the texts and study aids assigned for the examination for which you are preparing.

Using the LOMA Study Aid

LOMA has prepared a study aid designed to help students prepare for the LOMA 301 examination. LOMA recommends that you use this study aid. **Studies indicate that students who use LOMA study aids consistently perform significantly better on LOMA examinations than students who do not use these study aids**.

This study aid, LOMA's *Test Preparation Guide for LOMA 301*, is assigned reading for students preparing for the LOMA 301 examination. Used along with the textbook, the Test Preparation Guide (TPG) will help you master the course material. The TPG includes practice exam questions, a full-scale sample examination in both paper and electronic format, and answers to every question in the TPG.

Part 1: Introduction to Insurance Administration

chapter 1

Overview of Insurance Administration

Outline

Insurers' Ethical Duties to Customers
Equity in Risk Acceptance
Prompt and Equitable Claim Handling
Honest, Objective, and Fair Customer Service
Privacy and Confidentiality of Customer Information
Adequate Financial Resources

Insurance Administration Functions
Underwriting
Reinsurance
Claim Administration
Customer Service

Other Insurance Functions
Marketing
Actuarial
Accounting and Treasury
Legal and Compliance
Human Resources
Information Technology

Staffing

Administration Systems
Technology Components
Technologies that Enhance Insurance Administration Processes
Systems Integration
Security

Quality Control
Quantitative Performance Measurement
Qualitative Performance Measurement

Learning Objectives

After studying this chapter, you should be able to…

- Define the basic terms used to describe the people and entities involved in the creation and administration of an insurance policy
- Explain how an insurer fulfills its ethical duties pertaining to insurance administration
- Define the following insurance functions: underwriting, reinsurance, claim administration, customer service, marketing, actuarial, accounting, treasury, legal, compliance, human resources, and information technology
- Define the technology components of a computer-based insurance administration system
- Describe the functions of a database management system, data mining, predictive modeling, a business rules engine, a document management system, and an automated workflow system
- Define quality control and distinguish between quantitative performance measurement and qualitative performance measurement

Life and health insurance companies are complex organizations that engage in many diverse activities. In this textbook, we refer to those insurance company activities specifically associated with administering insurance policies—such as underwriting, reinsurance, claims, and customer service—as ***insurance administration***. The purpose of this text is to give an overview of these functions as they apply to individual and group life and health insurance. Note that in some countries, notably Canada, health insurance is referred to as ***living benefits*** because insurance benefits are paid while an insured is living. Also note that this text sets out those company practices, policies, and procedures typically found in the life and health insurance industry, but individual company practices, policies, and procedures vary widely.

We begin this chapter with a discussion of insurers' ethical duties regarding insurance administration. Then we provide an overview of the four insurance administration functions and the other areas of an insurance company with which those functions interact. Finally, we discuss staffing, computer-based systems used in insurance administration, and quality control.

Before proceeding, we need to clarify the terminology used throughout this text to describe the people and entities involved in the creation and administration of an insurance policy. In this text, the term ***producer*** refers to any person or entity that (1) sells insurance, including agents, brokers, financial advisors, and bank personnel or (2) is involved in insurance sales made through direct marketing or the Internet.

The ***applicant*** is the person or entity that submits an application for individual insurance and seeks to purchase the insurance coverage. The ***insured***, also known as the *assured* in some countries, is the person whose life, health, property, or income is covered by an individual insurance policy. During the underwriting process, this person often is referred to as the ***proposed insured***. The ***policyowner*** is the person or entity that owns an individual insurance policy. The applicant, insured, and policyowner of an individual insurance policy may be, and often are, the same person. If, for example, you apply for and are issued an insurance policy on your life, then you are the applicant, the insured, and the policyowner. If, however, your spouse applies for a policy on your life, then your spouse is the applicant and you are the insured. When the policy is issued, your spouse—the applicant—becomes the policyowner. When one person purchases an individual insurance policy on the life of another person, the policy is known as a ***third-party policy***.

In group insurance, the ***master group insurance contract***, also known as a *group insurance policy*, is an insurance contract that insures a number of people. The ***policyholder*** is the employer or other organization that decides what kind of coverage to purchase for the group and negotiates the terms of and enters into the master group insurance contract with the insurer. The policyholder usually helps administer and pays for part or all of the group coverage. During the underwriting process, a group that has applied, but has not yet been approved, for group coverage from an insurance company may be referred to as the ***group prospect*** or *proposed group*.

In the United States and Canada, the individuals covered by a master group insurance contract are referred to as the ***group insureds*** or *covered persons*. These individuals sometimes are referred to as *certificate holders* because they receive a document called a ***certificate of insurance*** that describes (1) the coverage that the master group insurance contract provides and (2) the group insured's rights under the contract.

If the event insured against occurs while an insurance policy is in force, the insurer pays the benefits provided under the terms of the policy. Life insurance policy proceeds usually are paid to the ***beneficiary***—the person or party the policyowner named to receive the policy benefit. The person or party to whom health insurance benefits are paid varies, depending on the type of health insurance policy. Medical expense insurance benefits usually are paid either to the insured or the hospital, doctor, or other health care provider. Disability and critical illness insurance benefits usually are paid to the insured. Long-term care insurance benefits are paid to either the insured or the provider of long-term care services.

Insurers' Ethical Duties to Customers

Ethics is a system of accepted standards of conduct and moral judgment that combines the elements of honesty, integrity, and fair treatment. Acting in an ethical manner involves behaving in accordance with accepted legal and moral principles of right and wrong. Every area of an insurance company, including those involved in insurance administration activities, is responsible for behaving ethically. Figure 1.1 sets forth some of an insurer's ethical duties pertaining to insurance administration functions.

Equity in Risk Acceptance

Equity in risk acceptance is maintained when the insurer evaluates every application for insurance consistently in accordance with the insurer's established underwriting guidelines and charges each policyowner a premium rate that is based solely on factors that affect the degree of risk the insurer is accepting by issuing a policy. For example, individual life insurance premium rates generally differ among insureds on the basis of factors such as the age, sex, health, occupation, and avocations of the insured because such factors affect the degree of risk the insurer is accepting. Note that the term *risk* can refer to not only the possibility of loss to an insurer, but also the actual person or persons being insured.

FIGURE 1.1 Ethical Duties for Insurance Administration

- Maintain equity in risk acceptance among all insureds
- Provide prompt and equitable claim handling
- Provide honest, objective, and fair customer service
- Preserve customers' privacy and confidentiality
- Maintain adequate financial resources

Prompt and Equitable Claim Handling

Insurers also have an ethical duty to process claims in a timely and equitable manner. Equitable claim handling includes assessing every claim in accordance with the terms of the policy and paying only eligible claims.

Honest, Objective, and Fair Customer Service

When a customer applies for new coverage, changes existing coverage, requests information, or interacts with the insurer in any other way, the customer deserves honesty, objectivity, and fairness from the insurer. The customer also expects prompt, accurate, and empathetic responses. Producers conducting business with the insurer also deserve such treatment.

Privacy and Confidentiality of Customer Information

Insurers have an ethical and sometimes legal duty to

- Use only lawful, reasonable, and ethical means of obtaining information
- Obtain authorization to collect information when required
- Use only accurate information
- Restrict access to personal information to only those people who have a lawful and business-specific need for it
- Establish written guidelines for information handling so that employees will know exactly how to safeguard confidential information

In Chapter 3, we discuss legislation that dictates how insurers must protect information they acquire about their customers.

Adequate Financial Resources

An insurer must have adequate financial resources to pay contractual benefits when covered events occur. Therefore, insurers must conduct business in a manner that allows them to remain financially stable and profitable. To strengthen their financial positions, insurers focus on using resources wisely, managing expenses, and becoming more efficient in serving their customers.

Insurance Administration Functions

Figure 1.2 introduces the insurance administration functions of underwriting, reinsurance, claim administration, and customer service. Later chapters of this text examine each of these functions in detail.

FIGURE 1.2 Insurance Administration Functions

UNDERWRITING

Investigates, assesses, and classifies degree of risk

Accepts or declines risk

REINSURANCE

Transfers a portion of the risk to another insurer

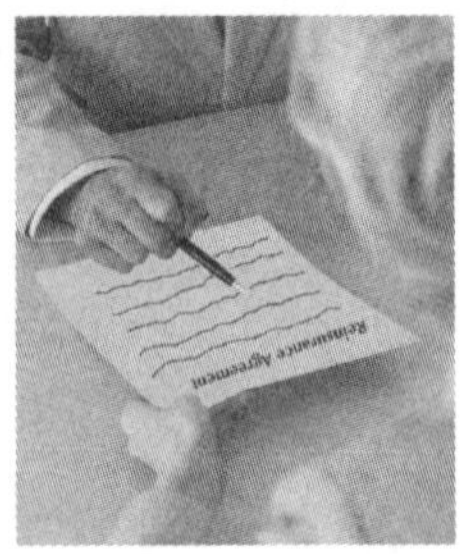

CLAIM ADMINISTRATION

Evaluates claims

Pays eligible claims

Denies ineligible claims

CUSTOMER SERVICE

Answers customers' questions

Provides requested information to customers

Processes customers' policy changes and transactions

Solves customers' problems

Underwriting

Underwriting is the process of (1) assessing and classifying the degree of risk represented by a proposed insured or group with respect to a specific insurance product and (2) making a decision to accept or decline that risk. An ***underwriter*** is an individual who (1) assesses and classifies the degree of risk represented by a proposed insured or group with respect to a specific insurance product and (2) makes a decision to accept or decline that risk. Note that producers in the United States historically have been known as *field underwriters*. In this text, however, the term *underwriter* refers to an insurance company home office or regional office employee who performs the risk assessment, classification, and selection process.

Sound underwriting decisions are extremely important to an insurer's financial strength. If an insurer accepts too many improperly assessed risks at premium rates that are not adequate for the true risks, the insurer will pay more in claims than it can afford. If an insurer fails to accept enough appropriate risks at appropriate rates, the insurer will not prosper.

Underwriting is one of the primary functions that make up the group of activities known as *new business*. The term new business can have a variety of meanings, including the policies an insurer underwrites and issues. In addition, producers may think of new business as potential clients, as all the activities they engage in to sell insurance, or as applications submitted. In this text, we use the term ***new business*** to refer to the activities an insurer undertakes in receiving applications, underwriting applications, and issuing policies. Chapter 2 begins with an overview of the entire new business process, including underwriting, and concludes with a discussion of underwriting principles, including risk assessment and risk classification. Chapter 3 covers the legal aspects of underwriting, and Chapters 4–8 describe the underwriting function in more detail.

Reinsurance

Reinsurance is insurance that one insurance company obtains from another insurance company on risks associated with insurance policies issued by the first company. In this context, risk refers to the possibility of financial loss. Briefly, reinsurance is insurance for an insurer. In a reinsurance arrangement, one insurer transfers a portion of a risk to a second insurer, which agrees to pay part of the claims of the first insurer in exchange for a reinsurance premium.

The discussion of reinsurance in Chapters 9–11 gives a thorough introduction to the subject of reinsurance, including the types of reinsurance coverage, the relationship between the parties in a reinsurance arrangement, the features of reinsurance agreements, and the administration of reinsurance.

Claim Administration

An insurer has a legal and an ethical obligation to pay all eligible claims promptly and to deny liability for all others. ***Claim administration*** is the process of evaluating each submitted claim, deciding whether or not the claim is eligible, informing the person who submitted the claim of the decision, and authorizing the payment of each eligible claim according to the terms of the policy. We discuss claim administration in Chapters 12–15.

Customer Service

A company has many customers, including policyowners, insureds, beneficiaries, and producers. Maintaining positive relationships with all its customers is essential for an insurance company. ***Customer service*** refers to the broad range of activities that a company and its employees perform to keep customers satisfied so they will continue doing business with the company and speak positively about it to potential customers. ***Policyowner service*** is a specific type of customer service that includes all the service activities performed for people or entities that own individual insurance policies. ***Member service*** is a specific type of customer service that includes all the service activities performed for group insureds. Chapters 16 and 17 focus on customer service activities.

Because customer service staff members typically have direct contact with customers, these employees often can provide feedback to other areas of the company about customer needs, wants, and problems. Such input assists the company in the design of products and processes that better meet the needs of customers.

Other Insurance Functions

Insurance administration staff members typically coordinate many aspects of their work with other insurance company staff working in such functional areas as marketing, actuarial, accounting and treasury, legal and compliance, human resources, and information technology. We introduce these functions now, and throughout this book we mention the ways that insurance administration staff interact with staff engaged in these other functions.

Marketing

Marketing is the functional area of an insurer that has primary responsibility for identifying the insurer's prospective customers and what they want, as well as planning the promotion and distribution of the insurer's products.

Marketing also seeks to improve the insurer's competitive position by (1) gathering information about the insurer's business environment, including data about its competitors; (2) assessing the insurer's sales performance in the marketplace; and (3) assisting in the development of competitive, profitable insurance products. Marketing typically has several units, one of which is devoted to providing support to producers.

Actuarial

Actuarial is the functional area composed of ***actuaries***—experts in financial risk management and the mathematics and modeling of insurance, annuities, and financial instruments. Among other activities, members of an insurer's actuarial staff

- Use statistics to predict the rates of illness, injury, disability, and death among insureds
- Calculate premium rates for insurance products
- Determine legal reserve liabilities
- Conduct research on trends in mortality and morbidity rates, policy lapses, policy loans, company expenses, and interest rates
- Engage in financial reporting activities

An insurer uses actuarial information to develop assumptions used in pricing new products and in selecting risks. Members of the actuarial staff also may be involved in developing new products and making reinsurance decisions.

Accounting and Treasury

Accounting is the functional area of an insurance company that collects, records, summarizes, analyzes, and reports data about a company's financial condition. Members of the accounting staff develop financial information that is used throughout the company to make decisions, measure financial performance, and satisfy internal and regulatory financial reporting requirements.

Treasury is the functional area of an insurance company that manages cash as it flows through the company. Treasury's responsibilities include setting up bank accounts, managing lockboxes for the collection of premium payments, and disbursing policy proceeds via checks or automatic deposits. In some companies, a separate unit in the customer service area handles premium billings.

Legal and Compliance

The ***legal*** area of an insurance company—also known as the *law department*—handles all legal matters for the company. Company lawyers may be called upon to advise life insurance claim personnel when claims are disputed; represent the company or supervise outside attorneys in any litigation involving the company; and develop or review policy forms, agency contracts, business contracts, and other legal documents used by the company.

Compliance is the functional area of an insurance company that is responsible for ensuring that an insurer adheres to all applicable laws and regulations in each jurisdiction in which the company does business. Some companies combine the legal and compliance functions into one department, while other companies have separate departments.

Human Resources

Human resources is the functional area of an insurance company that recruits and screens job applicants; helps select qualified employees; plans and presents appropriate orientation, training, and development for each employee; administers employee benefit programs; and maintains employee records. Human resources staff members also guide an insurer's management in conducting performance appraisals of employees and in determining compensation levels for various jobs. Finally, human resources personnel assist with employee separations resulting from resignation, layoff, retirement, or discharge.

Some companies have a separate training and development (T&D) area that helps employees plan their career paths and access education and training resources. As part of their T&D activities, some companies offer their employees tuition assistance for the completion of educational programs relevant to their jobs.

Information Technology

Information technology (IT) is the functional area of an insurance company that develops and maintains the company's information systems and oversees information management throughout the company. An ***information system*** is an interactive combination of technology, people, and processes that collects, manipulates, and disseminates information. ***Information management*** involves the use of information systems to provide a company's information users with the information they need to carry out their job responsibilities. These responsibilities include administering products, maintaining records, formulating strategy, and providing information to customers.

Staffing

Insurers are using telecommuting and outsourcing as creative responses to insurance administration staffing issues. To attract, reward, and motivate staff, some companies allow their employees to work from home, which is known as *telecommuting*. Insurers have employed telecommuting to great benefit in the underwriting, claims, and customer service areas. In the underwriting area, telecommuting is sometimes referred to as *remote underwriting*.

Companies must invest in the technical infrastructure that supports telecommuting, but they generally find that the increase in productivity and decrease in costs justify the investment. Some companies also are preparing for or implementing telecommuting as the threat of worldwide pandemics force them to seek ways to secure their business operations in times of catastrophe.

Outsourcing, which is described in Insight 1.1, is a departure from an insurer's traditional use of company employees to perform administrative functions.

INSIGHT 1.1 Outsourcing

Outsourcing is a business practice in which a company hires a vendor to conduct a specific activity that the company otherwise would perform itself, such as billing administration or customer contacts. The vendor is responsible for staffing and all of the related human resources issues. In the insurance industry, outsourcing was used first in the customer service area, but now it is used in many other areas, including underwriting, claims, accounting, and information technology.

On-shore outsourcing uses vendors within the company's country, while *off-shore outsourcing* uses vendors from other countries. While off-shore outsourcing can result in cost savings, cultural and language differences are obstacles.

The reasons companies use outsourcing vary. Some companies turn to outsourcing when they take on a new activity and do not have enough time to build the necessary expertise in-house. Some companies rely on outsourcing for temporary situations such as increases in workload due to new product launches. Other companies outsource to obtain access to technology they do not wish to purchase or develop in-house.

When a company outsources a function, it must work closely with the vendor to ensure that the vendor's performance meets company standards and customer expectations. Many companies obtain contractual guarantees in which the vendor agrees to forfeit a portion of its fees if it fails to meet specific performance standards. Furthermore, a company must obtain contractual assurances from the vendor to protect the privacy and security of customer information as well as the company's proprietary information.

Source: Adapted from Mark Adel and Barbara Foxenberger Brown, *Foundations of Customer Service* [Atlanta: LOMA (Life Office Management Association, Inc.), © 2003], 290. Used with permission. All rights reserved.

Administration Systems

Information systems are essential to the efficient and effective operation of insurance administration functions in today's insurance company. An information system that an insurer uses to manage information about insurance policies is referred to as an ***administration system***. Insurers typically have more than one administration system, as we discuss later in this chapter.

In this section, we discuss administration systems' technology components, enhancements, integration, and security.[1] We introduce this subject here because we provide examples throughout the text of how technology is used to improve the performance of administration functions.

Technology Components

The technology components of a computer-based administration system include a technology platform, application software, databases, and communications technology, as illustrated in Figure 1.3.

Technology Platform

A ***technology platform*** is the combination of hardware and operating system software on which an administration system runs. Whereas the broad definition of hardware is the equipment and mechanical devices included in a computer-based information system, in the context of a technology platform, ***hardware*** refers to the types of computers the insurer uses. ***Software*** consists of computer programs that provide the sequences of instructions for a computer and that govern its operation. One type of software, known as ***operating system software***, controls the basic operations of a computer. Among other functions, the operating system software performs common computer tasks, such as saving data to different storage mediums or devices. The most commonly used operating system for personal computers is Microsoft Windows®.

Application Software

Application software, also known as a *software application* or simply an *application*, is software used to perform specific tasks or solve particular types of problems. Word processing software that creates text documents and spreadsheet software that creates data tables and performs calculations are two types of application software. Insurers use many specialized types of application software to perform insurance-specific tasks. Examples include software that can

FIGURE 1.3 The Technology Components of an Administration System

TECHNOLOGY PLATFORM

- Hardware, e.g., mainframes, servers, and/or personal computers

AND

- Operating system software, e.g., Windows®*, UNIX, or Mac

APPLICATION SOFTWARE

- Software that performs specific, business-related tasks

DATABASES

- Organized collections of data and information

COMMUNICATIONS TECHNOLOGY

- Use of telecommunications to communicate and transfer data electronically

*Windows® is a registered trademark of Microsoft Corporation.

Source: Adapted from Mark Adel and Nicolas L. Desoutter, *Annuity Systems and Administration*, 2nd ed. [Atlanta: LOMA (Life Office Management Association, Inc.), © 2004], 177. Used with permission; all rights reserved.

- Prepare quotes for insurance policies
- Process the issuance of policies
- Administer policy loans and policy dividends
- Prepare policy value statements
- Calculate correct benefit payments
- Print benefit payment checks

Such software applications form one component of a ***transaction processing system***, which is an organized collection of procedures, software, databases, and devices used to perform high-volume, routine, and repetitive business transactions. A ***transaction*** is any business-related exchange—such as a death benefit paid in exchange for proof of death received or payment of a renewal premium for the continuation of coverage. Various transaction processing systems work together to perform the different processes involved in each insurance administration function.

Vendors offer many different types of software applications and many different varieties of each type. Insurers also can develop their own applications. Often, application software is purchased from a vendor and then customized by the insurer or vendor to better support the insurer's products and processes.

An insurer's choice of application software depends on each insurer's specific administration processes. An insurer seeks the application software that can best accomplish the tasks it performs. As we see in this text, administration processes are much the same from one company to the next, yet each insurer's processes are to some extent unique. An insurer's history, culture, business philosophy, corporate strategy, corporate structure, target markets, products, distribution channels, business policies, and business practices all shape its administration processes. Therefore, the ideal application software performs certain core administration processes and also meets an insurer's distinctive needs.

Databases

A ***database*** is an organized collection of data and information. Databases are vitally important for insurers that need to store, access, and process vast amounts of data about, for example, policyowners, insureds, claimants, producers, and policies. Insurers develop their own databases and use external databases developed and maintained by government agencies, industry associations, business partners, and other information providers.

Note that a distinction must be made between the terms *data* and *information*. The term ***data*** refers to unprocessed facts. A policyowner's name, address, and policy number are pieces of data. Data are combined, manipulated, and analyzed to create ***information***, which is a collection of data that has been converted into a form that is meaningful or useful for the accomplishment of some objective, such as performing a transaction, drawing a conclusion, or solving a problem.

Communications Technology

Communications technology makes use of ***telecommunications***, which is the electronic transmission of communication signals. Telecommunications enables organizations to link computer systems into networks. A ***network*** is a group of interconnected computers and computer devices, including the telecommunications equipment and software that connect them. The Internet is an example of a worldwide network among unrelated users. An ***intranet*** is an organization's internal computer network that uses Internet technology but is accessible only to people within the organization. An ***extranet*** is a portion of an organization's intranet that is accessible to people within the organization and to selected external parties. Insurers often establish extranets to allow home office employees and producers to communicate electronically.

Examples of how telecommunications and networks are useful to businesses are the commonly-known electronic mail (e-mail), electronic data interchange, and electronic commerce.

- ***Electronic mail (e-mail)*** is a form of telecommunication that allows a user to type a message into a computer and then send the message to other computers connected to a network.
- ***Electronic data interchange (EDI)*** is the computer-to-computer exchange of data between organizations using a data format agreed upon by the sending and receiving parties. Organizations that exchange data through EDI are called *trading partners* and are said to be part of an EDI network. The primary purpose of an EDI network is to allow an organization to transmit data directly from its computers to the computers of other organizations on the network. In the life insurance industry, EDI networks are used for many purposes, such as transferring medical laboratory results to underwriting departments, depositing policy benefits into a policyowner's bank account, and exchanging data with reinsurers.
- ***Electronic commerce (e-commerce)*** is the use of the Internet and other networks to deliver commercial information and to facilitate business transactions and the delivery of products and services. The sale of products over the Internet is the classic example of e-commerce. Other examples include electronic applications for insurance and electronic claim submittals.

Telecommunications equipment and telephone systems are especially important to the customer service function and are discussed in the customer service section of this text.

Technologies that Enhance Insurance Administration Processes

The previous section describes the technology components of a core administration system that an insurer uses to manage information about customers and policies. This section focuses on the role of technology in ***business process management (BPM)***, which is a strategy for optimizing business processes or adapting them to meet changing needs. The functions of underwriting, reinsurance, and claims in particular are very process oriented; business process management seeks to combine proven management practices with technology to automate and improve these processes. Some software vendors sell BPM suites (BPMSs), which are collections of software tools that support and manage the design, modeling, construction, deployment, monitoring, and refinement of business processes.

The goal of many insurers that focus on business process management is ***straight through processing (STP)***, which is the electronic processing of every step of a transaction without manual intervention. For example, STP can enable the completely electronic processing of new business from the submission of the application for insurance to the actual issuing of the policy. A potential policyowner and a producer can complete and submit an application electronically, and then the insurer's administration system can do everything else necessary to produce a policy, including underwriting and printing the policy. Pure STP would result in a paperless environment in which all forms and records are maintained electronically.

Insurers desire straight through processing for the following reasons:

- Increased efficiency and, thus, reduced expenses
- Decreased error rate because of the decreased need for data entry and other human input
- Improved consistency and quality
- Increased productivity
- Faster service to customers and producers

STP is not yet a single product that an insurer can buy off the shelf. It is composed of many available applications that can interface with one another to produce a straight through process. Critical components of STP include database management systems, data mining, predictive modeling, business rules engines, document management systems, and workflow automation systems. In this section, we discuss how these software tools and applications automate processes. Of course, these tools and applications can be used independently of STP. Figure 1.4 illustrates the components of STP.

Database Management Systems and Data Mining

Insurance companies collect and store a tremendous amount of data about customers and their policies, and many areas of the company need to use this data. Rather than replicating this data in separate database files for each separate function, the insurer typically uses a ***centralized data repository***, a database that houses all the relevant data contained in the

FIGURE 1.4 Components of Straight Through Processing

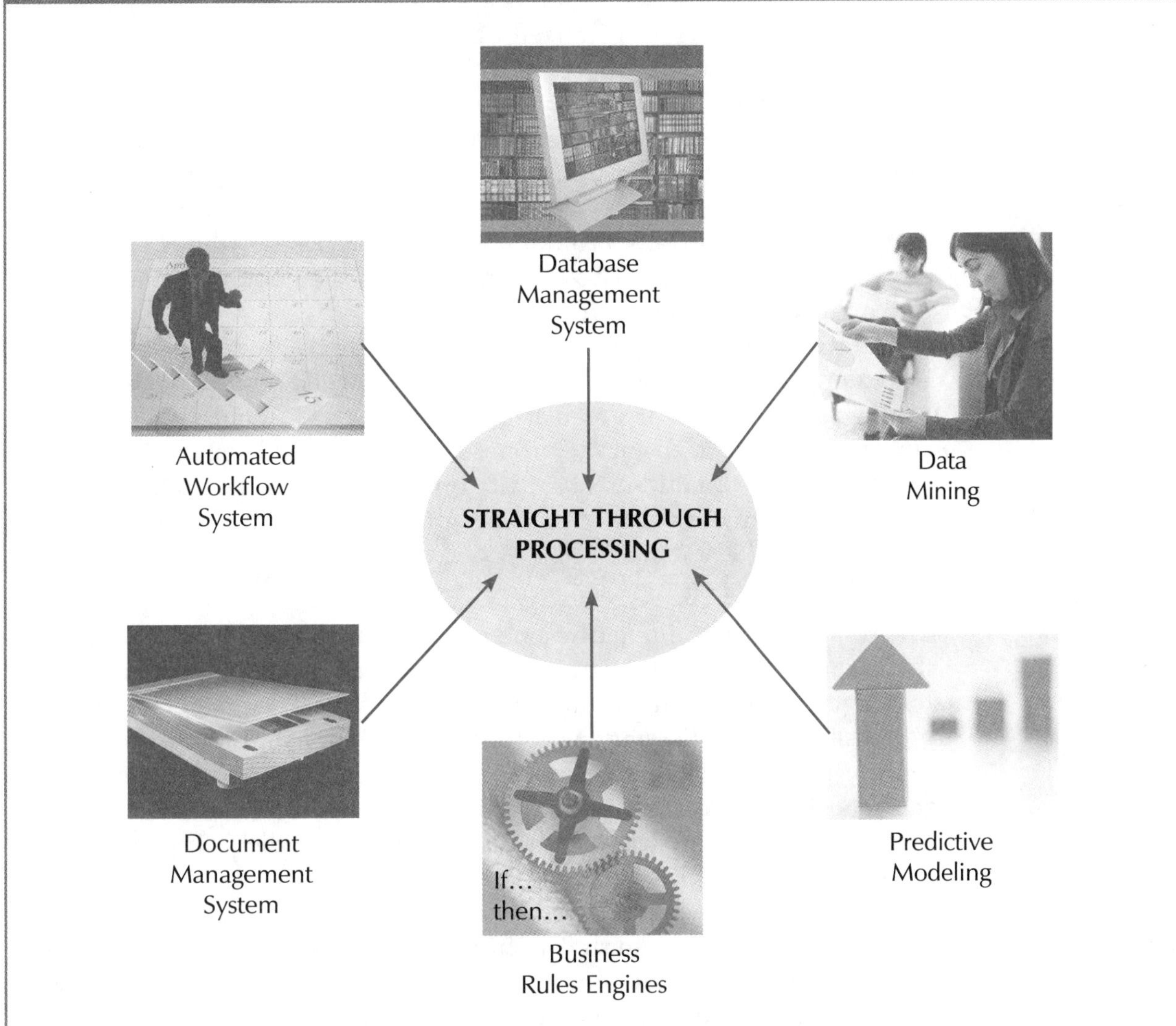

insurer's separate administration systems. To access the centralized data repository or other databases, insurance company employees typically use a ***database management system (DBMS)***, which is a group of computer programs that organizes data in a database and allows users to obtain the information they need. A DBMS manipulates the data in response to queries from users in different functional areas of the company and allows them to access and share the data in the centralized data repository. For example, underwriters can obtain data on policy applications, claim staff can access data on benefits and policy terms, and customer service representatives can retrieve information necessary to answer customers' questions.

A ***data warehouse*** is a type of DBMS that collects data from the company's existing databases and possibly from sources outside the company, screens and edits the data, puts the data in a standard format, and then stores the data in the centralized data repository. An insurer can analyze the data in its data warehouse, as well as data from other sources, through ***data mining***, which is the analysis of large amounts of data to discover previously unknown trends, patterns, and relationships. As an example, data mining technology might bring together payment history data and claims experience on all of an insurer's covered insureds to reveal relationships that profile a potentially profitable segment of people who then could be targeted for marketing. These characteristics also could be incorporated into an insurer's underwriting guidelines.

Data mining systems can analyze data from internal and external sources. For example, information on other policies owned by a proposed insured would come from the insurer's internal records; additional data, such as the current financial status of the proposed insured, could come from external sources, such as credit bureaus. Data mining systems are often Web-based, allowing information gathering to be automatic and instantaneous.

Predictive Modeling

The results of data mining can generate even more useful information when they are used as the input in ***predictive modeling***, which is an automated technique for predicting future behavior or events. The predictive modeling process involves collecting the patterns and relationships unearthed by data mining, formulating a statistical model, and generating predictions based on the model.[2] For example, using predictive modeling, insurers can develop company-specific models that take into account the company's policy, underwriting, and claim data, as well as data from outside sources. Such models can forecast mortality and morbidity by predicting the development of medical conditions and the onset of illnesses, as well as the likelihood of losses due to risky professions and avocations. Thus, predictive modeling improves risk evaluation and selection, as well as premium rating.

As new data become available, predictive models are validated or revised.[3] For example, scientific progress in the field of genetic testing will lead to improvements in disease prevention. These improvements become new data inputs into the models and thus lead to improved predictions.

Business Rules Engines

A ***business rules engine (BRE)*** is application software that automates the decision-making process by creating and applying rules to all available information. Any decision-making process that can be stated in an "if… then…" format can be automated. For example, a business rules engine would be able to make the decision that *if* a proposed insured has a certain number of medical conditions, *then* she should be declined coverage.

Business rules engines are particularly useful in the underwriting decision-making process, which is characterized by the application of certain rules to data and combinations of data. In fact, hard copy underwriting manuals are nothing more than business rules books. However, whereas an underwriter using an underwriting manual can evaluate quite a few variables, business rules engines—supported by data mining and predictive modeling—can consider hundreds of variables. In addition, BREs can ensure the consistent processing of these variables, leading to more equitable underwriting decisions.

By using BREs, insurers can engage in exception-based underwriting in which rules are applied to process all applications electronically, except the most difficult ones that require an underwriter to apply human judgment in the decision-making process. A jet issue electronic system is an example of how business rules engines are used in the underwriting process. A ***jet issue electronic system*** uses business rules engines to determine that certain criteria are met and the application is approved for issue; or the rules engine determines that the criteria are not met, and the application is either declined or sent to an underwriter. Thus, BREs free underwriters from the more routine cases, leaving them to handle those cases that are particularly complex or call for a particular expertise.

Business rules engines also can identify missing pieces of information necessary to make the underwriting decision and can order this information from people and systems both inside and outside of the company. For example, the software can request data, such as payment history and claims, on other policies owned by the applicant. It also can request data over the Internet from third parties.

Increasingly, insurers are using BREs in more and more functional areas. They are frequently used to process claims. Routine claims can be processed automatically by the system, leaving the more challenging ones for the claim analysts to handle. Insurers also use BREs to guide employees through the benefit enrollment process, assist in ordering supplies, evaluate investment alternatives, and help a policyowner make an address change via the Internet.

Document Management Systems

A ***document management system*** is a type of technology that stores, organizes, and retrieves documents that have been converted to digital images. Insurers can enter documents into a document management system either by creating documents electronically and converting them to digital images or by converting paper documents to digital images through imaging.

Document imaging, also known as *scanning*, is a process of converting printed characters or graphics into digital images on a computer by inserting paper documents in a type of hardware called a *scanner*. The scanner "reads" the documents and "translates" them into electronic files, which are then converted to digital images, indexed, and stored in the insurer's document management system. Employees can use a document management system to search for, view, print, and share the digitized documents when processing applications or transactions.

Document management systems provide staff members with computer access to a variety of company-specific forms and documents, such as completed applications. In addition, these systems can provide computer access to correspondence and other documents—such as credit scores—from outside the company.

The advantages of document management systems include

- Eliminating the expense of storing thousands—if not millions—of paper documents that can instead be stored electronically
- Avoiding the complicated logistics of storing paper documents
- Increasing efficiency, as processors never have to wait for a paper document to be pulled from a paper file or passed from processor to processor
- Reducing frustration, delays, and wasted time that result from lost and misfiled documents
- Facilitating document sharing because several employees in different locations can view the same document at the same time on their computer screen

Automated Workflow Systems

Document management systems often are used in conjunction with automated workflow systems. An ***automated workflow system***, also called a *workflow application*, is a technology used to create computer-based records pertaining to the status and processing of specific transactions. Basically, an automated workflow system can be thought of as a tracking sheet that accompanies a transaction through the entire workflow process from initial receipt through completion and filing. The automated workflow system shows the type of transaction, the person to whom it was assigned, when it was received, questions that arose, actions taken, documents created, completion dates and times, and so on. Rather than include this information in a paper file, an automated workflow system stores it electronically.

An automated workflow system can route documents automatically to staff members for processing, placing the jobs in a work queue so that the jobs are available when staff members are ready to work on them. After a staff member has finished working on a case, the workflow system then routes the job to the next staff member who needs to work on the case. Automated workflow systems can use business rules engines for purposes such as 1) gauging the priority of a work item and placing high priority items in the front of queues and 2) determining what skill set is needed for a particular work item and then routing the work to an employee with those particular skills.

Automated workflow systems can increase accuracy by creating an ***audit log***, which is a record of the work that has been completed on a case. The insurer can use the audit log to make sure that all the proper procedures are followed on each case.

Systems Integration

Many insurers maintain more than one administration system, using different systems to administer different portions of their business. For example, an insurer may have a life insurance administration system and a disability income insurance administration system. In addition, individual business and group business typically are administered on separate systems. Furthermore, an insurer that has acquired or merged with another insurer may maintain two sets of systems—one from each insurer.

If an insurer administers different portions of its business on different systems, the different systems may not work well together or they might not work together at all. In these situations, the insurer takes steps to integrate the otherwise incompatible systems. One way insurers integrate incompatible systems is by using ***middleware***, which is a type of software used to enable two or more systems to work together.

Another way to integrate systems involves a centralized data repository, which, as we mentioned earlier, is a database that houses all the relevant data contained in the insurer's separate administration systems. On a regular basis—usually daily—the various administrative systems update the centralized database. The centralized database then can provide the systems with updated data as required for processes or transactions. This process allows each of the various administration systems to retain data in a format that works best for them, while providing a centralized, holistic view of data from all of the systems. The downside of this method of integrating systems is the expense of maintaining multiple copies of the same data, along with the complexity of keeping multiple copies in sync. Once a centralized database is established, insurers can begin modifying their administration systems to use data directly from the centralized database, as opposed to the database unique to the administration system. However, this can prove to be a long and expensive project.

As an example of how middleware and a centralized data repository operate, consider the information a customer service representative (CSR) might view on his computer monitor when he receives a telephone call. The insurer might use middleware to search all the systems, retrieve the relevant information, and present it to the CSR. Alternatively, if the insurer's customer information resides on several systems, the CSR might actually be seeing data contained in a centralized data repository made up of data from all of the insurer's administrative systems.

Security

One of the challenges insurers face when they maintain and exchange data and information electronically is providing adequate security. ***Security*** refers to the physical, technical, and procedural steps a company takes to prevent the loss, wrongful disclosure (accidental or intentional), or theft of data or information. Security is to be distinguished from *privacy* of data and information, which we discuss in Chapter 3.

Figure 1.5 lists the major types of security risks that insurers face and the technological tools they use to combat such risks.

Quality Control

Quality control is the process of ensuring that an organization accomplishes its objectives and follows its standards. Organizations set objectives both to measure their own performance and guide their activities. Periodically, organizations evaluate their activities to see how well their performance meets their objectives. If an organization is not meeting its objectives, then the organization can determine the causes and can implement changes to improve its performance.

Most insurers evaluate the quality of their administrative activities by measuring results and then comparing actual performance to set standards. ***Performance measurement*** is a process through which a company (1) decides what activities are key to the achievement of the company's goals and objectives, how to measure the performance of those activities, and what performance standards it hopes to achieve, (2) gathers the information, and (3) communicates the results. A ***performance standard*** is an established level of performance against which a company or an individual compares actual performance. ***Benchmarks*** are performance standards, often based on standards achieved by leading companies, that represent a company's goals for performance.

As part of a company's quality control program, the company creates written documentation of its policies, processes, and procedures. These written documents define how the processes work and give employees clear guidance on how they should accomplish administrative tasks. The documents also provide a basis for monitoring compliance with the established procedures.

FIGURE 1.5 Security Risks and Technological Tools

Security Risk: Unauthorized persons might intercept data traveling over the Internet or a private network.

Technological Tools:

Encryption. Technology that encodes data so that only an authorized person, who possesses the required hardware and/or software that contains the decryption key, can decode the data.

Virtual private network (VPN). An organization's network that uses public telecommunications infrastructure such as the Internet to provide authorized individual users or remote offices with secure access.

Security Risk: Hackers might gain access to company databases and view, manipulate, or steal data.

Technological Tools:

Firewall. A combination of hardware and software that creates an electronic barrier between the public and private areas of a company's systems. Only those individuals who know the appropriate security procedures can access the areas behind the firewall.

Intrusion detection software. Software that monitors system traffic and identifies sequences of commands that indicate an unauthorized user is attempting to access the organization's systems or databases.

Security Risk: Unauthorized persons might gain access to private customer information by impersonating authorized persons.

Technological Tools:

Authentication. A combination of technology and procedures designed to verify a user's identity before giving the user access to a system or database. The typical authentication procedure calls for someone trying to access the system or database to provide a user name and password.

Cookies. A file that the Web server—a computer that contains shared resources—places on a user's personal computer that enables the server to recognize the personal computer. The user can access the protected file only from a computer containing the cookie.

Biometric authentication. Technology that identifies users by "reading" a physical trait that is unique to each user, such as the user's fingerprint or retina.

Security Risk: A virus or worm might destroy data and/or programs or disable computers.

Technological Tool:

Antivirus software. A software application that detects viruses and prevents them from infecting a computer and/or helps an infected computer recover.

Security Risk: A natural or manmade disaster might destroy data or the system's ability to function.

Technological Tools:

Data backup software. Companies use systems to back up data to the Internet or intranets while the data is being created and then store the back-up copies off site.

Disaster recovery software. Software applications are available that can aid insurers in developing disaster recovery plans. Insurers regularly conduct disaster recovery tests to practice the recovery of key systems and data.

Most insurers evaluate their processes and procedures by using quantitative and qualitative performance measurement, although usually with a greater emphasis on quantitative measurement.

Quantitative Performance Measurement

Quantitative performance measurement is a type of performance measurement that relies on numerical methods to track and report results to determine how quickly, often, accurately, and profitably processes and transactions are completed. Quantitative measures might indicate the number of transactions handled per day, the average length of time spent on a process, or the number of customer complaints and compliments responded to in a month. In this section, we explain the quantitative performance measurements of service level, number of processes completed, timeliness, and quality rate.

Service Level

Service level is the percentage of inbound customer contacts answered within a specified time frame—for example, 90 percent of telephone calls answered within 20 seconds. In this context, *responded to* does not mean that the customer's request was handled, but simply that someone responded to the request. Reports on service level help an insurer determine how accessible it is to its internal and external customers.

Processes Completed

The number of ***processes completed*** measures how many transactions are handled within a specified period of time, such as the number of telephone calls answered, applications processed, claims adjudicated, or checks released within a month. This measurement indicates how quickly and efficiently a process is working.

Timeliness

Turnaround time, also known as *average handling time*, indicates the time necessary to complete a customer-initiated request or transaction, such as processing a loan or responding to a policyowner's or producer's request for information.

Quality Rate

Quality rate measures the accuracy of a particular type of transaction. It is often expressed as a percentage of the total number of transactions that were handled or processed without errors, such as 98.4 percent of account transactions having no reported errors.

Qualitative Performance Measurement

Qualitative performance measurement is a type of performance measurement that focuses on behaviors, attitudes, or opinions to determine how efficiently and effectively processes and transactions are completed. For example, qualitative performance measurement can be used to evaluate interactions with customers. The customer may be asked to complete a survey in which he assesses the company representative's level of courtesy and clarity of communication. Note that some qualitative performance measures require an evaluator to make subjective judgments. Consequently, qualitative performance measurement is more difficult to administer and interpret than quantitative measurement.

Key Terms

insurance administration
living benefits
producer
applicant
insured
proposed insured
policyowner
third-party policy
master group insurance contract
policyholder
group prospect
group insured
certificate of insurance
beneficiary
ethics
underwriting
underwriter
new business
reinsurance
claim administration
customer service
policyowner service
member service
marketing
actuary
accounting
treasury
legal
compliance
human resources
information technology (IT)
information system
information management
outsourcing
administration system
technology platform
hardware
software
operating systems software
application software
transaction processing system
transaction
database
data
information
telecommunications
network
intranet
extranet
electronic mail (e-mail)
electronic data interchange (EDI)
electronic commerce (e-commerce)
business process management (BPM)
straight through processing (STP)
centralized data repository

Key Terms (*continued*)

database management system (DBMS)
data warehouse
data mining
predictive modeling
business rules engine (BRE)
jet issue electronic system
document management system
document imaging
automated workflow system
audit log
middleware
security
quality control
performance measurement
performance standard
benchmark
encryption
virtual private network (VPN)
firewall
intrusion detection software
authentication
cookie
biometric authentication
antivirus software
quantitative performance measurement
service level
processes completed
turnaround time
quality rate
qualitative performance measurement

Endnotes

1. This section is adapted from Miriam A. Orsina and Gene Stone, *Insurance Company Operations*, 2nd ed. [Atlanta: LOMA (Life Office Management Association, Inc.), © 2005], 309–324; Mary C. Bickley et al., Barbara Foxenberger Brown, Jane Lightcap Brown, and Harriett E. Jones, *Life and Health Insurance Underwriting*, 2nd ed. [Atlanta: LOMA (Life Office Management Association, Inc.), © 2007], 95–100; and Mark Adel and Nicholas L. Desoutter, *Annuity Systems and Administration*, 2nd ed. [Atlanta: LOMA (Life Office Management Association, Inc.), © 2004], 177–187. All sources used with permission; all rights reserved.
2. LOMA, *Predictive Modeling: Life and Health Insurance Underwriting and Risk Analysis*, Information Center Brief (August 2003), 1. Used with permission; all rights reserved.
3. Ibid.

Part 2: Underwriting

chapter

2

Overview of the New Business Process and Underwriting

Outline

New Business Process
Field Underwriting
Teleunderwriting
Data Entry and Review
Underwriting
Policy Issue

New Business/Underwriting Quality Control

Underwriting Principles
Risk Assessment
Risk Classification
Underwriting Philosophy and Underwriting Guidelines

Underwriting Organization
Job Positions
Authority Levels
Organizational Systems

Learning Objectives

After studying this chapter, you should be able to...

- Describe the new business process
- Explain common quality control methods used in the new business/underwriting area
- Explain the importance of risk assessment and risk classification and describe the factors that insurers consider when they evaluate a risk
- Distinguish among the preferred, standard, substandard, and declined risk classes
- Explain how an insurer ensures that it approves and issues coverage that is equitable to the insureds, equitable to the insurer, and deliverable by the producer
- List typical underwriting job positions and authority levels and define the different approaches that insurers use to organize the work within underwriting units and list examples of each approach

As we mentioned in Chapter 1, underwriting is the process of (1) assessing and classifying the degree of risk represented by a proposed insured or group with respect to a specific insurance product and (2) making a decision to accept or decline that risk. Underwriting is part of the new business process—activities an insurer undertakes in receiving applications, underwriting applications, and issuing policies. In some companies, underwriting and new business are part of the same unit; in other companies, they are separate units.

We begin this chapter with an overview of the entire new business process, including underwriting, and a brief explanation of new business/underwriting quality control. We then begin our focus on underwriting with a discussion of its principles, including risk assessment and risk classification. We also explain how an insurer's underwriting philosophy and underwriting guidelines affect risk assessment and classification. We conclude with a survey of how an underwriting department is staffed and organized. Throughout this chapter, we discuss the use of technology in new business and underwriting, which we also covered in Chapter 1.

New Business Process

Individual and group insurance applications go through basically the same new business process before a policy is issued. In general, (1) information is gathered and entered into an administration system; (2) additional information is acquired, if necessary; (3) information is assessed; (4) the decision is made whether to accept the risk; and, (5) if the decision is favorable, a policy is issued. However, the processes for underwriting individual and group coverage differ in many respects. In this section, we describe the individual life and health insurance new business process. In Chapter 8, we cover the group life and health insurance new business process.

Figure 2.1 illustrates the steps an individual application goes through from field underwriting to policy issue. Although field underwriting is not technically a part of new business, it is included because of its importance in the underwriting process. Note that we explain some of the terminology used in this figure in the text that follows.

Field Underwriting

Underwriting an application for insurance often begins well before the application reaches the insurer's home office underwriters. ***Field underwriting*** is the practice of gathering initial information about applicants and proposed insureds and screening proposed insureds to determine if they are likely to be approved for a specific type of coverage. Effective field underwriting

FIGURE 2.1 Processing of An Application

1 Field underwriting
- ✓ Gather information
- ✓ Screen applicant and proposed insured (if different from applicant)

2 Teleunderwriting
- ✓ Gather information

3 Data entry and review
- ✓ Create case file
- ✓ Enter data
- ✓ Conduct good order check
- ✓ Conduct suitability check
- ✓ Search records for information on applicant and proposed insured (if different from applicant)

4 Underwriting
- ✓ Assess risk
- ✓ Classify risk
- ✓ Make underwriting decision

5 Policy Issue
- ✓ Enter data
- ✓ Assemble policy
- ✓ Facilitate policy delivery
- ✓ Collect post-issue requirements

- Reduces the insurer's costs by eliminating the need for home office processing and underwriting of clearly unacceptable applications
- Helps ensure that underwriters have the information they need to assess each proposed risk
- Assures that applicants are applying for an appropriate amount and type of coverage at an appropriate premium rate, which fosters better relations with applicants because false expectations are not created.

Sometimes producers submit informal applications to several insurers to determine which company offers the best terms and rates for a specific proposed insured. Producers expect insurers to respond within a matter of days with a rate quote. Such informal applications typically are shorter than the formal application and do not require the applicant or proposed insured to authorize the collection of additional information, although some companies do require such authorization. When the producer finds the offer that is best for the client, he will submit a formal application to the insurer that made that offer. The application then is fully underwritten.

Traditionally, formal applications for individual life and health insurance have consisted of two sections—Part I and Part II. Part I contains questions designed to identify the applicant and proposed insured (if different from the applicant), specify the amount and type of coverage requested, and provide the insurer with basic information about the proposed beneficiary and proposed insured. Figure 2.2 lists the types of information typically sought in Part I of an application for individual life insurance.

Part II of the application, which we describe in Chapter 4, provides the insurer with medical information about the proposed insured. Note that some insurers no longer divide the insurance application into Part I and Part II, although nearly all insurers ask basically the same types of questions.

Most individual life and health applications also include a section called the ***agent's statement***, in which the producer can comment on any factors relevant to the case and the risk it involves. When an underwriter knows that a producer tends to submit quality business, the agent's statement can be particularly valuable in explaining circumstances that may otherwise cause delays in underwriting when it appears that more information is needed to ensure a sound decision. Unlike the rest of the application, the agent's statement is not made a part of the insurance contract. The insurer keeps the agent's statement confidential so that producers will feel free to comment honestly on elements that affect the risk represented by each proposed insured. A typical agent's statement includes the following questions:

- How long has the producer known the applicant/proposed insured?
- How well does the producer know the applicant/proposed insured?
- What is the producer's impression of the applicant's/proposed insured's financial worth and annual income?
- Does the producer have any additional information about the proposed insured that could affect the proposed insured's insurability?
- Did the producer actually see the proposed insured when the application was completed? If so, did the proposed insured appear to be in good health and free from any defect, deformity or abnormality that might affect the underwriting decision?

FIGURE 2.2 Information Sought in Part I of an Individual Life Insurance Application

- The proposed insured's name, government identification number (for example, Social Security number in the United States and social insurance number in Canada), date of birth, place of birth, age, sex, address, telephone number, length of time at the current residence, marital status, driver's license number, occupation, current employer, income, and length of time with the current employer
- The applicant's name (if the policy is applied for by someone other than the proposed insured), government identification number, address, and relationship to the proposed insured
- The policyowner's name (if the policy is to be owned by someone other than the applicant or proposed insured), government identification number, address, and relationship to the proposed insured
- The plan of insurance, face amount, and premium payment mode requested
- Dividend options and special features or riders desired
- Name of the beneficiary and relationship to the proposed insured
- The proposed insured's
    - Avocations and aviation activities, including hazardous activities such as sky diving, hang-gliding, and scuba diving
    - International residence and travel
    - Driving history
    - Tobacco use
    - Criminal convictions
    - Insurance history, including
        - The total amount of insurance already in force on the life of the proposed insured with any insurance company and the purpose of such coverage
        - Whether any applied-for insurance is pending at the time of this application
        - Whether any in-force insurance coverage will be replaced by the coverage applied for
        - Whether the proposed insured ever has been declined for insurance coverage, been offered coverage with restricted benefits or other than standard rates, or applied for or received insurance benefits because of ill health or injury

Source: Adapted from Mary C. Bickley et al., *Life and Health Insurance Underwriting*, 2nd ed. [Atlanta: LOMA (Life Office Management Association, Inc.), © 2007], 82. Used with permission; all rights reserved.

- Did the producer solicit the business or did the applicant initiate the purchase?
- What is the applicant's reason for buying the requested coverage?
- Is the producer a full-time representative of another insurance company?
- Has the producer submitted an application on the proposed insured to any other insurer within the past six months?
- Does the policy replace another policy?
- Are the proposed insured and a family member applying for insurance at the same time?
- Is the proposed insured applying for two policies (for example, life and disability income) at the same time?

To help producers perform field underwriting, most insurers develop a ***field underwriting manual***, which is a document that (1) presents specific guidance for a producer's assessment of the risk represented by a proposed insured and (2) guides the producer in assembling and submitting the application and any other information needed for the underwriter to evaluate the risk. For example, the field underwriting manual typically contains an ***age and amount requirements chart***, also known as *table of underwriting requirements*, for each product that specifies the kinds of information the underwriter must obtain and review in assessing the insurability of a proposed insured. Producers are responsible for ordering the appropriate underwriting requirements listed in this chart. We discuss the age and amount requirements chart in more detail in Chapter 4.

Most insurers also provide producers with an ***impairment guide***, which is a list of common impairments and the probable underwriting decision for proposed insureds who have each type of impairment. An ***impairment*** is a physical or psychological abnormality or loss of function. The impairment guide may be part of an insurer's field underwriting manual. By using the impairment guide, a producer can inform a proposed insured about coverage types and amounts for which she is most likely to be approved.

The typical contents of a field underwriting manual are listed in Figure 2.3.

Traditionally, the producer helps the applicant complete a paper application and mails or faxes it to the home office. Some companies encourage producers to use imaging for the submission of applications. Using an imaging system, the producer scans the application so it can be stored in and retrieved from the insurer's document management system.

When a producer submits an application by mail, fax, or imaging, a new business case analyst must enter the information from the application into the insurer's new business administration system.[1] This double-entry process

FIGURE 2.3 Typical Contents of a Field Underwriting Manual

- The insurer's ***underwriting philosophy***, also known as an *underwriting objective*, which is a set of objectives that guides all of an insurer's underwriting actions, generally reflects the insurer's strategic business goals, and includes its pricing assumptions for products
- An outline of the producer's responsibilities, including compliance issues
- Specific guidance on completing applications and on submitting changes and reinstatements
- Brief definitions of common medical terms and common impairments to help the producer describe impairments revealed by a proposed insured
- Lists of questions related to common impairments so that the producer can obtain sufficiently detailed information about them
- Age and amount requirements charts
- Impairment guide
- Criteria for a preferred rating
- Criteria for qualifying as a tobacco nonuser

means that, in effect, two different people—the producer and a new business case analyst—each perform the same function, which creates additional work, adds to processing time, and increases the likelihood of errors.

To reduce the amount of time insurers spend on new business processing and improve accuracy, some companies use an ***electronic application system***, which is a technology that allows producers or applicants to enter application information into a computer, rather than on paper, and transmit the information to the insurer over a computer network. Some insurers who use electronic applications have built rules engines into their systems. Such rules engines can determine if the information submitted is incomplete or inaccurate and will require the producer and applicant to correct the problem before they can proceed with filling out the application. When the electronic application is complete, the system transfers the information directly into the insurer's new business administration system. Electronic application systems can form part of the straight through processing systems that we described in Chapter 1.

Applicants and proposed insureds are required to sign applications, as well as authorizations for the release, collection, use, and disclosure of information. Obviously, with an electronic application system, signatures cannot be in ink on paper. Some insurers obtain "wet" signatures after the electronic application has been submitted. Others accept an ***electronic signature***, which is a unique personal identifier that makes a legally binding contract using electronic communications media like the Internet. The ***Electronic Signatures in Global and National Commerce (E-SIGN) Act***, a federal law in the United States, gives electronic signatures the same legal status as hard-copy signatures. Although this law clarifies the legal status of electronic signatures, insurers have to develop appropriate policies, procedures, and technological capabilities before accepting applications with electronic signatures.

E-SIGN does not dictate what form an electronic signature should take. In fact, the law states that an electronic signature can take almost any form, as long as the person affixing the signature intends to sign the document in question. Electronic signature pads that an applicant signs with a pen-like instrument are rare because of the cost involved. Often, the signature consists of the applicant clicking on an "I agree" or "I accept" icon.

Teleunderwriting

Teleunderwriting is a method by which the insurer, rather than a producer, takes responsibility for gathering from the proposed insured most of the information needed for underwriting. When teleunderwriting is used, the producer and the applicant complete an abbreviated application that includes only basic information about the proposed insured and the coverage applied for. An underwriter, a specially-trained employee of the insurer, or an employee of a vendor then interviews the proposed insured to gather the additional information required for underwriting.

Typically, the interview is conducted by telephone, but some insurers conduct such interviews online via their Internet sites. The interviewer may use a software application that presents him with a prepared script of questions similar to those that appear on the application and that are customized for the product being underwritten. The software incorporates a business rules engine that guides the interviewer through the questions in the interview. Based on the proposed insured's answer to a question, the business rules engine determines the follow-up questions the interviewer should ask. Voice signatures in which an applicant simply voices his agreement that he has honestly and fully answered the questions often are acceptable for teleapplications.

Data Entry and Review

When an application is received in the home office, it is assigned to a new business case analyst, who assigns the application a number or code for identification and tracking purposes and creates a case file. The application then goes through a manual or an automated *good order check* process to verify that the

- Application form is the proper one for the issuing jurisdiction

- Application form has received state regulatory approval, if required
- Other forms required by the insurer or state regulatory authority have been completed and received
- Producer and the insurer are licensed to sell the type of coverage requested in the applicable jurisdiction
- Application is complete

If a new business case analyst discovers that an application is incomplete, she will contact the producer to rectify the problem, although the underwriter contacts the producer in some companies.

Applications for some products also must undergo a *suitability check* in which a determination is made whether the amount and type of coverage applied for are appropriate, considering the age and circumstances of the proposed insured. Producers are expected to submit only suitable applications, but the new business unit typically is responsible for confirming suitability.

Next, a new business case analyst or an automated system searches the insurer's records for information about the applicant and proposed insured, such as previous life and/or health insurance applications or claims.

Some companies assign applications to case managers, who are responsible for overseeing the entire new business process from receipt of application to policy issuance for those cases assigned to them. A case manager's duties may include assuring that all underwriting requirements are obtained and submitted to underwriting, along with the application and any other internal information gathered by the new business case analyst. A case manager usually also is responsible for communicating with producers in order to allow underwriters more time to underwrite. Typically, new business case analysts still are assigned to certain tasks such as data entry, and policy issue analysts still are responsible for assembling policies.

Some companies tier their new business service by providing the highest level of service from the most experienced and competent new business personnel to the most successful producers. Other companies provide the highest level of service to new producers to entice them to perform well and to train them, even though new business staff members are not responsible for training producers.

Underwriting

The goal of underwriting is neither to deny insurance coverage to proposed insureds who have impairments nor to verify every statement presented on an application. The goal of underwriting is to accept the greatest number of qualified proposed insureds while keeping the insurer financially stable and profitable. Thus, the underwriter analyzes as much information as seems necessary to assess and classify the risk adequately. We cover the assessment and classification of risk in greater detail later in this chapter.

After evaluating the degree of risk represented by a proposed insured, the underwriter decides whether to

- **Issue the policy as applied for.**
- **Rate the policy.** ***Rating*** a policy means approving a higher-than-average risk by charging a higher-than-usual premium rate for the coverage applied for.
- **Modify the extent or amount of coverage.** The insurer may issue a policy with an ***exclusion rider***, also known as an *impairment rider*, which is a policy amendment that specifies that benefits will not be paid for any loss that results from the condition specified in the rider. For example, an individual life insurance policy may exclude death benefits for a death resulting from an aviation accident. The insurer also may issue the insurance with a lower amount of coverage than applied for. Individual medical expense policies can be modified by increasing the amount of eligible expenses the insured must pay, and all individual health policies can be modified by increasing the period of time that an insured must wait before benefits are payable.
- **Decline to issue the policy.**
- **Postpone offering coverage for a specified period of time (usually 6, 12, or 24 months) until the level of risk is reduced to one that the underwriter can evaluate on a reasonable basis.** For example, an underwriter might postpone offering coverage on a proposed insured with pending cardiac surgery until the surgery has been completed and the level of risk can be determined.

Policy Issue

When an underwriter has made a decision to approve a case, he forwards the file—electronically or manually—to the policy issue unit of new business. ***Policy issue*** is the insurance company unit that prepares the insurance contract and facilitates the delivery of the policy to the customer. A policy issue analyst enters the policy's rating and other necessary information into the administration system. Although some insurers allow some producers to print and bind policies, most insurers rely on policy issue analysts to print and bind the correct policy with any required forms, which may include the application and amended illustrations. Some insurers rely on their compliance department to maintain an updated list of all forms required for each product in each jurisdiction.

Most insurers use automated systems to produce policy documents promptly and accurately. In addition, an insurer's administration system typically verifies that the initial premium payment has been received and that all policy requirements have been met. For individual coverages, the policy issue analyst typically then mails the policy to the producer for delivery to the policyowner.

Most companies require the producer to be informed of the underwriting decision *in advance* of the producer's receipt of the policy, especially if the policy is issued other than as applied for. The new business case manager, the underwriter, or a member of the underwriting staff may communicate the underwriting decision to the producer. In some companies, producers may learn the fate of applications through online status reports that the insurer uses to advise producers of activity on all cases they have handled.

Some jurisdictions also require that the insurer inform the applicant in writing of the reason the coverage was rated, modified or declined; even when not required to do so by law, insurers typically send such a letter to the applicant and the proposed insured. Because of privacy concerns, the applicant's letter will contain generic information, such as "The application was declined due to medical reasons." The proposed insured's letter will contain more specific information, such as "The application was declined due to cardiac test results."

If an underwriter rates a policy, adds a rider, or modifies coverage, typically the policy is still issued and delivered to the producer, who then attempts to deliver it to the policyowner. In such a situation, the policyowner usually must sign a document saying that he understands that the policy was not issued as applied for.

The policy issue unit verifies that all delivery requirements are met, such as obtaining a policy delivery receipt and any amendments to the application.

New Business/Underwriting Quality Control

In Chapter 1, we introduced the subject of quality control, which is the process of ensuring that an organization accomplishes its objectives and follows its standards. Insurers employ many quantitative measurements on a regular basis to judge performance in the new business/underwriting area. Some turnaround times averages used to judge the efficiency of new business/underwriting activities are listed in Insight 2.1.

In the underwriting area, audits are a frequently used quality control tool. An ***audit*** is an evaluation of a company's records and operations to ensure the accuracy of the records and the effectiveness of operational policies and procedures. However, the underlying purpose of all underwriting audits is to strengthen risk assessment, classification, and acceptance.

INSIGHT 2.1 New Business/Underwriting Turnaround Times Averages

The following information is taken from the North American version of the 2007 LOMA Service Turnaround Times Survey in which 38 companies participated. The overall averages of the number of calendar days reported on the survey are based on both paper and electronic submission and reporting systems.

Metric	Definition	Overall Average Number of Calendar Days
Mail Times	Average number of calendar days from application date before application is received in home office	5.8
Time to Underwriter	Average number of calendar days from date received in house to first review by underwriting	3.0
Pending Requirements	Average number of calendar days elapsed from first underwriting review to date that last medical requirement is received	21.1
Time to Underwrite Case	Average number of calendar days elapsed from receipt of last underwriting requirement to date underwriting decision is made	2.4
Time to Issue Case	Average number of calendar days elapsed from underwriting approval to date policy is generated	1.7
Delivery Requirements	Average number of calendar days elapsed from date policy is mailed to producer to date all delivery requirements are received back in the home office	18.7
Total Time	Average number of calendar days from application date to the date that all delivery requirements are received back in the home office	48.9

Source: Ted Hatcher and Jim Huffman, *Time Flies When You're Having Fun: Underwriting and Issue Service Times*, Presentation at The Life Insurance Conference, Atlanta, GA, (April 2007). Used with permission;

Audits employ qualitative and quantitative performance measurements, and they can reveal whether underwriters are

- Making appropriate and consistent decisions
- Complying with applicable laws and regulations
- Documenting cases clearly and completely

Audits can be internal or external. An ***internal audit*** is an audit conducted by a company's own staff. Typically, insurers conduct internal audits of their underwriting operations not only to ensure the accuracy of their records and the effectiveness of their procedures and policies, but also to judge the quality of their underwriters' work.

An ***external audit*** is an audit conducted by a third party who is not employed by the company being audited. Insurers are subject to regular external audits by regulatory authorities. One of the most important quality control tools for insurers, though, is the external audit conducted by its reinsurance partners. Reinsurers periodically conduct external audits of most insurers with which they do business, and insurers are subject to separate audits by each reinsurer with which they do business. Reinsurers audit not only an insurer's reinsurance operations, but also an insurer's underwriting and claim operations.

In auditing underwriting, the reinsurer determines whether the insurer is following its practices, policies, and procedures, which the insurer agreed to do when it entered into the reinsurance agreement. Reinsurers audit an underwriting area's compliance with the insurer's age and amount requirements charts and preferred criteria, as well as how often cases are referred to the medical staff. Reinsurers are especially interested in how often underwriters make exceptions to their underwriting guidelines because of a perceived business reason to do so. We discuss reinsurance audits in more detail in Chapter 11.

Underwriting Principles

Risk assessment and risk classification are the foundations of underwriting individual and group insurance. A basic understanding of how an insurer determines its premium structure is essential to understanding how important risk assessment and risk classification are to an insurer.

Insurance company actuaries design premium structures so that the premium rate charged to each insured person or group is based on the amount of risk that each represents relative to others insured by the same product. A ***premium rate*** is a charge per unit of insurance coverage. Note that this term does not refer to the total amount paid for the requested coverage;

rather, it refers to the rate charged for one *unit*, or specific amount of coverage specified in a premium rate. For example, the unit specified in an individual life insurance premium rate typically is $1,000. If an insurer charges individual insureds who exhibit the same amount of risk $3.25 per year per $1,000 of term life insurance coverage, then the premium rate for that coverage is $3.25 and the unit is $1,000 of coverage. The ***annual premium amount*** is the amount the insurer charges annually for the total amount of coverage provided. Thus, if the premium rate for a certain individual term life insurance policy is $3.25 per unit of $1,000 of coverage and a policy provides $50,000 of coverage, the annual premium amount is $162.50.

A person or group that represents a higher amount of risk is charged a proportionately greater premium rate for coverage than a person or group that represents a lesser amount of risk. A ***risk class*** is a group of insureds who represent a similar level of risk to an insurance company. Insureds in the same risk class are charged the same premium rate. When setting premium rates, actuaries also predict and factor into the calculation the probable rate of loss—the *loss rate*—that a given group of insureds will experience. To predict the loss rate for a given group of insureds, the actuary must predict the number and timing of covered losses that are likely to occur in that group of insureds.

Underwriters bear the responsibility of assessing and classifying risks appropriately to ensure that (1) each person or group is placed in the appropriate risk class and (2) the insurer's claim experience is as close as possible to the assumed loss rate used to establish premium rates. Underwriters obtain guidance for risk assessment and risk classification from an insurer's underwriting philosophy and underwriting guidelines.

Risk Assessment

Risk assessment is the process of determining the degree of risk represented by each proposed insured person or group using a number of factors established when the insurance product was designed and priced. Risk assessment for life insurance is particularly concerned with mortality, and risk assessment for health insurance is particularly concerned with morbidity.

- ***Mortality*** is the incidence of death among a specified group of people. A ***mortality rate*** is the rate at which death occurs among a specified group of people during a specified period, typically one year.
- ***Morbidity*** is the incidence of sickness and injury among a specified group of people. A ***morbidity rate*** is the rate at which sickness and injury occur among a specified group of people during a specified period.

Underwriters assess proposed insureds and groups for coverage and evaluate the level of risk by reviewing proposed insureds' risk factors and proposed groups' characteristics. For individual insurance underwriting purposes, a ***risk factor*** is any aspect of a proposed insured's present health, medical history, family history, health habits (such as tobacco use), financial condition, reputation, driving record, criminal record, occupation, or activities that increases the likelihood that the person will suffer a covered loss. In third-party policy situations, the underwriter also takes into account the applicant's financial condition to determine whether the applicant has the ability to pay for the coverage. Individual insurance risk factors typically are categorized as medical risk factors, personal risk factors, and financial risk factors, which are explained in Figure 2.4.

In assessing the degree of risk represented by a proposed insured, an underwriter also considers the possibility of antiselection, which produces a high degree of risk. ***Antiselection*** is the tendency of people who believe they have a greater-than-average likelihood of loss to seek insurance protection to a greater extent than do those who believe they have an average or a less-than-average likelihood of loss. For example, a person who believes she has a serious illness may be more likely to purchase insurance than a person who believes he is in good health.

Another risk factor that underwriters must be aware of is moral hazard. ***Moral hazard*** is a characteristic that exists when the reputation, financial position, or criminal record of an applicant or proposed insured indicates that the person may act dishonestly in the insurance transaction. Moral hazard exists, for example, when a person applies for disability income coverage with the intention of submitting a claim in order to be supported by insurance benefits while not working. If an underwriter suspects that an applicant or proposed insured presents a moral hazard to the insurer, the underwriter may have reason to believe that the applicant or proposed insured has not answered questions on the insurance application honestly. Therefore, the underwriter verifies as much information as possible.

Risk Classification

During risk assessment for individual life insurance and certain types of health insurance, underwriters classify proposed insureds into risk classes. Each insurer defines the parameters of its own risk classes. The terms insurers use for these classes may differ; however, most insurers identify risk classes as preferred, standard, substandard, and declined.

- ***Preferred classes*** designate proposed insureds whose anticipated mortality or morbidity rates are lower than average and who represent the lowest degree of mortality or morbidity risk. Proposed insureds who fall in the preferred classes typically are the healthiest and are charged lower-than-average premium rates.

FIGURE 2.4 Individual Insurance Risk Factors

- A ***medical risk factor*** is a physical or psychological characteristic that may increase the likelihood of loss. For example, a history of emphysema is a medical risk factor because a person who has this disease is more likely to die prematurely or incur increased medical expenses than is a person of the same age and sex who does not have a history of emphysema.

- A ***personal risk factor*** is a lifestyle choice that can significantly affect a person's health or longevity. For example, a proposed insured with a record for reckless driving poses a greater risk than does a proposed insured with a clean driving record.

- A ***financial risk factor*** is financial information that an underwriter considers to determine whether a person is applying for more insurance than he reasonably needs or can afford. For example, if a person is seeking life insurance to replace his income so that his dependents will continue to have financial support after his death, the amount of insurance applied for must bear a reasonable relationship to the amount of income to be replaced. Furthermore, proposed insureds who buy more insurance than they can afford tend to let their policies lapse.

Source: Adapted from Mary C. Bickley et al., *Life and Health Insurance Underwriting*, 2nd ed. [Atlanta: LOMA (Life Office Management Association, Inc.), © 2007], 12. Used with permission; all rights reserved.

- ***Standard classes*** designate proposed insureds whose anticipated mortality or morbidity rates are average. The mortality or morbidity risk of people in standard classes is higher than the mortality or morbidity risk for people in preferred classes, but lower than the mortality or morbidity risk for people in substandard classes. Traditionally, most proposed insureds fell within standard classes; today in some companies, most proposed insureds for individual life insurance fall within preferred classes.

- ***Substandard classes***, also called *special classes*, designate proposed insureds whose anticipated mortality or morbidity rates are higher than average, but who are still considered to be insurable. Many insurers assign to substandard classes those proposed insureds who are recovering from serious illnesses or accidents, whose occupations or avocations produce a significant risk of illness or accident, or who have permanent significant medical conditions. Thus, insurers charge higher premium rates to people in the substandard classes than they charge to people in standard classes.
- The ***declined class*** designates proposed insureds whose anticipated mortality or morbidity rates are so great that the insurer cannot provide coverage at an affordable cost or whose mortality or morbidity risk cannot be predicted because of recent or unusual medical conditions or other risk factors.

Risk assessment for group life or health insurance generally does not involve risk classes.

Underwriting Philosophy and Underwriting Guidelines

As we mentioned in Figure 2.3, an insurer's underwriting philosophy is a set of objectives that guides all of an insurer's underwriting actions, generally reflects the insurer's strategic business goals, and includes its pricing assumptions for products. An insurer's underwriting philosophy describes in general terms the types of risks that the company will and will not accept. An insurer's underwriting philosophy strongly influences its underwriting guidelines.

Underwriting guidelines are general standards that underwriters follow as they establish the level of risk presented by a proposed insured or group. For individual life insurance, an insurer's underwriting guidelines specify the parameters within which an applicant may be assigned to one of the risk classes established for each insurance product. Figure 2.5 sets forth the most common factors considered in underwriting guidelines.

In establishing its underwriting philosophy and underwriting guidelines, an insurer may consider ***industry experience***, which is the collective data about insurance claim experience generated by industry-wide studies. For instance, studies on mortality and morbidity rates, policy lapse rates, impairments, and demographics contribute to industry experience. These studies generally are conducted by large insurers, reinsurance companies, and industry associations. An insurer also uses the experience data from its own insurance products. Industry experience and an insurer's own experience are useful guides for the insurer's future actions and decisions, especially for establishing underwriting requirements, risk classes, and premiums rates for new coverages.

FIGURE 2.5 Factors Typically Considered in Underwriting Guidelines

Individual life and health insurance underwriting guidelines typically focus on factors relating to the proposed insured such as

- Age
- Height and weight
- Blood pressure
- Cholesterol levels
- The presence of specific impairments (such as coronary artery disease, diabetes, and cancer) or ***comorbidity***, which is the simultaneous appearance of two or more unrelated illnesses or conditions that may act in conjunction with one another (such as alcoholism and depression)
- Medical history
- Family medical history
- Financial circumstances
- Occupation
- Indications of specific behaviors (such as tobacco use, substance abuse, poor driving record, and participation in certain avocations)
- The type and amount of coverage applied for
- The purpose of the insurance

Group life and health insurance underwriting guidelines typically focus on factors relating to the group such as the

- Size of the group
- Nature of the group's business
- Employee occupational classes
- Type and amount of coverage requested

Source: Adapted from Mary C. Bickley et al., *Life and Health Insurance Underwriting*, 2nd ed. [Atlanta: LOMA (Life Office Management Association, Inc.), © 2007], 15. Used with permission; all rights reserved.

Because insurers' underwriting guidelines differ, insurers may classify a proposed insured differently from one another. One insurer might classify a risk as preferred, while another classifies it as standard. This disparity in classifications leads some producers to "shop" applications by applying for insurance with several insurers and then seeing which comes back with the best offer, as we mentioned earlier.

As an insurer's experience changes over time, the insurer may modify its underwriting philosophy and underwriting guidelines. Despite changes to the insurer's underwriting philosophy and underwriting guidelines, underwriters always must focus on approving and issuing coverage that is

- Equitable to the insureds
- Equitable to the insurer
- Deliverable by the producer

Equitable to the Insureds

Risk classification maintains equity among insureds and groups by ensuring that each insured or group pays a premium rate that reflects the degree of risk that the insured or group represents. For example, an insurer assigns a person who represents a standard risk to a standard risk class and charges a standard premium rate for a person of that age and sex. The insurer usually assigns a person who represents a significantly greater-than-average risk to a substandard risk class and charges that person a higher premium rate than the standard premium rate. A person who represents an unacceptable level of risk is not issued coverage.

Similarly, an insurer may accept two groups of employees for long-term disability income coverage but may charge the groups different premium rates because the two groups' work involves different levels of risk. By charging higher rates for higher risks and by declining risks it cannot afford to cover, an insurer is better able to protect its long-term financial well-being, thus enabling it to provide coverage for all the risks it does accept.

To maintain equity among insureds, risk assessment and risk classification must be as objective as possible—that is, the risks must be evaluated fairly, without bias or prejudice. Being objective in underwriting is sometimes difficult, however, because an underwriter makes decisions under considerable pressure from producers, actuaries, and company management. Producers want underwriters to issue coverage quickly and assign proposed insureds to preferred or standard classes. Actuaries want underwriters to use risk classification methods that keep actual mortality and morbidity rates very close to those on which the pricing assumptions for the insurance product are based. The insurer's management wants underwriters to accomplish both these objectives—fast issue and favorable mortality and morbidity results—while keeping underwriting costs as low as possible.

Equitable to the Insurer

An insurer's underwriting guidelines and premium rates help ensure that the underwritten coverage will be equitable to the insurer. If an insurer's underwriting guidelines are too strict or its premium rates are not competitive with other companies, insurance producers are less likely to submit applications to the company; and, therefore, the insurer will lose potential premium income. If an insurer's underwriting guidelines are too lax or its premium rates are too low in relation to the level of the risks accepted, over time the insurer might not have sufficient funds to pay all legitimate claims. Eventually, the insurer could become financially impaired or insolvent, which would be inequitable to the insurer, as well as the insureds, policyowners, and shareholders.

Deliverable by the Producer

An individual insurance applicant makes the final decision whether to accept an insurance policy at the time the policy is delivered. If an applicant chooses not to accept a policy when a producer attempts to deliver it, the policy is said to be ***undeliverable***. A policy may be undeliverable because the underwriter has rated the policy or modified the extent or amount of coverage.

For group coverage, the policy is not prepared and delivered until after the sale is finalized, except perhaps for small groups. Thus, although an undeliverable group policy is rare, the same principle applies: a group prospect may refuse to purchase a policy offered with a premium rate greater than or coverage less than anticipated.

One of the greatest challenges facing the underwriter is explaining tactfully and persuasively to a producer the reasons for rating, modifying, or declining an application for insurance so that the producer will be satisfied that the underwriting decision was equitable and in turn will be able to explain the decision to the applicant and place the policy. A successful underwriter not only makes equitable decisions, but also earns the confidence and respect of producers in doing so. Underwriters form a productive relationship with producers by

- Completing work on each application in a timely manner
- Assessing each application in a consistent manner
- Keeping producers informed of progress in cases that are delayed because of requirements for additional information
- Communicating with producers about rating, modifying, or declining an application without disclosing confidential information
- Making use of opportunities to educate producers and their staffs about the insurer's underwriting philosophy and guidelines

Underwriting Organization

The underwriting departments of life and health insurance companies may have variations, but they all are composed of different ranks of underwriters who have different authority levels and are organized in certain ways.

Job Positions

The typical underwriting job positions include underwriting trainee, junior underwriter, intermediate underwriter, senior underwriter, and chief underwriter. An individual is promoted from one rank to another as his knowledge, skills, and abilities improve.

The chief underwriter is the highest ranking underwriter in an insurance company. This individual is an expert in risk selection and also is quite knowledgeable about reinsurance, claim administration, and customer service. The chief underwriter's typical responsibilities include

- Establishing the insurer's underwriting philosophy and guidelines
- Monitoring the cost and quality of underwriting
- Assisting with underwriting large or unusually difficult cases
- Deciding which products, services, and vendors to use
- Overseeing the training of all underwriters
- Reviewing contestable claims
- Serving as a liaison with the insurer's other functional areas, including working with
    - Legal staff to create contract wording
    - Information technology staff to develop underwriting systems
    - Actuaries to establish appropriate pricing, preferred risk criteria, and other product characteristics

The chief underwriter typically also is involved with the negotiation and administration of reinsurance agreements.

Note that in some companies, underwriting managers—rather than the chief underwriter—may have responsibility for workflow and personnel issues. In addition, in some companies, the chief underwriter is the highest-level technical underwriter; the vice president of underwriting has responsibility for managerial and executive duties.

Most insurers also use physicians as underwriting medical experts. They consult with underwriters on cases with unusual or difficult medical histories and may be responsible for developing and updating the insurer's medical underwriting guidelines. Large insurers usually appoint a medical director to lead a medical underwriting staff composed of physicians and other medical personnel.

Authority Levels

In general, an underwriter's authority to approve, rate, or decline applications increases as the underwriter's level of experience increases and as her demonstrated ability and quality of judgment improve. An underwriter's level of authority is specified by (1) the maximum coverage amount that the underwriter can approve and (2) the degree to which the underwriter may rate or decline a policy without approval or review by a more experienced underwriter.

Authority to Approve Specified Coverage Limits

Most individual life insurers develop charts or schedules of underwriting authority to specify the highest amount of coverage that can be approved by each level of underwriter. Figure 2.6 provides an example of authority levels to approve specified coverage limits for individual life insurance and critical illness insurance.

The approval authority of disability income underwriters may be based on the monthly benefit amount applied for. For example, disability income underwriters may have the following authorization limits whether the coverage is to be issued as standard or substandard:

Level of Underwriter	Monthly Benefit Limits
Junior	Up to $2,000
Intermediate	Up to $5,000
Senior	Up to $8,000
Chief	All amounts

Other health insurance underwriters typically have product-type authority limits rather than monetary authority limits.

Authority to Rate or Decline Cases

As Figure 2.6 indicates, some insurers require underwriting decisions to rate a policy, add an exclusion rider, or decline a case to be reviewed and approved by a higher-level underwriter. In other words, the underwriter's authority to approve a case as applied for does not also permit the underwriter to rate, modify, or decline the case without review by a higher-level underwriter.

FIGURE 2.6 Example of Case Authority Levels

Underwriter Level	Approve Standard Cases up to	Approve Substandard Cases or Cases with Exclusions up to	Decline Cases up to
Junior Underwriter with less than 1 year of experience at this level	$100,000	Not authorized without review	Not authorized without review
Junior Underwriter with 1 year or more of experience at this level	$400,000	$100,000	Not authorized without review
Intermediate Underwriter with less than 1 year of experience at this level	$500,000	$200,000	Not authorized without review
Intermediate Underwriter with 1 year or more of experience at this level	$750,000	$500,000	Not authorized without review
Senior Underwriter with less than 1 year of experience at this level	$1,000,000	$500,000	$200,000
Senior Underwriter with 1 year or more of experience at this level	$1,500,000	$1,000,000	$500,000
Chief Underwriter	ALL AMOUNTS	ALL AMOUNTS	ALL AMOUNTS

Note: The dollar amounts stated in the figure are used for illustration only. Specific amounts and the number of levels of coverage approval authority vary from one insurer to another.

In some insurance companies, all rated and declined cases are reviewed by an underwriter one level higher than the original underwriter. Other insurers require the chief underwriter to perform this kind of review. The review is performed to

- Ensure the appropriateness of the original underwriting decision
- Ensure the consistency of underwriting actions
- Evaluate the underwriter's job performance
- Train the underwriter
- Enhance producers' confidence in the insurer's underwriting practices

Organizational Systems

Some insurers establish separate underwriting units to handle various types of applications—life, medical expense, disability income, and other types of coverage. For individual coverages, insurers may organize the work within these units according to a case assignment system, a work division system, or a combination of the two systems. Group insurers may organize their underwriting departments by case size, geographic location, or producer. Typically, senior group underwriters will work on larger, more complex groups. Some group underwriting departments prefer to assign groups randomly to give their group underwriters a wide variety of experience.

Figure 2.7 outlines some organizational systems for organizing underwriting of individual coverages. Note that the organization of the underwriting function comes in dozens of permutations, not all of which are listed here.

Case Assisgnment System

A ***case assignment system*** is a method of assigning cases to underwriters based on the characteristics of the case. The benefit of this system is that it enables an underwriter to specialize in certain types of cases. The basis used to assign case files to underwriters varies depending on the size of the insurer, the number of applications usually received, and the difficulty of the cases to be underwritten.

An advantage of the case assignment system is that the underwriters may become more productive and effective through specialization. A drawback of this system is that underwriters can become well informed about only their own areas of specialization. As a result, employees' vacations and absences may cause other underwriters to work temporarily—and probably less productively—with "unfamiliar" cases. Insurers control this problem, however, by periodic rotation of assignments and cross-training so that several underwriters become familiar with the characteristics of other types of cases.

Type of Application or Policy Change. When cases are based on the type of application or policy change requested—usually an increase in the coverage amount or the addition of a rider—one life insurance underwriter may be assigned only nonmedical applications that don't require medical proof

FIGURE 2.7 Systems for Organizing Individual Underwriting

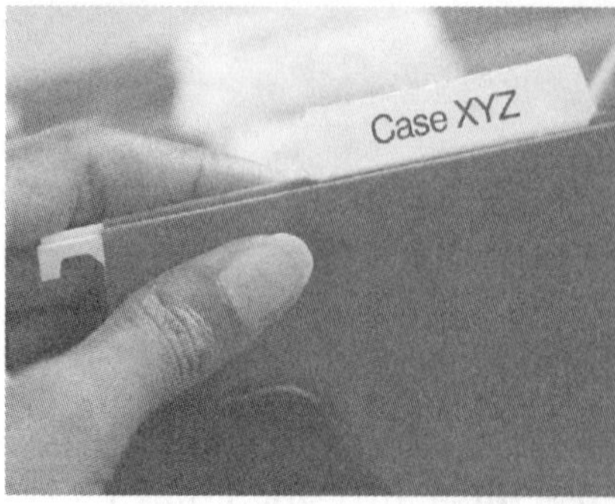

Case Assignment System

- Type of application or policy change
- Geographic origin
- Producer submitting application

Work Division System

- Independent underwriting
- Team underwriting
- Jet unit underwriting
- Committee underwriting

of insurability, a second underwriter may handle only applications requiring a medical examination report, and a third underwriter may be responsible only for requests for accidental death benefit coverage.

Medical expense insurers typically assign cases to underwriters based on the type of coverage involved. For example, junior underwriters usually will handle accident only, hospital and surgical, or specified benefit policies, while senior underwriters will handle major medical policies.

Geographic Origin. If the geographic origin of the application is the basis of an insurer's case assignment system, the underwriting department is divided into regional sections, with each section handling all business submitted from a specific geographic area. Case assignment on the basis of geographic origin enables underwriters to become more knowledgeable about legislative and regulatory requirements within specific jurisdictions, learn more about impairments or occupations that may be peculiar to a certain geographic region, and operate in the same time zones as their customers.

Producer Submitting Application. Alternatively, some insurers assign specific producers to each underwriter, regardless of the producers' geographic locations. This case assignment method enables an underwriter to become familiar with the quality of the producers' business and develop effective working relationships with the producers.

Work Division System

A ***work division system*** is a method of assigning cases to underwriters that divides cases according to the person or group that underwrites them.

Independent Underwriting. In many insurance companies, applications are assigned according to a work division system known as ***independent underwriting*** in which underwriters work alone to assess each risk. Some insurers assign only cases requiring extensive research to independent underwriters.

Team Underwriting. ***Team underwriting*** is a work division system in which underwriters are divided into small groups. The team usually includes one or more senior underwriters who handle large-amount or complex cases and one or more lower-level underwriters who handle simpler cases.

Team underwriting usually enables team members to exercise considerable autonomy in making underwriting decisions. Members of the team are responsible for setting work assignments and establishing priorities for themselves. Team members make recommendations to the supervisor or chief underwriter on such issues as team training and development, work and vacation schedules, solutions to production problems, and conflict resolution. Compared to other underwriting methods, team underwriting can be more cost effective and can provide producers with faster service because if one team member is out of the office, another team member can handle the case.

Jet Unit Underwriting. Designed to underwrite simple cases quickly, ***jet unit underwriting*** is a work division system in which a separate group of employees is authorized to approve certain types of individual insurance applications for immediate policy issue. For example, individual life insurance applications with the following characteristics are typically eligible for consideration by a jet unit:

- Proposed insured's age, height, and weight are within specified ranges
- Proposed insured has no significant health problems
- Proposed insured has an acceptable occupation
- Application is being made for an amount of insurance below a specified limit, depending on the proposed insured's age and the insurer's requirements
- Applicant has not made an unusual beneficiary designation
- Applicant has answered all questions on the application
- Insurer's records contain no adverse underwriting information on the proposed insured

A jet unit usually is not authorized to request further information or to rate or decline an application except for certain specified impairments. All applications that are not issued for immediate coverage are sent from the jet unit to other underwriters, who gather additional information and make the final decisions on the cases.

The jet issue process can take only days when completed manually and even less when done electronically by a jet issue system. However, some insurers are able to underwrite policies in only minutes by engaging in ***real-time underwriting***, or *instant-issue underwriting*, which is a straight through processing system that evaluates insurance applications quickly and almost instantly provides the applicant or producer with an underwriting decision. With real-time underwriting, applications typically are submitted over the Internet.

Committee Underwriting. Cases involving large coverage amounts or special problems, such as unusual occupations, may require committee evaluation. ***Committee underwriting*** is a work division system in which a committee of highly qualified people from inside and outside the underwriting function is called together for case assessment.

Usually the committee is composed of the chief underwriter, the medical director, and representatives from the legal and actuarial functions. By pooling their technical expertise, the committee members can reach an appropriate decision on cases that otherwise might have to be passed from person to person in a less efficient manner.

Combination System

Some insurers combine a case assignment system with a work division system. For example, a jet unit may handle only nonmedical applications that don't require medical proof of insurability, or an underwriting team may handle only term life insurance applications from a specific geographic area or certain producer.

Key Terms

field underwriting
agent's statement
field underwriting manual
age and amount requirements chart
impairment guide
impairment
underwriting philosophy
electronic application system
electronic signature
Electronic Signatures in Global and National Commerce (E-SIGN) Act
teleunderwriting
rating
exclusion rider
policy issue
audit
internal audit
external audit
premium rate
annual premium amount
risk class
risk assessment
mortality
mortality rate
morbidity
morbidity rate
risk factor
antiselection
moral hazard
preferred class
medical risk factor
personal risk factor
financial risk factor
standard class
substandard class
declined class
underwriting guidelines
industry experience
comorbidity
undeliverable
case assignment system
work division system
independent underwriting
team underwriting
jet unit underwriting
real-time underwriting
committee underwriting

Endnote

1. This section is adapted from Mark Adel and Nicholas L. Desoutter, *Annuity Systems and Administration*, 2nd ed. [Atlanta: LOMA (Life Office Management Association, Inc.), © 2004], 197–198. Used with permission; all rights reserved.

chapter 3

Legal Aspects of Underwriting

Outline

Valid Contract Requirements
Mutual Assent
Legally Adequate Consideration
Contractual Capacity
Lawful Purpose

Regulatory Compliance Issues Affecting Individual Insurance Underwriting
Privacy Protection
Nondiscrimination
Medical Testing
Replacements
Money Laundering and Financing Terrorists

Regulatory Compliance Issues Affecting Group Insurance Underwriting
U.S. State Regulatory Requirements
U.S. Federal Regulatory Requirements
Canadian Regulatory Requirements

Underwriting Standards
Reviewing Applications for Proper Completion
Processing Applications Promptly
Documenting Underwriting

Learning Objectives

After studying this chapter, you should be able to…

- Define the terms *valid contract*, *void contract*, and *voidable contract* and identify the requirements for the creation of a valid insurance contract
- Distinguish between binding insurance receipts and conditional premium receipts
- Describe how U.S. and Canadian federal, state, and provincial governments regulate privacy
- Describe how U.S. and Canadian federal, state, and provincial governments regulate discrimination, medical testing, replacements, money laundering, and financing terrorists during the individual life and health insurance underwriting process
- Describe how U.S. and Canadian federal, state, and provincial governments regulate group life and health insurance policies during the underwriting process
- Recognize the importance of an underwriter's responsibility to review applications, act promptly on applications, and document underwriting

During most of the underwriting process, underwriters focus on evaluating the insurability of the proposed insured—who typically is the applicant for insurance—or on the characteristics of the proposed group. However, in reviewing applications, underwriters also must take into account certain legal considerations. Underwriters must

- Ensure that legal requirements for the formation of a valid contract are met
- Adhere to the requirements of various laws and regulations
- Abide by certain standards to ensure that proposed risks are evaluated fairly and the company's interests are protected

In this chapter, we address these legal aspects of underwriting.[1]

Valid Contract Requirements

An insurance policy is a contract between the insurer that issued the policy and the individual or organization that purchased the policy. A ***contract*** is a legally enforceable agreement between two or more parties. When an insurer issues an insurance policy, the insurer makes a contractual promise to pay a stated benefit amount if the event insured against occurs while the policy is in force. Underwriting is an important part of the process of forming an insurance contract, and an underwriter's actions can affect the insurer's contractual rights and duties.

Not all contracts are legally enforceable. In describing the legal status of a contract, the words *valid*, *void*, and *voidable* often are used. These terms are defined in Figure 3.1.

In most jurisdictions in the United States and Canada, to form a valid insurance contract, the parties must

- Mutually assent (agree) to the terms of the contract
- Exchange legally adequate consideration
- Have contractual capacity
- Form the contract for a lawful purpose

An underwriter must ensure that these requirements are met before a policy is issued to either an individual or a group. The parties to a group contract meet these requirements in much the same way as the parties to an individual contract. The primary difference is in how the lawful purpose requirement is met, as we note later in this section.

FIGURE 3.1 Valid, Void, and Voidable Contracts

- ***Valid contract.*** A contract that satisfies all legal requirements and, thus, is enforceable at law.
- ***Void contract.*** A contract that does not satisfy one or more of the legal requirements to create a valid contract and, thus, is never enforceable at law. The term *void* is used in law to describe something that was never valid.
- ***Voidable contract.*** A contract under which a party has the right to avoid his obligations under the contract without incurring legal liability.

Source: Reprinted from Mary C. Bickley et al., *Life and Health Insurance Underwriting*, 2nd ed. [Atlanta: LOMA (Life Office Management Association, Inc.), © 2007], 52. Used with permission; all rights reserved.

Mutual Assent

Mutual assent requires that the parties (1) intend to be bound to the contract's terms and (2) clearly show the intent to be bound by making some outward expression of that intent. The parties show their mutual assent to a contract when one party makes a definite offer to contract and the other party accepts that offer unconditionally. As a general rule, applicants for individual insurance make an offer to enter into an insurance contract by completing an application for insurance and submitting it to an insurer along with payment of the initial premium. The insurer accepts an applicant's offer by (1) issuing a policy that contains the same terms as those contemplated by the applicant's offer and (2) delivering the policy to the applicant, who then becomes the policyowner, or to the individual the applicant has named as the policyowner.

When an underwriter approves an application for individual insurance in a manner that is other than the coverage was applied for, the insurer has rejected the applicant's offer and made a counteroffer to the applicant. The applicant accepts the insurer's counteroffer by accepting delivery of the policy and paying any additional premium, if applicable. Underwriters may be involved in this process of offer and acceptance, especially with large-amount individual life insurance policies. We discuss the process for group policies in Chapter 8.

Legally Adequate Consideration

Consideration is whatever a promisor asks for and receives in exchange for making a contractual promise. As a general rule, consideration is legally adequate if it was bargained for and exchanged between the parties. When an insurer issues an insurance policy, the insurer makes a legally enforceable promise to pay policy benefits if the event insured against occurs while the policy is in force. The applicant gives the insurer the application and initial premium as consideration in exchange for the insurer's promise.

If the applicant for an individual policy pays the initial premium with the application, the insurer generally issues the applicant a ***premium receipt***, which is a written acknowledgment that an insurer has received the initial premium submitted with an application for insurance. Insurers issue premium receipts with individual life insurance applications more often than with individual health insurance applications. Figure 3.2 explains the various types of premium receipts issued by insurers in the United States.

Underwriters must be aware of the type of premium receipt issued with a given application and the amount of coverage provided by such a receipt. Some insurers use the same type of premium receipt for all types of policy applications, and other companies use specific premium receipts with specific policy applications.

To protect the insurer against liability for a risk it otherwise would not have accepted, the underwriter must make an underwriting decision quickly on a proposed insured covered under the terms of a premium receipt. If the underwriter's decision is to decline an application, the insurer returns the initial premium paid and coverage under the premium receipt terminates.

Contractual Capacity

The parties to a contract must have ***contractual capacity***—the legal capability to make a contract—for the contract to be binding. Insurers that are licensed and authorized to conduct an insurance business by the appropriate regulatory authority have the contractual capacity to enter into insurance contracts. Individuals also are presumed to have the legal capacity to enter into a valid contract, but most jurisdictions limit the contractual capacity of individuals who (1) are minors or (2) lack mental capacity. Organizations that have been created in accordance with the laws of the applicable jurisdiction are presumed to have contractual capacity to apply for insurance on the life of an individual or for group life or health insurance coverage. If any question arises as to the contractual capacity of an organization or individual, the underwriter must investigate.

Minors

A ***minor*** is a person who has not attained the age of majority, which is the age at which a person is given by law the rights and responsibilities of an adult. Individuals generally have the capacity to enter into contracts when they reach the age of majority. In most jurisdictions, including most states of the United States, the age of majority is 18. In Canada, the age of majority in the various provinces and territories is fairly evenly split between 18 and 19.

FIGURE 3.2 Premium Receipts in the United States

When an applicant pays the initial premium with the application, the insurance producer gives the applicant a premium receipt that acknowledges the premium payment and often includes a ***temporary insurance agreement (TIA)***, which is a contract between the insurer and the applicant that provides temporary coverage on the proposed insured before a policy is issued and delivered, although such coverage may be subject to certain conditions.

A premium receipt that provides temporary insurance coverage states when that coverage becomes effective, the conditions that must be met for the coverage to become effective, and when the coverage will end. Premium receipts also usually state that the temporary insurance coverage is provided subject to the terms for the insurance policy for which the applicant applied. For example, if the policy applied for contains a suicide exclusion provision, then the temporary insurance agreement also contains that suicide exclusion provision, even if the premium receipt is silent concerning suicide. By contrast, when the terms of a premium receipt conflict with the terms of the policy applied for, then the terms of the premium receipt control. For example, premium receipts often limit the amount of life insurance benefits available to a stated dollar amount, which is often less than the amount of insurance that the applicant applied for. If the proposed insured dies while insured under a temporary insurance agreement, the amount of the death benefit payable is limited to the amount specified in the premium receipt.

Three basic types of premium receipts with temporary insurance agreements are issued: binding premium receipts, insurability premium receipts, and approval premium receipts.

A ***binding premium receipt*** provides temporary insurance coverage that becomes effective from the time the applicant receives the receipt. Temporary coverage under a binding premium receipt generally remains effective until the earliest of the following occurrences:

- The insurer issues the applicant a policy
- The insurer declines the application
- The insurer terminates or suspends coverage under the receipt
- A specified time—usually 45 to 60 days—expires

Insurability premium receipts and approval premium receipts are known as ***conditional premium receipts*** because they specify certain conditions that must be met before the temporary insurance coverage provided by the receipt becomes effective.

- An ***approval premium receipt*** is a conditional premium receipt that provides temporary insurance coverage only when the insurer approves the proposed insured as a standard or better-than-average risk. If the insurer approves the risk, the insurance coverage is effective on the date of the insurer's approval. If the proposed insured dies before the application is approved, the receipt provides no coverage. U.S. insurers rarely issue approval premium receipts.
- An ***insurability premium receipt*** is a conditional premium receipt that provides temporary insurance coverage on condition that the insurer finds that the proposed insured was insurable as a standard risk on a certain date specified in the premium receipt. The date is typically that of the premium receipt, application, or medical examination. Should a proposed insured die before the application is approved, the insurer completes the underwriting process as if the proposed insured were still alive. If the underwriter determines that the proposed insured was insurable at the time specified in the receipt, then a death benefit is payable.

Source: Adapted from Harriett E. Jones, *Business Law for Financial Services Professionals* [Atlanta: LOMA (Life Office Management Association, Inc.), © 2004], 206-209. Used with permission; all rights reserved.

With a few exceptions, a contract entered into by a minor is voidable by the minor. Thus, if an insurer sells an insurance policy to a person who is younger than the permissible age to purchase insurance, the insurer has to provide the promised insurance protection. The minor policyowner, however, can avoid the insurance contract; and the insurer would have to return the premiums the minor policyowner paid on the policy. Thus, the insurer will have provided insurance protection, yet will forgo receiving premiums for providing that coverage.

Most Canadian provinces have enacted laws that allow minors of a stated minimum age—typically 16—to enter into valid insurance contracts that they cannot avoid. Some jurisdictions in the United States have enacted such laws that allow minors who are 16, 15, and sometimes even younger to enter into enforceable life insurance contracts, subject to certain conditions. For example, some states permit minors to purchase life and health insurance on their own lives, while other states permit minors to purchase life and health insurance on any individual in whose life or health the minor has an insurable interest. (We discuss insurable interest in the next section.) In addition, laws vary as to who may be named as the beneficiary of a life insurance policy purchased by a minor on her own life. For example, many states require the beneficiary of such a policy to be the minor's parent, spouse, child, brother, or sister.

Mental Incapacity

A person has the required mental capacity to contract if he understands the nature of the agreement and the legal effect of entering into the agreement. Whether a person lacks such capacity is a question of fact that must be decided on a case-by-case basis. Two situations arise in which mental capacity affects a person's contractual capacity.

- A contract entered into by a person who has been declared insane or mentally incompetent by a court is usually void.
- A contract entered into by someone whose mental competence is impaired but who has not been declared insane or mentally incompetent by a court is generally voidable by the impaired person. If the person later regains mental competence, she may either avoid the contract or require that it be carried out. The other party to the contract does not have the right to avoid the contract and must carry out its terms if required to do so. For example, a person who is drugged may be mentally impaired and may enter into a contract that she can later avoid, but the other party must abide by the terms of the contract.

Although cases in which an applicant for insurance lacks mental capacity are rare, producers and underwriters must be alert for them.

Lawful Purpose

If an agreement's purpose is illegal or against public policy, the agreement is void. Laws in each jurisdiction define the agreements that are illegal; in most jurisdictions, wagering agreements are illegal. A ***wagering agreement*** is an agreement under which either party may gain or lose depending on the outcome of an uncertain event, such as the timing of an individual's death.

To guard against the purchase of insurance contracts as wagering agreements that allow a person to profit from another person's death, laws in many jurisdictions impose an insurable interest requirement on the issuance of individual insurance. An ***insurable interest*** exists when a person is likely to suffer a genuine loss or detriment should the event insured against occur. Group life and health insurance contracts are not required to meet the insurable interest requirement because the group policyholder's interest in the contract does not induce wagering as does a policyowner's interest in an individual insurance contract. The lawful purpose requirement for a group insurance contract is met if the group policyholder purchases the coverage to provide a benefit to covered group members.

For an individual insurance contract to be valid, an insurable interest must exist at the time of contracting. If an insurer issues an individual insurance policy and the policyowner—and in some cases, the beneficiary—did not in fact have an insurable interest in the insured when the contract was created, then the agreement is void. Most jurisdictions do not require an insurable interest to continue throughout the life of the policy. For example, if spouses purchase life insurance policies on each other's lives and then the spouses subsequently divorce, the policies typically are not voided at the time of the divorce because of lack of insurable interest.

Insurable interest requirements vary depending on whether a policy insures the policyowner or someone other than the policyowner. According to laws in most jurisdictions, a person has an unlimited insurable interest in his own life. Thus, an applicant who seeks to insure his own life may lawfully name anyone he wishes as beneficiary. Even though the beneficiary's insurable interest is not required by law when a person seeks to insure his own life, insurers' underwriting guidelines typically require the proposed beneficiary to have an insurable interest in the proposed insured's life in all cases.

In the case of a third-party policy, the applicant generally must provide the insurer with evidence that she has an insurable interest in the proposed insured's life. An insurable interest is presumed to exist

- Between certain close family members, such as a proposed insured's spouse, mother, father, child, grandparent, grandchild, brother, and sister. For example, a sibling would have an insurable interest in a proposed insured, but an aunt, uncle, cousin, or in-law would not have an insurable interest.

- When someone has a financial interest in the continued life of the insured.

Typically, a person who purchases insurance on another's life names herself as the policy beneficiary. Thus, the person who will benefit from the policy after the insured's death is also the policyowner. When an applicant for a third-party policy has an insurable interest in the proposed insured's life and has named herself as the policy beneficiary, then the insurable interest requirement is met. However, if the applicant for a third-party policy names another person as the policy beneficiary, then laws in many jurisdictions require both the applicant and the person named as policy beneficiary to have an insurable interest in the proposed insured's life. Insurers carefully scrutinize applications for third-party coverage for insurable interest.

Insurable interest requirements are included in underwriting guidelines, and underwriters verify that the insurable interest requirement is met before they issue a policy. In fact, many insurers' underwriting guidelines impose insurable interest requirements that are more stringent than the requirements imposed by law. An insurer that fails to exercise reasonable care in evaluating whether the insurable interest requirement is met for a given policy could be subject to liability for any harm that befalls an insured as a result of that failure.

In addition to imposing an insurable interest requirement, many jurisdictions, including most states in the United States, require a proposed insured to consent to the issuance of a policy on his life. Without such consent, a policy taken out on the life of another person is void. As an exception to this rule, a parent generally may insure the life of a minor child without the child's consent. A few states permit one spouse to insure the life of another spouse without obtaining the insured's consent.

Regulatory Compliance Issues Affecting Individual Insurance Underwriting

Laws in many countries impose requirements that affect the life and health insurance underwriting process. In this section, we discuss such laws concerning privacy protection, nondiscrimination, medical testing, replacements, money laundering, and financing terrorists. We focus on U.S. and Canadian federal, state, and provincial laws and regulations. Insight 3.1 briefly introduces the insurance regulatory systems in the United States and Canada.

INSIGHT 3.1 Insurance Regulatory Systems

Insurance Regulation in the United States

The U.S. federal government has constitutional authority to regulate the business of insurance, but Congress has agreed that the states should have primary authority to regulate insurance as long as Congress finds such state regulation to be adequate. Although the states have primary authority, Congress has enacted a number of laws and regulations that regulate how all businesses—including insurers—conduct business.

Each state has established an administrative agency, often referred to as the *state insurance department*, that is responsible for enforcing the state insurance laws and regulations and making sure that insurers conducting business within the state comply with all state insurance laws and regulations. The head of the state insurance department typically is referred to as the *insurance commissioner*.

Insurance laws and regulations vary from state to state; however, laws in the states are somewhat consistent because they often are based on model laws adopted by the ***National Association of Insurance Commissioners (NAIC)***, which is a private, nonprofit association of insurance commissioners from all 50 states and the District of Columbia that promotes uniformity of state insurance regulation within the United States. The NAIC adopts model laws and regulations that each state can choose to adopt, use as the basis for its own laws and regulations, or ignore altogether. A ***model law*** is a sample law that legislatures are encouraged to enact. A ***model regulation*** is a sample regulation that state insurance departments are encouraged to adopt.

Insurance Regulation in Canada

In Canada, constitutional authority to regulate insurance is shared between the federal and provincial governments. The federal government has the authority to incorporate insurers that conduct business in more than one province. The federal ***Office of the Superintendent of Financial Institutions (OSFI)*** regulates the solvency of federally incorporated insurers, insurers incorporated in other countries, and specified provincially incorporated insurers in accordance with the federal *Insurance Companies Act*.

The provincial governments have the authority to incorporate insurers that operate only in that province. In addition to overseeing the solvency of provincially incorporated insurers, each provincial government regulates how all insurers—federally and provincially incorporated—and producers carry on business within the provinces. However, just as in the United States, the Canadian federal government has enacted a number of laws that regulate how all businesses—including insurers—conduct business.

Each province has established an executive agency that is responsible for administering the province's insurance laws and regulations, sometimes in conjunction with laws pertaining to all other financial institutions. The titles of these agencies vary widely, although the most common are variations of *Financial Services Commission* and *Office of the Superintendent of Insurance*. The most common variations on the titles of the individuals who head these offices are *Superintendent of Financial Services* and *Superintendent of Insurance*.

The provincial regulators have formed a body known as the ***Canadian Council of Insurance Regulators (CCIR)*** that recommends uniform insurance legislation to the provincial legislatures. The ***Canadian Life and Health Insurance Association (CLHIA)***, a voluntary association with member companies that account for 99 percent of Canada's life and health insurance business, adopts guidelines—referred to as the ***CLHIA Guidelines***—with which member companies are expected to comply although they are not law.

In all provinces and territories of Canada except Quebec, laws based on the model ***Uniform Life Insurance Act (Uniform Act)*** govern both individual and group life insurance contracts,

continued on next page...

INSIGHT 3.1 *continued* **Insurance Regulatory Systems**

while the model ***Uniform Accident and Sickness Insurance Act*** governs both individual and group health insurance contracts. Quebec's insurance laws are similar to those in the other provinces.

Canadian residents receive health insurance benefits through government-mandated insurance programs. The federal ***Canada Health Act*** affirms the Canadian government's commitment to providing a universal, accessible, comprehensive, portable, and publicly administered health insurance system.[3] Provinces that establish medical expense insurance plans that meet conditions set out in the act qualify to receive federal funding for their plans.

For medical expense coverage, Canadian provinces require that, if a certain medical service or treatment is covered under the provincial health care plan, then group or individual private insurance plans cannot offer benefits for that service or treatment. For instance, if a provincial health care plan provided coverage for inpatient hospital services such as radiological procedures, an insurer could not offer coverage for those procedures under a private health care plan. An insurer can offer only supplemental health coverage for services that are not covered—or not fully covered—by the government plan. However, in 2005, in a case arising from Quebec, the Supreme Court of Canada ruled that the prohibition on private insurance for the payment of medical or hospital services that are covered under the province's health care plan contravened Quebec's Charter of Human Rights and Freedoms.[4] As a result, some observers are of the view that the use of private insurance to cover health care benefits is likely to expand in the future.

Source: Adapted from Mary C. Bickley et al., *Life and Health Insurance Underwriting*, 2nd ed. [Atlanta: LOMA (Life Office Management Association, Inc.), © 2007], 61.

Privacy Protection

To conduct business, insurers need to acquire, store, and use a great deal of personal information about their customers. Such personal information can include facts about a person's health, medical history, financial situation, credit history, occupation, and avocations. To protect the privacy of customers and the confidentiality of personal information, most jurisdictions have passed laws regulating the use and disclosure of that information. Insurance underwriting is subject to these laws.

U.S. Federal Fair Credit Reporting Act

When assessing the risk represented by a proposed insured, an underwriter often obtains a consumer report. The U.S. federal ***Fair Credit Reporting Act (FCRA)*** regulates the reporting and use of consumer information and seeks to ensure that consumer reports contain only accurate, relevant, and recent information.[2] For purposes of the FCRA, a ***consumer report*** is any communication of information by a consumer reporting agency that (1) bears on a consumer's creditworthiness, credit standing, credit capacity, character, general reputation, personal characteristics, or mode of living and (2) is used or collected as a factor in establishing a consumer's eligibility for insurance or credit. A ***consumer reporting agency*** is a private business that assembles or evaluates information on consumers and furnishes consumer reports to third parties in exchange for a fee. Under the FCRA, only individuals are considered to be consumers; corporations and other types of businesses are not protected by this act.

Consumer reporting agencies usually obtain information contained in a consumer report directly from the consumer or his creditors. An ***investigative consumer report*** is a consumer report that contains information obtained through personal interviews with an individual's neighbors, friends, associates, or others who may have information about the individual.

The FCRA regulates not only consumer reporting agencies, but also third parties that obtain consumer reports, such as insurance companies and banks. To comply with FCRA requirements regarding investigative consumer reports, underwriters must notify an applicant and the proposed insured that this type of report may be ordered. This "pre-notice" must

- Be in writing
- Be mailed or otherwise delivered to the applicant no later than three days after the date on which the report was first requested
- Include a statement informing the applicant of her right to obtain a report on the nature and scope of the investigation

The insurer must respond no later than five days after receiving a request from the applicant regarding the nature and scope of the investigation. In addition, when an insurer takes an adverse action based on information contained in any consumer report, the insurer must send a "post-notice" to the applicant and insured notifying them of

- The name, address, and telephone number of the consumer reporting agency that provided the consumer report to the insurer
- Her right to obtain a free copy of the consumer report from the consumer reporting agency
- Her right to dispute with the consumer reporting agency the accuracy or completeness of any information contained in the consumer report
- The fact that the consumer reporting agency did not make the adverse decision and is unable to inform the consumer why the adverse decision was made

For insurance purposes, an ***adverse action*** means a denial or revocation of insurance coverage, a change in the terms of existing insurance coverage, or a refusal to grant insurance in substantially the amount or on substantially the terms requested.

In 2003, the U.S. federal Fair and Accurate Credit Transactions Act (FACTA) was enacted.[5] This law amends the FCRA and places new responsibilities on insurers who order consumer credit reports on applicants. Insurers now must allow customers an opportunity to opt out of the sharing of information in consumer reports with the insurer's affiliates. Insurers also must safeguard consumer information when it is being disposed of to help prevent identity theft.

U.S. Federal Health Insurance Portability and Accountability Act

The ***Health Insurance Portability and Accountability Act (HIPAA)*** is U.S. federal legislation that sets forth requirements that insurers, managed care organizations, and employer-sponsored group insurance plans must meet in providing individual and group medical expense insurance coverage.[6] The following HIPAA provisions are designed to ensure the privacy of protected health information:

- Health care providers must obtain an individual's written consent to use health information for purposes of treatment, payment, or health care; but health insurers can use protected information for their own operations without obtaining the individual's consent.
- Sharing of health information without the individual's written consent generally is prohibited for purposes other than treatment, payment, or health care operations.
- Individuals are allowed to request that restrictions be placed on access to and use of their health information.

Entities subject to HIPAA's provisions must establish privacy policies and procedures and must institute ongoing training programs for employees. In addition, covered entities must implement administrative, physical, and technical safeguards, as well as relevant policies and procedures to assure the confidentiality and security of individually identifiable health information that is electronically maintained or used in an electronic transmission. Underwriters must comply with the insurer's policies, procedures, and safeguards.

Life and health insurers typically ask proposed insureds to sign a HIPAA-compliant authorization for the release of health-related information at the time of application, but no later than when the underwriter must order medical information. This HIPAA authorization is separate from the application's general authorization and is not part of the application. Note that under HIPAA, the insurer is restricted in what can be disclosed to the producer and applicant.

U.S. Federal Gramm-Leach-Bliley Act

The ***Gramm-Leach-Bliley (GLB) Act*** is U.S. federal legislation that removed many of the barriers to affiliations among institutions in the various segments of the financial services industry.[7] A purported benefit of the GLB Act is the ability of various industry segments to share customer information. However, the GLB Act requires financial institutions, including insurance companies, to respect customers' privacy and to protect the security and confidentiality of those customers' nonpublic personal information. Under the GLB Act, ***nonpublic personal information*** is personally identifiable information about a consumer that is not publicly available.

Subject to certain exceptions, the GLB requires insurers to

- Disclose their policies for obtaining and sharing customers' nonpublic personal information at the beginning of the relationship and at least annually thereafter
- Provide the customer with an opportunity to opt out of information sharing with nonaffiliated third parties
- Explain to the customer how to opt out of the information sharing
- Maintain policies to protect the security and confidentiality of nonpublic information

Note that the GLB Act does not restrict insurers from sharing information with affiliated parties that are related to the insurer by common ownership or control.

U.S. State Laws and Regulations

Insurance privacy laws in many states are based on the NAIC's ***Insurance Information and Privacy Protection Model Act (Model Privacy Act)***, which establishes standards for the collection, use, and disclosure of information gathered in connection with insurance transactions. Note the Model Privacy Act applies only to personal insurance and not to insurance for business or professional needs, and the act primarily governs underwriting and claim evaluation. Figure 3.3 sets forth the Model Privacy Act's requirements on insurers.

The privacy provisions of the GLB Act preempt state privacy laws unless a state's laws provide for stricter protections of the privacy of consumer information than does the GLB Act. In response to the GLB Act, some states amended their privacy laws by including additional provisions consistent with the GLB Act. Other states responded by adopting new regulations based on the NAIC's ***Privacy of Consumer Financial and Health Information Regulation (Model Privacy Regulation)***, which includes requirements similar to those contained in the GLB Act, including limits on an insurer's right to disclose nonpublic personal information about a consumer without the consumer's consent.

Figure 3.3 Model Privacy Act's Privacy Requirements

An insurer must provide a consumer with a written notice of the insurer's information practices when the insurer (1) intends to collect information about a consumer who has applied for insurance, policy renewal, or policy reinstatement and (2) will collect that information from sources other than the consumer or public records.

- With a few exceptions, an insurer may disclose personal or privileged information only if it first obtains the individual's written authorization. For purposes of the Model Privacy Act, ***personal information*** is information gathered about an individual in connection with an insurance transaction and from which judgments can be made about the individual's personal characteristics, such as character, habits, finances, credit, and health. ***Privileged information*** is information that relates to either an insurance claim or a court proceeding.
- Insurers may use investigative consumer reports in connection with insurance transactions, but they must inform the individual who is the subject of the report that he may request to be interviewed in connection with the investigative consumer report and may obtain a copy of the report.
- With one exception, insurers are prohibited from conducting pretext interviews in connection with insurance transactions. A ***pretext interview*** is an interview in which one person attempts to gain information from another person by (1) pretending to be someone he is not, (2) pretending to represent someone he does not represent, (3) refusing to identify himself, or (4) misrepresenting the purpose of the interview. The exception is that, within stated limits, an insurer may conduct pretext interviews during the investigation of a claim only if the insurer has a reasonable basis to suspect criminal activity, fraud, or material misrepresentation in connection with the claim.
- Individuals have the right to access recorded personal information that an insurer has collected about them by submitting a written request to the insurer. An insurer that receives such a written request has 30 days in which to (1) provide the information to the individual, (2) identify the persons to whom the information has been disclosed, and (3) inform the individual how to request that the information be corrected, amended, or deleted.

Canadian Federal and Provincial Laws

In Canada, the federal ***Personal Information Protection and Electronics Document Act (PIPEDA)*** governs the collection, use, and disclosure of personal information by organizations in the private sector.[8] Figure 3.4 sets forth the principles of PIPEDA.

Like other commercial organizations, insurance companies are governed by PIPEDA, except in Quebec, British Columbia, and Alberta, where substantially similar provincial privacy legislation applies. In addition, some provinces have enacted laws dealing specifically with the collection, use, and disclosure of health information by health care organizations. These laws set forth rules that apply when such organizations disclose health information to other organizations, such as health insurers.

FIGURE 3.4 PIPEDA Privacy Principles

Organizations subject to Canada's Personal Information Protection and Electronics Document Act (PIPEDA) are responsible for complying with the following 10 principles:

Be accountable. Develop policies and procedures for the safeguarding of personal information and appoint an individual responsible for assuring compliance.

Identify purpose. Before or at the time of collecting personal information, identify the purpose for doing so.

Obtain consent. Inform the individual from whom personal information is collected of the purpose of the collection and obtain the individual's consent for the collection, use, or disclosure of the information.

Limit collection. Limit the collection of information to the purpose for which it was intended.

Limit use, disclosure, and retention. Use or disclose information only for the purpose for which it was collected, unless the individual consents or the law provides for broader use or disclosure. Establish policies and procedures for retention and destruction of information.

Be accurate. Ascertain that information is accurate, complete, and up to date as is necessary for the purpose for which it is to be used.

Establish and use appropriate safeguards. Protect information against loss and theft, as well as unauthorized access, disclosure, copying, use, or modification.

Be open. Make policies and procedures easily understandable and available to customers and employees.

Give individuals access. Give individuals access to their information at minimal or no cost, subject to certain exceptions.

Provide recourse. Develop and inform customers of simple-to-use and easily accessible complaint procedures.

Source: Adapted from Mary C. Bickley, *Canadian Supplement to Business Law for Financial Services Professionals* [Atlanta: LOMA (Life Office Management Association, Inc.), © 2006], 70. Used with permission; all rights reserved.

On the provincial level, the Canadian Life and Health Insurance Association has issued Right to Privacy Guidelines. Insurers may either adopt these guidelines or develop their own stricter guidelines.

Nondiscrimination

An underwriter's responsibility is to distinguish risks that are acceptable from risks that are unacceptable by carefully examining the facts about proposed insureds. Such discrimination among risks is usually legal when it is based upon (1) recognized actuarial principles or (2) actual or reasonably anticipated experience. However, many U.S. jurisdictions have enacted laws that prohibit insurers from using the following factors as underwriting criteria:

- Sex
- Marital status
- Sexual orientation
- Blindness or partial blindness
- Status as a victim of physical abuse
- Race

Underwriters in Canada generally may not discriminate among proposed insureds for life and health insurance coverage on the basis of whether a person is male or female. In addition, some provinces specifically prohibit discrimination on the basis of physical and mental impairments, marital status, and sexual orientation.

Medical Testing

Acquired immune deficiency syndrome (AIDS) and genetic testing present insurers with unique underwriting challenges.

HIV Testing

Proposed insureds with the human immunodeficiency virus (HIV) or AIDS have increased mortality and morbidity risks. Thus, insurers typically include questions about those physical conditions on applications for individual life and health insurance.

A variety of issues about the collection and use of medical testing information in the underwriting process have been raised because (1) certain segments of the population—homosexual and bisexual men and intravenous drug users—have been most affected by HIV and AIDS, (2) AIDS can be a fatal disease, and (3) maintaining confidentiality is essential. Many states have adopted regulatory guidelines that insurers must abide by when they request and use information about AIDS-related conditions in the underwriting process. In accordance with these guidelines, insurers must

- Conduct testing for AIDS-related conditions on a nondiscriminatory basis; an insurer must not single out certain segments of the population or specific applicants for such testing.
- Notify the proposed insured that an AIDS-related blood test will be performed and obtain the proposed insured's written consent.

- Base an adverse underwriting decision on an HIV blood test that is positive—that is, a test that indicates that HIV is present—or indeterminate only if the test was conducted in accordance with an established test protocol. Such a test protocol involves repeated testing to ensure that a positive test result is accurate.
- Maintain the confidentiality of medical information.

In Canada, according to the CLHIA *Guidelines with Respect to AIDS for the Sale and Underwriting of Life and Health Insurance*, a proposed insured must give written consent before his blood or other bodily fluid is taken to test for the presence of HIV. If a proposed insured refuses to consent to such a test, then the insurer may decline the application for insurance. Questions contained in applications for insurance should not be directed toward determining the proposed insured's sexual orientation. Questions may relate to past instances of sexually transmitted diseases and past testing for HIV or AIDS; however, the proposed insured must be given the opportunity to explain any affirmative answers to these questions. An insurer cannot base an adverse underwriting decision on (1) the proposed insured's sexual orientation, (2) previous testing for HIV if the result of such a test was negative or is unknown, or (3) an unconfirmed positive test result.

Tests for HIV must follow a current standard protocol, which involves a screening test and a confirmatory test. For an insurer to consider a test result as proof of the presence of the virus, (1) two screening tests must indicate the presence of HIV and (2) the positive results then must be confirmed by a more refined test.

Genetic Testing

Although the term is defined in numerous ways, basically a ***genetic test*** is a test of human DNA used to indicate a person's predisposition to a certain illness or disease. Researchers have developed genetic tests for a variety of life-threatening diseases, and the information gained from such testing obviously would be useful to life and health insurers in their underwriting process.

Nevertheless, many jurisdictions have enacted laws that limit insurers' ability to use genetic testing results. These restrictions exist for a number of reasons: (1) regulators have made policy decisions that genetic material is personal and confidential, (2) genetic testing is still new and its results are not always reliable, (3) regulators fear that insurance decisions made on the basis of genetic information will be unfairly discriminatory, and (4) regulators do not want to force individuals to learn that they have a predisposition to a certain disease or illness if the person does not want to have such testing. Also, insurers fear that antiselection will occur if individuals learn they are predisposed to a genetic condition and do not reveal that information to the insurer.

Legislation is pending in the U.S. Congress that would bar health insurers and group health plans from using genetic testing in underwriting decisions or setting premiums. Many states already impose some limits on an insurer's right to use the results of genetic testing in underwriting. Figure 3.5 illustrates how state laws imposing limits on an insurer's right to use genetic testing vary widely.

Reflecting a policy promulgated by the Canadian Life and Health Insurance Association, life and health insurers in Canada do not require applicants to undergo genetic testing. Furthermore, no laws in Canada specifically address the issue of genetic testing used for insurance underwriting.[9]

Replacements

A ***replacement*** is the purchase of one life insurance policy or annuity contract to take the place of another. Although replacement of an existing life insurance policy is not illegal, the replacement may not be in a policyowner's best interest. Because most producers earn high first-year commissions on new sales, producers sometimes are tempted to place their own financial interests above the interests of their clients and of the insurers they represent by recommending replacements that are adverse to the client's interests.

FIGURE 3.5 Regulation of Genetic Testing

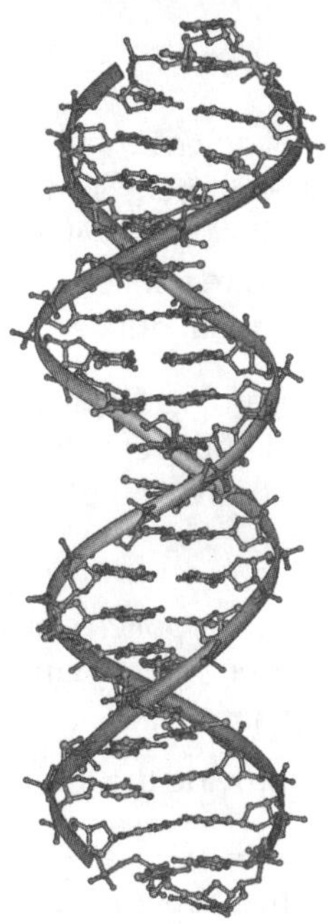

Although laws vary widely, the following examples illustrate U.S. state laws on genetic testing:

- Only a few states permit insurers to require a proposed insured to undergo genetic testing and to deny coverage to proposed insureds who refuse to undergo such testing.
- Most states that have enacted genetic testing laws permit insurers to use the results of genetic testing for purposes of underwriting life insurance and disability income insurance, but they prohibit insurers from using such information in underwriting medical expense insurance. Some states prohibit the use of genetic testing results in underwriting life insurance, disability income insurance, and medical expense insurance.
- Some states permit insurers to use the results of genetic testing only if those results are actuarially significant.
- Laws in some states focus on consumers' privacy rights and impose restrictions on the ability of insurers to access genetic information that consumers have obtained for themselves.

Source: Adapted from Mary C. Bickley et al., *Life and Health Insurance Underwriting*, 2nd ed. [Atlanta: LOMA (Life Office Management Association, Inc.), © 2007], 69. Used with permission; all rights reserved.

When an application involves a replacement, an underwriter must be alert to evidence that producers are engaged in twisting or churning. ***Twisting*** occurs when a producer misrepresents the features of a policy to induce a client to purchase a policy. ***Churning*** occurs when a producer induces a customer to replace one policy after another so that the producer can earn a series of first-year commissions on the replacements.

To help prevent unethical replacement, most states have adopted some version of the NAIC's ***Replacement of Life Insurance and Annuities Model Regulation***, which states that replacement of policies is generally permissible if the replacing insurer provides full and fair disclosure and no deceptive practices are involved. State replacement regulations usually do not govern certain types of policies, including group policies, conversion policies, and temporary coverage issued under a premium receipt.

Producers have certain duties under these replacement regulations, and underwriters may be required to verify that producers have fulfilled these duties, which are set forth in Figure 3.6.

When another insurer's policy will be replaced, most states require the replacing insurer to send a written notification to the insurer that issued the policy that may be replaced. Along with such notification, the replacing insurer must provide the original insurer with certain information about the new policy for which the applicant has applied. The original insurer then may contact its policyowner to offer additional information about the

FIGURE 3.6 U.S. State Replacement Requirements

U.S. state regulations typically provide that in the issuance of any new policy, the producer must submit to the insurer a replacement statement signed by the applicant and producer indicating whether an in-force policy will be replaced. If no policy is to be replaced, the producer's duties are fulfilled. If a policy will be replaced, the producer has the following additional duties:

- Provide the applicant with a Notice to Applicants Regarding Replacement, which provides general information about the potential effects of a replacement and advises the applicant to receive all the relevant facts before making a replacement.
- Obtain a list of all existing life insurance policies that will be replaced and ensure those policies are listed on the notice regarding replacement. For each such policy, the notice must identify the name of the insurer, the name of the insured, and the policy number or other identifying number.
- Submit to the insurer the completed and signed notice regarding replacement and provide the applicant a copy of the completed notice.
- Leave with the applicant copies of all sales materials that the producer showed the applicant and provide the insurer with a list of all such materials.

existing policy and to attempt to conserve its existing business. Underwriters may bear the responsibility of contacting the original insurers, but in most companies, a new business case analyst handles this task.

In Canada, provincial regulations govern replacements. These regulations call for full and accurate disclosure and mandate that certain disclosure forms be used.

Money Laundering and Financing Terrorists

The ***USA Patriot Act of 2001*** was designed to strengthen the federal government's ability to investigate, prosecute, and seize the assets of terrorists.[10] This act extended anti-money laundering requirements to all financial institutions, including insurers, and prohibited doing business with known terrorists. ***Money laundering*** is the practice of engaging in financial transactions to hide the identity, source, and/or destination of money associated with criminal activity.

While criminals traditionally used accounts in banks and other depository institutions to launder money, they now sometimes use products issued by insurance companies. As a result, many jurisdictions have enacted laws requiring insurers to establish anti-money laundering programs if they issue products with features that allow them to be used to launder money, such as cash value life insurance policies.

Underwriters must be alert to cases that could involve money laundering activities, such as when a customer

- Applies for an insurance product that seems inconsistent with the customer's needs
- Indicates a desire to use an unusual method of paying premiums, such as paying in cash
- Shows little concern for the financial performance of a product but a great deal of concern about the product's early termination features
- Is reluctant to provide identifying information when purchasing a product or provides minimal or seemingly fictitious information

The U.S. Treasury's Office of Foreign Assets Control (OFAC) maintains a list of countries, individuals, and organizations that participate in or sponsor terrorism and other illegal acts. Insurers must monitor OFAC's list constantly to guard against doing business with prohibited entities or people. New business staff or underwriters typically bear responsibility for making sure that applicants, policyowners, proposed insureds, and beneficiaries are not on the list. Policyowner service staff must not approve any kind of policy changes, such as a change of beneficiary or assignment of ownership, if the change involves any entity or person on the list. Claim staff must be certain that no payments are made to anyone on the list.

Insurers typically comply with OFAC's requirements by using software designed to automatically check transactions for the involvement of any prohibited entity or individual.

In Canada, the ***Proceeds of Crime (Money Laundering) and Terrorist Financing Act*** requires companies, including life insurers, to report every financial transaction that occurs for which there are reasonable grounds to suspect that the transaction is related to money laundering or financing terrorists.[11]

Regulatory Compliance Issues Affecting Group Insurance Underwriting

In the United States and Canada, group insurance underwriters must comply with many of the same laws that affect individual insurance underwriting, as well as laws that specifically affect group insurance underwriting.

U. S. State Regulatory Requirements

The NAIC's ***Group Life Insurance Definition and Group Life Insurance Standard Provisions Model Act (Group Life Insurance Model Act)*** and the NAIC's ***Group Health Insurance Definition and Group Health Insurance Standard Provisions Model Act (Group Health Insurance Model Act)*** define the types of groups eligible for group life insurance and group health insurance, respectively, as well as set forth provisions that such group policies must contain. Most states have adopted laws based on the Group Life Insurance Model Act, but fewer states have adopted laws based on the Group Health Insurance Model Act. Thus, group life insurance regulation is more uniform in the United States than is group health insurance regulation.

Underwriters must ensure that groups applying for coverage are eligible to do so under the applicable state laws. Group underwriters also must be familiar with policy provisions that are required in those jurisdictions in which the insurer does business. The provisions that both group life and group health insurance policies must include under the Group Life Insurance Model Act and the Group Health Insurance Model Act are summarized in Figure 3.7.

Group Life Insurance Conversion Provisions

In addition to the provisions listed in Figure 3.7, most states require group life insurance policies to contain a ***conversion provision*** that gives a group insured who meets specific conditions the right to obtain an individual life insurance policy without providing evidence of insurability. Some individual life policies also contain such a provision. The conversion provision in group life insurance applies in the following situations:

FIGURE 3.7 Provisions Required in Group Life and Group Health Insurance Policies

- **Grace period provision.** Gives the policyholder a grace period of 31 days for the payment of renewal premiums.
- ***Incontestability provision.*** States that, after the policy has been in force for two years, the insurer may not contest the validity of the group contract except for nonpayment of premium. The provision also limits the insurer's ability to contest the validity of a group insured's coverage under a group policy after that coverage has been in force for two years during the group insured's lifetime.
- **Entire contract provision.** States that a copy of the application shall be attached to the policy when issued; that all statements made by the policyholder or the group insureds shall be deemed representations—statements that will invalidate the contract if not substantially true—and not warranties—statements that will invalidate the contract if not literally true; and that no statement made by a group insured shall be used in any contest unless a copy of the document containing the statement has been furnished to the group insured.
- **Evidence of insurability provision.** Specifies the conditions, if any, under which the insurer reserves the right to require a person eligible for insurance to furnish evidence of insurability satisfactory to the insurer as a condition to part or all of her coverage.
- **Misstatement of age provision.** Specifies an equitable adjustment of premiums, benefits, or both premiums and benefits if the age of a group insured is misstated.
- **Certificate of coverage provision.** States that the insurer will issue a certificate of insurance to the policyholder for delivery to each group insured.

Source: Adapted from Mary C. Bickley et al., *Life and Health Insurance Underwriting*, 2nd ed. [Atlanta: LOMA (Life Office Management Association, Inc.), © 2007], 243. Used with permission; all rights reserved.

- If a group insured's coverage terminates because the insured's employment terminates or the insured is no longer a member of a class eligible for coverage, then the insured must be given the right to purchase any type of individual policy the insurer is then issuing at the insurer's customary premium rate for that policy based on the insured's age. The exception is that the group policy may exclude the option of purchasing term life insurance. The amount of insurance provided by the individual policy is limited to the amount of group life insurance that terminated, less any amount of group life insurance for which the insured becomes eligible within 31 days after termination of the group life coverage.

- If a covered dependent of a group insured no longer qualifies for group coverage, then the dependent must have the right to obtain an individual life insurance policy on the same terms described in the previous bullet point.
- If an individual insured under a group life policy dies, then the insured's surviving dependents who were covered under the group plan at the insured's death must have the right to obtain an individual life insurance policy on the same terms we described in the first bullet point.
- If a group policy terminates or is amended so as to terminate the coverage of any class of group insureds, then each group insured—including dependents—whose coverage terminates is entitled to obtain an individual life insurance policy provided the group insured has been insured under the group policy for at least five years. The amount of insurance that must be provided by the individual policy is limited to the smaller of (1) $10,000 or (2) the amount of group life insurance that terminated less the amount of group life insurance for which the group insured becomes eligible within 31 days after termination of the group policy.

To convert group coverage to an individual policy, the group insured must complete an application for the individual policy and pay the premium to the insurer within 31 days after becoming ineligible for group coverage. If a person applies for coverage in accordance with the conversion provision, the insurer's policyowner service department verifies the applicant's eligibility and the benefit amount that can be approved, and then issues an individual life insurance policy. However, if an applicant requests coverage of a different type or amount than what was provided under the group policy, then the application usually is forwarded to an underwriter who specializes in underwriting individual life insurance coverage and who evaluates the application in accordance with the insurer's usual underwriting guidelines for the requested policy.

Group Health Insurance Conversion Provisions

Most states require group policies that provide hospital, surgical, or major medical expense coverage to include a conversion provision that gives a group insured the right to obtain an individual health insurance policy from the insurer without providing evidence of insurability if the following conditions are met:

- The group insured was insured under the group policy for at least three months

- The group policy is discontinued and is not replaced with similar coverage within 31 days or the group insured's coverage under the group policy is terminated for reasons other than the individual's failure to pay a required premium
- The group insured applies in writing for a conversion policy and pays the first premium for that policy within 31 days after termination of group coverage

The insurer is not required to issue an individual policy with the same benefits and rates as the group policy. Furthermore, the insurer is not required to issue an individual policy if the group insured is covered by Medicare or is eligible for—regardless of whether she is covered by—other medical expense coverage and the benefits provided by that coverage together with the benefits provided by the converted policy would result in the insured's being overinsured according to the insurer's underwriting guidelines.

U.S. Federal Regulatory Requirements

In this section, we describe some of the U.S. federal laws that affect the design and operation of group life and health insurance policies.

Employee Retirement Income Security Act

The ***Employee Retirement Income Security Act (ERISA)*** regulates employee retirement plans and specifies minimum requirements that employee welfare benefit plans must meet.[12] For purposes of ERISA, group life and health insurance plans established by employers are welfare benefit plans that must meet ERISA requirements, which include

- Establishing and maintaining the plan in accordance with a written plan document
- Meeting reporting and disclosure requirements
- Providing a summary plan description to each plan participant

Consolidated Omnibus Budget Reconciliation Act (COBRA)

The federal ***Consolidated Omnibus Budget Reconciliation Act of 1986 (COBRA)*** imposes requirements on group insurance plans that provide medical expense benefits and that are sponsored by employers with 20 or more employees.[13] COBRA requires such group medical expense plans to provide covered employees and their covered spouses and dependent children the right to continue their group insurance coverage for a limited time in specified situations, known as ***qualifying events***, in which group coverage would otherwise terminate. Covered individuals who are eligible to continue their group insurance coverage following a qualifying event are referred to as ***qualified beneficiaries***. When an individual elects to continue group coverage under COBRA, the group coverage often is referred to as ***COBRA continuation coverage***.

Health Insurance Portability and Accountability Act (HIPAA)

The Health Insurance Portability and Accountability Act (HIPAA) imposes a number of requirements on health insurance companies and employer-sponsored group medical expense insurance plans with which underwriters should be familiar.

Pre-Existing Conditions. Individual and group health insurance plans often include a ***pre-existing conditions provision*** which states that benefits will not be paid for a pre-existing condition until the insured has been covered under the policy for a specified length of time. HIPAA places limits on the pre-existing condition exclusion that a group medical expense plan may include. These limits are designed to allow group insureds who have a pre-existing condition to change jobs without losing coverage for their pre-existing conditions. HIPAA defines a ***pre-existing condition*** as a physical or mental condition for which medical advice, diagnosis, care, or treatment was recommended or received within the six-month period preceding an individual's enrollment date in a group medical expense insurance plan. The ***enrollment date*** is the date the individual becomes covered under the group medical expense insurance plan or the first day of the probationary period for enrollment, whichever occurs earlier.

Nondiscrimination. HIPAA prohibits discrimination among individuals covered by a group medical expense plan by restricting such plans from establishing eligibility rules for group coverage based on any of the following factors:

- Health status
- Medical condition, including physical and mental illnesses
- Claim experience
- Receipt of health care
- Medical history
- Genetic information
- Evidence of insurability, including conditions arising out of acts of domestic violence
- Disability

Guaranteed Availability Requirements. HIPAA requires the guaranteed availability of individual medical expense insurance coverage to certain individuals who have had group medical expense insurance coverage. In Figure 3.8, we identify those eligible individuals who must be provided such coverage. HIPAA prohibits an insurer from declining to cover an eligible individual or imposing any pre-existing condition exclusion on the coverage of an eligible individual. Health insurers, however, are exempt from this requirement if the state in which they conduct business implements an acceptable alternative mechanism by which such eligible individuals may obtain coverage. Most states have implemented such an acceptable alternative mechanism, as we discussed earlier.

HIPAA contains another guaranteed availability requirement. Subject to certain exceptions, in every state in which an insurer offers medical expense coverage to small groups, HIPAA requires the insurer to accept every small employer that applies for such coverage. HIPAA defines a ***small employer*** as an employer that had an average of at least 2 but not more than 50 employees during the preceding calendar year and had at least 2 employees on the first day of the group plan year.

Guaranteed Renewability Requirement. HIPAA requires insurers that offer group medical expense coverages to renew such coverage at the option of the group policyholder, subject to certain exceptions.

FIGURE 3.8 HIPAA's Definition of Eligible Individuals

For purposes of the Health Insurance Portability and Accountability Act's (HIPAA) guaranteed availability requirement, an eligible individual is someone who meets all of the following requirements:

- The individual is not eligible for coverage under a group health plan, Medicare, or Medicaid.
- The individual has at least 18 months of ***creditable coverage***, which is coverage under virtually any type of individual or group health care plan without a break in coverage of 63 days or more.
- The individual's most recent creditable coverage must have been provided by a group health plan, governmental plan, or church plan.
- The individual's most recent coverage was not terminated because of fraud or nonpayment of premium.
- The individual has no other health coverage and has exhausted the benefits to which he was entitled under COBRA.

Source: Adapted from Mary C. Bickley et al., *Life and Health Insurance Underwriting*, 2nd ed. [Atlanta: LOMA (Life Office Management Association, Inc.), © 2007], 253. Used with permission; all rights reserved.

Federal Employment Laws

U.S. federal employment laws have been enacted to ensure that all employees are treated fairly in the workplace. Employment laws prohibit discrimination regarding hiring, advancement, wages, and other terms and conditions of employment. Employer-sponsored plans that provide employee benefits, such as group life and group health insurance plans, must comply with all applicable federal employment laws. The following federal laws impose nondiscrimination requirements on most employers and, thus, affect the design of employee benefit plans:

- The ***Civil Rights Act of 1964*** prohibits employment discrimination on the basis of race, color, sex, religion, or national origin.[14] The act applies to employers that are engaged in interstate commerce and have 15 or more employees.
- The ***Pregnancy Discrimination Act*** is a part of the Civil Rights Act and requires employers to treat pregnancy, childbirth, and related medical conditions the same as any other medical condition.[15]
- The ***Americans with Disabilities Act (ADA)*** protects disabled individuals against all types of discrimination, including employment discrimination.[16] The ADA applies to all employers with 15 or more employees.
- The ***Age Discrimination in Employment Act (ADEA)*** protects workers who are age 40 and older from being discriminated against because of their age.[17] The ADEA, which applies to employers with 20 or more employees, permits an employer to reduce the level of group life insurance benefits provided to older employees if the employer's premium contributions for those benefits is at least equal to its contributions provided to fund the benefits provided to younger workers. Similarly, employers are permitted to reduce disability income benefits of workers who are age 65 and older if the cost of providing benefits for older workers is more than the cost of providing benefits for younger workers. By contrast, employers are required to make the same medical expense coverages available to older workers and their covered dependents as are available to younger workers and covered dependents, and older employees cannot be required to pay more for the coverage than younger employees pay.

Canadian Regulatory Requirements

In Canada, most group medical expense insurance plans provide group members and their dependents with benefits that are supplementary to the provincial health care plan available to all provincial residents. Group disability income benefit plans typically take into account the benefits provided by the Canada Pension Plan or the Quebec Pension Plan, so the private group disability plans may offset the amounts paid by the governmental programs.

The ***Canada Pension Plan (CPP)*** is a federal program that provides a pension for wage earners who have contributed money into the plan during their working years. The CPP covers workers in all provinces except Quebec, which has elected to establish its own provincial plan. The ***Quebec Pension Plan (QPP)*** functions in the same manner as the CPP except that the QPP applies only to wage earners in Quebec. The CPP and QPP are coordinated closely and tend to operate as one plan. In addition to pension benefits, the CPP and QPP provide survivorship benefits, lump-sum death benefits, benefits for orphans, and long-term disability income benefits. To know what supplemental benefits can be offered to prospective customers, underwriters become familiar with the provisions of relevant laws.

Group life insurance and group health insurance are governed in most provinces by legislation based on the Uniform Life Insurance Act and the Uniform Accident and Sickness Insurance Act. Quebec has its own insurance regulations to cover group life and health insurance.

In addition, CLHIA's Guideline G-3: Group Life and Group Health Insurance (Group Guidelines) provides important details about group life and health insurance regulation, such as required policy provisions in regard to policy termination and conversion, as well as the contents of group certificates.

Underwriting Standards

Insurers establish certain standards to ensure that applications are processed properly and risks are evaluated fairly, without bias or prejudice. By adhering to these standards, underwriters protect the insurer should the policy become the subject of a legal action.

Reviewing Applications for Proper Completion

Applicants and proposed insureds have a duty to answer completely and honestly any questions contained in the application for insurance, asked during a physical examination, or furnished to the insurer by any other means as evidence of insurability. Thus, in addition to ascertaining whether the requirements for a valid contract have been met, an underwriter must evaluate an application to ensure that it provides complete, accurate, and consistent information and is signed. If an insurer allows an application with missing or incomplete information to proceed to policy issue, the insurer may lose its right to contest the policy based on the missing or incomplete information.

Courts typically will permit an application as evidence in a lawsuit only if it is the original, unaltered document signed by the applicant. Thus, no one can alter an application after the applicant submits it to the insurer unless the applicant affirms the change in writing. Most insurers use an amendment, signed by the applicant, to modify or complete the answer to a question on the application. Such an amendment then becomes part of the application.

Sometimes an application contains an untrue statement of a fact, known as a ***misrepresentation***. Some misrepresentations do not affect the underwriter's decision, but others do. A ***material misrepresentation*** is a misrepresentation that induces the other party—in this case, the insurer—to enter into a contract that it would not have entered into as written had it known the truth. In general, a misrepresentation is material to the formation of an insurance contract if an insurer that knew the true facts would have

- Declined to issue the policy
- Increased the premium rate charged for the policy
- Excluded coverage for certain risks

Figure 3.9 lists some potential warning signs that might indicate material misrepresentation in an application for insurance.

If the insurer finds material misrepresentation, the insurer may rescind—or avoid—the policy, subject to certain limitations. ***Rescission*** is a remedy provided by law to an insurer that discovers that it has issued a policy based on material misrepresentation. If a contract is rescinded, it is void

FIGURE 3.9 Material Misrepresenation Warning Signs

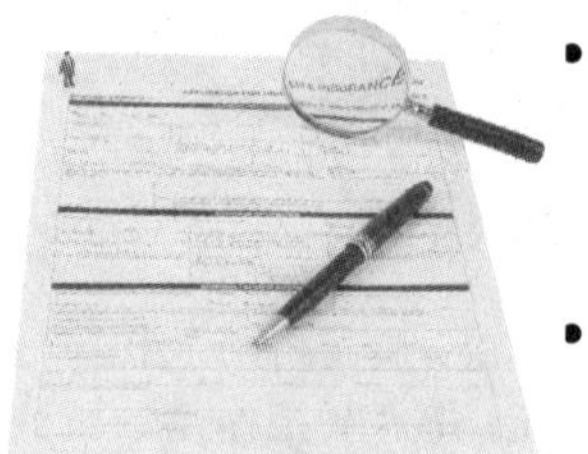

- The applicant requested an amount of coverage that is slightly less than the amount of coverage that would require the proposed insured to undergo a physical examination.
- The applicant's signature on the application does not match the applicant's signature on other documents, such as a physical examination report.
- Answers to questions on the application have been changed or covered by correction fluid.
- The applicant requested an unusually large amount of coverage for her occupation and income.

Source: Adapted from Mary C. Bickley et al., *Life and Health Insurance Underwriting*, 2nd ed. [Atlanta: LOMA (Life Office Management Association, Inc.), © 2007], 58. Used with permission; all rights reserved.

from the beginning. In the United States, the parties are returned to the positions they would have been in had no contract ever been created. Thus, rescission obligates the insurer to return the premiums paid for the policy. In Canada, whether the insurer repays the premiums depends on the terms of the contract.

Insurers are limited in their right to rescind policies by a policy's *incontestability provision*, which in individual insurance policies denies the insurer the right to avoid the contract on the grounds of a material misrepresentation in the application after the contract has been in force for a stated period during the life of the insured. In the United States, this ***contestable period***—the time period within which the insurer has the right to avoid a life insurance policy on the grounds of a material misrepresentation in the application—typically is two years from the date the policy was issued. In Canada, an insurer loses the right to contest the validity of a contract after the contract has been in force for two years during the lifetime of the insured unless the misrepresentation was fraudulent. In some U.S. states, an insurer still can contest the validity of a contract after the contestable period if the misrepresentation was fraudulent.

Processing Applications Promptly

Underwriters process applications promptly not only to assure that the applicant does not change his mind, but also to avoid a court ruling that the insurer is liable for paying benefits if the event insured against occurs before the underwriting decision is made. If the insurer is held liable for not acting with reasonable promptness in processing an application, the insurer will have to pay benefits under the policy regardless of the proposed insured's insurability. The courts have been especially strict in holding an insurer liable when an applicant submits a premium with the application. Consequently, insurers typically issue premium receipts, which we discussed earlier, to set forth their own terms of liability before the court does so for them.

Documenting Underwriting

Insurers create a case file for each application, and underwriters working on the case must be careful to note in the file all communications and actions concerning the application. Each notation must be specific and should include the date and time, the exact action taken or requested, and the underwriter's full signature. The file must be precise and thorough because it may become evidence in a court proceeding.

In addition, all comments included in a case file must be relevant to the risk assessment and classification process and must not indicate personal bias against an applicant or proposed insured. Thus, underwriters must avoid writing unsubstantiated or personal comments in a case file such as

"Applicant probably drinks more than he indicated on his application," which could be interpreted as showing an underwriter's bias against an applicant. Underwriters must be able to demonstrate effectively that their decisions were based on objective criteria and not on personal judgments.

Most insurers require underwriters to use a worksheet to keep track of the information requested and received, as well as to record the final decision on each case. An ***underwriting worksheet*** is a document that contains records of telephone calls, letters, and other communications; documentation of requests for reinsurance; lists of reports and other information requested; and other notations that will explain clearly the manner in which the underwriter has handled the case beginning with the submission of the application to the insurer. If the underwriter responsible for the case is out of the office, another underwriter usually will be able to answer inquiries on the case by reviewing the underwriting worksheet. The worksheet also explains to the insurer's internal auditors unusual or exceptional handling of a case. We explain more about the use of an underwriting worksheet in Chapter 5.

Key Terms

contract
valid contract
void contract
voidable contract
consideration
premium receipt
contractual capacity
minor
temporary insurance agreement (TIA)
binding premium receipt
conditional premium receipt
approval premium receipt
insurability premium receipt
wagering agreement
insurable interest
National Association of Insurance Commissioners (NAIC)
model law
model regulation
Office of the Superintendent of Financial Institutions (OSFI)
Canadian Council of Insurance Regulators (CCIR)
Canadian Life and Health Insurance Association (CLHIA)
CLHIA Guidelines
Uniform Life Insurance Act (Uniform Act)
Uniform Accident and Sickness Insurance Act
Canada Health Act
Fair Credit Reporting Act (FCRA)
consumer report
consumer reporting agency
investigative consumer report
adverse action
Health Insurance Portability and Accountability Act (HIPAA)
Gramm-Leach-Bliley (GLB) Act
nonpublic personal information
Insurance Information and Privacy Protection Model Act (Model Privacy Act)
Privacy of Consumer Financial and Health Information Regulation (Model Privacy Regulation)

Key Terms (*continued*)

personal information
privileged information
pretext interview
Personal Information Protection and Electronics Document Act (PIPEDA)
genetic test
replacement
twisting
churning
Replacement of Life Insurance and Annuities Model Regulation
USA Patriot Act of 2001
money laundering
Proceeds of Crime (Money Laundering) and Terrorist Financing Act
Group Life Insurance Definition and Group Life Insurance Standard Provisions Model Act (Group Life Insurance Model Act)
Group Health Insurance Definition and Group Health Insurance Standard Provisions Model Act (Group Health Insurance Model Act)
conversion provision
incontestability provision
Employee Retirement Income Security Act (ERISA)
Consolidated Omnibus Budget Reconciliation Act of 1986 (COBRA)
qualifying event
qualified beneficiary
COBRA continuation coverage
pre-existing conditions provision
pre-existing condition
enrollment date
small employer
creditable coverage
Civil Rights Act of 1964
Pregnancy Discrimination Act
Americans with Disabilities Act (ADA)
Age Discrimination in Employment Act (ADEA)
Canada Pension Plan
Quebec Pension Plan
misrepresentation
material misrepresentation
rescission
contestable period
underwriting worksheet

Endnotes

1. Portions of this chapter are adapted from Mary C. Bickley et al., *Life and Health Insurance Underwriting*, 2nd ed. [Atlanta: LOMA (Life Office Management Association, Inc.), © 2007], 49–75 and 237–256. Used with permission; all rights reserved.
2. 15 U.S.C. § 1681 et seq. (2001).
3. R.S. 1985, c. C-6 (2004).
4. Chaoulli v. Quebec (Attorney General), [2005] S.C.C. 35.
5. Public Law No. 108–159.
6. Public Law 104–191 (21 August 1996).
7. 15 U.S.C. 6801(a) (2001).
8. S.C. 2000, c. 5.
9. Genetic Testing and Screening, HumGen International, http://www.humgen.umontreal.ca/int/faq.cfm?Idcat=7 (6 December 2006).
10. Public Law 107–56.
11. S.C. 2000, c. 17.
12. 29 U.S.C. 1001 et seq. (2000).
13. 26 U.S.C. 4980 D (2000).
14. 42 U.S.C. 1981 et seq. (1999).
15. 42 U.S.C. 2002 (e)(k) et seq. (1999).
16. 42 U.S.C. 12101–213 (1999).
17. 29 U.S.C. 621–634 (2000).

chapter

4

Underwriting Individual Life Insurance: Assessing Mortality Risk

Outline

Medical Risk Factors
Sources of Medical Information
Assessing Medical Factors

Personal Risk Factors
Sources of Personal Information
Assessing Personal Factors

Learning Objectives

After studying this chapter, you should be able to…

- Describe the sources of information about medical risk factors used in underwriting individual life insurance
- Distinguish among a nonmedical supplement, a paramedical report, and a medical report
- Identify the requirements imposed on insurers requesting information from MIB, Inc.
- Discuss the importance of the following factors for underwriting individual life insurance: impairments, age, sex, and build
- Describe the sources of information about personal risk factors used in underwriting individual life insurance
- List and describe personal risk factors used in underwriting individual life insurance
- Describe how an underwriter assesses personal risk factors used in underwriting individual life insurance

As we mentioned in Chapter 2, risk assessment is the process of determining the degree of risk represented by each proposed insured person or group using a number of criteria established when the insurance product was designed and priced. Risk assessment for life insurance is particularly concerned with mortality, which is the incidence of death among a specified group of people.

In this chapter, we discuss how an individual life underwriter assesses a proposed insured's mortality risk by evaluating the proposed insured's medical and personal risk factors. As mentioned earlier, a medical risk factor is a physical or psychological characteristic that may increase the likelihood of loss; a personal risk factor is a lifestyle choice that can significantly affect a person's health or longevity.

Medical Risk Factors

We begin this section by describing the sources of medical information that an individual life underwriter reviews in evaluating a proposed insured's mortality risk. We then discuss the assessment of medical risk factors.

Sources of Medical Information

The most common sources of medical information used by an individual life underwriter are

- The application for insurance
- MIB Group, Inc.
- Physicians
- Medical tests
- Personal history interviews
- Inspection reports
- Pharmaceutical databases

An underwriter's goal in gathering information about a proposed insured's health status is to have enough data to assess the risk fairly without accumulating unnecessary information, incurring excessive costs, or taking too much time.

Application for Insurance

The insurance application is one of the underwriter's most important risk assessment tools. As we noted in Chapter 2, the application traditionally consists of two parts. Part I contains questions designed to identify the applicant and the proposed insured (if different from the applicant), specify the amount and type of coverage requested, and provide the insurer with basic information about the proposed beneficiary and the insurability of the proposed insured. Part II asks for the proposed insured's medical information.

Part II may take one of three forms: (1) a nonmedical supplement, (2) a paramedical report, or (3) a medical report. The type of Part II application used depends on the insurer's age and amount requirements chart for the product, which specifies the kinds of information the producer must submit and the underwriter must review in assessing the insurability of a proposed insured. Generally, applications that represent a greater degree of risk—for example, large amounts of coverage or insurance for older people—require greater amounts of information about insurability than do applications representing less risk. Information about insurability is also known as *evidence of insurability*.

Figure 4.1 shows a portion of an age and amount requirements chart developed by one insurer for a specific individual life insurance product. As the amount of insurance applied for increases within each age group, the amount of underwriting information required also increases. For example, a person between the ages of 31 and 40 can apply for up to $99,999 of life insurance on a ***nonmedical basis***—that is, without providing medical proof of insurability. To apply for up to $300,000 of life insurance, that person would need a blood profile; to apply for up to $1,000,000 of coverage, that person would need a paramedical report and a blood profile. An underwriter might request even more information if the applicant had certain impairments.

The proposed insured answers questions about her medical history in all three types of Part II application. Such questions ask about her current and past medical conditions, diseases, and injuries; the extent of her drug, tobacco, and alcohol use; her family's history of medical impairments; the ages of her parents and any siblings; and, if a parent or sibling is deceased, the cause of death. The type of individual who records the answers to these questions depends on which type of Part II application is used. However, in all three types of applications, the proposed insured signs the medical history portion to verify that the information given was correctly recorded. This medical history portion then becomes part of the contract.

Nonmedical Supplement. A ***nonmedical supplement*** is a type of Part II application for individual life insurance that contains the proposed insured's answers to medical history questions recorded by a producer or teleunderwriter but that does not require the proposed insured to undergo a

FIGURE 4.1 Portion of an Age and Amount Requirements Chart for Individual Life Insurance

Age at Last Birthday	Amount of Coverage Applied For	Underwriting Requirements
0–15	Up to $499,999	Nonmedical
	$500,000 to $1,500,000	Paramedical, Attending Physician's Statement (APS)
	$1,500,001 to $3,000,000	Medical, APS
	$3,000,001 and up	Medical, APS, electrocardiogram (ECG)
16–30	Up to $99,999	Nonmedical
	$100,000 to $400,000	Nonmedical, blood profile
	$400,001 to $1,500,000	Paramedical, blood profile
	$1,500,001 to $3,000,000	Paramedical, blood profile, ECG
	$3,000,001 and up	Medical, blood profile, ECG, inspection report
31–40	Up to $99,999	Nonmedical
	$100,000 to $300,000	Nonmedical, blood profile
	$300,001 to $1,000,000	Paramedical, blood profile
	$1,000,001 to $2,000,000	Paramedical, blood profile, ECG
	$2,000,001 and up	Medical, blood profile, ECG
41–45	Up to $99,999	Nonmedical
	$100,000 to $500,000	Paramedical, blood profile
	$500,001 to $1,500,000	Paramedical, blood profile, ECG
	$1,500,001 to $3,000,000	Medical, blood profile, ECG
	$3,000,001 and up	Medical, blood profile, ECG, X-ray, inspection report
46–50	Up to $49,999	Nonmedical
	$50,000 to $100,000	Paramedical
	$100,001 to $200,000	Paramedical, blood profile
	$200,001 to $1,000,000	Paramedical, blood profile, ECG
	$1,000,001 to $3,000,000	Medical, blood profile, ECG
	$3,000,001 and up	Medical, blood profile, ECG, X-ray, inspection report
51–60	Up to $99,999	Paramedical
	$100,000 to $750,000	Paramedical, blood profile, ECG
	$750,001 to $2,000,000	Medical, blood profile, ECG
	$2,000,001 and up	Medical, blood profile, ECG, X-ray, inspection report
61–70	Up to $49,999	Paramedical
	$50,000 to $100,000	Paramedical, ECG
	$100,001 to $1,000,000	Medical, blood profile, ECG
	$1,000,001 and up	Medical, blood profile, ECG, X-ray, inspection report
71 and up	Up to $49,999	Paramedical, ECG, APS
	$50,000 to $100,000	Medical, ECG, APS
	$100,001 to $500,000	Medical, blood profile, ECG, APS
	$500,001 and up	Medical, blood profile, ECG, APS, X-ray, inspection report

physical examination. Based on the information provided in the nonmedical supplement, though, the underwriter may need to confirm information or investigate further. Thus, the underwriter may request a paramedical exam, a medical exam, or an attending physician's statement, which we discuss later in this chapter.

An underwriter uses a nonmedical supplement when the proposed insured qualifies for coverage issued on a nonmedical basis, which means he does not have to present medical proof of insurability by undergoing any type of physical examination, either paramedical or medical. Typically, insurers require an exam when a face amount applied for exceeds a set limit. An insurer's ***nonmedical limit*** is the total amount of insurance that the insurer will permit to be issued on a proposed insured without requiring the proposed insured to undergo a physical examination. For example, an insurer may specify the following nonmedical limits for a specific insurance product:

Age	Limit of Nonmedical Coverage
0–30	$250,000
31–40	200,000
41–45	100,000
46–50	75,000
51–60	50,000

Nonmedical limits usually apply to the total of (1) insurance being applied for and (2) insurance already in force. That is, if a proposed insured already has a certain amount of life insurance coverage in force and applies for an additional amount of life coverage, the total amount of in-force and applied-for coverage cannot exceed the insurer's nonmedical limits if the applicant wants to apply on a nonmedical basis. For example, if a 43-year-old applicant already has $50,000 of life insurance coverage in force and is applying for an additional $100,000 of coverage, the total of $150,000 would exceed the nonmedical limits specified in the preceding table. In such a case, the proposed insured typically would undergo a medical examination to apply for the $100,000 additional coverage.

Note that some insurers consider only in-force coverage that has been issued in the last 6 to 12 months when determining whether total coverage exceeds the nonmedical limit. Furthermore, some insurers consider only in-force coverage issued by their own company, while other companies take into account coverage issued by other companies.

Paramedical Report. Another type of Part II application is the ***paramedical report***, which contains the proposed insured's answers to medical history questions recorded by a paramedical examiner and the results of a paramedical examination conducted by a paramedical examiner. The proposed insured signs the section of the paramedical report that contains answers to medical history questions, and this section becomes a part of the insurance contract. However, the proposed insured does not sign the portion of the paramedical report containing paramedical examination results, and this portion does not become a part of the insurance contract.

A paramedical examiner typically measures and records height, weight, blood pressure, pulse, and chest and waist measurements (for men only). Sometimes the paramedical examiner also collects a blood or urine sample.

A paramedical examination generally is used when the face amount of coverage is too high for the insurer to rely on a nonmedical supplement alone. If the information on a paramedical report indicates a possible medical impairment, an underwriter can request a medical examination of the proposed insured by a physician. More and more insurers use paramedical examinations instead of medical examinations because paramedical exams are less expensive and faster for the insurer and more convenient for the proposed insured. Furthermore, in many cases, paramedical exams provide all the information needed for accurate underwriting.

Medical Report. The third type of Part II application is a ***medical report***, which contains the proposed insured's answers to medical history questions recorded by a physician and the results of a medical examination conducted by a physician. Unlike the answers to the medical history questions, the results of the medical examination do not become part of the contract.

During a medical examination, the physician collects the same medical information as obtained in a paramedical examination, plus the physician examines the proposed insured, including her heart, lungs, liver, eyes, ears, nose, and throat. The main differences between a medical report and a paramedical report are (1) the medical exam is more extensive, (2) the physician may comment on any symptoms noted, and (3) the medical report is completed and signed by a physician. Figure 4.2 presents an example of a medical report.

MIB Group, Inc.

An underwriter in the United States or Canada may be able to request information about a proposed insured from ***MIB Group, Inc. (MIB)***, a not-for-profit membership corporation established to provide coded information to insurers about impairments that applicants have disclosed or other insurance companies have detected in connection with previous applications for insurance. MIB maintains information about people applying for coverage with MIB-member life and health insurance companies. MIB members may request information to find out whether proposed insureds

FIGURE 4.2 Example of a Medical Report

Questions to be Answered by the Proposed Insured and Recorded by a Physician

Proposed Insured ______________________ (First Name, Middle Initial, Last Name) | Birth Date ______________ (Day, Month, Year)

1. a. Name and address of your personal physician ______________________
(*If none, so state*)
b. Date and reason last consulted? ______________________
c. What treatment was given or medication prescribed? ______________________

2. Have you ever had medical treatment for: YES NO
a. Disorder of eyes, ears, nose, or throat? ☐ ☐
b. Dizziness, fainting, convulsions, headache; speech defect, paralysis or stroke; mental or nervous disorder? ☐ ☐
c. Shortness or breath, persistent hoarseness or cough, blood spitting; bronchitis, pleurisy, asthma, emphysema, tuberculosis or chronic respiratory disorder? ☐ ☐
d. Chest pain, palpitation, high blood pressure, rheumatic fever, heart murmur, heart attack or other disorder of the heart or blood vessels? ☐ ☐
e. Jaundice, intestinal bleeding; ulcer, hernia, appendicitis, colitis, diverticulitis, hemorrohoids, recurrent indigestion, or other disorder of the stomach, intestines, liver, or gall bladder? ☐ ☐
f. Sugar, albumin, blood or pus in urine; veneral disease; stone or other disorder of kidney, bladder, prostate, male or female reproductive organs, breasts? ☐ ☐
g. Diabetes; thyroid or other endocrine disorders? ☐ ☐
h. Neuritis, scintica, rheumatism, arthritis, gout, or disorder of the muscles or bones, including the spine, back, or joints? ☐ ☐
i. Deformity, lameness or amputation? ☐ ☐
j. Disorder of skin, lymph glands, cyst, tumor, or cancer? ☐ ☐
k. Allergies; anemia or other disorder of the blood? ☐ ☐
l. Excessive use of alcohol, tobacco, or any habit-forming drugs? ☐ ☐
m. Any mental or physical discorder not listed abvoe? ☐ ☐

3. Are you now under observation or taking treatment? ☐ ☐

4. Have you had any change in weight in the past year? ☐ ☐

5. *Other than the foregoing,* have you within the past 5 years:
a. Had a checkup, consultation, illness, injury, surgery? ☐ ☐
b. Been a patient in a hospital, clinic, sanatorium, or other medical facility? ☐ ☐
c. Had electrocardiogram, X-ray, other diagnostic test? ☐ ☐
d. Been advised to have any diagnostic test, hospitalization or surgery which was not completed? ☐ ☐

6. Have you ever had military service deferment, rejection or discharge because of a physical or mental condition? ☐ ☐

7. Have you ever requested or received a pension, benefits or payment because of an injury, sickness, or disability? ☐ ☐

8. Family History: Tuberculosis, diabetes, cancer, high blood pressure, heart or kidney disease, mental illness or suicide ☐ ☐

	Age if Living?	Cause of Death	Age at Death?
Father			
Mother			
Brothers and Sisters			
No. Living ______ No. Dead______			

9. Have you been diagnosed by a member of the medical profession for:
a. AIDS (Acquired Immune Deficiency Syndrome), ARC (AIDS Related Complex) or any other immunological disorder? ☐ ☐
b. Enlargement of lymph nodes (glands), chronic diarrhea, unusual or persistent skin lesions or unexplained infections? ☐ ☐

Please give details of all "Yes" answers. Include diagnoses, dates, duration, and names and addresses of all attending physicians and medical facilities. ______________________

It is hereby represented that the statements and answers in all parts of this application are true, complete, and correctly recorded, to the best of my knowledge and belief.

I hereby authorize ANY PHYSICIAN, HOSPITAL, CLINIC, INSURANCE COMPANY OR OTHER ORGANIZATION, INSTITUTION OR PERSON, that has any records or knowledge of me or my health, to give to the Company any and all information about me with reference to my health and medical history and any hospitalization, advice, diagnosis, treatment, disease or ailment. A photographic copy of this authorization shall be as valid as the original.

Date ____________ Witness ______________ M.D. ______________
Medical Examiner *Signature of Proposed Insured*

continued on next page…

FIGURE 4.2 *continued* Example of a Medical Report

To be completed by a Physician

1. HEIGHT (IN SHOES) WEIGHT (CLOTHED) CHEST (FULL INSPIRATION) CHEST (FORCED EXPIRATION) ABDOMEN AT UMBILICUS RELAXED

FT. _____ IN. _____LBS. _____IN. _____IN. _____IN.

Details of "Yes" answers. (Identify Item.)

Did you weigh? ❑ Yes ❑ No Did you measure? ❑ Yes ❑ No
Weight change in past year?______lbs. ❑ Gain ❑ Loss – Cause?
Is appearance unhealthy or older than stated age? ❑ Yes ❑ No

2. Blood Pressure (Take three readings at rest—3 minutes apart)

	1st	2nd	3rd
Systolic			
Diastolic			

3. Pulse:

	BEFORE EXERCISE	AFTER EXERCISE	AFTER REST
Rate			
Irregularities			

4. Heart:
   a. Is there any cyanosis, dyspnea, edema, arteriosclerosis, peripheral vascular or other cardiovascular disorder? ❑ Yes ❑ No
   b. Is heart enlarged? ❑ Yes ❑ No (If yes, describe)
   c. Is murmur present? ❑ Yes ❑ No (If yes, complete 4d)
   d. Murmur is:
      Timing: ❑ Stystolic ❑ Prestyolic ❑ Diastolic
      Intensity: ❑ Faint ❑ Moderate ❑ Loud
      Quality: ❑ Soft ❑ Blowing ❑ Rough
      Location: ❑ Apex ❑ Base
   e. How is murmur affected by:
      Respiration? ____________________
      Exercise? ____________________
      Recumbency? ____________________
   f. Is murmur transmitted? .... Yes ☐ No ☐
      If yes, where ____________________
   g. Degree of hypertrophy:
      ❑ None ❑ Slight ❑ Moderate ❑ Marked
   h. Is there evidence of decompensation? .... Yes ☐ No ☐
   i. Is there a thrill? .... Yes ☐ No ☐
   j. Is murmur: ❑ Organic ❑ Functional ❑ Unsure

   Show location of
   Apex by **X**
   Area of murmur by ◌
   Point of greatest intensity by ○
   Transmission by ⟶

   Your impression?

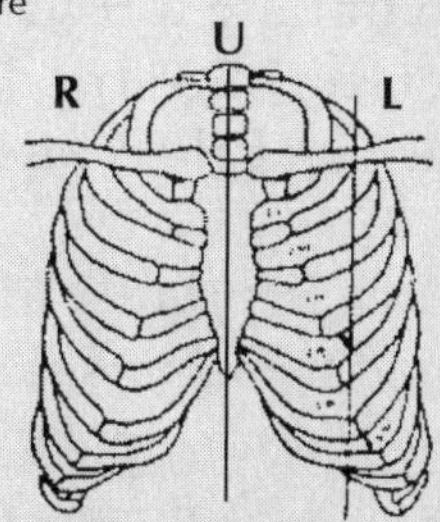

5. Do you FIND any evidence of past or present abnormalities or disease of: (Check applicable items and give details.) YES NO
   a. Eyes, ears, nose, or throat? .... ☐ ☐
      (If vision or hearing markedly impaired, indicate degree and correction.)
   b. Brain or nervous system (Test pupillary and patellar reflexes. Note gait. Any paralysis?) .... ☐ ☐
   c. Glands? (thyroid, lymph, endocrine) ....
   d. Lungs or other respiratory organs? .... ☐ ☐
   e. Heart or blood vessels? .... ☐ ☐
   f. Stomach or other abdominal organs? .... ☐ ☐
   g. Genito-urinary system? (including prostate) .... ☐ ☐
   h. Bones, joints, or skin? .... ☐ ☐

continued on next page…

FIGURE 4.2 continued Example of a Medical Report

6. IS THERE — YES NO
   - a. Hernia.......... ☐ ☐
     - If "Yes" is it reducible?.......... ☐ ☐
   - b. Evidence of varicose veins or ulcers?.......... ☐ ☐
   - c. Deformity, loss of limb or lameness?.......... ☐ ☐

7. GENERAL
   - a. How well do you know examinee?.......... ☐ ☐
   - b. Have you ever treated the examinee or been consulted by him/her? .. ☐ ☐
   - c. Do you find that the examinee has any physical or mental defect, or is in ill health?.......... ☐ ☐
   - d. Do you believe the examinee is older than the age given?.......... ☐ ☐
   - e. Have you reason to suspect that the examinee is or has been an intemperate user of alcohol or a user or narcotics?.......... ☐ ☐

8. URINALYSIS	Specific Gravity	Albumin	Sugar

9. Have you any pertinent information not brought out above?.......... ☐ ☐

Dated this___ day of_____________, 20____ Signature of Examiner ________________ M.D.

____
(Please Print or Stamp Name)

____
Address

____

have significant impairments or avocational risks that they did not disclose on their current applications for insurance. Such information is provided as an alert to initiate further investigation, not to use as the sole basis for denying coverage. MIB strictly prohibits its member companies from using MIB information as the sole basis of an unfavorable underwriting decision or action.

MIB operates to protect life and health insurance companies—and, ultimately, life and health insurance purchasers—from proposed insureds who knowingly or unknowingly omit information about their insurability. If underwriters had no means of detecting and investigating these unadmitted impairments, some people with uninsurable medical conditions might obtain insurance coverage, and other people might purchase insurance at insufficient premium rates.

In interacting with MIB, underwriters of MIB-member companies engage in two primary activities: reporting and requesting impairment information. MIB has established procedures for each of these two activities, as well as requirements for underwriting on the basis of MIB information and for ensuring confidentiality.

Reporting Information to MIB. MIB furnishes its members with a confidential list of factors that are considered important to risk selection and a code that identifies each factor. Member companies are required to report these codes to MIB when they find evidence of these factors in the course of underwriting. The codes may be described as brief summaries of medical and avocational information that may have a bearing on health or longevity. These reports are encoded to protect confidentiality. Codes that have been reported already should not be reported again unless some new, intervening factor has been disclosed or has developed.

Member companies are required to notify MIB if they have reason to believe that an MIB report contains inaccurate or incomplete information. For example, if a proposed insured has been rated in the past but tests conducted during a more recent application process show that the rating is no longer justified, the member company reports this information to MIB to benefit the proposed insured. Member companies do *not* send MIB any actual medical reports or information about (1) specific amounts of insurance applied for or issued, (2) underwriting decisions, or (3) claim decisions.

Requesting Information from MIB. Before an underwriter at a member company can ask MIB to search its files for coded information about a proposed insured, the company must

- Obtain the proposed insured's written authorization to release medical information to the member company on a form expressly naming MIB as an authorized source of such information.
- Furnish the proposed insured for individual life or health insurance with a written pre-notice specifying that a report regarding the person's insurability may be made to MIB and further, that if he later applies for life or health insurance (or files a claim for benefits) with an MIB member company, then MIB may supply such company with an MIB report. The notice also indicates that the person has a right to contact MIB for a copy of his MIB file under the procedures specified in the Fair Credit Reporting Act (FCRA).

Note that authorization forms are subject to various state and federal laws and regulations, including the NAIC Insurance Information and Privacy Protection Model Act, the Gramm-Leach-Bliley Act and its progeny, and the Health Insurance Portability and Accountability Act (HIPAA). Among other things, the authorization should cover nonmedical as well as medical sources. The authorization should not imply to the consumer that MIB information may be given to another consumer reporting agency. Further, no authorization can permit any organization other than an MIB member to obtain MIB record information.

Some MIB members use a single document that combines the MIB authorization together with the MIB pre-notice, the Fair Credit Reporting Act pre-notice, and the NAIC Insurance Information and Privacy Protection Model Act "Notice of Information Practices." The combined document may be incorporated into the company's application form or a separate form.

If the search of the MIB files shows that an insurer previously reported coded information as a result of underwriting an application on the proposed insured, the codes are sent to the inquiring insurer.

Underwriting on the Basis of MIB Information. Any coded information received from MIB may be used only to alert members to the possible need for further investigation of a proposed insured's insurability. In the interest of sound underwriting and to avoid unfair competitive practices in the underwriting of risks, MIB-coded information cannot be used as the basis for establishing a proposed insured's eligibility for insurance.

Adverse actions (for example, declined or rated coverages or postponed applications) must not be based solely on an unverified MIB report without an independent investigation. MIB deems it inappropriate for a member to make an underwriting decision based on an MIB report where the identities of the proposed insured and the person about whom the MIB report relates have not been clearly matched and where the coded information has not been verified by independent investigation. Furthermore, the laws in several states that have adopted the NAIC Insurance Information and Privacy Protection Model Act (or some version of it) prevent insurance companies from making an adverse underwriting decision on the sole basis of information received from an "insurance support organization."

If the underwriter is unable to find medical information consistent with the reported codes for the proposed insured in the application or in other documents submitted by the applicant or producer, then the underwriter typically will make an effort to obtain more comprehensive medical information from a variety of sources.

If an underwriter's investigation does not verify coded information from MIB and if the underwriter has met specific MIB requirements, the underwriter can ask MIB to provide details about the coded information, and MIB then asks the reporting insurer for further information. The reporting insurer is encouraged but not obligated to furnish such information, which typically consists of the documents (or document summaries) that were the basis of the reporting insurer's report to MIB, such as an attending physician's statement or medical test result. The underwriter then can use this information as the basis of her own decision.

Confidentiality Procedures. According to current MIB rules, all MIB information must be kept absolutely confidential. Only authorized medical, underwriting, and claim personnel of member companies are allowed access to MIB information. Member companies also must establish and maintain internal security procedures that will prevent unauthorized people and entities from seeing or using MIB information. To ensure confidentiality, an insurer's MIB code books are locked in desks or cabinets when not in use, and underwriters do not discuss information about MIB codes with other employees, producers, or other unauthorized people or entities. Among the people and entities considered unauthorized in this sense are companies that are not members of the MIB, brokers, nonmember corporate affiliates of member companies, and consumer reporting agencies.

Physicians

A physician, whether he is a primary care physician or a specialist, who has provided medical care for a proposed insured usually is called an ***attending physician***. A physician who performs an examination of a proposed insured at the request of the insurance company usually is called an ***examining physician***. When an underwriter reviews an application on which the health information requires clarification or amplification, the underwriter can (1) request an attending physician's statement, (2) ask the physician to complete a specialized medical questionnaire, or (3) talk to the physician. Although the proposed insured signs a HIPAA-compliant authorization for the physician's release of health care information to the insurer at the time of application, some doctors now require their own HIPAA-compliant authorization to be signed.

The ***attending physician's statement (APS)*** is a report by a physician who has treated or is currently treating the proposed insured. The APS contains a proposed insured's medical records. In traditional underwriting, an APS is one of the most frequently ordered additional sources of medical information. Underwriters typically order an APS when

- The insurer's age and amount requirements specify that an APS is required for the proposed insured.
- The application mentions a specific illness or medical history. For example, histories of coronary artery disease and cancer usually require at least one APS from the primary physician and perhaps additional APSs from specialists, such as the cardiologist or oncologist.
- The application reports a recent visit to a doctor and the underwriter wants to confirm the absence of antiselection.
- Information on the application isn't consistent with information from MIB.

An underwriter also might gather more detailed information about certain conditions such as coronary artery disease, chest pain, or diabetes by using a ***specialized medical questionnaire***, which is a document that requests detailed information about a specific illness or condition from a proposed insured's attending physician or examining physician. Figure 4.3 is an example of a specialized medical questionnaire requesting detailed information about a neuropsychiatric condition.

FIGURE 4.3 Specialized Medical Questionnaire for a Neuropsychiatric Condition

NEUROPSYCHIATRIC QUESTIONNAIRE

Please complete from patient's existing medical records. A current medical exam is NOT required.

Patient's Name ____________________

Application Number ____________________

1. Please classify the disorder
   ____ Affective Disorder ____ Personality Disorder
   ____ Anxiety Disorder ____ Psychotic Disorder
   ____ Organic Brain Disorder
2. What is the appropriate DSM IV American Psychiatric Diagnostic Code? __________
3. Date of onset? __________
4. Please classify the degree of impairment
   ____ Mild ____ Moderate ____ Severe
5. Please indicate if any of the following have occurred
   ____ Substance Abuse ____ Suicide Ideation
   ____ Suicide Attempt
6. Indicate dates of psychiatric care
   In-patient (hospitalization) __________
   Out-patient __________
7. Please specify the type of treatment prescribed
   ____ Individual Counseling
   ____ Electroconvulsive Therapy
   ____ Medication (include name and dosage of drug)
   ____ Group Counseling
   ____ Other (please specify) __________
8. Is the condition under effective control?
   ____ Yes If yes, for how long? __________
   ____ No
9. Date of full recovery and return to work or school __________
10. Is there any reason to believe that psychiatric care may be necessary in the future? __________

Date ____________________

Physician's Name (signature not required) ____________________

An underwriter sometimes contacts an attending or examining physician or the physician's staff to gather additional information on a proposed insured's specific disorder, verify dates and details of treatment, or clarify the reasons for certain diagnoses and medications. In addition, sometimes an underwriter finds that information obtained from a source such as an APS or an MIB report discloses a medical impairment or condition that was not reported on the application for insurance. Because the third-party information may be incorrect, the underwriter is careful not to reach a conclusion before contacting the physician. Underwriters may call the physician, but written communication may be required to properly document the file. Sometimes the underwriter finds it more efficient for a doctor on the insurer's staff to call the physician on behalf of the underwriter.

Medical Tests

Usually producers are the ones to order medical tests in accordance with the insurer's published age and amount requirements. However, an underwriter also may order medical tests in addition to those ordered by the producer. Figure 4.4 provides a brief description of four common tests. Note that a urinalysis, a blood chemistry profile, and an oral specimen (saliva) test commonly are referred to as *laboratory tests*.

Insurers keep medical test results confidential and only disclose the results to those with a legitimate need to know them.

Personal History Interviews

The insurer also may require a ***personal history interview (PHI)***, which is a conversation between an underwriter or another insurance company employee and the proposed insured in which the underwriter verifies the accuracy of information already received about the proposed insured and obtains any additional information needed for underwriting. The personal history interview is conducted by telephone or in person and is sometimes used in teleunderwriting.

Some companies have a special PHI unit that conducts PHIs. If the underwriter has additional questions, she may ask the PHI unit to follow up with the applicant or proposed insured.

Inspection Reports

An ***inspection report*** is a type of investigative consumer report that a consumer reporting agency prepares about a proposed insured. The consumer reporting agency's inspector gathers the information for an inspection report from public records, including court records, bankruptcy records, motor vehicle records, credit reports, documents verifying business ownership, and interviews with the proposed insured, as well as some of his friends, neighbors, and business associates.

FIGURE 4.4 Four Medical Tests Commonly Ordered for Underwriting

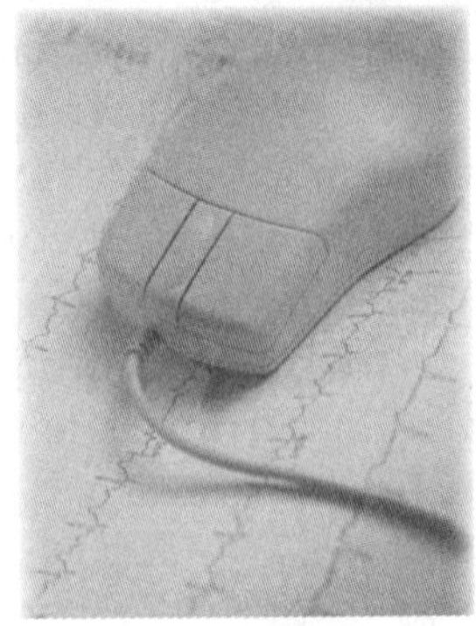

Electrocardiogram. An ***electrocardiogram (ECG)*** is a graphic record of the electrical forces produced by the heart and is a diagnostic tool for detecting a disease or an abnormality of the heart.

- A *resting ECG* is taken when a proposed insured is at rest and the heart is beating at its normal rate.
- A *stress ECG*, also known as an exercise ECG, is the same test taken during and after a proposed insured has engaged in a strictly defined amount of exercise.

In cases that call for ECGs, general industry practice is to obtain a resting ECG. A resting ECG reveals past heart damage while a stress ECG signals potential future heart problems. Although a stress ECG provides a more detailed analysis of a proposed insured's cardiac condition than does a resting ECG, underwriters usually request a stress ECG only at higher age and amount combinations because the test is expensive and time consuming.

Urinalysis. ***Urinalysis*** is the analysis of a urine specimen. A urinalysis is frequently required because it can detect the presence of protein, sugar, blood cells, and hypertension, as well as prescription medication and certain other drugs. Because urinalysis also can detect cotinine (a byproduct of nicotine that stays in the body far longer than nicotine) in urine, insurers use this test to verify whether a declared nonuser of tobacco is qualified for nonuser rates. A urinalysis also may test for human immunodeficiency virus (HIV). A required urine specimen typically is collected during the paramedical or medical examination, and insurance industry laboratories produce detailed reports of the findings. Urinalysis is performed in a laboratory chosen by the insurer.

Blood chemistry profile. A ***blood chemistry profile*** is a group of laboratory tests that analyze a sample of blood to identify factors that point to possible chronic and acute diseases. The standard blood profile has 15 to 18 components related to liver function, kidney function, glucose/diabetes, blood lipids, and serum proteins. In addition, as we mentioned in Chapter 3, some insurers require genetic and/or HIV testing. Blood also can be tested for cotinine. Blood specimens typically are collected during paramedical or medical examinations and are analyzed in insurance industry laboratories.

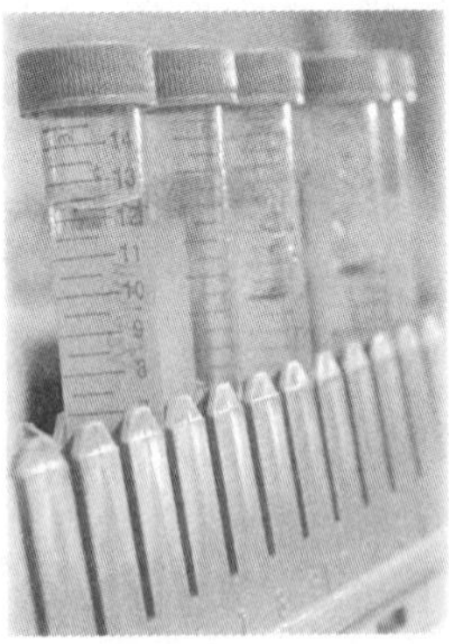

Oral specimen (saliva) test. An ***oral specimen (saliva) test*** is a means of screening proposed insureds for habitual use of nicotine or cocaine and the presence of HIV antibodies by testing a specimen of the proposed saliva. The specimen typically is collected by the producer at the time of application and sent to a laboratory to be tested. Oral specimen testing is usually more convenient and less expensive and invasive than blood or urine testing. However, oral specimen tests cannot be used to test for as many substances as blood or urine tests can.

Generally, an inspection report gathers more personal and financial information than it does medical information. The medical information collected on an inspection report includes

- The proposed insured's height and weight
- The proposed insured's health history
- The names and addresses of the proposed insured's attending physicians and other medical caregivers
- The date and cause of death of the proposed insured's parents if either is deceased

This information is the same as that requested on the application. In the event the information provided by the proposed insured on the application conflicts with information on the inspection report, the underwriter will be alerted to the need for further investigation.

Insurers typically establish age and amount limits above which underwriters routinely order inspection reports. Below such limits, the underwriter may use a PHI instead. When ordering inspection reports, insurers must abide by the provisions of the Fair Credit Reporting Act that we discussed in Chapter 3.

Pharmaceutical Databases

Pharmacy benefit managers (PBMs), which are clearinghouses that manage health care prescription benefit programs, maintain pharmaceutical databases that contain records of prescriptions filled by the persons enrolled in such benefit programs. These prescription histories are valuable to underwriters because the prescriptions taken by a proposed insured may be indicative of the conditions he has and the treatment he is receiving.

Insurers contract with vendors known as *prescription drug profiling services* that access these databases. Some insurers obtain prescription histories rather than APSs because obtaining a prescription history can be less expensive and time consuming than getting an APS. However, note that these histories are not available if the proposed insured is not enrolled in a health care prescription benefit program. If the proposed insured is enrolled in such a program, the underwriter must obtain his written consent to access this information. As with MIB information, information in a pharmaceutical database cannot be the sole factor for the underwriting decision.

Assessing Medical Factors

Individual life underwriters must have a high degree of medical knowledge because of the importance of medical factors in the assessment of mortality risk. While a detailed discussion of impairments is beyond the scope of this text, in this section we briefly mention the most common impairments that affect mortality risk. We also discuss age, sex, and build. While age and sex are not medical factors, per se, we discuss age here because of its correlation with impairments and importance in the individual life insurance underwriting decision; we touch upon sex because of its correlation with mortality rating and impact on pricing.

Impairments

To accurately assess a proposed insured's mortality risk, an individual life insurance underwriter needs to know about the human body's systems, possible impairments of those systems, treatments of those impairments, and interactions of multiple impairments. Impairments that typically are of particular concern to underwriters are listed in Insight 4.1.

INSIGHT 4.1 Typical Impairments of Concern to Underwriters

- Heart disease
- Lung disease
- Kidney disease
- Liver disease
- Cerebrovascular disease
- Gastrointestinal disorders
- Congenital heart defects
- Neurological impairments
- Diabetes
- Cancer
- Psychiatric impairments
- Alcohol and drug abuse
- AIDS

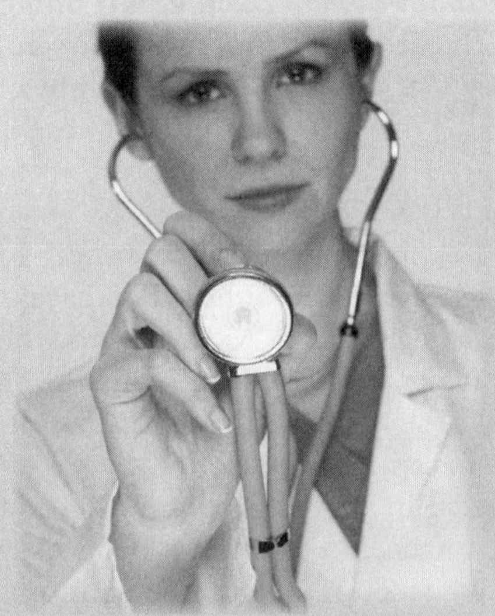

Source: Adapted from Mary C. Bickley et al., *Life and Health Insurance Underwriting*, 2nd ed. [Atlanta: LOMA (Life Office Management Association, Inc.), © 2007], 123. Used with permission; all rights reserved.

Age

Current age is the most important factor indicating a proposed insured's expected longevity because, as people age, the chance that they have an impairment increases. With young proposed insureds—generally ages 15 through 39—underwriters are more concerned about accidental death than they are with impairments. The situation changes if the proposed insured is middle-aged, which traditionally has been defined as ages 40 through 60, but which some companies now define as ages 50 to 70. At these ages, many proposed insureds develop health problems. At ages above 60 or 70, the chance that a proposed insured has or soon will develop an impairment is fairly high. A 72-year-old woman who does not admit to having seen any doctors during the previous five years or who lists only minor or very few injuries or illnesses is not typical. An underwriter probably would conduct a very thorough review of such a case, and some companies would require that the woman undergo a full medical examination.

Age also can be an indication of antiselection. For example, a 60-year-old man purchasing life insurance for the first time is statistically a greater risk for possible antiselection than is a 60-year-old man who has purchased insurance throughout his adult life. The fact that the first man has decided to purchase coverage only at an older age, perhaps as a result of sudden concern for his declining health, indicates the possibility of antiselection.

The underwriter may approve first-time coverage for a proposed insured of an advanced age if the underwriter determines that the reason for the insurance purchase is legitimate. For example, the proposed insured may have come to the realization belatedly that his family lacks adequate means of support upon his death. In addition, some older people who previously felt they lacked the financial means to purchase life insurance may apply for it to pay their final expenses.

Nearly all life insurers establish maximum age limits beyond which the insurer will not issue coverage. The maximum age limits usually vary according to the insurance product applied for and are generally lower for term insurance (about 75) and higher for whole life insurance (about 80). Some insurers now issue policies to proposed insureds up to age 85, and a few insurers issue policies up to at least age 90.

Sex

Individual life insurance underwriters typically disregard the sex of the proposed insured in determining the amounts and types of coverage issued because of laws and competitive pressure. However, many insurers do use sex-based actuarial tables to determine premiums rates because, statistically, females live longer than males.

Build

Build is the shape or form of the body, including the relationships among height, weight, and distribution of the weight. To evaluate build, underwriters typically use a ***build chart***, which is a chart that indicates average weights for various heights, along with the mortality debits associated with increases in weight. (We discuss mortality debits and credits in Chapter 5 under the section titled "Classification of Risks.") Some companies now rate the policy if the proposed insured is underweight, which is a particular concern when underwriting proposed insureds who are suffering from anorexia or are elderly. Underwriters also consider whether the proposed insured has gained or lost weight recently, because substantial or rapid gains or losses in weight may indicate medical impairments.

Underwriters typically use separate male and female build charts, as well as separate adult, child, and infant build charts. Figure 4.5 illustrates a typical adult build chart for an adult female.

Some underwriters now use body mass index (BMI) instead of build charts to evaluate build. BMI measures body fat and is based on height and weight. The BMI formula for male and female adults, teens, and children is

$$\frac{\textbf{Weight (lb)}}{\textbf{Height (in)}^2} \times 703$$

For example, if an adult male is 5′10″ tall and weighs 170 pounds, his BMI is $170/70^2 \times 703 = .035 \times 703 = 24.6$. According to the adult BMI chart set forth below, this adult male's weight is normal for his height.

BMI	Weight Status
Below 18.5	Underweight
18.5–24.9	Normal
25.0–29.9	Overweight
30.0 and above	Obese

BMI charts that categorize weight status differ for adults, teens, and children.

Personal Risk Factors

Individual life underwriters have a wide variety of sources of information about a proposed insured's personal risk factors. In this section, we discuss these sources and how an underwriter assesses personal risk factors, which are listed in Figure 4.6.

FIGURE 4.5 Adult Female Build Chart

Adult Female Build Chart
Age 16 and Over

Height	Avg. Female Wt.	Mortality Debits								
		+25	+50	+75	+100	+125	+150	+200	+250	+300
4'8"	105 lbs	180 lbs	190 lbs	200 lbs	215 lbs	220 lbs	230 lbs	240 lbs	245 lbs	255 lbs
4'9"	108	185	195	205	215	225	235	245	255	260
4'10"	112	190	200	210	220	230	240	250	255	265
4'11"	116	195	205	215	225	235	245	255	260	270
5'0"	118	195	205	220	230	240	250	255	265	275
5'1"	122	205	210	225	235	245	250	260	270	280
5'2"	125	205	215	230	235	245	255	265	275	285
5'3"	129	210	220	230	245	255	265	275	280	290
5'4"	132	220	225	240	250	260	270	280	290	300
5'5"	135	225	235	245	255	265	275	285	295	305
5'6"	138	230	240	250	260	270	285	295	305	315
5'7"	143	235	245	255	270	280	290	300	310	320
5'8"	146	240	250	265	275	285	300	310	320	330
5'9"	151	250	260	270	285	295	305	320	330	340
5'10"	154	255	265	280	290	305	315	325	335	345
5'11"	158	260	275	285	300	310	325	335	345	355
6'0"	162	270	280	295	305	320	330	340	355	365
6'1"	166	275	290	300	315	325	340	350	360	370
6'2"	169	285	300	310	325	335	345	360	370	380
6'3"	173	290	305	320	330	345	355	365	380	390

Sources of Personal Information

To assess a proposed insured's personal risk factors, an underwriter may consult many sources of information, including the application for insurance, the producer, the proposed insured's motor vehicle record (MVR), the inspection report, and personal questionnaires.

FIGURE 4.6 Personal Risk Factors Considered in Underwriting

- Occupation
- Driving history
- Avocations
- Tobacco use
- Alcohol use
- Drug abuse
- Subject of physical abuse
- Criminal history
- Civilian and military aviation
- Military status
- International residence and travel
- Foreign citizenship

Source: Adapted from Mary C. Bickley et al., *Life and Health Insurance Underwriting*, 2nd ed. [Atlanta: LOMA (Life Office Management Association, Inc.), © 2007], 161. Used with permission; all rights reserved.

The Application for Insurance

Some of the questions on the application for insurance are so personal that they could not be asked in other situations. For example, during a job interview, a prospective employer cannot make direct queries about marital status, weight, physical handicaps or defects, past illnesses, number and ages of children, net worth, and outstanding loans. However, such personal information helps an underwriter not only make an accurate assessment of the risk, but also view the proposed insured as an individual rather than just as another request for coverage.

The insurance application typically requests such information as the proposed insured's

- Date and place of birth
- Marital status

- Length of time at current residence
- Occupation
- Driving history, including driver's license suspension or revocation, driving convictions, pending charges, or more than a specified number (usually two or three) of moving traffic violations during a specified time period
- Participation in hazardous avocations that could result in physical injury (including motor vehicle racing, scuba or sky diving, hang gliding, parachuting, mountain climbing, and participating in rodeos)
- Tobacco use
- Alcohol use
- Drug abuse
- Criminal history information, including arrests and convictions for any criminal offenses
- Aviation activities other than as a passenger on scheduled commercial airline flights
- Residence or travel outside the country in which coverage is being sought

If any of the information provided on the application indicates the possibility of an increased risk—for example, if the proposed insured participates in a dangerous avocation, uses tobacco, or has a criminal history—the underwriter gathers sufficient information to decide whether to issue, rate, modify, or decline the requested coverage.

Also, if information on the application appears contradictory—for instance, if business travel seems inconsistent with the proposed insured's occupation—the underwriter seeks additional information to clarify the apparent inconsistencies. An underwriter also might seek additional information if information on the application indicates that the proposed insured has unexplained gaps in her employment history.

Producer

Because the producer may interact with and know the proposed insured personally, the producer is often in a unique position to provide first-hand knowledge about the proposed insured to the life underwriter. Thus, the underwriter carefully examines the agent's statement and any letter the producer may have submitted with the application.

Motor Vehicle Record

A ***motor vehicle record (MVR)*** is a report that contains information about a person's driving history, including information about traffic violations, arrests, and convictions. The underwriter uses information in the MVR to assess the degree of risk represented by a proposed insured's driving habits. Note that the MVR may not be available to underwriters in all jurisdictions, as some jurisdictions will not release the MVR to insurers due to privacy regulations and some states have increased fees to obtain a MVR to a prohibitive level.

Inspection Report

An inspection report may include some or all of the following information concerning personal risk factors:

- The type and frequency of the proposed insured's tobacco, alcohol, and drug use
- The proposed insured's avocations, driving history, and police record, including arrests and convictions
- The type of business in which the proposed insured has been employed, the length of time employed, and typical work duties

Personal Questionnaires

Personal questionnaires typically ask for information about the proposed insured's participation in a specified activity that is known to increase the risk of injury or death. Examples include personal questionnaires about avocations, alcohol usage, and drug usage. Avocation questionnaires ask if the proposed insured is licensed or certified to take part in the specified activity and by whom. Figure 4.7 is an example of a personal questionnaire requesting information about a proposed insured's participation in scuba diving.

The questions in a personal questionnaire are based on statistical information about the relationship of specific activities to injury and death. Many insurers rely on standard questionnaires that have been used in the industry for years and have been proven to be helpful in gathering information needed for underwriting.

Insurers verify the quality of specialized personal questionnaires in two ways. First, insurance regulatory authorities must approve questionnaire forms that are to be signed by proposed insureds and will become part of the application for insurance. Second, insurance companies doing business with reinsurers usually ask the reinsuring companies to review and revise the questionnaires to assure that the questionnaires ask the questions necessary to assess each risk correctly.

FIGURE 4.7 Scuba Diving Questionnaire

SCUBA DIVING QUESTIONNAIRE

Purpose of diving ____ Business ___ Pleasure

Type of diving (if applicable) ___ Instruction ___ Construction ___ Salvage
___ Research ___ Night diving

Where do you dive? ___ Inland waters ___ Ocean or sea

Diving History

	Last 12 months		Next 12 months	
Depth (in ft.)	No. of Dives	Average Duration of Dives	No. of Dives	Average Duration of Dives
<50				
50–100				
>100				

Maximum depth obtained ________________

Are you a member of a diving organization? ___ Yes ___ No

Are you a certified diver? ___ Yes ___ No

If yes, please list certification(s) and level(s):

____

Have you ever had a diving-related accident? ___ Yes ___ No

If yes, please give details:

____

I declare that the above information is true and complete and shall form part of my application to ABC Assurance Company.

Signature__________________________

Date __________________________

Note that if the insurer discovers that the proposed insured made a material misrepresentation of fact in a questionnaire that has been filed with the appropriate regulatory authority and is considered to be part of the policy, then the insurer has the right to rescind the policy during the policy's contestable period.

Assessing Personal Factors

In this section, we consider how each of the personal risk factors listed in Figure 4.6 affects the underwriting of individual life insurance.

Occupation

A proposed insured's occupation usually is not a factor in underwriting individual life insurance unless the insurer considers the occupation to be hazardous. An underwriter typically assesses two kinds of occupational hazards: *accident hazards* (such as working on high-rise construction) and *health hazards* (such as exposure to toxic chemicals). Accident hazards are more common among some workers, such as lumber workers and demolition experts, while health hazards are more common among other workers, such as those involved in radium analysis. Moreover, some workers—coal miners, for example—are subject to both types of hazards. Figure 4.8 lists and describes some occupations that many insurers consider hazardous.

Within certain categories of occupations, some policies generally are issued as standard and others generally are rated, depending on the proposed insured's actual job duties. For example, a coal miner who is an above-ground machinist might be issued a standard policy, while an underground worker typically would be issued a rated policy.

FIGURE 4.8 Occupations That Many Insurers Consider Hazardous

Occupation	Description of Risk
Building demolition	**Accident hazards**: collapse of unsound structures, explosions, blasting
Open mining and quarrying	**Accident hazards**: rock falls, cave-ins, quarrying fire, explosions **Health hazards**: asphyxiation, poisonous gases
Stunts in films	**Accident hazards**: high-speed driving, leaps and dives, fire, explosions
Radium analysis	**Health hazards**: radioactive poisoning, potential carcinogenic effects

Source: Adapted from Mary C. Bickley et al., *Life and Health Insurance Underwriting*, 2nd ed. [Atlanta: LOMA (Life Office Management Association, Inc.), © 2007], 165. Used with permission; all rights reserved.

A rating for occupation may be reduced or removed when the insured's occupation changes. Generally, insurers require that an insured person who has previously been in a hazardous occupation must work for at least one year in a less hazardous occupation and must not be likely to return to the former, more hazardous occupation for the rating to be reduced or removed. Some ratings also may be removed automatically when the insured reaches a certain age, such as age 65.

Driving History

Because accidental deaths frequently result from motor vehicle accidents, underwriters pay considerable attention to a proposed insured's driving history. Underwriters consider the number, type, and timing of traffic violations, as well as whether alcohol or drugs were involved in any of the violations. Proposed insureds who have many traffic violations generally pose greater risks for fatal motor vehicle accidents.

Most insurers attempt to identify poor drivers by including in the application a question asking if the proposed insured has been convicted of a moving traffic violation or been charged with driving under the influence (DUI) within a certain period of time. To obtain additional information about a proposed insured's driving record, an underwriter may request a MVR.

For people who have unfavorable driving histories, most insurers rate the policy, modify the benefit amounts to compensate for the extra risk, postpone making a decision, or decline the application. For example, a proposed insured who has had two DUIs within the last five years probably would be denied coverage.

Avocations

To gather information about an applicant's avocations, or leisure activities, underwriters use specialized personal questionnaires such as the one shown in Figure 4.7. Such a questionnaire may focus on just one activity or may gather information on several avocations.

In underwriting avocations, underwriters consider the proposed insured's age, training, and type and quality of equipment to determine whether the policy should be rated for participation in a potentially risky avocation. Underwriters usually distinguish between people who pursue activities as an occupation (professional) and those who do it as an avocation (amateur). As examples, automobile racing, boxing, wrestling, and rodeo riding can be either avocations or occupations.

Tobacco Use

People who use tobacco in any form show greater mortality at every age than people who do not. As a result, life insurers generally charge higher premium rates for tobacco users than for nonusers. Insurers accomplish this premium rate differential in a number of ways, including

- Developing separate premium rate schedules for tobacco users and nonusers.
- Assigning higher ratings for impairments that are sensitive to tobacco use, such as coronary artery disease, cancer, and lung disease, than the impairments would be assigned if the proposed insured didn't use tobacco.
- Placing tobacco users in a standard classification and nonusers in a preferred classification.
- Adjusting premium rates for tobacco users and nonusers. Under this approach, tobacco use and nonuse are considered risk factors that have a negative or positive impact, respectively, on mortality risk.
- Offering discounted premiums for tobacco nonusers.

Answers to tobacco-use questions are some of the most frequently misrepresented answers on applications for insurance because most proposed insureds who use tobacco know that answering truthfully about their use will increase their premium rates. Therefore, when a proposed insured undergoes a physical examination, underwriters usually ask the paramedical or medical examiner to test a sample of the proposed insured's blood, urine, or saliva for the presence of cotinine. Underwriters also can require a tobacco questionnaire or an inspection report that includes comments on the proposed insured's use of tobacco.

Alcohol Use

Underwriters investigate a proposed insured's use of alcohol to ascertain the potential for alcohol abuse or alcoholism, both of which can increase a proposed insured's mortality risk. An underwriter decides whether to rate or decline a policy for alcohol use depending on the degree of use.

Obtaining information about a proposed insured's use of alcohol can be very difficult. Underwriters usually gather information from inspection reports, alcohol usage questionnaires, MVRs, APSs, and liver function tests. In addition, underwriters can order two specific laboratory tests that can indicate heavy drinking—HAA and CDT, which are known as "alcohol markers."

An alcohol usage questionnaire asks a proposed insured to provide information on his consumption of alcoholic beverages, as well as details about the effects of alcohol use on his health, driving, and occupation.

Drug Abuse

Drug abuse generally refers to the excessive or inappropriate use of prescription drugs or the use of illegal drugs. Drugs subject to abuse include marijuana, narcotics, hallucinogens, stimulants, and sedatives. Figure 4.9 lists the most commonly used illicit drugs in the United States in 2006. People who abuse these drugs may have or may develop psychological impairments, physical dependence, or personality disorders that can constitute additional risk.

When investigating the possibility of drug abuse, underwriters try to ascertain what drugs are being used and to what extent. Life insurers typically decline coverage for any proposed insured who currently engages in drug abuse, although some companies will offer coverage to proposed insureds who admit to moderate marijuana use.

A distinct difference between alcohol abuse and the abuse of some drugs is that alcohol is legal and, if used in moderation, acceptable in our society; whereas the use of some drugs is illegal. As a result, gathering information about a proposed insured's drug abuse often is difficult, especially because positive answers to questions concerning a person's use of illegal drugs can be incriminating. Additionally, the fact that a proposed insured uses illegal drugs raises the question of moral hazard.

FIGURE 4.9 Most Commonly Used Illicit Drugs in the United States in 2006

Drug	Percentage of U.S. Population (Age 12 or Older) Who Admitted Use
Nonmedical Use of Prescription Drugs	6.6
Marijuana and Hashish	10.3
Cocaine	2.5
Hallucinogens	1.6
Inhalants	0.9

Source: Substance Abuse and Mental Health Services Administration, Office of Applied Studies, *Results from the 2005 National Survey on Drug Use and Health: National Findings*, http://www.oas.samhsa.gov/NSDUH/2k6NSDUH/tabs/Sect1peTabs1to46.htm#Tab1.1B (6 September 2007).

When drug abuse is suspected and the amount of insurance applied for is sufficient to warrant such an extensive investigation, the underwriter may order an APS, a urine test, a drug usage questionnaire, and an inspection report focused on drug abuse. The underwriter verifies that any tests for the presence of illegal drugs are conducted properly and that the test results are kept confidential.

Subject of Physical Abuse

The risk that results from the physical abuse of a proposed insured by a spouse, partner, or other family member is a sensitive issue for underwriters. Recall from Chapter 3 that several U.S. jurisdictions have enacted legislation that prohibits insurers from requesting or using information about whether a proposed insured is abused in making an underwriting decision.

However, in states where the law permits insurers to consider abuse status when making an underwriting decision, assessing the risk posed by potential abuse requires the underwriter to evaluate impartially the level of risk that the abuse represents and to determine the degree to which the risk is acceptable or unacceptable to the insurer. Insurers typically try to insure subjects of abuse unless the abuse constitutes a grave risk of serious injury or death.

To investigate abuse, an underwriter may focus on hospital emergency room records that indicate treatment for traumatic injuries. Also, because physical abuse often is accompanied by alcohol and/or drug abuse, as well as severe depression, the underwriter checks medical records, inspection reports, producer's comments, and other sources for evidence of such conditions.

Criminal History

Underwriters carefully investigate proposed insureds who have a history of criminal or illegal activities. Although an underwriter cannot predict that criminal activity will recur, such a case requires a thorough review of the facts, an extensive inspection report, and detailed interviews with people who are likely to know the current activities and character of the proposed insured.

Generally, an underwriter considers the following factors in evaluating a proposed insured's criminal activity:

- The length of time the proposed insured was involved in crime
- The length of time that has elapsed since the proposed insured was involved in crime
- The proposed insured's history in relation to police, courts, and correctional institutions
- The nature of the offense or offenses committed

Recent criminal activity in the history of a proposed insured usually causes underwriters to rate or decline the case. Proposed insureds who have been arrested for multiple or violent crimes, have been involved in criminal activity over a period of time, or have a history of criminal activity coupled with alcohol abuse, drug abuse, compulsive gambling, extreme aggression, or severe psychological problems are rarely, if ever, accepted for coverage. Insurers generally give more lenient consideration to proposed insureds who have no history of violent crime and have noncriminal family members, consistent work records, and associates and friends who are not involved in criminal activity. In addition, insurers may be more lenient when the crime was in the distant past and the proposed insured appears to be rehabilitated.

Civilian and Military Aviation

Although civilian and military aviation are underwritten somewhat differently, the primary sources of information for both include the application for insurance, aviation questionnaire, inspection report, and personal history interview. Typically, if a proposed insured indicates on the application that he is involved in aviation activities, the insurer requires the proposed insured to complete an aviation questionnaire.

Civilian Aviation. Civilian aviation includes air ambulance, ballooning, commercial aviation, crop dusting, fire fighting, power line and pipe inspecting, mail service, mapping, policing, racing, sightseeing, and weather or traffic control. Civilian aviation also includes flying for pleasure.

For most civilian aviation, the proposed insured's total hours of flying experience and the number of hours that the person plans to fly annually are important information. Another factor that an underwriter considers is the aviation certificate or ratings that the proposed insured holds. Studies show that proposed insureds with high levels of flying certification or ratings, as well as extensive flying experience, have a greater degree of skill and are less likely to be involved in aviation accidents than proposed insureds with lower levels of certification or ratings or less experience.

An underwriter also considers the medical certificate held by a proposed insured. The medical certificate is the only proof required for a pilot to be medically certified to fly. However, underwriters are also aware that, even if a person is denied a medical certificate, numerous appeal mechanisms enable a person with even severe medical impairments, such as alcoholism or a history of coronary bypass surgery, to obtain medical certification. In short, a proposed insured who holds an aviation medical certificate is not necessarily a standard risk for insurance.

Insurers typically issue individual life insurance coverage at standard rates to most civilian pilots who apply for coverage. However, the underwriter may rate a policy for the aviation hazard if she determines that the pilot represents a greater-than-standard risk. Another approach to insuring a greater-than-standard risk is to issue the policy with an aviation exclusion rider, although some jurisdictions limit or prohibit such riders. Generally, aviation exclusion riders are used only in cases in which (1) the aviation hazard is greater than the insurer is willing to accept, (2) the aviation hazard cannot be measured, or (3) the pilot has a history of certain medical impairments, such as depression, stroke, or heart disease.

In assessing risk for pilots flying employer-owned aircraft, an underwriter ascertains whether the pilot has either an airline transport certificate or a commercial certificate with an instrument flight rating, indicating that the pilot is qualified to fly in all weather conditions. Insurers typically rate policies issued to pilots who do not hold one of these certificates.

Military Aviation. When underwriting military aviation, underwriters consider many of the same factors evaluated in underwriting civilian aviation. In addition, underwriters look carefully at the duty area of all proposed insureds who are military aviators, as well as the type of aircraft in which they fly. In most military aviation cases, proposed insureds who serve for specified periods in a hazardous place are not acceptable risks; underwriters typically will not issue coverage until the proposed insured returns from the dangerous assignment and has no pending hazardous assignments.

Life insurers typically rate policies for proposed insureds engaged in military aviation. Generally, the extra charges for military aviation are higher for people under the age of 30 than for people age 30 and older. Also, the extra amounts charged for military pilots are usually higher than the extra amounts charged for aviation crew members.

Military Status

If a country is not at war or involved in a military conflict, most insurers approve most military personnel for coverage at standard rates. Underwriters generally consider most career military personnel as good risks and underwrite them as if they were civilians. However, many insurers do not issue coverage to noncareer military personnel from the lower pay grades because those people have statistically higher-than-average lapse rates and accidental death rates.

If an armed conflict occurs, most insurers will refuse an application from military personnel for as long as the conflict lasts or will attach a rider to the policy excluding losses as a result of war. Some insurance companies, however, issue individual life insurance coverage at standard rates to all military personnel who do not exhibit extraordinary risk other than that associated with military service.

International Residence and Travel

Many insurers in the United States and Canada do not approve coverage for proposed insureds who reside abroad for extended periods because of the difficulty of gathering complete underwriting information and, if coverage is issued and death occurs, of conducting an adequate, cost-effective claim investigation. Insurers that conduct considerable business in foreign countries and have established foreign offices, however, typically do issue insurance to people residing there either temporarily or permanently. The rates for such coverage are generally higher than for similar people not living abroad.

Vacation trips of three to six weeks duration are usually of no concern to the underwriter unless a proposed insured plans to travel to an area with great political unrest, military activity, or known, widespread deadly disease. If the proposed insured plans to travel to such a high-risk area, the underwriter may approve coverage at a higher premium or decline to issue the coverage. Alternatively, the underwriter may postpone the decision to issue coverage until the proposed insured returns to her home country. Most U.S. and Canadian insurers remove extra premiums after an insured has been home for a period or one to two years.

One of the most important factors in all applications that involve foreign residence and travel is the type of insurance requested. In general, when a proposed insured requests the lowest premium term insurance and wishes to make monthly payments for it, the underwriter considers the coverage to be "trip insurance" which the applicant probably has no intention of maintaining after the trip is completed. Therefore, the underwriter usually declines the risk.

Note that at the time this publication went to press, the U.S. Congress was considering legislation that would prohibit life insurance underwriters from rating or declining coverage based on a proposed insured's foreign travel plans. In addition, similar legislation has passed or is pending in several states. Because of the uncertainty surrounding the legality of asking about foreign travel, some companies do not ask about foreign travel. Other companies keep track of legislation in each jurisdiction and underwrite accordingly.

Foreign Citizenship

Underwriting life insurance for recent immigrants and residents who are citizens of foreign countries is based on individual consideration of the class of risk presented, the reason for the insurance purchase, the reputation of the submitting producer, and the quality of the producer's previously submitted business. Generally, insurers give favorable consideration to foreign citizens who

- Intend to become permanent residents of the country in which the insurer does business

- Possess a permanent resident visa
- Own property or have bank accounts in the country in which the insurer does business

If a proposed insured is a foreign citizen who has lived in the new country for less than one year, most insurers require a medical examination and a complete blood profile for any amount of life insurance coverage. Certain factors in developing countries can contribute to higher morbidity and mortality in people who leave those countries and establish residence elsewhere. These factors include

- Scarcity of medical resources
- Malnutrition
- Unsafe water and provisions for sanitation
- Inadequate education about healthful practices

Most North American insurers do not issue coverage to foreign nationals who are only visiting or temporarily living in North America because such a person has little apparent reason to own a policy issued outside the native country. Insurers are concerned that the policy may lapse upon the person's departure and that claims may be difficult to investigate should the insured die in his native country.

Key Terms

nonmedical basis
nonmedical supplement
nonmedical limit
paramedical report
medical report
MIB Group, Inc. (MIB)
attending physician
examining physician
attending physician's statement (APS)
specialized medical questionnaire
personal history interview (PHI)
inspection report
electrocardiogram (ECG)
urinalysis
blood chemistry profile
oral specimen (saliva) test
pharmacy benefit manager (PBM)
build
build chart
motor vehicle record (MVR)

chapter

5

Underwriting Individual Life Insurance: Financial Underwriting and Risk Classification

Outline

Financial Underwriting

Risks Deterred by Financial Underwriting

Sources of Financial Information

Assessing Life Insurance Needs and Financial Factors

Tools to Determine the Appropriate Amount of Insurance

Risk Classification

Numerical Rating System

Charging for Substandard Risks

Learning Objectives

After studying this chapter, you should be able to…

- Describe the risks deterred by financial underwriting
- List and describe the sources of financial information used in underwriting individual life insurance
- List and describe financial factors used in underwriting individual life insurance
- Explain how an underwriter assesses financial need for individual life insurance
- Use a factor table and the percentage-of-income rule to calculate the maximum amount of coverage a proposed insured with a specified income could qualify for
- Explain how underwriters use the numerical rating system to classify individual life insurance risks and calculate the total risk represented by a proposed insured
- List and describe three methods of charging for substandard individual life insurance risks and identify which method is most appropriate based on whether a risk is expected to increase, decrease, or remain constant over time

In Chapter 4, we saw how individual life insurance underwriters assess medical and personal factors to determine mortality risk. In this chapter, we begin by discussing why and how individual life underwriters assess a proposed insured's financial condition.

Although financial factors are relevant in underwriting both personal and business life insurance, we postpone the discussion of their relevance to business life insurance until Chapter 6. In this chapter, we focus on personal insurance, which is insurance that fulfills the needs of an individual rather than a business. The term *personal insurance* includes property and liability coverages that meet the needs of an individual, but we limit our discussion to individual life insurance that meets such needs.

Having covered the assessment of medical and personal risk factors in Chapter 4 and the financial risk factors in the first part of this chapter, we conclude this chapter with a discussion of risk classification. We explain the typical process for calculating and classifying risk and approaches for charging premiums for substandard risks.

Financial Underwriting

An individual life insurance underwriter assesses the proposed insured's financial condition to determine whether 1) the proposed insured needs the coverage, 2) a reasonable relationship exists between the need for the coverage and the amount of coverage applied for, and 3) the premiums are affordable. This assessment of the proposed risk based on financial factors is known as ***financial underwriting***. Note that when we refer to the proposed insured's financial condition, we assume that the proposed insured, applicant, and policyowner are the same person. If the proposed insured is not the policyowner, who typically is the person responsible for paying premiums, the underwriter also will assess the policyowner's financial condition in terms of his ability to afford the premium payments.

We begin this section by discussing risks that financial underwriting is designed to detect and deter. We then examine the sources of financial information used for underwriting individual life insurance. Next, we explain an underwriter's assessment of need and financial factors. We conclude by describing tools an underwriter uses to determine the appropriate amount of individual life insurance to issue.

Risks Deterred by Financial Underwriting

By engaging in financial underwriting, an underwriter can detect and protect against the risks of lapse, antiselection, speculation, and money laundering.

Lapse

Insurers know from experience that proposed insureds who buy more insurance than they can afford tend to let their policies lapse, and lapses negatively affect an insurer's financial statements. Underwriters are concerned with maintaining an excellent ***persistency rate***, which is the percentage of a specified group of contracts that remain in force during a specified period, such as a year. Thus, underwriters engage in financial underwriting to ensure that the proposed insured can afford the premiums and that the policy does not lapse. However, when the application is for relatively inexpensive term insurance, underwriters forego examining the proposed insured's ability to pay but not the need for the amount applied for.

Antiselection

Underwriters are unable to properly assess risk when antiselection is involved; thus, the premium charged for any coverage that is issued will not be adequate to cover the risk, resulting in a financial loss to the insurer. Underwriters therefore engage in financial underwriting to ensure that the proposed insured needs the coverage because they know that people who buy more life insurance than they appear to need may be engaging in antiselection.

For example, if a person who has never applied for life insurance does so at an advanced age and the application indicates that the person has no impairments, the underwriter may suspect antiselection and investigate for undisclosed impairments. The underwriter's investigation may reveal facts that will prompt her to decline the coverage. However, if the underwriter determines that the proposed insured never had any dependents and thus had no need for insurance to support them upon his death but that he now needs the insurance proceeds to pay the estate taxes on his large estate, the underwriter is less likely to suspect antiselection.

Note that insurers' experience has shown that the possibility of antiselection tends to be greater for large policies. In underwriting an application for a substantial amount of coverage, the underwriter needs to know considerably more about the proposed insured's financial background than is necessary for smaller-amount cases.

Speculation

In terms of insurance, ***speculation*** is the unethical purchase of insurance to make a profit on the proceeds rather than to protect against the risk of financial loss. The possibility of speculation may arise when the amount of insurance applied for exceeds the potential financial loss that a beneficiary might suffer if a proposed insured were to die. Thus, underwriters engage in financial underwriting to ensure that the amount of coverage applied for is consistent with the potential financial loss.

For example, an application made by an adult child for insurance on an aged, dependent parent requires special examination, because such an application may present an element of speculation. Upon the death of the proposed insured, the adult child not only would receive the death benefit, but also would be relieved of the expenses of supporting the parent. The underwriter might, however, approve coverage on the life of an elderly parent who provides a service, such as babysitting for grandchildren for which the adult child would have to pay. Note that in the case of a third-party policy, the policyowner's lack of an insurable interest in the proposed insured can indicate speculation. Without an insurable interest, the policyowner, who is usually the beneficiary, would benefit rather than suffer a loss from the proposed insured's death.

Some believe that a life settlement is another example of speculation. A ***life settlement*** is the sale of a life insurance policy to a third party for a discount from the policy's face amount. While some see life settlements as a viable way of funding end of life costs, others feel they are speculative because the company purchasing the policy (generally known as a *life settlement provider*) expects to earn a profit by receiving the full death benefit from a life insurance policy for which it paid a discounted amount.

Money Laundering

As we noted in Chapter 3, money laundering is a crime involving hiding the identity, source, and/or destination of money associated with criminal activity. If a proposed insured applies for more cash value coverage than she needs or if she is hesitant to provide financial information, an underwriter may suspect money laundering. However, the large amount applied for may be the result of an exaggerated financial needs analysis.

Insight 5.1 illustrates how an underwriter would analyze a case for lapse, antiselection, speculation, and money laundering from a financial underwriting point of view.

Sources of Financial Information

An underwriter relies on three main sources of information to assess a proposed insured's financial situation: (1) the application for insurance, (2) the producer, and (3) the inspection report. If additional information is needed, an underwriter may consult tax documents, financial questionnaires, and financial statements. The amount and type of financial information gathered generally are determined by the amount of coverage requested. To manage and organize financial information, an underwriter may use a ***financial worksheet***, which is a document that enables an underwriter to organize financial information and develop a clear picture of a person's financial situation.

INSIGHT 5.1 Analysis for Lapse, Antiselection, Speculation, and Money Laundering

Joanna Ingstrom's aunt, Emma, has lived with Joanna and her two children for three years. During that time, Emma has been in good health and has volunteered at Joanna's antique shop three days a week. Joanna pays for Emma's living expenses. After Emma suffered a fall that broke her arm, Joanna applied for a $50,000 life insurance policy on her aunt, with herself as the policyowner and beneficiary.

In reviewing this case, the underwriter engaged in the following analysis to detect the possibility of lapse and the presence of antiselection, speculation, and money laundering:

- **Lapse**. The underwriter will analyze Joanna's financial condition to determine if she can afford the premiums.
- **Antiselection**. Although Emma had never been insured before, the underwriter recognized that this was the first time that her death would result in a financial loss to anyone. Emma was healthy at the time of the application, as the broken arm was a minor injury from which she was expected to fully recover. Thus, antiselection is probably not a factor.
- **Speculation**. Even though, upon Emma's death, Joanna would be relieved of paying Emma's living expenses, the death benefit Joanna would receive would serve to offset the salary she now would have to pay an employee to replace Emma's volunteer services. Thus, Joanna is protecting against the risk of a financial loss rather than trying to make a profit.
- **Money Laundering**. The amount of coverage requested in relation to the loss suffered is not great enough for suspicions of money laundering to arise.

The Application for Insurance

The application for insurance provides the underwriter with an initial picture of the proposed insured's ***financial status***. A person's financial status includes his (1) current income expressed in terms of amount, sources, and permanency and (2) ***net worth***, which is the difference between the person's assets and liabilities. Figure 5.1 summarizes and gives examples of the significant financial information an underwriter can obtain from the insurance application.

In examining the application information, the underwriter determines whether an insurable interest exists and whether the amount of insurance requested is appropriate. For example, if a proposed insured already has several small-amount life insurance policies that have been in force for years and now wishes to purchase a large additional amount of coverage, the underwriter determines whether the new coverage can be justified according to the proposed insured's current income, ability to pay for the coverage, and the need for insurance.

Figure 5.1 Information on the Insurance Application of Significance to Financial Underwriting

Information	Underwriting Significance
Age of proposed insured	Years of future employment
Occupation	Future potential income
Income	Current income
Insurance in force and amount of requested coverage	Current and requested coverage compared to total needed coverage
Relationship between proposed insured and policyowner, if not the same person	Presence of insurable interest
Relationship between proposed insured and beneficiary	Presence of insurance interest Justification of amount of coverage
Net worth	Determination of appropriate amount of coverage needed to preserve a proposed insured's estate

Source: Adapted from Mary C. Bickley et al., *Life and Health Insurance Underwriting*, 2nd ed. [Atlanta: LOMA (Life Office Management Association, Inc.), © 2007], 136. Used with permission; all rights reserved.

Producer

A producer who has established a strong relationship with an insurer and who generally requests coverage only for qualified proposed insureds is likely to be considered a reliable source of financial information during underwriting. If the underwriter has questions or doubts about the justification for requested insurance, the underwriter typically communicates with the producer to clarify the submitted information. For underwriting large-amount cases, the underwriter might request a letter from the producer explaining the proposed insured's need for a large amount of insurance. If doubts persist, the underwriter then may request more information from the producer, the proposed insured, or a consumer reporting agency.

Inspection Report

The information in an inspection report can be useful in verifying information from the application and the producer and in gathering further information. For example, the underwriter may ask the consumer reporting agency to check for any liens—which are claims on the proposed insured's property in connection with outstanding debts—bankruptcies, poor credit history, outstanding lawsuits, and other significant debts in the proposed insured's financial history. The underwriter also may ask the consumer reporting agency to interview the proposed insured's attorney, tax adviser, and/or accountant to verify or gather further details about financial information on the application.

Tax Documents

An underwriter can gather valuable information from a proposed insured's W-2 form (in the United States) or T4 form (in Canada), which provides the underwriter with information about the amount of money paid to the proposed insured by an employer.

An underwriter can assess many aspects of a proposed insured's insurability using information from income tax returns, including all schedules to such returns. For example, when a proposed insured has listed alimony paid or large amounts of business expenses, the underwriter may question whether the proposed insured has sufficient funds to pay for insurance. Moreover, if the proposed insured lists a considerable deduction for medical or dental expenses, the underwriter may seek further information about the proposed insured's health.

For large-amount applications, some insurers use statements from a proposed insured's banker or certified public accountant instead of or in addition to information from tax documents. The statements typically cover several years and report gross income, net income, net worth, and financial losses.

Financial Questionnaire

For a large-amount application, the insurer may require the proposed insured to complete and sign a financial questionnaire. Each insurance company typically designs its own financial questionnaire to gather detailed information about proposed insureds. In handling financial questionnaires, the underwriter is especially careful to adhere to the insurance company's rules of confidentiality.

If a proposed insured is requesting personal life insurance as a means of paying a future estate tax liability, the underwriter may use a financial questionnaire to gather such information as the value of the proposed insured's estate, the composition of the estate (for instance, property, investments, and other sources of assets), the estimated value and the dates of all gifts made from the estate, the estimated amount of estate tax payable, and the name of the person who is liable for paying the estate tax after the proposed insured's death.

Financial Statements

When a proposed insured who owns a business wishes to purchase a considerable amount of life insurance, the underwriter usually requests financial statements—that is, standardized reports summarizing the business's finances—to determine the stability of the business. In assessing financial statements, an underwriter usually considers the following information:

- The historic trend of profit or loss in the business, typically for a period of at least the three to five years prior to the date of application for insurance
- Financial obligations to which the business is or will be committed
- Evidence of plans to expand, restructure, or sell the business

The debt of a business can rise and fall substantially during the year. Therefore, in analyzing the amount of debt a company carries, underwriters typically use annual financial statements, rather than recent quarterly reports, which could present a distorted view of the company's financial strength or weakness. Figure 5.2 describes the types of financial statements an underwriter may examine.

Some businesses—typically those that sell stock to the public—produce annual reports that may be helpful to an underwriter. An ***annual report*** is a financial document that a corporation issues to its stockholders to report the business's activities and financial status for a specified period, which is usually the preceding year. The annual report includes independently audited financial statements, along with information from the business's management team concerning the organization's current and future business position and performance.

Assessing Life Insurance Needs and Financial Factors

An underwriter evaluates a proposed insured's financial situation in part to assess that person's need for insurance. An underwriter must determine that the need for the coverage is legitimate and the amount of insurance requested to cover this need is reasonable and affordable. In other words, the amount of insurance applied for and in force must make sense and not create a situation in which the proposed insured is worth more dead than alive.

Some generally accepted financial purposes for purchasing personal life insurance include

- **Family income protection.** Funds needed to pay the ordinary living expenses of a family that were formerly paid by the income of a deceased person. Underwriters generally approve coverage for family income protection if the need for the amount requested is shown clearly.

FIGURE 5.2 Financial Statements Used by Underwriters

Statement of owners' equity (also known as a *statement of changes in owners' equity*). A financial statement that shows the changes in owners' equity during a specified period. In the context of valuing a business, ***equity*** is the amount of the business owned—and not financed—by the owners. The underwriter uses the statement of owners' equity to determine the dollar amount of the owners' shares in a business.

Balance sheet. A financial statement that shows the business's financial position on a certain date. The balance sheet includes information on the business's *assets*, which are all things of value owned by the business; the business's *liabilities*, which are the business's debts and future obligations; and the *equity* of the owners of the business, which represents the value of the business as determined by deducting liabilities from assets.

Income statement. A financial document, (also known as a *profit and loss statement*), that reports the business's revenues and expenses during a specified period and indicates whether the business experienced net income or a net loss during the period. The income statement attempts to match the revenues—or income—for the specified period with the expenses—or costs of doing business—during that period.

Statement of cash flows. A financial statement that indicates the amounts of cash received and paid in the operating, investing, and financing activities associated with the business. A statement of cash flows helps an underwriter to assess a firm's ability to produce adequate future cash flows. This statement also helps the underwriter determine the reason for any gaps that exist between a company's net income and the amount of cash received. A company that shows increasing deficiencies in cash flow from year to year may be in financial difficulty.

- **Estate settlement.** The process of paying debts after a person's death. Estate settlement typically requires funds to pay taxes, medical expenses not covered by insurance, funeral costs, attorneys' fees and other expenses incurred to settle the estate, as well as funds to repay debts owed by the deceased person. Life insurance can provide the funds needed to pay these expenses. Underwriters usually approve coverage intended to pay such expenses when evidence of the obligations is clear.
- **Charitable contributions.** The naming of a charitable institution as the beneficiary in an application for life insurance. A person who has made regular contributions to a charitable organization may wish to continue to support that organization after her death. Life insurance proceeds can be used to replace the future contributions she would have made. Even if a person has made no previous contributions, using life insurance proceeds to benefit a charity is a legitimate and widely recognized way of making charitable gifts.

Life insurance is designed to meet the needs of insureds by providing policy proceeds that compensate for a financial loss but do not represent a profit to the beneficiary. Most proposed insureds demonstrate a clear need for the requested coverage and can afford the premiums, especially in these days of low-cost term insurance. However, determining whether the amount of coverage is appropriate—in other words, whether the coverage will compensate for a loss but will not be so great as to represent a profit to the beneficiary—may be a challenge to underwriters.

In this section, we discuss the financial factors underwriters assess in determining whether the proposed amount of coverage is appropriate based on the proposed insured's need and ability to pay for the coverage. Such factors include the proposed insured's financial status and other life insurance in force.

Financial Status

A proposed insured's financial status includes his income and net worth. In addition bankruptcies can affect the proposed insured's financial status.

Current Income. *Current income*, also referred to as *annual income*, is one of the elements used to determine the appropriate amount of coverage to issue. Current income may be earned or unearned. *Earned income* is income that will not continue after the insured dies—such as salary from a full- or part-time job, regular bonuses and commissions, and stock options—and is a measure of the financial loss that family members would suffer in the event of a person's death. *Unearned income* is income that may continue after the person dies, such as interest income, dividends, and capital gains. Many insurance companies will consider only the proposed insured's earned income when determining the need for insurance, but will consider both the earned and unearned income when determining ability to pay for the coverage.

Potential Income. Besides looking at current income, the underwriter considers the *potential income* of a proposed insured. The person may be in the process of establishing a career and may not yet have reached her full potential for earning income.

If a proposed insured has an irregular or unstable income—for instance, if a person has little business experience and is starting a new company—the underwriter may have difficulty estimating the person's potential income. Consultation with the chief underwriter and research into the performance of similar business enterprises can help the underwriter develop the information needed to make a sound decision on the case.

Net Worth. Underwriters use net worth—the difference between the person's assets and liabilities—to determine the appropriate amount of coverage needed to preserve a proposed insured's estate. Keep in mind that while the amount of life insurance in force is *not* considered as part of a person's net worth, the cash value of any cash value life insurance policy in force *is* considered as an asset when calculating the person's net worth.

Bankruptcy. An underwriter who discovers that a proposed insured has been or is involved in a bankruptcy must assess the increased risks of antiselection and lapse. An underwriter also must investigate whether a proposed insured who has been involved in a bankruptcy still has the legal ability to enter into an insurance contract involving the payment of premiums.

For a proposed insured who has been or is involved in a bankruptcy, the producer submitting the application should provide the underwriter with a letter explaining what caused the bankruptcy, how the proposed insured has settled or is settling the bankruptcy, and how the proposed insured is managing his current finances. If the proposed insured is involved in an ongoing bankruptcy proceeding, many insurers postpone making an underwriting decision until the proposed insured has been discharged from bankruptcy for a certain period of time, usually one to seven years.

Insurance in Force

To rule out the risks of antiselection, speculation, and money laundering, the underwriter makes certain that the proposed insured is not overinsured. ***Overinsurance*** refers to an amount of applied-for insurance that, together with in-force insurance, is excessive in relation to the need for which coverage is being purchased. Therefore, the underwriter evaluates the amount of insurance that a proposed insured currently has in force with all insurers and the amount of insurance for which the person is applying. Typically, the various purposes of coverage also are considered. If the proposed insured is replacing one policy with another, the underwriter subtracts the amount of the policy being replaced from the proposed insured's total amount of coverage. Each insurer sets its own limits for the total acceptable amount of in-force coverage.

In some insurance companies, the calculation of the amount of insurance in force includes any accidental death benefit (ADB), which provides a death benefit above the face amount of the policy if the insured dies in an accident as defined in the policy. Some insurers establish separate limits for face amount coverage and for ADB coverage.

When reviewing an application for personal insurance, an underwriter typically does not consider as in-force coverage any business life insurance coverage paid for by the proposed insured's employer and for which the employer is the beneficiary. In addition, the death benefits of pensions and Social Security are usually small and generally are not included in the calculation of in-force coverage. Group life insurance generally is not considered either because the amount is small and coverage terminates when employment does.

Tools to Determine the Appropriate Amount of Insurance

As we discussed, when assessing the appropriate amount of insurance to issue, an underwriter must consider the need for which the coverage is being purchased and the proposed insured's ability to pay for the coverage. In making this determination, the underwriter typically uses one or both of the following tools:

- Factor tables
- Percentage-of-income rule

Underwriters use these tools as guidelines, not as rigid decision-making rules, and may consider other factors in determining an appropriate amount of insurance for a specific case.

Factor Tables

A ***factor table*** is a chart that shows the maximum amount of insurance—expressed in multiples of a person's salary or current gross earned income—that an insurer typically will approve in each of several age ranges. Because each insurer develops its own factor tables, the amount of insurance a person can buy may vary from one insurer to another. Figure 5.3 shows a typical factor table for life insurance; the table specifies the amount of insurance, figured as a multiple of a proposed insured's current gross earned income that may be purchased at specified ages.

An underwriter usually is not bound absolutely by the numbers in a factor table. Higher amounts of coverage can be approved for proposed insureds whose current income is low, but who can be expected to have higher earnings in later years. For example, young doctors, attorneys, financial consultants, and sales people generally can be expected to earn considerably more money as they gain experience and develop larger practices and more

FIGURE 5.3 A Typical Factor Table for Whole Life Insurance

Age	Multiple of Current Gross Earned Income
20–40	20
41–50	15
51–60	10
61–64	5
65 and over	4

clients. For such proposed insureds, an underwriter often requests documentation indicating the proposed insured's potential future earnings.

Percentage-of-Income Rule

To determine the ability to pay premiums, some insurers use a ***percentage-of-income rule***, which stipulates the amount of money a proposed insured can afford to spend on insurance annually according to a specified percentage of the proposed insured's current gross earned and unearned annual income. The percentage generally varies between 6 percent and 20 percent, depending on the level of the person's current gross earned and unearned annual income and the type and amount of coverage requested. Each insurer stipulates its own percentages for each insurance product.

As an example, one insurer's percentage-of-income rule specifies that a proposed insured for a certain life insurance product can afford premiums no greater than 7 percent of the first $10,000 of her current gross earned and unearned annual income, 11 percent of the next $15,000, and 18 percent of the remainder. According to this insurer's percentage-of-income rule, a proposed insured whose current gross earned and unearned annual income is $100,000 a year can afford to pay a maximum premium of $15,850 annually for life insurance coverage, computed as follows:

$700	[0.07 × $10,000]
+ 1,650	[0.11 × $15,000]
+13,500	[0.18 × $75,000]
$15,850	

Because $15,850 a year is the maximum amount of premiums that the proposed insured can afford to pay, the underwriter may not approve more coverage than that amount will purchase.

Keep in mind that whatever the result is under a factor table or the percentage-of-income rule, the underwriter will consider in-force and applied for coverage in determining the amount of insurance to approve. In addition, note that underwriters typically do not consider a proposed insured's liabilities as a separate factor when determining the amount of coverage to issue. Underwriters generally feel that the large multiples used in factor tables and under the percentage-of-income rule already take into account certain liabilities, such as mortgages.

Risk Classification

In making an underwriting decision for individual life insurance, an underwriter assesses the risk presented by a proposed insured by examining medical, personal, and financial information concerning the proposed insured.

An underwriter then classifies the proposed insured as a preferred, standard, or substandard risk or declines to approve coverage. In this section, we discuss how an underwriter determines a proposed insured's appropriate risk class. We also explain different approaches to charging premiums for substandard risks. Note that typically financial risk factors are not rated. Rather, unfavorable financial information may cause the underwriter to lower the amount of coverage offered or decline to issue the policy.

Numerical Rating System

Most individual life insurance underwriters use the numerical rating system to place the proposed insured in the appropriate risk class. The ***numerical rating system*** is a risk classification method in which an underwriter calculates a numerical value for the degree of risk a proposed insured presents to the insurer; the underwriter then places the proposed insured in a risk class according to the numerical value. The higher the numerical value, the higher the degree of risk presented by the proposed insured.

Insurers set the numerical value of the average, or standard, mortality risk accepted for coverage at 100. The underwriter then assigns a positive or negative number to each medical and personal factor that has been determined statistically to have a positive or negative impact on the mortality risk presented by a proposed insured.

A proposed insured's medical and personal risk factors that have an unfavorable effect on mortality or morbidity are assigned "plus" values (such as +25) and are called ***debits***. Debits increase the numerical value indicating an applicant's predicted percentage of standard mortality.

In contrast, a proposed insured's medical and personal risk factors that have a favorable effect on mortality or morbidity are assigned "minus" values (such as –25) and are called ***credits***. Credits lower the numerical value indicating an applicant's predicted percentage of standard mortality.

Combining debits and credits with the basic standard value of 100 produces the total numerical value of the risk represented by an individual proposed insured. For example, suppose Alfredo de Santo's medical records indicate that he has a slightly enlarged heart. The insurer from which Mr. de Santo is requesting coverage typically assigns a debit of +50 to such an impairment, indicating that this type of impairment represents 150 percent of the mortality rate for standard risks. On the other hand, the insurer may assign a credit of -10 if both Mr. de Santo's parents are alive, healthy, and in their 80s. If Mr. de Santo has no other impairments or personal factors that decrease or increase his predicted mortality, then the total numerical value of the risk Mr. de Santo represents is equal to 140 (100 points representing standard mortality, plus 50 points representing the additional risk of his enlarged heart, minus 10 points representing the better than average risk posed by the health status of his parents). Figure 5.4 presents a typical life underwriting worksheet showing debits and credits assigned. Note that the debits and credits and the extra ratings that insurers assign to mortality risks vary from one insurer to another because of differences in assumptions about expected mortality.

FIGURE 5.4 Typical Life Insurance Worksheet Showing Debits and Credits

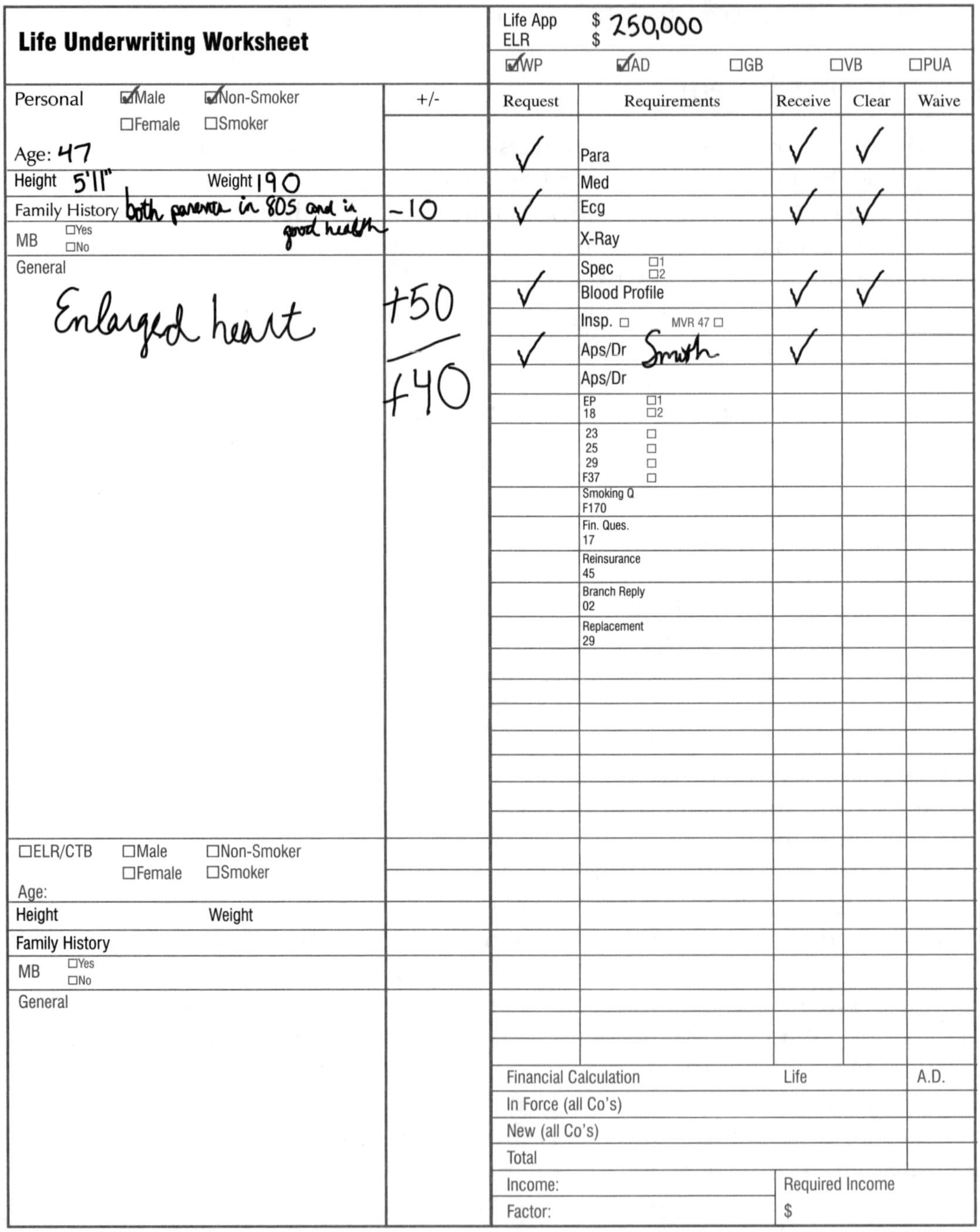

Life Underwriting Worksheet

Life App $ 250,000
ELR $
☑WP ☑AD ☐GB ☐VB ☐PUA

Personal ☑Male ☑Non-Smoker ☐Female ☐Smoker Age: 47	+/-
Height 5'11" Weight 190	
Family History both parents in 80s and in good health	−10
MB ☐Yes ☐No	
General: Enlarged heart	+50
	+40
☐ELR/CTB ☐Male ☐Female ☐Non-Smoker ☐Smoker Age:	
Height Weight	
Family History	
MB ☐Yes ☐No	
General	

Request	Requirements	Receive	Clear	Waive
✓	Para	✓	✓	
	Med			
✓	Ecg	✓	✓	
	X-Ray			
	Spec ☐1 ☐2			
✓	Blood Profile	✓	✓	
	Insp. ☐ MVR 47 ☐			
✓	Aps/Dr Smith	✓		
	Aps/Dr			
	EP 18 ☐1 ☐2			
	23 ☐ 25 ☐ 29 ☐ F37 ☐			
	Smoking Q F170			
	Fin. Ques. 17			
	Reinsurance 45			
	Branch Reply 02			
	Replacement 29			

Financial Calculation	Life	A.D.
In Force (all Co's)		
New (all Co's)		
Total		
Income:	Required Income	
Factor:	$	

Note: The total of the debits and credits equals 40, but the number representing the proposed insured's mortality risk is 140, representing the standard mortality of 100 plus the total of the debits and credits.

The information an insurer uses to assign numerical values—that is, debits and credits—to life and health insurance medical and personal risks is contained in a document known as an ***underwriting manual***, which also typically provides descriptive information on impairments and serves as a guide to underwriting action. Whereas in the past underwriting manuals were provided in paper form, now they typically are provided to the underwriting staff on a CD-ROM or are located on the insurer's intranet.

Each underwriting manual includes an index listing synonyms and derivative terms for characteristics, with page references. Most manuals also include a laboratory section that lists basic laboratory test data and a "normal" range of values for the most commonly used laboratory tests. To help underwriters interpret medical information, many manuals contain a glossary of symptoms and medical terms, as well as a list of medical abbreviations. Most insurers emphasize that the suggested actions and ratings listed in their underwriting manuals are intended to be flexible and may be modified by an underwriter according to individual circumstances.

In addition to descriptions of various impairments associated with each organ and system of the body, the underwriting manual may include

- A list of debits or credits, or both, for specific impairments and personal factors
- Extra-percentage tables to be used for table ratings, which we discuss in the next section
- A statement of the amount of flat extra premium to be charged for certain impairments and personal factors

Note that in today's highly technical environment, most companies have the extra-percentage tables automated within their policy issue systems, such that an underwriter would indicate the case is rated at 150 percent and the policy issue system would calculate the premium based on actuarially derived extra-percentage tables.

Charging for Substandard Risks

For individual life insurance, insurers compensate for the extra mortality represented by substandard risks by charging a premium based on a table rating, a flat extra premium, or a combination of the two. The approach to charging for a particular substandard risk depends on whether the mortality risk of a given medical or personal factor is assumed to remain constant, increase with age, or decrease with age.

Table Rating Method

The ***table rating method*** is a method for adjusting individual life insurance premium rates to compensate for extra mortality that divides substandard risks into broad groups—or tables—according to their numerical value. The extra mortality for each substandard group is expressed as a percentage added to standard mortality as has been shown by the insurer's actual mortality experience. The total mortality for each substandard group is presented in an ***extra-percentage table***, which is a document that lists all the tables used in the table rating method. Each table is labeled by either a number or a letter of the alphabet. Underwriters calculate a proposed insured's numerical rating and determine which table the rating falls within. As indicated earlier, typically the table rating is then entered into the administrative system, which automatically calculates the appropriate premium rate.

The table rating method is appropriate when extra mortality increases with age, as is found in diabetic and overweight people. Underwriters use table ratings for the majority of substandard risks, and the table ratings are generally the same from one insurer to another. Typically, underwriters classify numerical total mortality values of up to approximately 125 as preferred or standard, and the numerical values above that number are classified as substandard or declined. Figure 5.5 shows an example of an extra-percentage table.

According to Figure 5.5, the total mortality for each class is figured as 100 (representing standard mortality) plus the total of debits (representing extra mortality) and credits (representing favorable mortality). For exam-

FIGURE 5.5 Typical Extra-Percentage Table

Table (or Substandard Class)	Total Mortality (Standard Mortality + Extra Mortality)
1 or A	125
2 or B	150
3 or C	175
4 or D	200
5 or E	225
6 or F	250
8 or H	300
10 or J	350
12 or L	400
16 or P	500

Note: Tables 7, 9, 11, 13, 14, and 15 do exist and each increases by 25 debits over the prior table, but underwriters rarely use these tables.

ple, Table 1's (or A's) total mortality of 125 equals 100 for standard mortality plus 25 debits for the extra mortality. The 25 debits for extra mortality actually could be composed of 50 debits for extra mortality offset by 25 credits for favorable mortality.

Each table represents an increase in extra mortality of 25 debits. Therefore, a case rated Table 1 has a mortality rating of 125, or 1.25 times the standard mortality; a case rated Table 2 has a mortality rating of 150, or 1.5 times the standard mortality; and so on.

Another way to calculate the amount of extra mortality represented by each table is to multiply the table number by 25, then add 100 (which represents standard mortality). For instance, a case rated Table 4 has a mortality rating of 200 [(4 × 25) + 100] or 2 times the standard mortality, and a case rated Table 5 has a mortality rating of 225 [(5 × 25) + 100] or 2.25 times the standard mortality.

Flat Extra Premium Method

The ***flat extra premium method*** is a method of charging for substandard risk in which the insurer adds to the standard premium a specified extra dollar amount. In individual life insurance, the insurer adds to the standard premium a specified extra dollar amount for every $1,000 of insurance. The flat extra premium method is used mainly in cases involving extra mortality that is considered to be either constant or decreasing with age.

The amount of extra premium charged under this method varies according to the amount of risk represented by the medical impairment or personal factor, but does not vary from year to year during the time the extra premium is charged. For example, an insurer may charge $2 per $1,000 for a mild impairment, but $7 or $15 per $1,000 for a more serious impairment. Whatever the amount charged, it will remain the same ($2 or $7 or $15) throughout the period that the flat extra premium is charged.

An insurer may charge either a temporary or a permanent flat extra premium. A ***temporary flat extra premium*** is an amount added to the premium for cases in which a risk factor is expected to decrease and eventually disappear over a limited time period. A temporary flat extra premium is charged for such impairments as cancers in remission and heart conditions from which the proposed insured is recovering. Most insurers program their administration systems to remove this type of premium automatically at the appropriate time. When insurers do impose a flat extra premium for a medical impairment, the extra premium is almost always temporary.

A ***permanent flat extra premium*** is an amount added to the premium for cases in which a personal risk factor is expected to remain constant throughout the life of the policy. This type of rating is most commonly used for hazardous occupations, dangerous avocations, or unfavorable driving records.

Combining Methods

Insurers often use a combination of a flat extra premium and a table rating when the risk of death is expected to increase during a certain period and to decrease after that period. For example, experience has shown that a person who has been treated for certain cancers has the greatest risk of recurrence during the first 10 years following the initial treatment. After 10 years, the risk of recurrence is much lower, although it still exists. Thus, a proposed insured who was treated for cancer six years before applying for life insurance might be accepted with a table 4 rating (200 percent), plus a $15 flat extra premium per $1,000 of coverage for each of the next four years. After four years, the $15 flat extra premium would be removed automatically, but the table rating would continue.

Key Terms

financial underwriting
persistency rate
speculation
life settlement
financial worksheet
financial status
net worth
annual report
statement of owners' equity
equity
balance sheet
income statement
statement of cash flows
overinsurance
factor table
percentage-of-income rule
numerical rating system
debits
credits
underwriting manual
table rating method
extra-percentage table
flat extra premium method
temporary flat extra premium
permanent flat extra premium

chapter

6

Underwriting Individual Life Insurance: Niche Policies, Business Life Insurance, Replacements, and Supplemental Benefits

Outline

Underwriting Niche Policies
Multi-Life Policies
Juvenile Insurance Policies
Monthly Debit Ordinary Policies
Direct Response Policies

Underwriting Business Life Insurance
Financial Assessment of a Business
Underwriting Considerations for Various Types of Business Life Insurance

Underwriting Policy Replacements

Underwriting Supplemental Benefits
Waiver of Premium for Disability Benefit
Accidental Death Benefit
Family Benefit
Guaranteed Insurability Benefit
Accelerated Death Benefit

Learning Objectives

After studying this chapter, you should be able to...

- Describe the typical underwriting considerations for multi-life policies, juvenile insurance policies, monthly debit ordinary policies, and direct response policies
- Identify the warning signs that indicate a business is in financial difficulty or may be engaging in commercial fraud
- Define the three methods an underwriter can use to estimate the value of a business
- Explain how an underwriter assesses the financial condition of a business by examining solvency, liquidity, and profitability
- Describe the typical underwriting considerations for life insurance used to fund a buy-sell agreement, key-person life insurance, split-dollar life insurance, and creditor insurance
- Describe underwriting considerations for policy replacements
- Describe the typical underwriting considerations for a waiver of premium for disability benefit, an accidental death benefit, a family benefit, a guaranteed insurability benefit, and an accelerated death benefit

Chapters 4 and 5 of this text deal with the underwriting of basic individual life insurance policies designed to be sold by producers to individuals to meet traditional personal needs. We begin this chapter by discussing the underwriting of individual life insurance policies designed to meet other personal needs. We then explore how underwriters analyze individual life insurance policies that meet business needs. We conclude with sections on underwriting replacement policies and ***supplemental benefits***, which are benefits added to the coverage specified in the basic insurance policy.

Underwriting Niche Policies

Niche personal life insurance policies are life insurance policies that an insurer designs to fulfill the needs of a specific marketing segment. Niche policies that serve personal insurance needs include

- Multi-life policies
- Juvenile insurance policies
- Monthly debit ordinary policies
- Direct response policies

Underwriters of niche policies assess many of the same factors assessed in underwriting traditional individual life policies that meet personal needs. In this section, we discuss the unique aspects of underwriting niche policies.

Multi-Life Policies

A life insurance contract that is written on two or more lives is a ***multi-life policy***. Some insurers write policies on as many as 10 to 20 lives. Although some policies pay some benefits when each of the insured persons dies, the two most common types of multi-life policies are the

- ***First-to-die life insurance policy***, also known as a *joint life insurance policy*, which provides that proceeds will be paid when the first of two (or more) insureds covered by the policy dies
- ***Survivorship life insurance policy***, also known as a *second-to-die life insurance policy*, which provides that proceeds will be paid when the second (or last) of two (or more) insureds covered by the policy dies

An underwriter makes a separate evaluation of each life to be covered under a multi-life policy. If an underwriter determines that one of the proposed insureds represents a ratable risk, the policy typically can be issued at an increased premium rate. Some insurers allow a multi-life policy to be issued even if one of the proposed insureds is uninsurable.

Juvenile Insurance Policies

A ***juvenile insurance policy*** is an insurance policy issued on the life of a child but owned and paid for by an adult—usually the child's parent, grandparent, or legal guardian—who typically is also the beneficiary. Most insurers will approve coverage after a full-term, newborn child has been released from a hospital. However, most insurers decline coverage for infants born prematurely, although most insurers will consider coverage again when the infant has reached a certain weight or age, depending on the insurer's underwriting requirements. Insurers cover adopted children in the same manner as biological children, but insurers do not issue coverage until the adoption is final. Note that some jurisdictions limit the amount of coverage that can be issued on a juvenile.

Underwriters use most of the same information sources to assess a juvenile proposed insured as those used to assess an adult. Some insurers offer a special, nonmedical juvenile application that is similar to an adult nonmedical application and is completed by the adult applying for coverage on the child's life.

In assessing an application for juvenile insurance, underwriters consider many of the same factors considered for risk appraisal of an adult. These factors include the age and medical history of the child, as well as the financial status of the policyowner. However, underwriters regard the policy face amount and policy ownership differently when evaluating an application for juvenile insurance than when evaluating an application for an adult.

In evaluating the appropriateness of the face amount requested, an underwriter considers the insurance in force or applied for on the parents or guardian. Typically, the amounts for the "breadwinners" must be at least equal to or, in some companies, twice that of the amount applied for on the child.

An underwriter also looks at whether other children in the family are similarly insured. If only one child of several is insured, or if one child is being insured for a larger amount of coverage than are the other children, the underwriter investigates the reason for such unusual treatment of one child. Singling out one child for life insurance coverage may be justified if that child brings in an income, for example, as a child star. However, disparate treatment of children when applying for life insurance coverage may indicate the presence of antiselection. Insuring only one child also could indicate the presence of speculation because the death of a seriously ill child who requires expensive medical treatments would relieve the family of a financial burden rather than create a need for compensation for a financial loss.

Underwriters also consider who will be the owner and the beneficiary of a juvenile policy. Usually, only parents, grandparents, or legal guardians are considered to have an insurable interest in the life of a child. Therefore, insurers usually require that one of these parties be either the owner or the beneficiary of the policy, or both. When grandparents purchase a juvenile policy, an underwriter also considers insurance in force and applied for on all other grandchildren for the same reasons mentioned above.

When parents are not the owners of a policy covering a child, the underwriter typically obtains the parents' written consent to the issuance of the coverage and requires them to attest to the accuracy of responses to medical questions because they should have first-hand knowledge of the child's current state of health. The parental consent is kept on file with the application or is made a part of the policy.

Insurers may not require a physical examination for juvenile insurance for two reasons: (1) after the first year of life, the mortality rate for children is very low; and (2) most juvenile insurance applications do not involve large sums of money and therefore do not justify the expense of a physical examination. If the information provided on the juvenile application indicates that the child has a health problem or if the parent or legal guardian cannot complete the nonmedical portion of the application, then the underwriter usually requests an APS.

Some juvenile policies include a ***waiver of premium for payor benefit***, which is a supplemental benefit that provides that an insurer will waive payment of the policy's premiums if the *payor*—the person paying the policy premium—becomes disabled or dies prior to the insured child's attainment of a specified age, usually 21. Insurers usually require modest evidence of insurability from the payor before approving this benefit. Typically, the payor's age, occupation, height and weight, and a brief medical history are sufficient evidence of the payor's insurability. The payor usually provides this information as part of the regular application for juvenile coverage. Insurers seldom require a medical examination of the payor unless the payor's medical history indicates that an examination is warranted. Insurers normally issue the waiver of premium for payor benefit only if the payor is rated a preferred, standard, or slightly substandard risk.

Monthly Debit Ordinary Policies

A ***monthly debit ordinary (MDO) policy*** is an individual life insurance policy that is marketed under the home service distribution system and paid for by monthly premium payments. The ***home service distribution system*** is a method of selling and servicing insurance policies through commissioned producers, known as ***home service agents***, who sell a range of products and provide specified policyowner services, including the collection of renewal premiums, within a specified geographic area. MDO policies tend to be sold in smaller face amounts than other life insurance policies.

MDO policies are underwritten like other types of personal life insurance policies. Underwriters refer to an age and amount requirements chart and determine whether the policy will be underwritten on a nonmedical, paramedical, or medical basis depending on the age of the proposed insured and the amount of applied-for coverage. If the application is for more than a certain amount of coverage, the underwriter seeks information about the proposed insured from MIB.

Direct Response Policies

Some insurers sell some or all of their products through a ***direct response distribution system***, which is a type of distribution channel in which customers purchase products directly from a company by responding to advertisements, Internet Web sites, or telephone, e-mail, or fax solicitations. Policies distributed through a direct response system, known as ***direct response policies***, may be fully underwritten, underwritten on a nonmedical basis, or underwritten on a guaranteed-issue basis.

When products are offered on a ***guaranteed-issue basis***, no individual underwriting takes place; every eligible proposed insured who applies and meets specified conditions is automatically issued a policy. The term *guaranteed-issue* does not imply that everyone who applies is approved but that if the proposed insured meets the eligibility requirements for applying for the policy, he will be approved. The eligibility requirements are relatively liberal and typically concern the insured's age or the amount of coverage already in force with the insurer.[1]

Some direct response policy applications ask a proposed insured to respond to certain medical history inquiries, such as

- Within the past five years, have you consulted a doctor or received medical treatment for any of the following conditions? (A list follows, containing impairments such as heart trouble, stroke, cancer, lung disease, diabetes, chest pains, cancer, tumors, convulsions, and diabetes.)
- Within the last five years, have you tested positive for the human immunodeficiency virus (HIV) or been told you have acquired immune deficiency syndrome (AIDS)?
- Within the last three years, have you consulted a doctor, been hospitalized, or taken prescription medication?

Most insurers that use such direct response policy applications either accept or reject the application solely on the basis of the answers to these questions, and some insurers even consider these to be guaranteed-issue policy applications.

After reviewing the answers to these medical questions, some insurers will go on to request additional medical information before accepting or rejecting the application for the direct response policy, in which case the policy definitely is not offered on a guaranteed issue basis. In some companies, if the underwriter determines that the proposed insured falls outside the parameters of the direct response policy applied for, the underwriter may suggest another product to the proposed insured. In such a case, the underwriter would request additional medical information and underwrite in accordance with that product's guidelines.

Underwriting Business Life Insurance

Business insurance is insurance that serves the needs of a business organization rather than those of a person. Note that whereas the term *business insurance* includes property and liability coverages that meet the needs of a business organization, the scope of our discussion is limited to life insurance that meets the needs of a business. Figure 6.1 describes some of the needs met by business life insurance.

Unlike most personal life insurance, business life insurance is usually third-party insurance. Thus, the proposed insured is not the applicant and will not be the policyowner if a policy is issued. An exception is a policy issued to the sole owner of a business under which the proposed insured, applicant, and policyowner are the same individual.

For business life insurance purposes, an insurable interest is present if the premature death of the insured party in a business relationship would result in a financial loss to the surviving parties or to the business. For example, insurable interest generally is considered to exist when partners in a partnership wish to insure each other's lives or a business wishes to insure the lives of certain key employees who are essential to the continued success of the company.

When underwriting individual life insurance that serves business needs, underwriters examine the same risk factors pertaining to the proposed insured—medical, personal, and financial—as they do when underwriting individual life insurance that serves personal needs. However, if an applicant is purchasing life insurance for business reasons, the underwriter will focus more closely on the business's finances than she would if evaluating the risk represented by an applicant who owns a business and is buying insurance for personal reasons. In this section, we explain how an

FIGURE 6.1 Needs Met by Business Life Insurance

BUSINESS CONTINUATION NEEDS

A business owner may need a means of assuring that the business will continue to operate after his death. Thus, he may establish a ***business continuation insurance plan***, which is an insurance plan designed to enable a business to continue operations upon the death or disability of an owner or other person important to the business. Two types of business continuation insurance plans are the buy-sell agreement and key person life insurance.

- A ***buy-sell agreement*** is an agreement in which one party agrees to purchase a second party's financial interest in a business following the second party's death, and the second party agrees to direct his estate to sell his interest in the business to the purchasing party. If an individual life insurance policy is used to fund the buy-sell agreement, the first party takes out a life insurance policy on the second party's life; and upon the death of the second party, the first party uses the life insurance proceeds to purchase the business interest from the estate of the second party.
- ***Key-person life insurance*** is individual life insurance that a business purchases on the life of a ***key person***, who is a person whose continued participation in the business is necessary to its success and whose death would cause substantial financial loss to the business. A key person can be almost anyone important to the business, including an owner, a top salesperson, or an employee possessing special skills, knowledge, or abilities.

EMPLOYEE BENEFITS NEEDS

To attract and retain quality employees, an employer may need to provide an ***employee benefit plan***, which is a program under which an employer provides its employees with various benefits in addition to their wages. Group life and group health insurance, which we discuss later in the text, are popular employee benefit plans. Another such employee benefit plan is a ***split-dollar life insurance plan***, which is "any arrangement between an owner of a life insurance contract and a non-owner of the contract under which either party to the arrangement pays all or part of the premiums, and one of the parties paying the premiums is entitled to recover (either conditionally or unconditionally) all or any portion of those premiums and such recovery is to be made from, or is secured by, the proceeds of the contract."[2] For example, under such an arrangement, a business might provide individual cash value life insurance policies for certain employees, who share in paying the cost of the policies. The employer pays the portion of each annual premium that is equal to the amount by which the policy's cash value will increase that year, and the employee pays the remainder of the annual premium. The policy can be owned by the employer or the employee. If the employee dies while still an employee and while the policy is in force, the employer receives proceeds equal to the policy's cash value, and the beneficiary named by the employee receives the rest of the proceeds.

CREDITOR PROTECTION NEEDS

Sometimes creditors need assurance that they will be repaid if a key person of a business borrower dies. ***Creditor insurance***, also known as *loan coverage* or *debt coverage*, is coverage designed to pay for the economic loss suffered by a creditor when a key person of a debtor business dies before the debt is paid. To maintain the principle of insurable interest, the proceeds of creditor insurance cannot be greater than the unpaid debt.

Source: Adapted from Mary C. Bickley et al., *Life and Health Insurance Underwriting*, 2nd ed. [Atlanta: LOMA (Life Office Management Association, Inc.), © 2007], 182–183. Used with permission; all rights reserved.

underwriter assesses a business's finances when underwriting a business life policy. We then look at the unique aspects of underwriting various business life insurance coverages.

Financial Assessment of a Business

When underwriting business life insurance, underwriters assess the value and financial well-being of a business to ensure 1) a legitimate need for the insurance exists, 2) the amount of coverage requested is appropriate, and 3) the business will be able to pay the premiums.

Many of the sources of financial information used in underwriting business life insurance are the same as those used in underwriting personal life insurance. These sources of financial information include the application for insurance, the agent's statement, an inspection report, the business's income tax returns, and the business's financial statements. In addition, if a business's creditor has required the proposed insured to be covered by a specific amount of insurance, the underwriter usually asks the producer to obtain copies of relevant loan documents.

A business life insurance underwriter also may use a specialized questionnaire called a ***business financial supplement***, which is a document that requests information about the type of business, the current financial condition of the business, and the purpose for which the insurance is being requested. This type of supplement also is used occasionally for underwriting personal life insurance when the value of a proposed insured's business is important in assessing that person's financial worth. Figure 6.2 illustrates a typical business financial supplement.

An underwriter assesses financial documents for business life insurance in much the same way as for personal coverage applications. However, one special consideration for business coverages is that a business's audited financial statements sometimes require investigation because of variations in acceptable methods of valuing assets and liabilities and of reporting profits and earnings. An underwriter also can have difficulty assessing the financial strength of nondomestic corporations whose accounting practices differ considerably from those generally applied to domestic organizations. Underwriters may ask the insurer's accounting area for help with investigating and understanding business-related financial documents.

Underwriters who specialize in business life insurance look for indications that a business is in financial difficulty. Such indications include

- Negative cash flow from operations and inadequate financing
- Excessive debt that probably cannot be paid within a reasonable time or without reducing the funds that the business needs for maintenance and expansion

FIGURE 6.2 Business Financial Supplement

BUSINESS FINANCIAL SUPPLEMENT

I. NAME OF COMPANY ______________________________

II. TYPE OF ORGANIZATION ❐ Corporation ❐ Partnership ❐ Sole Proprietorship

III. Please attach a copy of your company's latest audited financial statements. If not available, please provide the requested information.

A. CURRENT COMPANY BOOK VALUE

Assets $________
Liabilities $________
Net Worth $________

B. CURRENT COMPANY MARKET VALUE

Market Value $________
Insured's % Ownership ________%
Market Value of Insured's Ownership $________

C. COMPANY NET PROFIT—Past Three Years (before taxes and bonuses)

20____ $__________
20____ $__________
20____ $__________
This year (est.) $__________

D. What other stockholders, partners, or key persons also are being insured in favor of the company? (Please name.)

____
____
____

IV. (Check at least one box and provide details.)

❐ **KEY PERSON**

A. Why is the person to be insured important to the company? What special skills, knowledge, or abilities does he/she possess that make insurance necessary?______________________________

____
____

B. How is it expected that the proceeds will be utilized? ______________________________

____

❐ **BUY AND SELL**

A. Is there a written agreement: In effect? ❐ Yes ❐ No (If in effect, attach signed copy.)
Contemplated? ❐ Yes ❐ No
(If contemplated, give expected finalization date.)__________

B. How is the business being valued in the agreement?______________________________

____

❐ **BUSINESS LOAN**

A. Name and address of the lender ______________________________
B. Amount of loan $ __________________ **C.** Date of loan __________________
D. The repayment terms are ______________________________
E. The purpose of the loan is ______________________________
F. Is lender requiring the insurance? ❐ Yes ❐ No

I understand that ABC Life Insurance Company will rely on the above statements in determining the need and justification for the insurance applied for, and I represent that all answers are true and accurate statements to the best of my knowledge and belief as of the date of application for life insurance. A photographic copy of this statement may be attached to and made part of any insurance contract issued.

Signature of Proposed Insured __________________ Date __________________
Signature of Owner __________________ Date __________________
Witnessed by __________________ Date __________________

- Unusual financing arrangements, such as loans from family members, subsidiaries, or clients
- Dependence on only a few projects or clients instead of a wide variety of projects or clients
- A trend of declining sales or revenues
- A history of defaults on loans or debts, denial of credit by lenders, or recent financial restructuring
- Unexplained or illogical sale of substantial assets
- Bankruptcy
- Labor strife
- Recent or substantial litigation
- Large losses that were not covered by insurance

Because a large percentage of new businesses fail within the first two to three years of existence, underwriting coverage for a new company that will own the business life insurance policy is more conservative than for businesses with a longer history of operation. The insurer is concerned that a new business might fail before the insurer has collected enough premiums to cover the expenses of underwriting, issuing, and administering the policy.

An underwriter also is trained to look for signs of commercial fraud. Figure 6.3 lists some of the warning signs of commercial fraud.

FIGURE 6.3 Warning Signs of Commercial Fraud

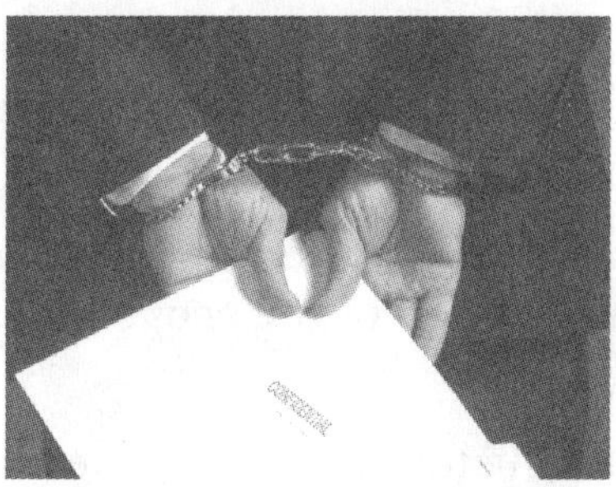

- Evidence that the ownership of a company is being concealed
- A partner or other key person has worked for a number of companies that are no longer in business
- A partner or other key person is unable to provide information concerning her business history and past associations
- An overly complex organizational or partnership structure, or a confusing web of subsidiaries and conglomerates
- Trade, bank, or business references that appear fraudulent or unbelievably positive
- Financial statements that have been issued at irregular intervals, list assets that cannot be confirmed by other sources, use round figures instead of specific amounts, or list accounts receivable that are inconsistent with other figures such as inventory and purchasing records

Business Valuation

Sometimes a certified public accountant (CPA) who supplies a business's financial statements also submits an assessment of a business's value to the underwriter. If no valuation is provided, the underwriter assesses the value of the business himself. Underwriters typically employ one or more of the following approaches to valuing a business:

- **Asset-based approach.** The underwriter places a value on the business by calculating the book value of the business, which is the excess of the business's assets over its liabilities.
- **Income-based approach.** The underwriter places a value on the business by focusing on the earning capacity of the business.
- **Market approach.** The underwriter places a value on the business by researching the selling prices of comparable businesses. General guidelines have been established to aid an underwriter in the valuation of businesses using a market approach. For example, on average, dental practices sell for 70 percent of annual gross sales.

When using one of these three approaches to valuing a business, an underwriter may consider one or more of the following factors:

- Tangible assets (such as buildings, equipment, and inventory)
- Intangible assets (such as goodwill, an established customer base, favorable industry reputation, market presence, franchise value, name recognition, a desirable location of the business, logos, copyrights, trademarks, and patents)
- Historic trend of profit or loss, especially the average earning capacity over a period of at least three to five years prior to the date of application for insurance
- Performance of the business relative to its industry during the same three- to five-year period
- Current economic conditions and the future outlook of the business sector in which the business operates and of the economy as a whole
- Availability of qualified employees and customers so that the business may maintain its present position and/or continue to grow and strengthen itself
- Current price and recent sales of the company's stock, if any, and the dividend-paying capacity of the business

- Financial obligations to which the business is or will be committed
- Evidence of plans to expand, restructure, or sell the business

Solvency, Liquidity, and Profitability

An underwriter also may assess a business's financial condition by examining the business's solvency, liquidity, and profitability. Such an evaluation may employ financial ratios. A ***ratio*** is a comparison of two numeric values that results in a measurement expressed as a percentage or fraction. ***Financial ratio analysis*** consists of calculating the relationships between various pairs of financial values for the purpose of assessing a company's financial condition.

Considered in isolation, the ratios concerning solvency, liquidity, and profitability mean little, if anything. Underwriters typically compare these ratios for a business to the range of acceptable values established for other businesses in the same or similar industries.

Solvency. ***Solvency*** is an entity's ability to meet its financial obligations on time. A business that is unable to maintain sufficient funds to pay its debts not only may be unable to pay insurance premiums, but also may be likely to suffer financial failure. In either situation, such a company is not a sound candidate for business coverage.

Generally, solvency analysis compares the amount of an entity's financial obligations with its resources available to meet those obligations. One measure of solvency is a ***debt-to-equity ratio***, also known as a *debt ratio*, which is calculated by dividing a company's total debt by its owners' equity. As we mentioned in Chapter 5, owners' equity is the amount of the business owned outright—and not financed. The formula for the debt-to-equity ratio is

$$\textbf{Debt-to-Equity Ratio} = \frac{\textbf{Total Debt}}{\textbf{Owners' Equity}}$$

The greater the owners' equity in relation to total debt, the more resources the company has to pay its debts. A financially sound company should have more owners' equity than debt. In other words, the value of a company's debt-to-equity ratio should certainly be less than 1. An underwriter's comfort with any given level of debt depends on many factors; in general, the greater the margin of equity over debt, the more confident an underwriter should be with a company's financial position.

For example, suppose owners' equity is $4,750,000 and total debt is $4,500,000. When we divide the total debt by owners' equity, the result is 0.947, as shown:

$$\textbf{Debt-to-Equity Ratio} = \frac{\$4{,}500{,}000}{\$4{,}750{,}000} = 0.947$$

In this example, the value of the debt-to-equity ratio is less than 1, so the company is technically solvent.

If the total debt were increased to $4,900,000 and owner's equity remained $4,750,000, the value of the ratio would be greater than 1, indicating a lack of solvency, as shown:

$$\textbf{Debt-to-Equity Ratio} = \frac{\$4{,}900{,}000}{\$4{,}750{,}000} = 1.03$$

Liquidity. ***Liquidity*** is a company's ability to readily convert its assets to cash for an approximation of their true value. To determine a company's liquidity, many insurers calculate a ***current ratio*** by dividing current assets by current liabilities as shown:

$$\textbf{Current Ratio} = \frac{\textbf{Current Assets}}{\textbf{Current Liabilities}}$$

Current assets usually are items that the company presently has or owns that can be readily converted to cash at a close approximation of their true value. Examples include cash, cash equivalents such as money market accounts, and inventory. If a current appraisal of asset values is available, the underwriter uses it. If such information is not available, the underwriter estimates the market values of the assets. Current liabilities are all the debts and obligations due and payable within the next accounting period. ***Current liabilities*** include salaries payable and interest payable.

Although the minimum acceptable value for the current ratio varies greatly among industries, underwriters generally require at least $2 in current assets for every $1 in current liabilities. That is, current assets should be at least two times as great as current liabilities.

Underwriters also sometimes assess a company's liquidity by examining its ability to pay its debts immediately. Immediate debt payment requires cash or its equivalent rather than proceeds from selling such assets as inventory, which may sell slowly, at a lower-than-expected price, or not at all. A company's ability to liquidate debt immediately can be measured using a ***quick ratio***, also called a *quick liquidity ratio* or an *acid-test ratio*. The quick ratio is calculated by dividing a company's most liquid current assets—consisting of cash, liquid investments, and accounts receivable, which are also known as *quick assets*—by the company's current liabilities, as shown:

$$\textbf{Quick Ratio} = \frac{\textbf{Liquid Assets}}{\textbf{Current Liabilities}}$$

The range of acceptable values for the quick ratio also varies greatly by industry; but in general, the greater the excess of liquid assets over current liabilities, the more liquid a company would be. Compared to the current ratio, the quick ratio provides a more realistic view of a company's debt-paying ability because the quick ratio eliminates any reliance on noncash assets that are not immediately available to meet emergency needs for cash.

Profitability. A company's ***profitability*** is the degree to which it is successful in consistently generating returns to its owners and measures the productivity of the company's assets and its return on the owners' investment in the company. One ratio for evaluating profitability is the ***return-on-equity (ROE) ratio***, which is determined by dividing net income by owners' equity as shown:

$$\textbf{Return-on-Equity (ROE) Ratio} = \frac{\textbf{Net Income}}{\textbf{Owners' Equity}}$$

Acceptable return on equity varies with the risk involved in a business. Underwriters expect companies operating in higher risk businesses to produce a higher ROE ratio, whereas underwriters expect companies operating in lower risk businesses to produce a comparatively lower ROE ratio. Note that the general state of the economy also influences acceptable values for return on equity.

Underwriting Considerations for Various Types of Business Life Insurance

The approaches used to assess risks are basically the same for every type of business life insurance. However, each type of business life insurance coverage has slightly different underwriting considerations. In this section, we examine these considerations for the business coverages defined in Figure 6.1.

Buy-Sell Agreements

When the applied-for insurance is intended to fund a buy-sell agreement, an underwriter evaluates the proposed insured's medical, personal, and financial factors and makes an estimation of the business's value and the proposed insured's financial interest in the business. The underwriter also confirms that the insurance is being purchased to continue the business and verifies the ability of the prospective purchaser to run the business. Life insurance can be used to fund buy-sell agreements for sole proprietorships, partnerships, and small corporations.

Sole Proprietorship. A ***sole proprietorship*** is a business owned by one person (or, in some jurisdictions, by a husband and wife). The owner of a sole proprietorship may enter into a buy-sell agreement with another person, typically an employee. This other person then may purchase life insurance coverage on the sole proprietor's life and may use the proceeds to purchase the business from the sole proprietor's estate. The underwriter typically determines the amount of insurance to issue based on the value of the business. An individual has an insurable interest in the owner of a sole proprietorship if the individual has entered into a buy-sell agreement with the sole proprietor and the insurance is intended to fund the buy-sell agreement.

Partnership. Although a partnership dissolves by law in most jurisdictions upon the death of a partner, partners often plan for the funding of the business's continuation after the death of a partner by entering into a buy-sell agreement that sets out the terms under which a deceased partner's interest in the partnership will be purchased. Surviving partners then may continue the business as a new partnership; or, if only one partner remains, he may continue as a sole proprietor. Two kinds of buy-sell agreements can accomplish this purpose—a cross-purchase agreement and an entity agreement.

A ***cross-purchase agreement*** is a type of buy-sell agreement in which each partner agrees to purchase a share of a deceased partner's interest in the partnership. Each partner funds the buy-sell agreement by purchasing an insurance policy on the life of each of the other partners. Thus, each partner owns, pays the premiums on, and is the named beneficiary of a policy on the life of each of the other partners. If one partner dies, each surviving partner will receive the proceeds of a life insurance policy and can use those proceeds to purchase a share of the deceased partner's ownership interest in the partnership.

An ***entity agreement*** is a type of buy-sell agreement under which the partnership—rather than the individual partners—agrees to purchase the share of any partner who dies. The partnership also agrees to distribute a share of that ownership interest to each of the surviving partners. The partnership purchases an insurance policy on the life of each of the partners, pays the premiums, and is the named beneficiary of each policy. If a partner dies, the partnership uses the life insurance policy proceeds to purchase the deceased partner's share in the business from the deceased's estate.

With either the cross-purchase or the entity method of funding a buy-sell agreement, all partners' lives should be insured unless a strong reason exists not to do so. Each partner is considered to have an insurable interest in the lives of the other partners.

To determine the amount of insurance to approve, the underwriter needs to know the value of the partnership and the value of the proposed insured's interest in the partnership. An underwriter uses a financial questionnaire that focuses on the partnership to obtain initial figures on these values, as well as other information about the partnership and partners. Figure 6.4 illustrates such a partnership questionnaire.

FIGURE 6.4 Partnership Questionnaire

1. Name of applicant ____________________
2. Name of proposed insured ____________________
3. How many partners are there? ____________________
   3a. What are the partners' names and what percentage of the business do they each own?
   ____________________ ________%
   ____________________ ________%
   ____________________ ________%
4. What is the nature of business transacted? ____________________
5. How long has the partnership been in existence? ____________________
6. What has been the profit/loss of the partnership over each of the last three years?
   20 ______ $______
   20 ______ $______
   20 ______ $______
   This year (est) $______
7. What has been the proposed insured's salary/share of profits over each of the last three years?
   20 ______ $______
   20 ______ $______
   20 ______ $______
   This year (est) $______
8. What is the current value of the partnership? $____________________
   8a. How was the value established? ____________________
9. What is the proposed insured's percentage share of the partnership? ________%
10. Does a buy-sell agreement exist? ____________________
    10a. If not, is one to be executed in the near future? ____________________
11. Are policies to be purchased on the lives of all other partners? ____________________
    11a. If not, please give reasons ____________________
    ____

Signature ____________________

Date ____________________

Small Corporation. Stockholders of a small corporation may enter into a buy-sell agreement using either funding method described in the preceding section on partnerships. However, in a corporate setting, the entity method of funding a buy-sell agreement is known as a *stock redemption agreement*; the corporation redeems, or retires, the deceased's stock rather than redistributing the shares to the surviving stockholders.

Stockholders of a small corporation each have an insurable interest in the lives of the other stockholders, and a small corporation has an insurable interest in its stockholders. To guard against antiselection, the underwriter makes sure that the lives of all major stockholders are covered by insurance.

In deciding the appropriate amount of insurance coverage to issue in connection with a buy-sell agreement involving a small corporation, an underwriter determines the present and projected value of the stock and the business's net worth. Another underwriting concern for stock repurchase insurance is the proportion of the total amount of stock owned by a proposed insured. If the proposed insured's stock holdings represent a significant portion of the company's equity, a need for the coverage exists. However, no real need for the coverage may exist if the proposed insured's stock holdings represent an insignificant portion of the company's equity.

Key-Person Life Insurance

As noted in Figure 6.1, key-person life insurance is coverage that a business purchases on the life of a person whose continued participation in the business is necessary to its success and whose death would cause substantial financial loss to the business. Such loss can include the value to the business of a person's skills, knowledge, patents, business contacts, and involvement in corporate financing.

Although the insurable interest that a business has in the life of a key person is usually obvious, certain situations may prompt the underwriter to look more closely for insurable interest. If the proposed insured is nearing retirement age and has not been insured by that business previously, the underwriter questions why that person has become important to the company. If a company applies for a large amount of coverage on a proposed insured who holds what appears to be only a moderately important position in the company, the underwriter may investigate further to determine insurable interest.

The size of a business is important for underwriting key-person coverage. Generally, the more people a business employs, the less likely the loss of one person is to produce a significant loss to the business. If a business appears to have other equally valuable employees who are not being proposed for key-person coverage, the underwriter usually questions why the business is singling out the proposed insured.

In evaluating the amount of coverage requested on a key person, the underwriter determines the monetary value of the proposed insured to the company, which generally is based on the amount of her compensation multiplied by a factor that represents the cost to recruit and train a replacement and to recover from the loss of her skills, special knowledge, and other benefits to the business. This monetary value of the proposed insured usually is set at 5 to 10 times the proposed insured's current annual salary, but the underwriter also may include the monetary value of other compensation, whether in cash (such as bonuses) or in fringe benefits (such as employer-provided health insurance or use of a company car).

Underwriters pay particular attention to applications for insurance for key persons in multinational companies—those that operate in two or more countries. The financial documents may be written in another language, may be abridged or unaudited, and/or may use accounting terms with different meanings from those in the underwriter's country.

Figure 6.5 illustrates a typical questionnaire used to gather information necessary to assess the risk for key-person life insurance.

Split-Dollar Life Insurance Plans

The individual life insurance policies that are part of split-dollar plans are underwritten in basically the same manner as individual life insurance policies purchased to fulfill personal insurance needs. The underwriter takes into account medical, personal, and financial factors in assessing the risk presented by the proposed insured. Also, the underwriter analyzes the employer's financial condition, but the extent of the analysis depends on the employer's ownership interest in the policy and the amount of coverage requested.

Creditor Insurance

As mentioned earlier, creditor insurance provides benefits to compensate a creditor for the economic loss suffered when a key person of a debtor business dies before the debt is paid. The debtor business takes out a life insurance policy on the key person, and the policy provides a death benefit amount that is never greater than the amount of the unpaid debt. A creditor has an insurable interest in the life of such a person. In this discussion, we consider only business loans and not consumer loans that finance the purchase of a house or a personal vehicle.

A potential overlap exists between creditor insurance and key-person insurance. In a creditor insurance situation, the creditor typically has inserted a clause in a loan agreement requiring immediate payment upon the death of the key person. The death of such a person could present a loss so severe that the debtor business may not survive without sufficient life insurance on the key person to pay off the loan. In a key person insurance situation, the business may purchase life insurance on the key person in an amount sufficient to pay off the loan upon the key person's death, plus an amount to compensate the business in other ways for the key person's death. This example illustrates the potential overlap between creditor insurance, which only pays off the loan, and key-person insurance, which does more than pay off the loan.

FIGURE 6.5 Key-Person Life Insurance Questionnaire

1. Name of applicant ______________________________
2. Name of proposed insured (key person) ______________________________
3 What is the key person's precise occupation and nature of duties? ______________________________

____

4. What is the nature of the business transacted by the key person's employer? ______________________________

____

5. How long has the employer been in business? ______________________________
6. How many other employees are there? ______________________________
7. How long has the key person been employed by the employer? ______________________________
8. What has been the key person's gross salary over each of the last three years? This figure should include bonuses and commissions.
   20_______ $_______
   20_______ $_______
   20_______ $_______
   This year (est) $_______
9. What has been the net profit/loss of the employer over each of the last three years?
   20_______ $_______
   20_______ $_______
   20_______ $_______
   This year (est) $_______
10. Is the key person a shareholder in the employer's business? ______________________________
    10a. If so, what percentage of shares does the key person hold? ______________________________%
11. What special abilities does the key person possess to justify classification as a key person? __________

____

12. What existing coverage is in force on the key person's life? ______________________________

____

____

13. Why has the amount of insurance applied for been chosen? ______________________________

____

14. What is the nature of the risk that is subject to loss?
    - Future earnings or sales jeopardized ______________________________
    - Investment jeopardized ______________________________
    - Forced liquidation of assets ______________________________
    - Working capital jeopardized ______________________________
    - Loss of management expertise ______________________________
    - Other ______________________________
15. Will the employer insure the lives of other employees as key persons? If so, how many lives and what amounts of coverage are proposed? Include lives already insured under key-person coverage. ________

____

Signature ______________________________

Date ______________________________

In analyzing the application for a business insurance policy on a person who is already insured under another business insurance policy, the underwriter must be sure that the total amount of coverage does not exceed the total need. For example, if a key person is insured under a creditor insurance policy and the debtor business applies for a key person policy on this key person, the underwriter must be sure that the key person policy is not intended to provide funds for payment of the outstanding amount of the loan.

In underwriting creditor insurance, an underwriter determines whether a borrower has means other than insurance to repay the debt. An underwriter investigates whether money from the loan is being used to purchase something that can serve as collateral for the loan, and, if so, whether the collateral will continue to produce income to pay off the loan. If it seems likely that the borrower will have to rely on the life insurance proceeds to pay off the loan, then the underwriter declines the case.

An underwriter also may want to see the loan repayment schedule. Generally, issuing creditor insurance for short-term loans is not in an insurer's best interest because a short-term creditor policy may lapse before the insurer can recover the costs of underwriting, issuing, and administering the policy.

If a company applies for creditor insurance a significant amount of time after a loan was granted, an underwriter guards against antiselection by investigating whether a debtor's financial situation or the health of the proposed insured has deteriorated since the loan was granted. Therefore, the underwriter verifies that loan payments have been made in a timely fashion, the debtor's financial condition is sound, and the proposed insured is healthy.

Underwriting Policy Replacements

In Chapter 3, we defined replacement as the purchase of one life insurance policy or annuity contract to take the place of another. Policyowners can replace personal and business life insurance policies.

Replacements can be internal or external. In an ***internal replacement***, the new policy is purchased from the same insurer that issued the original policy. In an ***external replacement***, the new policy is purchased from an insurer other than the insurer that issued the original policy. Most replacing insurers underwrite internal and external replacements in accordance with their current underwriting requirements, but sometimes insurers will offer special programs with reduced underwriting requirements that allow replacements—typically internal only—of policies issued fairly recently.

In evaluating an application for a policy replacement, an underwriter considers the possibility that antiselection has motivated the request for the replacement, particularly when the proposed insured is of an advanced age. The underwriter also must be wary of twisting and churning when a policy is being replaced, especially when the producer does a high volume of replacement business. Recall that twisting occurs when a producer misrepresents the features of a policy to induce a client to purchase a policy, and churning occurs when a producer induces a customer to replace one policy after another so that the producer can earn a series of first-year commissions on the replacements.

In the United States, an underwriter also must be aware of whether a policy replacement involves a 1035 exchange. Named after Section 1035a of the United States Internal Revenue Code, a ***Section 1035 exchange*** is a tax-free replacement of a life insurance or annuity contract for another contract insuring the same person and meeting conditions specified in the tax code.

Many policyowners in the United States use a 1035 exchange to avoid paying income tax on any gain realized from surrendering a policy and receiving its cash surrender value. Any portion of the cash surrender value that exceeds the cost basis for the policy is considered a gain and is taxable as ordinary income. Usually, the ***cost basis*** of an insurance policy is equal to the total premiums paid minus paid or credited policy dividends. In a 1035 exchange, the policyowner receives no financial gain on the transaction because the cash surrender value of the original policy is used to pay premiums on the new policy. Because the policyowner experiences no gain, no tax is due.

Generally, a policy issued as part of a 1035 exchange is underwritten in the same manner as any other individual life insurance policy. However, if the new policy—whether or not a 1035 exchange is involved—must be issued with a less desirable rating than the original policy, the underwriter obtains from the applicant a letter stating that the applicant understands that a higher premium will be required if the face amount of the new policy remains the same as that of the original policy. Alternatively, the applicant may elect to receive a lower face amount of coverage rather than pay a higher premium than he was paying for the original policy.

Underwriting Supplemental Benefits

As mentioned earlier, supplemental benefits are benefits added to the coverage specified in the basic insurance policy. Although insurers can provide some or all of these benefits through standard policy provisions, usually insurers add the benefits by means of riders, which are policy amendments. By using riders, the insurer can customize a basic life insurance policy prior to policy issue or adapt an existing policy to meet the policyowner's changing needs. Insurers typically charge a premium for these benefits.

If an applicant desires supplemental coverage, the request is considered during underwriting. If a current policyowner asks for supplemental coverage, the insurer's policyowner service staff usually considers the request first. When such a request involves only a slight increase in the insurer's risk, policyowner service staff can approve the request. However, if the supplemental benefit may cause the insurer to bear a greater degree of risk, the policyowner service staff forwards the request to underwriting for more detailed consideration.

In this section, we discuss five important supplemental benefits:

- Waiver of premium for disability (WP) benefit
- Accidental death benefit (ADB)
- Family benefit
- Guaranteed insurability (GI) benefit
- Accelerated death benefit

Waiver of Premium for Disability Benefit

A ***waiver of premium for disability (WP) benefit*** is a supplemental insurance benefit that provides that, in the event an insured is totally disabled as defined in the WP benefit, the insurance company will waive the payment of all premiums that become due during the period of disability. Note that the WP benefit is designed for policies issued to a policyowner who also is the policy's insured. The WP benefit reduces the possibility of the policyowner/insured canceling her policy when she experiences a loss of income from disability. The insurer pays the premiums waived by the WP benefit.

When underwriting the WP benefit, an underwriter considers medical and personal factors, but rarely financial factors. Because the risk of disability increases with age, issuance of the benefit is normally limited to proposed insureds below age 55 or 60, and the WP benefit usually covers only disabilities that begin before the insured reaches a specified age, such as age 65.

If a proposed insured's mortality rating is standard according to health history and physical condition, an underwriter usually will approve the WP benefit. In some situations, however, even if the policy was issued as a standard mortality risk, the insured's avocation or occupation may present enough of a disability hazard that a higher-than-usual premium will be required for the WP benefit or the underwriter may decline to approve it.

Accidental Death Benefit

An ***accidental death benefit (ADB)*** is a supplemental benefit that provides a death benefit above the face amount of the basic policy if an insured's death occurs as the result of an accident. This additional amount can be a multiple of the amount of the basic life coverage or an unrelated amount. The amount of ADB coverage approved usually depends on the amount of life insurance in force and the amount of coverage requested.

In underwriting ADB coverage, the underwriter usually adheres to the same principles used in underwriting basic personal life insurance. In certain business life insurance cases, the ADB may not be justified. For example, if a business needs $100,000 to fund a buy-sell agreement, the amount is fixed and specific. The business has no reason to receive a multiple of that amount simply because the insured's death is accidental. However, personal insurance needs—as well as some business insurance needs, such as key-person coverage—are not fixed and specific and are not as easily measured. Accidental death benefit coverage may be an appropriate supplement to life insurance to cover the beneficiary's increased economic loss that results from an accidental death.

Age is an important factor considered in underwriting ADB coverage because as people age, they are prone to more accidents. Insurers rarely issue such coverage to insureds over age 55 or 60, and most ADB riders expire when the insured reaches age 65 or 70.

Rather than trying to assess each case individually, most insurers establish underwriting guidelines that specify a mortality rating range in which the underwriter can accept proposed insureds for coverage. For example, underwriting guidelines may state that the accidental death benefit may be issued at standard rates to proposed insureds rated at 200 percent mortality or below, but will be rated or denied for those who exceed 200 percent mortality.

ADB riders usually are not available to proposed insureds rated for alcohol or substance abuse. In addition, proposed insureds with certain hazardous occupations or avocations may have to pay an extra premium for ADB coverage, or the underwriter may deny them the ADB coverage.

Family Benefit

A ***family benefit*** is a supplemental benefit that insures the lives of the insured's spouse and children. After a policy with such a benefit is issued, children who are born or adopted into the family, or who become part of the family by marriage, usually are covered when they reach the age of at least 15 days (or whatever minimum age the benefit provision or rider specifies). A family benefit usually covers a child from a previous relationship but generally does not cover foster children.

To underwrite family benefit coverage, the underwriter requires insurability information for all family members, but usually the basic information on the application fills this need. An underwriter generally accepts a spouse and children, including those with slight impairments, as standard risks if the mortality rating of each family member is no higher than 200 percent. Underwriters usually decline to issue family benefits for mortality risks higher than 200 percent.

Some insurers establish age requirements for family benefit coverage. For example, an insurer might require that a spouse be at least 17 years old and no more than 10 to 15 years younger than the proposed insured. The insurer also might establish an upper age limit for a spouse. To be accepted for coverage, children typically must be under 18 years old at the time of policy issue. Furthermore, unless a child has a physical disability and is a dependent, coverage on the child ends when the child reaches age 21 or 25.

Guaranteed Insurability Benefit

A ***guaranteed insurability (GI) benefit*** is a supplemental benefit that gives the policyowner the right to purchase additional insurance of the same type as the basic life insurance policy—for an additional premium amount—on specified option dates during the life of the policy without supplying evidence of the insured's insurability. If the policyowner does not exercise the option under the GI benefit to buy additional insurance at the time specified, that opportunity is lost; the policyowner cannot purchase the amount of insurance available under those circumstances at a subsequent option date. The purpose of the requirement to exercise options promptly is to avoid antiselection.

If a GI benefit is not included in the basic policy when the policy is issued, a policyowner usually may add a GI benefit up to 60 days after issue. The underwriter's main concern is to determine the probability of a change in insurability during the 60-day post-issue period. Some insurers allow the addition of the GI rider more than 60 days after issue if the insured presents acceptable evidence of insurability.

An important underwriting factor for the GI benefit is age. Usually, the maximum age for issuing a GI benefit is 40 or 45. Aside from age, the risk selection factors involved in underwriting a GI benefit are typically the same as those considered in underwriting the basic policy. The additional coverage provided by the GI benefit has the same risk class rating as the policy. Note that insurers typically do not add a GI benefit to a basic policy that was issued substandard.

Accelerated Death Benefit

Some policies offer life insurance policyowner-insureds the option of taking an ***accelerated death benefit***, also known as a *living benefit* in the United States, which is a supplemental benefit that gives a policyowner-insured the right to receive all or part of the policy's death benefit before her death if certain conditions are met.[3] When the policyowner-insured dies, the amount of the death benefit payable under the policy to the named beneficiary is reduced by the amount of the accelerated death benefit that was paid out to the policyowner-insured.

Life insurers generally offer accelerated death benefit coverage only on policies with large face amounts, such as $100,000 or $250,000 and above. The three most common types of accelerated death benefits are the terminal illness benefit, the dread disease benefit, and the long-term care insurance benefit.

Terminal Illness Benefit

A ***terminal illness (TI) benefit*** is an accelerated death benefit under which the insurer pays a portion of the policy's death benefit to a policyowner-insured if he suffers from a terminal illness and has a physician-certified life expectancy of 12 months or less. The underwriter obtains a statement from an attending physician that establishes evidence of the terminal condition and certifies that the insured is likely to die within the time period specified by the benefit.

Dread Disease Benefit

A ***dread disease (DD) benefit***, also known as a *critical illness benefit*, is an accelerated death benefit under which the insurer agrees to pay a portion of the policy's death benefit to a policyowner-insured if he suffers from one of a number of specified diseases. The specified diseases usually include

- Life-threatening cancer
- AIDS
- End-stage renal (kidney) failure
- Myocardial infarction (heart attack)
- Stroke
- Coronary bypass surgery

Most insurers provide DD coverage only to insureds who are under the age of 70 and who have no serious health problems.

Long-Term Care Insurance Benefit

A ***long-term care (LTC) insurance benefit*** is an accelerated death benefit under which the insurer agrees to pay periodic benefits to a policyowner-insured if he requires care in his own home or a qualified facility. The types of care given and medical condition required to qualify for the LTC benefit are specified in the LTC policy provision or rider.

Key Terms

supplemental benefit
multi-life policy
first-to-die life insurance policy
survivorship life insurance policy
juvenile insurance policy
waiver of premium for payor benefit
monthly debit ordinary (MDO) policy
home service distribution system
home service agent
direct response distribution system
direct response policy
guaranteed-issue basis
business continuation insurance plan
buy-sell agreement
key-person life insurance
key person
employee benefit plan
split-dollar life insurance plan
creditor insurance
business financial supplement
ratio
financial ratio analysis
solvency
debt-to-equity ratio
liquidity
current ratio
current asset
current liability
quick ratio
profitability
return-on-equity (ROE) ratio
sole proprietorship
cross-purchase agreement
entity agreement
internal replacement
external replacement
Section 1035 exchange
cost basis
waiver of premium for disability (WP) benefit
accidental death benefit (ADB)
family benefit
guaranteed insurability (GI) benefit
accelerated death benefit
terminal illness (TI) benefit
dread disease (DD) benefit
long-term care (LTC) insurance benefit

Endnotes

1. Adapted from Sharon B. Allen et al., *Life and Health Insurance Marketing*, 3rd ed. [Atlanta: LOMA (Life Office Management Association, Inc.), © 2003], 349–350. Used with permission; all rights reserved.
2. IRS Final Regulations, 17 September 2003.
3. Adapted from Harriett E. Jones, *Principles of Insurance: Life, Health, and Annuities*, 3rd ed. [Atlanta: LOMA (Life Office Management Association, Inc.), © 2005], 124–126. Used with permission; all rights reserved.

chapter

7

Underwriting Individual Health Insurance

Outline

Information Sources for Individual Health Underwriting

Risk Factors for Individual Health Underwriting
Age
Health History
Family History
Occupation
Avocations
Driving History
Alcohol and Drug Abuse
International Residence and Travel
Foreign Citizenship
Finances
Existing Health Coverage

Underwriting Substandard Health Risks
Premium Rating Methods
Policy Modifications

Underwriting Individual Disability Income Insurance
Antiselection
Health History
Occupation
Finances

Underwriting Individual Critical Illness Insurance

Underwriting Individual Long-Term Care Insurance
Field Underwriting
Sources of LTC Underwriting Information
Risk Factors

Learning Objectives

After studying this chapter, you should be able to…

- Identify the information sources an individual health insurance underwriter uses
- Describe the importance of age, health history, and other risk factors in underwriting individual health insurance
- List the options an underwriter has that enable a policy to be issued to a substandard risk
- Explain how the factors of antiselection, health history, occupation, and finances affect the underwriting of individual disability income coverage
- Discuss the factors involved in underwriting critical illness insurance
- Describe the differences between underwriting long-term care insurance and underwriting other types of health insurance

As we have mentioned, individual life insurance underwriting focuses on the proposed insured's *mortality risk*—the risk of dying—whereas individual health insurance underwriting focuses on the proposed insured's *morbidity* risk—the risk of becoming sick or being injured. Despite this difference in focus, the general principles and activities of underwriting we described in Chapter 2 apply to both individual life and health insurance.

The sources of information consulted and the risk factors assessed during underwriting vary depending on the type of health insurance applied for. In this chapter, we focus on the following types of individual health insurance:

- ***Medical expense insurance***, which pays benefits for the treatment of sickness and injury
- ***Disability income (DI) insurance***, which provides periodic benefits to replace income if the insured is unable to work as a result of sickness or injury
- ***Critical illness (CI) insurance***, which pays a lump-sum benefit if the insured is diagnosed with a specified critical illness or condition
- ***Long-term care (LTC) insurance***, which pays benefits for medical or other health-related services needed by the insured who, because of his advanced age or the effects of a serious illness or injury, needs care in his own home or in a qualified facility

Individual stand-alone critical illness policies are more common in Canada than in the United States, where CI coverage is issued more often as riders on life insurance policies. Long-term care coverage is increasingly being issued as riders on life and annuity policies.

Note that insurance terminology varies from country to country, and the terminology we use in this chapter is that used in the United States. For example, as we mentioned in Chapter 1, in Canada, the health insurance products listed above are referred to as *living benefits* because they provide insurance benefits that are paid while an insured is living.

In this chapter, we first look at the information sources that individual health insurance underwriters use most frequently. We then examine the risk factors assessed during the underwriting of individual health insurance. Next we explain the underwriting of substandard health risks. We conclude by describing some specifics about the underwriting of individual DI, CI, and LTC insurance. Again, keep in mind that company practices vary widely.

Information Sources for Individual Health Underwriting

Health underwriters consider the cost involved in relation to the underwriting benefit when deciding how much information to gather about a proposed insured. Depending on the type of coverage they are underwriting, health underwriters may use some or all of the information sources we described in Chapter 4—the insurance application, agent's statement, MIB, paramedical and medical examinations, APSs, specialized medical questionnaires, medical tests, personal history interviews, inspection reports, pharmaceutical databases, motor vehicle records, and personal questionnaires. Medical expense underwriters, for example, now typically rely on APSs and blood profiles more than medical exams, and they rarely use inspection reports. In addition, many medical expense policies are sold over the Internet with an e-application, so the agent's statement is not as important a sourcc of information as it traditionally was. Instead, expanded personal history interviews with the proposed insured are conducted by telephone. In fact, all types of health insurance are moving toward teleunderwriting and away from full applications and agent's statements.

Whether health insurance applications are completed on paper or electronically, they provide the insurer with medical, personal, and financial information about the proposed insured. However, applications vary among the different types of health products. For example, questions on an individual disability income insurance application typically place more emphasis on the proposed insured's occupational duties and income than do the questions on other types of health insurance applications.

The extent of the medical information a proposed insured must provide varies depending on the type of coverage being applied for and the age and amount requirements. When a physical examination is not required, insurers generally instruct producers—or the teleunderwriting interviewer—to furnish the following information about each impairment that a proposed insured acknowledges on the insurance application:

- Date and duration of each illness or injury
- For a chronic or recurrent condition, date the condition first manifested itself, frequency of recurrence, and date of most recent recurrence
- Aftereffects and complications, if any
- Nature of treatment or medication, date of last such treatment or medication, and whether future treatments are scheduled
- Names and addresses of physicians consulted, dates of visits, and sequence in which physicians were consulted

- If hospitalization occurred, dates of hospitalization, length of hospital stay, and name and location of hospital

Many individual health insurers still require a producer to meet personally with a proposed insured to complete the application for insurance and the agent's statement. The agent's statement can be very useful to a health insurance underwriter. For instance, a producer may notice that a proposed insured has difficulty moving from one chair to another or has trouble communicating verbally. By communicating this type of information to the underwriter, the producer plays a key role in helping an underwriter evaluate each risk appropriately.

To assist producers in interviewing proposed insureds and gathering complete information about a proposed insured's health history, most insurers provide producers with a field underwriting manual. As we noted in Chapter 2, the field underwriting manual typically includes age and amount requirements charts and an impairment guide—a list of common impairments and the probable underwriting decision for proposed insureds who have each type of impairment. Figure 7.1 presents sample entries in one insurer's impairment guide. Note that the health underwriting decisions for a specific impairment differ from the life underwriting decisions for the same impairment. Also, the typical underwriting decisions will not be the same for every insurer.

Risk Factors for Individual Health Underwriting

Medical expense, disability income, critical illness, and long-term care underwriters assess many of the same medical, personal, and financial risk factors when evaluating an application. Remember, though, that health insurance underwriters assess the risks differently depending on the type of coverage. Medical expense underwriters focus on impairments and avocations that may result in future medical expenses. Disability income underwriters focus on the likelihood the proposed insured will become disabled. Critical illness underwriters focus on the probability that the proposed insured will develop an illness or condition covered by the policy. Note that one such condition can be paralysis, so avocations are of importance to critical illness underwriters. Long-term care underwriters focus on the likelihood the proposed insured will need care in his own home or a qualified facility.

In this section, we discuss medical, personal, and financial risk factors as they apply to underwriting individual health insurance in general. In later sections, we focus on the some of the unique aspects of underwriting disability income insurance, critical illness insurance, and LTC insurance.

FIGURE 7.1 Entries in One Insurer's Impairment Guide

Impairment	Type of Coverage	Typical Underwriting Decision
APPENDICITIS	Health	Unoperated—exclusion rider
		Operated within one month—decline
		One month after successful, uncomplicated operation—probably standard
	Life	Usually standard
ASTHMA	Health	Mild, occasional—usually standard
		Moderate to severe—rate, exclude, or decline
	Life	Mild—usually standard
		Moderate to severe—rate to decline
DIABETES	Health	Mild—individual consideration
		Others—decline
	Life	Depending on age, duration and other medical factors—standard to decline
EPILEPSY	Health	Individual consideration
	Life	Depends on history—rate to decline
		Some types after five years—standard
FRACTURES	Health	According to location, severity, complications, and recovery—standard, exclusion rider, or both
	Life	After recovery—standard

Age

A proposed insured's age significantly affects the degree of risk the proposed insured presents for health insurance. Morbidity rates generally increase with age. As people grow older, they are more likely to become ill, and the average duration of their illnesses increases. Further, the length of time required to recuperate from an injury also increases with age.

Because women generally experience a higher morbidity rate than men of the same age, the cost of providing health insurance coverage to women is generally higher than the cost of providing similar coverage to men. As with life insurance, sex affects the premium rate but not whether a risk is accepted.

Health History

The health underwriter is responsible for assessing the probable impact of each impairment and combination of impairments on the health of a proposed insured. That assessment includes consideration of the likelihood the proposed insured will suffer a covered loss in the future. For example, certain impairments—such as arthritis, back pain, or recurring kidney stones—can be of considerable significance in health underwriting because those impairments have been shown statistically to result in higher-than-average medical expense and disability claims.

The health underwriter focuses special attention on the timing of the diagnosis and the treatment of health conditions because some conditions, especially certain types of cancer, are considered more serious when they have been recently diagnosed or treated. However, health insurance underwriters can accept some proposed insureds for coverage after specified periods of time following the last treatment for some impairments.

Certain conditions that have been stable for a number of years may not negatively impact the issuance of coverage because the conditions are not considered to have a significant potential effect on the proposed insured's future health. Even a history of acute illness, such as pneumonia, may not be significant in health underwriting if the proposed insured has recovered fully.

Moreover, health underwriters do not consider each impairment in isolation, but try to obtain a clear understanding of the possible connections between various impairments and their combined effect on the proposed insured's health. For example, a proposed insured who has been treated for gangrene (tissue death) may have suffered the effects of an isolated incident of exposure to extreme cold; because the gangrene is unlikely to recur, it may not increase the proposed insured's risk of loss. In contrast, a proposed insured who has been treated for gangrene associated with diabetes or another medical condition presents a significant risk of loss.

Health underwriters also consider medical conditions that may present a higher-than-average probability of resulting in accidents. Some impairments, such as epilepsy, vertigo, and impaired eyesight and hearing, often are associated with accidents and are examined thoroughly in health underwriting.

Finally, health underwriters pay special attention to personal factors that can decrease or increase the probable effect of an impairment on the proposed insured's health. For example, a proposed insured who has been diagnosed with mild to moderate asthma and who also smokes is underwritten more cautiously than one who has asthma and does not smoke.

Family History

Health insurance underwriters also consider a proposed insured's family history of health conditions because many health conditions have a genetic component. For example, a proposed insured whose mother or sister died as a result of breast cancer is at higher risk of having breast cancer than is a proposed insured with no such family history.

Occupation

In general, occupation has a greater effect on morbidity than on mortality. Health underwriters are particularly concerned about occupations that produce greater-than-average accident rates and health hazards.

Some health underwriters classify occupations according to the type and degree of risk presented by each occupation. In deciding the proper occupational classification for a proposed insured, the underwriter typically considers the job duties performed rather than the job title. The degree of risk presented by a specific occupation is based on the most hazardous duty performed and the proportion of the work time spent performing that duty. Medical expense and disability income underwriters will decline certain occupations automatically due to a high degree of risk.

Avocations

Occasional exposures to common avocation risks are generally acceptable for health underwriting purposes. However, if a proposed insured participates more frequently than average in some avocations—for example, scuba diving, mountain climbing, and stock car racing—the underwriter usually excludes from coverage any losses that result while the insured is engaged in the dangerous avocation. In some cases, the risk resulting from a dangerous avocation is so great that the application is declined.

An interesting example of how avocations are underwritten differently depending on the type of coverage is a proposed insured who skydives and who applies for both life and disability coverage. Whereas a life insurance policy issued to such an individual may be rated, a disability policy may be issued on a standard basis. The reasoning is that if anything went wrong, the insured would be killed instead of disabled. Thus, skydiving is not a high-risk factor for disability insurance.

Driving History

Each insurer sets its own guidelines for rating or declining coverage based on a proposed insured's driving history, but if a proposed insured has a poor driving record—as shown by numerous traffic violations, arrests, or accidents on his MVR—most insurers severely limit benefits or decline coverage. Some insurers set general guidelines, such as charging a flat extra premium for a proposed insured with one driving violation during the past year and declining coverage for a proposed insured with more than one violation within the past year. Other insurers consider each application on a case-by-case basis. Generally, the underwriter considers the type of driving offenses that occurred, how recently they occurred, and how frequently multiple offenses occurred.

Underwriters pay special attention to any indication that a proposed insured has a record of driving under the influence (DUI) of alcohol or drugs. Some insurers will not approve coverage for proposed insureds who have been convicted of driving under the influence during the past three years.

Alcohol and Drug Abuse

Comments in an APS or agent's statement or evidence from a motor vehicle record that a proposed insured has abused alcohol and/or drugs are clear indications that the underwriter should thoroughly investigate for alcohol and/or drug abuse. Underwriters who find evidence of past alcohol or drug abuse typically obtain specific tests, such as a urinalysis or blood profile, to check for current use. The underwriter also can require the proposed insured to complete an alcohol- or drug-use questionnaire. Some health underwriters—disability income in particular—may order an inspection report that focuses on alcohol- or drug-use habits.

If a proposed insured has been free of alcohol and drug abuse for a considerable period of time—usually a minimum of five years—and has undergone treatment, most insurers will issue a policy, although probably with a high premium. Abuse of alcohol or drugs within the past five years, however, typically results in an underwriting decision to decline coverage.

International Residence and Travel

Many insurers do not approve health insurance for proposed insureds who reside abroad or travel abroad for extended periods. Insurers that do consider issuing health insurance coverage in such cases pay particular attention to the prevalence of diseases peculiar to a given area and may increase the premium charged for the coverage or impose other requirements. For example, some insurers require a proposed insured to spend at least nine months of each year in her own country of residence. Some insurers obtain an inspection report that focuses on the location and frequency of the travel or duration of residence.

As we mentioned in Chapter 4, legislation has passed in several U.S. states prohibiting underwriting on the basis of foreign travel for life insurance; such legislation is pending in the U.S. Congress. At the time this text went to press, legislation applied only to life and not health insurance.

Foreign Citizenship

Most insurers in the United States will consider issuing health insurance to a proposed insured who is not a U.S. citizen if he

- Resides in the United States for one to two years before applying for health insurance
- Supplies a permanent resident visa
- Provides the name of a medical practitioner in the United States who can supply adequate medical records
- Shows intent to remain in the United States

Proposed insureds who meet these requirements typically are eligible for coverage and are underwritten in other respects according to the same guidelines that are applied to applicants who are U.S. citizens.

Finances

Most health insurers require that a proposed insured have a minimum level of annual income to qualify for certain types of insurance. Each insurer establishes its own eligibility requirements.

Existing Health Coverage

To avoid overinsurance, the underwriter checks the application to determine the amount and type of health insurance that the proposed insured already has in force. Some insurers deny coverage or limit the amount of coverage issued if a proposed insured is already covered under another policy of the same type being applied for.

Underwriting Substandard Health Risks

Ideally, an individual health insurance underwriter decides to accept an application as applied for at the requested premium rate. However, if a proposed insured represents a greater-than-average risk, an underwriter may take the actions outlined in Figure 7.2, depending on the insurer and the type of coverage. In some cases, the insurer may issue a policy with a combination of a higher premium rate and coverage modifications.

FIGURE 7.2 Underwriting Substandard Health Risks

	Medical Expense	Disability Income	Critical Illness	Long-Term Care
Issue the coverage at a higher-than-standard premium rate	X	X	X	X
Modify the coverage requested by taking one or more of the following actions:				
• Increase the amount of eligible expenses the insured must pay	X			
• Decrease the amount of coverage applied for	X	X	X	X
• Decrease the benefit period available		X		X
• Increase the waiting period		X	X	X
• Add an exclusion rider		X	X	
Decline to issue coverage	X	X	X	X

Premium Rating Methods

All insurers offering individual coverages use some type of premium rating method that involves a point system (debits and credits) being translated into a percentage increase in the standard premium. However, the type of method will vary depending on the type of coverage and the insurer. As we discussed in Chapter 5, insurers use a numerical rating system for life insurance. Some insurers also use this system for health insurance coverages.

Medical expense underwriters often use a percentage rating method to establish the premium rate for a proposed insured who presents a substandard risk. The ***percentage rating method*** is a method of establishing the health insurance premium rate to charge for substandard risks in which the insurer adds to the standard premium rate an extra percentage of that standard premium rate to reflect the additional risk.

Using the percentage rating method, an underwriter first assigns to each proposed insured a numerical rating that indicates the degree of risk presented by the proposed insured. According to a typical percentage rating system, the average, or standard, morbidity risk is set at 0 percent. An underwriter assigns debits for impairments that unfavorably affect the morbidity risk presented by a proposed insured. Unlike a life underwriter, a health underwriter typically does not assign credits for factors that reduce the level of risk presented by a proposed insured.

After assigning debits to a proposed insured, the underwriter uses a rating schedule to determine the extra percentage of the standard premium rate to charge for a proposed insured. A ***rating schedule*** is a table that lists the rating percentages that are to be assigned to proposed insureds based on the total debits assigned to them by the underwriter. Each insurer develops its own rating schedule. An example of a typical rating schedule is shown in Figure 7.3.

Using the rating schedule, the underwriter calculates the premium rate to charge for a proposed insured as follows:

Premium Rate = Standard Premium Rate × Rating Percentage

For example, suppose a proposed insured has 30 debits. According to the rating schedule in Figure 7.3, an underwriter assigns a rating percentage of 25 to a proposed insured who has 30 debits. This proposed insured will be charged a premium rate that is 25 percent greater than the standard premium rate. If the standard premium rate for the applied-for coverage is $3,000 a year, the premium this proposed insured will be charged for the coverage is $3,750 ($3,000 × 1.25).

FIGURE 7.3 Example of a Rating Schedule

Debits	Rating Percentage
0–5	0
10–15	10
20–35	25
40–60	50
65–85	75
90–110	100
115–135	125
140–165	150
170–185	175
190–200	200
220 and up	Declined

When a proposed insured has more than one ratable impairment and when no other instructions are given in the health underwriting manual, the health underwriter usually sums the debits. If the sum of the debits appears to overstate the risk anticipated, only a portion of the debits for the second or third impairment may be appropriate for the total risk presented. For certain impairments occurring together, however, the risk is higher than the sum of the debits. For instance, diabetes occurring with hypertension presents a much higher risk than the debits for diabetes and the debits for hypertension added together would indicate.

Certain medical impairments when found in conjunction with certain personal factors also may increase risk significantly. For example, a proposed insured who has a respiratory disease and smokes or a cosmetologist who is sensitive to certain chemical solutions used in performing her job present significantly increased risks because their personal factors directly affect their medical impairments. An underwriter considers such combinations of medical and personal factors to reach an appropriate rating.

Occasionally, health underwriters use flat extra premiums, which we discussed in Chapter 5, to establish premium amounts for individual health insurance coverage.

Policy Modifications

Proposed insureds sometimes present such an increased morbidity risk that the underwriter must modify the coverage originally requested before accepting the risk. The health coverage issued to a high-risk proposed insured can be modified in a variety of ways depending on the type of coverage being underwritten.

Expenses, Benefits, and Benefit Period

For proposed insureds that present an increased morbidity risk, underwriters may increase the amount of eligible expenses the insured must pay, decrease the amount of benefits applied for, and/or decrease the length of the benefit period, depending on the type of coverage.

- Individual medical expense coverage can be modified by increasing the amount of eligible expenses the insured must pay. For example, the insurer can increase the amount of the (1) ***deductible***, which is the flat monetary amount of eligible medical expenses the insured must pay before the insurer will begin making any benefit payments, (2) ***coinsurance***, which is the percentage of all eligible medical expenses in excess of the deductible the insured must pay, and/or (3) ***copayment***, which is a specified, fixed amount that an insured pays for a specified medical service at the time the service is rendered. The insurer also can impose a dollar limit, or a cap, on the amount of benefits that are payable each calendar year and/or over the life of the policy. Policy provisions that describe deductibles, coinsurance, and copayments are known as *expense participation requirements*.
- Individual disability income coverage can be modified by reducing the periodic benefit applied for and/or reducing the length of the policy's benefit payment period.
- Individual critical illness coverage typically is either issued as applied for or rejected, although the coverage can be modified by reducing the amount of benefits applied for.
- Individual long-term care coverage can be modified by reducing the amount of benefits applied for and/or reducing the length of the benefit period.

Waiting Period

When allowed by applicable regulatory requirements, an insurer may modify an individual health insurance policy as applied for by increasing the length of the ***waiting period***, which is a stated period of time that must pass before benefits are payable.

- For individual medical expense coverage, the waiting period typically is 30 days and begins on the policy issue date.
- For individual disability income coverage, the applicant can select the waiting period, which begins on the date of the onset of the disability. Typical options are 30, 60, 90, and 120 days. The shorter the waiting period that the applicant selects, the higher the premium he pays.
- For individual critical illness coverage, the waiting period typically is 30 to 90 days, depending on the condition to which it applies. The waiting period begins on the date of policy issue.
- For individual long-term care coverage, the applicant can select the waiting period, which begins when the insured requires long-term care. Typical options range from 0 to 100 days. The shorter the waiting period that the applicant selects, the higher the premium he pays.

Exclusions

If the proposed insured's health history presents the possibility of the recurrence of a serious illness, if the proposed insured has a chronic condition for which future treatment seems likely, or if the proposed insured has a particularly hazardous avocation, an exclusion rider typically is attached to a disability income or critical illness policy. Exclusion riders are not used with medical expense and long-term care policies.

Insurers typically do not exclude from coverage any loss that arises from a temporary condition. For instance, if a proposed insured has sprained his shoulder or has undergone shoulder surgery a month before applying for coverage, but has no previous history of shoulder problems (and if any surgery is considered to have resolved the current problem), most insurers would issue health insurance coverage without excluding shoulder or joint problems. Other temporary conditions that generally are not excluded by riders include eye and ear injuries that do not permanently impair sight and hearing and nonmalignant skin tumors that can be removed successfully and that do not require more extensive treatment.

An insurer may use the rider for a condition not manifested but indicated as being strongly possible in the future. For example, suppose that a proposed insured with a family history of breast cancer has no identified breast cancer, but has developed fibrocystic disease, certain forms of which are associated with a higher risk of breast cancer. In this case, the underwriter typically requires an exclusion rider for diseases of the breasts because the proposed insured currently has a condition that can increase risk.

A sample exclusion rider that specifies the limits of coverage is shown in Figure 7.4.

FIGURE 7.4 Sample Exclusion Rider

EXCLUSION RIDER

Name of insured ______________________________

Policy number ______________________________

Effective date of coverage ______________________________

This Exclusion Rider is attached to and forms a part of the above-referenced policy number.

It is agreed and understood, anything in the printed part of this policy notwithstanding, that the proposed insured expressly waives any benefits for any loss or disability resulting directly or indirectly, in whole or in part, from **arterial hypertension disease or disorder of the heart or stroke** on behalf of the proposed insured, and no benefits shall accrue on account of any loss resulting therefrom. Said waiver is a permanent waiver for the entire duration of this policy.

ABC Insurance Company

Signature of insured ______________________________

Date rider signed ______________________________

Signature of owner, if other than insured ______________________________

Date rider signed ______________________________

Source: Adapted from Mary C. Bickley et al., *Life and Health Insurance Underwriting*, 2nd ed. [Atlanta: LOMA (Life Office Management Association, Inc.), © 2007], 214. Used with permission; all rights reserved.

Most underwriting manuals provide the wording for many conditions that might warrant the use of an exclusion rider. Samples of such suggested wording for riders covering certain medical conditions are shown in Insight 7.1. If a case is unusual, the insurer's medical director or legal department can help an underwriter draft an appropriate exclusion rider.

Underwriting Individual Disability Income Insurance

Disability income (DI) insurance presents somewhat different underwriting considerations from those presented by other types of health insurance

INSIGHT 7.1 Examples of Wording for Standardized Exclusion Riders

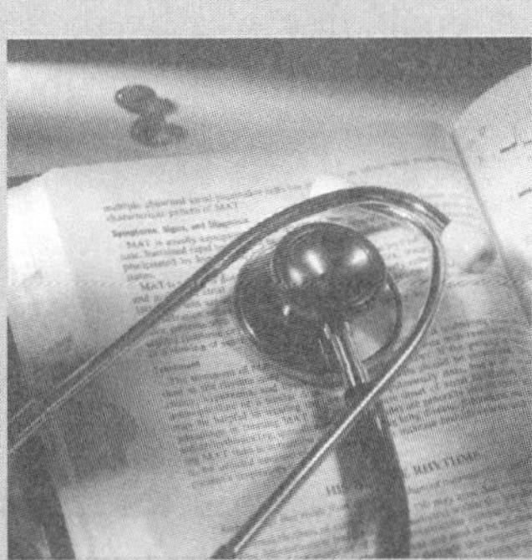

Condition Involved	Suggested Wording for Riders
Cataract	Cataract or disease of, or partial or complete loss of sight of, one or both eyes, a complication thereof, treatment or operation thereof
Phlebitis	Phlebitis, varicose veins, thrombosis, a complication thereof, treatment or operation therefor
Raynaud's disease	Raynaud's disease or other peripheral vascular disease, a complication thereof, treatment or operation therefor
Rheumatic fever	Rheumatic fever, including a complication or residual effects thereof, treatment or operation therefor

coverages. DI coverage is intended to replace only a portion of income that is lost during a period of disability so that the disability will not cause the insured to suffer serious financial harm.

Disability income underwriters seek information from many sources, including medical records, blood profiles, urinalysis, MVRs, and inspection reports. The greater the amount of DI coverage the proposed insured seeks, the more likely the underwriter is to require greater evidence of insurability in order to evaluate thoroughly all medical conditions.

The risk factors we described in the section entitled "Risk Factors for Individual Health Underwriting" are analyzed in underwriting all types of individual health insurance, including DI coverage. In this section, we describe some of the unique aspects of underwriting disability income insurance.

Antiselection

The potential for antiselection for DI coverage is greater than for other types of health insurance. Because DI insurance provides income benefits while an insured is not working, such coverage gives some insureds a financial incentive to "retire." Underwriters generally regard as suspicious any proposed insured who (1) intentionally includes erroneous information on the application, (2) withholds information on the application, (3) attempts to buy excessive amounts of DI coverage, or (4) is otherwise unethical. Such proposed insureds may present moral hazard and are investigated with extreme care. The DI underwriter guards against antiselection by seeking to approve an amount of DI coverage that is appropriate for the proposed insured's needs.

Health History

Generally, a medical condition is more likely to result in disability than in death. For example, if a proposed insured for life coverage mentions in a questionnaire that she has a history of back sprains, most life underwriters will not investigate further because back sprains usually do not result in death. A DI underwriter, however, typically investigates such a report because back sprains often result in disability.

In some cases, the proposed insured has a history of a physical condition, such as a nervous system disorder, that could make it difficult to determine whether a disability exists when a claim is made. In these cases, the underwriter usually does not approve DI coverage. However, in some cases, the underwriter approves coverage but adds an exclusion rider to the policy stating that benefits will not be paid for any disability that results from the condition.

Occupation

Disability benefits are paid when an insured is unable to work. Thus, a proposed insured's occupation is of particular importance in DI underwriting.

To be considered a standard risk, a proposed insured for DI coverage should have a favorable employment record—that is, steady employment and regular attendance—in a nonhazardous occupation. Proposed insureds whose work environment presents potential accident or disease hazards or whose employment is seasonal or otherwise irregular generally are viewed as undesirable risks for DI coverage. A proposed insured who is likely to be out of work may be more likely to apply for DI coverage and to develop or prolong a disability than a proposed insured with steady employment.

A proposed insured who works from his home sometimes is considered a questionable risk because if a disability occurs, the underwriter may find it difficult to determine if the person is still working and, thus, not eligible for DI benefits. In certain occupations, a self-employed proposed insured who works from home and who has no considerable net worth or other means of support also is considered a poor risk for DI coverage because the person may have little incentive to return to work after recovering from a disability.

The proposed insured's job duties or requirements also affect the anticipated duration of a disability and, thus, affect the underwriting decision. Insurance industry statistics show, for instance, that a white-collar worker who has suffered a heart attack is likely to return to work sooner than a blue-collar worker who has suffered a similar heart attack. Likewise, a relatively minor injury such as a broken wrist could prove incapacitating to a dentist or a doctor, but would not necessarily prevent a teacher, an office manager, or a minister from continuing to work.

DI insurers establish ***occupational rating classes*** into which they group occupations according to the relative degree of risk they present for DI coverage. Occupations that are rated as presenting less relative risk include those that present few physical dangers or psychological stresses and are stable, with little annual turnover. Occupational classes range from the least hazardous occupations to the most hazardous occupations, which are uninsurable. When assessing a proposed insured whose duties cross occupational lines, a DI underwriter usually applies the classification covering the most hazardous duties. One insurer's occupational rating classes are shown in Figure 7.5.

Although health underwriters in general do not often use inspection reports to gather information about a proposed insured, disability income underwriters do use such reports. Inspection reports are particularly helpful when underwriting disability income insurance because they provide information about the proposed insured's specific job duties, which enables the underwriter to classify the occupation properly.

Finances

A proposed insured for DI coverage typically submits detailed information about her finances to establish the amount of her income from all sources and the amount of disability income benefit for which she qualifies. The underwriter examines a proposed insured's net worth, net earned income (gross earned income minus taxes), and unearned income, such as income from investments, interest, or a trust fund. Insurers carefully limit the maximum amount of disability income benefit that a particular applicant can purchase.

DI insurance is not intended to replace 100 percent of an insured's predisability income. Without restrictions on the income amounts available under DI coverage, a disabled insured could receive as much income as he received when working. In such a case, the disabled insured would have no financial incentive to return to work.

DI insurers typically create an ***income replacement table***, which is a chart that states the limits on the amount of DI insurance—usually expressed as a monetary amount of monthly income benefit—the insurer will issue based on a proposed insured's net earned income. For example, according to Figure 7.6, which is a portion of one insurer's income

FIGURE 7.5 Occupational Rating Classes

CLASS 1 (STANDARD)

This class includes people in the least hazardous occupations—for example, attorneys, auditors, bookkeepers, drafters, insurance producers, librarians, meteorologists, pharmacists, administrative assistants, and stockbrokers.

CLASS 2

This class generally includes (a) people in certain nonhazardous occupations in which even a minor injury can result in a claim, such as most people working in medical professions, laboratory workers, and musicians for whom a minor injury could interrupt or end employment in that occupation; and (b) people having office and overall supervisory responsibility in manufacturing plants or at construction sites. Examples include architects, building contractors who inspect construction, medical technicians, and supervising plant managers.

CLASS 3

This class generally includes (a) blue-collar workers or people doing light manual labor, (b) people who drive passenger or light delivery vehicles, and (c) managers who directly supervise manual laborers on the job and who may occasionally assist in manual activity. Examples include athletic coaches, bus drivers, house painters, motor freight dispatchers, plumbers, taxi drivers, and waiters.

CLASS 4 (MOST HAZARDOUS)

This class includes people in the most hazardous insurable occupations, generally those in which the incidence of injury is high—for example, boilermakers, border patrol police, locomotive engineers, stevedores, structural steelworkers, and other heavy construction workers.

UNINSURABLE

This class includes people who are exposed to unusual hazards and are uninsurable for any disability income—for instance, certain professional and semiprofessional athletes, aerial photographers or surveyors, blasters, underground miners, steeplejacks, test pilots, and war correspondents.

Source: Adapted from Ernest L. Martin, *Intro to Underwriting* [Atlanta: LOMA (Life Office Management Association, Inc.), © 1999], 50.

FIGURE 7.6 Income Replacement Table

Annual Net Earned Income	Monthly Net Earned Income	Total DI Benefit
$20,000	$1,667	$1,150
$40,000	$3,333	$1,925
$50,000	$4,167	$2,250
$60,000	$5,000	$2,500
$70,000	$5,833	$2,750
$80,000	$6,667	$3,000
$90,000	$7,500	$3,250
$100,000	$8,333	$3,450

replacement table, a proposed insured who has an annual net earned income of $40,000 and receives approximately $3,333 monthly after taxes is eligible for approximately $1,925 in monthly benefits under DI coverage.

In calculating the amount of DI benefit a proposed insured is eligible to purchase, the underwriter considers both primary and secondary income sources if it is likely that a disability would result in the proposed insured losing both incomes. Such situations often arise when a proposed insured's primary and secondary sources of income require similar job duties. If, however, the proposed insured is unable to work at her primary job but is likely to be able to continue to earn income from the secondary source, the underwriter does not include the secondary income in calculating the amount of the DI benefit for which the insured is eligible.

An underwriter's decision whether to include secondary income is also based on how much of the total income that secondary source provides and whether the secondary source is a regular job or is just seasonal or a hobby. If the secondary income is a significant portion of the total income and the source is a regular job, then the secondary income probably will be included.

A DI underwriter also looks at a proposed insured's income stability over a recent period, typically the prior three years. The underwriter considers as favorable any indication that a proposed insured's income is consistent or increasing over this period. Conversely, if a proposed insured has suffered significant decreases in income over this period, the underwriter investigates further.

Income earned through seasonal or temporary employment generally is not considered stable, and a DI underwriter generally does not take such income into account in calculating the amount of periodic DI benefit a proposed insured is eligible to purchase. For example, a person who delivers new telephone directories once a year or who works at a retail store only during a holiday season is typically ineligible to have income from those sources protected under DI coverage.

An underwriter generally does not include unearned income in figuring the amount of income to be covered because unearned income typically continues when the insured is disabled.

If a proposed insured has a high net worth, the underwriter verifies that the proposed insured cannot completely replace the current net earned income by liquidating assets. For instance, if a proposed insured has a net worth of $3,000,000 and an annual net income of $20,000, most underwriters would conclude that this person does not need DI coverage. If this person were disabled so that he could not work, he has sufficient net worth to provide well for himself.

Underwriters also consider any other DI coverage protecting a proposed insured and use the income replacement table to assess whether a proposed insured is eligible for DI benefits. For instance, according to Figure 7.5, a proposed insured who has $60,000 in annual net earned income and who has no significant unearned income or excessive net worth would be eligible for $2,500 a month in DI benefits. If this proposed insured is covered already by DI insurance offered by her employer, the underwriter usually reduces the benefit amount available under the new policy so that the total of DI benefits paid—by all insurers—does not exceed $2,500 per month.

Underwriting Individual Critical Illness Insurance

As we mentioned at the beginning of this chapter, critical illness (CI) insurance is a type of health insurance that pays a benefit directly to the insured when the insured is diagnosed with a specified illness or condition. The benefit is typically paid in a lump sum and is paid without regard to expenses incurred. The conditions that are considered critical illnesses are specified in the policy using very specific definitions and usually include heart attack, stroke, and life-threatening cancer. The number of impairments covered can range from a minimum of 3 or 4 to 30 or more. An underwriter can exclude a condition if he feels the risk of that condition occurring is too great.

CI insurance is considered to be a survivor benefit, which means it is designed to provide for the insured's living needs. This type of coverage protects insureds against the financial hardship that can result from living with a serious illness, typically providing a fixed amount of coverage regardless of the insured's actual expenses. Benefit use is at the policyowner's discretion. Typical uses of the benefits include out-of-system or experimental care, non-reimbursed copayments, and pharmaceutical expenses; however, insureds can use the benefits in any way they want, including paying the mortgage or going on a vacation. Note, though, that financial underwriting of critical illness is done to minimize the potential of an excessive windfall in the event of a critical illness claim.

Some companies provide an insurability checklist for field underwriters to complete with the client before beginning the application process. This insurability checklist is a list of illnesses or conditions that a proposed insured has or has had that would indicate that an application should not be taken. If the proposed insured has not had any of the conditions listed on the insurability checklist, the producer can proceed with the application process.

Critical illness underwriting focuses on determining the risk of the proposed insured developing one of the insured critical conditions. Thus, CI underwriters must become very familiar with the medical and personal risk factors associated with the impairments covered by the policy. CI underwriters typically focus on similar risk factors and use similar sources of information as life underwriters. Medical underwriting for critical illness focuses on risk factors that may increase the incidence of a critical condition. Family history is also significant in determining the likelihood of future incidences of the impairments covered by critical illness products. For those policies that include paralysis as a covered condition, the underwriter carefully examines hazardous avocations and aviation activities.

Underwriting Individual Long-Term Care Insurance

Long-term care (LTC) insurance provides coverage for care an insured receives in a setting other than a hospital, such as in the insured's home or a nursing home facility. Care paid for by LTC coverage may include diagnostic, preventive, therapeutic, rehabilitative, maintenance, or personal care services. The benefit period for LTC insurance can be set for any length of time—from one year to a maximum of lifetime coverage.

Benefits generally are payable if an insured loses her physical functional capacity to perform the activities of daily living or has a cognitive impairment. The ***activities of daily living (ADLs)*** are the activities of eating, bathing, dressing, continence, toileting, and transferring into or out of a bed, chair, or wheelchair. A ***cognitive impairment*** is a reduction in a person's ability to think, reason, or remember. Cognitive impairment may result in forgetfulness, memory loss, decreased ability to think clearly, confusion or disorientation, delirium, or amnesia. Two of the most common types of cognitive impairment are

- ***Dementia***, which is a general term used to describe mental deterioration characterized by loss of essential intellectual abilities such as memory, judgment, and abstract thinking, of such a degree as to interfere with social functioning
- ***Alzheimer's disease***, also called *primary degenerative dementia*, which causes deterioration of a person's intellectual and cognitive functions, including memory, orientation, intellect, and judgment, and can cause deterioration of a person's speech and motor functions

Some people can manage the ADLs, but have difficulty with other, usually less essential, types of activities that are called ***instrumental activities of daily living (IADLs)*** and that include the following activities:

- Managing finances
- Cooking
- Doing laundry
- Shopping for food and clothing
- Transporting oneself in a car or on public transportation
- Using the telephone
- Taking medications

Some insurers consider ADLs and IADLs in underwriting proposed insureds for LTC coverage, but others consider only ADLs.

Possible underwriting actions on most LTC products are to issue the coverage at standard rates, modify the amount of coverage available, decrease the period during which benefits are payable, increase the premium amount or waiting period, or decline to issue the coverage. Most underwriters automatically decline LTC applications submitted by proposed insureds who have a history of a health condition that places severe limitations on the person's ability to function independently. In these cases, underwriters do not issue LTC policies because (1) the condition is fatal or recovery is rare or (2) the symptoms are severe and tend to be progressive. Figure 7.7 provides a partial listing of such uninsurable conditions.

Most underwriters also automatically decline LTC applications submitted by proposed insureds who

- Are receiving home health care or attending an adult day care center
- Are confined to a hospital or nursing home
- Have undergone an organ transplant (including a kidney transplant five or more years ago)
- Are scheduled or expected to undergo surgery (except for cataract surgery under local anesthesia)

FIGURE 7.7 Partial Listing of Conditions that Prevent Approval of LTC Coverage

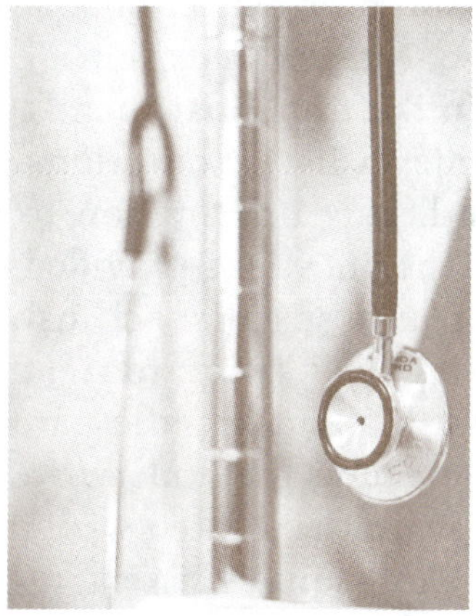

- Alzheimer's disease
- Amputation resulting from disease (for instance, from diabetes or atherosclerosis)
- Blindness resulting from disease or with ADL/IADL limitations
- Cancer with evidence of distant metastasis within past 10 years
- Cystic fibrosis
- Dementia, irreversible
- Emphysema, on oxygen
- Gangrene resulting from diabetes or peripheral vascular disease
- Memory loss within 12 months, including confusion, delirium, or disorientation, and any current use of medication for same
- Multiple sclerosis
- Muscular dystrophy
- Oxygen use, current
- Paralysis, paraplegia, or quadriplegia
- Senility, all forms
- Spinal cord injury
- Stroke (cardiovascular accident)

Field Underwriting

To help producers perform effective field underwriting of LTC proposed insureds, many insurers develop special field underwriting manuals that focus specifically on the requirements for this type of insurance. Generally, an ***LTC field underwriting manual*** is an insurer's guidebook that lists a number of medical conditions associated with aging and provides general underwriting criteria for those conditions. For each medical condition, the LTC field underwriting manual describes characteristics and complications and includes questions that the producer is expected to ask in gathering information from the proposed insured.

An LTC field underwriting manual is similar to an impairment guide in that both these documents list impairments. The documents differ in that an impairment guide provides very general information on a wide variety of impairments, whereas an LTC field underwriting manual provides more specific information on the types of conditions that people applying for LTC coverage can exhibit.

Unlike the impairment guide, the LTC field underwriting manual also provides a list of questions that a producer may ask a proposed insured in gathering information to submit with the application for LTC coverage. The questions provided for the producer to ask a proposed insured are often quite specific. For instance, in inquiring whether a proposed insured is using medication to treat pain associated with a fracture, the producer may ask about specific narcotics prescribed for pain. Such specific information helps the underwriter distinguish between mild aching or stiffness that might be treated with over-the-counter medications and more severe pain that requires strong, prescription medication.

In addition, an impairment guide gives very general information about the probable underwriting decision for each impairment, whereas an LTC field underwriting manual cites more specific information about the underwriting decision for specific types of impairments. For example, the listing for fractures in a typical LTC field underwriting manual, as shown in Figure 7.8, provides specific underwriting information for certain types of fractures and also identifies fractures for which no coverage will be issued.

Sources of LTC Underwriting Information

Typically, LTC underwriters receive the initial information needed to evaluate a proposed insured from the application, agent's statement, a paramedical examination, and an APS from each physician who has treated the proposed insured within the last three to five years. In addition, LTC underwriters sometimes obtain a specific type of inspection report tailored to provide information that is helpful in underwriting applications for LTC coverage, such as information about the proposed insured's living conditions, hobbies, activities, and travel, among other things. Furthermore, the LTC underwriter may receive information specifically designed to enable him to determine whether a proposed insured currently has a cognitive impairment or is unable to perform the activities of daily living and who is likely to be declined for coverage. The primary sources of such information are a personal history interview, a face-to-face assessment, and a cognitive screen.

Personal History Interview

As part of the PHI, the interviewer may ask a short list of questions designed to indicate the presence of cognitive impairment. For example, the interviewer may ask the current date, season, and location of the

FIGURE 7.8 Section of One Insurer's LTC Field Underwriting Manual

Fractures

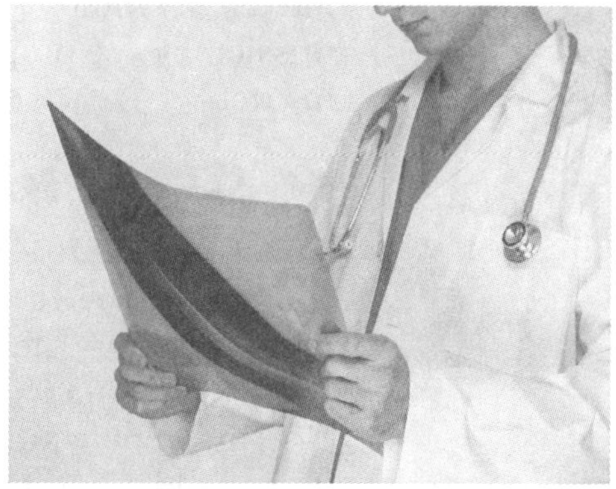

Fractures are more common in women than in men, probably because of post-menopausal osteoporosis and the tendency for women to outlive men. The presence of osteoporosis often determines whether a fall results in a fracture. Pathological fractures—those not associated with a fall or trauma—are common in the elderly.

The most common sites of fractures in our claim experience have been the hips, followed by compression fractures of the spinal column and fractures of the pelvis, shoulders, and wrists. Healing of fractures in the elderly is often delayed because of reduced blood supply to the area, arthritis, reduced nutrition, and decreased physical activity.

If a proposed insured has suffered a fracture, you should find out

- What bone was fractured and when?
- Has surgery been recommended?
- Has osteoporosis been diagnosed?
- Is there evidence of functional or movement limitations, or is human assistance required?
- Are narcotics such as Demerol, morphine, or Percodan being used to control pain?
- Is physical therapy currently required?
- Are assistive devices such as a wheelchair, walker, or crutches used?
- Does the proposed insured have a history of imbalance with falls and fractures?

Fractures are underwritten according to the following criteria:

- Hip replacement and fractures of the hip or tibia are acceptable six months after the person regains full functional status and release from medical follow-up
- Fractures of the pelvis or vertebra are acceptable twelve months after recovery

The following fractures are not acceptable for coverage:

- Three or more long bone, vertebral, or pelvic fractures due to falls or osteoporosis
- Any fracture where assistance is still required or a wheelchair or walker is used
- Curvature of the spine with secondary pulmonary problems

Source: Reprinted from Mary C. Bickley et al., *Life and Health Insurance Underwriting*, 2nd ed. [Atlanta: LOMA (Life Office Management Association, Inc.), © 2007], 230. Used with permission; all rights reserved.

proposed insured and other questions that people with a cognitive impairment might find difficult to answer.

For an LTC policy, the PHI may take place between the interviewer and the proposed insured's medical caregiver. To comply with privacy requirements, the interviewer must verify that each caregiver has been given permission by the proposed insured to discuss medical information with the insurer.

Face-to-Face Assessment

A ***face-to-face assessment*** involves a meeting between a proposed insured and an interviewer who observes and, to some extent, examines the proposed insured's physical and mental condition. The interviewer represents the insurance company and usually is employed by a vendor. Most LTC insurers require a face-to-face assessment for proposed insureds aged 70 and older; although if an application reveals the possibility of significant medical conditions, or if current medical records are unavailable, an insurer may require a face-to-face assessment for a proposed insured who is younger than 70. Typical questions asked during a face-to-face assessment are shown in Figure 7.9.

Cognitive Screen

As part of the face-to-face assessment, the interviewer also may administer a ***cognitive screen***, also known as a *cognitive test*, which is a test designed

FIGURE 7.9 Typical Questions Asked During Face-to-Face Assessment

To assess a proposed insured's mobility:

- Do you go outside your house at any time? If so, where do you go? Do you go alone or with someone else?
- Do you drive? If so, where do you drive? How often?
- Do you need support or help from another person when you go outside within walking distance of your home?
- Do you need to use any equipment such as a cane, walker, or wheelchair?

To assess the ability of a proposed insured to dress himself:

- Do you need help to dress or undress yourself?
- Are you able to get your clothes from the closet?
- Can you manage dressing with someone standing by in case you need help, or do you need frequent assistance?

to determine a person's powers of recollection or short-term memory. An underwriter also may receive the results of a cognitive screen in an APS or other health history report.

A ***delayed word recall (DWR) test*** is a type of cognitive screen that examines the ability of a proposed insured to remember several common words. The inability to recall between 3 and 5 words correctly from a list of 10 words is indicative of a cognitive impairment. If a proposed insured shows a significant degree of forgetfulness, the underwriter generally declines the application.

A ***backward number sequence test*** is a type of cognitive screen that examines the ability of a proposed insured to recall a series of numbers and name them in reverse sequence. For example, if an interviewer gives the numbers "45, 78, 17," the proposed insured is supposed to recall the numbers in this order: "17, 78, 45."

Risk Factors

In addition to the risk factors we described earlier in this chapter, the LTC underwriter considers whether a proposed insured has a medical condition that usually leads to functional incapacity over time, or has already suffered, or in the near future is likely to suffer, either the loss of functional capacity to perform the activities of daily living or a cognitive impairment. In addition, a proposed insured's age is of special significance to the LTC underwriter.

Functional Capacity

According to the terms of most LTC policies, an insured loses functional capacity and, thus, qualifies for LTC benefits, when he is not able to perform a stated number of activities of daily living without assistance. Generally, insurers deny coverage to anyone who, at the time of application, cannot personally perform all ADLs, but some insurers do offer limited coverage to people who are unable to fulfill only one or two such functions. Signs that a person currently may need, or soon will need, long-term care include

- Use of a walker, a quad cane, a wheelchair, an oxygen respirator, or kidney dialysis
- Current institutionalization in a nursing home, an assisted living facility, or a hospital
- Current use of home care services, skilled nursing care, adult day care, or hospice care
- Use of a catheter or other draining device, ostomy care, or a hospital bed

Cognitive Impairment

Certain types of cognitive impairment can limit one's ability to perform ADLs. For example, a person suffering from dementia may be physically able to feed himself, but may not remember to eat or may forget how to feed himself. He may be able to put on his own clothes, but may wear the same clothes day after day. People with significant cognitive impairment usually require assistance with ADLs.

Age

LTC coverage generally is available to individuals between the ages of 40 and 85. The older a proposed insured is, the more likely she is to have a physical or mental condition that makes her unable to perform the ADLs. Thus, age is one of the most important factors affecting the degree of risk a proposed insured presents. LTC underwriters must be knowledgeable about the physical and mental effects that the aging process has on insureds. Thus, they study ***geriatrics***, which is the branch of medicine that deals with the diagnosis and treatment of diseases and problems specific to the aged.

Accurate underwriting for LTC insurance requires consideration of the proposed insured's physiological age as well as his chronological age. A person's ***physiological age*** refers to the relative age or youthfulness of his vital organs and their functioning. A person who has a chronological age of 75 years may be in far better health than the average person of that age, so his physiological age may be closer to 60 or 65 than to 75. Conversely, another person who has a chronological age of 75 may be in such poor health that his physiological age may be closer to 85 or 90 than to 75.

Key Terms

medical expense insurance
disability income (DI) insurance
critical illness (CI) insurance
long-term care (LTC) insurance
percentage rating method
rating schedule
deductible
coinsurance
copayment
waiting period
occupational rating classes
income replacement table
activities of daily living (ADLs)
cognitive impairment
dementia
Alzheimer's disease
instrumental activities of daily living (IADLs)
LTC field underwriting manual
face-to-face assessment
cognitive screen
delayed word recall (DWR) test
backward number sequence test
geriatrics
physiological age

chapter 8

Underwriting Group Life and Health Insurance

Outline

Group Underwriting Process

Information Sources for Group Underwriting
Request for Proposal
Producer's Letter
ERISA Documents
The Master Application

Risk Factors for Group Underwriting
The Group Prospect
The Proposed Coverage

Rating Methods for Group Cases
Manual Rating
Experience Rating
Blended Rating
Rating Approaches for Small Groups

Post-Issue Underwriting for Group Insurance
Underwriting of Late Enrollees
Renewal Underwriting

Learning Objectives

After studying this chapter, you should be able to…

- Describe the group underwriting process and the documents prepared by the insurer and the group prospect
- Identify the sources of information for group underwriting
- Explain the enrollment process and compare the process for contributory and noncontributory plans
- List the risk factors pertaining to a group prospect and describe their effect on the risk presented by a group prospect
- List and describe risk factors pertaining to the proposed coverage
- Distinguish among manual rating, experience rating, and blended rating and calculate sample premium rates
- Describe how an insurer minimizes the risk associated with late enrollees
- Explain renewal underwriting

Group life and health insurance underwriters adhere to many of the same principles as do individual life and health insurance underwriters. However, some major differences exist between underwriting group and individual products, which we explore in this chapter.

We begin this chapter by discussing the group underwriting process. We then describe the sources of information that a group underwriter consults, as well as the risk factors that the group underwriter assesses, in evaluating a *group prospect*—a group that has applied for, but has not yet been approved for, group coverage from an insurance company. After discussing group insurance rating methods, we conclude the chapter with an explanation of post-issue underwriting.

Note that we refer to the individuals who are part of a group but are not covered by insurance as ***group members***, and we refer to the individuals covered by a group insurance policy as the *group insureds*.

Group Underwriting Process

The group life and health insurance underwriting process resembles the individual life and health insurance underwriting process in that group underwriters gather information, assess risk, and decide whether, and on what terms, to approve coverage just as do individual underwriters. Much of the initial information about a group comes from the individual who markets the policy to the group. Most group policies are marketed by ***group representatives***, who are salaried insurance company employees specifically trained in the techniques of marketing and servicing group products. Group representatives may work alone or in conjunction with producers. In some cases, the group representative initiates the sale to an organization and is the only contact between the group prospect and the insurer. In other cases, producers initiate contact with the group prospect and then call on the group representative for assistance in selling and implementing the plan.

A group prospect, often with the help of a producer or group representative, develops a ***request for proposal (RFP)***, which is a document that provides detailed information about the group and the requested coverage and solicits a bid from an insurer for providing that coverage. The producer or group representative sends the RFP to the underwriter, and the information in the RFP allows the underwriter to make an initial assessment of the risk and determine whether the group meets the insurer's underwriting guidelines for the requested coverage. If the underwriter determines that the insurer cannot offer the requested coverage to the group, he can propose changes in the coverage or decline to respond to the RFP.

If the underwriter decides that the group prospect represents an acceptable risk, he develops a proposal for insurance for the producer or group representative to present to the group prospect for consideration. A ***proposal for insurance*** is a document that details the specifications of a group insurance plan proposed by an insurer for a group prospect. Although each insurer develops its own format for a proposal for insurance, such a document usually includes the following information:

- A ***benefit schedule***, which is a table or schedule that specifies the types and amounts of coverage that will be provided for each class that is insured. A ***class*** is a group of group members categorized according to some nondiscriminatory characteristic for purposes of determining eligibility for coverage and benefit levels.
- A list of the premium rates required for each type of coverage.
- Underwriting principles and assumptions for the proposed coverage.
- Details of plan administration, including the responsibilities of the policyholder and the insurer.

A proposal for insurance enables a group prospect to examine the coverage that the underwriter has approved for the group and compare the cost and benefits of plans offered by several insurers. Because the group insurance market is highly competitive, group underwriters work closely with the producer or group representative to design a group insurance plan that is acceptable to the group prospect and the insurer.

After evaluating the proposals for insurance it has received, the group prospect may accept or reject an insurer's proposal or ask the insurer to modify it in some way. If the underwriter agrees to make modifications to the plan or to the rates, the underwriter makes those changes to the proposal for insurance and provides the revised proposal for insurance to the group prospect.

When a group prospect approves a proposal for insurance, the producer or group representative helps the group prospect complete and submit to the insurer a master application for final underwriting. The ***master application*** is an application for group insurance that contains the specific provisions of the requested plan of insurance and is signed by an authorized officer of the proposed policyholder. The underwriter examines the master application to ensure that all information is complete and is consistent with the coverage that the group prospect agreed to in the proposal for insurance. The underwriter has the opportunity to investigate any discrepancies or omissions, and the underwriter approves the coverage only after fully evaluating the case and finding the risk to be acceptable.

If the underwriter approves the coverage, information from the master application is used to develop the master group insurance contract, which is typically referred to as the group insurance policy, as we mentioned in Chapter 1. This legal document certifies the relationship between the insurer and the group policyholder and specifies the benefits provided and the terms of coverage. The group insureds are not parties to the contract.

Figure 8.1 shows the sequence of documents typically exchanged between the insurer and group prospect during group insurance underwriting. Note that some of the terms in the figure will be explained later in the text.

FIGURE 8.1 Sequence of Typical Group Underwriting Documents

	1 Request for Proposal (RFP)	2 Proposal for Insurance	3 Master Application	4 Master Group Insurance Contract
Person or entity who prepares the document	Group prospect or producer or group representative on behalf of the group prospect	Underwriter	Producer or group representative, on behalf of the group prospect	Insurer
Purpose of the document	To provide general information about the group prospect and to request a bid from the insurer for specified group coverage, including plan benefits and rates	To propose a plan for group coverage; may or may not match the coverage or rates requested in the RFP	To provide detailed information about the group prospect and the coverage being requested	To certify the relationship between the insurer and the policyholder and specify the benefits provided and the terms of coverage
Some of the information included in or provided with the document	• Coverage requested • Insurance history • Current benefits • Census • Producer's letter • List of current open claimants, if applicable	• Benefit schedule • Premium rates	• Name of the plan administrator • Enrollment card for each group member	• Terms of Coverage • Benefits

Source: Adapted from Mary C. Bickley et al., *Life and Health Insurance Underwriting*, 2nd ed. [Atlanta: LOMA (Life Office Management Association, Inc.), © 2007], 271. Used with permission; all rights reserved.

Information Sources for Group Underwriting

An underwriter uses various sources to find the information needed to assess the risk represented by a group prospect, including the request for proposal, attachments submitted with the RFP, the producer's letter, ERISA documents, and the master application.

Request for Proposal

An RFP usually includes the following information:

- Name and address of the group
- Characteristics of the group, such as size and industry
- Proposed effective date of coverage
- Types and details of coverage requested
- Administration information for premium billing and claims
- Classes of group members to be covered
- Percentage of the premium that the policyholder will contribute toward the cost of the coverage
- The group's previous insurance history, if any, including premium rates paid, claim experience, and duration of coverage
- The group's current benefits, if different from those being applied for
- Current or expected participation level, which is the percentage of group members who will enroll in the group plan

An RFP for a plan that provides disability income coverage or a waiver of premium for disability provision usually includes a list of current ***open claimants***, who are group insureds receiving short- or long-term disability income benefits. Closed claim information is also included. The information provided on the open claimant list includes each claimant's name, date of birth, date of the disability, expected date of return to work (if any), and gross and/or net monthly benefit amount. Some lists include the prognosis for each disability. The nature of each disability typically isn't revealed due to privacy regulations. The underwriter uses this information to assess the group's future claim liability. In general, the current insurer retains responsibility for making benefit payments to current open claimants.

Another typical RFP attachment is a ***census*** that lists demographic information about the group prospect as a unit and about individual members within the group. Figure 8.2 shows a portion of a typical census for an employer-employee group, which we refer to as an *employee census*. An employee census usually includes the following information:

FIGURE 8.2 Portion of a Typical Employee Census

Date of Birth	M/F	Salary	Classification	Date of Hire	Dependents	Life	*LTD	**WI
05/57	F	$33,904	0001	03/1990	Y	$68,000	$1,695	$435
01/67	M	$27,050	0001	04/1999	N	$55,000	$1,350	$347
10/49	M	$26,520	0002	01/2004	Y	$54,000	$1,325	$341
09/47	F	$41,600	0001	11/1988	Y	$84,000	$2,080	$534
03/52	M	$30,680	0003	09/1990	Y	$62,000	$1,534	$394
11/65	M	$33,280	0001	04/2000	Y	$67,000	$1,665	$427
10/45	F	$30,680	0003	03/1988	Y	$62,000	$1,534	$394
07/39	M	$70,000	0001	10/1980	N	$70,000	$3,500	$600

*The numbers in this column represent the amount of monthly long-term disability income benefits requested for the employee.
**The numbers in this column represent the amount of weekly income coverage (for short-term disability) requested for the employee.

- The total number of individuals in the group.
- Types and amount of coverage requested.
- The total number of group members to be insured by each type of coverage.
- Each group member's date of birth, sex, salary, and job classification.
- Whether each group member has dependents for whom coverage is requested. Group policies typically define a ***dependent*** as (1) a spouse, (2) an unmarried child who is under age 19 and who relies on the group member for financial support and maintenance, (3) a child older than 19—up to a stated maximum age, often 25—if she is a full-time student, and (4) a disabled child for as long as the disability exists, regardless of the child's age.

Producer's Letter

Along with the RFP, the producer or group representative may submit a letter, which includes observations and recommendations about the appropriateness of the requested coverage. The producer's letter is important to the group underwriter in deciding whether to submit a bid for providing the coverage.

An underwriter typically looks favorably upon recommendations submitted by a producer or group representative who consistently has submitted sound business to the insurer, especially if the producer or group representative has extensive experience selling the type of group product being underwritten. Figure 8.3 shows a sample producer's letter for group coverage.

In some cases, the producer also will give the insurer a letter from the group prospect indicating that the group prospect has authorized the producer to obtain proposals for insurance on its behalf.

ERISA Documents

The U.S. federal Employee Retirement Income Security Act (ERISA) imposes a number of reporting requirements on welfare benefit plans, including employer-sponsored group life and health insurance plans. Underwriters sometimes find the information contained in documents employers are required to file under ERISA to be helpful in risk assessment. Typically, underwriters evaluate such documents only in cases in which a group is currently self-insured and is requesting coverage under a fully insured group plan. A ***self-insured group plan*** is a plan for which the group sponsor rather than an insurance company is financially responsible for the claims incurred by group insureds. In contrast, a ***fully insured group plan*** is a plan for which an insurance company is financially responsible for incurred claims. Plans also may be partially insured and partially self insured.

The Master Application

Typically, the master application provides the group underwriter with the following information about the group prospect and the proposed plan of insurance:

FIGURE 8.3 Producer's Letter for Group Coverage

The ABC company has been in business for 47 years manufacturing and assembling movable windows. Its annual net profit has increased during the past 5 years from $1.3 million to $4.4 million. The current carrier has been underwriting coverage for 7 years; the anniversary date is June 1, 2008. Major claims over $10,000 in the past 24 months have been nonexistent. I feel that the strength of the business and the stability of the group, coupled with its moderate claim experience, make it a prime candidate for coverage under our policy.

- Identification of the individuals who are eligible for coverage under the plan, including the total number of eligible group members and dependents, if applicable
- Definition of the ***probationary period***, also known as a *waiting period*, which is the length of time—typically from one to six months—that a new group member must wait before becoming eligible to enroll in a group insurance plan
- A schedule of benefits, by class if applicable
- The percentage of the premium that the group policyholder will pay for the coverage requested
- The type of plan administration

In addition, the master application includes the name of the ***plan administrator***, who is the party responsible for handling the administrative aspects of a group plan. The plan administrator serves as the liaison with the insurer. In employer-employee groups, the plan administrator often is a member of the human resources department.

Along with the master application, the group prospect submits enrollment cards either in hard copy or electronically. An ***enrollment card***, also called a *group enrollment card*, an *enrollment application*, or an *employee application*, is a document that must be completed and signed by a group member to enroll in a group insurance plan. Figure 8.4 illustrates a typical employee enrollment card.

In addition to providing the group member's personal data, the enrollment card includes a statement that the group member signs to indicate that he understands the coverage offered and agrees to pay his portion of the premium if the plan is contributory. A ***contributory plan*** is a group insurance plan for which group insureds must pay some or all of the premiums for their coverage. An employee typically agrees to have his portion of the premium deducted from his salary.

A ***noncontributory plan*** is a group insurance plan for which the group insureds are not required to pay any part of the premium for the coverage; the premiums are paid entirely by the policyholder and all eligible group members are provided with coverage automatically. A group member who chooses not to participate in a contributory group plan signs a statement to that effect.

Risk Factors for Group Underwriting

Group life and health insurance underwriters usually do not assess individual group members. However, underwriters may require evidence of insurability from group members in accordance with age and amount

FIGURE 8.4 Typical Employee Enrollment Card

EMPLOYEE APPLICATION TO **ABC Life Insurance Company**

NAME OF EMPLOYEE (LAST) (FIRST) (MIDDLE)	GROUP NO.	SECTION NO.	CERT. NO
ADDRESS OF EMPLOYEE (STREET NO.)	(CITY)	(STATE)	(ZIP)

NAME OF EMPLOYER	SUBSIDIARY, AFFILIATE, OR MEMBER OF

DEPT.	DATE OF BIRTH (MO) (DAY) (YR)	DATE EMPLOYED (MO) (DAY) (YR)	SEX ▯ MALE ▯ FEMALE	BASIC SALARY FROM EMPLOYER $	▯ SEMI-MONTHLY ▯ HOURLY ▯ MONTHLY ▯ WEEKLY ▯ ANNUALLY

JOB TITLE—IF AMOUNT OF INSURANCE IS BASED ON TITLE BE SURE THAT TITLE GIVEN AGREES WITH POLICY.	SOCIAL SECURITY NO.	NO. OF HOURS WORKED IN NORMAL WEEK	MARITAL STATUS ▯ MARRIED ▯ WIDOWED ▯ SINGLE ▯ DIVORCED

BENEFICIARY'S LAST NAME	FIRST NAME	INITIAL	RELATIONSHIP	AGE

IF MORE THAN ONE BENEFICIARY IS DESIGNATED, INTEREST WILL BE EQUAL UNLESS OTHERWISE INDICATED

CLASS	OPTIONAL COVERAGE ENROLLED FOR (IF APPLICABLE)		
	DEPENDENT LIFE ▯ YES ▯ NO	OPTIONAL LIFE INSURANCE ▯ YES ▯ NO IF YES Amount $ _______	LTD ▯ YES ▯ NO

I hereby apply for group insurance as indicated above and authorize my employer to make the necessary deductions from my earnings to apply toward the premiums, if required. I understand that all insurance coverages will become effective according to the terms of the contract.

DATE ____________________ SIGNATURE ______________________________

Source: Reprinted from Mary C. Bickley et al., *Life and Health Insurance Underwriting*, 2nd ed. [Atlanta: LOMA (Life Office Management Association, Inc.), © 2007], 270.

requirements charts if the group is small and from those group members who enroll in a plan after the enrollment deadline.

Evidence of insurability also is required when excess coverage is requested. *Excess coverage* is coverage for which the group member is eligible but that exceeds a maximum limit above which the group member must provide evidence of insurability. For example, a group life plan may offer employees coverage in the amount of two times their salary; but if the coverage exceeds $75,000, the group member must provide evidence of insurability. If a group member makes $50,000 a year, she is entitled to only $75,000 without providing evidence of insurability. To obtain the remaining $25,000 in coverage, the group member provides whatever evidence of insurability the insurer requires based on the amount of coverage over the maximum limit and the employee's age.

FIGURE 8.5 Risk Assessment Factors for Group Insurance

CHARACTERISTICS OF THE GROUP PROSPECT

- Reason for existence
- Type of group
- Size
- Nature of business
- Description of the occupations and duties
- Geographic location(s)
- Age distribution
- Turnover of group membership
- Participation in the plan
- Classes
- Expected persistency
- Prior coverage
- Claim experience

CHARACTERISTICS OF THE PROPOSED COVERAGE

- Plan of insurance
- Plan administration

The factors that a group underwriter considers when assessing the risk presented by a group prospect fall into two major categories: characteristics of the group prospect and characteristics of the proposed coverage. Figure 8.5 lists the factors typically included under each category.

The Group Prospect

In evaluating a group prospect, the underwriter's goal is to accept only those groups that meet the established underwriting guidelines for the product and whose expected claim costs are reasonably predictable. Insurers have identified various risk characteristics of group prospects that most affect the likelihood a group's claim experience will be high.

Reason for Existence

Most insurance companies in the United States and Canada generally adhere to the principle that an eligible group must have been formed for a purpose other than to purchase insurance coverage. This requirement protects insurance companies from antiselection that would result if a number of people, most of whom are poor insurance risks, joined together for the purpose of obtaining insurance.

Type of Group

Insurers sometimes must comply with regulatory requirements that specify the types of groups that are eligible for group life and health insurance, and underwriters must ensure that policies are issued only to such groups. Figure 8.6 provides a brief explanation of the typical types of groups. For each of these types of groups, specific underwriting considerations influence risk assessment.

Size

Group size is one of the most important factors used to underwrite group life and health insurance because the size of a group affects an insurer's ability to accurately predict the group's expected claim experience. In general, the smaller the group, the less likely the group's actual claim experience will approximate its expected claim experience. When group insurance was first introduced, only groups with at least 50 or 100 members were approved for coverage. Today, because of increasing information about mortality and morbidity experience, the minimum group size has been reduced considerably. Some insurers, in fact, underwrite groups with as few as two members.

Each insurer establishes its own standards as to (1) the size of group it is willing to insure and (2) the procedures it will follow for different sizes of groups. Because small-group underwriting for life insurance and short- and long-term disability income coverage is similar to individual underwriting for these products, some companies send such small-group cases to an individual underwriter. After assessing the risk, if the case is acceptable, the individual underwriter forwards the case to a group underwriter, who performs the rate calculations.

Underwriting guidelines for small groups typically are more stringent than those used to underwrite large groups. Whereas insurers typically do not require that each large group member provide evidence of insurability, insurers may require that each small group member provide evidence of insurability. The evidence required ranges from a simple health questionnaire completed by each group member to APSs and other medical evidence. An underwriter might require APSs and additional evidence on only those group members whose health questionnaires indicate the possibility of a

FIGURE 8.6 Types of Groups

SINGLE-EMPLOYER GROUP

A ***single-employer group***, commonly referred to as an *employer-employee group*, consists of the employees of one employer. The single-employer group is the most common type of group.

MULTIPLE-EMPLOYER GROUP

A ***multiple-employer group*** consists of the employees of (1) two or more employers in the same industry, (2) two or more labor unions, or (3) one or more employers and one or more labor unions. The most common types of multiple-employer groups are (1) trade association groups, (2) labor union groups, and (3) multiple-employer welfare arrangements. A *trade association* is a group formed by several employers that are in the same industry and that are members of an association formed for a purpose other than to obtain group insurance. A *labor union group* is a group of workers in a given industry or group of industries who organize a union to improve the terms and conditions under which they work. A *multiple-employer welfare arrangement (MEWA)* is a group formed when two or more small employers—usually in the same industry—band together to provide group insurance benefits for their employees. MEWAs differ from other multiple-employer groups in that each MEWA is sponsored by an insurer or a third party, and the policy is issued to the trustees of a trust established for the purpose of purchasing the coverage.

ASSOCIATION GROUPS

An ***association group*** consists of the members of an association, which is an organization of employers or individuals formed for a purpose other than to obtain insurance. Two types of association groups are the professional association and the affinity group. A ***professional association group*** is a group of people who share the same type of occupation and who belong to the association. Professionals such as educators, health care workers, real estate agents, and police officers typically form an association, and often such professional associations purchase group insurance coverage for association members. An ***affinity group*** is a group of people who share a common bond, background, or interest and who belong to an association or organization. For example, a university alumni association and a fraternal organization are affinity groups, which sometimes purchase group insurance for group members.

DEBTOR-CREDITOR GROUP

A ***debtor-creditor group*** consists of individuals who have borrowed money from a specific lender or lenders.

high risk. Note that even though an underwriter might request evidence of insurability, a group underwriter does not rate or place impairment riders on individual group members. If an individual does not meet the insurability requirements, the underwriter declines coverage for that person.

Nature of Business

The type of work that group members perform affects the degree of risk the group presents to an insurer. Thus, in establishing underwriting guidelines, insurers use claim experience data concerning the likelihood of people in certain jobs to incur covered losses.

The underwriter also considers the economic strength or weakness of the industry in which a group prospect operates. When market trends cause businesses in certain industries to slow production or lay off workers, most insurers closely examine the ability of group prospects in those industries to pay premiums.

The strength and financial condition of a business are also important in underwriting group insurance as indications of the business's ability to pay premiums. Usually, a business or an organization must have been operating on a sound financial basis for at least two years before most insurers will consider the group prospect for insurance coverage because of the high percentage of new businesses that fail.

Geographic Location

The geographic location of a group can affect its mortality and morbidity rates. For example, certain locations are more susceptible to natural disasters or certain diseases. In addition, economic and living conditions vary, as do the availability and cost of adequate health care. Thus, an underwriter must be aware of the geographic location of a group and the impact it can have on risk.

If a group has members in various locations, an underwriter must consider the environmental, economic, and social conditions of all areas in which group members are living. In assessing groups that operate from multiple locations, an underwriter also must consider all applicable laws and regulations.

Age Distribution

Because mortality and morbidity rates tend to increase with age, a group composed mostly of older members is likely to present a higher degree of risk than a group composed mostly of younger members.

While underwriters cannot decline a group life or health case based on gender distribution, they do consider the ratio of males to females in a group because it affects the group's expected claim costs and, thus, the group's premium rate. Women as a group tend to have lower mortality rates, but higher morbidity rates, than men as a group. Thus, all other factors being equal, a predominantly female group will experience fewer life insurance claims than a group with a large proportion of males. On the other hand, a predominantly male group will experience fewer health insurance claims than a predominantly female group.

Turnover of Group Membership

Low turnover of group membership results in an increase in the average age of the group members. Because a group with low turnover and older employees probably will produce unusually high claim costs, an ideal group from an underwriting perspective has a steady flow of younger, new members to replace or at least balance the gradual aging of older members.

On the other hand, underwriters are wary of unusually high turnover rates because they produce unexpectedly high administrative costs. Unusually high turnover rates also may indicate problems within the organization, such as management issues and low morale, that lead to more employees submitting medical expense and disability claims as a result of the stressful work environment. In addition, a high turnover rate may indicate that people are joining the group for the purpose of obtaining insurance coverage for a short period of time because they know they are likely to experience a loss. This type of antiselection generally produces an undesirably high level of claim costs.

When the flow of new members into a group is not adequate to compensate for the aging of current members, the underwriter may increase the proposed premium rate to reflect the additional risk or may decline the risk.

A group's turnover rate also affects the length of the probationary period included in the group insurance policy. A probationary period reduces the administrative expenses involved in initiating and terminating coverage on employees who leave employment soon after hire. Typically, the probationary period is shorter if the policy insures a group that experiences low turnover and is longer if the policy insures a group that experiences high turnover.

Participation in the Plan

The more group members who enroll in a group insurance plan, the larger the insured group and the more likely an underwriter can accurately assess the group's mortality or morbidity risk. Although group insurance policies specify the minimum participation level a group must maintain to keep the coverage in force, an underwriter must factor the likely participation rate into his analysis.

With a noncontributory plan, enrollment is automatic; and insurers typically require a noncontributory plan's level of participation to be 100 percent of all eligible group members. By contrast, with a contributory plan, group members must choose whether to enroll, and some choose not to be insured. Consequently, insurers normally require that between 75 and 100 percent of eligible group members participate in a contributory plan, depending on the size of the group. In general, the larger the group, the lower the minimum participation level can be. The following table illustrates minimum participation requirements established by one insurer for groups of various sizes enrolled in contributory insurance plans:

Number of Eligible Employees	Minimum Participation Requirement
Less than 250	75 percent
250–499	65 percent
500–749	60 percent
750–999	55 percent
1,000 or more	Case-by-case evaluation

Classes

To prevent antiselection, group underwriting guidelines require that the level of benefits provided to each group insured must be determined automatically in accordance with the terms of the group policy. If group members were able to select their own benefit, group members with a higher-than-average degree of risk typically would elect higher benefit levels. Likewise, to ensure that benefit levels are determined fairly for all group insureds, the group policyholder is not permitted to select the benefit levels to be provided to specific individuals.

For purposes of determining eligibility for coverage and benefit levels, insurers usually require group prospects to assign group members to classes according to some nondiscriminatory characteristic. Note that laws in some jurisdictions prohibit classes based on marital status, sex, or age. Figure 8.7 illustrates some typical nondiscriminatory classes established for an employer-employee group.

Expected Persistency

An underwriter evaluates a group prospect's expected persistency because of the effect persistency can have on an insurer's profit. During the first year of a group insurance policy, commissions and administrative costs associated with covering the group greatly reduce—and sometimes eliminate—the insurer's profit. If the policyholder cancels the coverage soon

FIGURE 8.7 Typical Nondiscriminatory Classes for Group Insurance

CLASSES BASED ON SALARY

- All employees earning up to $100,000 per year
- All employees earning more than $100,000 per year

CLASSES BASED ON RANK

- All officers
- All managers who are not officers
- All other employees

CLASSES BASED ON HOURS WORKED

- All employees working 30 hours or more a week
- All employees working less than 30 hours a week

CLASSES BASED ON LENGTH OF SERVICE

- All employees with five or more years of service
- All employees with fewer than five years of service

after issuance, the insurer will not be able to recoup the costs of issuing the coverage. The longer a group policy remains in force, the more profitable the business is likely to be for the insurer. Insurers usually decline to cover or charge extra premiums to a group that has a history of poor persistency.

Prior Coverage and Claims Experience

In analyzing a group prospect's prior coverage, an underwriter generally requires at least three years' documentation of the group's previous benefits, premium rates charged, annual premiums paid, claims incurred, and claims paid. As we mentioned earlier, the underwriter also requests a list of open claimants for disability coverages. In addition, an underwriter may request a copy of the employee handbook or other document that describes the current benefit plan.

The Proposed Coverage

When assessing the coverage requested by a group prospect, an underwriter evaluates certain elements of the plan's design and how the plan is to be administered. Details of these elements vary from one plan to another.

Plan of Insurance

When evaluating the plan's design, the underwriter considers how the plan defines the people who are eligible for coverage and the benefit levels that those people are eligible to receive.

Eligibility Requirements. Each group policy identifies which members of the group are eligible for coverage. For example, most employer-employee policies state that an employee must meet the policyholder's definition of a full-time employee to be eligible for coverage. Policies issued to association groups typically provide that only people who are members of the association are eligible for coverage. Policies issued to a creditor provide that certain debtors of the creditor are eligible for coverage.

Group insurance policies often include additional eligibility requirements, including a probationary period. In the case of noncontributory plans, group members who meet other eligibility requirements are automatically enrolled in the plan at the end of the probationary period. In the case of contributory plans, the probationary period is followed by an eligibility period. The ***eligibility period***, also known as the *enrollment period*, is the period of time—usually 31 days—during which eligible group members may enroll for contributory group insurance coverage without having to provide evidence of insurability.

Employer-employee group insurance policies also include an ***actively at work provision***, which requires that, in order to be eligible for coverage, an employee must be actively at work—rather than ill or on leave—on the day the group coverage is to take effect. If the employee is not actively at work on the day coverage is to take effect, then the employee is not covered by the group policy until she returns to work.

Group insurance policies that provide coverage to the dependents of covered group members must define specifically which people qualify for dependent coverage. For example, the definition of group member's child may include an adopted child, stepchild, or foster child. Some policies permit dependent coverage on the partners of covered group members who are in unmarried relationships, including same-sex partners.

Benefit Levels. Benefit levels—the type and amount of coverage offered—determine in large part whether a plan will be financially successful for both the insured and the insurer. A plan with excessive benefits may be over-utilized so that claims experience will be too high, whereas a plan with too few benefits or with inequitable benefits for one or more classes may not appeal to group members and, therefore, will not achieve the desired participation level.

Plan Administration

Unlike individual insurance policies, many group plans require the owner of the policy to be actively involved in managing and administering benefits. Effective plan administration is critical to keeping plan costs low and helping ensure the long-term satisfaction of the policyholder—and the group insureds—and, thus, the persistency of the coverage.

A group insurance plan for which the insurer handles most of the administrative aspects of the plan is known as an ***insurer-administered group plan***, and such a plan for which the group policyholder handles most of the administrative aspects is known as a ***self-administered group plan***. Alternatively, a group plan may be administered by a ***third-party administrator (TPA)***, which is an organization that is not affiliated with an insurer and provides various administrative services to insurers and group policyholders.

As a general rule, the more administrative activities the policyholder performs, the lower the premium rate that will be charged for the coverage. Underwriters evaluate the willingness and ability of the policyholder and its plan administrator to administer the plan. Specifically, a group policyholder and plan administrator should be able to

- Promote the plan and encourage all eligible group members to enroll
- Certify the eligibility of each group member who will be covered by the plan
- Collect and keep accurate records of each group member's contributions to the plan
- Maintain accurate and complete records of costs and claims
- Record additions, terminations, and status changes accurately and promptly (for example, changes in marital status, class, and earnings)
- Assist with claims submissions

Rating Methods for Group Cases

Group insurance premium rates are established on a case-by case basis and typically are recalculated every policy year. The rate needs to be

- Adequate to cover the insurer's costs of paying claims, administering the group insurance plan, and conducting business, including paying commissions
- Equitable so that each insured group pays a premium amount that fairly reflects the group's risk
- Competitive enough to attract group prospects

Although the group premium rate will not change from month to month, the number of group insureds will change from month to month and that will impact the total monthly premium amount. Insight 8.1 gives a simplified example of how an insurer might determine a group's monthly premium amount.

The benefit unit for short-term disability income coverage typically is $10 of weekly benefit, and the benefit unit for long-term disability income coverage typically is $100 of covered monthly income. Because most group medical expense plans provide the same coverage for each group insured, U.S. insurers typically establish a different monthly premium rate for the following categories:

- Group member only
- Group member and spouse
- Group member and dependent children
- Group member, spouse, and dependent children

Most insurers now use computer-based rating systems to determine group premium rates. However, an underwriter may have information about a case that is not reflected in the computerized rate. For example, the underwriter may know that the producer or group representative submitting a case has a long history of submitting quality business to the insurer. This knowledge might enable the underwriter to charge the group a lower rate than the rate calculated by the automated system.

In calculating the premium rate to charge for group coverage, insurance companies generally use manual rating, experience rating, or a combination of the two. Other rating approaches may be used for small groups.

INSIGHT 8.1 Example of a Monthly Premium Calculation

In January, Zenotone Corporation has 100 employees, and it wants to provide each of its employees with $50,000 of term life insurance coverage. Eon Life Insurance Company determines that the premium rate for such coverage is $0.20 per month per $1,000 of coverage. To calculate the January monthly premium amount for the coverage, Eon takes the following steps:

$0.20	Premium rate per month per benefit unit of $1,000 of coverage
× 50	Number of benefit units per employee per month ($50,000 ÷ $1,000)
$ 10	Monthly premium amount per employee
×100	Number of covered employees
$1,000	Total monthly premium amount for all covered employees

If Zenotone hires three employees in February and the employees have gone through their three month probationary period, in May the monthly premium amount per employee of $10 would be multiplied by 103 (the number of employees), and the total monthly premium amount for all covered employees would be $1,030.

Manual Rating

Manual rating is a method of establishing group insurance premium rates under which the insurer establishes rates for very broad classifications of group insureds using its own experience with the product and information collected by various governmental and trade associations. Typically, group underwriters use manual rating to determine the initial premium to charge a small group prospect. Group underwriters also use manual rating to calculate the initial premium for a large group prospect that has no recorded or reliable claim experience.

Experience Rating

Experience rating is a method of establishing group insurance premium rates using a group's own claim experience. Underwriters typically use experience rating to calculate (1) initial premium rates for large groups that have been previously insured and have credible claim experience and (2) renewal premium rates for currently insured groups that have credible experience.

An important assumption underlying experience rating is that a group's claim experience is likely to remain relatively constant from year to year. When using experience rating to establish a premium rate, the underwriter usually examines the group prospect's claim experience as follows:

- For group life insurance and long-term disability income coverage, the underwriter examines the group's claim figures for the past five years, if available.
- For medical expense and short-term disability income coverage, the underwriter examines the group's claim figures for the past three years, if available.

In addition to taking into account the group prospect's claim experience, an underwriter calculates the group prospect's ***expected claim experience***, which is the monetary amount of claims that the insurer estimates the group will submit during the upcoming policy year. In addition to the group's claim experience, the following factors affect the calculation of a group's expected claim experience:

- A change in the number of group insureds
- Changes in the group's average age or predominant sex
- Changes in the covered expenses, benefit schedules, benefit maximums, and expense participation requirements

- A significant change in the employee mix (for example, shifting from mostly white-collar to mostly blue-collar employees)
- A reassignment of employees to new job duties that pose significant additional hazards
- Changes in the group's industry or business segment
- Economic conditions affecting the financial strength of the group policyholder

The terms of some group life and health insurance policies provide that a portion of the premiums paid during the year may be refunded to the group policyholder at the end of the policy year. An ***experience refund*** is the portion of a group insurance premium that is returned to a policyholder if the group's claim experience during the year was more favorable than expected when the premium was calculated.

All experience refunds are payable to the group policyholder, even if the plan is contributory. If the amount of the refund to the policyholder of a contributory plan is greater than the portion of the group premium that was paid out of the policyholder's funds, then the excess must be used for the benefit of the group insureds. For example, when an employer receives an experience refund that is larger than the amount the employer paid out of its own funds for the policy year, the employer may apply the excess refund to pay a portion of the employees' contributions during the next year or to pay for additional benefits for group insureds.

Blended Rating

Some groups are too large for an insurer to rely totally on manual rating, but they do not have enough claim experience information for the insurer to rely on experience rating. In such cases, insurers sometimes use ***blended rating***, which is a premium rating method that uses a combination of manual rating and experience rating. In blended rating, the underwriter assigns a credibility factor to the group's experience. A ***credibility factor*** is a percentage that represents the amount of weight given to a group's actual claim experience for premium rate calculation purposes. For example, an underwriter who assigns a 25 percent credibility factor to a group's claim experience assumes that 25 percent of the group's expected claim experience will be based on the group's prior experience. The remaining 75 percent of the group's expected claim experience will be based on the insurer's manual rating of the group.

An underwriter determines the blended rate by (1) multiplying the premium calculated using experience rating by the credibility factor assigned to the rating, (2) multiplying the premium calculated using manual rating by the remaining percentage of the group's expected claim experience, and (3) adding the two resulting numbers. For instance, suppose an underwriter arrives at the following information for a group:

- Premium calculated by experience rating = $250
- Credibility factor for experience rating = 15%
- Premium calculated by manual rating = $300

The underwriter calculates the premium using blended rating as follows:

($250 × 0.15) + ($300 × 0.85) = $37.50 + $255.00 = $292.50

Rating Approaches for Small Groups

Developing equitable rates for small groups requires the underwriter to exercise particular caution because each group insured's age, health, and other risk factors increase in importance as group size decreases. In a group of eight people, for example, one person who represents a high level of risk can have a strong effect on the risk represented by the group. However, in a group of 500 people, that same person would have much less effect on the group's level of risk.

Insurers use the following methods to calculate equitable premium rates for small groups:

- Manual rating.
- ***Pooling***, which is a rating method by which the insurer combines several small groups into one large group, or pool. The more individuals grouped together in the pool, the better the underwriter's chances of accurately estimating the entire group's expected claim costs.
- Step rates, especially for insurance that provides a limited number of benefits and limited amounts of coverage. ***Step rates*** are group insurance premium rates based on an insurer's experience expressed in age-graded, and sometimes sex-specific, tables. If step rates are used, then the group policyholder and/or group member generally is charged the actual step rate. On the other hand, manual rating calculates a rate for each group insured and then determines a composite rate for the group. With step rates, a composite group rate is used only in evaluating the group's experience.

Figure 8.8 provides a sample table of step rates and illustrates how an underwriter uses step rates to calculate a premium for an employee group with five members. Group members with spouses usually pay an additional amount for coverage for their spouses.

FIGURE 8.8 Sample Step-Rate Table and Calculation of Small Group Premium

Type of coverage: Comprehensive major medical, $200 deductible

Name	Age	Step Rate (Monthly)
Paula Griffin	26	$215
Terri Young	29	$225
Hugh Small	43	$240
Aaron Stein	51	$275
Rowan Neill	32	$235

To calculate the group's premium rate, the underwriter adds the step rates to determine the total monthly cost of coverage for the five employees.

($215 + $225 + $240 + $275 + $235)
= $1,190

Source: Adapted from Mary C. Bickley et al., *Life and Health Insurance Underwriting*, 2nd ed. [Atlanta: LOMA (Life Office Management Association, Inc.), © 2007], 278. Used with permission; all rights reserved.

Post-Issue Underwriting for Group Insurance

Unlike individual insurance underwriting, group insurance underwriting does not end when a policy is issued. In this section we explain group underwriting that occurs post-issue: underwriting of late enrollees and renewal underwriting.

Underwriting of Late Enrollees

Under a noncontributory group insurance plan, all group members are enrolled automatically in the plan. Under a contributory plan, however, only those group members who want group coverage and who complete an enrollment card during the eligibility period are covered. As mentioned earlier, by enrolling during the eligibility period, the group member does not have to provide evidence of insurability. Similarly, group members must enroll their eligible dependents during the eligibility period. If a group member acquires a new dependent after the eligibility period, the group member can add that dependent without having to provide evidence of insurability as long as the dependent is added within 31 days of first becoming eligible. For example, an adopted child may be added within 31 days of being adopted without having to provide evidence of insurability.

Group members and eligible dependents who are not enrolled when coverage is first offered and later decide to enroll in the plan are known as ***late enrollees*** and are required to provide the insurer with evidence of insurability before being allowed to enroll in the plan. In addition, if a group member withdraws from a plan while still employed and then later applies to re-enroll in the plan, the insurer usually requires the group member to provide evidence of insurability. In such cases, the underwriter must be alert to the possibility of antiselection because a group member may be seeking to enroll in the group plan only after discovering that she has a health problem.

The evidence an underwriter requires from late enrollees varies from insurer to insurer and varies depending on the plan of insurance. As a general rule, however, the more extensive the benefits a plan provides, the more detailed the evidence must be. Most insurers require late enrollees to complete a health questionnaire; some also require a medical examination and documentation of medical treatments received by the late enrollees. The insurer has the right to refuse to permit a late enrollee to enroll in a group insurance plan if satisfactory evidence of insurability is not provided.

Renewal Underwriting

Unlike individual policies, group policies must be renewed at the end of the contract term, which typically is every year or two. ***Renewal underwriting*** is the process by which an underwriter assesses the risk presented by a group that has requested to renew its group insurance contract. As we noted in Chapter 3, U.S. insurers are required by the Health Insurance Portability and Accountability Act (HIPAA) to guarantee renewal of all group medical expense policies, except under stated conditions. Although the insurer must renew a group medical expense policy if the policyholder requests renewal, the insurer has the right to adjust the premium rate charged for the coverage. For group coverages other than medical expense coverage, the underwriter may decline to renew the coverage, increase or decrease the premium rate, or require that the plan design be changed.

In renewal underwriting, the underwriter reviews all the risk assessment factors considered when the group was originally underwritten and determines whether the characteristics of the group have changed in ways that affect the degree of risk the group presents. In addition, the underwriter assesses how efficiently the policyholder has administered the plan during the year. If the underwriter identifies administrative problems, he brings them to the attention of the group policyholder along with suggestions for corrective action.

For most groups, the insurer uses experience rating or a blend of manual rating and experience rating to calculate the renewal premium rate. However, insurers sometimes use manual rating to calculate renewal premium rates for groups that are very small or do not have credible experience.

Generally, if a group's claim experience and administrative costs fall within acceptable limits, the underwriter renews the coverage without changing the premium rate. When a group's claim experience has been very favorable—that is, significantly less than expected—and other factors are equal, the underwriter may approve the renewal and reduce the premium rate required for the coverage. However, demographic changes in the group—and medical cost inflation for medical expense insurance—are a couple of factors that may lead to a premium rate increase. In addition, if a group's claim experience or administrative costs have exceeded the policy's projected costs, the underwriter likely will increase the premium rate for the coverage as a condition of the renewal. Before proposing a higher rate, however, the underwriter first tries to determine the reasons for the excessive claims or administrative costs and factor these reasons into her decision on the renewal premium rate.

Because a group policyholder may decide not to renew a group policy if the premium rate increases significantly, the underwriter typically suggests ways the group plan can be changed so as to modify or eliminate any proposed premium rate increase:

- Change the benefit design by, for example, reducing the benefit.
- Require a larger premium contribution from group insureds, thus passing part or all of the premium rate increase along to group insureds.
- Pool a small group's experience with other small groups' experience, thereby creating a more acceptable level of risk overall.
- Investigate the cause of the poor experience and take measures to eliminate it. For example, if a group has poor long-term disability experience, the insurer may introduce early intervention whereby an employee who has been on leave for more than two weeks (but is not yet eligible for long-term disability) is assessed to see what can be done sooner rather than later to improve his situation.

With the rapid rise in health insurance premiums, some employers have terminated some coverages and raised the employee contribution level on others. Some employers are now offering coverages on a voluntary basis where the employee pays 100 percent of the premiums. Life, disability income, and dental are popular voluntary benefits. In recent years, the voluntary benefit market has grown to include critical illness and long-term care. These coverages are underwritten as individual products, although the group still needs to meet some basic group underwriting guidelines.

Key Terms

group member
group representative
request for proposal (RFP)
proposal for insurance
benefit schedule
class
master application
open claimant
census
dependent
self-insured group plan
fully insured group plan
probationary period
plan administrator
enrollment card
contributory plan
noncontributory plan
single-employer group
multiple-employer group
association group
professional association group
affinity group
debtor-creditor group
eligibility period
actively at work provision
insurer-administered group plan
self-administered group plan
third-party administrator (TPA)
manual rating
experience rating
expected claim experience
experience refund
blended rating
credibility factor
pooling
step rates
late enrollee
renewal underwriting

Part 3: Reinsurance

chapter

9

Overview of Reinsurance

Outline

Roles of Insurance Companies in Reinsurance Arrangements
Types of Reinsurance Providers
Reciprocal Arrangements
Reinsurance Pools

Assumption and Indemnity Reinsurance
Assumption Reinsurance
Indemnity Reinsurance

Basic Financial Aspects of Indemnity Reinsurance

Purposes of Indemnity Reinsurance for the Direct Writer
Managing Capacity
Easing Surplus Strain
Reducing Fluctuations in Claim Payments
Obtaining Information and Expertise

Documentation of Reinsurance Arrangements

Cession Arrangements in Reinsurance
Automatic Reinsurance
Facultative Reinsurance
Facultative-Obligatory Reinsurance
Comparison of Cession Bases

Reinsurance Activities

Reinsurance Staffing
Reinsurance Analysts
Other Staff Involved in Reinsurance Activities

Reinsurance Information Systems

Regulation of Reinsurance
Licensing
Monitoring Financial Condition
Reserves

Learning Objectives

After studying this chapter, you should be able to…

- Identify the roles that insurance companies can take in a reinsurance transaction
- Describe reciprocal arrangements and reinsurance pools
- Contrast assumption reinsurance with indemnity reinsurance
- Describe the basic financial aspects of an indemnity reinsurance arrangement
- Describe several purposes—in addition to spreading risk—that reinsurance can serve for direct writers
- Compare and contrast the automatic, facultative, and facultative-obligatory bases for reinsurance cessions
- Explain the role that each of the following functional areas within an insurance company plays in the insurer's reinsurance business: marketing, actuarial, underwriting, legal and compliance, accounting, auditing, and claims
- Describe the primary types of laws and regulations affecting reinsurance in the United States

The purchase of insurance represents a transfer of risk from a customer to an insurance company.[1] Recall from Chapter 1 that in the context of reinsurance, *risk* refers to the possibility of financial loss. One primary tool insurers use to manage the risks they assume is reinsurance, which is insurance that one insurance company obtains from another insurance company on risks associated with insurance policies issued by the first company. The term *reinsurance arrangement* generally refers to the business deal that the two companies make for the transfer of risk from one company to the other.

The business of reinsurance involves vast amounts of money, many insurance companies, and countries around the globe. Reinsurance is available for virtually every line of life, health, property, and liability insurance. Our focus is on reinsurance for individual and group life and health policies. The same basic concepts of reinsurance generally apply to both life and health reinsurance. However, the exact structure and operation of each reinsurance arrangement depend in great part on the type of insurance—individual or group, life or health—involved.

A reinsurance arrangement may involve one policy, a group of policies, a block of business, a line of business, or any combination of policies, policy groups, or blocks or lines of business. A *block of business* is a number of similar insurance policies. The term *case,* in a reinsurance context, can refer to a single policy or a group of policies.

In this chapter, we first introduce some fundamentals of reinsurance, including the parties to reinsurance arrangements and types of reinsurance providers. We then explain two main types of reinsurance—assumption reinsurance and indemnity reinsurance—and the purposes of indemnity reinsurance. Next, we explore the documentation of reinsurance arrangements and different cession bases for reinsurance—that is, different methods for the transfer and acceptance of risk. We also discuss activities, staffing, and information systems for reinsurance. Finally, we describe the regulation of reinsurance, including requirements related to licensing, financial condition monitoring, and policy reserves.

Roles of Insurance Companies in Reinsurance Arrangements

An insurer can act as a buyer of reinsurance in one transaction and a seller of reinsurance in another transaction. With respect to any given reinsurance arrangement, though, each company takes on one of the following specific roles:

- A ***direct writer***, also called a *ceding company* in a reinsurance arrangement, is an insurer that sells insurance coverage to the public. A direct writer can transfer—or *cede*—its insurance risks by obtaining reinsurance on those insurance risks. In this textbook, a reference to a direct writer in a reinsurance transaction means the company that cedes the risk. A ***cession*** is the unit of insurance risk that a direct writer transfers to a reinsurer. The term *cession* also can refer to the document used to record the transfer of risk from a direct writer to a reinsurer. Cessions and other documents related to reinsurance typically are in electronic form rather than paper form.
- A ***reinsurer***, also called a *reinsurance company* or an *assuming company*, is an insurer that provides reinsurance coverage by accepting, or *assuming*, insurance risk from a direct writer or another reinsurance company.
- Under some circumstances, a reinsurer can be the ceding company. A reinsurer can transfer some of the risks it has assumed from a direct writer by obtaining reinsurance from a third insurance company. In such a situation, the third insurer is a ***retrocessionaire***, which is an insurance company that accepts risks from—and provides reinsurance to—a reinsurer. A reinsurer that transfers insurance risk to a retrocessionaire is called a *retrocedent*. A ***retrocession*** is the unit of reinsurance that a reinsurer cedes to a retrocessionaire. The term *retrocession* also can refer to the document used to record the transfer of risk from a reinsurer to a retrocessionaire.

Figure 9.1 illustrates the roles of reinsurance buyers and sellers.

Reinsurance is a global business activity. In general, any direct writer can enter into arrangements and do business with any properly licensed or authorized reinsurer, regardless of where each company is located. Major reinsurers maintain offices on multiple continents and actively seek to disperse risk geographically.

Types of Reinsurance Providers

In the United States, virtually any licensed insurance company can sell reinsurance. Although some insurance companies act as both direct writers and reinsurers, other insurance companies deal only or mainly in reinsurance, as shown in the following table:

	Professional	Occasional
Reinsurer	***Professional reinsurer***	***Occasional reinsurer***
	An insurance company whose sole or primary line of business is selling reinsurance to direct writers	An insurer that accepts some reinsurance business but is not a professional reinsurer
Retrocessionaire	***Professional retrocessionaire***	***Occasional retrocessionaire***
	A reinsurer whose sole or primary business is providing reinsurance to reinsurers	A reinsurer whose primary business is not retrocessions but who accepts retrocessions

An insurance company that acts as both a direct writer and a reinsurer may create a subsidiary company that is dedicated to reinsurance business. A ***captive reinsurer*** is a reinsurer that was formed by an insurer for the purpose of providing reinsurance and that is controlled by the insurance company that formed it. Depending on its corporate charter, a captive reinsurer may offer reinsurance to only the organization that formed it, or to the organization that formed it and other insurers within the same line of business.

Reciprocal Arrangements

A ***reciprocal arrangement***, also called *reciprocity*, is a two-way reinsurance arrangement in which two insurance companies cede business to each other and assume risk from each other. ***Premium-based reciprocity*** is a reciprocal arrangement that involves the exchange of blocks of reinsurance business representing approximately the same amount of gross premium on the reinsured risks. ***Results-based reciprocity*** is a reciprocal arrangement that involves the exchange of blocks of reinsurance business representing approximately the same projected monetary amount of claims experience on the reinsured risks.

FIGURE 9.1 Roles of Reinsurance Buyers and Sellers

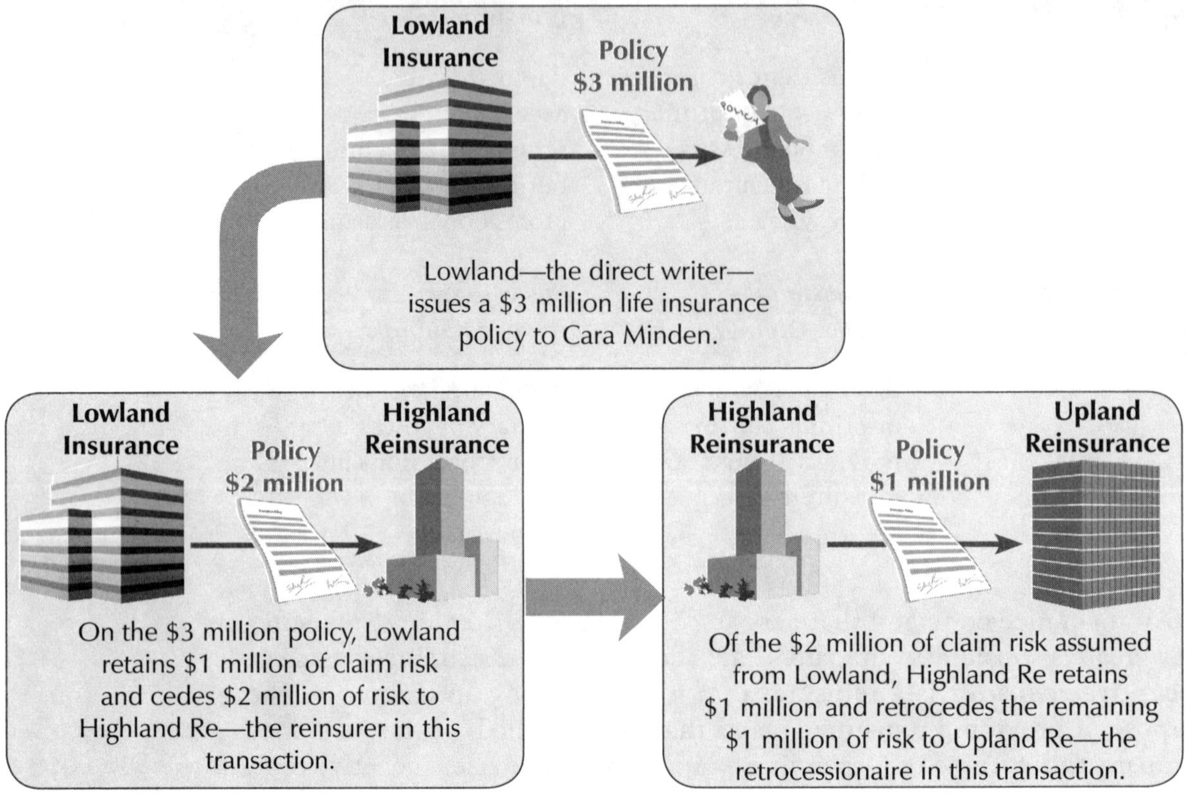

Source: Adapted from Jane Lightcap Brown and Jennifer W. Herrod, *Reinsurance Administration* [Atlanta: LOMA (Life Office Management Association, Inc.), © 2000], 5. Used with permission; all rights reserved.

In a reciprocal arrangement, both insurance companies take on the roles of direct writer and reinsurer. For example, suppose that the Sonora Insurance Company and the Ahab Insurance Company have entered into a reciprocal arrangement in which each company has agreed to provide reinsurance on $40 million of the other company's directly written business.

Sonora Insurance		Ahab Insurance
Sonora as Direct Writer Issues insurance and transfers $40 million in risk to Ahab	→	**Ahab as Reinsurer** Assumes $40 million in risk from Sonora
Sonora as Reinsurer Assumes $40 million in risk from Ahab	←	**Ahab as Direct Writer** Issues insurance and transfers $40 million in risk to Sonora

Several types of insurers may participate in a reciprocal arrangement. For example, a direct writer and a reinsurer may reciprocate; a reinsurer and a retrocessionaire may reciprocate; two reinsurers may reciprocate; and so on. Two direct writers can reciprocate only if both are *authorized* reinsurers. We discuss authorized reinsurers later in this chapter. In a given transaction, though, one insurer acts as a direct writer and the other acts as a reinsurer.

One purpose of a reciprocal arrangement is to diversify risks. The insurance companies that exchange business through reciprocal arrangements usually issue the same type of business, but they typically do not compete against each other in the same geographic areas. International reinsurance transactions often involve reciprocal arrangements.

Reinsurance Pools

A ***reinsurance pool*** is a group of two or more insurance companies who jointly reinsure ceded risks. Each participant in a reinsurance pool has an individual liability and is not responsible for the liabilities of other pool members. The reinsured risk usually is spread between or among the pool members according to specified portions, known as quota shares. In general, a ***quota share*** in reinsurance is each insurance company's—direct writer's or reinsurer's—fixed percentage share of the total risk being divided between or among companies. In the context of reinsurance pools, a *quota share,* also known as a *subscription,* is the amount each reinsurance pool member accepts as its liability under a specific reinsurance arrangement.

As an example, the following table shows the quota share (portion of risk) assumed by each member of a reinsurance pool. These shares need not be divided equally among the pool members.

100% of Reinsured Risk
Divided among pool members

Quota Share	Reinsurance Pool Members
30%	Reinsurer A
20%	Reinsurer B
40%	Reinsurer C
10%	Reinsurer D

Assumption and Indemnity Reinsurance

Reinsurance can be divided into two broad classifications: assumption reinsurance and indemnity reinsurance. Although this book primarily focuses on indemnity reinsurance arrangements, assumption reinsurance also has important roles in the insurance industry.

Assumption Reinsurance

Assumption reinsurance, also known as *portfolio reinsurance*, is reinsurance designed to permanently and entirely transfer blocks of existing insurance business from one company to another. In assumption reinsurance, the reinsurer assumes the entire legal obligation formerly borne by the insurer that issued the business. The assuming company (reinsurer) issues new insurance certificates—known as ***assumption certificates***—to all affected policyowners. These assumption certificates show policyowners that the assuming insurer has taken responsibility for all risk under their insurance policies. Under an assumption reinsurance arrangement, the direct writer, the reinsurer, and the policyowners are parties to the reinsurance transaction.

Assumption reinsurance is the most common method of buying and selling blocks of insurance business. Insurers sometimes use assumption reinsurance to exit a line of business by ceding the business to a reinsurer or to enter a new line of business by assuming a line of business from another insurer. An assumption transaction can be used to complete the purchase and sale of an entire insurance company.

Indemnity Reinsurance

Indemnity reinsurance is the type of reinsurance most commonly used to transfer risk. Under indemnity reinsurance, a reinsurer is obligated to reimburse a direct writer only after the direct writer pays benefits under reinsured policies. Indemnity reinsurance includes traditional indemnity reinsurance and finite reinsurance; however, a discussion of finite reinsurance is beyond the scope of this text. ***Traditional indemnity reinsurance*** is a reinsurance arrangement that is used to transfer a portion of a direct writer's accepted risk on an ongoing basis and that is intended to be a permanent transfer. The parties to a traditional indemnity reinsurance arrangement—the direct writer (ceding company) and the reinsurer—negotiate the terms of the arrangement, which vary from one arrangement to another, to meet the specific needs of both parties.

Direct writers sometime cede blocks of in-force business, but traditional indemnity reinsurance typically transfers risk on a direct writer's new business rather than its in-force business, Traditional indemnity reinsurance arrangements create an ongoing contractual relationship between the parties to the arrangement.

Although the parties to a traditional indemnity reinsurance arrangement intend for the risk transfer to be permanent, traditional indemnity reinsurance arrangements typically include a means for the direct writer and reinsurer to end or otherwise modify the reinsurance arrangement. For example, traditional reinsurance arrangements usually allow the direct writer to take back—or *recapture*—specified reinsured risks, and may allow the reinsurer to return—or *commute*—specified reinsured risks. Traditional indemnity reinsurance arrangements also allow for termination of the entire arrangement either through mutual agreement or automatically due to the inability of one of the parties to the arrangement to meet its financial obligations on time.

Unlike assumption reinsurance transactions, a traditional indemnity reinsurance arrangement is not disclosed to the direct writer's customers, who are not parties to the agreement. Under traditional indemnity reinsurance, the direct writer retains the entire legal liability to its customers whose policies are reinsured.

Figure 9.2 summarizes the primary characteristics of assumption and traditional indemnity reinsurance arrangements. The remainder of this chapter and Chapters 10 and 11 focus on traditional indemnity reinsurance. Unless specified otherwise, the term *indemnity reinsurance* or simply *reinsurance* refers to traditional indemnity reinsurance.

FIGURE 9.2 Characteristics of Assumption and Traditional Indemnity Reinsurance

	Assumption Reinsurance	Traditional Indemnity Reinsurance
Is the arrangement intended to be temporary or permanent?	Permanent	Permanent
Is recapture permitted?	No	Yes
Does the reinsurer become a party to the underlying reinsured policies?	Yes	No
Is the arrangement used to reinsure new business or in-force business?	In-force	New
What are the primary purposes of the reinsurance arrangement?	Transfer the risk	Share risks
Who administers the reinsured insurance policies?	Reinsurer	Reinsurer or direct writer or both

Source: Adapted from Susan Conant, *Capital Management for Insurance Companies* [Atlanta: LOMA (Life Office Management Association, Inc.), © 2001], 149. Used with permission; all rights reserved.

Basic Finanical Aspects of Indemnity Reinsurance

In indemnity reinsurance, the direct writer makes periodic payments, known as ***reinsurance premiums***, to the reinsurer as compensation for the reinsurance coverage. In return, the reinsurer agrees to reimburse the direct writer for a stated amount or portion of policy benefits the direct writer has paid to customers under the reinsured policies. Under many reinsurance arrangements, the reinsurer agrees to establish similar policy reserves for the reinsured portion of the risk as the direct writer establishes for its portion of the business. ***Policy reserves*** are a liability amount that, together with future premiums and investment income, the insurer estimates it will need to pay contractual benefits as they come due under in-force policies.

Some reinsurance arrangements also include an allowance for the direct writer. An ***allowance***, also known as an *expense allowance*, a *reinsurance allowance*, a *ceding commission*, or a *reinsurance commission*, is an amount paid by the reinsurer to the direct writer and that is designed to recognize the direct writer's acquisition, maintenance, and other expenses.

- ***Acquisition expenses*** are the costs a direct writer incurs in developing, marketing, and issuing new business. Examples of acquisition expenses covered in the reinsurance allowance are first-year commissions, underwriting costs, new business processing costs, and policy issue costs.

- ***Maintenance expenses***, also known as *renewal expenses* or *administration expenses*, are the direct writer's ongoing expenses for administering and servicing a policy or a block of business after it has been placed in force.

The amount of the allowance usually depends on the policy duration and generally is larger in early policy years and lower in later policy years. The reinsurer deducts the allowance from the reinsurance premium that the direct writer must pay to the reinsurer. A gross reinsurance premium is the reinsurance premium before the allowance is deducted. A net reinsurance premium is the cost that the direct writer pays for reinsurance coverage, after allowances. The following formula illustrates these relationships:

Reinsurance Gross Premium	–	Allowance	=	Reinsurance Net Premium

Under some reinsurance arrangements, when the actual financial outcome from operations is better than the parties anticipated, the reinsurer shares its profits by reimbursing the direct writer for a portion of the reinsurance premiums. An ***experience refund*** is an amount the reinsurer credits the direct writer as compensation for favorable risk experience.

The reinsurer also may share the direct writer's expenses for ***premium taxes***, which are amounts of tax that governments levy on a direct writer's premium income. The reinsurer typically pays a portion of the direct writer's premium taxes by refunding part of the reinsurance premiums to the direct writer.

Purposes of Indemnity Reinsurance for the Direct Writer

The principal purpose of indemnity reinsurance is to share the risk represented by insurance policies issued by the direct writer. Generally, the use of reinsurance also serves other purposes for the direct writer, such as helping to

- Manage capacity
- Ease surplus strain
- Reduce fluctuations in claim payments
- Obtain product, underwriting, claim, and reinsurance information and experience

Managing Capacity

Many direct writers use reinsurance to strengthen their financial positions. Every insurance company has a limit on (1) the amount of coverage it can approve or afford to pay on a single risk and (2) the total amount of risk it can accept. Generally, a direct writer's ***underwriting capacity*** or risk-taking capability is the highest monetary amount of risk that the company will accept on an individual insured so that unusual fluctuations in claims will not damage the ongoing solvency of the company. Underwriting capacity includes (1) the amount of risk a direct writer transfers to reinsurers plus (2) the direct writer's retention limit. A ***retention limit*** is a specified maximum monetary amount of insurance that an insurer is willing to carry at its own risk without transferring some of the risk to a reinsurer. Direct writers and reinsurers have retention limits.

An insurer's ***financial capacity*** is the total monetary amount of risk the company can accept based on the investable funds it has available to write new business. If a direct writer's marketing efforts cause the company to sell larger policies or more total insurance coverage than its financial position can support, the direct writing company can transfer the excess risk to a reinsurer.

Easing Surplus Strain

In the early years of an insurance policy, the premium payments often are not adequate to cover the expenses associated with selling and issuing the policy and maintaining the required policy reserves. To establish the required reserves for the policy, the direct writer must use some of its ***surplus***, which, for an insurer, is the amount of assets the company has over and above its policy reserves and other financial obligations. However, laws in the United States and Canada establish minimum surplus standards that insurers must maintain to conduct business. The use of surplus to establish policy reserves can cause a direct writer's surplus level to fall close to the minimum level.

This decrease in surplus caused by the high initial costs and reserve requirements associated with issuing new insurance policies is called ***surplus strain***, or *new business strain*. The direct writer may be able to reduce surplus strain through the purchase of reinsurance. In some reinsurance arrangements, when the reinsurer assumes a portion of the direct writer's risk, the reinsurer establishes reserves for the reinsured portion of the risk, thus reducing the amount of reserves the direct writer must provide. A decrease in potential surplus strain—which is known as ***surplus relief***—strengthens an insurer's financial position.

Reducing Fluctuations in Claim Payments

The timing and amount of insurance claims received by an insurer can fluctuate greatly. Reinsurance cannot control the frequency of claims, but it can smooth the impact of extreme fluctuations because the reinsurer pays a portion of the policy benefits. Thus, reinsurance protects the direct writer from the financial stress that could result from unexpectedly large or early claims or a larger-than-expected number of claims in a single period.

Obtaining Information and Expertise

Reinsurers have exposure to the underwriting, claim, and reinsurance administration policies and practices of many direct writers, so reinsurers are aware of challenges that many direct writers face and of successful responses to those challenges. Reinsurers also develop extensive databases of mortality and morbidity statistics based on the collective experience of their direct writer clients and their own reinsurance cases. As a result, reinsurers typically have a great deal of information and expertise to share with direct writers.

A reinsurer can provide expertise on establishing sound policies and practices for many areas—notably product development, underwriting, reinsurance administration, and claim administration. Although the need to protect client confidentiality and proprietary information prevents a reinsurer from sharing the specific details of any direct writer's business practices, the reinsurer can offer general advice to a direct writer about administrative systems, workflows, control mechanisms, best practices, and procedures.

Direct writers often obtain a reinsurer's advice in developing underwriting and claim administration manuals, determining premium rates, and wording policy provisions. A reinsurer can assess the strength of a direct writer's proposed new product by evaluating the product's underwriting standards, administration method, system requirements, pricing assumptions, premium rate structure, commission plan, and marketing approach. However, reinsurers cannot share specific financial design information obtained from direct writers with other direct writers.

Reinsurers' statistics on impairments, such as heart disease, hypertension, and diabetes, can help direct writers more accurately underwrite proposed insureds with these impairments. Typically, if the direct writer requests advice on a particular underwriting or claim case, a reinsurer will review the case and give an opinion on the underwriting or claim issue.

Documentation of Reinsurance Arrangements

When a direct writer and a reinsurer enter into an indemnity reinsurance arrangement, they typically create a written *reinsurance agreement*, which also historically has been called a reinsurance treaty. The reinsurance agreement documents the terms of the business to be conducted, including the nature of the risk transfer, reinsurance administration procedures, information exchanges, and the rights and duties of each party under the reinsurance arrangement. A reinsurance agreement is a contract that is binding on the parties to the agreement. Individual reinsurance agreements can vary greatly in terms of length, level of detail, and the scope of risks covered. However, most include certain standard provisions. One of these provisions states the cession basis for the arrangement.

Cession Arrangements in Reinsurance

The *cession basis*, or cession arrangement, identifies the direct writer's obligations and rights to cede risks, as well as the reinsurer's obligations to accept risk and rights to accept or reject risk. A direct writer can cede reinsurance risk on an automatic, a facultative, or a facultative-obligatory (fac-ob) basis.

Automatic Reinsurance

Automatic reinsurance is a reinsurance cession basis in which the direct writer agrees in advance to cede and the reinsurer agrees in advance to assume all risks that meet the specifications in the reinsurance agreement. For a risk that meets all agreement specifications, automatic reinsurance allows a direct writer to *automatically* bind a reinsurer to a risk without first providing the reinsurer with underwriting evidence for the risk and without asking the reinsurer's approval in advance.

The automatic cession is the only cession basis in which the direct writer must cede and the reinsurer must assume a qualifying risk based on only the direct writer's underwriting evaluation. If a risk meets the requirements for automatic cession, then the direct writer generally must reinsure the risk and the reinsurer must accept the risk, without question.

Automatic reinsurance arrangements may limit cessions based on factors such as the plan of insurance, age of the insured, policy issue date, and underwriting class (standard or substandard). Direct writers and reinsurers also have financial limits for automatic reinsurance cessions. Figure 9.3 lists several types of financial limits on risk amounts transferred that may apply to an automatic reinsurance arrangement.

Insurers sometimes exceed the retention limit for a particular policy by using *corridors*. In this context, a ***retention limit corridor*** is a monetary amount greater than the company's retention limit that a direct writer is willing to retain to avoid ceding small amounts of coverage. Because small cessions are relatively expensive to administer, direct writers typically use a corridor to limit the number of small cessions and, thus, to make reinsurance more cost-effective.

For example, suppose that the Wisteria Insurance Company has a retention limit of $500,000 on its whole life policies and a retention limit corridor of $25,000. If Wisteria issues a policy for an amount greater than $525,000, Wisteria retains $500,000 and cedes the remainder. However, if Wisteria issues a policy for an amount between $500,000 and $525,000, Wisteria retains the entire amount to avoid the expense of ceding a very small amount of coverage.

Facultative Reinsurance

Facultative reinsurance is a reinsurance cession basis in which a direct writer chooses whether to cede a risk and the reinsurer chooses whether to accept that risk. Facultative reinsurance is the only cession basis in which the reinsurer performs an independent underwriting evaluation and has the option to reject risks on the basis of the underwriting. For a facultative case, a reinsurer underwrites the case, assigns the case a risk classification, and can quote a reinsurance price based on its own underwriting guidelines

FIGURE 9.3 Limits on Risk Amounts Transferred Under Automatic Reinsurance Agreements

- A retention limit is a specified maximum monetary amount of insurance that an insurer is willing to carry at its own risk without transferring some of the risk to a reinsurer.
- A reinsurer's ***automatic binding limit*** represents the maximum monetary amount of risk the reinsurer will obligate itself to accept automatically on a given policy or case without making an independent underwriting assessment. The reinsurer must accept the entire ceded risk on all policies when that risk does not exceed the automatic binding limit.
- A reinsurer's ***minimum cession*** is the smallest monetary amount of risk the reinsurer will accept in an automatic cession. For a direct writer, a minimum cession is the smallest monetary amount of risk the direct writer will cede in an automatic cession. Having a minimum cession allows a direct writer to avoid the obligation to cede and a reinsurer to avoid the obligation to accept amounts of risk that are relatively small in comparison to the administrative costs associated with the risk amounts. An example of a commonly used minimum cession is $25,000.
- A ***jumbo limit*** is the maximum allowable monetary amount of total insurance—in force and yet-to-be-placed—with all companies on any one life that a reinsurer will accept for automatic cession. Many companies vary the basic definition of a jumbo limit by specifying whether the allowable amount includes replacement of existing coverage. A jumbo limit on life reinsurance protects a reinsurer from excessive risk resulting from the accumulation of several policies on the same life. Only automatic reinsurance arrangements for life insurance or critical illness coverage are subject to jumbo limits.

Source: Adapted from Susan Conant and Miriam A. Orsina, *Principles of Reinsurance* [Atlanta: LOMA (Life Office Management Association, Inc.), © 2006], 42. Used with permission; all rights reserved.

and terms. A reinsurer has no obligation to submit a quote for a risk submitted on a facultative basis. Also, a direct writer is under no obligation to accept a quote from a reinsurer on a facultative case.

Many direct writers choose facultative reinsurance because facultative reinsurance allows them to obtain the benefit of the reinsurer's underwriting judgment before accepting a case. Automatic reinsurance agreements often include provisions that allow the direct writer to submit certain applications—such as applications that do not comply with automatic reinsurance limitations—on a facultative or facultative-obligatory basis to its reinsurance partner and to other reinsurers.

Facultative-Obligatory Reinsurance

Facultative-obligatory (fac-ob) reinsurance is a reinsurance cession basis in which (1) the direct writer may choose to submit specific cases to the reinsurer and (2) the reinsurer must accept the cases based on the direct writer's underwriting, up to a stated maximum amount, if the reinsurer has available financial capacity. Under a fac-ob arrangement, the reinsurer determines whether the requested coverage exceeds the reinsurer's capacity. If the reinsurer lacks financial capacity and therefore cannot accept the risk, it immediately notifies the direct writer. If the reinsurer fails to notify the direct writer within a specified period, the reinsurer automatically is bound to the risk within the agreed-upon acceptance limits. If the reinsurer lacks capacity to cover the case, the reinsurer may be able to retrocede the excess risk to its own reinsurers.

Comparison of Cession Bases

For life and health reinsurance in North America, automatic reinsurance is more common than facultative or facultative-obligatory reinsurance. The three cession bases have the following similarities and differences:

- The direct writer ideally should perform an underwriting evaluation of every application for insurance under all three cession arrangements.
- The direct writer must cede and the reinsurer must assume a qualifying case based on only the direct writer's underwriting evaluation under only the automatic cession basis.
- Only the automatic cession basis includes both an automatic binding limit and a jumbo limit.
- The reinsurer performs an independent underwriting evaluation and, on the basis of that risk evaluation, has the option to reject qualifying cases under only the facultative arrangement.
- All other factors being the same, the direct writer's cost of administering reinsurance facultatively generally is higher than the cost of administering reinsurance automatically.
- The reinsurer has the same rights and obligations under a fac-ob cession basis as under an automatic cession basis, with the additional right to reject a case if the reinsurer lacks financial capacity.

The following table summarizes the typical options or requirements for the direct writer and the reinsurer under the various cession arrangements we have discussed:

	Direct Writer	Reinsurer
Automatic	Must cede all qualifying cases	Must assume all qualifying cases Does not perform any underwriting evaluation before its assumption of risk
Facultative	Has the option to cede or retain qualifying cases	Has the option to reject cases Performs an underwriting evaluation before accepting a risk
Fac-Ob	Has the option to cede or retain qualifying cases	Must assume all qualifying cases if financial capacity is available May reject qualifying cases if financial capacity is not available

Reinsurance Activities

From the time a direct writer decides to seek reinsurance to the time that all reinsurance coverage under a reinsurance agreement is ended, employees of the direct writer and the reinsurer perform a wide variety of reinsurance-related activities, including

- Selecting a reinsurance partner and negotiating a reinsurance agreement
- Ceding or assuming specific risks
- Administering in-force reinsurance
- Terminating the reinsurance agreement

A large proportion of these activities can be classified as ***reinsurance administration***, which includes all of the day-to-day activities conducted by the direct writer and the reinsurer to process and manage each risk that the direct writer cedes automatically or submits for facultative or facultative-obligatory consideration. Under some reinsurance agreements, the direct writer accepts primary responsibility for administration; under other agreements, the reinsurer accepts primary responsibility; and in yet others, the reinsurance parties share administrative duties. Generally, the company that is primarily responsible for administering the reinsurance carries out the following tasks:

- Determining the amount of reinsurance coverage

- Interpreting and complying with the requirements of existing reinsurance agreements and helping to provide administrative specifications for new agreements
- Handling reinsurance premiums, billing, and payments
- Administering the effects of policy changes and policy terminations on reinsurance coverage
- Maintaining comprehensive records and developing reports
- Ensuring quality control and timeliness of all reinsurance administration activities
- Administering reinsurance agreement terminations

Reinsurance Staffing

Although most reinsurance companies have designated functional areas that handle reinsurance administration activities, the organization of reinsurance operations varies greatly among direct writers. Some direct writers have a reinsurance department, but others do not. Direct writers without reinsurance departments typically assign reinsurance administration responsibilities to staff in departments such as underwriting, new business, or customer service. In this text, we refer to all the units or staff involved in reinsurance administration as the *reinsurance administration unit*.

Reinsurance Analysts

The staff members who administer reinsurance may have various titles, such as reinsurance analyst, client administrator, and reinsurance specialist. For consistency in this text, we use the term ***reinsurance analyst*** to refer to any direct writer or reinsurer employee—except the person holding top leadership responsibility—who is involved in any phase of reinsurance administration. Reinsurance analysts are responsible for handling many of the activities required to conduct reinsurance transactions between reinsurers and direct writers. However, a reinsurance analyst's job duties may vary from company to company and depending on the reinsurance analyst's level of experience. Reinsurance analysts typically perform some or all of the activities listed in Figure 9.4.

Other Staff Involved in Reinsurance Activities

In addition to the reinsurance administration unit, various other operational units of direct writers and reinsurers perform reinsurance-related activities. Other functional areas typically involved in reinsurance-related

FIGURE 9.4 Typical Activities of Reinsurance Analysts

- Verifying that the correct reinsurance agreement is used to guide administration of a specified risk and set the effective date of reinsurance coverage
- Researching reinsurance agreements to verify that administrative activities for a given risk meet agreement requirements
- Researching and administering changes to reinsurance agreements and the reinsurance coverage on individual policies or blocks of business
- Ensuring that facultative coverage complies with the reinsurer's underwriting decision
- Calculating the portion of each risk that is retained and the portion that is ceded
- Calculating and generating payments for funds due to or from the reinsurance parties
- Reconciling reinsurance billing statements and payments with company records
- Recordkeeping and preparing detailed reports regarding reinsured policies for use by the reinsurance parties
- Meeting financial and regulatory reporting requirements
- Collaborating with other company staff and outside organizations as necessary

Source: Adapted from Susan Conant and Miriam A. Orsina, *Principles of Reinsurance* [Atlanta: LOMA (Life Office Management Association, Inc), © 2006], 162–163. Used with permission; all rights reserved.

activities include marketing, actuarial, underwriting, legal and compliance, accounting, auditing, and claim administration.

Marketing

Some professional reinsurers use reinsurance marketing officers to help them establish reinsurance agreements. A ***reinsurance marketing officer***, also known as a *reinsurance account executive*, is a reinsurer's employee who sells reinsurance and coordinates the marketing process for the reinsurer. Such employees visit the home offices of current and potential clients—usually direct writing companies and other reinsurers—and gather information about new reinsurance arrangements that clients need or adjustments they would like to make to existing arrangements.

Although not required to be licensed as insurance producers, most reinsurance marketing officers have extensive experience in the insurance industry. Typically, direct writers consider reinsurance marketing officers to be valuable sources of information and advice concerning developments in the insurance and reinsurance markets.

Actuarial

Actuaries who deal with reinsurance calculate appropriate pricing structures and policy reserves for reinsurance ceded and assumed, and they project future liabilities, such as amounts needed to pay future claims. Actuaries also assist in setting retention limits and conduct mortality and morbidity trend analysis.

Direct writers' actuaries also submit requests for proposals for new reinsurance agreements, evaluate the proposals that are submitted, and—with input from employees working in other functional areas of the company—select reinsurers and negotiate reinsurance agreements. In addition, they evaluate new reinsurance products and services.

Underwriting

Underwriting plays an important role in reinsurance for both direct writers and reinsurers. Evaluating the risks associated with policies to be reinsured is the central reinsurance-related task of underwriting. If changes occur to ceded or assumed risks, or if a direct writer wishes to modify ceded coverage, underwriters for either reinsurance partner may need to underwrite the changes in risk. Underwriters also may participate in negotiating reinsurance agreements.

Legal and Compliance

The legal department typically helps develop and interpret reinsurance agreements and provides advice when reinsurance agreement negotiations become particularly complex. Many reinsurers and retrocessionaires have separate departments that develop and negotiate reinsurance agreements.

The compliance unit typically has the following responsibilities with respect to reinsurance:

- Studies current and proposed laws to determine their effects on the insurer's reinsurance activities
- Educates company employees about applicable regulatory requirements and company compliance policies for reinsurance activities
- Monitors the conduct of employees and marketers affiliated with the insurer to verify that they are complying with applicable regulatory requirements and company compliance policies for reinsurance activities
- Oversees internal control procedures for reinsurance activities

Accounting

Reinsurance accounting involves (1) maintaining accurate records of the numerous financial transactions associated with administering reinsurance, such as the payment of reinsurance premiums to reinsurers and the receipt of reinsurance claim benefits from reinsurers, and (2) preparing financial statements and summarizing the company's reinsurance-related accounts. Each insurer's accounting unit provides advice to other units within the company about accounting requirements and assists those units in setting up procedures to fulfill the requirements. The accounting requirements may vary by the company's role in a particular reinsurance agreement—direct writer or reinsurer—and by the type of reinsurance arrangement. We discuss types of reinsurance arrangements in Chapter 10.

The accounting unit can offer assistance to reinsurance analysts as they perform accounting tasks, such as budget planning and control, management information reporting, and maintaining financial records on reinsured business—for example, records of reinsurance premium and claim payments.

Auditing

In a reinsurance audit, auditors examine the company's reinsurance records and procedures and recommend improvements to those procedures. Reinsurance audits typically focus on underwriting, claim administration, and reinsurance administration.

Claim Administration

The direct writer's claim analysts notify the company's reinsurance administration unit when a claim under a reinsured policy is received. In some cases, a claim analyst can settle the claim without consulting the reinsurer for an opinion on the claim. The claim analyst then passes the information about the settlement on to a reinsurance analyst, who prepares reports of claims submitted and paid and sends the reports to the reinsurer to obtain reimbursement for all or a portion of each paid claim.

However, in certain circumstances such as anticipated denials of claims or large contestable claims, the direct writer must send the claim documentation to the reinsurer for a claim recommendation or opinion prior to settling a claim. Also, the direct writer's claim analyst may contact the reinsurer's claim department for advice on any large or unusual claims. Reinsurers' claim analysts typically have experience with claims submitted under a wide variety of products and complex circumstances.

Reinsurance Information Systems

Due to the current high volume of reinsurance business and the global nature of the reinsurance industry, computer-based information systems are essential to efficient, effective administration of reinsurance. Negotiating reinsurance agreements, requesting facultative coverage, sending underwriting advice and information, checking agreements for details of implementation, calculating the amount of risk to be ceded or assumed on a particular policy or a group of policies, calculating premium and claim amounts due and paid, producing innumerable reports on all sorts of administrative transactions, and checking the quality of every aspect of reinsurance operations—these activities demand rapid, accurate information in a form that can be collected, organized, corrected, modified, and communicated to those who need it.

Information system technologies—such as spreadsheet software and database management systems—allow reinsurance analysts to organize, analyze, and report information in almost any configuration desired. Reinsurers in particular need flexible, sophisticated systems to manipulate and report data related to a variety of products provided by a large number of direct writers, each of which has its own information system. Some companies also use computer systems for reinsurance decision making and strategic planning. For example, a reinsurance information system for automatic reinsurance can check the direct writer's retention and cede any excess of retention to the appropriate reinsurer.

Telecommunications plays a major role in reinsurance. Voicemail, e-mail, videoconferencing, and e-commerce all facilitate reinsurance partnerships and transactions. An important application of e-commerce for the reinsurance industry is ***business-to-business (B2B) e-commerce***, which is the electronic transmission of data or information between organizations to perform or facilitate business transactions. B2B e-commerce for reinsurance often involves communications and transactions between

- Direct writers and reinsurers
- Reinsurance parties and reinsurance intermediaries (which we discuss later in this chapter)
- Reinsurance parties and vendors, such as consumer reporting agencies
- Reinsurance parties and other financial institutions, such as banks
- Reinsurance parties and regulatory bodies

B2B e-commerce between direct writers and reinsurers facilitates the negotiation and preparation of reinsurance agreements, the submission of underwriting information to reinsurers, the payment of reinsurance premiums, claim administration, and many other administrative procedures.

Regulation of Reinsurance

Whether in the role of direct writers or reinsurers, insurance companies with reinsurance activities are regulated by the laws that govern all other insurance companies. Additionally, specific reinsurance regulations apply to their reinsurance activities. Because the parties to a reinsurance arrangement are business entities that are assumed to be able to protect themselves legally, reinsurance regulation is less extensive and less detailed than is the regulation governing insurance transactions in which an individual or group is a party to the insurance contract.

In the United States, the National Association of Insurance Commissioners (NAIC) has adopted various model laws and regulations related to reinsurance practices. Most states have enacted versions of these model laws and regulations. As a result, regulation of reinsurance is fairly uniform throughout the country. The U.S. federal and state privacy protection laws and regulations described in Chapter 3 also apply to reinsurers and reinsurance activities.

In Canada, sections of the federal Insurance Companies Act deal with reinsurance and the Office of the Superintendent of Financial Institutions (OSFI)—the federal office responsible for regulating the solvency of federally incorporated insurers, insurers incorporated in other countries, and specified provincially incorporated insurers—publishes guidelines that specifically address reinsurance. In addition, the ***Canadian Reinsurance Guidelines***, which are under the governance of the Canadian Life and Health Insurance Association (CLHIA), are a set of common reinsurance principles that companies can use voluntarily as a basis for writing and interpreting reinsurance agreements. Insurance companies regard these guidelines as official standards of practice for the industry.

The regulation of reinsurance primarily focuses on solvency issues. Recall that solvency is an entity's ability to meet its financial obligations on time. ***Insolvency*** is a condition in which an entity is consistently unable to meet its financial obligations on time. ***Solvency laws*** are designed to ensure that insurance companies are financially able to meet their debts and to pay policy benefits when they come due. To protect their financial stability, insurance companies with reinsurance activities must meet requirements for licensing, financial condition and reporting, and reserves.

Licensing

In the United States, licensing requirements apply to direct writers, reinsurers, and reinsurance intermediaries.

Licensing Requirements—Direct Writers

To conduct business within a state, a direct writer must obtain a license from the state insurance department. Each state establishes its own licensing standards, which are designed to (1) make sure that companies can meet their financial obligations when they become due and (2) establish a mechanism for regulatory oversight of insurer operations. Figure 9.5 lists typical requirements for licensing a direct writer.

Licensing Requirements—Reinsurers

The states also have established systems to license professional and occasional reinsurers.

Authorized Reinsurers. An ***authorized reinsurer***, also called an *admitted reinsurer*, is a reinsurer that is licensed or otherwise recognized by the insurance department in a given state. Just as the licensing process for a direct writer subjects the company to the jurisdiction's regulation, when a reinsurer is authorized or admitted, the reinsurer becomes subject to regulation by the authorizing jurisdiction's insurance laws and is subject to that jurisdiction's courts. Some reinsurance arrangements require the reinsurer to establish policy reserves for the ceded portion of the direct writer's risk. A direct writer usually can take reserve credit on its financial statements for the policy reserves established by an authorized reinsurer. A ***reserve credit*** is the accounting entry a direct writer uses to record an offset of its required reserves due to the use of reinsurance.

Accreditation for Reinsurers. Most states in the United States offer a status of *accreditation* for reinsurers. An ***accredited reinsurer*** is a reinsurer that is not licensed in a given state but that meets specified financial

FIGURE 9.5 Direct Writer Licensing Requirements in the United States

State laws and regulations typically require a direct writer to

- Hold a minimum dollar amount of capital and surplus
- Deposit in trust a minimum dollar amount of securities or other liquid assets
- Name the state's insurance commissioner as the insurer's attorney-in-fact for service of process in any legal action filed against the insurer in that state

and reporting requirements of that state and is licensed to transact insurance or reinsurance in at least one other state. Because solvency regulation is relatively uniform across the United States, requiring a reinsurer to be licensed in at least one other state provides assurance to regulators in other states that the reinsurer is subject to solvency requirements that are similar to those imposed by such other states. A direct writer usually can take reserve credit on its financial statements for the policy reserves established by an accredited reinsurer.

Unauthorized Reinsurers. An ***unauthorized reinsurer***, also known as a *nonadmitted reinsurer*, is a reinsurer that is not authorized or accredited in a given state. Regulators may not be able to adequately monitor an unauthorized reinsurer's solvency. An unauthorized reinsurer could become insolvent and harm the financial condition of a direct writer. For this reason, many states prohibit direct writers incorporated in the state from taking a reserve credit for reinsurance with an unauthorized reinsurer without at the same time obtaining security for the ceded risk.

Licensing Requirements—Reinsurance Intermediaries

Most reinsurance is marketed by marketing representatives who are employees of a reinsurer and who are not required to meet typical insurance agent or broker licensing requirements. However, a ***reinsurance intermediary*** is a third party who is not employed by a licensed insurer or reinsurer, but who acts on behalf of a direct writer or reinsurer to place reinsurance. The parties to a reinsurance arrangement typically use a reinsurance intermediary when the direct writer lacks reinsurance experience with a particular product. Reinsurance intermediaries usually handle reinsurance for health coverage, but they occasionally handle life reinsurance, particularly for cases involving very high face amounts, unusual underwriting circumstances, or complex product designs.

State laws based on the NAIC ***Reinsurance Intermediary Model Act*** regulate the activities of reinsurance intermediaries and the companies that use the services of reinsurance intermediaries. The Model Act identifies two types of reinsurance intermediaries:

- A ***reinsurance intermediary—broker*** is any person, firm, or corporation that solicits, negotiates, or places reinsurance cessions or retrocessions on behalf of a direct writer, but that is not authorized to enter into a binding reinsurance contract on behalf of the direct writer.

- A ***reinsurance intermediary—manager*** is any third party that acts as an agent of a reinsurer and either has authority to bind the reinsurer to a reinsurance contract or manages all or part of the reinsurer's assumed business.

The Model Act, which has been enacted by almost all of the states, is designed to (1) ensure that reinsurance intermediaries are qualified to perform their services and (2) enable regulators—in the event of the insolvency of a reinsurer—to account for any funds the intermediary may have handled. The Model Act requires each reinsurance intermediary to be licensed as a reinsurance broker or reinsurance manager in each state in which the intermediary has an office.

Monitoring Financial Condition

Regulators monitor the solvency and liquidity of insurers and reinsurers by (1) examining required financial reports from each company, (2) conducting on-site financial condition examinations to identify and monitor threats to a company's solvency, and (3) setting capital and surplus requirements and monitoring compliance with those requirements.

Capital and surplus are the amounts remaining after liabilities are subtracted from assets. Capital and surplus reflect a company's value. Generally, ***capital*** refers to an amount of money invested in a company by its owners or to a company's long-term financial resources. As we mentioned earlier, surplus is the amount of assets the company has over and above its policy reserves and other financial obligations. By convention, though, *surplus* alone or *capital* alone can refer to capital and surplus.

In the United States, all insurers must meet the following types of capital and surplus requirements:

- ***Minimum capital and surplus requirements***, also known as *statutory minimum capitalization requirements*, are solvency requirements that set a required minimum flat dollar amount of capital and surplus for a company as a whole and for each of the company's product lines. Each jurisdiction sets its own minimum capital and surplus requirements.

- The ***risk-based capital (RBC) ratio*** is a requirement for insurers to use a specified formula to demonstrate to state regulators the adequacy of an insurer's capital relative to the riskiness of the insurer's operations. In its most basic form, a ***capital ratio*** is a ratio that expresses the relationship between an insurer's capital and surplus and its liabilities. The RBC ratio, which was developed by the NAIC, involves a more complex formula. An insurer must meet or exceed the minimum ratio value—which is 100 percent—to be considered solvent. Generally, the greater the value of the capital ratio, the better an insurer's solvency.

Reserves

Each state in the United States requires policy reserves that meet NAIC standards. Regulators use information from required financial statements to monitor insurers' policy reserve levels. ***Required reserves***, also called *statutory reserves*, are the reserves calculated according to regulatory requirements.

Insurers have some latitude in determining the size of their reserves. Each insurer adopts appropriate reserves based on a combination of legal requirements, its own circumstances, and its business objectives. In addition, some reserve calculations incorporate the insurer's claim projections. In the United States, statutory requirements set a minimum reserve amount, but no maximum amount.

Reinsurance arrangements that require the reinsurer to establish reserves for the reinsured portion of the direct writer's risk can decrease the direct writer's required policy reserves and, as a result, ease the direct writer's surplus strain through the use of a reserve credit. Taking reserve credit may improve a direct writer's financial condition if the benefit of the reserve credit exceeds the cost of the reinsurance.

However, the availability of reserve credit to the direct writer depends in great part on the reinsurer assuming the ceded risk in a particular reinsurance arrangement. The NAIC ***Credit for Reinsurance Model Law*** specifies requirements for taking reserve credits, including requirements that the reinsurer must meet. Thus, direct writers typically seek to cede risks to reinsurers meeting those requirements.

Key Terms

direct writer
cession
reinsurer
retrocessionaire
retrocession
professional reinsurer
occasional reinsurer
professional retrocessionaire
occasional retrocessionaire
captive reinsurer
reciprocal arrangement
premium-based reciprocity
results-based reciprocity
reinsurance pool
quota share
assumption reinsurance
assumption certificate
traditional indemnity reinsurance
reinsurance premium
policy reserves
allowance
acquisition expense
maintenance expense
experience refund
premium tax
underwriting capacity
retention limit
financial capacity
surplus
surplus strain
surplus relief
automatic reinsurance
retention limit corridor
facultative reinsurance
automatic binding limit
minimum cession
jumbo limit
facultative-obligatory (fac-ob) reinsurance
reinsurance administration
reinsurance analyst
reinsurance marketing officer
business-to-business (B2B) e-commerce
Canadian Reinsurance Guidelines
insolvency
solvency law
authorized reinsurer
reserve credit
accredited reinsurer
unauthorized reinsurer
reinsurance intermediary
Reinsurance Intermediary Model Act
reinsurance intermediary—broker
reinsurance intermediary—manager
capital and surplus
capital
minimum capital and surplus requirements
risk-based capital (RBC) ratio
capital ratio
required reserves
Credit for Reinsurance Model Law

Endnote

1. Portions of this chapter are adapted from Susan Conant and Miriam A. Orsina, *Principles of Reinsurance* [Atlanta: LOMA (Life Office Management Association, Inc.), © 2006], 4–19, 21–32, 39–44, 135–140, 148–153, 155–156, 159–177. Used with permission; all rights reserved.

chapter 10

Types of Reinsurance and Reinsurance Agreements

Outline

Nonproportional and Proportional Reinsurance
Nonproportional Reinsurance
Proportional Reinsurance

The Cession Amount in Proportional Reinsurance
Excess-of-Retention Arrangements
Quota Share Arrangements

Plans of Reinsurance
Coinsurance
Modified Coinsurance
Yearly Renewable Term Reinsurance

Reinsurance Agreements
Defining the Reinsurance Coverage
Reinsurance Administration Procedures
Financial Arrangements

Learning Objectives

After studying this chapter, you should be able to…

- Contrast nonproportional reinsurance with proportional reinsurance and give examples of each
- Describe the excess-of-retention and quota share methods for risk-sharing in proportional reinsurance
- Compare and contrast the basic plans of reinsurance, including coinsurance, modified coinsurance (modco), and yearly renewable term (YRT) reinsurance
- Describe the general characteristics of a reinsurance agreement and the main provisions typically included in an agreement
- Describe the reinsurance agreement provisions that address the scope of the agreement, the termination of the agreement, and the reinsurance coverage
- Describe the reinsurance agreement provisions that address procedures for beginning reinsurance coverage, administration of policy changes, and claim administration
- Define the following methods of reinsurance record administration: individual cession administration, self-administration, and bulk administration
- Discuss the methods available to handle potential problems between the direct writer and the reinsurer

Indemnity reinsurance arrangements are quite complex and can take a variety of forms. For example, in Chapter 9, we discussed three different cession bases for indemnity reinsurance: automatic, facultative, and facultative-obligatory. Reinsurance arrangements also can vary according to the way that risk is shared by the direct writer and the reinsurer—proportionally or nonproportionally—and the plan of reinsurance—coinsurance, modified coinsurance, or yearly renewable term reinsurance.

The cession basis, the risk-sharing arrangement, and the reinsurance plan are just a few of the elements documented in reinsurance agreements. Reinsurance agreements also describe the coverage to be ceded and assumed, procedures for reinsurance administration and problem solving, and financial arrangements.

In this chapter, we describe different types of risk-sharing arrangements for reinsurance, methods for determining the amount of risk the direct writer will cede, and specific plans of reinsurance. We also discuss the provisions typically included in reinsurance agreements.

Nonproportional and Proportional Reinsurance

Reinsurance arrangements generally can be classified as either nonproportional or proportional, depending on how the sharing of risk between the direct writer and reinsurer is structured.[1] Indemnity reinsurance for life, disability income, critical illness, and long-term care coverage typically is proportional; reinsurance for property, liability, and medical expense coverage generally is nonproportional.

Nonproportional Reinsurance

Nonproportional reinsurance is a type of reinsurance in which neither the reinsurer nor the direct writer knows in advance what share of a risk the reinsurer ultimately will assume. Under nonproportional reinsurance, the reinsurer's liability depends on the actual claims the direct writer pays, so the amount of the reinsurer's liability is not precisely known in advance. The reinsurer establishes a portion of the policy reserves under some nonproportional arrangements; however such nonproportional reinsurance arrangements may not qualify for reserve credit.

Nonproportional health reinsurance can apply to the risk represented by a single insurance policy or the risk represented by a group of policies or a block of business. Under many nonproportional reinsurance arrangements, the reinsurer begins to reimburse a direct writer for claim payments when the direct writer's losses on a specified policy or a specified group of policies exceed a specified monetary limit within a specified period, such as one year. The specified monetary limit at which the reinsurer becomes obligated to reimburse the direct writer for claim payments is known as the reinsurer's ***attachment point***. For example, for a specified block of the direct writer's business within a specified calendar year, a reinsurer agrees to cover the direct writer's total claim payments greater than $50 million.

The most common plans of nonproportional reinsurance include excess-of-loss reinsurance, stop-loss reinsurance, and catastrophe coverage. Less commonly used plans of nonproportional reinsurance are spread-loss coverage and extended-time reinsurance.

Excess-of-Loss Reinsurance

Excess-of-loss reinsurance is a type of nonproportional reinsurance in which a reinsurer is responsible for paying a specified amount of a direct writer's claim benefits paid on a single loss, within a specified range of monetary amounts. In this context, a *single loss* could refer to the monetary loss per policy, per person, or per occurrence. An excess-of-loss plan generally specifies both a lower and an upper limit on the reinsurer's monetary obligation for a single loss. The reinsurance coverage extends to each loss that falls within the specified range or *layer* of monetary amounts. Excess-of-loss reinsurance typically covers the entire monetary amount of the loss within the coverage range.

For example, on reinsurance for an individual medical expense policy, the direct writer retains the risk for the first $15,000 of claims paid per policy per year. The reinsurer assumes the risk for claim benefits greater than $15,000, up to a maximum of $100,000. If the direct writer pays claims totaling $50,000 under the policy during the year, the reinsurer is responsible for reimbursing the direct writer for $35,000 ($50,000 – $15,000 = $35,000). If the direct writer's claim payments under the policy during the year are $80,000, the reinsurer's claim liability is $65,000 ($80,000 – $15,000 = $65,000). The risk assumed by the reinsurer is not proportional and the amount of the reinsurer's claim liability is not known in advance of receiving claims.

Stop-Loss Reinsurance

Stop-loss reinsurance, also known as *stop-loss ratio reinsurance* or *excess-of-loss ratio reinsurance*, is a type of nonproportional reinsurance in which the reinsurer agrees to pay for a portion of total claims on a block of business in an amount between stated lower and upper limits for a specified operating period. In stop-loss reinsurance, the stated lower limit could be either (1) an agreed monetary amount or (2) an agreed percentage of some other monetary measure of business volume, such as (a) aggregate net premiums over the same period or (b) average insurance in force for the same period.

For example, on reinsurance for all coverage issued under a medical expense insurance plan, the direct writer retains responsibility for paying the first $250,000 of benefits in the year. The reinsurer will be responsible for the remainder of benefits, up to a maximum of $1,000,000. Thus, if the direct writer paid a total of $400,000 in claims under the plan, the reinsurer would be liable for $150,000 of the benefits. The risk assumed by the reinsurer is not proportional, and the amount of the reinsurer's liability is unknown before the claim occurs.

Both stop-loss and excess-of-loss reinsurance cover situations in which unexpectedly large claims would cause a financial strain for the direct writer. Note that the main difference between excess-of-loss and stop-loss reinsurance is that excess-of-loss reinsurance applies to a single loss, whereas stop-loss reinsurance typically applies to a block of business within a stated period of operations.

Catastrophe Coverage

Catastrophe coverage, commonly known as *cat cover*, is a type of nonproportional reinsurance designed to partially protect direct writers from (1) a single catastrophic event resulting in multiple claims or (2) an annual total of claims in a catastrophic amount. Cat cover usually is a backup for accident or casualty coverages. However, cat cover can be applied to life insurance, medical expense insurance, disability income insurance, critical illness insurance, or long-term care insurance coverages. Cat cover usually requires the reinsurer to reimburse the direct writer for claims when the direct writer's total claims exceed a stated amount, subject to (1) a minimum number of qualified claims or minimum amount of claim benefits and (2) a maximum total reinsurance payout. Examples of such single catastrophic events involving multiple claims are building fires, earthquakes, volcanic eruptions, commercial airplane crashes, environmental accidents, epidemics, and tsunamis. Typically, a cat cover arrangement for a single catastrophic event requires a minimum of three claims from the same event.

Spread-Loss Coverage

Spread-loss coverage is a nonproportional reinsurance arrangement—similar to a loan—between a direct writer and a reinsurer. In spread-loss coverage, if the direct writer's total claims for a specified block of business in a stated period exceed a stated attachment point, the reinsurer pays a specified amount of the excess claims. In return, the direct writer is required to repay the reinsurer's funds over time with interest payable according to specified terms.

Extended-Time Reinsurance

Extended-time reinsurance, also called *excess-of-time reinsurance*, is a type of nonproportional reinsurance in which the reinsurer reimburses the direct writer for all claims paid under reinsured policies after the direct writer has paid claims for a specified amount of time. An extended-time reinsurance plan may or may not set an upper limit on the reinsurer's obligation. Extended-time reinsurance is commonly used with disability income and long-term care insurance. In contrast to spread-loss coverage, the direct writer is not required to repay the reinsurer.

For example, suppose that a long-term care insurance policy provides a maximum benefit period of five years. Under the reinsurance arrangement for that plan of insurance, the direct writer retains the liability for the first two years of each claim. If any claim extends longer than the first two years, then the reinsurer reimburses the direct writer for all claims that become payable after the first two years, up to the policy maximum of five years.

Figure 10.1 lists essential characteristics of the five nonproportional reinsurance plans just described.

Proportional Reinsurance

Proportional reinsurance is a type of reinsurance under which the direct writer and reinsurer agree to share premiums and claim obligations according to a specified amount or percentage. A key characteristic of proportional reinsurance is that the reinsurer's portion of the premiums and claim liability is known in advance of any claims. In proportional business, the direct writer and reinsurer share the policy reserve proportionately.

The proportional arrangement may express the reinsurer's share of the claim risk and direct writer's premiums as a percentage or ratio of the face amount of life insurance issued. For example, a proportional reinsurance agreement states that the reinsurer will accept the risk for 60 percent of the face amount of each of the direct writer's whole life claims. For a claim on a $1 million policy, we can calculate the direct writer's and reinsurer's proportionate claim responsibilities, as follows:

	Proportionate Share	×	Face Amount	=	Liability
Direct Writer	0.40	×	$1,000,000	=	$400,000
Reinsurer	0.60	×	$1,000,000	=	$600,000

FIGURE 10.1 Types of Nonproportional Reinsurance Plans

Plan	Amount of Reinsurer's Liability for Covered Business	Upper Limit on Reinsurer's Liability?
Excess-of-loss reinsurance	A specified monetary amount of the direct writer's claims on a single loss, within a specified range of monetary amounts	Yes
Stop-loss reinsurance	A portion of the direct writer's total claims on a block of business in a monetary amount between stated upper and lower limits for a specified operating period	Yes
Catastrophe coverage	The direct writer's total claims above a stated amount, subject to (1) a minimum number of qualified claims or a minimum amount of claim benefits and (2) a maximum total reinsurance payout	Yes
Spread-loss coverage	Benefits on a specified block of business that exceed a specified monetary amount in a stated period; direct writer repays the reinsurer for benefits the reinsurer has paid, plus interest	No
Extended-time reinsurance	The entire amount of claims that become payable after the direct writer has paid benefits for a specified amount of time	Sometimes

Source: Adapted from Susan Conant and Miriam A. Orsina, *Principles of Reinsurance* [Atlanta: LOMA (Life Office Management Association, Inc.), © 2006], 45–47. Used with permission; all rights reserved.

The timing of the monetary exchanges under proportional reinsurance depends on the plan of proportional reinsurance—for example, coinsurance, funds withheld coinsurance, or modified coinsurance. We discuss these reinsurance plans later in this chapter. Figure 10.2 compares some of the characteristics of nonproportional and proportional reinsurance.

The Cession Amount in Proportional Reinsurance

A proportional reinsurance arrangement generally specifies a method for determining the amount of risk the direct writer will cede. The two most common methods are excess of retention and first-dollar quota share.

FIGURE 10.2 Comparison of Nonproportional and Proportional Reinsurance

	Nonproportional	Proportional
Arrangements for Assumption of Risk	The reinsurance arrangement does not describe the reinsurer's specific share of the risk. After a direct writer's losses exceed a specified maximum limit, the reinsurer begins to share in claim liabilities.	The direct writer and the reinsurer agree to share the direct writer's premiums and claim liabilities in a specified monetary amount or percentage.
Predictability of Reinsurer's Liability	The reinsurer's liability depends on the level of claims and is not known precisely in advance of the loss.	The reinsurer's liability is defined in advance of a loss in terms of a specified monetary amount or percentage of claims.
Treatment of Policy Reserves	Policy reserves are shared nonproportionally. The sharing of policy reserves under nonproportional reinsurance arrangements may not qualify for reserve credit.	Policy reserves are shared proportionally, with reserves held by the direct writer and reinsurer. The direct writer takes a reserve credit for the proportion of the risk ceded to the reinsurer.
Primary Types of Business Reinsured	Property and liability insurance Medical expense insurance	Life insurance Annuities Disability income insurance Long-term care coverage Critical illness insurance

Source: Adapted from Susan Conant and Miriam A. Orsina, *Principles of Reinsurance* [Atlanta: LOMA (Life Office Management Association, Inc.), © 2006], 50.

Excess-of-Retention Arrangements

An ***excess-of-retention arrangement*** is a method for assigning risk in proportional reinsurance in which the direct writer establishes a monetary amount as a retention limit and the reinsurer agrees to assume monetary amounts greater than the direct writer's specified retention limit, up to the reinsurer's automatic binding limit. The excess-of-retention arrangement is used with automatic reinsurance cessions.

For example, the Shasta Insurance Company has a retention limit of $500,000 per policy on its whole life insurance policies. Shasta has a reinsurance agreement with Inyo Reinsurance Company under which Inyo Re has agreed to take the excess of retention up to $2 million on Shasta's whole life products. If Shasta sells a $1.5 million policy, Shasta will retain $500,000 of the risk and cede the remaining $1 million of risk to Inyo Re.

The ***excess of retention*** is the monetary amount of risk remaining after the direct writer's retention limit is subtracted from the net amount at risk on a case. Generally, the ***net amount at risk (NAR)*** is the difference between the face amount of a life insurance policy—other than a universal life policy—and the policy reserve (or cash value) at the end of any given policy year. Thus, the excess of retention for a case is the amount of risk the direct writer cedes and the reinsurer assumes.

Direct Writer's Excess of Retention	=	Direct Writer's Net Amount at Risk	–	Direct Writer's Retention Limit

For example, for a particular life insurance policy, the face amount is $100,000 and the NAR is $90,000. If the direct writer's retention limit for this type of policy is $25,000, then the direct writer's excess of retention for the case is $65,000, as follows:

$90,000 – $25,000 = $65,000

Quota Share Arrangements

A ***quota share arrangement*** is a method for assigning risk in proportional reinsurance in which the direct writer retains a specified monetary amount or percentage of the risk on a case and cedes the remaining risk to one or more reinsurers. Quota share arrangements usually are used with automatic cessions, but they can be used with facultative cessions.

Two types of quota share arrangements are excess quota share and the more popular first-dollar quota share. An ***excess quota share arrangement*** is a method for assigning risk in proportional reinsurance in which the direct writer keeps its full retention limit and cedes the remaining risk to two or more reinsurers on a percentage basis.

For example, the Montrose Insurance Company has a $200,000 retention limit on its whole life insurance policies. Montrose has the following reinsurance agreements with excess quota share arrangements on these products:

- The Heliotrope Reinsurance Company agrees to assume 40 percent of specified risks in excess of Montrose's retention limit

FIGURE 10.3 Excess Quota Share Arrangements with Two Reinsurers

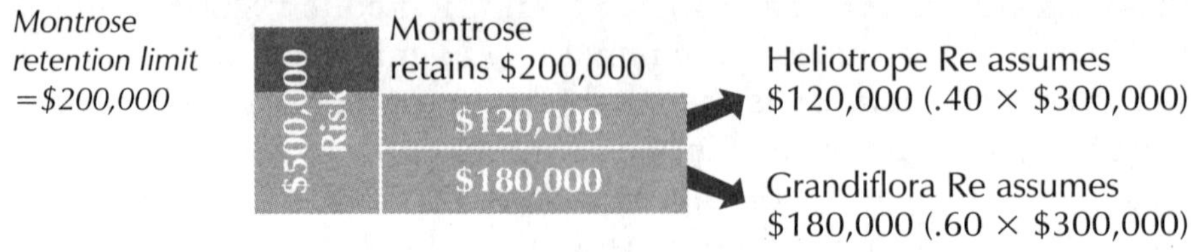

Source: Adapted from Jane Lightcap Brown and Jennifer W. Herrod, *Reinsurance Administration* [Atlanta: LOMA (Life Office Management Association, Inc.), © 2000], 26. Used with permission; all rights reserved.

- The Grandiflora Reinsurance Company agrees to assume 60 percent of specified risks in excess of Montrose's retention limit

For a policy with a face amount of $500,000, Montrose would retain its retention limit of $200,000 of risk and cede $300,000 to its reinsurers according to the previously stated quota shares. Figure 10.3 illustrates the division of risk among the three companies.

A ***first-dollar quota share (FDQS) arrangement*** is a method for assigning risk in proportional reinsurance in which the direct writer retains a stated percentage of the risk for each policy in a given block of business, up to its retention limit, and cedes the remaining risk to one or more reinsurers. In FDQS arrangements, the direct writer generally cedes coverage from the "first dollar" on all policies. However, some FDQS arrangements have a minimum cession requirement. The FDQS arrangement usually states a maximum monetary amount of risk that the reinsurer is willing to accept.

For example, the Green River Insurance Company has a first-dollar quota share arrangement with the Sandy Shores Reinsurance Company and the Tall Trees Reinsurance Company. In this arrangement, Green River agrees to retain 20 percent of each risk, Sandy Shores Re agrees to assume 35 percent of each risk, and Tall Trees Re agrees to assume 45 percent of each risk. Figure 10.4 illustrates the division of risk among the three companies for a policy with a face amount of $500,000.

Compared to excess quota share arrangements, FDQS arrangements give the reinsurer greater participation in the direct writer's risks. Under FDQS, the direct writer cedes a fixed percentage of the risk on each policy, assuming that the resulting amount meets any minimum cession requirements in the reinsurance arrangement. Thus, in FDQS, the reinsurer may share the risk on policies that do not have an excess of retention.

FIGURE 10.4 First-Dollar Quota Share Arrangements with Two Reinsurers

On a $500,000 policy, Green River retains $100,000 (.20 × $500,000)

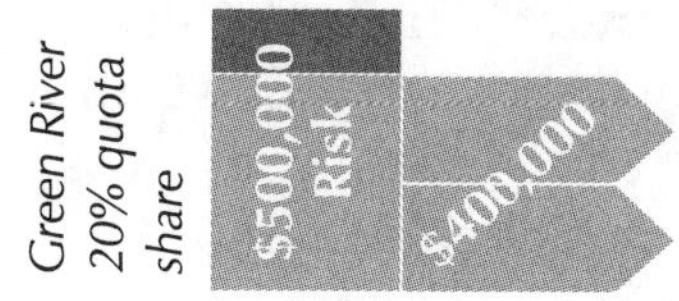

Sandy Shores Re assumes $175,000 (.35 × $500,000)

Tall Trees Re assumes $225,000 (.45 × $500,000)

Source: Adapted from Jane Lightcap Brown and Jennifer W. Herrod, *Reinsurance Administration* [Atlanta: LOMA (Life Office Management Association, Inc.), © 2000], 29. Used with permission; all rights reserved.

Plans of Reinsurance

Reinsurers offer several standard plans of reinsurance and variations of those standard plans. Coinsurance, funds withheld coinsurance, and modified coinsurances (modco) are plans of proportional reinsurance. Industry opinion is divided as to whether yearly renewable term (YRT) reinsurance is proportional. This text uses the definition of proportional reinsurance that excludes YRT reinsurance.

Coinsurance

Coinsurance is a plan of proportional reinsurance under which the direct writer and reinsurer proportionately share monetary responsibility for almost every aspect of each policy covered under the arrangement. The coinsurance agreement may specify each party's proportion of the monetary responsibility as either (1) a percentage of risk—for example, 45 percent of a risk—or (2) a monetary amount of risk—for example, the first $50,000 of a risk.

The direct writer and reinsurer share the premiums and various obligations of the primary coverage—any death benefit, other policy benefits, nonforfeiture values, and policy reserves. The reinsurer, however, very rarely shares in the direct writer's responsibility for the amounts of outstanding policy loans. In addition, the reinsurer proportionately shares in the direct writer's expenses—for commissions, administration, and sometimes premium taxes—in the form of a ***coinsurance allowance***, also known as a *ceding allowance*. The reinsurer receives a proportionate share of the direct writer's gross premiums, less the coinsurance allowance withheld by the direct writer.

Coinsurance transfers to the reinsurer the surplus strain of the reinsured portion of newly issued policies. Coinsurance is suitable for life insurance, medical expense insurance, disability income insurance, long-term care insurance, and annuity coverages.

Funds withheld coinsurance is a variation on basic coinsurance and, thus, is similar to basic coinsurance in many ways. ***Funds withheld coinsurance*** is a plan of proportional reinsurance under which the direct writer and reinsurer proportionately share responsibility for almost all aspects of a reinsured policy, but the direct writer retains the initial gross reinsurance premium and the reinsurer retains the initial coinsurance allowance. This plan allows the direct writer and reinsurer to limit cash flows between them over the life of the reinsurance arrangement. Both parties maintain accounting records and, thus, track changes in the net balance of the withheld funds. The net balance is the difference between the amounts the direct writer and the reinsurer owe each other.

For all coinsurance, the direct writer and the reinsurer have responsibility for their portion of the policy reserves. However, in funds withheld coinsurance and modified coinsurance (which we discuss in the next section), the direct writer holds the reserves, invests the corresponding assets, and credits the reinsurer's reserve fund with the reinsurer's portion of the investment earnings.

Modified Coinsurance

Modified coinsurance (modco) is a plan of proportional reinsurance under which (1) the direct writer and reinsurer share proportionately in the policy reserve obligation, the direct writer's gross premiums, and the risks of loss from expenses for death, surrender, or other benefits or from lapse, and (2) the direct writer holds the entire reserve for each reinsured policy. The reinsurer deposits its proportionate share of the policy reserves with the direct writer and the direct writer pays the reinsurer its share of interest earnings on the reserves. Modco requires a periodic adjustment to the policy reserves to reconcile changes in the reserve amount due to earnings or losses on the assets underlying the reserves.

For any given period, the value of a modco reserve adjustment may be positive or negative.

- A positive modco reserve adjustment value indicates that the reinsurer owes funds to the direct writer.
- A negative modco reserve adjustment value indicates that the direct writer owes funds to the reinsurer.

When a claim is made on a policy, the reinsurer reimburses the direct writer for the benefit on the reinsured portion of the policy, minus the amount of the reinsurer's reserve deposit for that policy. Modco typically is used for cash value life insurance and annuity products, and it is particularly appropriate for interest-sensitive products.

Figure 10.5 compares features of basic coinsurance and modco arrangements.

Yearly Renewable Term Reinsurance

Yearly renewable term (YRT) reinsurance is a plan of reinsurance that is used to reinsure only the mortality portion of a life insurance risk. For YRT reinsurance, the direct writer pays a one-year term insurance premium to the reinsurer on the anniversary date of each reinsured policy. The direct writer remains responsible for paying policy dividends and cash values and for holding most reserves on the reinsured business. Thus, YRT reinsurance does not significantly reduce the direct writer's surplus strain.

FIGURE 10.5 Comparison of Basic Coinsurance and Modco

Method	Types of Coverage Reinsured
Basic Coinsurance	Suitable for life, medical expense, disability income, and long-term care insurance and annuities
Modco	Suitable for annuities and cash value life insurance products and particularly appropriate for interest-sensitive products
	Reinsurer's Obligations
Basic Coinsurance	Proportionate share in the policy reserve obligation, the direct writer's gross premium, and expenses for death, surrender, or other benefits or lapse
Modco	Proportionate share in the policy reserve obligation, the direct writer's gross premium, and expenses for death, surrender, or other benefits or lapse
	Treatment of Policy Reserve Obligation
Basic Coinsurance	Direct writer and reinsurer proportionately share responsibility for the policy reserve obligation and maintain the reserves within their companies
Modco	Direct writer and reinsurer proportionately share responsibility for the policy reserve obligation, but the direct writer holds the entire policy reserve and pays the reinsurer its share of the interest earned on the reinsured portion of the reserve

Source: Adapted from Susan Conant and Miriam A. Orsina, *Principles of Reinsurance* [Atlanta: LOMA (Life Office Management Association, Inc.), © 2006], 55. Used with permission; all rights reserved.

Under YRT reinsurance, the reinsurance liability amount equals the NAR on the reinsured portion of a policy. The NAR for a cash value life insurance policy is calculated as

Cash Value Life Policy's Net Amount at Risk (NAR)	=	Policy's Death Benefit	−	Policy Reserves (or Cash Value)

Because a cash value policy's cash value and reserves typically increase over time, the NAR, and thus the amount of the YRT reinsurance coverage a direct writer needs, typically decrease each policy year. When a whole life insurance policy reaches maturity, the direct writer's accumulated reserves equal the entire mortality risk, leaving no NAR, and the YRT reinsurance terminates. Figure 10.6 illustrates how the NAR decreases over time.

However, because the mortality risk for a policy increases every year as the insured ages, the mortality cost and YRT reinsurance premium rate for a cash value life insurance policy increase every year. For YRT reinsurance arrangements, these important elements change in the following directions as time passes:

With the passage of time,	
The following amounts increase...	**The following amounts decrease...**
Policy reserve	Net amount at risk
Policy cash value	Reinsurer's liability
Age of insured	
YRT reinsurance premium rate	
Mortality risk	
Mortality cost	

Reinsurance Agreements

An indemnity reinsurance agreement addresses many different aspects of the business conducted between the reinsurance parties during the effective period of the agreement and even after the termination of the agreement. Although oral reinsurance agreements can be valid and binding on the parties, the parties to a reinsurance arrangement typically create a written document that specifies the terms of the arrangement. The principal reason for having a written reinsurance agreement is to document the terms of the arrangement. Because reinsurance may remain in effect for many years, a written agreement allows not only the current but also

FIGURE 10.6 Decreasing Net Amount at Risk on Life Insurance Policies

Policy Year	Anniversary Date	NAR (Net Amount at Risk)
1	11/26/07	$2,900,000
2	11/26/08	$2,700,000
3	11/26/09	$2,500,000
4	11/26/10	$2,300,000
5	11/26/11	$2,150,000
6	11/26/12	$1,900,000
. . . Maturity	11/26/XX	$0

Source: Adapted from Jane Lightcap Brown and Jennifer W. Herrod, *Reinsurance Administration* [Atlanta: LOMA (Life Office Management Association, Inc.), © 2000], 23. Used with permission; all rights reserved.

the next generation of reinsurance analysts to understand how to handle a reinsured policy.

Ideally, the reinsurance partners establish a written reinsurance agreement before any reinsurance cessions occur under the reinsurance arrangement. In practice, however, the formal agreement can take effect before, during, or after the initial transfer of risk from the direct writer to the reinsurer.

Either the direct writer or reinsurer may develop the written reinsurance agreement. The party that does not draft the agreement must review and approve the document. Some jurisdictions require the reinsurance parties to file reinsurance agreements with insurance regulators before implementing the agreements. Most jurisdictions do not require approval of reinsurance agreements by insurance regulators.

Because a direct writer and a reinsurer negotiate each agreement to meet their specific needs, no two reinsurance agreements are exactly alike. In addition, some reinsurance agreements—particularly those between reinsurance parties that have had a long-term, ongoing relationship—describe the reinsurance arrangement in broad terms that give both parties considerable discretion in implementing and administering the agreement. Other reinsurance agreements are quite specific concerning the accountabilities of each party and the procedures the parties agree to follow.

Regardless of the amount of detail expressed in an agreement, every reinsurance agreement contains certain provisions that protect the interests of the parties. Figure 10.7 describes the basic provisions found in most indemnity reinsurance agreements.

FIGURE 10.7 Basic Provisions in a Reinsurance Agreement

DEFINING THE REINSURANCE COVERAGE

Scope of the Agreement

- Names the direct writer and the reinsurer as the sole parties to the reinsurance agreement
- Specifies that the agreement articles, schedules, and amendments constitute the entire agreement between the parties
- States the effective date and duration of the reinsurance agreement
- Describes the process by which a direct writer takes back some or all of the ceded business from a reinsurer

Termination of the Reinsurance Agreement

- Identifies the terms and conditions under which the reinsurance agreement may end
- Describes the procedures for notification of termination
- Describes the handling of the reinsurance in force under the agreement upon termination

Reinsurance Coverages

- Identifies the plans of insurance to be reinsured, such as whole life products or disability income products, including any policy riders; the cession basis of reinsurance, such as facultative or automatic; the method for determining the amount of risk the direct writer will cede, such as first-dollar quota share or excess of retention; and the plan of reinsurance coverage, such as YRT or coinsurance
- Describes any limits on the reinsurance, including exclusions from automatic coverage
- Includes amount of reinsurance and any related limits, such as retention limits

REINSURANCE ADMINISTRATION PROCEDURES

Procedures to Begin Coverage

Describes the notification process for automatic, facultative, and facultative-obligatory reinsurance

Reporting

- Describes the procedures for reporting reinsurance transactions and the types of reports required
- Describes the timing of reporting and the consequences of late reporting

Records Inspection

States that either party to the agreement can inspect the other party's records relating to the agreement

Changes to the Reinsurance

States the procedures required for notification and handling of changes to reinsurance coverage as a result of changes to reinsured policies, such as increases or decreases in benefits, continuations, conversions, reinstatements, and terminations

continued on next page...

FIGURE 10.7 *continued* Basic Provisions in a Reinsurance Agreement

REINSURANCE ADMINISTRATION PROCEDURES *(continued)*

Claims

- States the circumstances under which a reinsurer will pay claims and outlines the procedures required for notification, settlement, and denial of claims
- Describes how the reinsurance parties will handle claim expenses in various situations
- Discusses contests of claim denials

Rescission

Describes the notification and handling procedures required when the direct writer rescinds a reinsured policy

Errors and Omissions

States that, under certain circumstances, if an unintentional administrative error occurs because of misunderstanding or oversight, both parties normally are restored to the positions they would have occupied if the error had not occurred

Arbitration

Describes the arbitration process to be used if a dispute arises that the parties to the agreement cannot resolve to their mutual satisfaction

Insolvency

Describes the procedures that will be followed if either party to the reinsurance agreement becomes unable to meet its financial obligations on time

REINSURANCE RATES AND PAYMENTS

Describes the calculation of reinsurance premiums, allowances, and other payments and specifies when the payments are due

Source: Adapted from Jane Lightcap Brown and Jennifer W. Herrod, *Reinsurance Administration* [Atlanta: LOMA (Life Office Management Association, Inc.), © 2000], 84–85. Used with permission; all rights reserved.

The body of the reinsurance agreement is made up of ***articles***, which are relatively standard contract provisions. The parties tailor the reinsurance agreement by adding ***schedules***, also known as *exhibits* or *conditions*, which are parts of the reinsurance agreement that cover the more variable elements of the agreement. Figure 10.8 lists information typically presented in schedules in a reinsurance agreement. Note, though, that because each reinsurance agreement is unique, details may be in an article in one agreement and in a schedule in another agreement.

FIGURE 10.8 Typical Reinsurance Agreement Schedules

- Description of the percentage or monetary amount of risk retained and ceded per type of policy reinsured
- Description of the policies reinsured (policy forms or product names)
- Direct writer's retention schedule
- Automatic binding limits and jumbo limits
- Exclusions to automatic reinsurance coverage
- Types of reports required
    - In-force policy reports
    - Policy exhibits
    - Policy change reports
    - Billing statements
    - Policy reserve listings
- Premium taxes
- Details concerning reinsurance premiums and allowances, including
    - Rates for reinsurance premiums and allowances on reinsured policies
    - Rates for additional benefits—such as waiver of premium or accidental death benefit—if reinsured

Source: Adapted from Jane Lightcap Brown and Jennifer W. Herrod, *Reinsurance Administration* [Atlanta: LOMA (Life Office Management Association, Inc.), © 2000], 86. Used with permission; all rights reserved.

The remainder of this chapter provides further information about many of the reinsurance agreement provisions and schedules listed in Figures 10.7 and 10.8.

Defining the Reinsurance Coverage

Reinsurance agreement provisions that define the reinsurance coverage describe the (1) scope of the agreement, (2) termination of the agreement, and (3) specific insurance to be ceded and the reinsurance coverage to be provided.

Scope of the Agreement

The provisions that describe the scope of the reinsurance agreement include the parties to the agreement provision, the entire agreement provision, the duration of the agreement provision, and the recapture provision.

Parties to the Agreement Provision. In an indemnity reinsurance agreement, the ***parties to the agreement provision*** typically states that the reinsurance agreement exists solely between the direct writer and the reinsurer. The reinsurance agreement does not create any legal relationship between the reinsurer and the insured, the policyowner, any beneficiary, any assignee, or any party other than the direct writer.

Entire Agreement Provision. The ***entire agreement provision*** states that the written agreement articles, schedules, and any amendments represent the whole agreement between the parties, which have no further agreement than that stated in the written document. Only the reinsurance arrangements that are specifically stated in the written document and its amendments are binding on the parties. Arrangements not stated in the written document, even though they may be typical in the industry, are not binding on the parties. If a reinsurer cedes to a retrocessionaire part of the risk it has assumed from a direct writer, such a retrocession does not affect the agreement between the direct writer and the reinsurer in any way.

Duration of the Agreement Provision. The duration of the agreement provision addresses when the reinsurance agreement becomes effective and when it ends. Most reinsurance agreements provide that the agreement takes effect on an agreed-upon date, known as the agreement effective date. The ***agreement effective date*** may be either (1) the date on which the written agreement is signed by authorized representatives of the direct writer and the reinsurer and a copy of the agreement is delivered to each party or (2) any agreed-upon date when the direct writer submits policies to the reinsurer for automatic reinsurance or the reinsurer approves policies for facultative or facultative-obligatory reinsurance.

Each reinsurance agreement also specifies how the reinsurance effective date will be determined. The ***reinsurance effective date*** is the date on which the reinsurance coverage for a specific risk takes effect. Some agreements specify that reinsurance coverage for a given policy begins on the date the application for the policy is submitted to the direct writer; other agreements state that reinsurance coverage begins on the policy issue date.

Although some reinsurance agreements state when the agreement will end, most agreements specify that, when the agreement has taken effect, it continues to be effective for an unlimited period of time unless canceled by one or both parties.

Recapture Provision. *Recapture* is the process by which a direct writer takes back some or all ceded business from a reinsurer. The reinsurance agreement generally permits the direct writer to increase its retention limit. Usually, if a direct writer chooses to increase its retention limits, the agreement allows the company to recapture some of the reinsured risk so that the company maintains full retention on the reinsured policies.

Typically, for a policy to be eligible for recapture, the direct writer must have (1) retained its full retention at the time it originally ceded the case and (2) reinsured the case with the reinsurer for a specified period of time (often 10 to 15 years). Generally, the agreement does not allow the direct writer to cede the recaptured business to another reinsurer.

If the direct writer recaptures risk on any single policy, then the direct writer also must recapture risk in a similar manner on all ceded policies that are eligible for recapture. By preventing the direct writer from selectively recapturing only the lowest risks and leaving the highest risks covered by the reinsurer, this provision protects the reinsurer from adverse selection by the direct writer.

Keep in mind that recapture of ceded business typically is optional—the direct writer does not have to recapture the ceded business. If the direct writer elects not to recapture, the higher retention limit would apply only to newly issued policies. If a direct writer chooses to recapture business, this recapture results in a reduction of the amount reinsured and, typically, a decrease in the direct writer's total reinsurance costs.

Termination of the Reinsurance Agreement

Most reinsurance agreements—particularly those that cover life insurance—stay in effect indefinitely until the agreement is canceled by one or both parties to the contract. The complete cancellation of a reinsurance agreement for both new business and in-force business is called a ***termination***. The parties mutually can agree to cancel the agreement at any time. Also, most reinsurance agreements allow the reinsurer to unilaterally cancel the agreement for new business and in-force business if the direct writer fails to pay reinsurance premiums owed to the reinsurer within the timeframe specified in the agreement.

If one of the parties to a reinsurance agreement notifies the other party of a ***termination for new business***, the parties no longer cede or assume new business under that agreement, but reinsurance coverage continues on business already in place. Either party to a reinsurance agreement has the right to cancel the agreement with regard to new business, assuming that the canceling party provides proper notification—usually 30 to 90 days in advance of the intended termination—to the other party. However, unless the parties mutually agree to completely end the entire arrangement established under a written reinsurance agreement, existing reinsurance typically remains in force until the natural termination or expiration of the reinsured policies. That is, an in-force policy remains reinsured until the policy terminates due to lapse, surrender, payment of a life insurance claim, or—for term insurance—until the term of coverage has ended. Thus, under a termination for new business, reinsurance coverage issued earlier than the termination date is still in force, unless other arrangements are made to discontinue that coverage.

Each jurisdiction determines the circumstances under which the parties may terminate a reinsurance agreement. Insurance regulators may limit policy reserve credit for direct writers whose reinsurance agreements allow the reinsurer to terminate in-force coverage for reasons not deemed acceptable.

Reinsurance Coverages

A reinsurance agreement describes the plans of insurance to be reinsured and the reinsurance coverage to be provided. The articles included in a reinsurance agreement define in general terms the

- Plans of insurance to be covered by the reinsurance—for example, whole life, term life, or universal life
- Reinsurance cession basis or bases—for example, automatic, facultative, or automatic and facultative
- Method for determining the amount of risk the direct writer will cede—for example, an excess-of-retention or a quota share arrangement
- Type of reinsurance plan—for example, YRT, modified coinsurance, or coinsurance

The articles generally refer to schedules for the specifics pertaining to these general topics.

As a general rule, an automatic reinsurance agreement contains more specific and restrictive parameters than does a facultative agreement. Because the reinsurer *must* accept policies that are automatically reinsured, an automatic reinsurance agreement specifies the parameters under which the direct writer can submit a risk to the reinsurer. For example, the agreement may specify that only "individual life insurance policies issued to standard or preferred risks" may be submitted for automatic reinsurance. In contrast, a facultative reinsurance agreement can contain more general parameters because the reinsurer has the opportunity to underwrite each policy individually and then to accept or decline each risk.

An automatic reinsurance agreement specifies the lower and upper issue ages and the acceptable risk level for each type of coverage. For instance, a reinsurance agreement for term life insurance may state that no one under the age of 6 or above the age of 70 and no one with a mortality rate greater than a specified level can be reinsured under the agreement.

In describing the reinsurance to be provided, an automatic reinsurance agreement may specify certain risks that are excluded from coverage. Figure 10.9 lists situations in which most agreements exclude automatic coverage.

An automatic reinsurance agreement typically states that the direct writer may facultatively submit to the reinsurer any risks that do not qualify for automatic reinsurance as long as the plan of insurance is covered

FIGURE 10.9 Typical Exclusions from Automatic Coverage

Most automatic reinsurance agreements exclude a specific risk if the

- Direct writer intends to retain less than its available retention for the insured's age and mortality rate under an excess-of-retention agreement
- Total amount of life insurance in force on a life in all companies plus the amount yet-to-be-placed with all companies exceeds the jumbo limit
- Total amount of life insurance previously reinsured and currently applied for and to be reinsured under the agreement exceeds the specified automatic binding limit
- Substandard underwriting rating assigned by the direct writer to the risk exceeds a specified level
- Plan of reinsurance requested by the direct writer is not included in the agreement
- Direct writer is issuing the insurance in a manner not specified in the agreement—for example, as a conversion of group insurance or as a policy exchange
- Underwriting guidelines used by the direct writer differ from the agreed-upon selection criteria specified in the agreement
- Full length of the policy's suicide exclusion period and/or contestable period do not apply because the policy to be reinsured is a continuation or conversion of another policy
- Policy is a continuation of coverage of a previously issued policy that has been reinsured under another agreement or that was fully retained by the direct writer
- Insured does not meet criteria set by both parties—for example, the insured is not a resident of a specified jurisdiction or the insured exceeds the maximum age allowed

Source: Adapted from Jane Lightcap Brown and Jennifer W. Herrod, *Reinsurance Administration* [Atlanta: LOMA (Life Office Management Association, Inc.), © 2000], 94. Used with permission; all rights reserved.

under the arrangement. In addition, the direct writer may submit a policy facultatively because it prefers to have the reinsurer's underwriters review the risk.

A schedule—or in some cases, an article—in the reinsurance agreement specifies the method to be used to calculate the reinsured policy's NAR and the direct writer's retention limits. Most automatic reinsurance agreements also state a minimum cession. Figure 10.10 shows a retention limits schedule in a reinsurance agreement.

For nonproportional reinsurance, the reinsurance agreement generally includes a schedule that specifies the amount the reinsurer will pay based on the number or amount of claims paid under the coverage.

The reinsurer's binding limits typically are listed in a schedule, which also typically specifies the jumbo limit. Figure 10.11 shows an example of a binding limits schedule.

FIGURE 10.10 Schedule of Retention Limits

LIMITS OF RETENTION: RIGHTWAY LIFE INSURANCE COMPANY

Whole Life Insurance

Issue Age	Standard–Table 4	Table 5–Table 8	Table 9–Table 16
0–60	$100,000	$50,000	$25,000
61–70	$50,000	$25,000	$25,000
71–80	$25,000	$25,000	$25,000

Waiver of Premium

Same as Whole Life Insurance

Source: Adapted from Jane Lightcap Brown and Jennifer W. Herrod, *Reinsurance Administration* [Atlanta: LOMA (Life Office Management Association, Inc.), © 2000], 96. Used with permission; all rights reserved.

Reinsurance Administration Procedures

Indemnity reinsurance agreements typically include provisions regarding

- Procedures for beginning reinsurance coverage
- The method of reinsurance record administration
- Reporting requirements
- Records inspections
- Administration of changes to reinsured policies
- Claim administration
- Rescissions
- Potential problems between the direct writer and reinsurer
- Insolvency

Procedures for Beginning Reinsurance Coverage

Reinsurance agreements generally include a provision describing the procedures that the direct writer should use to notify the reinsurer of automatic or fac-ob reinsurance liability or to request facultative reinsurance. The provision specifies information the direct writer must send to the reinsurer and the form this information should take.

FIGURE 10.11 Schedule of Binding Limits

AUTOMATIC ACCEPTANCE LIMITS OF EXCEPTIONAL RE

Life Insurance

Exceptional Re will automatically accept ceded assumed business, subject to the following maximums:

Issue Ages	Standard	Substandard 125%–300%	Substandard 301%–500%	Substandard 501%+
0–80	$1,000,000	$1,000,000	$500,0000	0

Under no circumstances will the reinsurer automatically accept any risk when the total face amount of the life insurance in force and yet-to-be-placed with all companies exceeds $65,000,000.

Source: Adapted from Jane Lightcap Brown and Jennifer W. Herrod, *Reinsurance Administration* [Atlanta: LOMA (Life Office Management Association, Inc.), © 2000], 95. Used with permission; all rights reserved.

The ***notification for automatic reinsurance provision*** specifies (1) the details about each policy that a direct writer must send to a reinsurer to begin automatic reinsurance coverage and (2) how frequently the direct writer must notify the reinsurer of new automatic cessions. The provision states the effective date of the reinsurance for each reinsured policy and describes the effects of conditional premium receipts and temporary insurance agreements.

The ***notification for facultative reinsurance provision*** specifies the (1) information the direct writer must provide to notify the reinsurer of a request for facultative reinsurance coverage, (2) procedures the reinsurer must follow to make an offer of reinsurance to the direct writer, and (3) procedures the direct writer must follow to accept the reinsurer's offer.

The ***notification for fac-ob reinsurance provision*** specifies the (1) information the direct writer must provide to notify the reinsurer of risks ceded on a facultative-obligatory basis and (2) maximum time periods allowed for the reinsurance parties to respond to each other concerning capacity available and the amount of risk ceded and accepted.

Method of Reinsurance Record Administration

The reinsurance parties typically use one of three methods to administer their reinsurance records: individual cession administration, self-administration, or bulk administration.

- ***Individual cession administration*** is a method of reinsurance record administration under which the reinsurer prepares its own cession records based on detailed information about individual cessions provided by the direct writer. Under this method, the reinsurer has complete information about the risks that it assumes and primary control over reinsurance administration.
- ***Self-administration*** is a method of reinsurance record administration in which the direct writer maintains detailed records for each ceded policy and sends the reinsurer periodic reports outlining the risks ceded and reinsurance premiums due for each policy. The reinsurer uses the information provided by the direct writer to manage the risks assumed.
- ***Bulk administration*** is a method of reinsurance record administration in which the direct writer periodically submits summarized reports—such as reinsurance premium and policy summaries—to the reinsurer, but does not provide detailed information about individual risks reinsured other than an annual detailed in-force listing. Bulk administration does not provide the reinsurer with adequate information to perform retention management or mortality studies.

Reporting Requirements

The party that administers the reinsurance records must submit periodic reports to the other party. The reports serve as a basis for reinsurance premium and allowance payments, retention management, and financial reporting. The reinsurance agreement specifies the reports to be submitted, the party responsible for submitting the reports, the timing for each report, and the consequences of submitting reports late. The reports required depend on the method of reinsurance record administration specified in the agreement and the requirements of the financial statements that the companies must file with regulatory authorities.

Records Inspection

The ***records inspection provision*** states the rights of each party to inspect the other party's records and documents relating to the reinsurance provided under the agreement. The provision typically limits the right of record inspection by allowing inspection at any reasonable time for any reasonable purpose and at the respective parties' offices during normal business hours.

Administration of Changes to Reinsured Policies

Because reinsurance arrangements may remain in force for years, the reinsurance agreement provides specific instructions for handling changes to reinsured policies. Some of these changes are increases and reductions in benefits and continuations, conversions, reinstatements, and terminations of reinsured policies.

An automatic reinsurance agreement addresses most of these changes. As a result, the direct writer is allowed to make changes to a reinsured policy without obtaining the reinsurer's consent, as long as the changes fall within the parameters of the agreement. Under facultative reinsurance agreements, however, the direct writer is required to obtain prior approval from the reinsurer before making policy changes that increase coverage or increase underwriting ratings.

Provisions for Increasing and Reducing Death Benefits. Increases in death benefit amounts can be contractual—that is, payable in accordance with the terms of a life insurance policy—or noncontractual—that is, requested by the policyowner, although not required under the terms of the policy. Under automatic reinsurance, the reinsurer generally must accept contractual increases up to the amount of the reinsurer's automatic binding limits.

Noncontractual increases generally require new evidence of insurability. The reinsurance agreement typically requires the reinsurance partners to handle the increased amount like new business, and all the requirements for reinsuring new business apply.

When a life insurance policyowner reduces a reinsured policy's face amount or exercises a nonforfeiture option that decreases the value of the policy, the direct writer must reduce the reinsurance on that policy or on other policies covering the insured life, according to the provisions of the applicable reinsurance agreement. A ***reduction of reinsurance*** is the process of reducing the amount of reinsurance covering an insurance policy.

Continuation Provision. The ***continuation provision*** in a reinsurance agreement addresses which reinsurer(s) should provide the reinsurance, the amount of reinsurance, and the effective date of reinsurance for continued policies. A ***continuation*** of an insurance policy occurs either when (1) the provisions of an in-force policy are significantly modified or (2) a policy replaces an existing policy from the same direct writer, but differs from a new insurance policy in at least one of the following ways:

- The policy is not subject to the direct writer's new business underwriting requirements
- The direct writer does not pay full first-year commissions to the insurance producer
- The policy does not introduce a new suicide exclusion period
- The policy does not introduce a new contestable period

An internal replacement can be a continuation, assuming that the replacement policy satisfies one of the preceding conditions. However, an external replacement does not qualify as a continuation because the two policies involved are issued by different companies. A conversion of a policy usually qualifies as a continuation. The reinstatement of a policy is not a continuation because only one policy is involved and that policy is not modified. We discuss conversions and reinstatements in the next section of this chapter.

Type of Policy Change	Can Qualify as a Continuation?
Internal replacement	Yes
External replacement	No
Conversion	Yes
Reinstatement	No

Conversion Provision. A ***conversion*** is a new policy that is issued on the basis of the policyowner's contractual right to change the policy form, as provided in the original policy. For example, some life insurance policies allow a policyowner to convert a term policy to a whole life policy. Conversions do not require additional evidence of insurability.

The ***conversion provision*** in a reinsurance agreement typically states (1) that the direct writer must continue the reinsurance on converted policies with the original reinsurer unless the reinsurer releases its right to reinsure the policies and (2) any conditions under which the direct writer or the reinsurer can cancel the reinsurance on conversions.

Reinstatement Provision. ***Reinstatement*** is the process by which an insurer puts back into force an insurance policy that has lapsed due to nonpayment of premiums. The ***reinstatement provision*** in a reinsurance agreement typically specifies that when a reinsured policy lapses for nonpayment of premium, the reinsurance can be reinstated if certain conditions regarding the timing of the request for reinstatement and the payment of reinsurance premiums due are met.

Provision for Termination of Reinsurance. A ***termination of reinsurance*** is the process by which a direct writer cancels the reinsurance covering a policy issued by the company. A termination of reinsurance on a life insurance policy can occur because a reinsured policy expires, matures, is surrendered, or lapses due to nonpayment of premiums or because the insured dies. The reinsurance agreement typically states that the reinsurer's liability ends when the reinsured policy is no longer in effect.

Claim Administration

A ***claim provision*** in an indemnity reinsurance agreement states the terms and conditions of the reinsurer's liability for claims submitted under reinsured policies. Figure 10.12 summarizes the information typically included in a claim provision.

FIGURE 10.12 Information in a Claim Provision

- The extent of the direct writer's authority to handle claims, including any limits on that authority
- The procedures the direct writer must follow to be reimbursed by the reinsurer for paid claims, including the manner and timing in which claims will be reported to the reinsurer
- How the direct writer and reinsurer will share responsibility for expenses related to claims and adjustments to the benefit amount
- The conditions under which the reinsurer will be liable to share in paying claim expenses other than the benefits payable under the insurance policy

Source: Adapted from Jane Lightcap Brown and Jennifer W. Herrod, *Reinsurance Administration* [Atlanta: LOMA (Life Office Management Association, Inc.), © 2000], 136.

For life reinsurance, the reinsurance claim provision typically states that, within a specified time period after receiving notice that the direct writer has paid a death claim under a reinsured policy, the reinsurer will pay the reinsurance benefits in a lump sum, even if the reinsured policy calls for the benefit to be paid to the beneficiary in installments. The reinsurer typically reimburses the direct writer for the reinsurer's share of medical expense and critical illness claim payments in a lump sum. However, for disability income reinsurance or long-term care reinsurance, the reinsurer periodically disburses reinsurance benefit payments to the direct writer throughout the benefit payment period in proportion to the benefit amounts paid by the direct writer.

Under some circumstances, a facultative reinsurance agreement requires the direct writer to obtain an opinion from the reinsurer before settling a claim, or else the reinsurer may not be bound to participate in paying the claim. The claim provision in an automatic or a fac-ob reinsurance agreement typically states that the direct writer has the authority to make decisions on claims and that the reinsurer is bound by the direct writer's decisions. However, an automatic reinsurance agreement also usually requires the direct writer to consult with the reinsurer before settling a claim in some or all of the following situations:

- A claim occurs during the reinsured life insurance policy's contestable period
- The reinsurer has assumed more than 50 percent of the risk covered by a reinsured policy

- The total amount of a claim or the amount of risk ceded to the reinsurer exceeds the limits stated in the reinsurance agreement
- The direct writer has retained less than its published retention limit on a reinsured policy
- A claim involves an insured's death in a foreign country
- The direct writer suspects that a claim involves ***fraud***, which is an act by which someone intentionally deceives another party and induces that other party to part with something of value

In addition, the reinsurance agreement claim provision usually requires the direct writer to provide the reinsurer the opportunity to review the claim file of any claim that the direct writer plans to deny. This provision also addresses the rights and responsibilities of the direct writer and the reinsurer regarding claim contests. A ***contest*** of an insurance claim is a court action to determine the validity of the claim. A claim contest generally occurs when an insurer denies liability to pay a claim, and the beneficiary or policyowner files a lawsuit seeking to force the insurer to pay the claim.

Rescissions

The ***rescission provision*** in a reinsurance agreement describes the notification and administrative procedures required when a direct writer rescinds a reinsured policy. This provision generally requires the direct writer to make decisions regarding rescission in good faith and to inform the reinsurer in a timely manner of any rescission of a reinsured policy. ***Good faith*** refers to a party's honesty of intention and avoidance of attempts to deceive or take unfair advantage of another party to an agreement.

Potential Problems between a Direct Writer and a Reinsurer

The parties to a reinsurance agreement anticipate the potential for occasional problems by stating in the reinsurance agreement the procedures the parties agree to use to resolve such problems. These procedures address errors and omissions that may occur in administering the reinsurance agreement and more serious disputes that cannot be solved through negotiation.

Errors and Omissions. Unintentional errors or omissions of information may occur during the administration of a reinsurance agreement. The ***errors and omissions provision*** of a reinsurance agreement states that if either party to the agreement fails to comply with the terms of the agreement through unintentional administrative mistake or clerical error, then both parties will be restored to the position they would have occupied if the mistake or error had not occurred. Unintentional administrative errors and omissions will not affect the rights and obligations established by the agreement as long as both parties work to handle errors and omissions appropriately.

The errors and omissions provision typically applies only to clerical errors, not to errors involving decisions that one of the parties deliberately made. Although the errors and omissions provision applies to situations in which the direct writer fails to cede a risk that it is required to cede under an automatic reinsurance agreement, this provision does not cover policies that the direct writer cedes automatically even though they exceed the reinsurer's jumbo or automatic binding limits.

Arbitration. ***Arbitration*** is a method of dispute resolution in which impartial third parties—known as ***arbitrators***—evaluate the facts in dispute and render a decision that usually is binding on the parties to the dispute. Reinsurance agreements usually include an ***arbitration provision***, which requires the reinsurance parties to submit disputes that they cannot resolve through negotiation to an arbitration panel rather than to a court of law. Insight 10.1 describes why arbitration often is preferable to ***litigation***, which is the process or act of resolving a dispute by means of a lawsuit.

The arbitration provision also describes the procedures the parties must use to select arbitrators and conduct the arbitration process. Typically, the arbitrators must be current or former officers of insurance or reinsurance companies and can have no present or former affiliation with either party or their subsidiaries. The arbitrators are required to base their decisions on their interpretation of the terms and conditions of the reinsurance agreement and on the customs of the insurance industry. The majority decision of the arbitrators is final, and no appeal process is available to the parties.

INSIGHT 10.1 Reasons for Using Arbitration Instead of Litigation

Arbitration often is preferable to litigation for the following reasons[2]:

- Arbitration helps ensure that the intentions of the parties when the reinsurance agreement was established are taken into consideration.
- The parties to a reinsurance agreement typically view arbitration as a more appropriate way to handle disagreements than litigation because insurance industry experts can assess the specific technical issues involved more fairly than can civil courts.
- Arbitration generally is less costly, faster, easier, and more flexible than litigation. In the United States, many reinsurance agreements base the requirements for the arbitration process on the American Arbitration Association of New York City *Rules of Arbitration* or the guidelines of the AIDA Reinsurance and Insurance Arbitration Society.[3] These rules and guidelines allow for more freedom in the procedures and the types of information accepted as admissible than do courts of law.
- Unlike litigation, arbitration allows the parties to keep confidential business information from becoming a matter of public record.

Insolvency

Although the insolvency of either party to a reinsurance agreement is unlikely, reinsurance agreements typically include an ***insolvency provision*** that describes the rights and responsibilities of the direct writer and the reinsurer in the event that either party becomes insolvent. The provision also may specify circumstances under which a party to the agreement will be deemed insolvent.

Under a typical insolvency provision, if the direct writer becomes insolvent, the reinsurer becomes obligated to pay any amounts owed on reinsured policies immediately upon receiving verification that such amounts are rightfully due. Thus, the reinsurer must pay its reinsurance liability in full, even if the direct writer has failed to pay all or a portion of any claim. The reinsurer pays the amounts due into the trust held by the direct writer's receiver. In an insurance context, a ***receiver*** is an individual who is appointed by a court to hold and administer an insolvent insurer's assets and liabilities.

The insolvency provision requires a reinsurer that becomes insolvent to notify the direct writer immediately of the insolvency and provide the direct writer with any applicable documentation of its financial situation. The insolvency provision generally gives the direct writer the right to terminate the reinsurance agreement immediately as a consequence of the reinsurer's insolvency and to recapture all reinsured risks within a specified period of time.

Financial Arrangements

Reinsurance agreements contain financial provisions designed to ensure the accuracy and timeliness of financial exchanges between a direct writer and a reinsurer. Among the elements addressed by financial provisions are reinsurance premiums, allowances, policy cash values, policy dividends, experience refunds, and premium tax refunds.

Key Terms

nonproportional reinsurance
attachment point
excess-of-loss reinsurance
stop-loss reinsurance
catastrophe coverage
spread-loss coverage
extended-time reinsurance
proportional reinsurance
excess-of-retention arrangement
excess of retention
net amount at risk (NAR)
quota share arrangement
excess quota share arrangement
first-dollar quota share (FDQS) arrangement
coinsurance
coinsurance allowance
funds withheld coinsurance
modified coinsurance (modco)
yearly renewable term (YRT) reinsurance
article
schedule
parties to the agreement provision
entire agreement provision
agreement effective date
reinsurance effective date
recapture
termination
termination for new business
notification for automatic reinsurance provision
notification for facultative reinsurance provision
notification for fac-ob reinsurance provision
individual cession administration
self-administration
bulk administration
records inspection provision
reduction of reinsurance
continuation provision
continuation
conversion
conversion provision
reinstatement
reinstatement provision
termination of reinsurance
claim provision
fraud
contest
rescission provision
good faith
errors and omissions provision
arbitration
arbitrator
arbitration provision
litigation
insolvency provision
receiver

Endnotes

1. Portions of this chapter are adapted from Susan Conant and Miriam A. Orsina, *Principles of Reinsurance* [Atlanta: LOMA (Life Office Management Association, Inc.), © 2006], 45–49, 65–67, 69–104, 109–125, 130, 136–140. Used with permission; all rights reserved.
2. John E. Tiller, Jr., and Denise Fagerberg Tiller, *Life, Health and Annuity Reinsurance*, 3rd ed. (Winsted, CT: ACTEX Publications, 2005), 213.
3. The AIDA is the Association Internationale de Droit des Assurances, an international association of professionals interested in insurance law and regulation.

chapter

11

Reinsurance Administration

Outline

Administering New Business
Preplacement of Reinsurance
Placement of Reinsurance

Administering In-Force Business
Reporting on In-Force Business
Processing Changes in Reinsurance Coverage
Processing Billing Statements
Recording Policy Reserves

Administering Terminations of Reinsurance

Administering Claims under Reinsured Policies
Establishing the Claim File
Verifying Claim-Related Information
Approving the Claim Liability
Settling the Claim Liability
Notifying Retrocessionaires of a Claim Liability

Auditing Reinsurance Operations
Internal Audits
External Audits by the Reinsurer

Learning Objectives

After studying this chapter, you should be able to…

- Describe the activities involved in preplacement and placement of reinsurance coverage
- Explain the process for reserving capacity for requested coverage
- Explain how the process for placing individual new business cessions differs among automatic, facultative, and facultative-obligatory reinsurance
- Describe five types of reinsurance reports
- Describe the procedures followed to administer changes in reinsurance coverage, reinsurance premiums and other amounts included on a billing statement, policy reserves, and terminations of reinsurance
- Describe the steps a reinsurer takes to examine, approve, and settle a request from a direct writer for claim payment reimbursement
- Describe how reinsurance operations are audited

Reinsurance administration starts when the direct writer seeks reinsurance for a risk and lasts until the reinsurance is no longer in force.[1] Reinsurance administration can involve three or all four of the following stages:

- In the *preplacement stage*, the reinsurer reviews the direct writer's request for facultative or fac-ob reinsurance coverage and either offers to reinsure the risk or declines it. If the reinsurer decides to offer coverage, it establishes a reservation for the capacity needed to reinsure the case.
- In the *placement stage*, also known as the *submission stage*, the direct writer and reinsurer activate reinsurance for automatic, facultative, and fac-ob cessions.
- In the *in-force stage*, the direct writer pays the reinsurance premiums to the reinsurer to keep the coverage in force. The reinsurance parties make adjustments to the reinsurance coverage as changes are made to the reinsured policies. The reinsurer receives claim notices from the direct writer, reviews and approves or rejects the requests for claim payment reimbursement, and settles valid claim liabilities. Because the payment of a death claim results in the termination of the policy and the termination of the reinsurance on that policy, some direct writers and reinsurers view claim administration as part of the termination stage.
- In the *termination stage*, the direct writer notifies the reinsurer of any terminations of reinsured policies, and the reinsurer processes the termination of reinsurance on each case.

Because reinsurance administration can vary greatly from one reinsurance agreement to another and from one company to another, the procedures described in this text may be somewhat different from the procedures that your company uses. Keep in mind that most reinsurance administration activities are automated to some extent. Direct writers and reinsurers typically use administration systems to maintain their reinsurance records and telecommunications systems to exchange information.

Administering New Business

Reinsurance administration for new business includes the preplacement stage, if applicable, and placement.

Preplacement of Reinsurance

Preplacement is the process by which a reinsurer (1) reviews a direct writer's request for coverage, (2) establishes appropriate records and reserves capacity for the case, and (3) as necessary, follows up on reservations for capacity that have been inactive for a specified period of time. ***Reserved capacity*** is the portion of a reinsurer's financial capacity that the reinsurer sets aside to fund its financial obligations under anticipated new business. Preplacement begins when a direct writer requests coverage, and it continues until either (1) the reinsurance coverage begins, (2) the reinsurer denies the direct writer's request for coverage, or (3) the direct writer withdraws its request for coverage.

As a general rule, preplacement is required only for facultative and fac-ob cases. Preplacement typically is not necessary for automatic cases because the direct writer and reinsurer have agreed in advance that the direct writer will place certain types of risk with the reinsurer. Thus, administration of automatic reinsurance generally begins at the placement stage. Note that all reinsurance cases, regardless of the basis of submission, go through the stages of placement, in-force administration, and termination.

Reviewing a Request for Coverage

Under facultative and fac-ob reinsurance agreements, the direct writer requests reinsurance coverage on a particular insured or group of insureds by sending the reinsurer a document known as a ***request for coverage*** or *facultative application*. For each preplaced case, the direct writer maintains a file that includes a copy of the request for coverage, reinsurers' requests for additional information on the case, and any offers received. The direct writer's reinsurance analyst responds to any questions or requests from reinsurers about the request for coverage. Some direct writers outsource the submission of requests for coverage and the tracking of offers to third-party administrators.

Figure 11.1 shows an example of a request for coverage. Upon receiving a request for coverage with all of the required information, the reinsurer establishes the appropriate records and reserves the necessary capacity.

For facultative cases, sending a request for coverage to a reinsurer does not guarantee that the direct writer will cede the case to that reinsurer. The direct writer may be shopping—that is, submitting cases facultatively to several reinsurers. Direct writers sometimes shop cases to obtain the best reinsurance coverage for the most competitive price. Thus, sometimes a reinsurer reviews a case that the direct writer eventually places with another reinsurer.

Reinsurance agreements sometimes include time limits to protect a direct writer from the risk resulting from a reinsurer's failure to respond to a request for coverage in a timely manner. As mentioned in Chapter 9,

FIGURE 11.1 Example of a Request for Coverage

BOWDOIN
INSURANCE COMPANY

Request for Reinsurance

To Joel Guildan, Syracuse Reinsurance Company

From Kelly Dawson

Date 1/19/2007

Name Tattersall, Marc T. **Age** 54 **Sex** M

Policy Number 367822 **Tobacco Use** No

Date and Place of Birth 12/6/1950, NY

Residence 2247 Main St., East Dalton, NY

Insurance applied for $500,000 in USD

Insurance retained $200,000

Reinsurance requested $300,000

Total insurance in force or applied for with us $1,000,000

Rating 100.00 standard

Please reserve your maximum and advise amount. No aviation or avocation concerns. Related papers are enclosed.

Regards,

Kelly Dawson

Kelly Dawson
(555) 555-5555 Fax (555) 555-5556

Source: Adapted from Jane Lightcap Brown and Jennifer W. Herrod, *Reinsurance Administration* [Atlanta: LOMA (Life Office Management Association, Inc.), © 2000], 166. Used with permission; all rights reserved.

a fac-ob reinsurance agreement may state that, if the reinsurer does not respond to a request for coverage within a specified time limit, then the direct writer can assume that reinsurance on the policy will take effect.

Establishing Records and Reserving Capacity

A reinsurer establishes a paper or an electronic case file for each submitted case. Reinsurers use status codes—such as those listed in Figure 11.2—to enable them to track the current status of each case. The status code terminology varies from one reinsurer to another. Also, note that some of these codes—*replaced*, *claim*, *paid*, and *terminated*—apply to in-force business rather than to new business.

For example, when a reinsurer makes an offer on a facultative case, the reinsurer codes the case's status as *pending*. If the direct writer subsequently sends a cession, the reinsurer updates the case's status to *placed*,

FIGURE 11.2 Sample Status Codes

Reserved — The reinsurer has set aside reinsurance capacity.

Waiting — The reinsurer has requested additional information from the direct writer. Also known as *pending underwriting* or *outstanding requirements*.

Pending — The reinsurer has made an offer on a facultative case and is waiting for a response from the direct writer.

Placed — The direct writer has ceded the case to the reinsurer. Also known as *active*, *premium paying*, or *in-force*.

Declined — The reinsurer has declined the facultative case.

Withdrawn — The direct writer has not accepted the reinsurer's facultative offer. Also known as *not taken*.

Replaced — The policyowner has replaced the original policy with or converted the original policy to a different policy.

Claim — The direct writer has notified the reinsurer of a claim filed under the reinsured policy.

Paid — The reinsurer has paid a claim liability under the reinsured coverage.

Terminated — The policy has lapsed, been surrendered, or otherwise ceased being reinsured.

Source: Adapted from Jane Lightcap Brown and Jennifer W. Herrod, *Reinsurance Administration* [Atlanta: LOMA (Life Office Management Association, Inc.), © 2000], 167. Used with permission;

showing that the reinsurance is in force. Alternatively, if the direct writer places the case with another reinsurer, the reinsurer changes the case file's status from *pending* to *withdrawn*.

In the process of establishing case files and reserving capacity, the reinsurer's staff perform the following activities, which may not always occur in the sequence shown:

- Comparing the request for coverage to the reinsurance agreement
- Checking the reinsurer's retention and financial capacity
- Assessing the risk
- Arranging retrocession as needed
- Placing the reservation of capacity

Comparing the Request for Coverage to the Reinsurance Agreement. The reinsurance analyst verifies that the direct writer and reinsurer have a reinsurance agreement for the type of coverage requested and that the agreement is in effect for new business. The reinsurance analyst then determines the types and amounts of reinsurance, if any, it is obligated to provide to the direct writer under that agreement and evaluates whether the request for coverage meets all of the agreement's requirements—for example, age limits and residency requirements for the proposed insured, the amount of coverage to be ceded, and the underwriting classification of the proposed insured—for risks to be reinsured.

Verifying Retention and Financial Capacity. The reinsurer checks the amount of its current retention on the insured and its financial capacity. The reinsurer's reinsurance analyst then compares the amount of risk already retained on an insured to the retention limits listed in its retention schedules to determine the amount of additional risk it can accept on that insured and, if necessary, the amount of risk to cede to a retrocessionaire. Some reinsurance administration information systems automatically perform these calculations for the reinsurer.

Assessing the Risk. The first step in assessing a reinsurance risk is determining whether the case requires an underwriting decision. Facultative cases typically require underwriting approval from the reinsurer. For each case submitted on a facultative basis, the reinsurer's underwriters evaluate the underwriting documents that the direct writer sends with the request for coverage and decide whether to make an offer, decline the case, or ask the direct writer to provide additional information. This evaluation and decision-making process usually is called *facultative reinsurance underwriting*.

The process for facultative reinsurance underwriting is very similar to primary underwriting, which is the underwriting process performed by a direct writer. However, reinsurance underwriters tend to work more often with unusual or problematic cases—such as those involving very large face amounts, complicated medical factors, unusual avocations, or celebrities—than do primary underwriters. Also, in primary underwriting, the underwriter's judgment of an insurance producer's integrity traditionally has played a role in the underwriting decision. A reinsurance underwriter is concerned primarily with the quality of the direct writer's underwriting department and is less concerned with the producer.

Although reinsurance analysts do not assess reinsurance risks, a reinsurance analyst may be responsible for collecting the required underwriting documents and information, organizing those documents appropriately in a case file, and referring the file to the reinsurer's underwriters. Typically, a case file includes two types of underwriting-related documents: (1) documents received from the direct writer and (2) documents generated by the reinsurer's information systems. Figure 11.3 provides a list of underwriting-related documents often included in an individual life reinsurance case file. An individual health reinsurance case file also may include information on family members covered under the policy to be reinsured.

A reinsurance case file for a group life or health insurance case includes information about the proposed insured group, such as the group's name, size, location, and industry; the scope of coverage; the basis for determining the amount of coverage for each individual; and each group member's sex, date of birth, and salary. Disability income reinsurance case files are similar to life case files for either individuals or groups. However, disability income reinsurance case files include more information about the proposed insured's occupation and income than do life case files.

In North America, case files often include information obtained from MIB. Each MIB-member direct writer and reinsurer has guidelines for obtaining MIB reports. Many reinsurers require MIB reports for all life cases underwritten on a medical basis. Other reinsurers may require MIB reports for facultative cases, for fac-ob cases in which retrocessionaires will be used, or for insureds who are over a certain age—for example, 65—or for whom a particularly large amount of reinsurance has been requested.

The reinsurer's underwriter notifies the direct writer of the decision to accept or decline the facultative case. If the underwriter declines the case, the reinsurance analyst or underwriter changes the status of the case file to *declined*.

Arranging Retrocession. Most reinsurers have established multiple automatic retrocession agreements with professional retrocessionaires, other reinsurers, or retrocession pools. A ***retrocession pool***, also called a *retro pool*, is a group of two or more professional retrocessionaires or reinsurers that jointly reinsure retroceded risks.

If the amount that the reinsurer needs to retrocede exceeds the amount covered by the reinsurer's established automatic retrocession arrangements, the reinsurer generally has four options:

FIGURE 11.3 Underwriting-Related Documents Often Included in a Case File

Documents Provided by the Direct Writer

- Cover page containing information about the insured and the reinsurance applied for, including the insured's name, residence, date of birth, underwriting classification, and amount of reinsurance
- Letter from the direct writer to the reinsurer
- Insurance application
- Nonmedical supplement
- Medical questionnaires, such as questionnaires for asthma and diabetes
- Personal questionnaires, such as questionnaires for aviation and scuba diving
- Medical or paramedical report
- Laboratory and x-ray reports
- Physician and hospital reports
- Results of an electrocardiogram
- Inspection report
- Statements describing the insured's financial position
- Motor vehicle records/driving history
- Correspondence with the proposed insured, applicant, producer, medical personnel, and others with relevant information
- Documentation that the direct writer has confirmed that the insurance applicant, policyowner, insured, and beneficiary are not included on any applicable government lists of suspected terrorists

Documents Generated by the Reinsurer

- Reinsurer's underwriting worksheet
- Documentation of the retention check
- Status code documentation
- The underwriting decision sent to the direct writer and worksheets compiled by reinsurance analysts
- Documentation that the reinsurer has confirmed that the insurance applicant, policyowner, insured, and beneficiary are not included on any applicable government lists of suspected terrorists

Source: Adapted from Jane Lightcap Brown and Jennifer W. Herrod, *Reinsurance Administration* [Atlanta: LOMA (Life Office Management Association, Inc.), © 2000], 177. Used with permission; all rights reserved.

- Pursue retrocession coverage with a retrocessionaire or retrocession pool with which the reinsurer currently does not have a reinsurance agreement
- Ask retrocessionaires or retro pool members to increase the amount they are willing to accept facultatively
- Accept a smaller amount of the risk and notify the direct writer to seek additional reinsurance
- Decline to reinsure the case (for facultative and fac-ob cases only)

Placing the Reservation. If the reinsurer offers to reinsure the case, the reinsurer codes the status of the file as *reserved*. This reserved status holds the required capacity for a specified period of time, such as 90 days. The reinsurer assigns the reservation a ***date of expiry***—the date on which the reinsurer will cancel the reservation of reinsurance capacity if the reinsurer does not receive a cession or other placement information from the direct writer. Typically, the date of expiry falls between 90 and 120 days after the date the reservation was made.

Following Up on Reserved Capacity

A direct writer's reinsurance administration system may track the capacity the company has reserved with reinsurers and contact each reinsurer as appropriate regarding potential offers, cessions, delays in processing cases, or cancellations of reserved capacity. Reinsurers also periodically check for reservations that are near their dates of expiry. Follow-up on reserved capacity helps the reinsurer avoid maintaining reserved capacity that the direct writer does not need.

Most reinsurers' administration systems generate lists of outstanding cases for which (1) the date of expiry is near and (2) the direct writer has not sent a cession, a drop notice, or an extension request.

- A ***drop notice***, or *close notice*, is a written notification from a direct writer to a reinsurer stating that the direct writer no longer needs reinsurance that it previously requested and asking the reinsurer to cancel the reservation.
- An ***extension request*** is a request from a direct writer to a reinsurer to extend the direct writer's reservation of capacity for a specified period so that the direct writer can gather all information needed to move the case from *reserved* to *placed* status.

To follow up on reserved capacity, the reinsurer sends a notice of expiry to each direct writer that has outstanding cases close to their dates of expiry. A ***notice of expiry*** is a document the reinsurer uses to notify the direct writer that an offer to reinsure is due to expire and to request additional information, a cession, a drop notice, or an extension request from the direct writer. The direct writer marks on the notice of expiry the status of each case listed and returns the notice to the reinsurer, along with any cessions, drop notices, requests for extensions, or requested information.

Placement of Reinsurance

Placement is a process in which the direct writer and reinsurer activate reinsurance coverage for a new automatic, facultative, or fac-ob cession. To begin placement, the direct writer verifies which reinsurer should receive the cession and provides specified information about the risk to the reinsurer. Figure 11.4 identifies the information that a direct writer typically provides to a reinsurer for cession of coverage on an individual life insurance policy.

FIGURE 11.4 Information Included in a New Business Cession for an Individual Life Insurance Policy

- Full name of insured
- Date of birth
- Issue age
- Issue date (for self-administered reinsurance)
- Age basis (last or nearest birthday)
- Sex
- Residence
- Underwriting classification
- Tobacco use/nonuse
- Policy number
- Effective date of policy
- Face amount of policy
- Plan name or code (with a reference list)
- Automatic/facultative indicator
- YRT/coinsurance indicator
- Amount ceded to reinsurer, separated by primary coverage, waiver of premium, accidental death benefit, and so on
- Reinsurance premiums, separated by primary coverage, waiver of premium, accidental death benefit, and so on (for self-administered reinsurance)
- Annual waived premium, if applicable
- Amount of any allowances (for self-administered reinsurance)
- Extra premium (e.g., $5/1000/5 years) or underwriting rating
- Net amount at risk for the first five years, if not level
- Currency in which reinsurance records will be kept
- Effective date of reinsurance, if different from policy effective date

Source: Adapted from Jane Lightcap Brown and Jennifer W. Herrod, *Reinsurance Administration* [Atlanta: LOMA (Life Office Management Association, Inc.), © 2000], 183. Used with permission; all rights reserved.

After receiving a new business cession, the reinsurance analyst marks the case as *placed*, updates the reinsurance administration system, and sends reinsurance certificates as necessary. A ***reinsurance certificate*** is a document that notifies the direct writer that reinsurance is officially in force. A reinsurance certificate includes information about the insured, the reinsured policy, and the terms of the applicable reinsurance agreement. Reinsurers generally send reinsurance certificates only for individual cession reinsurance and not for self- or bulk-administered reinsurance.

Administering In-Force Business

The party administering the reinsurance records provides the information needed for in-force administration through a variety of reports. For simplicity, we refer to the reinsurance party that administers the reinsurance records and reports as the *reporting party*. The reinsurance parties use the information in reinsurance reports to

- Verify that reinsurance transactions comply with the terms of the applicable reinsurance agreement
- Prepare statements and reports for financial and management accounting
- Produce policy reserve reports for various regulatory and accounting bodies
- Study lapse experience
- Detect unusual trends
- Conduct profitability and mortality studies
- Maintain historical data to use for future pricing

Reporting on In-Force Business

To provide information related to changes in risk, revenue, expenses, and policy reserves, the reporting party typically prepares five types of reports: in-force policy report, policy exhibit, policy change report, billing statement, and reserve listing. Although the format of reinsurance reports varies from agreement to agreement, the information included in such reports generally is the same. Most reinsurance reports are in electronic form.

In-Force Policy Report

An ***in-force policy report*** is a reinsurance report that lists all in-force reinsured policies as of a given date and provides detailed information about each policy. The in-force policy report allows the direct writer and reinsurer to verify that they are keeping accurate, parallel records. For self-administered reinsurance, the direct writer typically provides the report to the reinsurer monthly, quarterly, or annually.

Figure 11.5 shows a section of an in-force policy report. Note that an actual in-force policy report would include additional columns for the policy number, underwriting rating or class, tobacco use status, plan of insurance, face amount of the policy, and proportion of risk reinsured.

For group life insurance, the in-force policy report includes the policy number; effective date; plan of insurance; information about the group, such as the group name, number of group insureds, and amount of coverage for each class; total insurance coverage provided by the policy; the amount or proportion of risk reinsured; and the amount of reinsurance in force.

Policy Exhibit

A ***policy exhibit*** is a reinsurance report that summarizes and reconciles the changes that have occurred in reinsured policies during the reporting period. Such changes may include new business, increases and decreases in policy face amounts, conversions, lapses, deaths, terminations, and reinstatements. The policy exhibit usually presents a beginning total policy count and reinsured risk amount, any increases or decreases in the policy count and reinsured risk amount, and a final total policy count and reinsured risk amount for that reporting period. A portion of a policy exhibit is shown in Figure 11.6.

FIGURE 11.5 Portion of an In-Force Policy Report

Individual In-Force Report

Agreement	Cession	Insured	Effective Date	DOB	Issue Age	Sex	Auto/ Fac	Reinsurance NAR ($)
200300	12334	Rosen, David	05/05/1998	11/02/1944	53	M	F	200,000
200500	14558	Cooper, Jalen	12/12/2000	03/22/1945	55	M	A	75,000
200500	14611	Abrams, Martin	10/01/2000	07/10/1960	40	M	A	16,161
300200	16199	Nalibotsy, Sophie	12/13/2001	05/05/1955	46	F	A	200,000

Source: Adapted from Jane Lightcap Brown and Jennifer W. Herrod, *Reinsurance Administration* [Atlanta: LOMA (Life Office Management Association, Inc.), © 2000], 190. Used with permission; all rights reserved.

FIGURE 11.6 Portion of a Policy Exhibit

Reinsurance Policy Exhibit
Ceded to: Mid-state Reinsurance Company
For the Period of: 04/01/07–06/30/07
Agreement #: 24653

	Count	Reinsured Amount ($)	Risk Amount ($)	Reinsurance Premium ($)
Beginning In-Force	15	8,320,000	8,320,000	90,231.38
New Business	2	350,000	350,000	4,885.11
Reinstatements	0	0	0	0
Conversions On	0	0	0	0
Other Increases	0	0	0	0
Deaths	0	0	0	0
Maturities	0	0	0	0
Expiries	0	0	0	0
Surrenders	0	0	0	0
Lapses	1	100,000	100,000	598.50
Conversions Off	1	500,000	500,000	5,120.00
Recaptures	0	0	0	0
Rescissions	0	0	0	0
Other Decreases	0	0	0	0
Ending In-Force	15	8,070,000	8,070,000	89,397.99

Source: Adapted from Jane Lightcap Brown and Jennifer W. Herrod, *Reinsurance Administration* [Atlanta: LOMA (Life Office Management Association, Inc.), © 2000], 191. Used with permission; all rights reserved.

Policy Change Report

A ***policy change report***, also known as a *transaction report*, is a reinsurance report that shows details for all policies that, during the reporting period, have changed in a way that affects the amount of the reinsurance coverage, the reinsurance premium, or the allowance. Policy terminations due to death or policy lapse, increases or decreases in the face amount, and reinstatements are examples of changes typically listed on a policy change report. Figure 11.7 shows a portion of a policy change report. A policy change report also may show any changes in reinsurance premiums associated with the policy changes.

FIGURE 11.7 Portion of a Policy Change Report

Policy Changes for February 1, 2008 to February 29, 2008

Reinstatements

Agreement	YRT/ COI	Insured	DOB	Plan	Cession Number	Auto/ Fac	Policy	Change Date	Amount ($)
100	COI	Kennison, Gary	6/26/1962	XX	32334	A	59959934	2/13/2008	300,000
100	COI	Lapcevich, Alvin	1/25/1956	XY	32699	A	60259887	2/24/2008	200,000
200	YRT	Prince, Dawson	4/30/1950	XZ	32788	A	60265888	2/14/2008	240,000

Lapses

Agreement	YRT/ COI	Insured	DOB	Plan	Cession Number	Auto/ Fac	Policy	Change Date	Amount ($)
200	COI	Cook, Demetrius	5/22/1955	XX	32445	A	60001242	2/20/2008	280,000
300	COI	Sehra, Azad	9/23/1948	XY	33699	A	60002545	2/02/2008	135,000

Terminations

Agreement	YRT/ COI	Insured	DOB	Plan	Cession Number	Auto/ Fac	Policy	Change Date	Amount ($)
100	COI	Thayer, Alyssa	9/10/1950	XX	31454	A	60000112	2/06/2008	250,000

Decreases

Agreement	YRT/ COI	Insured	DOB	Plan	Cession Number	Auto/ Fac	Policy	Change Date	Amount ($)
300	YRT	Sanchez, Guillermo	2/12/1957	XF	35799	F	60021450	2/07/2008	8,000
400	YRT	Baker, Gretchen	8/02/1960	XJ	36002	A	60001234	2/05/2008	12,000

Source: Adapted from Jane Lightcap Brown and Jennifer W. Herrod, *Reinsurance Administration* [Atlanta: LOMA (Life Office Management Association, Inc.), © 2000], 192. Used with permission; all rights reserved.

Billing Statement

A ***billing statement*** is a reinsurance report that lists the amounts owed by and due to each party to the reinsurance agreement. (The policy change report also may show this type of information.) If the reporting party owes money to the other reinsurance party, the reporting party usually sends payment of the amount owed along with the billing statement. If the nonreporting party owes money to the reporting party, the billing statement notifies the nonreporting party of the amount that it owes. A portion of a simplified billing statement is shown in Figure 11.8. Note that an actual billing statement (1) divides reinsurance premiums and allowances into first-year and renewal amounts and (2) includes information about any refund of premiums, policy dividends, and cash surrender value reimbursements.

The reporting party typically uses a separate statement to bill amounts that are calculated on a collective basis rather than on a per-policy basis. Such amounts include modco reserve adjustments and experience refunds.

Reserve Listing

A ***reserve listing*** is a reinsurance report that shows all policies reinsured and the reserve held for each policy. The reserve listing helps the parties determine the appropriate amount of reserves to maintain for the reinsured portion of each policy in force at the end of the reporting period. Figure 11.9 shows a portion of a reserve listing.

Processing Changes in Reinsurance Coverage

Certain changes to a reinsured policy or a block of reinsurance business can increase or decrease the amount of risk assumed by the reinsurer. New business, recapture, increases or decreases in a policy's face amount, claims, surrenders, lapses, reinstatements, conversions, and maturity are all examples of changes that can affect the amount of risk covered by reinsurance. The direct writer must notify the reinsurer promptly of any such

FIGURE 11.8 Portion of a Billing Statement

Policy	Insured	Date	Cession	Initial Amount ($)	NAR ($)	Reinsurance Premium ($)	Allow-ances ($)	Net Amount Owed to the Reinsurer ($)
10201	Hanson, Emily	1/08/2007	23454	200,000	200,000	230.00	46.00	184.00
10324	Best, Kyle	1/18/2007	23535	240,000	240,000	691.20	138.24	552.96
10402	Nagpal, Sailesh	1/20/2007	25699	400,000	400,000	848.00	135.68	712.32
10498	Strausser, Joan	1/29/2007	25780	90,000	90,000	574.20	765.68	(191.48)

Source: Adapted from Jane Lightcap Brown and Jennifer W. Herrod, *Reinsurance Administration* [Atlanta: LOMA (Life Office Management Association, Inc.), © 2000], 193. Used with permission; all rights reserved.

changes. Other changes—such as corrections to an insured's name—may not affect the amount at risk under a reinsured policy, but such changes still require administration.

The direct writer's reinsurance analyst generally is responsible for updating reinsurance administration records to reflect changes to a reinsured policy and for notifying the appropriate staff at both the direct writer and the reinsurer of the changes. The direct writer may report changes to reinsured policies on a collective basis—as is the case with a policy exhibit—or on a policy-by-policy basis, under which the reinsurer receives detailed updates on each policy reinsured and not just a summary of total results. In either case, direct writers and reinsurers typically use automated systems to process and transmit or receive changes to the reinsurance coverage.

The reinsurer may require approval from its underwriting department for certain types of risk changes to policies reinsured on a facultative basis. Examples of such changes that may require an underwriter's approval are reinstatements, changes from smoker to nonsmoker status, or reinsurance increases not specified in the reinsurance agreement. The reinsurer's reinsurance analyst also may need to verify that the agreement provides for certain types of changes, such as recaptures, policy reductions, and conversions. For an increase in the face amount of a reinsured policy, the reinsurance analyst checks the reinsurer's retention to determine if the reinsurer needs to retrocede some of the additional risk to avoid becoming over-retained.

Processing Billing Statements

Billing statements usually involve the receipt or payment of funds. A direct writer that uses self-administration or bulk administration produces the billing statements for its reinsurance arrangements and includes the statements with its reinsurance premium payments to reinsurers. The reinsurer produces billing statements for (1) individual cession reinsurance

FIGURE 11.9 Portion of a Reserve Listing

Statutory Reserves

Policy	Plan Code	Effective Date	Age	Attained Age	Sex	Name	Face Amount ($)	Ceded Amount ($)	NAR ($)	Factor	Amount Reserve ($)
122467	XX	5/15/1996	37	48	F	Howell	100,000	94,242	44,272	4.45	8.21
122678	XZ	8/25/1997	43	53	M	Ryan	500,000	370,555	320,555	9.19	122.75
123566	XX	1/14/1998	31	40	M	Hemphill	100,000	95,768	45,768	3.42	6.52

Source: Adapted from Jane Lightcap Brown and Jennifer W. Herrod, *Reinsurance Administration* [Atlanta: LOMA (Life Office Management Association, Inc.), © 2000], 193. Used with permission; all rights reserved.

arrangements and (2) retrocessionaires to whom the reinsurer cedes business. The nonreporting party processes the billing statements provided by the reporting party. Note that direct writers and reinsurers typically use automated systems to prepare and process billing statements and that many or all of the processing activities we attribute to reinsurance analysts actually are performed by computerized reinsurance administration systems.

If a payment accompanies a billing statement, the nonreporting party's reinsurance analyst verifies that the amount due according to the statement matches the amount of the enclosed payment. If the nonreporting party owes money, the analyst verifies that the amount requested by the reporting party is accurate and arranges for the payment to the reporting party. For each payment made or received, the reinsurance analyst updates the corresponding record in the reinsurance administration system. Depending on the direct writer's or reinsurer's practices, the reinsurance analyst may enter information for each individual policy or only summarized information for blocks of policies.

If a billing statement from a direct writer indicates that the reinsurer owes amounts for premium tax refunds, experience refunds, or cash value or policy dividend payment reimbursements, the reinsurer's reinsurance analyst first verifies that, in the applicable reinsurance agreement, the reinsurer agreed to participate in the requested type of refund or reimbursement. The reinsurance analyst then proceeds to determine or verify the amount due and request the appropriate payment to the direct writer.

Premium Tax Refunds

The determination of the amount of a premium tax refund depends on the requirements in the applicable reinsurance agreement. The direct writer calculates the refund as either an exact percentage based on the premium taxes the direct writer actually paid or as an estimated percentage specified in the agreement.

Experience Refunds

A reinsurance agreement that provides for payment of experience refunds to the direct writer also specifies the formula for calculating the refund. The reinsurance analyst confirms that the direct writer has used the specified formula to calculate the refund and verifies the accuracy of the amount requested.

Cash Value and Policy Dividend Payment Reimbursements

A ***cash value reimbursement*** is a monetary amount the reinsurer reimburses the direct writer under a coinsurance or modco reinsurance agreement when a life insurance policyowner surrenders a reinsured policy in exchange for the policy's cash value. The result of this surrender is termination of the reinsurance on the policy. Reinsurance agreements generally require the direct writer to inform the reinsurer as soon as possible when policies terminate and the direct writer has disbursed cash values.

Also, a reinsurance agreement may require the reinsurer to reimburse the direct writer for a portion of policy dividend payments made to the policyowners of participating policies. In general, under a coinsurance or modco agreement, the reinsurer participates in cash value and policy dividend payments, whereas the reinsurer in a YRT agreement does not.

To process a request for cash value reimbursement or policy dividend payment reimbursement, the reinsurance analyst verifies the accuracy of the amount requested according to the terms of the reinsurance agreement. The amount due for policy dividend reimbursement also depends on the direct writer's current scale for policy dividends. For cash value reimbursements, the reinsurance analyst terminates the corresponding policy records in the reinsurer's administration system.

Recording Policy Reserves

When a reinsurer receives policy reserve calculations from a direct writer that self-administers its business, or when the reinsurer's actuaries calculate reserves for business that the reinsurer administers, the reinsurance analyst is responsible for updating the information in the reinsurance administration records.

Administering Terminations of Reinsurance

Reinsurance coverage can be terminated as a result of recapture; the lapse, surrender, expiration, or maturity of the reinsured policy; and, for life insurance, the death of the insured. The process for terminating reinsurance is similar for terminations due to recapture, lapse, surrender, expiration, or maturity. However, terminating reinsurance coverage due to recapture requires an extra administrative step for the reinsurer. If a reinsurer receives notice that a direct writer wishes to recapture part or all of a reinsured risk, the reinsurance analyst first must verify that the reinsurance agreement allows recapture at that time. If the agreement does not allow the recapture, the reinsurance analyst arranges for approval of the request for recapture before terminating the reinsurance in the reinsurance administration records.

After the direct writer notifies the reinsurer of a termination due to recapture, lapse, surrender, expiration, or maturity, the reinsurer's analyst verifies the effective date for the termination of reinsurance; the policies included in the termination; the current net amount at risk; any premium refund that may be applicable; and—for any case involving coinsurance or modco reinsurance—expense allowances, policy dividends, or cash value. For recaptures, the analyst also determines whether the direct writer owes any recapture fee.

For all types of terminations, (1) the direct writer must transfer all reinsurance premiums and information due, (2) the reinsurer must process all statements from the direct writer, and (3) the direct writer's current in-force listing must match the reinsurer's records. The reinsurer then terminates the reinsurance administration records for the affected policies and arranges for the refund of any unearned reinsurance premium to the direct writer.

Administering Claims Under Reinsured Policies

The direct writer makes the decisions on whether to pay claims submitted under reinsured policies. Typically, the direct writer informs the reinsurer of such claim decisions and requests the reinsurer's payment for its portion of any benefits paid or due to the policy beneficiary. The reinsurer's claim analysts—with assistance from the company's reinsurance analysts—then decide whether to reimburse the direct writer the requested portion of the claim payment. A reinsurer's claim analysts and reinsurance analysts collaborate to

- Ensure that the reinsurer pays only valid claims that are reinsured under a valid reinsurance agreement
- Respond to claims promptly, accurately, and professionally by meeting all internal guidelines and all external legal and regulatory requirements
- Ensure that the reinsurer records accurate information for claims and processes claim payments in an accurate and timely manner

For most reinsurers, a reinsurance analyst has the following administrative responsibilities for claims:

- Establishing a claim file
- Verifying information related to the reinsured policy and the claim
- Securing approval for the claim
- Settling the claim in some companies

The reinsurance analyst also may notify the retrocessionaire of a claim on which the reinsurer has retroceded a portion of the risk. At some reinsurers, claim analysts handle some of the responsibilities we assign to reinsurance analysts.

Establishing the Claim File

The reinsurance claim administration process begins when the direct writer's reinsurance analyst sends the reinsurer a claim notice with information about the

- Insured
- Loss incurred—for example, medical expenses incurred
- Reinsured policy or policies that the direct writer has in force on the insured
- Reinsurance arrangements for the applicable policy or policies
- Status of the claim—for example, *under investigation*, *approved but not paid*, or *paid*
- Amount of payment requested for the claim

The analyst also sends the reinsurer a copy of the following documents:

- A copy of the claim submitted to the direct writer by the claimant—usually the insured, a healthcare provider who treated the insured, or the beneficiary of a life insurance policy—or a representative of the claimant, such as a producer
- A copy of the proof of loss, such as an itemized list of health services provided to the insured and the charges for those services or an official document verifying the insured's death
- A copy of the proof of claim payment, if the direct writer has already paid the claim

The reinsurance analyst then monitors the time required for the reinsurer to settle its claim liability for the case.

The reinsurer's reinsurance analyst establishes a ***claim file***, which is an organized collection of all the information relevant to a claim. For example, an individual life reinsurance claim file typically includes the following information:

- Insured's name, sex, and date of birth
- Date of the insured's death, if known
- Name of the direct writer
- Policy number assigned by the direct writer

- Name of and contact information for the person at the direct writer who can provide further information about the claim
- Date the reinsurer received the claim

The claim file also includes the copies of the claim submitted to the direct writer, the proof of loss, and, if applicable, the proof of claim payment. The reinsurance analyst makes notes in the claim file about the applicable reinsurance arrangement, the reinsured risk for the policy, and any reinsurance claim activities in progress or completed.

Verifying Claim-Related Information

Next, the reinsurer's reinsurance analyst—or in some cases, a claim analyst—performs a variety of activities to determine if the reinsurer has a liability under the claim and, if so, the amount of that liability.

Verifying the Policy Status and the Reinsurance Agreement

The reinsurance analyst verifies

- That a reinsurance agreement covers the policy under which the claim was submitted
- That the policy and the reinsurance on the policy were in force at the time of the loss
- Whether any policy changes—such as reinstatements and increases—affected the cession.

The reinsurance analyst then determines whether the reinsurer has reinsured other policies from any other direct writer on this insured. If the reinsurer is covering other policies for the same insured, the analyst notes these policies and direct writers in the claim file. The reinsurance analyst also checks for any amounts retroceded on the case. If the claim involves retroceded coverage, the reinsurance analyst creates a ***retrocession claim file***—that is, a file containing all the information relevant to the claim, plus information about the retrocession—to use when the reinsurer notifies its retrocessionaires of the claim.

Verifying Payment of Reinsurance Premiums

The reinsurance analyst confirms that the direct writer has paid the reinsurance premiums on the case and adds the premium-related information to the claim file. The reinsurance analyst also calculates any premium refunds due if the reinsurance coverage terminates as a result of the claim.

Verifying Claim Compliance with the Reinsurance Agreement

The reinsurance analyst or, at some companies, the claim analyst confirms that the reinsurer is responsible for paying the requested claim amount to the direct writer, based on the criteria set forth for reinsured claim risks in the applicable reinsurance agreement. Figure 11.10 lists the types of reinsurance agreement specifications with which a claim submitted under a reinsured policy typically must comply.

The reinsurance analyst also determines whether any special instructions or arrangements govern the policy. For example, the reinsurance analyst notifies the claim analyst if the reinsurer has the right to review the claim and offer its opinion to the direct writer on whether to pay the claim, known as the ***right of recommendation***. If any discrepancies exist between the claim and the terms of the reinsurance agreement, the reinsurance analyst refers the case to a claim analyst for further examination.

Reviewing the Proof of Loss

The reinsurance analyst or claim analyst verifies that the direct writer has provided a proper proof of loss to the reinsurer. For a disability income insurance claim, for example, the direct writer submits a physician's statement that confirms the disability. The reinsurance analyst reviews the proof documents and confirms that they apply to the insured and adds the proof documents to the claim file.

FIGURE 11.10 Reinsurance Agreement Specifications for Claim Liability

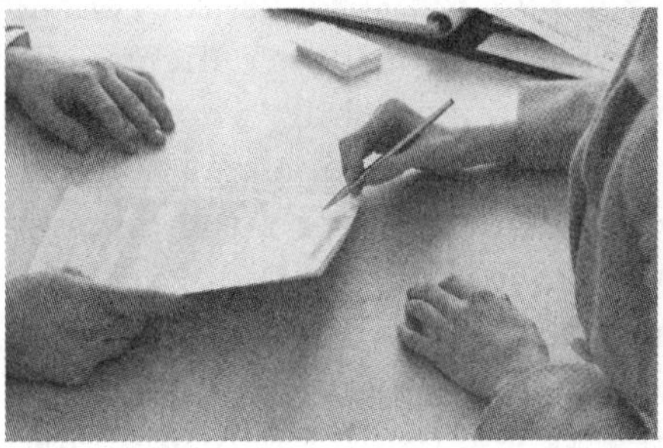

The claim must comply with the reinsurance agreement's specifications for the

- Type of policy
- Information used to underwrite the policy
- Underwriting classification of the insured
- Age limits for policy issue
- Effective date of the policy
- Allowable coverage
- Maximum amount of risk to be ceded per policy
- Jumbo limit
- Quota share arrangements

Determining Whether the Claim Is Fraudulent or Contestable

Both reinsurance analysts and claim analysts of the reinsurer check claims for signs of fraud. The reinsurance and claim analysts also check each life insurance claim to determine if it is contestable. A ***contestable claim*** is a claim for life insurance policy proceeds following the death of an insured during the policy's contestable period.

If a claim is not contestable, the reinsurance analyst typically refers the claim to the claim analyst for approval. If a claim is contestable, the reinsurance analyst notes the length of time the policy has been in force, checks MIB records if the reinsurer is a member of MIB, and sends the claim to the claim analyst for further investigation.

Determining the Reinsurer's Claim Liability

For coinsurance or modco reinsurance, the reinsurance analyst uses the information found in the reinsurance agreement and reinsurance administration records to determine the reinsurer's claim liability. The reinsurance administration records for a policy reinsured under quota share reinsurance may not provide the reinsurer's claim liability. In this case, the analyst calculates the reinsurer's claim liability by multiplying the direct writer's claim liability by the quota share percentage.

For example, if the direct writer has $200,000 of claim liability under a policy, and the reinsurer has reinsured the policy using a 60 percent quota share, the reinsurer's claim liability on the policy is $120,000, calculated as follows:

$$\$200,000 \times 0.60 = \$120,000$$

For YRT reinsurance, the reinsurer's claim liability is based on the reinsurer's NAR. For some policies—such as traditional whole life policies—the direct writer generally knows at the time of policy issue the policy reserve amounts for future years. When a policy's future policy reserve amounts are known in advance, the reinsurance administration records for the policy often include a schedule that shows the reinsurer's NAR. However, the direct writer typically cannot predict accurately the future policy reserves and resulting NAR for products with flexible or indeterminate premium rates. When a policy's future policy reserves and NAR are not predictable in advance, the reinsurance analyst generally refers to the most recent billing statement for the reinsurer's current NAR.

If the reinsurer's claim liability calculated by the reinsurance analyst is the same as the reinsurer's claim liability specified on the direct writer's claim notice, the reinsurance analyst updates the claim file to show the reinsurer's claim liability. If the two amounts are not the same, the reinsurance analyst refers the case to the claim analyst for investigation of the discrepancy.

Approving the Claim Liability

As mentioned earlier, the reinsurer's claim analysts typically evaluate all requests for claim payment reimbursements and make the decisions regarding claim liabilities owed to the direct writer. Each reinsurer establishes guidelines specifying which staff can approve various amounts and types of reinsurance claim liabilities. In some companies, reinsurance analysts have the authority to approve claim liabilities up to certain amounts under particular circumstances. However, the same reinsurance analyst that verified the information related to a claim generally cannot approve that claim liability. For simplicity, we assume that the person responsible for approving or denying a reinsurance claim liability is a claim analyst.

After approving a reinsurance claim liability, the claim analyst either settles the claim liability or instructs a reinsurance analyst or another claim analyst to settle the liability. After denying a claim, the claim analyst generally notifies the direct writer of the decision and advises the reinsurance analyst who verified the claim-related information how to update the reinsurance administration records.

Settling the Claim Liability

The reinsurance analyst or claim analyst settling the claim liability usually communicates the amount of the payment to the direct writer and arranges for the payment to be made. Some bulk-administered reinsurance arrangements allow the direct writer to net off claims from billing statements. ***Netting off*** is a process by which a direct writer subtracts the claim amount owed to it by a reinsurer from the amount that the direct writer owes the reinsurer for premiums. If the reinsurance agreement allows netting off, the direct writer notifies the reinsurer of a claim through the billing statement, which shows claim amounts that the direct writer has netted off.

Notifying Retrocessionaires of a Claim Liability

If the reinsurer retroceded a portion of the reinsured risk to a retrocessionaire, the reinsurer sends the retrocessionaire a copy of the proof of loss, the claim form, and the proof of the claim liability payment to the direct writer, along with a request for payment from the retrocessionaire. The retrocessionaire then examines the claim, secures approval for the claim liability to the reinsurer, and settles the claim liability with the reinsurer.

Auditing Reinsurance Operations

Direct writers and reinsurers undertake quality control activities, including quantitative and qualitative performance measurements, to ensure that their staffs are following appropriate procedures for reinsurance operations. Auditing is one of the primary methods that direct writers and reinsurers use for quality control. The purpose of an audit is to examine the effectiveness of interrelated objectives, procedures, personnel, records, and process controls. A ***process control*** is a procedure that allows an organization to monitor the accuracy of its processes on a regular, ongoing basis.

Both direct writers and reinsurers conduct internal audits of their companies' own reinsurance activities. In addition, reinsurance agreements typically grant the reinsurer the right to conduct periodic external audits of the direct writer.

Internal Audits

The purpose of an internal audit of reinsurance activities is to verify that the company's employees are meeting service standards; recording accurate, complete, and current data in the company's records; and following established procedures as defined by the company and its reinsurance agreements. For example, a direct writer's internal audit might include the following questions:

- Do the staff members transmit information about new cessions and changes to in-force policies to the reinsurer in an accurate and timely manner?
- Do the direct writer's employees adhere to the reinsurance agreement provisions regarding retention limits and recapture?

A reinsurer's internal audit might evaluate how accurately the reinsurer's staff members calculate reinsurance premiums and other financial amounts.

Each direct writer's or reinsurer's auditors review the procedural documentation for reinsurance and selected reinsurance cases to determine whether the company's staff followed documented procedures regarding recordkeeping and administrative processes. Internal audits can help to identify any potential shortcomings and opportunities for improvement in a company's process controls.

An internal audit may focus on a single aspect of reinsurance, such as claims or underwriting, or it may cover several or all aspects of reinsurance operations. After an internal audit is completed, the company's auditors summarize the audit findings in a report for the company's managers.

External Audits by the Reinsurer

Reinsurance agreements contain an ***access to records provision***, which gives the reinsurance company the authority to examine the direct writer's records related to the business conducted between the companies. Reinsurers typically conduct external audits of a direct writer every two to three years. Both the direct writer and the reinsurer have a right to request additional unscheduled external audits of the direct writer. The direct writer may request an external audit to obtain the reinsurer's objective opinion about any aspect of the direct writer's operations, such as its underwriting processes or its information systems. The reinsurer may request an unscheduled external audit if it discovers irregularities in reinsurance administration by the direct writer. The audits provide information for the reinsurer and the direct writer, and the results are not made public.

In a reinsurer's external audit of a direct writer, the reinsurer's representatives visit the direct writer and examine various aspects of the direct writer's operations, documents, and data. An external audit may include interviews, examination of records, observation of operations, calculation of various values, and review of procedures manuals. An external audit also typically involves negative testing. In this context, ***negative testing*** is the process of ensuring that the direct writer ceded all of the policies that met the qualifications specified in the reinsurance agreement and no policies that were not covered by the agreement.

Typically, the reinsurer's audit team focuses on the following tasks:

- Understanding the direct writer's operations, workflows, and procedures
- Evaluating the direct writer's administrative processes
- Identifying weaknesses in the direct writer's process control systems
- Evaluating the direct writer's compliance with the reinsurance agreement
- Reviewing cases to verify the accuracy of amounts retained and reinsured, reinsurance premiums charged, policy terminations and lapses, and billing
- Evaluating the timeliness of the direct writer's reporting, particularly for changes to reinsured policies
- Reviewing the direct writer's administration systems

Preparing for an External Audit

Generally, the reinsurer gives the direct writer two to three months' advance notice of an external audit to allow both companies time to prepare for the audit. After negotiating the schedule for the audit, the reinsurer notifies the direct writer about the purposes of the audit, the members of the reinsurance audit team, and the needs of the audit team during the audit. Such needs typically include access to the direct writer's reinsurance computer systems and documentation of processes and process controls for specified administrative activities. For some external audits, the direct writer sends the reinsurer information in advance to allow the reinsurer to conduct a desk audit prior to the on-site evaluation. Insight 11.1 describes the use of desk audits.

The team chooses a sample of reinsured case files to examine on site. The team next prepares a policy audit questionnaire for each policy included in the audit sample. A ***policy audit questionnaire*** is a document that allows an audit team to examine the accuracy and timeliness of data about insureds, compliance with the reinsurance agreement, premium rates, and other elements by comparing the reinsurer's data with the direct writer's data.

INSIGHT 11.1 Desk Audits

In reinsurance, a ***desk audit*** is a reinsurer's systematic review of the quality of the direct writer's reinsurance administration that is performed by the reinsurer's staff at the reinsurer's own offices. Desk audits verify that the information a reinsurer has received from a direct writer is accurate, timely, and in compliance with the applicable reinsurance agreements. A desk audit may replace an external audit or trigger the need for a full external audit if the desk audit reveals significant issues.

When conducting a desk audit, the reinsurer obtains from the direct writer copies of reinsurance case files for a mix of policy types. Typically, the reinsurer requests sample cases that represent standard and substandard underwriting classifications; insureds of both sexes and various ages; various plans and amounts of insurance coverage; facultative, fac-ob, automatic, YRT, and coinsurance cessions; and new business, in-force business, and terminations.

The desk audit is limited in scope because the reinsurer does not have all of the direct writer's resources available as it would during an on-site evaluation, nor does the reinsurer examine information on risks that the direct writer retained. A reinsurer may conduct a very detailed one-time desk audit due to concerns about a particular direct writer. Other desk audits occur at regular intervals or are even ongoing.

Auditors report the findings of a desk audit in detail to the direct writer, including suggestions for correcting noted errors or checking policies needing investigation.

Sources: Adapted from Jane Lightcap Brown and Jennifer W. Herrod, *Reinsurance Administration* [Atlanta: LOMA (Life Office Management Association, Inc.), © 2000], 225–226 and Susan Conant and Miriam A. Orsina, *Principles of Reinsurance* [Atlanta: LOMA (Life Office Management Association, Inc.), © 2006], 243–244. Used with permission; all rights reserved.

Gathering Information and Reviewing Records

At the beginning of the audit, the direct writer's staff instructs the external audit team on how to use the computer system to access needed files. The direct writer's staff may demonstrate policy administration workflow, their billing process, and controls to monitor timeliness, accuracy, and completeness of data.

Next, the external audit team reviews the selected sample files, investigates any special circumstances it encounters, and examines the direct writer's retention management, audit processes, and technology. The external audit team audits the direct writer's underwriting administration by interviewing the direct writer's staff to determine whether they

- Understand automatic binding limits, jumbo limits, and other constraints, so that cases are assigned to appropriate reinsurers
- Understand retention limits and follow appropriate procedures for determining cession amounts
- Follow appropriate procedures for updating files and other system records

In an audit of a direct writer's claim administration, the external audit team ensures that the direct writer's procedures for administering claims are properly documented and that the direct writer's staff applies claim procedures in a timely and accurate manner. The external audit team also evaluates the expertise of the claim staff. The sample files used for auditing claims generally include files of contestable claims, uncontested but large claims, foreign claims, claims involving errors and omissions, claims involving conversions and reinstatements, and any other unusual claims.

Documenting the Audit

At the end of the audit visit, the audit team meets with the direct writer's staff and presents the audit team's initial findings and recommendations. The audit team may help the direct writer solve problems or improve its processes. To document its findings, the audit team prepares a written ***audit report*** that includes the following types of documentation:

- **An analysis of problems.** A brief description of the problems uncovered; an assessment of the severity of each problem; whether the problem is a one-time error or a systemic error; the estimated financial impact of the problem; and the proposed resolution for each problem
- **An internal trip report.** A detailed review of the audit, intended for the reinsurer's management team
- **The audit report.** A document created for the direct writer, communicating the audit's significant findings and recommendations

The direct writer prepares an action plan documenting corrective steps the company has agreed to take.

Following Up after the External Audit

After the direct writer receives the report, the direct writer and reinsurer complete actions agreed to during the audit and correct data and processes as needed. As a part of the follow-up, the direct writer and reinsurer collaborate to resolve problems.

Key Terms

preplacement
reserved capacity
request for coverage
retrocession pool
date of expiry
drop notice
extension request
notice of expiry
placement
reinsurance certificate
in-force policy report
policy exhibit
policy change report
billing statement
reserve listing
cash value reimbursement
claim file
retrocession claim file
right of recommendation
contestable claim
netting off
process control
access to records provision
negative testing
policy audit questionnaire
desk audit
audit report

Endnote

1. Portions of this chapter are adapted from Susan Conant and Miriam A. Orsina, *Principles of Reinsurance* [Atlanta: LOMA (Life Office Management Association, Inc.), © 2006], 179–225, 232, 235–245. Used with permission; all rights reserved.

Part 4: Claim Administration

chapter 12

Overview of Claim Administration

Outline

Claim Philosophy and Practices

Claim Evaluation Process

Claim Staffing and Organization
Staffing
Authority Levels
Organizational Systems

Relationships with Other Insurer Functions

Legal Issues Affecting Claim Administration
Unfair Claims Settlement Practices
Privacy
Financing Terrorists
Fraud

Technology

Claim Administration Quality Control

Learning Objectives

After studying this chapter, you should be able to…

- Explain the importance of an insurer's claim philosophy in guiding its claim practices
- Describe the steps in the claim evaluation process
- Describe the typical staffing, authority levels, and organization of a claim department
- Describe a claim department's relationship with other insurance company functional areas
- Distinguish between compensatory and punitive damages
- Discuss the requirements imposed on insurers by the NAIC Unfair Claims Settlement Practices Act and the NAIC Unfair Life, Accident and Health Claims Settlement Practices Model Regulation
- Identify situations in which an insurer can and cannot conduct a pretext interview
- Identify the warning signs of a fraudulent claim
- Discuss legal requirements related to insurance fraud
- Discuss claim administration quality control

Claim administration is the process of evaluating each submitted claim to determine whether the claim is eligible for payment, informing the person who submitted the claim of the decision, and authorizing the payment of each eligible claim according to the terms of the policy. Effective claim administration fulfills the insurer's responsibilities to its customers (1) to pay all valid claims promptly and accurately and (2) to deny any claim that is not covered under the terms of the policy or is fraudulent.

This chapter serves as an introduction to claim administration. We first explain the importance of an insurer's claim philosophy in guiding its claim practices. Next, we examine the basic activities involved in claim evaluation. Then we describe a typical claim department's staffing, authority levels, and organizational systems and the claim department's relationship with other insurance company functional areas. We also review the primary legal issues affecting claim administration. We conclude with discussions of technology and claim administration quality control.

Claim Philosophy and Practices

An insurer's ***claim philosophy*** is a statement of the insurer's objectives for administering claims. An insurer's senior management typically develops the claim philosophy, which is focused on timely, accurate, equitable, and courteous administration of claims. For example, an insurer's claim philosophy may be "To act promptly, equitably, and courteously in paying all eligible claims and denying all ineligible claims."

Using the insurer's claim philosophy as a foundation, claim administration senior management develops claim practices, which are statements that guide the day-to-day handling of claims. Most insurers' ***claim practices*** include commitments to

- Process claims on a timely basis and notify a claimant if an extended time period is necessary to make a claim determination
- Apply the provisions of policies consistently
- Train claim staff so that they can perform their duties professionally and accurately and can document claim handling appropriately
- Investigate questionable claims
- Obtain medical and legal advice when needed to make a decision on a claim

- Process all claims in compliance with state, provincial, and federal regulations
- Provide claimants with courteous, prompt, and complete explanations of claims for which benefits are not payable or are limited
- Permit claimants to submit additional supporting information on a denied or limited claim
- Provide satisfactory means for appeal of denied claims

The International Claim Association (ICA) has developed and distributed a *Statement of Principles* that companies must adhere to as a condition of membership. Insight 12.1 presents the ICA's *Statement of Principles.*

INSIGHT 12.1 The International Claim Association's Statement of Principles

The International Claim Association, in recognition of the need to continue public trust and confidence in the insurance industry, reaffirms the following principles:

- Any individual who has, or believes he has, a claim is entitled to courteous, fair and just treatment; and shall receive with reasonable promptness an acknowledgment of any communications with respect to his claim.
- Every claimant is entitled to prompt investigation of all facts, an objective evaluation and the fair and equitable settlement of his claim as soon as liability has become reasonably clear.
- Claimants are to be treated equally and without considerations other than those dictated by the provisions of their contracts.
- Claimants shall not be compelled to institute unnecessary litigation in order to recover amounts due, nor shall the failure to settle a claim under one policy or one portion of a policy be used to influence settlement under another policy or portion of a policy.
- Recognizing the obligation to pay promptly all just claims, there is an equal obligation to protect the insurance-buying public from increased costs due to fraudulent or nonmeritorious claims.
- Procedures and practices shall be established to prevent misrepresentation of pertinent facts or policy provisions, to avoid unfair advantage by reason of superior knowledge, and to maintain accurate insurance claim records as privileged and confidential.
- Reasonable standards shall be implemented to provide for adequate personnel, systems and procedures to effectively service claims. These standards shall be such as to eliminate unnecessary delays or requirements, overinsistence on technicalities, and excessive appraisals or examinations. Claim personnel shall be encouraged and assisted in further developing their knowledge, expertise, and professionalism in the field of claim administration.

Source: Reprinted from Statement of Principles, International Claim Association, http://www.claim.org (15 March 2007). Reprinted with permission.

Claim Evaluation Process

When an insurer is notified of a loss, the insurer must provide the claimant with a claim form or another means of supplying notification of loss such as electronic filing through an insurer's Web site. A ***claim form***, also called a *claimant's statement*, is a document containing information about a loss under an insurance policy that is submitted to an insurance company to begin the claim evaluation process. In the case of some health insurance claims, the insurer provides the health care provider with the claim form. The claimant or health care provider then is responsible for completing the claim form and submitting it, along with evidence supporting the claim, which is known as *proof of loss*, to the insurer's claim department. Many health insurers accept standardized electronic claims transmissions from health care providers for medical expense claims.

A ***claim analyst***, also known as a *claim examiner* or *claim adjuster*, is an insurance company employee who reviews claims and determines the company's liability under each claim. When a claim analyst receives the claim form, she begins the claim evaluation process. This process may differ somewhat depending on the type of claim, but it typically is composed of the steps listed in Figure 12.1. The process applies to individual and group claims.

Note that a claim analyst does not always take these steps in the order they are presented here because she may have to wait for information pertaining to some of the steps. Also note that any or all of these steps, which will be discussed further in coming chapters, may be fully automated.

Whether an insurer uses paper or electronic claim files, or a combination of both, the claim analyst is responsible for maintaining a complete record of the progress and disposition of every claim. Particularly when a claim analyst reaches a decision to deny a claim, clear and complete written documentation outlining the claim history and supporting the denial must be made a part of the claim file, because such documentation may be of great value in the event of a legal action on the denial.

Although many claims are received, processed, and completed within a short time, other claims—for example, those for long-term disability—can continue for months or years. The claim analyst must update such claim files and ensure that their contents are current. In many such cases, more than one claim analyst works on a case. Claims analysts find automated workflow systems to be particularly helpful in processing ongoing claims in which multiple claim analysts are involved.

FIGURE 12.1 Steps in the Claim Evaluation Process

1

Verify that the coverage was in force when the loss occurred. The claim analyst must verify that premiums have been paid. For example, if the policy was issued and delivered but the initial premium was never paid, then the policy was never in force and no benefit is payable.

2

Verify that the deceased or the claimant is covered. The claim analyst must determine whether the policy actually covers the deceased under a life insurance policy or the claimant under a health insurance policy. This step is especially important when benefits are claimed under a policy that covers more than one person, such as a family policy or a group policy. Insureds under such policies occasionally mistakenly submit claims for a person who is not covered by the policy. In addition, the claim analyst must verify the identity of the deceased or the claimant as the insured.

3

Verify that the loss occurred. To pay policy benefits, the claim analyst must examine evidence that the reported loss occurred.

4

Determine whether the policy is contestable. If the policy's contestable period has not expired, the claim analyst generally investigates whether the insured made a material misrepresentation on the application. If so, the claim analyst must determine whether the policy should be considered void.

5

Determine whether the loss is covered by the policy. As part of this step, the claim analyst must ensure that the loss is not excluded from the policy's coverage. For example, if a person insured under a life insurance policy died as a the result of suicide during the policy's suicide exclusion period, then the policy's death benefit is not payable; the insurer generally is obligated only to return the premiums paid for such a policy.

6

Calculate the amount of the benefit payable. The claim analyst must apply the policy's method of calculating benefits to the claim.

7

Determine who is entitled to receive the benefit. The claim analyst must determine if the person claiming the benefits is the person entitled to the benefits under the policy.

Source: Adapted from Harriett E. Jones and Monica R. Maxwell, *Regulatory Compliance: Companies, Producers, and Operations*, 2nd ed. [Atlanta: LOMA (Life Office Management Association, Inc.), © 2002], 163–164. Used with permission; all rights reserved.

Claim Staffing and Organization

Insurers have many different systems for ranking their claim personnel, setting authority levels, and assigning claims to claim personnel. The systems used by a particular insurer typically depend on that insurer's size and the variety of products it offers.

Staffing

The day-to-day operations of claim administration are performed by claim analysts and support staff, who are managed by claim supervisors. A vice president or director of claim administration usually oversees the entire claim administration function.

Claim analysts typically are responsible for performing all of the steps in the claim evaluation process listed in Figure 12.1. In addition, claim analysts may explain claim payments, denials, and contract provisions to claimants, providers, and producers.

When claims arrive, most claim departments have support staff who order information needed for a claim decision, establish files, assign case or file numbers to claims, exchange information with other functional areas of the insurance company, and perform other routine actions designed to facilitate the decision-making process. When a claim is approved, the analyst authorizes that payment be made to the person or entity who is to receive benefits; support staff may facilitate the payment process. In some insurance companies, support staff also handle some communications with claimants, providers, and producers.

A claim supervisor, also known as a claim manager, oversees several claim analysts and support staff. Figure 12.2 lists the typical duties of a claim supervisor. Note that a claim supervisor's duties will vary depending on the size of the company and the sophistication of the claim administration system.

Large companies usually assign several supervisors to handle a particular type of product or line of business. For instance, some insurers appoint supervisors for life claims, medical expense claims, and disability income claims, whereas other insurers establish supervisors for individual claims and group claims. Group insurers might assign each group to a specific supervisor.

Authority Levels

Like underwriters, claim analysts receive increasing amounts of decision-making authority as they gain experience and demonstrate enhanced ability and quality of judgment. A new claim analyst usually handles small-amount,

FIGURE 12.2 Typical Duties of a Claim Supervisor

- Assigns cases to claim analysts in the absence of or in addition to workflow systems
- Consults with and advises claim analysts on cases with which the analyst needs assistance
- May handle difficult and large amount cases personally
- Monitors the training and performance of each claim analyst
- Responds to or assists in handling any state insurance department complaints
- Assists with claim audits
- Produces periodic production reports that show the quantity and quality of claims processed by claim analysts or reviews such reports if they are produced by the claim administration system
- Serves as liaison with the insurer's medical director and legal staff

routine claims that present few difficulties or unusual circumstances. A more senior claim analyst or a claim supervisor normally reviews the new claim analyst's work. As the claim analyst gains more experience, he is assigned more decision-making authority; handles less routine, more challenging cases that involve higher coverage amounts or more complex policy forms; and performs his work without the review of a more experienced person. Experienced claim analysts and claim supervisors usually process claims that require extensive investigation or consideration.

Organizational Systems

Some insurers have one claim department that handles claims for all lines of business offered by the company, while other insurers establish separate claim units to handle specific types of coverages, such as life, medical expense, and long-term care. Within these units, an insurer might choose to allocate claims to claim analysts according to a case assignment system, a work division system, or a combination of the two systems. These claim organizational systems are similar to underwriting organizational systems we described in Chapter 2.

Under a case assignment system, the claims typically are divided among claim analysts by alphabet, region, producer, or amount of coverage.[1] The claims received from group insureds under large group policies can be assigned to one or more claim analysts who specialize in handling only those claims.

Under a work division system, claim analysts might work independently to investigate and make decisions on claims, or they might be organized into teams similar to those used for underwriting. Complicated claims may be referred to a committee composed of a claim supervisor and representatives from other functional areas such as underwriting, legal, and medical. However, the role of representatives from other functional areas is to provide counsel rather than to make decisions.

Some insurers also establish a group of claim analysts who are authorized to approve routine or uncomplicated claims in much the same manner that the jet underwriting unit approves routine applications for insurance.

Some insurers hire a third-party administrator to administer claims. Other insurers establish branch offices whose primary purpose is to administer claims. One of an insurer's branch offices might handle only claims submitted under one line of business, and other branch offices might handle claims submitted under other lines of business. Alternatively, an insurer might send simple claims for small amounts of coverage to branch offices or regional service centers, where the claims can be handled electronically and benefit payments can be sent quickly to claimants.

Relationships with Other Insurer Functions

Claim analysts are occasionally in contact with the insurer's underwriters, especially when the analyst suspects misrepresentation or fraud. Claim analysts utilize the underwriters' risk appraisal expertise to review any information first discovered in a claim evaluation and determine how that information would have affected the risk appraisal process. Claim analysts and underwriters also may interact on complex beneficiary designations to make sure that potential problems can be addressed before a policy is issued. Claim analysts also may consult with underwriting regarding the impact that riders have on coverage.

Insight 12.2 outlines some of the approaches insurers have used to foster cooperation between claim administration and underwriting.

Claim analysts also consult with the insurer's medical and legal staff on problematic claims and with producers or vendors who can help gather or verify information related to a claim. Actuaries use statistical information generated by the claim department in setting premium rates for existing and new products, and the insurer's auditors use claim statistics to see if any improvements can be made not only to the claim process, but also to the underwriting process. The insurer's product development staff also uses claim information in developing new products.

INSIGHT 12.2 Fostering Cooperation Between Claim Administration and Underwriting

A firm understanding of the claim administration and underwriting functions improves the accuracy and quality of both underwriting and claim decisions, therefore enhancing the insurer's ability to compete successfully in a highly competitive environment. Recognizing the importance of these functions, insurers foster cooperation between claim administration and underwriting by

- Involving staff from underwriting and claim administration in the development of new insurance products and using data from both functions to evaluate the probable success of new products
- Using staff from both functions to review potential new policy documents, including application forms and claim forms, to check for potential underwriting and claim problems
- Providing cross training so that staff gain a deeper knowledge and better understanding of the work requirements and challenges of both functions

Legal Issues Affecting Claim Administration

Life and health insurance policies are contracts under which the insurer promises to pay policy benefits when those benefits are due. In carrying out this obligation, the insurer has the right to evaluate thoroughly all policy claims that it receives and to enforce the contract terms that govern which losses are covered by the policy. However, if the insurer fails to pay eligible claims when due, the claimant has the right to file an appeal with the insurer. The policy typically states that the claimant must complete the appeal process, which includes a hearing before an appeals committee, before proceeding to a lawsuit against the insurer for breach of contract. Some insurers mandate arbitration instead of a lawsuit.

Whether the lawsuit goes to court or is settled out of court, insurers must pay attorney's fees and other expenses in defending the case; these fees and expenses can be quite substantial. The insurer also suffers a loss of productivity because of the time employees must dedicate to helping the attorneys with the case.

If an insurer is found to have denied a claim improperly, the court can require the insurer to pay ***compensatory damages***, which are monetary awards intended to compensate an injured party for the amount of the monetary losses that resulted from the defendant's improper conduct. In the case of a claim lawsuit, compensatory damages typically consist of the policy benefits and, in some instances, interest.

In addition to compensatory damages, a claimant might receive ***punitive damages***, which are awarded in addition to compensatory damages when a defendant's conduct meets the jurisdiction's standards for behavior that is so egregious as to warrant such damages. The purpose of a punitive damage award is to punish the defendant and to deter others from similar conduct.

Some insurers establish a claim committee to review claim denials that potentially may result in legal action. The claim committee generally consists of senior claim analysts, a management representative, and a law department representative. The claim committee also may be responsible for replying to insurance department complaints and monitoring lawsuits filed to obtain benefits.

Unfair Claims Settlement Practices

In the United States, most states have enacted laws based on or similar to the NAIC model ***Unfair Claims Settlement Practices Act***, which lists a number of actions that are considered unfair claims practices if committed by an insurer (1) in conscious disregard of the law or (2) so frequently as to indicate a general business practice. Figure 12.3 lists some actions that can qualify as unfair claims settlement practices.

State unfair claims settlement practices laws require insurers to establish reasonable standards for the prompt investigation and settlement of claims and to settle claims promptly and fairly when their liability becomes reasonably clear. Some states have adopted regulations based on the NAIC ***Unfair Life, Accident and Health Claims Settlement Practices Model Regulation***, which establishes minimum standards that insurers must meet in handling life and health insurance claims. Many of these standards concern the maximum amount of time an insurer has to take a certain action. For example, under the Unfair Life, Accident and Health Claims Settlement Practices Model Regulation, an insurer has

- 15 days to provide claim forms after receiving notification of a claim
- 15 days to begin any necessary investigation of a claim after receiving proof of loss
- 30 days to pay a claim after determining it is liable
- 15 days to send the claimant a written notice of the denial after deciding to deny a claim

Note that these time limits may differ among states. Also note that most jurisdictions have regulations requiring the insurer to pay interest on claim benefits if the benefits are not paid in a timely manner.

FIGURE 12.3 Actions that Can Qualify as Unfair Claims Settlement Practices

The following actions can be considered unfair claims settlement practices if done (1) in conscious disregard of the law or (2) so frequently as to indicate a general business practice:

- Knowingly misrepresenting to claimants or insureds relevant facts or policy provisions relating to coverages at issue
- Failing to acknowledge with reasonable promptness the receipt of communications that are pertinent to claims
- Failing to adopt and implement reasonable standards for the prompt investigation and settlement of claims
- Not attempting in good faith to settle claims promptly, fairly, and equitably when it is reasonably clear the insurer is liable to pay such claims
- Compelling claimants to institute lawsuits to recover amounts due under policies by offering substantially less than the amounts those claimants ultimately recovered in their lawsuits
- Refusing to pay claims without conducting a reasonable investigation of those claims
- Failing to affirm or deny coverage of claims within a reasonable time after completion of the claim evaluation
- Settling or attempting to settle claims for less than the amount that a reasonable person would believe the claimants were entitled to receive according to the terms of advertising material that accompanied or was part of the application for insurance
- Settling or attempting to settle claims on the basis of an application that was materially altered without notice to, or the knowledge or consent of, the policyowner
- Making claims payments without indicating the coverage under which each payment is being made
- Unreasonably delaying the investigation or payment of claims by requiring both a formal proof of loss form and subsequent verification that would result in duplication of information and verification appearing in the formal proof of loss form
- In the case of a claim denial or an offer of a compromise settlement, failing to promptly provide a reasonable and accurate explanation of the reason for such actions
- Failing to provide forms necessary to present claims within 15 calendar days of a request for such forms with reasonable explanations regarding their use

Source: Adapted from NAIC, *Unfair Claims Settlement Practices Act*, Section 4, 1997. Reprinted with permission from the National Association of Insurance Commissioners.

Privacy

As we discussed in Chapter 3, to protect the privacy of customers and the confidentiality of personal information, most jurisdictions have passed laws regulating how insurers collect, use, and disclose that information. Such laws include

- U.S. state laws based on the Model Privacy Act
- U.S. state regulations based on the Model Privacy Regulation
- U.S. federal Fair Credit Reporting Act (FCRA)
- U.S. federal Fair and Accurate Credit Transactions Act (FACTA)
- U.S. federal Health Insurance Portability and Accountability Act (HIPAA)
- U.S. federal Gramm-Leach-Bliley (GLB) Act
- Canadian federal Personal Information Protection and Electronics Document Act (PIPEDA)
- Various Canadian provincial laws

When conducting a claim investigation, claim analysts must comply with the privacy provisions of all of these laws that apply to a particular jurisdiction. In addition, companies that are members of the Canadian Life and Health Insurance Association must adopt and abide by the CLHIA's Right to Privacy Guidelines unless they have developed their own guidelines that are stricter than the CLHIA's.

In the United States, the Model Privacy Act's general prohibition of pretext interviews directly affects how a claim analyst conducts a claim evaluation. Recall from Chapter 3 that a pretext interview is an interview in which one person attempts to gain information from another person by (1) pretending to be someone he is not, (2) pretending to represent someone he does not represent, (3) refusing to identify himself, or (4) misrepresenting the purpose of the interview. An insurer may conduct a pretext interview during a claim investigation only if the insurer has a reasonable basis to suspect criminal activity, fraud, material misrepresentation, or material nondisclosure in connection with the claim. The insurer may not conduct a pretext interview with any person who has a protected relationship with the person who is the subject of the interview. Such protected relationships include husband and wife, lawyer and client, and doctor and patient.

Financing Terrorists

As we discussed in Chapter 3, the U.S. Treasury's Office of Foreign Assets Control (OFAC) maintains a list of countries, individuals, and organizations that participate in or sponsor terrorism or other illegal acts. Claim analysts must be on guard against making any payments to anyone on the OFAC list. Typically the claim administration system will run such a check.

Fraud

Recall from Chapter 10 that fraud is an act by which someone intentionally deceives another party and induces that other party to part with something of value. ***Insurance fraud*** is any fraud that involves an insurance company, whether committed by consumers, insurance company employees, producers, health care providers, or anyone else connected with an insurance transaction.

Many perpetrators of insurance fraud view it as a victimless crime, but that is far from the case. In fact, the cost of insurance fraud is borne by all of an insurer's policyowners in the form of increased premiums. Those who submit fraudulent claims drive up the costs for insurance companies and thus the cost of insurance for everyone.

Insurance fraud is a crime in many jurisdictions, and the governments in such jurisdictions can prosecute those who commit fraud. In addition, victims of insurance fraud can file civil lawsuits against the perpetrator of the fraud in an attempt to recover any financial losses that resulted from the fraudulent acts.

In the United States, the NAIC has adopted the ***Insurance Fraud Prevention Model Act***, which is designed to permit the state insurance departments to

- Investigate and discover fraudulent insurance acts more effectively
- Halt fraudulent insurance acts
- Receive assistance from state, local, and federal law enforcement and regulatory agencies in enforcing laws that prohibit fraudulent insurance acts

Almost all states have enacted either a law based on the Insurance Fraud Prevention Model Act or a law with similar provisions designed to prevent and prosecute insurance fraud.

The Insurance Fraud Prevention Model Act requires insurers to undertake measures to prevent and detect insurance fraud. Some states require each insurer licensed to sell insurance in the state to develop and maintain an antifraud plan that establishes procedures to

- Prevent insurance fraud
- Review claims to detect insurance fraud and investigate claims where fraud is suspected
- Report fraud to appropriate law enforcement authorities and cooperate with such authorities in prosecuting cases of insurance fraud
- Pursue civil actions against persons who commit insurance fraud
- Train employees and producers to detect and prevent fraud

The Insurance Fraud Prevention Model Act also requires persons engaged in the business of insurance who know or reasonably believe that insurance fraud is being committed to report the fraud to the state insurance department. Some states impose a time limit within which the report must be made after the individual discovers insurance fraud, while other states require that the report be made "immediately" or "promptly" after the discovery. Failure to report fraudulent activities to the insurance department can subject such an individual to civil and, in some cases, criminal penalties.

Some people are reluctant to report suspected insurance fraud to the state insurance department for fear that the accused might file a lawsuit saying that by filing the report, the accuser has engaged in defamation or invasion of privacy. ***Defamation*** is a civil wrong that occurs when a person makes false statements that tend to damage the reputation of another. ***Invasion of privacy*** is a civil wrong that occurs when a person (1) appropriates someone's name or personality, (2) publicizes someone's private affairs, (3) intrudes into someone's private affairs and the wrong causes mental suffering, shame, or humiliation, or (4) places someone in a false light in the public eye. To encourage the reporting of suspected insurance fraud, most states have laws that protect from civil liability anyone who in good faith reports such information to the insurance department.

Claim fraud—a subset of insurance fraud—is an action by which a person intentionally uses false information in an unfair or unlawful attempt to collect benefits under an insurance policy. Claim fraud can be committed by any person who is in a position to influence a claim decision or benefit from a claim payment, including an insured, a beneficiary, a medical care provider, a caregiver, a producer, or an employee of an insurance company.

In an effort to prevent claim fraud specifically, the Insurance Fraud Prevention Model Act requires insurers to include a fraud warning statement on all applications for insurance and claim forms. This statement notifies the applicant or claimant that knowingly presenting false information in an application or presenting a fraudulent claim is a crime.

Most people who submit insurance claims are honest. Claimants occasionally make mistakes in providing information on claims, but generally their intent is to submit eligible claims and to receive only benefits to which they are legitimately entitled. Unfortunately, some people try to manipulate the claim system to obtain benefits to which they are not entitled. From false billings and bribes to unnecessary and overpriced medical services, the varieties of fraud are limited only by the ingenuity of those who intend to take advantage of insurance companies. Figure 12.4 provides some of the warning signs of a potentially fraudulent claim.

FIGURE 12.4 Warning Signs of a Potentially Fradulent Claim

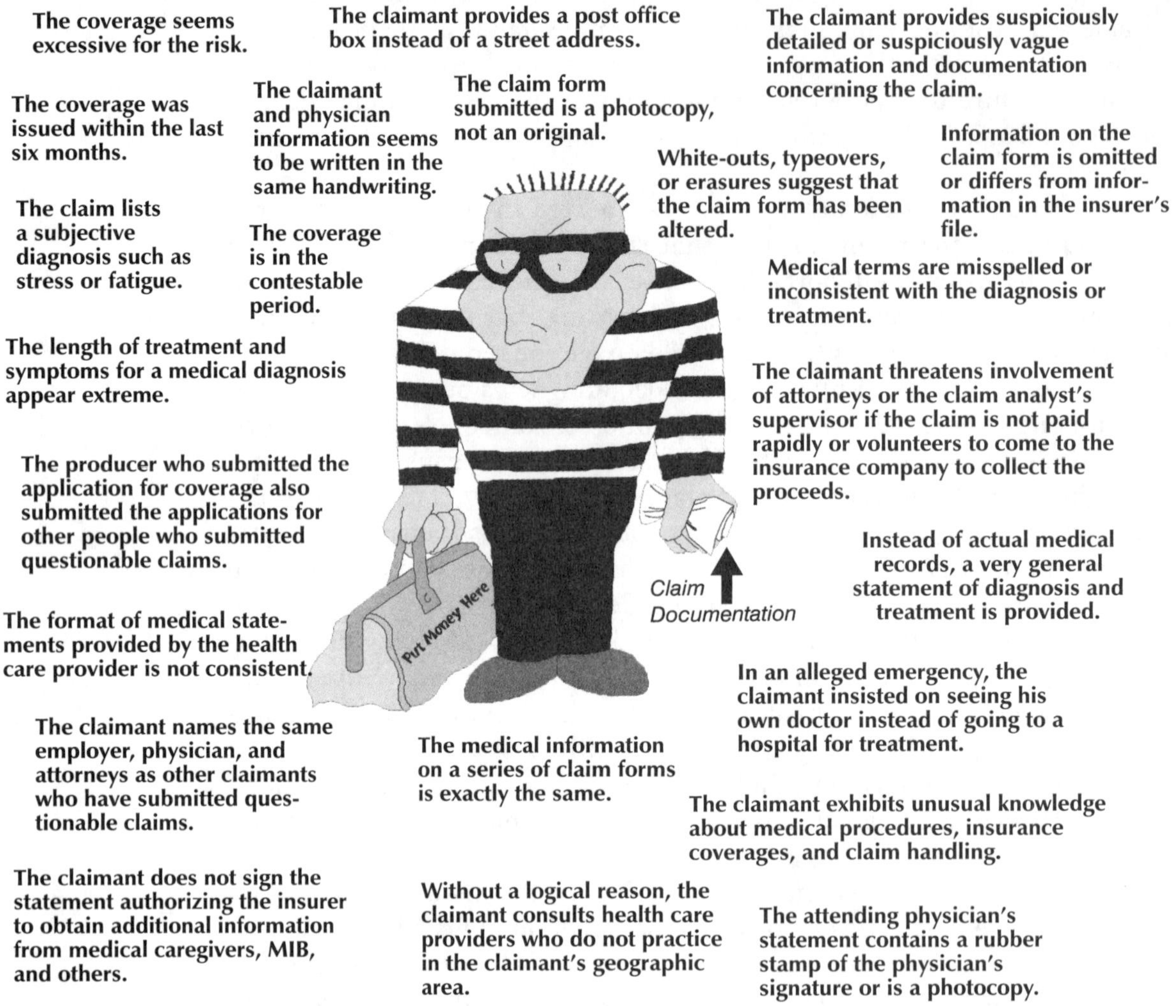

Source: Adapted from Jane Lightcap Brown and Jennifer W. Herrod, *Reinsurance Administration* [Atlanta: LOMA (Life Office Management Association, Inc.), © 2000], 211. Used with permission; all rights reserved.

Some states require insurers to establish a department to investigate suspected cases of insurance fraud. A ***special investigative unit (SIU)*** is a group of individuals who are employed by an insurance company and are responsible for detecting, investigating, and resolving cases involving insurance fraud. When a claim analyst suspects fraud of any kind, she contacts the SIU and works with this unit in investigating the case.

MIB's Claims Activity Index (CAI) can assist in detecting fraud and overinsurance. The CAI is a shared, industry-wide data exchange from which claim analysts can learn whether other claims have been filed for the same insured with other insurers. The CAI is available to all life, disability, long-term care, and credit life insurers on a subscription basis.

Technology

In the first chapter of this textbook, we explained the importance of information systems in enhancing the activities involved in insurance administration. Information systems are used to great advantage in the claims area, and particularly with medical expense claims. Many medical expense claims are submitted to insurers via electronic data interchange (EDI). Claims that fit certain parameters specified for electronic handling then can be processed by ***auto-adjudication***, which is an electronic claim processing system. Such a system not only can verify information about the coverage and the insured, but also can make claim decisions, calculate benefit amounts, authorize payment of benefits, produce checks or transfer funds electronically to pay benefits, and generate printed explanations of benefits so that each policyowner receives specific information about the amount of benefits paid for each claim—all without human intervention.

Even if a claim is submitted on paper, as life insurance claims typically are, an insurer may use imaging technology to convert it to an EDI format and then process the claim via the auto-adjudication system. Claims that do not fit the parameters specified for electronic handling are assigned to claim analysts for processing. Note that in this text when we refer to the claim analyst processing the claim, the information system actually may be doing so.

Insurers also use technology to detect and deter fraud. Rules-based systems and predictive modeling are particularly effective in determining whether fraud has occurred, especially when a pattern can be detected.

Claim Administration and Quality Control

Insurers judge the quality of their claim function using qualitative and quantitative performance measurements such as those we discussed in Chapter 1. Most companies review a percentage of claims every week or month to confirm that employees are maintaining turnaround time objectives and accuracy standards. Management reviews these reports, as well as reports of "old" pending claims, large dollar claims, names of payees who appear on the OFAC list, and any claim denial appeals.

Sometimes these measurements are taken and reviewed as part of an internal audit by the insurer or an external audit by reinsurers. Audits by reinsurers of claims and claim department operations typically focus on reinsurance agreement compliance and procedures and processes for reviewing and investigating claims, as we discussed in Chapter 11. In addition, regulatory authorities sometimes conduct external audits.

In the United States, insurers are subject to regular ***market conduct examinations***, which are formal investigations of an insurer's nonfinancial operations that are carried out by one or more state insurance departments and are designed to determine whether the insurer's market conduct operations comply with applicable laws and regulations. A market conduct examination typically covers many of an insurer's functional areas, including new business, underwriting, and claim administration. However, market conduct examinations typically place a great deal of emphasis on the claim function because matters pertaining to claims are near the top of the list of complaints that state insurance departments receive.

In a market conduct examination, the state examiners determine whether the insurer has complied with standards for doing business found in state statutes and regulations, such as those based on the NAIC's Unfair Claims Settlement Practices Act and the Unfair Life, Accident and Health Claims Settlement Practices Model Regulation. For example, a life claim standard may be "The company will pay interest at no less than 8 percent from the date of death until payment is made on the claim when the decedent is a resident of Washington at the time of death."[2] Of course, many companies already have adopted these regulatory standards as their own internal performance measurements. Thus, insurers have experience in complying with such standards.

Market conduct examiners also verify that an insurer has processed claims in compliance with policy terms and claim procedures manuals. They select a sample of claim files and review them to evaluate

- The length of time required to investigate and settle claims
- Whether files contain adequate and accurate documentation
- Whether the amounts of claim payments made are accurately calculated
- Whether claims are paid to the correct payee

Examiners also review claim files that have resulted in lawsuits to determine whether the insurer has improperly denied claims. Examiners also determine whether the insurer conducts its own meaningful internal audits.

Key Terms

claim philosophy
claim practices
claim form
claim analyst
compensatory damages
punitive damages
Unfair Claims Settlement Practices Act
Unfair Life, Accident and Health Claims Settlement Practices Model Regulation
insurance fraud
Insurance Fraud Prevention Model Act
defamation
invasion of privacy
claim fraud
special investigative unit (SIU)
auto-adjudication
market conduct examination

Endnotes

1. Joy Horrocks, *Claim Center Organization*, ICA Life Reports 2004, http://www.claim.org/pdf/2004_life.pdf (8 March 2007).
2. RCW 48.23.300, as quoted in Leslie A. Krier, *Life, Health & Disability Claims Under the Microscope: A State Market Conduct Examiner's Perspective*, Presentation at ICA 2006 Annual Conference (October 2006).

chapter 13

Administering Life Insurance Claims

Outline

Evaluating Life Insurance Claims
Verifying the Coverage Was in Force
Verifying that the Deceased Is Covered
Verifying the Death Occurred
Determining Whether the Policy Is Contestable
Determining Whether the Death Is Covered
Calculating the Amount of the Policy Proceeds and How They Are Payable
Determining Who Is Entitled to Receive the Policy Proceeds

Handling Supplemental Benefits
Waiver of Premium for Disability Benefit
Accidental Death Benefit
Family Benefit
Accelerated Death Benefit

Learning Objectives

After studying this chapter, you should be able to…

- Explain how claim analysts verify coverage was in force at the time of death
- Describe how claim analysts verify that the deceased is the insured
- Explain how claim analysts verify that the death occurred
- Describe how claim analysts determine whether the policy is contestable
- Explain how claim analysts determine whether the death is covered
- Calculate the amount of the policy proceeds payable in a specific situation
- Discuss the various settlement options available to the policyowner and beneficiary
- Explain how claim analysts determine who is entitled to receive policy proceeds
- Describe how claim analysts evaluate claims for waiver of premium for disability benefits, accidental death benefits, family benefits, and accelerated benefits

As we mentioned in Chapter 12, claim analysts go through the same basic steps in handling all types of claims. In this chapter, we explain how claim analysts handle each of the steps in the life insurance claim evaluation process. Group and individual life insurance claims are handled in basically the same manner, but we note where the group procedures differ from individual procedures.

Evaluating Life Insurance Claims

In the case of individual life insurance, the beneficiary, an heir, or the producer usually notifies an insurer of the insured's death. In the case of group life insurance, the employer usually notifies the insurer or third-party administrator of the group insured's death. The insurer then provides a claim form to the claimant to complete and asks the claimant to submit proof of loss, which in the case of life insurance is referred to as *proof of death*. A life insurance claim form asks for information about the deceased insured, including the date and place of birth, as well as the date, place, cause, and circumstances of death. The claim form also asks for information concerning the claimant, including her relationship to the insured, date of birth, contact information, and Social Security or taxpayer identification number.

Some companies' claim forms also ask for the names and contact information of all physicians or other health care providers who attended to the deceased insured within the past five years if death occurred during the contestable period. A HIPAA authorization must be obtained if information is to be obtained from these sources. This document typically is signed by the next of kin or an authorized representative of the deceased insured or his estate. Figure 13.1 shows a typical claim form for individual life insurance.

When a claim analyst receives a completed claim form, the analyst can have difficulty acquiring detailed information from some sources. Concerns about patient privacy and confidentiality cause some health care providers to delete information from the medical records before releasing the information to the insurer. In some situations, attorneys or claimants request that all information be sent to them before it is sent to the insurer. If the claim analyst becomes aware of this request, she challenges it to maintain the chain of custody of the medical records.

Claim analysts attempt to obtain all information necessary to evaluate a claim as soon as possible because they are required legally to process claims promptly. In addition, in many U.S. states, interest continues to accrue on the policy proceeds until the claim is resolved. Furthermore,

FIGURE 13.1 Typical Claim Form for Life Insurance

VERY IMPORTANT: BEFORE COMPLETING THIS FORM, PLEASE READ ALL INSTRUCTIONS ON THE INSTRUCTION PAGE

NOTE: Any person who knowingly and with intent to defraud any insurance company or other person a) files a claim form containing any materially false information or b) conceals information concerning any fact material thereto for the purpose of misleading, commits a fradulent insurance act, which is a crime. Such person may be subject to fines and/or confinement in prison.

PART ONE—To be completed in full

Name of Deceased (Print in Full)		Policy Number(s)
Date and Place of Birth	Date and Place of Death	Cause of Death

If your proceeds exceed the current applicable minimum set by the Company (currently $15,000), an interest bearing checking account will be opened for you, and you will promptly receive your personalized checks. You may immediately utilize all or a portion of those funds by writing checks against that account. The funds in the account, meanwhile, will earn interest at a competitive variable rate.

I certify, under penalty of perjury, the following is my correct Taxpayer Identification Number.

Beneficiary's Social Security Number	Taxpayer Identification Number **if the beneficiary is an Employer/Corporation/Trust/Estate**
| |	|

Name of Beneficiary* (Print in full)	Date of Birth (MM/DD/YY) / /	Your Relationship to Deceased
Address (Street, City, State, Zip)		Telephone Number ( ) –
Beneficiary/Payee Signature (Required)		Date

***If there is more than one beneficiary, each must complete his or her own claim form. Copies of the form are acceptable.**

continued on next page…

FIGURE 13.1 *continued* Typical Claim Form for Life Insurance

PART TWO—To be completed only IF: Death has occurred within two (2) years of original issue or reinstatement of the policy

1. **Please fully complete claim authorization form XYZ and submit with this claim form.**
2. **Fully complete information below and on the following page with signature and date**

Deceased driver's license number	Deceased driver's license state of issue	Date deceased first consulted a physician for last illlness / /
Date deceased last worked at his/her regular occupation / /	Did the deceased **ever** use tobacco in any form? ❑ Yes ❑ No If **Yes**, date last used from__________ to __________	

Name and addresses of **all** physicians (include personal physician) who attended to deceased and hospitals where treated for past **(5) five** years.

Name	Address (Street, City, State, Zip) & Telephone Number	Dates	Disease or Condition

List **all** Life and Health insurance of the Deceased

Company	Policy Number(s) and Amount(s)	Policy Issue Date(s)

SIGNATURES

Signature of Next of Kin/Authorized Representative	Date
Address (Street, City, State Zip)	Witness Signature

many U.S. states have regulations specifying that the insurer must take follow-up action according to a specified timetable, which may be every 30, 45, or 90 days. ERISA requires that such a timetable be followed for group claims. Compliance with such regulations becomes more difficult and costly the longer a claim is pending.

During the course of evaluating the claim, the claim analyst sends the claimant letters about the status of the evaluation. If the claim analyst denies the claim, he sends the claimant a denial letter explaining why the claim was denied. Many states and ERISA require the denial letter to include information on how a claimant can appeal a denial. Typically, the letter also states that if the claimant can provide additional information that might refute the information on which the denial was based, the insurer will consider such information in reexamining the claim. In some companies, the claim analyst sends such a letter prior to making a final decision to deny a claim so that the claimant may provide input prior to the final decision. In many companies, the claim supervisor—and sometimes the law department—must review and approve of each denial. The special investigative unit also may review the claim if fraud is suspected.

Verifying the Coverage Was in Force

The claim analyst usually can verify that coverage was in force when the death occurred by checking the administration system's record of the policy's premium payments made to date. However, if the policy has been applied for but not yet issued, the claim analyst must investigate whether coverage nonetheless was effective on the date of death. If the deceased paid a premium, then the insurer most likely issued a premium receipt. The claim analyst then may need to refer the claim to the law department to evaluate the terms of the premium receipt, applicable state and federal regulations, and applicable case law governing such matters.

The question of whether coverage was in force on the date of death also may arise if the policy was in the grace period or in the process of being reinstated. During the grace period, the loss typically will be covered even if the renewal premium had not yet been received. If death occurred during the reinstatement process, generally the loss will be covered only if the policyowner had completed all requirements for the reinstatement and the company had approved the application for reinstatement.

When a claim is submitted under a group life insurance policy, the claim analyst verifies that premiums have been paid for the group insured. If the deceased is a dependent under a group policy, the claim analyst verifies that the group insured was paying premiums for the dependent's coverage.

Verifying That the Deceased Is Covered

The life insurance claim analyst must verify that the policy actually covered the deceased at the time of death, which is especially important under multi-life, family, and group policies when claims may be submitted for individuals who actually were not covered. When a claim is submitted under a group life insurance policy, the insurer requires the employer to verify the insured's status as a covered member of the group. If the claim analyst determines she needs more proof of the deceased group member's status, the claim analyst examines payroll records and the employee's enrollment card. If the deceased is a dependent under a group policy, the claim analyst verifies that the dependent is on the group insured's enrollment form.

With life insurance, a claim analyst also must be careful to verify the identity of the deceased as the insured. To do so, the claim analyst compares the deceased's name and other vital information, such as date and place of birth, found on the claim form and documentation submitted as proof of death with the insured's name and information found in the insurer's records. However, difficulties may arise if the deceased is a woman who has changed her name along with her marital status. In such a case, the claim analyst typically would examine the marriage certificate.

Identifying the deceased as the insured may be complicated if the death occurred in a foreign country, the insured is missing and presumed dead, or the insured's body was badly deformed in the event causing the death. In such cases, autopsy reports, police reports, and interviews with those involved may give clues to the identity of the insured.

Verifying the Death Occurred

A typical proof of death for life insurance is a ***death certificate***, which is a document that attests to the death of a person and bears the signature—and sometimes the seal—of an official authorized to issue such a certificate. Because of concerns about protecting the privacy of individuals and ensuring the confidentiality of sensitive information, death certificates in some jurisdictions list only "natural causes" rather than specifying the cause of death as being from a particular disease.

Most insurers in the United States accept either an original or a certified copy of the official death certificate as proof of death. Most Canadian insurers accept an official death certificate, a coroner's certificate of death, or a hospital's certificate of death as proof of the death of an insured.

Certain jurisdictions have held that an insurer must accept as proof of death a document that attests to the death of an insured and that is signed by a person with knowledge of the insured's death. Nonetheless, in such circumstances, the insurer generally tries to obtain official death records, if any are available, to corroborate information in the unofficial document.

Death Outside North America

Typically when a death of a U.S. citizen occurs outside the United States, the local authorities issue a death certificate in the local language. The U.S. Consular Officer then usually issues a "Report of Death of an American Citizen Abroad" based on the death certificate. Most insurers require this report as proof of death instead of the death certificate. In addition, most insurers ask the claimant or next of kin to complete and sign a foreign death questionnaire.

Claim analysts sometimes have difficulty establishing how, or even if, a death occurred when the insured died outside North America. Because formalities and procedures for registration of death in other countries are not always as rigorous as those in the United States and Canada, situations in which the insured dies abroad introduce the possibility of fraud. Therefore, additional investigation and care usually are required to verify the validity of the claim. For example, the claim analyst may check to see if the insured's passport or return airline tickets were cancelled.

Disappearance of the Insured

Occasionally, a claim analyst must presume that an insured is dead because the insured has disappeared and the body has not been found. If an insured was exposed to a specific peril that can account for the insured's disappearance, and if no other suspicious circumstances exist, the claim analyst generally approves the claim after an appropriate investigation into the circumstances of the case if a death certificate is provided. For example, if a troop of Boy Scouts on a hike sees their leader swept away in a torrent during a thunderstorm but the troop leader's body is never found, the claim analyst more than likely would approve the claim after a reasonable period if no evidence of fraud was found.

If an insured disappears without exposure to a specific peril or any presentation of other definite proof of death, the insurer may determine that the burden of proof of death has not been met and may conclude that it is unable to pay the policy benefits. However, if an insured has been absent from her home continuously for a specified period—seven years in most jurisdictions—an insurer or a claimant can apply to a court for an order presuming death. If the court evaluates the evidence and is satisfied that the insured is more than likely deceased, the court issues a ***presumptive death certificate***, which is a court-issued document stating that a person is presumed to be dead. Figure 13.2 lists the four elements that the court considers before issuing a presumptive death certificate. When a claim analyst receives a presumptive death certificate, he calculates the policy proceeds as of the date of death shown on the court order.

If the claim analyst locates an insured person who does not want to have her location revealed, the claim analyst respects the insured's wishes. However, the claim analyst can justify nonpayment of insurance benefits only by obtaining a signed, dated, and notarized statement from the insured attesting to identifying information, such as date of birth, place of birth, and the names of such people as the insured's parents, spouse, and children.

Reappearance of the Insured

If an insured reappears after being declared dead by a court and after the insurer has paid the policy proceeds in full, the insurer usually has the right to recover the money because it was paid under a mistake of fact. If the insurer paid less than the full amount of benefits in a compromise settlement, however, the insurer generally cannot recover the benefits because courts will not disturb a compromise settlement.

Determining Whether the Policy is Contestable

If an individual life insurance claim is submitted during a policy's contestable period, the claim analyst investigates whether the application contains a material misrepresentation. Typically, the claim analyst refers the claim

FIGURE 13.2 Considerations for Issuing a Presumptive Death Certificate

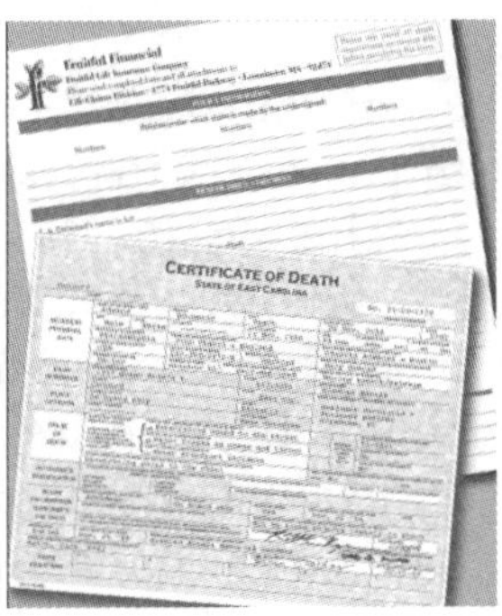

Before issuing a presumptive death certificate, a court will consider whether

1. The insured has been missing from his home or usual residence for the period of time required in the jurisdiction
2. The insured's absence has been continuous and whether any factors such as large debts, marital problems, or criminal indictments exist that would give cause for the disappearance
3. A diligent search for the insured has been conducted
4. The people most likely to hear from the insured have not heard from her

to the underwriting department if he suspects that material misrepresentation has occurred. Information on the insured's medical and personal risk factors is obtained and anything that predates the application is compared to the application to ensure the risk factor was disclosed during the underwriting process. If any medical or personal risk factor was not disclosed and if it would have been considered material to the issuance of the policy because the underwriter would not have issued the policy as written had he been fully informed, the claim analyst then may refer the claim to the law department or the special investigative unit to determine the validity of the policy and/or whether the company is required to report a fraud to the state in which the policy was issued.

Determining Whether the Death Is Covered

In deciding whether the loss is covered under the terms of an individual life insurance policy, the claim analyst examines all policy exclusions, including those for aviation, avocations, and suicide. The claim analyst also verifies that no changes in the insured's health or other material information submitted at the time of application have occurred between the time of application and policy delivery.

Aviation, Avocation, and Suicide Exclusions

Aviation and avocation exclusions typically are found in riders, whereas the suicide exclusion is part of the basic policy. Benefits payable under an aviation or avocation exclusion rider differ in accordance with the terms of the rider, which may provide that the insurer will

- Pay no benefit if death is a result of the activity excluded
- Return the premiums paid
- Pay the cash surrender value

If an insured person dies as a result of suicide, the claim analyst checks the policy's suicide exclusion provision. Insurance companies try to protect themselves against the possibility of antiselection by excluding suicide as a covered risk for a specified period—usually two years—following the date the policy is issued. If the policy lapses and is reinstated, the period still is considered to have begun on the date when the original policy was issued in most jurisdictions. In Canada, if a policy has been reinstated, the suicide exclusion period typically begins again on the date the policy is reinstated. The length of the new suicide exclusion period is the same as the length of the original period.

If the claim analyst determines that an insured died by suicide within the exclusion period, the insurer returns the premiums paid and does not pay full policy benefits. Returning the premiums paid is considered to be payment of the limited benefit agreed upon when the application for insurance was submitted and when the insurer accepted the risk. Returning the premiums is not considered to be a refund, and the insurer is not considered to have rescinded the coverage. By invoking the suicide exclusion, the insurer is not contesting the policy or attempting to rescind it, but instead is affirming the validity of the contract by applying the limited-benefit-for-death-by-suicide provision in the contract.

To determine what action to take if a proposed insured commits suicide during underwriting, most insurers rely on the language of the premium receipt. The receipt should state clearly that coverage under the receipt will be effective subject to the limitations contained in the policy applied for—and such a policy would contain the suicide exclusion provision.

If an insurer denies a claim for basic death benefits under a life insurance policy based on the suicide exclusion and is sued, most jurisdictions require that the insurer bear the burden of showing that the insured committed suicide. Most jurisdictions have a legal presumption that the insured did not commit suicide, and the insurer must overcome this presumption.

Change in Health Statement

Most individual life insurance applications and premium receipts contain a ***change in health statement*** that requires a proposed insured to notify the insurer in writing if his health or any material information in the application changes before the policy is delivered. Some insurers require the producer and/or the policyowner-insured to sign another change in health statement at the time the policy is delivered. A typical change in health statement as it appears in an application is shown in Figure 13.3.

FIGURE 13.3 Typical Change in Health Statement

I understand that no policy based on this application will be effective unless all of my statements and answers in the application continue to be true as of the date I receive the policy. I understand that if my health changes or any of my answers or statements change prior to delivery of the policy, I must so inform the insurer in writing.

If the insured does not notify the insurer of a change in health prior to delivery of the policy and a policy is issued, the insurer may deny a subsequent claim if it occurs during the contestable period. In most jurisdictions, to deny payment of policy proceeds because of a change in the insured's health between application for and delivery of the policy, the insurer must show that (1) the change in health directly affected the degree of risk for the case, (2) the proposed insured knew of the change in health, and (3) the change in health statement was unambiguous. On the other hand, if a proposed insured dies as a result of a sudden event, such as an accident or an acute condition about which the proposed insured had no prior knowledge, benefits may be payable under the policy depending on the terms of any premium receipt.

Calculating the Amount of the Policy Proceeds and How They Are Payable

In calculating the total amount of individual life insurance policy proceeds due the beneficiary, the claim analyst reviews the policy and policy records to determine (1) the basic death benefit, (2) any additions to the basic death benefit, and (3) any deductions from the basic death benefit. A group insured's death benefit is defined in the group master policy's benefit schedule. When the claim analyst has calculated the total amount of the policy proceeds, he then must determine how the proceeds are to be paid.

Basic Death Benefit

The amount of the basic death benefit due upon the insured's death is based on the face amount of the policy. However, most policies specify that the death benefit will be adjusted if the claim examiner finds that the policy application contained a misstatement of age or sex.

The claim analyst verifies the age and sex of the deceased insured to be certain that the premiums paid have reflected accurately the amount of risk borne by the insurer. If the age of a deceased insured is in question—for example, if the age on the death certificate is different from the insured's age according to the application—the claim analyst asks the claimant for acceptable proof of age. Proof of an insured's age can be established by various documents, including the insured's birth certificate or a document that establishes the insured's age at the time of a ceremony, such as a certificate of baptism, bar or bat mitzvah, or other religious ceremony.

If the claim analyst determines that the age or sex of the insured was misstated on the application and if a different age or sex on the application would have resulted in a different premium being charged, then the analyst adjusts the amount of the basic death benefit appropriately. Such an adjustment is permitted throughout the life of the policy and is not affected by the incontestability clause.

Generally, an adjustment for misstatement of age or sex results in a death benefit amount equal to the death benefit that the premiums paid would have purchased at the correct age or sex, according to the insurer's published premium rates at the time of policy issue. Insight 13.1 provides an example that illustrates how an insurer typically calculates the death benefit if an insured's age was misstated.

If a claim analyst discovers that an insured's age was misstated on the application, he must bring this to the claimant's attention. The burden of showing a misstatement of age or sex that results in a lower basic death benefit than the stated face amount rests with the insurer. The burden of showing a misstatement of age or sex that results in a higher basic death benefit than the stated face amount rests with the claimant.

In addition to increasing or decreasing the basic death benefit payable, an adjustment for age sometimes causes an insured to be ineligible to receive certain supplementary benefits. For example, if the accidental death benefit is payable only until an insured reaches a specified age, usually 65 or 70, then an insured whose age at death exceeds the limit probably will not be eligible for the accidental death benefit.

Additions to the Basic Death Benefit

After determining the basic death benefit payable, the claim analyst may add certain amounts, if applicable. Examples of such amounts are listed in Figure 13.4.

Insight 13.1 Calculating the Death Benefit with a Misstatement of Age

Genevieve Montague mistakenly stated her age as 34 when she applied for $150,000 of whole life insurance. She was charged an annual premium of $1.42 per thousand, or $213 ($1.42 × 150).

When Genevieve died and her beneficiary submitted a claim, the claim analyst discovered a discrepancy between Genevieve's age according to the application and her age at time of death. The insured actually was 43 years old when she applied for coverage. According to the insurer's published premium rates at the time of policy issue, the paid premium of $213 a year would have purchased $136,000 of whole life insurance. Therefore, the amount of the basic death benefit is $136,000.

If Genevieve actually had been less than 34 years old at the time of application, the premiums she paid while the policy was in force would have purchased more than $150,000 of coverage; in that situation, the claim analyst would adjust the amount of the death benefit upward accordingly.

FIGURE 13.4 Possible Additions to the Basic Death Benefit

- Paid-up additional insurance
- Accidental death benefits
- Excess premiums paid in advance
- Policy dividends declared but not yet paid
- Policy dividends left with the insurer to earn interest, plus the interest
- Interest on delayed claims payment
- Loan interest paid in advance

Deductions from the Basic Death Benefit

The claim analyst also deducts certain amounts from the basic death benefit, if applicable, including

- Premiums due but unpaid during the grace period
- Policy loans
- Interest on any policy loans
- Accelerated death benefits that have been paid

Insight 13.2 provides an example that illustrates additions to and deductions from a death benefit.

Settlement Option Administration

Life insurance policy proceeds typically are paid to the beneficiary in a lump sum upon the insured's death. The insurer can pay this sum by check, or the insurer can deposit the policy proceeds into an interest-bearing checking or money market account that the insurer establishes in the beneficiary's name. Because the beneficiary has the ability to withdraw the entire amount at one time, depositing the proceeds into such an account constitutes a lump-sum payment.

In addition to lump-sum settlements, insurers provide alternative methods of receiving the proceeds of a life insurance policy, which are known as ***settlement options***. Some group policies offer settlement options if the proceeds payable are at least a stated minimum amount.

During the lifetime of the insured, the policyowner can choose one of the settlement options. When the policy proceeds become payable, the beneficiary can select a settlement option if the policyowner has not done so or change the option selected by the policyowner unless the policyowner

INSIGHT 13.2 Calculating Additions to and Deductions from a Death Benefit

Malcolm Wright purchased a nonparticipating life insurance policy in the amount of $200,000, plus a $150,000 accidental death benefit rider. Malcolm subsequently bought $60,000 of additional coverage. At the time of Malcolm's death, which resulted from an accident, he had paid $500 in advance premiums and had an outstanding policy loan of $22,000 plus $1,500 of interest on that loan. The claim analyst would calculate the total benefit payable under this policy in the following manner:

	Face value of policy	$200,000
+	ADB rider	+ 150,000
+	Additional coverage	+ 60,000
+	Premium paid in advance	+ 500
	Death benefit plus additions	**$410,500**
–	Unpaid policy loan	– 22,000
–	Unpaid interest on policy loan	– 1,500
Total death benefit payable		**$387,000**

made the settlement mode irrevocable. The insurance company and the beneficiary then enter into a settlement agreement. The person or entity who is to receive the policy proceeds under a settlement option is referred to as the ***payee*** rather than a beneficiary. The typical settlement options are listed in Figure 13.5.

Determining Who Is Entitled to Receive the Policy Proceeds

Perhaps one of the most challenging tasks facing the claim analyst is determining the proper payee of the policy proceeds because of the risk of being subjected to making duplicate claim payments. If the insurer mistakenly pays proceeds to someone who is not entitled to them and the proper payee later asserts a valid claim to the proceeds, the insurer is obligated to pay the claim again. The insurer then can seek to recover the proceeds from the original payee.

In Canada, an insurer must be notified in writing of any person's right to receive policy proceeds. Therefore, when an insurer pays policy proceeds to a person who appears entitled to them according to the insurer's records, the insurer is fully discharged of all liability for payment of the proceeds. A person who claims he is entitled to the proceeds but didn't notify the insurer may seek to recover the proceeds only from the person who received them.

FIGURE 13.5 Typical Settlement Options

- The ***interest option*** under which the insurance company invests the policy proceeds and periodically pays interest on those proceeds
- The ***fixed-period option*** under which the insurance company agrees to pay policy proceeds in equal installments to the payee for a specified period of time
- The ***fixed-amount option*** under which the insurance company pays equal installments of a stated amount until the policy proceeds, plus the interest earned, are exhausted
- The ***life income option*** under which the insurance company agrees to pay the policy proceeds in periodic installments over the payee's lifetime

The claim analyst also must verify the payee's identity. In addition, because a payee generally must have attained the age of majority to provide an insurer with a valid discharge of liability, the insurer requires proof of the payee's age.

Usually the payee is the beneficiary—a spouse, a child or children, an estate, a trust, a charity, or almost any other entity that has an insurable interest in the life of the insured—and is designated clearly on the insurance application. However, a number of circumstances can complicate the claim analyst's responsibility to ensure that the benefits are paid to the correct payee.

No Named Beneficiary

If a policyowner does not name a beneficiary, the terms of the policy specify the recipient of the policy proceeds. In such cases, policies typically direct the claim analyst to pay the policy proceeds to the policyowner or to the policyowner's estate if the policyowner is deceased.

Alternatively, some policies—typically group—state that if no beneficiary has been named, the insurer will pay the policy proceeds in a stated order of preference, such as to the spouse of the insured, if living; then to the children of the insured, if living; then to the parents of the insured, if living. If no one on the list is living, then the insurer pays the policy proceeds to the insured's estate.

Death of the Beneficiary

If the beneficiary named in an insurance policy has predeceased the insured, the claim analyst checks its records to determine whether an alternate beneficiary was named. Such a beneficiary, called a ***contingent beneficiary*** or *secondary beneficiary*, is the person or entity designated to receive the proceeds of a life insurance policy following the insured's death if the primary beneficiary dies before the insured.

Disqualification of the Beneficiary

A beneficiary who intentionally kills the insured without legal justification, such as self defense, is disqualified by law from receiving the policy proceeds. If the beneficiary did not intend to kill the insured when the policy was applied for, the insurer pays the policy benefits to the contingent beneficiary. If the policyowner-beneficiary obtained the policy with the intent of causing the insured's death, then the contract is void from its inception; the insurer is required to return only the amount of premiums paid with interest, less any outstanding policy loans along with unpaid interest on those loans.

The insurer usually delays payment of the proceeds until the investigation into the insured's death is complete. If the investigation continues for a long period, the insurer generally deposits the amount of policy proceeds with the court for disbursement after a legal decision has been reached concerning the beneficiary's guilt or innocence. Note that a criminal court does not have to convict the beneficiary of intentionally killing the insured without legal justification for the beneficiary to be disqualified. If either a criminal or civil court finds that the beneficiary intentionally and wrongfully killed the insured, the beneficiary will not be eligible to receive the policy proceeds.

Disappearance of the Beneficiary

If a beneficiary has disappeared and cannot be located within a reasonable period, the insurer generally follows the laws of the state or province in which the beneficiary last resided. Most states have adopted variations of the NAIC Uniform Disposition of Unclaimed Property Act, which requires an insurer to hold the proceeds for a specified period—typically five to seven years—and then deposit with the state all proceeds that cannot be paid to a missing beneficiary. The state holds the money in trust for such a beneficiary, who may petition the state for the proceeds. After the state has held the money for a specified number of years, the proceeds then escheat to the state—which means the proceeds become the property of the state.

In all the Canadian provinces except Quebec, an insurer deposits unpayable proceeds with a court, which then determines the proper payee. In Quebec, three years after proceeds become payable, insurers are required by law to deposit proceeds payable to untraceable beneficiaries with the ***public curator***, a person authorized to handle the affairs of missing people.

Change in Beneficiary

At the time a claim is made, the claim analyst verifies that any change of beneficiary made by the policyowner was done so accurately and that the new beneficiary is eligible to receive the policy proceeds. A policyowner's right to change a revocable beneficiary is greater than his right to change an irrevocable beneficiary. A ***revocable beneficiary*** is a life insurance policy beneficiary who has no right to the policy proceeds during the insured's lifetime because the policyowner has the unrestricted right to change the beneficiary designation during the insured's lifetime. During the insured's lifetime, a revocable beneficiary's interest in the life insurance policy is said to be a mere expectancy. An ***irrevocable beneficiary*** is a life insurance policy beneficiary who has a vested interest in the policy proceeds even during the insured's lifetime because the policyowner has the right to change the beneficiary designation only after obtaining the beneficiary's consent or upon the beneficiary's death.

In Canada, claim analysts must be aware that policyowners of in-force policies issued prior to July 1, 1962 in common law jurisdictions have limitations on their ability to change the beneficiary designations of ***preferred beneficiaries***—certain family members of the insured. The policyowner cannot change the beneficiary to anyone outside this group of family members. In addition, the policyowner cannot obtain a policy loan, surrender the policy for its cash surrender value, or assign the policy benefits if doing so would diminish the rights of the preferred beneficiary, unless the preferred beneficiary consents in writing. The rights of a preferred beneficiary continue until that beneficiary dies, is divorced from the spouse-insured, or signs a release.

In both the United States and Canada, if the claim analyst determines that a policyowner was mentally incompetent when he made a beneficiary change, then the change is legally ineffective, and the original beneficiary receives the policy proceeds. If a former beneficiary wishes to challenge a change of beneficiary, the burden is upon the former beneficiary to prove the incompetence of the policyowner to make the change. The claim analyst is not legally bound, however, to question the competence of every policyowner who changes a beneficiary. If an insurer pays the policy proceeds to a new beneficiary and then discovers later that the policyowner was incompetent when he made the beneficiary change, the insurer usually is not required by law to pay the proceeds a second time to the original beneficiary.

Assigned Policy

The claim analyst checks whether an individual life insurance policy has been assigned. An ***assignment*** is an agreement under which a policyowner—the *assignor*—transfers some or all of her ownership rights in a particular policy to another party—the *assignee*. Most individual life insurance policies include an assignment provision stating that the insurer accepts no responsibility for determining the validity of an assignment and that the policyowner must notify the insurer of an assignment. If the insured dies without the insurer receiving notice of the assignment, the insurer may pay the policy proceeds to the designated beneficiary; the assignee will not be able to enforce a claim against the insurer.

An ***absolute assignment*** is an irrevocable transfer of all of a policyowner's ownership rights in a life insurance policy to the assignee. A ***collateral assignment*** is the transfer of some of a policyowner's rights in a life insurance policy to provide security for a debt. A collateral assignment gives the assignee the right to share in the policy proceeds to the extent of the policyowner's outstanding debt at the insured's death.

A claim analyst handling a claim involving an assigned policy must be aware that the rights of the policy beneficiary vary when a life insurance policy is assigned depending on the type of assignment, whether the beneficiary is revocable or irrevocable, and the laws of the applicable jurisdiction.

An absolute assignee has the right to change a revocable beneficiary designation; and when he does so, proceeds are payable to the new beneficiary. If an absolute assignee does not change the beneficiary designation and the policy is silent on this matter, some insurers pay the assignee the proceeds in accordance with court decisions that hold that the absolute assignment of a policy revokes the revocable beneficiary designation automatically. Other insurers, in keeping with contrary court decisions, pay the original beneficiary the policy proceeds.

The collateral assignee's rights in the policy are superior to the revocable beneficiary's rights regardless of whether the revocable beneficiary consents to the collateral assignment. Thus, the collateral assignee is entitled to be repaid from the policy proceeds.

According to the terms of most policies, the policyowner cannot assign ownership of the policy without obtaining the irrevocable beneficiary's consent. If the irrevocable beneficiary consents to an absolute assignment, he remains the beneficiary unless he consents to a change of beneficiary.

If the irrevocable beneficiary consents to a collateral assignment, the collateral assignee may be paid his appropriate share of the policy proceeds upon the death of the insured. However, if the irrevocable beneficiary does not consent to a collateral assignment, he generally has a superior right to the policy proceeds than does the assignee.

Adverse Claimants

When a claim analyst receives two or more conflicting claims on the proceeds of a policy, the analyst (1) conducts a thorough claim investigation according to the insurer's established procedures for handling adverse claimants and (2) consults with the insurer's legal department. During the investigation, the claim analyst notifies the adverse claimants of the conflicting claims. If the claimants can resolve the conflict between themselves, the claim analyst should obtain written notice of their decision and pay the policy proceeds in accordance with that decision. If the claimants cannot resolve the matter and the insurer pays the proceeds to one claimant but the other claimant later proves to have a superior claim, the insurer may have to pay the proceeds a second time.

When faced with adverse claimants who cannot agree on the disposition of the policy proceeds, the insurer typically initiates a legal process known in the United States as interpleader. ***Interpleader*** is a procedure by which the insurer pays the policy proceeds to a court, advises the court that the insurer cannot determine the correct recipient of the proceeds, and asks the court to determine the proper recipient or recipients. The insurer initiates an interpleader action only when the insurer acknowledges that it is liable for paying benefits, not when it is contesting a claim. By using interpleader, the insurer can avoid the risk of having to pay the policy proceeds more than once. In Canada, a procedure similar to interpleader is known as *payment into court*.

Community Property Laws

In some U.S. states, property ownership between spouses is governed by ***community property laws*** that provide that a spouse is entitled to receive an equal share of earned income and an equal share of property acquired by the other spouse during a marriage. However, some property is considered separate property and belongs solely to one spouse. Separate property includes property acquired by one spouse

- Before marriage.
- During marriage with separate property. For example, if a spouse put money in a savings account prior to marriage and uses that money to make a purchase during her marriage, the acquisition is her separate property.
- During marriage as a gift or inheritance.

As a general rule, both spouses must agree before ownership of community property may be transferred to a third party. When one spouse dies, the surviving spouse is entitled to half of the community property; the other half generally belongs to the estate of the deceased spouse.

When a spouse applies for and is issued an insurance policy on her life during marriage and pays the premiums with community property funds, the policy is considered to be community property. If the beneficiary is the insured's spouse, the proceeds usually are considered the spouse's separate property on the theory that the deceased spouse made a gift to the surviving spouse. If a third party is the beneficiary, the claim analyst is relieved of determining the rights of the beneficiary versus those of the surviving spouse by statutes passed in the community property states. ***Exculpatory statutes*** are laws that permit an insurer to pay life insurance proceeds according to the terms of a policy without fear of double liability. Unless the insurer has received prior written notice of a conflicting claim, the insurer may pay the policy proceeds to the named beneficiary and will be excused from making any payment that might have been due to a surviving spouse. To prevent possible conflict resulting from appearing to ignore or avoid a spouse's legal property rights, however, insurers generally obtain a release from a surviving spouse before paying policy proceeds above a certain amount to anyone other than the spouse.

Divorce

Sometimes a policyowner-insured who has named her spouse as the beneficiary fails to change the beneficiary designation after getting a divorce. Under the laws of most jurisdictions, the claim analyst must pay the proceeds to the former spouse. However, some states have divorce statutes that automatically remove a former spouse as beneficiary unless the former spouse is renamed as beneficiary after the divorce or in the divorce decree.

If a divorce decree specifies that a policyowner-insured must continue to pay premiums on the life insurance policy and retain the divorced spouse as beneficiary, no problem exists if the policyowner-insured complies with the decree requirements. However, sometimes the policyowner-insured continues to pay premiums but wants someone other than the former spouse as the beneficiary. If the claim analyst has received no notice of a new beneficiary and pays the policy proceeds to the former spouse as beneficiary according to the insurer's records, the insurer typically is not liable to pay benefits a second time if the new beneficiary later submits a claim. If the claim analyst receives notice of the existence of a rival claimant to the policy benefits before paying the benefits, the insurer typically files an interpleader action.

Simultaneous Deaths

If an insured and the beneficiary die in a common disaster and the claim analyst cannot determine with certainty the order of death, the claim analyst generally will rely on the jurisdiction's ***simultaneous death act***, which is a law that says if both the insured and the beneficiary die under circumstances which make it impossible to determine which of them died first, the insurer is to presume that the insured survived the beneficiary, unless the policy provides otherwise. Thus, the claim analyst is to pay the policy proceeds to a contingent beneficiary.

A simultaneous death act does not affect how the insurer pays policy proceeds when proof exists that a beneficiary survived the insured, even if only for a few minutes. In such a case, the insurer would pay the proceeds to the beneficiary's estate. Because this outcome may not be what the policyowner desires, some policies include a ***survivorship clause*** that states that the beneficiary must survive the insured by a specified period, usually 30 or 60 days, to be entitled to receive the policy proceeds. If the beneficiary does not survive for the stated period of time, the proceeds are paid as if the insured survived the beneficiary.

Handling Supplemental Benefits

As we explained in Chapter 6, the insurance protection provided by most individual life insurance policies can be expanded by supplemental benefits, including a waiver of premium for disability (WP) benefit, an accidental death benefit (ADB), a family benefit, and an accelerated death benefit. If such supplemental benefits are involved in a claim, the claim analyst goes through the claim evaluation process for the supplemental benefit in the same manner as he does for the policy's benefit. If a policy has a guaranteed insurability benefit and the policyowner has exercised options to purchase additional insurance, the claim analyst will include the additional benefits in the calculation of the policy proceeds.

Waiver of Premium for Disability Benefit

If a person becomes totally disabled and is insured under a life insurance policy that includes a waiver of premium for disability (WP) benefit, the claim analyst first verifies that the claimant has satisfied the waiting period, if any is required, and then verifies that the claimant is in fact disabled according to the WP benefit's definition. To make this determination, the claim analyst typically uses such tools as the claim form, disability information form, medical records—including the attending physician's statement—financial records, and information from the claimant's employer. In addition, the claim analyst verifies that the cause of the disability is not excluded from coverage.

The disability information form submitted by the claimant includes such information as

- The initial date of disability

- The cause of the disability and the medical diagnosis
- The claimant's occupation and job duties
- Additional sources, if any, of disability income, including names and addresses of providers of such benefits
- The expected return-to-work date

Most insurers review each active waiver of premium case at least annually to determine whether the claimant is still eligible for the waiver of premium. For example, some group WP benefits will terminate or be reduced when the group insured reaches a certain age.

Claim analysts typically review claims for disabilities that the insurer's experience has shown are usually short-term every three to six months. A claim analyst may require the claimant to complete a form to document continued disability periodically, and he may require an APS at least annually. In addition, the claim analyst may telephone the claimant to ask about the claimant's medical condition. If a claimant does not supply proof of continued disability, most insurers notify the claimant that she is being removed from waiver status and that she will be responsible for paying future life insurance premiums if she wants the coverage to remain in force.

Accidental Death Benefit

The purpose of the accidental death benefit (ADB) is to provide a death benefit in addition to the policy's basic death benefit if the insured dies as the result of an accident. A claim analyst must verify that the accidental death benefit was still in force when the insured died, as most such benefits expire when the insured reaches age 65 or 70.

An ADB is payable if the insured's death was caused, directly and independently of all other causes, by an accidental bodily injury. The claim analyst may find it difficult at times to determine the precise cause of an insured's death. For example, an insured might have suffered a heart attack that resulted in a fatal vehicle accident or other mishap. In such a case, the claim analyst may examine the autopsy report and medical records to ascertain the immediate cause of death. If the death resulted from the heart attack, no accidental death benefits would be payable.

Some ADBs specify that the insured's death must occur within a stated time—such as 90 days—after the accident for the benefit to be payable. However, some states now prohibit insurers from including such a time span limitation in ADBs.

An ADB claim may be quite complex due not only to the facts, but also to varying regulations and case law. Claim analysts may consult with the law department on such claims.

Family Benefit

An individual life insurance policy with a family benefit insures the lives of the insured's spouse and children. When a life insurance claim is submitted under a family benefit, the claim analyst verifies that the deceased meets the definition of a spouse or child and that the deceased meets the age requirements specified in the benefit provision or rider. The documents that the claim analyst typically uses for such verification include a marriage certificate, a birth certificate, or an adoption certificate.

Accelerated Death Benefit

An accelerated death benefits give a policyowner-insured the right to receive all or part of the basic policy's death benefit before her death if certain conditions are met.[1] When the policyowner-insured dies, the amount of the death benefit payable under the policy to the named beneficiary is reduced by the amount of the accelerated death benefit that was paid out to the policyowner-insured. Thus, before paying an accelerated death benefit, claim analysts may require the irrevocable beneficiary and any assignee to sign a release acknowledging that the policy's death benefit will be reduced by the amount paid to the policyowner-insured under the accelerated death benefit provision. Because only a portion of the death benefit is accelerated, the policy continues to provide some degree of protection for beneficiaries and assignees.

In administering claims for an accelerated death benefit, the claim analyst must establish the policyowner-insured's eligibility to receive benefits by determining if the policyowner-insured meets the insurer's definition for having a terminal illness, dread disease, or condition requiring long-term care, depending on the type of accelerated death benefit involved. The claim analyst also must be wary of fraudulent claims if a policyowner-insured wants to receive accelerated death benefits during a policy's contestable period.

The amount of the terminal illness (TI) benefit that is payable varies from insurer to insurer. Some TI benefits permit payment of the full face amount prior to the insured's death. Generally, however, the maximum TI benefit payable is a stated percentage—usually between 25 and 75 percent—of the policy's face amount up to a specified maximum dollar limit such as $250,000. The benefit usually is paid in a lump sum to the policyowner, and the remainder is paid to the beneficiary following the insured's death.

Dread disease benefits usually are paid in a lump sum, but some insurers pay the benefit in monthly installments over a period of 6 to 12 months. Some insurers do not make payments for multiple or recurring events.

The amount of each monthly LTC benefit payment generally is equal to a stated percentage of the policy's death benefit. For example, the benefit may state that 2 percent of the policy's death benefit will be paid each month if the insured requires nursing home care and 1 percent of the death benefit will be paid each month if the insured requires home health care. The insurer usually pays monthly benefits until a specified percentage of the policy's basic death benefit has been paid out. This percentage typically falls between 50 and 100 percent of the policy's face amount. Any remaining death benefit is paid to the beneficiary after the insured's death.

Most LTC benefits impose a 90-day waiting period before accelerated death benefits are payable; no benefits are payable until 90 days following the date on which the insured becomes eligible for benefits. According to the terms of some LTC benefits, however, coverage must be in force for a given period of time, usually one year or more, before the insured will qualify for LTC benefits.

Key Terms

death certificate
presumptive death certificate
change in health statement
settlement option
payee
interest option
fixed-period option
fixed-amount option
life income option
contingent beneficiary
public curator
revocable beneficiary
irrevocable beneficiary
preferred beneficiary
assignment
absolute assignment
collateral assignment
interpleader
community property laws
exculpatory statute
simultaneous death act
survivorship clause

Endnote

1. Adapted in part from Harriett E. Jones, *Principles of Insurance: Life, Health, and Annuities*, 3rd ed. [Atlanta: LOMA (Life Office Management Association, Inc.), © 2005], 124–126. Used with permission; all rights reserved.

chapter

14

Administering Medical Expense, Critical Illness, and Long-Term Care Insurance Claims

Outline

Processing Medical Expense Insurance Claims
Verifying the Coverage Was in Force
Verifying the Claimant Is Covered
Verifying Medical Expenses
Determining Whether the Policy Is Contestable
Determining Whether a Medical Expense Is Covered
Calculating Policy Benefits Payable
Determining Who Is Entitled to Receive the Benefits

Processing Critical Illness Insurance Claims

Processing Long-Term Care Insurance Claims
Long-Term Care Benefits
Verifying the Coverage Was in Force
Verifying the Claimant Is Covered
Verifying the Insured Needs Long-Term Care
Determining Whether the Policy Is Contestable
Determining Whether Long-Term Care Is Covered
Calculating Policy Benefits Payable
Determining Who Is Entitled to Receive the Benefits

Learning Objectives

After studying this chapter, you should be able to…

- Describe how claim analysts verify that a policy is in force and whether an allowable medical expense has occurred
- Discuss coverage and limitations and exclusions for medical expense policies that determine whether a medical expense is covered by a policy
- Describe how claim analysts calculate medical expense benefit amounts and calculate the benefit payable in specific situations
- Describe the policy provisions and methods that insurers use to pay benefits appropriately and to avoid making duplicate medical expense payments
- Describe the processing and payment of critical illness policy claims
- Describe the procedures used to determine whether a long-term care insurance loss has occurred
- Describe the benefit triggers for long-term care policies
- Describe the typical exclusions and limitations found in long-term care policies
- Describe the methods insurers use to pay long-term care benefits appropriately

Dozens of claims may be submitted for each insured under a medical expense policy, and it is possible for more than one claim to be submitted under a critical illness policy and a long-term care policy. Furthermore, medical expense and long-term care claim analysts typically receive a high volume of claims in a single day. Each claim must be handled promptly, accurately, and completely, in accordance with the insurer's claim philosophy, its other business practices, and legal requirements. In this chapter, we discuss how claim analysts process medical expense, critical illness, and long-term care claims.

Processing Medical Expense Insurance Claims

In Chapter 1, we explained the importance of information systems in enhancing the activities involved in insurance administration. Because of the volume of medical expense claims submitted, most insurers have implemented sophisticated medical expense claim administration systems that not only verify information about the coverage and the insured, but also calculate benefit amounts, produce checks or transfer funds electronically to pay benefits, and generate printed explanations of benefits so that each policyowner receives specific information about the amount of benefits paid for each claim. In many insurance companies, only those medical expense claims requiring special examination are handled individually by a claim analyst. However, the steps involved in evaluating claims are generally the same, whether the claim is automated or processed manually. In this chapter, we refer to a claim analyst as the one handling a claim, although in many cases it is the claim administration system doing so.

Medical expense claims usually are submitted either (1) manually on paper claim forms completed by insureds and their health care providers or (2) electronically by health care providers. The medical expense claim form asks the insured and his health care provider for basic information. Figure 14.1 lists the information requested from the insured and health care provider on a typical medical expense claim form. The claim form also asks for authorization from the patient (or from the insured parent if the person is a minor dependent) for all physicians, hospitals, health care providers, pharmacists, or other agencies and organizations to release information concerning the patient's records.

Generally, medical expense policies include a provision requiring that a claim be submitted within a specified period—usually 30 to 90 days—from the date the expense was incurred. Because claim analysts need to gather additional information for certain claims, insurers prefer to receive claims

FIGURE 14.1 Information Requested on a Typical Medical Expense Claim Form

INFORMATION REQUESTED FROM THE INSURED

- The name, address, sex, and date of birth of the patient
- The relationship of the patient to the primary insured (self or dependent)
- The name, address, sex, and date of birth of the primary insured
- The nature of the illness or injury on which the claim is based and the date on which the illness first manifested itself or the injury occurred
- Whether the patient is covered by other insurance
- Whether the illness or injury resulted from the patient's occupation
- Whether the claim is the result of an accident and, if so, whether the claimant expects to receive or has received payment for medical expenses from another source as the result of a lawsuit or settlement

INFORMATION REQUESTED FROM THE HEALTH CARE PROVIDER

- The name, address, and Taxpayer Identification Number (TIN) of the health care provider
- The name of the patient
- The nature of the illness or injury, including appropriate diagnostic codes
- The type of services rendered, including appropriate treatment codes
- The dates on which services were delivered
- The locations at which services were delivered
- The itemized charges for those services

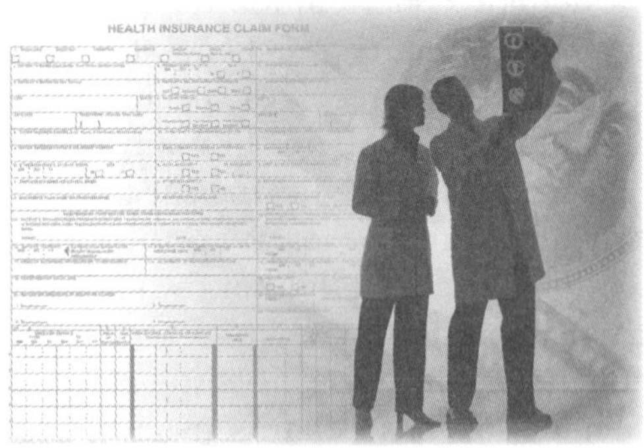

promptly so that such information can be gathered as soon as possible after the expense has been incurred.

In the United States, whether a paper or electronic claim is submitted, most insurers offering medical expense coverage use uniform claim forms. From the insurer's perspective, uniform claim forms enable claimants to provide complete and accurate information, enabling claim analysts to administer claims rapidly and correctly.

Verifying the Coverage Was in Force

The claim analyst verifies that an individual medical expense policy was in force when the medical expense was incurred by ensuring that the premium payments were current. For group medical expense coverage, the analyst verifies that the group insured's premiums were paid.

Verifying the Claimant Is Covered

If the claimant is the primary insured, the claim analyst typically has little difficulty determining whether the person is covered under the policy by checking the administration system. For family or group insurance, if the claimant is not the primary insured, the claim analyst must determine whether the claimant is a covered dependent of the primary insured. Typically, this information also is provided by the claim administration system.

In the United States, before approving benefits for an employee or covered dependent who has left a group, a claim analyst administering a group claim determines whether the employee has elected to continue his medical expense coverage under the provisions of the Consolidated Omnibus Budget Reconciliation Act (COBRA) of 1985. COBRA mandates that employees and their dependents who become ineligible for group medical expense coverage as a result of a specified qualifying event be allowed to continue their group coverage for a specified period following termination of their group coverage.

In addition, as discussed in Chapter 3, the laws of most states in the United States require all group medical expense insurance policies to include a conversion provision that grants a group insured who is leaving the group the right to purchase an individual policy offered by the same insurer without presenting evidence of insurability. The right is limited in that the insurer can refuse to issue the individual policy if the coverage would result in the insured group member becoming overinsured. The benefits provided by individual converted policies generally are more restrictive than those provided by group policies. In most states, if a person continues coverage with COBRA, the conversion provision applies at the end of the COBRA continuation period. Some individual medical expense policies also include a conversion provision.

Verifying Medical Expenses

The claim analyst determines whether a medical expense has been incurred by reviewing the itemized receipts that health care providers give patients or submit directly to the insurer. The information on such a receipt usually includes the name of the health care provider, a specific diagnosis, the expenses involved in diagnosis and treatment, and the date on which those expenses were incurred. If the insured files the claim rather than the health care provider, most insurers require original itemized receipts, not photocopies, as proof of loss. Itemized receipts may be given by any health care provider, including a physician, a paramedic, a laboratory, a hospital, or an outpatient clinic.

Figure 14.2 illustrates a portion of a typical receipt from a physician specializing in obstetrics and gynecology.

Most itemized receipts include ***diagnostic codes***, which are numbers and words that represent specific medical diagnoses. A common system of describing typical medical diagnoses is the ***International Classification of Diseases and Related Health Problems (ICD)***. Claim analysts refer to the ICD by its most current edition. For example, the 9th edition of the ICD, which is the most current edition in use in the United States, is called the ICD-9.

Itemized receipts also include ***treatment codes***, which are numbers and words that represent specific medical treatments. A common system of describing typical medical treatments is the ***Physicians' Current Procedural Terminology (CPT)***.

FIGURE 14.2 Portion of a Typical Medical Receipt

Date of Service ____________________

Name ____________________

Address ____________________

Social Security No. ____________________

DOB ____________________

PROCEDURES	LABORATORY	DIAGNOSIS
57500 Cervical Biopsy	82465 Cholesterol	D50 Iron Deficiency Anemia
58100 Endometrial Biopsy	82565 Creatinine	N80 Endometriosis
57511 Cautery of Cervix	82728 Ferritin	N83.0 Follicular Cyst of Ovary
59000 Amniocentesis	82947 Glucose	N97 Female Infertility
59050 Fetal Monitoring	86317 Hepatitis C	P70.2 Neonatal Diabetes Mellitus
58559 Hysteroscopy	84163 PAPP-A	R10.0 Acute Abdominal Pain

Remarks ____________________

____

Provider Signature ____________________

Diagnostic and treatment codes enable anyone familiar with the coding system to tell what information is being reported. These codes include (1) a number that identifies each diagnosis or treatment and (2) a brief, specific description of each diagnosis or treatment. However, if such a receipt contains only a written description of diagnosis or treatment, the claim analyst usually obtains clarification of the diagnosis or treatment from the health care provider. Figure 14.3 shows some of the codes commonly used to identify diagnoses and treatments associated with appendicitis.

In examining diagnostic and treatment codes, the claim analyst first determines whether the codes are accurate and complete. Suppose that a claim analyst received a claim for an appendectomy with the diagnosis coded 540.0 (acute appendicitis with peritonitis, including rupture of appendix) and the treatment coded 44960 (appendectomy; for ruptured appendix with abscess or generalized peritonitis). Because the diagnosis code and the treatment code appear to be consistent, the claim analyst would note no problem with that portion of the claim.

FIGURE 14.3 Codes Commonly Used for Diagnoses and Treatments of Appendicitis

Diagnosis

CODE	DIAGNOSIS
540.0	Acute appendicitis with peritonitis, including rupture of the appendix
540.1	Acute appendicitis with peritoneal abscess
540.9	Acute appendicitis without mention of peritonitis
542	Other appendicitis, including chronic or recurrent attacks

Treatment

CODE	TREATMENT
44900	Incision and drainage of appendiceal abscess; open
44955	Appendectomy; when done for indicated purpose at time of other major procedure (not as separate procedure)
44960	Appendectomy; for ruptured appendix with abscess or generalized peritonitis

But suppose instead that the diagnosis was coded 540.9 (acute appendicitis without mention of peritonitis) and the treatment was coded 44960 (appendectomy; for ruptured appendix with abscess or generalized peritonitis). In such a situation, because the codes appear to be inconsistent, the claim analyst obtains clarification from the health care provider.

Generally, when a claim analyst uncovers a problem with a diagnostic or treatment code, it indicates a simple human error that can be corrected by communicating directly with the health care provider. For example, when a claim analyst notices that a health care provider has reported overlapping codes—say, for both a surgical procedure and a postoperative checkup—the analyst notifies the health care provider and, unless unusual circumstances apply, does not approve benefits for postoperative visits because charges for such generally are included in the charge for the surgical procedure.

Determining Whether the Policy Is Contestable

The incontestability provision included in some individual health insurance policies is called the ***time limit on certain defenses provision***, and this provision states that after the policy has been in force for a specified period—usually two or three years—the insurer cannot use a material misrepresentation in the application to contest the policy or deny a claim unless the misrepresentation was fraudulent. If a claim analyst suspects misrepresentation or fraud, she follows the procedure we discussed in Chapter 13.

The incontestability provision in a group insurance policy limits to two years from the date of issue the period during which the insurer may use statements in the group insurance application to contest the validity of the master group insurance contract. Insurers rarely contest the validity of group insurance contracts, though, because material misrepresentation is a rare occurrence with these contracts.

The incontestability provision in a group insurance policy also allows the insurer to contest an individual group insured's coverage without contesting the validity of the master group contract itself. If a group insured is required to provide evidence of insurability in an application for group coverage and he makes a material misrepresentation, the insurer has the right to contest the individual's coverage for one or two years, depending on the policy provision, after the effective date of coverage.

Determining Whether a Medical Expense Is Covered

Insurers may offer many varieties of individual medical expense policies and may custom-design group medical expense policies. Because these policies contain various kinds and levels of coverages, limitations, and exclusions, the claim analyst usually refers to the policy to ensure that the medical expense is covered. Many insurers enter each policy's provisions into a database so that claim analysts can quickly check details of coverage for the policy in question.

Covered Services and Their Limitations

Policies specify as exactly as possible the medical services that they will and will not cover by defining certain elements of coverage:

- **The health care provider.** Most policies specify and define who may deliver health care. For example, the definition of a doctor may be a person who is licensed to practice the healing arts and who performs only those services permitted by his license. The policy may include in the definition that the insured or any relative will not qualify as a doctor under the terms of the policy.
- **The medical facility.** Most policies state that coverage extends only to certain types of facilities. For example, a policy that states that treatment must be provided in an accredited hospital would not cover certain treatments and procedures delivered in a patient's home, health care provider's office, or freestanding outpatient clinic.
- **The type of medical tests and procedures.** Policies indicate the types of medical tests and procedures that qualify for reimbursement. For example, some policies cover prostate specific antigen tests for males, but only annually for insureds age 45 and older.
- **The type of medical condition.** Most policies define the type of medical conditions for which treatment is covered. For example, an "injury" is typically defined as an accidental bodily injury that results in loss independently of sickness and other causes.
- **The type of services.** Policies list the services covered by the policy, subject to the conditions for coverage, limitations, benefit features, and exclusions. Figure 14.4 illustrates a typical list of services covered by a medical insurance policy.

The claim analyst must determine whether each claim meets the policy requirement that it is for a service or supply that is ***medically necessary***, which is a service or supply that is needed and appropriate for the diagnosis or treatment of an injury or sickness based on generally accepted current medical practice. In most policies, a service or supply will not be considered medically necessary if it meets any one of the following criteria:

- It is provided only as a convenience
- It is not appropriate for the diagnosis or symptoms

FIGURE 14.4 Typical List of Services Covered by a Medical Expense Insurance Policy

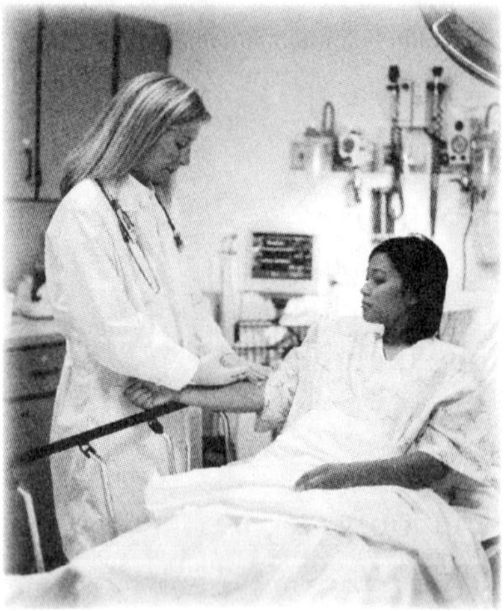

- Semiprivate room and board during necessary hospital confinement
- Confinement in an intensive care unit or cardiac care unit of a hospital
- Hospital services and supplies
- Treatment by a physician or surgeon
- Anesthesia and its administration
- X-ray and laboratory examinations
- Services of a radiologist for diagnosis or treatment
- Services of a professional physical or speech therapist acting under the direction of a physician
- Professional ambulance service for emergency transportation to the nearest hospital
- Services and supplies furnished by an ambulatory surgical facility
- Medical supplies such as blood and blood plasma, surgical dressings, casts, splints, crutches, oxygen, and approved drugs

- It exceeds in scope, duration, or intensity the level of care that is needed to provide safe, adequate, and appropriate diagnosis or treatment
- It is part of an experimental or investigational treatment

Some medical expense insurance policies require an insured to obtain precertification prior to hospitalization, and such policies may limit or exclude benefits if the insured does not obtain this precertification. ***Precertification*** is a statement from the insurer approving certain non-emergency inpatient and/or outpatient services or treatments. Policies differ as to what services and treatments require precertification, but precertification usually is required for surgical, maternity, substance abuse, and mental health hospital admissions.

To provide precertification, an insurer requires the claimant's attending physician to demonstrate, within a specified period of time prior to the time the proposed care is to be delivered, that the care is needed and appropriate. For a nonemergency inpatient admission, information required from the physician includes (1) the diagnosis or reason for hospital confinement, (2) the signs and symptoms indicating a need for such care, (3) the proposed treatment or surgical procedure, and (4) the expected number of days of confinement. Most insurers require a physician to provide this information at least two days before the hospital admission; many insurers allow the information to be transmitted to the insurer electronically or by telephone. If an insured must stay in the hospital longer than the period approved through precertification, the insurer usually obtains medical information from the physician to determine the medical necessity of the extended stay before approving payment for the extended period.

If an insured did not obtain precertification for a treatment for which precertification was necessary but still received the treatment, most policies require the insured to pay a greater portion of the eligible charges than he would if he had obtained precertification. If an insured was denied precertification for a treatment for which precertification was necessary but still received the treatment, most policies require the insured to pay all the expenses. In such cases, the insured can file an appeal with the insurer, as we mentioned in Chapter 12.

Exclusions

Medical expense policies typically exclude coverage for certain expenses, such as those resulting from

- Cosmetic surgery, other than corrective surgery required as a result of an accidental injury or other medical reason
- Treatment of a sickness or injury that occurs while the insured is in military service or that results from an act of war
- Treatment that is provided free-of-charge in a government facility
- Intentionally self-inflicted wounds or illness
- Wounds suffered in an assault on another person or in an attempt to commit a crime
- Experimental or investigational treatments
- Rest cures

In the United States, medical expense policies also exclude reimbursement of medical expenses that are covered by Medicare. In addition, if the claim is related to an occupational illness or injury, medical expenses typically would be covered by a government program such as workers' compensation, not by individual or group medical expense insurance. As mentioned in Chapter 3, most individual and group health insurance policies also contain a pre-existing conditions provision that states that until the insured has been covered under the policy for a certain period, the insurer will not pay benefits for a pre-existing condition. A ***pre-existing condition*** is typically defined in an individual health insurancc policy as an injury or illness that (1) occurred or manifested itself within a specified period before the policy was issued and (2) was not disclosed on the application. Group health insurance policies define pre-existing conditions in a variety of ways, although HIPAA dictates the definition for group medical expense policies, as we mentioned in Chapter 3.

Calculating Policy Benefits Payable

After a claim analyst determines that a claim should be paid, she then calculates the benefit payment according to the policy's schedule of benefits, which describes benefit features. The schedule of benefits includes expense participation requirements, which we discussed in Chapter 7. Thus, the claim analyst must determine whether the benefit amount should be reduced as a result of deductibles, coinsurance, or copayments. The claim analyst also must determine if benefits are limited (for example, for failure to obtain required precertification) or should be reduced under the terms of the coordination of benefits and/or subrogation provisions, both of which we explain later in this section.

Basic Policy Benefit

Medical expense policies typically state that after the insured meets his deductible (and/or copayment), the insurer will pay benefits by multiplying the coinsurance percentage by the usual, customary, and reasonable charges for the services listed in the policy, such as those shown in Figure 14.4. A ***usual, customary, and reasonable (UCR) charge***, also known as *usual and customary charge*, *reasonable and customary charge*, and *usual and prevailing charge*, is the amount that health care providers within a particular geographic region commonly charge for a particular medical service. Insight 14.1 describes how a claim examiner would calculate the basic policy benefit under a typical medical expense policy.

Of course, benefits are subject to all applicable policy limits, such as maximum limits on benefit amounts, hospital stays, and doctor's visits. For instance, a policy may limit the number of days of hospital stay for one period of confinement by stating that the insurer will pay 80 percent of the semi-private room charge up to a maximum of 30 days for any one accident or illness. As an example of policy limits on doctor's visits, a policy may state that the insurer will pay 80 percent of a mental health provider's charges for up to 20 outpatient visits in a calendar year.

INSIGHT 14.1 Calculation of Medical Expense Benefit Payable

Ralph Henson's medical expense policy has an annual $500 deductible and pays 80 percent of usual, customary, and reasonable charges billed by a doctor for a surgical procedure. Ralph undergoes the procedure, and submits a claim for $1,500. If the UCR charge for the procedure is $1,000, the insurer will limit the charge considered to $1,000. On the other hand, if the UCR charge for that treatment is $2,000, the insurer will consider the charge of $1,500 as acceptable for the treatment.

Assuming the UCR charge is $1,000, Ralph pays $600:

$1,000 – $500 (deductible Ralph pays) = $500 × 0.20 = $100

The insurer pays $400 in benefits:

$1,000 – $500 = $500 × 0.80 = $400

Some policies set a maximum limit on the amount of benefits for claims arising from a single injury or incident or for one period of sickness. Many medical expense insurance policies also contain a ***lifetime maximum benefit***, which is the maximum amount that the policy will pay for all eligible medical expenses an individual incurs while insured under the policy.

Coordination of Benefits

In the United States, many people are eligible for coverage under more than one group medical expense policy.[1] For example, spouses who both work may be covered under their own employer's group policy and under their spouse's group policy. Therefore, group medical expense policies usually include a ***coordination of benefits (COB) provision***, which is designed to prevent a group insured who is insured under more than one group medical expense insurance policy from receiving benefit amounts that are greater than the amount of medical expenses the group insured actually incurred. If a group insured is covered by more than one policy, the claim analyst checks the policy's COB provision to determine the insurer's responsibility for paying benefits.

The COB provision prevents duplicate benefit payments by defining the group medical expense policy that is the primary provider of benefits and the policy that is the secondary provider. Under the terms of most COB provisions, when a group insured requires medical care, the policy described as the primary provider is responsible for paying the full benefit amounts promised under the policy.

After the primary provider has paid the full benefit allowed under the policy, the group insured can submit the claim to the secondary provider along with a description of the benefit amounts the primary provider paid. The provider of the policy described as the secondary provider then determines the amount payable for the claim in accordance with the terms of that policy.

A policy's COB provision may take one of several approaches to determining the amount of benefits payable when the policy is functioning as the secondary provider. The most common approach is to first calculate the amount of the group insured's total allowable expenses and the amount of those expenses that the insurer would pay if it were the primary provider. ***Allowable expenses*** are those usual, customary, and reasonable expenses that a group insured incurred and that are covered under a group insured's medical expense policy. The secondary provider then compares this amount to the amount paid by the primary provider. If payment of the full amount provided by the secondary policy would result in the group insured receiving more in benefit payments from both policies than the total amount of allowable expenses, the secondary provider will pay only the difference between the allowable expenses incurred and the amount already paid by the primary provider. Under this type of COB provision, the group insured typically pays no portion of her covered medical expenses; the primary policy pays all benefits in excess of any deductible, copayment, and coinsurance requirements, and the secondary policy pays the portion of allowable medical expenses not paid by the primary policy, including reimbursing the insured for any deductible, copayment, and coinsurance amounts paid by the group insured.

Some group medical expense insurance policies include a special form of COB provision, generally called a nonduplication of benefits provision, that limits the amount payable if the policy is defined as the secondary provider. A ***nonduplication of benefits provision*** is a COB provision that limits the amount payable by the secondary policy to the difference, if any, between the amount paid by the primary policy and the amount that would have been payable by the secondary policy had that policy been the primary policy. A nonduplication of benefits provision requires the group insured to pay a portion of the cost of covered medical expenses.

Most COB provisions include rules for determining which policy is the primary policy. For example, most COB provisions state that when a group insured is also covered by another group policy that does not include a COB provision, the policy without a COB provision will be the primary provider of benefits. In addition, if spouses are covered by two separate policies, the primary policy for each spouse is the one of which that spouse is the group insured.

If an individual is covered as a dependent under more than one group policy, the policy that will be the primary provider can be determined in two ways. One method—the *birthday rule* or *earlier birthday method*—states that the policy covering the group insured whose birthday falls earlier in the calendar year will be considered the primary provider of benefits for a dependent. Note that the group insureds' actual ages are not a factor in determining the primary provider under this method. The second method states that the primary provider of benefits for a dependent is the policy that provides benefits for a male group insured rather than a female group insured.

Some individual health insurance policies contain an ***overinsurance provision***, which specifies that, under certain circumstances, policy benefits will be reduced if the insured has more insurance than needed to cover medical expenses.

Subrogation

The claim analyst also determines whether a policy contains a ***subrogation clause***, which gives the insurer a contractual right to recover payments made to an insured for medical care if that insured receives payment for damages through a legal action. Recall that a medical claim form asks a claimant to state whether she expects to receive or has received payment for medical expenses as the result of a lawsuit or settlement. If a claimant is reimbursed for medical expenses as the result of such a legal action, the insurer is eligible to recover whatever amount it has paid in medical benefits. For example, suppose an insured is involved in an automobile accident, and the insurer pays $15,000 for medical costs resulting from the accident. The insured later sues the person who caused the accident and is awarded $17,000 by the court for medical expenses incurred. If the insured's policy contains a subrogation clause, the insurer can recover up to $15,000 as reimbursement for the benefit amount paid to the insured.

Determining Who Is Entitled to Receive the Benefits

After calculating the benefit amount due on a claim, the claim analyst determines the appropriate recipient for the payment. In many situations, the claimant has signed an ***assignment of benefits***, which is a statement that directs an insurer to pay benefits directly to a health care provider rather than to the insured. For example, an assignment of benefits statement may say simply, "I authorize payment of medical benefits to the undersigned physician or supplier for service(s) described." If an insured has not signed an assignment of benefits statement, the claim analyst usually sends the benefit payment directly to the insured, unless the policy specifies otherwise. Most group policies specify that benefits will be sent directly to the provider.

When a claim payment is made, the claimant receives an ***explanation of benefits (EOB)***, which is a detailed statement showing

- Each treatment or medication submitted as part of a claim
- The insurer's decision concerning payment of benefits for each charge
- Any amount that is considered to be a deductible, copayment, or coinsurance
- An explanation of any nonpayment of part or all of a charge
- The total amount paid to the health care provider or the insured

Processing Critical Illness Insurance Claims

As with all types of coverages, the variations among critical illness policies are vast; as with processing other types of claims, processing critical illness claims involves certain activities. These activities include verifying that the coverage is in force and the claimant is covered under the policy. Premiums must be paid to date, and the insured must meet any policy requirement that he survive the critical illness for a certain period—typically 30 days—after diagnosis. Some insurers consider this survival period to be the same as the waiting period, and other insurers have separate survival and waiting periods. If the policy is in the contestable period, the claim analyst also follows the procedure outlined in Chapter 13 to determine if the policy is contestable.

The claim analyst's most important task is determining whether the insured actually has a medical condition that is defined as a critical illness in the policy. Critical illness policies list and give specific medical definitions for each covered illness and condition. For example, a heart attack might be defined as "the death of a portion of the heart muscle, as the result of cardiovascular interruption or event, and must be proved by presenting EKGs showing the abnormality, copies of lab reports showing elevated enzymes confirming cardiac damage, and a physician's report."

The claim analyst determines whether the illness or condition meets the policy's requirements by examining the documents that the policy requires be submitted along with the claim. As noted earlier, these requirements may be specified in the actual definition of the condition. The claim analyst also may need to verify certain information with the attending physician and/or obtain the advice of the insurer's medical director.

The claim analyst also determines whether the condition falls within the policy's limitations or exclusions. An example of a limitation would be if the policy covers a condition only if it is of a certain type or severity, which CI policies typically do. Thus, a non-life-threatening type of cancer may not be covered. Furthermore, some policies will not cover a condition if the insured did not adhere to her physician's treatment plan. In addition, an illness typically covered by a policy may be specifically excluded for a particular insured when the policy is issued if the underwriter determined that the individual's family history indicates a propensity to develop the condition. Finally, most policies do not cover pre-existing conditions.

Critical illness benefits typically are paid out in a lump sum. However, some insureds prefer to receive a partial benefit payment in a lump sum and leave the rest with the insurer in a deposit account or have the remainder paid in installments. If an insured recovers from the critical illness, he still is entitled to his entire amount of benefits. Note that if the insured dies of a condition not covered by the policy, some insurers will refund all premiums paid.

Processing Long-Term Care Insurance Claims

With the increased life expectancy in the United States and Canada, increasing numbers of people may require long-term care. Because the costs of long-term care can deplete savings quickly, many people are turning to long-term care (LTC) insurance to provide for that care. LTC coverage pays for medical or other health-related services required in a person's home or in a qualified facility, as we mentioned in Chapter 7.

People who have exhausted their savings and who do not have private LTC policies frequently rely on government health programs, such as Medicaid in the United States. However, the cost to government programs is such that in 1996 as part of HIPAA, the U.S. Congress provided tax breaks to encourage citizens to buy private LTC policies. HIPAA narrowly defines the kind of LTC insurance policy that is eligible for favorable tax treatment as a qualified LTC policy.

A ***qualified long-term care policy*** is a long-term care policy that provides all the features HIPAA requires. A ***nonqualified long-term care policy*** is a long-term care policy issued before or after 1996 that does not meet HIPAA requirements. Most LTC policies sold today are qualified, but nonqualified LTC policies also exist. However, qualified versus nonqualified status does not affect how LTC claims are administered. For both types of policies, the claim analyst determines whether a covered loss has occurred and, when applicable, calculates and pays the benefit amount.

LTC policies provide a variety of benefit types and amounts. Therefore, claim analysts for LTC products rely on the definitions in the policies to help them make claim decisions. In addition to communicating with insureds and physicians, LTC claim analysts frequently communicate with facility staff or home health care providers. In this section, we describe the LTC benefits typically provided and the way in which claims for such benefits are administered.

Long-Term Care Benefits

LTC policies generally provide coverage for nursing care; home health care; adult day care; and alternate care, including hospice care and assisted living facility care. Unlike individual LTC insurance policies, some group LTC policies may provide home health care and adult day care as options, rather than as standard features of a policy.

Nursing care provides basic nonmedical and medical care as necessary to patients, including

- ***Skilled nursing care***, which is 24-hour treatment, rehabilitation, and care at a special facility that provides the services of a registered nurse (RN) or a licensed practical nurse (LPN) under the supervision of a physician. Often, hospitalization is the only alternative to this kind of extensive care.
- ***Intermediate nursing care***, which is nursing care provided on less than a 24-hour basis that is usually rehabilitative in nature.
- ***Custodial care***, also known as *personal care*, which is the most basic level of nursing care, largely of a non-medical nature, provided by professionally trained nurses or other qualified people. In custodial nursing care, a patient receives assistance with the activities of daily living (ADLs).

Today, most LTC policies also include a benefit for long-term care provided in the insured's home. ***Home health care*** is care a patient receives at home—whether medical care or custodial care—including physical therapy, the services of a registered nurse, and homemaker services.

Adult day care is care provided to adults in a group setting during hours when primary caregivers are working. Candidates for adult day care are not bedridden and typically live at home under the care of an adult child or other relative who is not able to care for the patient during normal working hours. ***Adult day care centers*** are safe environments in which people in need of assistance with ADLs and IADLs can receive this help, associate with others in similar situations, and return home each day.

Most LTC insurance policies cover alternate care. ***Alternate care*** consists of plans of long-term care and services not otherwise covered under the policy that are developed cooperatively by a physician, the insured, and the insurer to substitute for more expensive nursing home care. Alternate care may include alternative sites of care or even medically necessary modifications to an insured's home.

Hospice care is care provided to terminally ill people, either in a facility or the patient's home. A ***hospice*** is a facility that specializes in the treatment of terminally ill people. Hospice care normally provides for meeting the special physical, emotional, social, and spiritual needs of dying individuals by providing palliative and supportive services during the illness to individuals who have no reasonable prospect of cure, including the services of doctors and nurses to care for a patient and provide pain relief. Hospice care typically is provided only if the insured has 12 months or less to live.

An ***assisted living facility*** is an inpatient residential facility designed to meet LTC needs for persons who are not in need of the level of care provided in a hospital or nursing home but who are in need of assistance with activities of daily living or are cognitively impaired. This care includes accommodations, board, and access to medical services. Assisted living facilities have become very popular because, besides offering accommodations for individual residents, these facilities allow elderly couples to stay together. An assisted living facility may offer several clustered residences, much like apartments or condominiums, with all residents of the assisted living community having access to personal care and meals.

For an assisted living facility to be covered under an LTC insurance policy, the insured typically must be under a plan of care prescribed by a physician. In other words, the individual needs to be in the assisted living facility, rather than choosing to be there, at least as it relates to LTC insurance coverage.

Additionally, many LTC insurance policies provide respite care and caregiver training benefits. ***Respite care*** is care provided by a nursing home or other qualified LTC facility or entity to allow a primary caregiver in the home a break from the day-to-day care of an insured receiving home health care. An LTC insurance policy that provides a respite care benefit typically limits the number of days—up to 21 to 30 days during the life of the policy—for which a benefit will be payable. A ***caregiver training benefit*** covers the cost of training the informal, non-paid caregiver to help care for a covered person who is to receive care at home. One common practice for determining the amount of the benefit is to set the total amount of the caregiver benefit as a multiple of the daily home health care benefit—that is, if the daily home health care benefit is $75 per day, the policy might provide that the maximum caregiver training allowance is four times the daily home health care benefit, or $300.

Verifying the Coverage Was in Force

Just as a claim analyst does to verify that medical expense coverage was in force when the claim is made, an LTC claim analyst ensures that the premium payments are current. If a claim analyst finds that a policy has lapsed, he must determine if the policy has an ***unintentional lapse provision***, which permits reinstatement of a lapsed policy if the reason for the lapse is that the policyowner has a cognitive impairment and that the reason for the missed premium payment was cognitive impairment, as defined in the policy. Many LTC insurers also include a ***third-party notification provision***, under which the policyowner provides the name of another person that the policyowner authorizes the insurer to contact in the event of a missed premium payment. In this way, an insurer can help prevent the unintentional lapse of an LTC insurance policy. If an insured has a third-party notification listed, the policy "extends" the grace period by another 30 or more days to allow time for the third party to either pay the premium or get in touch with the insured and remind him to pay the premium.

Group LTC policies typically offer one of two features not found in individual policies. The ***full portability option*** permits a group insured who leaves the group to take her coverage with her and continue to pay premiums. Before approving benefits for a group insured who has left a group, a claim analyst makes sure that the group insured has elected to use the portability feature and has paid all premiums due. If the group LTC policy does not offer the portability feature, the policy typically offers a conversion feature, which gives a group insured an opportunity to convert the group LTC insurance coverage to individual LTC insurance coverage with benefits substantially equivalent to those offered by the group LTC insurance policy.

Verifying the Claimant Is Covered

An LTC claim analyst verifies the claimant is covered by an LTC policy by verifying the claimant's identity as the insured. When checking to see if a claimant is covered by a group LTC policy, the claim analyst should be aware that under some policies not only are the group insured and his spouse eligible for coverage, but also the parents of the group insured and his spouse. Practically all employer-employee group LTC insurance policies also offer coverage for an employer's retirees.

Verifying the Insured Needs Long-Term Care

To request LTC benefits, the insured or a member of the insured's family must complete a claim form. Generally the claim form requests (1) general information, including the LTC policy number and contact information for the insured; (2) the insured's physician's contact information so that medical records may be obtained; and (3) information regarding the nature of services required or being received, including diagnoses and types of care required. Figure 14.5 illustrates a home health care, adult day care, and assisted living claim form.

LTC policies typically require that a licensed health care practitioner certify that the insured is eligible for benefits. The claim analyst also may speak directly with the insured and/or the insured's family, physician, and long-term care provider staff to understand the circumstances of the insured's case.

FIGURE 14.5 Home Health Care, Adult Day Care, and Assisted Living Claim Form

PART ONE: CLAIMANT'S STATEMENT

Applying for following benefits:

Home Health Care ❑ **Adult Day Care ❑** **Assisted Living ❑** **Other ❑**

Policyholder ______________ Patient's Name ______________

Policyholder's S.S. # ______________ Patient's S.S. # ______________

Policy # ______________ Date of Birth ___/___/___ Telephone # ______________

____

Address City/State Zip

Type of Residence—Check One:

Home ❑ **Apartment ❑** **Retirement Community ❑** **Other ❑** ______________

Name, address and telephone number of person assisting with claim (if any):

Name ______________ Relationship ______________

____

Address City/State Zip

Telephone # ______________

(Attach copy of Legal Instrument) Check one: **Power of Attorney ❑** **Guardianship ❑**

Describe condition for which claim is being made: ______________

____

Name of Attending Physician: ______________ Telephone # ______________

____

Address City/State Zip

Name of Hospital ______________ Date Admitted ___/___/___ Date Discharged ___/___/___

____

Address City/State Zip

It is a crime to knowingly provide false, incomplete, or misleading information to an insurance company for the purpose of defrauding the company. Penalties include imprisonment, fines, and denial of insurance benefits.

Please complete and return the HIPAA Authorization Form that accompanies this claim form.

Patient or Legal Representative

Signature ______________ Date ______________

continued on next page…

FIGURE 14.5 continued Home Health Care, Adult Day Care, and Assisted Living Claim Form

PART TWO:
ASSESSMENT FORM
To be completed by Case Manager, Social Worker, Registered Nurse or Physician

Patient Name: ______________________ **Date of Birth:** ____/____/____

Diagnosis: 1.__________ 2.__________
3.__________ 4.__________
5.__________ 6.__________

Was patient hospitalized? Yes ❑ No ❑ Dates of Confinement ___/___/___ To ___/___/___

Was patient in a Nursing Home Facility? Yes ❑ No ❑ Dates of Confinement ___/___/___ To ___/___/___

Date of Last Assessment ___/___/___ Date of Next Assessment ___/___/___

Period authorized from: ___/___/___ To ___/___/___ Medicare Coverage? Yes ❑ No ❑

The above listed patient requires care to perform the following **Activities of Daily Living** or **Instrumental Activities of Daily Living**:

I-Independent **S-Stand-by Assistance at arm's length** **U-Needs Hands-On to perform**

ADL	I	S	U	IADL	I	U
Bathing	❑	❑	❑	Medicine Admin	❑	❑
Dressing	❑	❑	❑	Personal Finances	❑	❑
Toileting	❑	❑	❑	Prepare/cook meals	❑	❑
Continence	❑	❑	❑	Use Telephone	❑	❑
Mobility	❑	❑	❑	Housework	❑	❑
Transfers	❑	❑	❑	Laundry	❑	❑
Feeding/Eating	❑	❑	❑			

Cognitive Impairment Yes ❑ No ❑ (If yes, attach clinical test/documentation.)

I hereby certify that the above listed patient will be chronically ill for a period of 90 days or more: Yes ❑ No ❑

Recommended Services Nurse ❑ Therapist ❑ Home Health Aide ❑ Homemaker ❑
Companion ❑ Other __________

Total Number of days per week __________ Number of hours per day __________

Where is care being provided? Check one: Home ❑ Apartment ❑ Retirement Community ❑ Facility ❑
Other __________

Name of Provider __________ **Tax ID/S.S. #** __________

Address __________ Telephone# __________

Type of License: Home Health Care Agency ❑ Adult Day Care Agency ❑ Hospice Agency ❑ Other __________

It is a crime to knowingly provide false, incomplete, or misleading information to an insurance company for the purpose of defrauding the company. Penalities include imprisonment, fines, and denial of insurance benefits.

(Print) Name __________ Degree ______ Telephone # __________

Street Address __________ City or Town __________ Zip Code __________

Signature __________ Date __________

ATTACH FOLLOWING DOCUMENTS: (1) Plan of Care (2) Itemized Billing Statement (3) Explanation of Medicare Benefits Statements (if Medicare is providing coverage on these services)

Determining Whether the Policy Is Contestable

If a claimant files a claim within the contestable period, the claim analyst obtains the underwriting department's advice if she suspects that a material misrepresentation has occurred. If the material misrepresentation is confirmed and the insured would not have been issued his policy as written had the underwriter known the true information, the claim analyst then may refer the claim to the law department or the special investigative unit to determine the validity of the policy contract and/or whether the company is required to report an instance of fraud to the state in which the policy was issued.

Determining Whether Long-Term Care Is Covered

After verifying the loss, the claim analyst verifies that the particular care or service is covered by the policy. To determine whether an LTC policy covers the care or service, the claim analyst must decide if the policy's benefit triggers have been met, whether any exclusion or limitation prohibits coverage, and whether coverage is affected by any other policy provision.

Benefit Triggers

A ***benefit trigger*** is a long-term care insurance policy requirement specifying the conditions that establish an insured's eligibility to receive LTC benefits. For qualified LTC insurance policies, the following two occurrences can serve as LTC benefit triggers:

1. Inability of the insured to perform a certain number of ADLs without assistance
2. Severe cognitive impairment of the insured

Some nonqualified LTC insurance policies include a third benefit trigger—a doctor's certification that the insured has a medical need for long-term care—but this benefit trigger is not common and is not allowed in qualified LTC insurance policies.

Inability to Perform Activities of Daily Living (ADLs). In Chapter 7, we defined activities of daily living to include eating, bathing, dressing, continence, toileting, and transferring into or out of a bed, chair, or wheelchair. Qualified LTC insurance policies define specifically what it means for a person to be unable to perform ADLs *without assistance*. A licensed health care practitioner must certify that the individual requires substantial assistance with at least two ADLs.

According to the Internal Revenue Service, *substantial assistance* means both hands-on assistance and standby assistance.

- ***Hands-on assistance*** is when an individual is unable to perform an activity of daily living without the physical assistance of another person such as a personal aide. For example, Mrs. Jones needs someone to help her get in and out of the bathtub or to help with bathing.
- ***Standby assistance*** is when the individual requires the presence of another person within arm's reach to prevent by physical intervention an injury to the individual while the individual is performing an activity of daily living. For example, an attendant stands nearby while Mrs. Jones is bathing so that Mrs. Jones will have immediate help in the event that she starts to fall as a result of weakness while she is getting in or out of a bathtub.

Cognitive Impairment. Also in Chapter 7, we defined cognitive impairment as a reduction in a person's ability to think, reason, or remember and discussed several tests specialists use to measure cognitive impairment. Cognitive impairment severe enough to require regular supervision or assistance to protect the insured and others around the insured triggers LTC benefits. Many policies treat severe cognitive impairment as a benefit trigger even if the insured can perform all of the ADLs without assistance.

Exclusions

Most LTC policies specify certain exclusions. Figure 14.6 lists a number of the situations and conditions for which insurers typically will not pay benefits.

In addition, LTC insurance policies exclude coverage of pre-existing conditions. The most common exclusion practice is the six-and-six test, which states that an insured's long-term care is not covered if (1) the insured was treated for a condition within six months prior to the effective date of coverage and (2) the condition becomes the cause of long-term care within six months after the effective date of coverage.

Many LTC policies have a waiting period, which, as we discussed in Chapter 7, is a stated period of time that must pass before benefits are payable. For LTC policies, the waiting period is referred to as the *elimination period*, which is the number of days after a person insured under an LTC insurance policy must receive qualified eligible care under the policy before benefit payments under the policy can begin. Almost all insurers permit a person applying for an individual LTC insurance policy to select the desired elimination period from choices typically ranging from 0 to 100 days, with some older policies having elimination periods of 180 and even 360 days. However, group LTC policies have a set waiting period, which typically is 90 days. The LTC claim analyst must verify that the elimination period has been met before he authorizes benefits to be paid.

FIGURE 14.6 Typical LTC Policy Exclusions

Benefits are not paid for

- Alcoholism, drug addiction, or chemical dependency, unless as a result of medication prescribed by a doctor
- Self-inflicted injury or attempted suicide
- Care received outside the country in which the policy was issued
- Care for which benefits are payable under Medicare or other government programs, except Medicaid, unless otherwise required by law
- Care in government nursing facilities unless a charge is made that the insured is obligated to pay.
- Services for which no charge is normally made in the absence of insurance

Many LTC insurance policies contain a restoration of benefits provision. The ***restoration of benefits provision*** allows an insured who has used some benefits under an LTC insurance policy to regain a full benefit period after a stated period of recovery time has passed following delivery of long-term care services. Insight 14.2 explains this provision.

Calculating Policy Benefits Payable

When the claim analyst determines the insured is entitled to an LTC benefit, he then determines the amount of the benefit payment based on the LTC policy provisions. Note that sometimes an applicant for an LTC insurance policy lists an incorrect age on the application, and the insurer issues a policy with premiums based on the misstated age. LTC insurance policies contain a misstatement of age provision like the one included in life insurance policies, in which LTC insurance policy benefits are adjusted to the level that the premiums paid would have bought based on the insured's correct age.

Benefits

The most common way of stating an LTC insurance policy's benefits is as a daily benefit amount. The ***daily benefit amount*** is the amount the insurer will pay for each day of an insured's long-term care at a care facility or in the insured's home. For instance, a policy may state that a benefit of $150 per day will be payable upon the insured's admission to a nursing home or other care facility that meets criteria specified in the policy.

INSIGHT 14.2 Restoration of Benefits Provision

Joan Bennett is covered by an LTC policy that provides a daily benefit of $300 for 24 months. Her policy has a restoration of benefits provision that specifies that her benefits will be restored to the full 24 months if she remains free from the need for long-term care for 6 months. Mrs. Bennett breaks her hip in a fall and receives long-term care in a nursing home for 8 months. Normally, Mrs. Bennett would have a maximum of 16 months left on the policy's 24-month benefit period. However, because her policy has a restoration of benefits provision, Mrs. Bennett's benefit period will be restored to a full 24 months if she remains free from the need for long-term care for 6 months following her release from the nursing home.

Long-term care policies generally determine the daily benefit amount according to either the indemnity benefit method or the reimbursement method. The ***indemnity benefit method*** pays a specified benefit regardless of the actual expenses for long-term care of the insured. Under the indemnity benefit method, if an insured enters a nursing home costing $150 per day and the policy provides for a daily benefit amount of $200 per day, then the insured will receive a benefit that is $50 greater than the actual nursing home cost. On the other hand, if the same nursing home charged $225 per day, then the insured will receive a benefit that is $25 less than the actual cost. In other words, an indemnity-type policy always pays the daily benefit amount for a day of services, no matter what the actual cost. If the policy stipulated a benefit period of three years, the benefits would be exhausted after exactly three years (1,095 days) of benefits have been paid.

Other LTC insurance policies use a reimbursement approach to benefit payments. Under the ***reimbursement method***, the insured receives reimbursement for approved LTC expenses up to a maximum limit specified by the policy. In no case, however, will the insured receive more in benefits than the actual charges for long-term care.

LTC policies may use methods other than the indemnity benefit method and the reimbursement method to describe the benefit amount for certain types of LTC benefits. For example, the benefit amount for home health care and for adult day care is typically 50 percent of the policy's daily benefit amount. Individual and group LTC policies typically have lifetime maximum benefits, and this maximum benefit payable also may be smaller for such benefits. For example, assume that Jamal Ahmad has an LTC policy that provides a benefit amount of $150 per day and a lifetime maximum benefit amount of $300,000. Mr. Ahmad's home health care benefit, however, specifies that the maximum daily amount is $75 per day, and the lifetime maximum benefit amount for this type of care is $150,000.

Payment of some benefits, such as alternate care benefits, reduces the maximum benefit amount payable under the LTC policy. For example, if the maximum benefit amount for an LTC policy is $200,000 and the insured receives $40,000 in alternate care benefits, the remaining maximum benefit amount for long-term care will be $160,000. For those benefits that have their own separate maximums, amounts paid are not counted toward the policy maximum.

LTC coverage may be offered as a rider to a life insurance policy, in which case the benefit amount usually is stated as a percentage of the death benefit of the life insurance policy, rather than as a flat amount per day. Although many insurers offer a lifetime benefit period under their life insurance policy LTC rider, most LTC riders include a limit to the total financial benefit for long-term care that will be paid. Long-term care benefits paid under a rider to a life insurance policy also reduce the life insurance benefit.

Inflation Protection

An ***inflation protection provision*** is an LTC insurance policy provision that either automatically increases the benefit amount each year by a specific percentage or allows the insured to opt for a higher daily benefit at specified intervals during the lifetime of the policy without having to show evidence of insurability. Inflation protection also may be provided by means of a rider to an LTC policy.

The two most common approaches to providing inflation protection in LTC insurance policies by automatically increasing the benefit amount each year are

- The ***simple inflation provision***, which increases the coverage amount for an LTC insurance policy each year by a specified percentage of the original daily benefit. For instance, a simple inflation provision might increase the daily benefit amount each year by 5 percent of the original daily benefit amount.

- The ***compound inflation provision***, which increases the coverage amount for an LTC insurance policy each year by a specified percentage of the compounded daily benefit amount. For example, if the policyowner of a new LTC insurance policy that provides a daily benefit amount of $100.00 chooses a compound inflation provision at a 5 percent interest rate, at the beginning of the second year, the benefit amount will be the same as for the simple inflation provision, or $105.00 [$100.00 + ($100.00 × 0.05)]. However, at the beginning of the third year, the base for calculating the daily benefit amount for the LTC insurance policy will now be $105.00, not $100.00 as is the case for the simple inflation provision. Thus, at the beginning of the third year, the daily benefit amount under a compound inflation provision will be $110.25 [$105.00 + ($105.00 × 0.05)], whereas the daily benefit amount under a simple inflation provision will be $110.00 [$105.00 + ($100.00 × 0.05)].

An inflation provision is an effective way to protect against the risk that a seemingly adequate benefit will become inadequate over time. Adding an inflation provision to an LTC insurance policy can be expensive, however. A simple inflation provision can increase an LTC insurance policy's premium by 25 to 30 percent. The compound inflation provision can almost double the premium. The compound inflation provision is more expensive because it creates significantly greater insurance coverage over a period of time.

To keep the cost of coverage reasonable, some insurers place a cap on the total increase in the LTC insurance policy's daily benefit amount that may occur during the lifetime of the policy as a result of an inflation provision. Many states allow for a cap with a simple inflation provision, but do not allow a cap with a compound inflation provision.

The second kind of inflation protection provision found in an LTC policy is the ***guaranteed purchase option***, which allows an insured person to add to the original daily benefit amount at intervals specified in the LTC insurance policy without having to provide evidence of insurability. For instance, at every third anniversary, an insured might have the right to buy an additional daily benefit amount up to the actual percentage increase during the three-year period in the . The ***()*** is a national measurement of the rate of inflation compiled monthly by the U. S. Bureau of Labor Statistics.

A few group LTC insurance policies provide a pre-funded protection option. Offered only at the time of application, a ***pre-funded inflation option*** typically provides that the group LTC insurance policy's daily benefit amount will increase by a certain amount or percentage each year after the insured reaches age 65, the cost of which is built into the policy's premium structure.

Determining Who Is Entitled to Receive the Benefits

Insurers pay benefits to the insured unless he has assigned them to the provider. Claims for LTC benefits sometimes involve an insured who has a family member or friend handling his finances and claim submission. In such a situation, the claim analyst obtains the appropriate documentation verifying this individual's legal authority to act on behalf of the insured. In addition, the claim analyst obtains a valid assignment of benefits from this individual if benefits are to be paid directly to a treatment provider. If benefits are not assigned, the insurer typically continues to pay benefits directly to the insured, but mails the payment to the person who is acting for the insured.

Key Terms

diagnostic code
International Classification of Diseases and Related Health Problems (ICD)
treatment code
Physicians' Current Procedural Terminology (CPT)
time limit on certain defenses provision
medically necessary
precertification
pre-existing condition
usual, customary, and reasonable (UCR) charge
lifetime maximum benefit
coordination of benefits (COB) provision
allowable expense
nonduplication of benefits provision
overinsurance provision
subrogation clause
assignment of benefits
explanation of benefits (EOB)
qualified long-term care policy
nonqualifed long-term care policy
nursing care
skilled nursing care
intermediate nursing care
custodial care
home health care
adult day care
adult day care center
alternate care
hospice care
hospice
assisted living facility
respite care
caregiver training benefit
unintentional lapse provision
third-party notification provision
full portability option
benefit trigger
hands-on assistance
standby assistance
restoration of benefits provision
daily benefit amount
indemnity benefit method
reimbursement method
inflation protection provision
simple inflation provision
compound inflation provision
guaranteed purchase option ()
pre-funded inflation option

Endnote

1. This section is adapted from Harriett E. Jones, *Principles of Insurance: Life, Health, and Annuities*, 3rd ed. [Atlanta: LOMA (Life Office Management Association, Inc.), © 2005], 351–355 and Mary C. Bickley, *Principles of Financial Services and Products* [Atlanta: LOMA (Life Office Management Association, Inc.), © 2004], 200–203. Used with permission; all rights reserved.

chapter 15

Administering Disability Income Insurance Claims

Outline

Sources of DI Insurance Claim Information
Claim Form
Medical Information
Personal Information
Financial Information
Employment Information

Processing DI Insurance Claims
Verifying the Coverage Was in Force
Verifying the Claimant Is Covered
Verifying a Disability Has Been Incurred
Determining Whether the Policy Is Contestable
Determining Whether the Disability Is Covered
Calculating Policy Benefits Payable

Administering Continuing DI Insurance Claims

DI Insurance Supplemental Benefits
Waiver of Premium for Disability Benefit
Cost-of-Living Adjustment Benefit
Rehabilitation Benefit
Transplant Donor Benefit
Future Increase Option Benefit

Terminating DI Insurance Benefits
End of Benefit Period
End of Disability
End of Eligibility for a Group Member or a Group

Settling DI Insurance Claims
Disputed Claims
Undisputed Claims

Learning Objectives

After studying this chapter, you should be able to…

- List the information sources claim analysts use for disability income (DI) insurance claims
- Explain the process for handling DI insurance claims
- Discuss how claim analysts handle continuing DI insurance claims
- Discuss supplementary benefits under DI insurance coverage
- Explain the procedures for terminating DI insurance coverage
- Discuss the methods insurers use to settle DI insurance claims

Disability income (DI) insurance provides periodic benefits to replace income if the insured is unable to work as a result of sickness or injury. Insurance companies issue both individual and group DI insurance policies. The coverage provided by such policies is classified as either short- or long-term coverage, depending on the length of the benefit period—the length of time during which DI benefits will be paid—which we discuss later in the chapter. Whether DI coverage is group or individual and short- or long-term has an impact on several aspects of claim administration.

Disability income insurance claims are processed using the same basic steps as life, medical expense, critical illness, and long-term care claims. However, DI claims frequently are more complex than these other types of claims. Evaluation of a DI claim involves not only establishing the presence of a disability, but also determining the probable length of that disability and its future impact on the ability of the insured to return to work. In addition, if a disability is long-term, the claim analyst must administer the claim over a period of time and possibly oversee the insured's rehabilitation.

We begin this chapter with a discussion of the sources of DI claim information, followed by an explanation of the DI claims process for new and continuing claims. We then discuss DI supplemental benefits. The remainder of the chapter covers the termination of DI benefits and the settlement of DI claims.

Sources of DI Insurance Claim Information

To gather the information needed to process a DI claim, a claim analyst refers to the claim form, as well as other sources of medical, personal, financial, and employment information.

Claim Form

When an insurer receives notice of a claim, a claim form is sent to the insured. Insurers typically ask the insured to complete and submit the claim form within a specified time—usually 30 to 90 days—after the onset of disability. However, most insurers allow an insured to submit a claim form at a later date, particularly if the nature of the disability prevented the insured from submitting the claim form in a timely manner.

DI claim forms contain a section that the insured completes, a section that the attending physician completes, and a section that the employer completes. Each insurer determines what information it needs to make a claim decision as accurately and efficiently as possible; thus, each insurer's claim form is different. Figure 15.1 provides an example of a disability income claim form.

Using information on the claim form, the claim analyst assesses the cause of the disability for the following three reasons:

1. The insurer's liability for coverage depends on whether the cause fits the policy's definition of sickness or injury.
2. The date on which benefits become payable may differ depending on whether the cause of the disability is sickness or injury because of the waiting period requirements. The waiting period begins on the date a covered disability begins. Group DI policies typically specify a seven-day waiting period for short-term DI claims caused by sickness, no waiting period for short-term disabilities caused by injury, and a 30- to 60-day waiting period for long-term DI claims caused by sickness or injury. Individual DI policies typically have waiting period options from which the insured can select, as we explained in Chapter 7.
3. If the cause of disability is a risk excluded from the policy, the claim will not be covered.

Medical Information

The physician's portion of the claim form may be considered an attending physician's statement (APS). The physician provides detailed information about the nature and cause of the disability, along with the physician's diagnosis, the results of laboratory and other tests, the types of treatment and medication recommended, and the places and dates of treatment. By reviewing the information provided by the physician, the claim analyst usually can determine a great deal about the nature and extent of the disability and the probable prognosis.

Some physicians are reluctant to state that an insured is disabled, usually because they do not know the details of an insured's occupation or the policy's definition of disability. However, most physicians will provide sufficient information for the claim analyst to determine whether the insured is disabled under the terms of the policy. Because a claim for disability is not as easily verifiable as a claim for death benefits or medical expense reimbursement, a DI claim analyst needs special training in evaluating the nature and extent of physical and mental impairments and in determining to what extent such impairments hamper the performance of specific job duties.

To encourage an attending physician to help determine the presence and extent of a disability, a claim analyst sometimes sends the physician information about the policy provisions relating to disability and a copy of the insured's job description from the employer. Using this information,

FIGURE 15.1 Disability Income Claim Form

CLAIMANT'S STATEMENT (PLEASE PRINT)

Your reply by __________ is appreciated and enables us to provide timely consideration of your claim. Mail Stop:

1. Claimant's Name (last, first, middle) | Social Security Number

Residence Address (Street, City, State, Zip)

Home Telephone Number ( ) | Business Telephone Number ( )

2. Policy Number(s)

3. Have you been at any of your places of business, or engaged in any work activity for payment, profit, or other compensation during your claimed period of disability? ❑ Yes ❑ No If yes, please give dates, hours worked, duties performed, and indicate how you were compensated.

Weekly or Monthly Earned Income Before Taxes $ **(please provide documentation of earnings)**

If you have not returned to work, when do you expect to return to work? Part Time: Full Time:

How does your injury or sickness continue to impede your ability to perform your occupational duties?

4. When was the last date you were treated by or consulted with a medical practitioner?

5. Describe your present activities.

Other than as described above, have there been any other changes in your daily activities or your condition since your last report? ❑ Yes ❑ No. If yes, describe.

6. Does your current condition prevent you from caring for yourself? ❑ Yes ❑ No Does someone provide assistance? ❑ Yes ❑ No If yes to either question, please explain how.

7. Since the last report, have you applied for or begun to receive any other Disability, Workers' Compensation, Unemployment, Social Security, Retirement, or Pension benefits? ❑ Yes ❑ No If yes, please provide us with detailed information for each benefit in the space provided below. Please also report any changes to previously reported benefits.

Source of Income	Name of Insurance Carrier (if applicable)	Policy or ID No.	Benefit Amount Weekly/Monthly	Date claim was filed	Date payments began	Date payments ended

If you have been approved or denied for any of these benefits, please submit a copy of Award or Denial letter(s).

The above statements are true and complete to the best of my knowledge and belief.
(Your signature is required for benefit consideration.)

Signature ____________________________ Date ____________

continued on next page...

FIGURE 15.1 *continued* Disability Income Claim Form

ATTENDING PHYSICIAN'S STATEMENT (PLEASE PRINT)

1. Name of Patient	Social Security Number	Height	Weight	Blood Pressure Last Visit

2. Primary Diagnosis Including ICD9 and/or DSM IV Multi Evaluation Nomenclature and Code Number

Date of most recent treatment: Date of next appointment: Frequency of visits:

PLEASE ATTACH ALL OFFICE TREATMENT NOTES SINCE LAST REPORT.

3. Objective Findings since last report (including current x-rays, EKGs, psychiatric testing, laboratory data, and any clinical findings)

Please describe symptoms since last report.

Are there secondary conditions impairing your patient's work capacity? ❑ Yes ❑ No If yes, what are they?

4. If cardiac condition, what is the patient's functional capacity? (American Heart Association)
❑ Class 1—No limitation ❑ Class 2—Slight limitation ❑ Class 3—Marked limitation ❑ Class 4—Complete limitation

5. Has the patient undergone surgery, been hospitalized, or been referred to a medical rehabilitation or therapy program? ❑ Yes ❑ No
If yes, give details. (Name and address of provider, facility, and dates of service or referral.)

6. Please list names and dosages of all medications that patient is currently taking.

7. Have you referred the patient for other types of consultations? ❑ Yes ❑ No If yes, give details (name and address of provider, facility, and date of referral).

8. Is return to work a focus of the treatment plan? ❑ Yes ❑ No If no, please explain.

9. Information About the Patient's Functional Capacity

Has patient been released to work in his/her occupation? ❑ Yes ❑ No In any occupation? ❑ Yes ❑ No If yes, provide date:
If no, when do you expect patient to be released to work in his/her occupation? Date: In any occupation? Date:

If the patient continues to demonstrate a loss of function, please provide current restrictions and limitations in the space provided below.

Fully describe restrictions and limitations.
RESTRICTIONS (what the patient should not do)

LIMITATIONS (what the patient cannot do)

Give details concerning any change (improvement or deterioration)

10. Additional Remarks

FRAUD NOTICE: Any person who knowingly files a statement of claim containing false or misleading information is subject to criminal and civil penalties. The above statements are true and complete to the best of my knowledge and belief.

Print or Type Name		Degree	Medical Specialty
Street Address			Phone Number ( )
City	State	Zip Code	Fax ( )
Signature of Physician			Date
SSN or Tax ID Number:			

continued on next page...

FIGURE 15.1 *continued* Disability Income Claim Form

EMPLOYER'S STATEMENT (PLEASE PRINT)

Type of Coverage (CHECK ALL THAT APPLY)

❑ Long Term Disability ❑ Individual Disability ❑ Waiver of Premium (Life Insurance) ❑ Voluntary Workplace Benefits

1. Employer Name	Employer's Phone Number ( )

Employer Address (Street, City, State, ZIP)

Policy Numbers	Division Number/Class Number	Division Description/Class Description

2. Claimaint's Name	Claimant's Phone Number ( )

Claimant's Address (Street, City, State, ZIP)

Social Security Number	Date of Hire	Effective Date of LTD Insurance	Effective Date of ID Insurance	Date Last Worked

Claimant's Work Status ❑ Full-time ❑ Part-time ❑ Exempt ❑ Non-exempt ❑ Bargaining ❑ Non-bargaining

Did the claimant's job duties and/or hours change prior to his/her last day worked due to disability? ❑ Yes ❑ No If yes, please explain.

Has the claimant's employment been terminated? ❑ Yes ❑ No If yes, please provide termination date.

3. Has claimant returned to work? ❑ Yes ❑ No | If yes, date ❑ Full-Time ❑ Part-Time Hours Per Week

4. Job Title/Major Job Duties **(Please attach a copy of claimant's job description)**

5. How was the LTD premium paid for the plan year in which the disability occurred?
Percentage paid by Employer _______ Was the premium amount paid by the employer included in the employee's W-2? ❑ Yes ❑ No
Percentage paid by Employee _______ ❑ Pre-tax ❑ Post-tax

6. How was the ID premium paid for the plan year in which the disability occurred?
Percentage paid by Employer _______ Was the premium amount paid by the employer included in the employee's W-2? ❑ Yes ❑ No
Percentage paid by Employee _______ ❑ Pre-tax ❑ Post-tax

7. Year to Date Earnings (for FICA % Deductions) $

8. How was the claimaint paid? (please check all that apply)

❑ Hourly ❑ Salary ❑ Overtime ❑ Bonus ❑ Commissions ❑ Other

What is the earnings figure you use to compute premium payments for this claimant on an annual basis ? $

Salary/Wage prior to date last worked ***(refer to Earnings definition in your contract.)***

❑ Hourly ❑ Weekly ❑ Bi-Weekly ❑ Semi-Monthly $	Bonuses (per week) $	Commissions (per week) $

9. Financial Documentation (please refer to your contract for your Earnings definition and attach the appropriate documentation).

Salary Only/Current Earnings definition: **Attach copy of payroll records or paystubs for 3 months just prior to disability.**

Bonus/Commissions Included: **Attach copy of payroll records for the 12 or 24 months (see definition) just prior to disability.**

Other Earnings definitions: **Attach referenced document per Earnings definition (W-2, K-1s, Schedule Cs, teacher's contract, etc.).**

continued on next page…

FIGURE 15.1 *continued* Disability Income Claim Form

Claimant Name | Social Security Number

10. Claimant Pre-Tax Withholdings (Indicate pre-tax withholdings in effect just prior to disbability.)

401(k)/403(b) %; Pre-tax medical and other insurance $ /week; Flexible spending account $ /week

11. Date of last Salary/Wage Increase | Work Schedule at time last worked Days/Week Hours/Day Hours/Week

Check off regular work days ❑ Sun ❑ Mon ❑ Tues ❑ Wed ❑ Thurs ❑ Fri ❑ Sat | Number of hours on date last worked

Date paid through For ❑ Salary Continuation ❑ Vacation Pay ❑ Accrued Sick Pay ❑ Other

Paid Time Off/Sick Leave balance as of last day worked

12. Does the claimant have an ownership interest in this business? ❑ Yes ❑ No If yes, what is the % of ownership? %

Type of business entity? ❑ Regular Corporation ❑ S Corporation ❑ Partnership ❑ Sole Proprietorship

13. If this is a Flexible Benefits Plan, indicate which option of coverage this claimant has chosen.

Previous Plan Year - Date of Open Enrollment Option ;Current Plan Year - Date of Open Enrollment Option

14. Prior LTD Carrier Name	Effective Date
Address (Street, City, State, ZIP)	Termination Date

15. Is claimant eligible for	Yes	No	If yes, weekly or monthly amount	Weekly	Monthly	When do benefits begin?	When do benefits end?
Salary Continuation	❑	❑	$	❑	❑		
State Disability	❑	❑	$	❑	❑		
Other Disability Benefits	❑	❑	$	❑	❑		
Social Security	❑	❑	$	❑	❑		
Worker's Compensation	❑	❑	$	❑	❑		

Is the claim the result of a work related injury or sickness? ❑ Yes ❑ No

If so, has Worker's Compensation claim been filed?	❑	❑	If yes, Name and Address of Carrier
Health Insurance	❑	❑	If yes, Name and Address of Carrier
Life Insurance	❑	❑	If yes, Amount of Coverage $

If Workers' Compensation claim has been denied, please submit a copy of denial with this claim.

16. Information about your pension plan (Please send copy of Plan Summary.) (Do not complete for maternity claim.)

Do you have a pension plan ❑ Yes ❑ No	If yes, what type? ❑ Defined benefit ❑ Defined contribution ❑ 401(k)/403(b) ❑ Profit Sharing ❑ Other (specify)	
Is claimant eligible for your pension plan? ❑ Yes ❑ No	If eligible, does the claimant participate? ❑ Yes ❑ No	What % does claimant contribute?

If the claimant is participating, when is he or she eligible for benefits under the plan?

17. If the claimant is released to return to work with restrictions and limitations, are you willing to accommodate?

The above statements are true and complete to the best of my knowledge and belief.

Name of Person Completing Form		Telephone Number ( )
Title of Person Completing Form	E-mail Address	Fax Number ( )
Signature		Date Signed

the physician can help the claim analyst determine whether the insured is (1) disabled under the terms of the policy and (2) capable of performing some or all of the specified job duties.

If a claim analyst would like more information on the cause and/or extent of the insured's sickness or injury, the claim analyst may require the insured to undergo an examination by an independent medical professional selected and compensated by the insurance company. The claim analyst also may consult the insurer's medical director, who can provide insight into medical diagnoses and treatments and advise the claim analyst during the investigation of a DI claim. None of these health care professionals—the attending physician, the independent medical professional, or the medical director—makes a final decision on a claim. After a review of all the information available along with consultation with these experts, the claim analyst is responsible for making that decision.

The claim analyst also can consult the Disability Insurance Records System (DIRS), which is managed by MIB and which provides MIB-member insurers with information designed to alert them to the presence of overinsurance. This information is especially important to a claim analyst who is evaluating an individual DI claim during the policy's contestable period.

Personal Information

The claim analyst can use the same kinds of investigatory techniques that an underwriter uses, including personal interviews with the insured. Although inspection reports are not widely used for investigations of DI claims, the analyst may order one. The usual information included in an inspection report compiled for DI claim purposes focuses on the degree of an insured's disability, the presence of overinsurance, and verification of information on income and employment. Claim analysts sometimes order surveillance to discover whether an insured is working at an undisclosed occupation or to verify the reported activity level of the insured. Surveillance is especially useful when an insured's claim is based on subjective complaints. In such a case, the surveillance is used to verify objectively the insured's limited activities.

Financial Information

If a claim analyst needs to verify a DI claimant's pre-disability income, she typically obtains and analyzes a W-2 form in the United States or a T4 form in Canada, as well as other tax forms that identify income from other sources. If a disabled insured is the sole proprietor of a business, the claim analyst usually obtains federal income tax returns for the business, along with a profit-and-loss statement, to verify the pre-disability level of income that the insured derived from the business. If a disabled insured is a partner in a business, a copy of the partnership tax return usually provides enough information for the claim analyst to establish the pre-disability income level of the insured. After a review of all the information available, claim analysts sometimes seek input from the insurer's accountants in analyzing financial records.

Employment Information

If a claim analyst needs more information concerning the insured's employment than is submitted on the claim form, the analyst usually asks the employer for the necessary information. The type of information usually requested includes details about an insured's job duties. Figure 15.2 illustrates a sample job analysis form for a long-term DI claim. The claim analyst also may need to determine whether the employer anticipates continuing to employ the insured if the insured is able to return to work.

Processing DI Insurance Claims

The steps taken by DI claim analysts to process claims are the same steps life, medical expense, critical illness, and long-term care claim analysts follow when processing claims. After completing the process, the claim analyst sends a letter to notify the claimant of the decision. If the decision is to deny the claim, the letter explains the basis for the denial. If the decision is to pay the claim in whole or in part, the letter specifies the benefits to which the claimant is entitled. With individual DI claims, the claim analyst usually notifies the producer who originally sold the DI policy of the decision.

Verify the Coverage Was in Force

The claim analyst verifies that premiums were paid to date when the disability began. If the policy has been applied for but not yet issued, the claim analyst must investigate any premium receipt that may have been issued to determine whether coverage nonetheless was effective on the date of disability.

If the insured under an individual disability income policy becomes disabled during the grace period, insurers typically will pay DI benefits and deduct all premiums due from the benefit payments. If the insured becomes disabled while the policy is being reinstated, policies differ. Under the terms of some policies, the insurer will pay DI benefits if the insured meets all the reinstatement conditions. Under the terms of other policies, the policy simply would not be reinstated.

FIGURE 15.2 Job Analysis Form for Long-Term Disability

JOB ANALYSIS FORM

To be completed by the employee's supervisor.

This claim is for (employee's name) ____________________

Employee's social security number ____________________

Date of disability (month, day, year) ____________________

A. General information about the employee's job

Job title ____________________

Minimum education or training required ____________________

Does the employee perform supervisory functions? ___ Yes ___ No

If yes, how many people are supervised? __________

Describe job duties ____________________

Check the items below that relate to the employee's job. Use these definitions for the frequency of occurrence:

Occasionally means the person does the activity up to 33% of the time.

Frequently means the person does the activity 34% to 66% of the time.

Continuously means the person does the activity 67% to 100% of the time.

ACTIVITY	OCCASIONALLY	FREQUENTLY	CONTINUOUSLY
_____ Relates to others	_____	_____	_____
_____ Written and verbal communication	_____	_____	_____
_____ Reasoning, math, and language	_____	_____	_____
_____ Makes independent judgments	_____	_____	_____

Which of the following describe the employee's working environment? Check all that apply.

_____ Unprotected heights ____ Changes in temperature or humidity ____ Exposure to dust, fumes, and gases

_____ Being near moving machinery _____ Driving automotive equipment ____ Other hazards

Is the employee required to travel? ____ Yes ____ No

If yes, complete the following information

How (automobile, plane, train, etc.) does the employee travel? ____________________

Where does the employee travel? ____________________

What percent of the time does the employee travel? ____________________

continued on next page…

FIGURE 15.2 *continued* Job Analysis Form for Long-Term Disability

B. Information about the physical aspects of the employee's job

Check the items below that relate to the employee's job and complete the information requested. Use these definitions for the frequency of occurrence:

Occasionally means the person does the activity up to 33% of the time.

Frequently means the person does the activity 34% to 66% of the time.

Continuously means the person does the activity 67% to 100% of the time.

ACTIVITY	OCCASIONALLY	FREQUENTLY	CONTINUOUSLY
_____ Standing	_____	_____	_____
_____ Walking	_____	_____	_____
_____ Sitting	_____	_____	_____
_____ Balancing	_____	_____	_____
_____ Stooping	_____	_____	_____
_____ Kneeling	_____	_____	_____
_____ Crouching	_____	_____	_____
_____ Crawling	_____	_____	_____
_____ Reaching/working overhead	_____	_____	_____
_____ Climbing	_____	_____	_____
_____ Stairs	_____	_____	_____
Number of stairs _____			
_____ Ladders	_____	_____	_____
Height of ladder _____			
_____ Pulling	_____	_____	_____
Describe activity and how many pounds pulled _____________________			
_____ Lifting/Carrying	_____	_____	_____
Describe activity and how many pounds lifted/carried _____________________			
_____ Pushing	_____	_____	_____
Describe activity and how many pounds pushed _____________________			

Can the job be performed by alternating sitting and standing?

____ Yes ____ No

Does the job require using the feet to operate foot controls?

____ Yes ____ No If yes, on what type of equipment? _____________________

continued on next page...

FIGURE 15.2 *continued* **Job Analysis Form for Long-Term Disability**

How important is good vision in the job? ______________________________

What are the major tasks requiring use of one or both hands?

	One Hand	Two Hands
______________________________	_____	_____
______________________________	_____	_____
______________________________	_____	_____

C. Information about the job as it relates to the disability

Can the job be modified to accommodate the disability either temporarily or permanently?
____ Yes ____ No

If yes, explain. ______________________________

Is it possible to offer the employee assistance in doing the job (through use of technology or personal assistance, for example)?
____ Yes ____ No

If yes, explain. ______________________________

D. Attachments and Signature (Attach a copy of the employee's job description.)

Name of person completing this form ____________________

Signature ______________________________

Title ______________________________

Date ______________________________

Telephone ______________________________

Fax ______________________________

Verify the Claimant Is Covered

The claim analyst must verify that the claimant is the insured under an individual DI policy and a covered member of the group under a group DI policy. As with other claims, the claim analyst's task of verifying the identity of the disabled individual as the insured typically involves comparing the disabled individual's name and other personal information found on the claim form with the insured's name and information found in the policy application and other policy records.

Verifying a Disability Has Been Incurred

Using the information submitted on a DI claim form and other medical information, the DI claim analyst determines whether the insured actually has incurred a disability or is still disabled. Some DI claims in particular raise questions about the existence or extent of the disability, and such questions must be answered before the claim analyst can make a decision to pay or deny the claim. In addition, claim analysts may find it particularly difficult to determine whether an insured is actually disabled when the cause of the purported disability is a mental disorder or substance abuse. Large DI insurers may have specially trained claim analysts to handle mental disorder and substance abuse cases.

Questionable Claims

A claim analyst investigates questionable claims or refers them for investigation to the special investigative unit if fraud is suspected. Additional information from the insured, the employer, health care providers, independent medical examiners, and the SIU typically enables the claim analyst to reach a decision. However, insurers sometimes get assistance on complex or highly unusual claims from an outside investigative agency. Ultimately, though, a claim analyst must make the decision and administer the claim.

Some of the most common circumstances in which claims may be considered questionable and may require additional investigation involve a late notice of claim, a problematic diagnosis, a problematic prognosis, and infrequent medical attention.

Late Notice of Claim. DI policies typically require written notice of a claim to be sent to the insurer within 30 days after a disability begins or as soon as reasonably possible. If the notice of claim is not submitted within a reasonable period of time after a disability is alleged to have begun, the notice is considered late. What constitutes a reasonable time varies considerably depending on the circumstances of the claim and whether the insurer can prove that the claim investigation was prejudiced by the late notice. Because most genuinely disabled insureds need money to replace lost income and, therefore, tend to notify the insurer of a DI claim promptly, a late notice of claim may indicate a suspicious claim. The claim analyst determines whether to order an investigative report of the claimant's activities during the period of alleged total disability.

Problematic Diagnosis. The diagnosis given for a claimant's disability is sometimes nonspecific or vague. For example, an attending physician may report symptoms, such as nausea or dizziness, rather than a specific diagnosis. These symptoms could be caused by any number of conditions, so the claim analyst undertakes an investigation to determine the exact diagnosis. Another example is a diagnosis that states only that a claimant suffers from anemia, arthritis, anxiety, pneumonia, hepatitis, or stroke with no accompanying explanation. Any of these conditions could be of minor or major concern, depending on how they limit the insured's activities. Given such a nonspecific or vague diagnosis, the claim analyst typically interviews or requests further written information from the physician to determine the exact cause of the claimant's disability and the severity of the condition.

Problematic Prognosis. An ambiguous or unreasonably extended prognosis usually requires careful investigation to determine the extent of a disability. Occasionally a physician indicates only that a claimant's prognosis is "unknown," "indefinite," or "uncertain" and refuses to state a date by which the claimant can be expected to return to work. Certain medical conditions do defy accurate estimates of continuing disability. However, for other conditions—particularly those for which the prognosis seems inconsistent with the cause of disability—the claim analyst persists in trying to learn from the physician a reasonable estimate of recovery time.

Sometimes an attending physician repeatedly extends the period of time during which a claimant will be disabled. If the physician changes the previous estimate of the date of return to work and the nature of the disability does not appear to warrant such an extended prognosis, the claim analyst generally attempts to elicit from the physician specific information about the disability and the work activities in which the claimant reasonably can be expected to take part.

Infrequent Medical Attention. In the case of a long-term disability claim, when a supposedly disabled claimant appears to need medical attention on a less frequent basis than would normally be required for his claimed condition, the claim analyst is alerted to the possibility that the reported disability should be investigated. An independent medical examination and an activities check of the claimant are two tools that may be used to determine whether the insured is still disabled.

Mental Disorders and Substance Abuse

When a claim indicates that the cause of the disability is a mental disorder or substance abuse, the claim analyst has to make decisions based on more subjective data than that which usually accompanies other sickness or injury claims. The most effective way to manage benefits for mental illness and substance abuse is to define in the policy the conditions that are covered, the level of coverage for each, and any other requirements for payment of benefits. The responsibility of the claim analyst is to verify that an insured applying for such benefits is disabled by a condition that meets the policy requirements and definitions.

Evaluating DI claims involving a mental illness diagnosis often calls for a work site assessment. During a ***work site assessment***, a claim analyst or an investigator interviews an employer and reviews the claimant's actual job duties and level of success in performing those duties. The claim analyst or investigator also obtains a specific job description for the claimant, learns the criteria by which the claimant's performance is evaluated, and determines whether such factors as downsizing or legal difficulties have affected the claimant's job. If a claimant is self-employed, the analyst or investigator obtains as much detail as possible about the claimant's work by using client appointment records, contracts, financial documents, and interviews with clients. The claim analyst then consults with the insured's physician to determine the extent to which the insured's mental disorder or substance abuse prevents him from performing his job duties.

Determining Whether the Policy Is Contestable

Most individual DI policies include an incontestability provision; if a claim is submitted during a policy's contestable period, the claim analyst investigates the possibility of a material misrepresentation in the application. Group DI contracts also contain incontestability provisions, but because most group DI insureds do not provide evidence of insurability, claim analysts rarely are concerned with the possibility of material misrepresentations in the application when a claim is made. However, claim analysts will check for material misrepresentations in the case of late enrollees, who must submit evidence of insurability. If that evidence includes material misstatements, the coverage can be voided; no benefits will be due if a claim is filed.

Determining Whether the Disability Is Covered

To qualify for benefits under a DI policy, an insured must have incurred a disability due to sickness or injury. The terms *sickness*, *injury*, and *disability* are all defined in the policy; the insured's condition must meet these definitions to be eligible for coverage. In addition, the cause of the disability must not be excluded from coverage.

Definitions of Sickness and Injury

In a DI policy, generally a ***sickness*** is an illness or a disease that (1) includes pregnancy unless it is specifically excluded under the contract and (2) begins while a person is insured under the policy. Usually an ***injury*** is defined as an accidental harm resulting from an unforeseen external force that (1) causes trauma to a person's body and (2) occurs while the DI policy is in force. An injury normally is defined as a condition resulting independently of sickness. A claim analyst uses the information on the claim form and in the medical records to ensure that an insured's condition meets the policy's definition of sickness or injury.

Definition of Disability

The claim analyst ascertains whether an insured has met the policy's definition of a particular level of disability, which may vary from one policy to another. The levels of disability covered under disability contracts typically include total disability, presumptive total disability, partial disability, and recurring disability.

Total Disability. Total disability is defined in several ways in insurance policies.

- Some older policies define total disability as a disability that prevents the insured from performing the duties of *any occupation*. Qualifying for DI benefits under this standard is relatively more difficult than qualifying under newer policies, and this definition is rarely used in policies any more.
- Most DI policies issued today use a two-part definition of total disability. An insured is considered totally disabled if, at the start of disability, the disability prevents him from performing the essential duties of his *regular occupation*. At the end of a specified period after the disability begins, usually two to five years, an insured is considered totally disabled only if the disability prevents him from working at *any occupation for which he is reasonably fitted by education, training, or experience*. Some policies that use this definition of total disability do not pay benefits if the insured voluntarily returns to work at any occupation.
- Some policies define total disability as the complete and continuous inability of an insured to perform the essential duties of his *own previous occupation*. Note that the typical *own occupation* definition specifies that a disability must prevent an insured from performing the *essential duties* of his occupation, while some policies specify that the disabled insured must be unable to perform *every one* of his job duties. Policies using the own previous occupation definition are typically individual DI policies sold to members of certain professional occupations. Such policies typically pay benefits even if the insured voluntarily returns to work at another occupation.
- Some policies sold primarily to upper-income professionals, called ***income protection insurance***, define total disability as the insured's loss of income as a result of disability. Such policies provide benefits when the insured is unable to work and even when she is working but, because of the disability, is earning less than she earned before being disabled.

Presumptive Total Disability. Some DI policies specify that if an insured suffers a presumptive total disability, that insured is eligible to receive DI benefits. A ***presumptive total disability*** is a stated condition that, if present, automatically causes the insured to be considered totally disabled; thus, the insured receives the full income benefit amount provided under the policy, even if he resumes full-time employment in a former occupation. Such a loss is usually severe, such as total and permanent blindness, loss of speech, loss of hearing in both ears, or loss of the use of any two limbs. For a presumptive total disability, the waiting period usually is waived.

Partial Disability. Under some DI contracts, an insured may receive benefits for a ***partial disability***, which is a disability that prevents the insured either from performing some of the duties of her usual occupation or from engaging in that occupation on a full-time basis. A partial disability benefit typically is either a specified flat amount or an amount determined by a formula specified in the policy. Using the formula method, the amount of the income benefit will vary according to the percentage of income that the insured has lost because of the partial disability.

Recurring Disability. Sometimes an insured experiences a period of total or partial disability, recovers from the disability, is able to return to work, and then suffers a recurrence of the condition that previously caused the disability, with the result that the insured is once again totally or partially disabled. A ***recurring disability*** is a disability that results from the same cause as a previous disability and that reappears after (1) the previous period of disability and (2) an intervening period of recovery.

Under most DI policies, if a disability (1) recurs within six months from the date the previous disability ended and (2) results from the previous sickness or injury, then the insurer will consider the benefit period to be a continuation of the previous benefit period. To the insured's advantage, the waiting period does not begin again at the start of a recurring disability. However, to the insured's disadvantage, the benefit period resumes running. For example, if an insured is disabled for 12 months, returns to work for 3 months, and then goes out on disability again for the same condition, the waiting period will not start again, but the first month of the recurring disability will be the 13th month of the benefit period. The period between the initial and recurring disabilities when the insured returned to work would not count toward the benefit period as the insured did not receive benefits during that period.

If more than six months has elapsed since the end of the previous disability and if the new disability results from the previous sickness or injury, most insurers consider the new disability *not* to be a continuation of the previous disability and, therefore, establish new waiting and benefit periods.

Exclusions

Most DI policies specify that DI benefits will not be paid for disabilities that result from certain specified causes, so claim analysts must verify that the cause of disability is not among such causes. Typical exclusions include

- Sicknesses or injuries that result from war, declared or undeclared
- Intentionally self-inflicted sicknesses or injuries
- Injuries received during the insured's commission of a felony

DI policies also exclude pre-existing conditions.

Some DI policies provide that, on the first day that an insured enters full-time active duty in any branch of the armed forces of any country, DI coverage is suspended until full-time active duty is completed. Generally, full-time active duty does not include active duty training that lasts for two months or less.

Disability policies also may have exclusion riders that exclude disabilities resulting from specified impairments or avocations. Some policies exclude sicknesses and injuries that are covered by workers' compensation, while other policies offset workers' compensation benefits against benefits payable under the policy. We discuss offset in the next section.

Calculating Policy Benefits Payable

Depending on the policy, the periodic benefit amount payable may be a specified flat amount or a percentage of the insured's pre-disability income calculated in accordance with a formula stated in the policy. Before calculating the benefits payable, though, the claim analyst verifies that any required waiting period has been satisfied.

Individual disability income policies usually specify a flat benefit amount that the insurer will pay periodically to an insured who becomes totally disabled. The flat amount is determined during underwriting using an income replacement table, as we discussed in Chapter 7; the amount usually equals 50 to 70 percent of the insured's net earned income at the time of the application for the policy. Even if the insured's income increases substantially after he purchases the policy, the benefit amount remains the same.

Most group DI policies include an income benefit formula that expresses the periodic benefit amount as a stated percentage of the insured's pre-disability earnings. Group short-term DI coverage typically replaces 90 to 100 percent of pre-disability earnings, and group long-term DI coverage typically replaces 60 to 75 percent of pre-disability earnings.

Most group and some individual DI policies provide that a long-term disability claimant may not receive more than 60 to 80 percent of pre-disability earnings from all sources of disability income combined. If an insured exceeds the specified limit of total coverage because of coverage from multiple sources, the claim analyst notifies the insured of any applicable ***offset***, which is the use of the benefits paid under one type of insurance coverage to reduce the benefits paid under another type of coverage. The types of coverage usually resulting in offsets to DI coverage, depending on the policy's language, include

- Workers' compensation
- Social Security in the United States
- Social insurance in Canada
- DI coverage under other insurance policies

When a claim analyst determines that a claimant is eligible for DI coverage from another source, the analyst sends the claimant a notice that an offset will be used in determining the amount of benefits that the insurer will pay. Some insurers provide a claimant with the options of the insurer (1) reducing the amount of monthly DI benefits by the amount of DI benefits paid by the other source or (2) paying the monthly DI benefits with no reduction until the claimant has time to claim her benefits from the other source. When the benefits from the other source begin, the claimant then is obligated to notify the insurer that such payments have begun and to repay the excess amount she has received from the insurer. Figure 15.3 shows a typical statement of long-term DI payment options.

Administering Continuing DI Insurance Claims

An insured may be disabled for a considerable period of time, during which the claim analyst remains informed about the insured's condition and his ability to return to some form of employment. Most insurers require a disabled insured to submit proof of continuation of the disability, usually at monthly intervals. Most proofs of a continuing DI claim are brief, consisting of a statement of continuing disability that is completed by the insured or by someone familiar with the insured's condition. Few insurers require a new APS each month, although if a disability appears to be short-term, the claim analyst may need APS information to determine that the disability is in fact continuing. If an insured is clearly totally disabled and his medical prognosis indicates little chance of recovery to near-normal functioning, most insurers require only semiannual or annual proof that an insured continues to be disabled and, therefore, eligible for benefits.

FIGURE 15.3 Statement of Long-Term Disability Payment Options

LONG-TERM DISABILITY PAYMENT OPTIONS

Insurer____________________________________ (herein referred to as "we" and "us")

Policy No.__________________Claim No. ______________

Date of disability ________________________________

Issued to ____________________________________

Address ____________________________________

Claimant ____________________________________

Address ____________________________________

The policy under which you are covered provides that Long-Term Disability benefits will be reduced by the amount of Social Security benefits that **you and your spouse and family** are eligible to receive. The policy also provides that if you do not apply for Social Security benefits, the policy benefits will be reduced by the amount of Social Security benefits **you and your spouse and family** would be eligible to receive if application had been made.

We understand that the Social Security Administration has not yet made a decision concerning your benefits. Until the Social Security Administration makes a decision, your Long-Term Disability benefits can be handled in one of two ways:

☐ 1. We can estimate the amount of Social Security benefits **you and your spouse and family** will receive and reduce your monthly policy benefit by this amount. If Social Security benefits are estimated, the monthly policy benefit will be adjusted when we receive proof of the amount awarded by Social Security or notification that Social Security benefits have been denied and the denial is not being appealed. If your Social Security application is denied and the denial is not being appealed, the amount estimated will be returned to you in a lump sum.

☐ 2. We can pay you a monthly benefit with no reduction for estimated Social Security benefits until Social Security makes a decision. This may result in an overpayment by us. You must supply us with a copy of the Social Security decision and repay any overpayment. In addition, if Social Security makes an award, we will reduce your monthly policy benefit by the amount of Social Security benefits **you and your spouse and family** receive according to the policy provisions. If you want to elect this option but have not yet applied for Social Security benefits, you must agree to apply for them immediately. If you do not apply for Social Security benefits, we will use approach #1.

Please tell us which approach you want to use by checking box #1 or box #2 and signing this form. If you make no selection, we will use approach #1. If you have any questions, please contact us.

____________________	____________________
(Policyowner-insured)	(Witness)
____________________	____________________
____________________	____________________
(Address)	(Address)
____________________	____________________
(Date)	(Date)

Estimating the length of time an insured will be disabled is one of a claim analyst's most important duties, but this task is difficult because the duration of the disability for a specified sickness or injury can vary widely. Most insurers develop information based on their experience and on published medical information about the typical disability period for injuries and sicknesses. Claim analysts use that information as a guide in assessing a claim. Such information might indicate, for example, that a person who undergoes a hip replacement typically is disabled for four to five months. The claim analyst should not consider this information to be absolute, however. Some insureds who suffer specified sicknesses or injuries may be able to return to work within a shorter time than the periods specified, whereas other insureds may require extensive treatment or physical therapy and may not be able to return to work for periods longer than those stated.

Depending on the definition of disability, claim analysts consider the job duties that an insured performs when determining the expected length of disability. For instance, if an insured who usually performs a job requiring sedentary activity undergoes surgical repair for a foot abnormality, the expected length of disability may range from three to four weeks. By contrast, a person whose work requires light to medium physical activity may be expected to be disabled from the same surgery for four to six weeks.

In addition to job duties, many other factors can affect the duration of a disability. For example, an insured's previous medical condition can affect the length of disability. A person who was quite healthy prior to becoming disabled may recover more rapidly than a person who was not in good health before becoming disabled. Other factors that can affect the length of a disability include the insured's age, the severity of the disability, the presence of complications and other physical and mental conditions, and the type of treatment available for the disability. In addition to these factors, an insured may or may not be motivated to return to work, may have a greater or lesser economic need to return to work, or may not be able to find work suitable for his present physical and mental condition.

Note that the Americans with Disabilities Act (ADA) provides that if an employee suffers a disability, the employer must make certain reasonable accommodations to enable the employee to continue employment. For example, if a disabled employee must work from a wheelchair, the employer is obligated to make certain changes in the employee's workstation to accommodate the wheelchair. If an employee has developed an ongoing disease such as diabetes, the employer is obligated by the ADA to make allowances in the employee's work schedule so that the employee can make periodic glucose level checks and eat if necessary. In some companies, the claim analyst, aided by the insurer's legal staff and/or vocational staff, may verify or assist in making sure that reasonable accommodations have been made for a disabled employee who wishes to return to work.

DI Insurance Supplemental Benefits

Supplemental benefits that may be available as DI policy provisions or riders include waiver of premium for disability benefit, cost-of-living adjustment benefit, rehabilitation benefit, transplant donor benefit, and future increase option benefit. When a claim is submitted, the claim analyst must determine which, if any, of these supplemental benefits are in force and process the claim accordingly.

Waiver of Premium for Disability Benefit

DI policies typically include a waiver of premium for disability provision. These provisions usually require a waiting period of 60 to 90 days. Some of these provisions state that after the waiting period has been satisfied, all future premiums will be waived as long as the insured remains disabled. Other provisions waive future premiums and grant refunds for premiums paid between the beginning of the disability and the satisfaction of the waiting period. DI policies require premium payments that have been waived to resume when the insured is no longer disabled, and some policies require payments to resume after age 65, even if the insured is still disabled and the policy provides lifetime DI benefits.

Cost-of-Living Adjustment Benefit

A ***cost-of-living adjustment (COLA) benefit*** provides for periodic increases in the disability income benefit amount that the insurer will pay to a disabled insured; these increases usually correspond to increases in the cost of living. An increase in the cost of living typically is defined in terms of a standard index, such as the Consumer Price Index.

The assumption underlying a cost-of-living adjustment benefit is that an employed person probably would continue to receive periodic salary increases. If a policy contains a cost-of-living adjustment provision and the insured continues to be disabled, the claim analyst authorizes an increase in the benefit amount according to the terms of the provision. In some companies, this adjustment is applied automatically by the insurer's administration system.

Rehabilitation Benefit

Rehabilitation is the process of helping a disabled person return to work, either at her own occupation or at another occupation if she is unable to perform the duties of her own occupation. Some policies offer a ***rehabilitation benefit***, which provides that an insurer will reimburse the insured for the expenses associated with participation in a rehabilitation program during any period in which an insured is receiving total or partial disability benefits.

Rehabilitation can provide a valuable service to an insured by enabling him to reenter the work force. Rehabilitation also benefits an insurer by saving a significant amount in claim costs. Thus, some insurers offer rehabilitation reimbursements to some insureds even if the DI policy does not contain this type of provision, particularly if the insured seems to be motivated to work and if rehabilitation will cost less than projected DI benefits.

Because rehabilitation is so important to both insureds and insurers, many insurance companies have established specialized teams of highly trained rehabilitation specialists who assist claim analysts in handling all such cases. In addition, vendors specializing in rehabilitation can help an insurer manage many rehabilitation activities, including evaluating the skills of disabled people, providing career counseling, performing job market surveys, and designing and building the devices needed to enable disabled people to return to work.

The definition of a rehabilitation program is specified in the benefit provision or rider and may include physical and occupational therapy, vocational training, educational assistance, job placement, and any other activities that help a disabled insured return to gainful employment. Insurers typically require that any such program must be operated by a federal, state, or provincial government or must be offered by a licensed hospital, vocational school, business school, or accredited college.

Most insurers approach disabled insureds early in the period of disability to assess the prospects of an insured's being able to return to work. Generally, the longer a claimant receives disability payments, the more difficult it is for that person to take the steps necessary to prepare herself for active participation in the workplace and the less likely she is to be motivated to return to work.

Most insurers require an insured who desires such rehabilitation benefits to agree with the insurer in advance on the type and extent of rehabilitation services that will be reimbursed. In addition, most policies set a monetary limit on the total amount of rehabilitation benefits. The monetary limit is usually a multiple, such as 24 or 36, of the policy's maximum monthly disability benefit. For example, if a DI policy pays a maximum monthly disability benefit of $1,000 and the rehabilitation limit is 24 times the maximum monthly disability benefit, the total amount that the policy will pay for rehabilitation services will not exceed $24,000.

To guide planning for the insured's rehabilitation, the claim analyst typically asks the insured to complete a brief questionnaire regarding the insured's training, education, and experience. Figure 15.4 illustrates such a rehabilitation information questionnaire.

FIGURE 15.4 Rehabilitation Information Questionnaire

REHABILITATION INFORMATION QUESTIONNAIRE

Name ______________________________

Policy number ______________________________

We are currently interested in receiving your response to the following questions so that we may continue to evaluate your claim and to understand your circumstances and needs. Please complete these questions and return the questionnaire to us in the enclosed postage-paid envelope.

1. Educational background

Circle highest grade completed 1 2 3 4 5 6 7 8 9 10 11 12

Did you attend college? _____Yes _____No

Major field of study ______________________________

Degree(s) received ______________________________

Were you in the armed forces? _____ Yes _____No

Branch of service ______________________________

Highest rank ______________________________

Specialty ______________________________

Please list any additional education or training you have had (carpentry, auto repair, sales, etc.).

____

____

2. Work experience

Please list chronologically all the jobs you have had. Include dates, type of work, physical requirements, and supervisory experience, if any.

____

____

3. How do you spend your time during the day? ______________________________

____

4. How do you feel about returning to work? ______________________________

____

5. If work was available that met your abilities and limitations, would you be interested in exploring the possibility of doing it? Please explain.

____

____

6. Do you have a special interest in specific occupations or work activities? Please explain.

____

____

7. Have you made efforts to explore work-related possibilities? Please explain.

____

____

Please feel free to make any additional comments on the reverse side of this questionnaire. We appreciate your cooperation.

______________________________ Signed ______________________________ Date

Many DI policies provide that a disabled insured who wishes to return to work will be granted a trial period, usually of one year, during which benefits will continue to be paid, typically in an amount that is reduced by some percentage according to the amount the insured is able to earn during that period. For example, if an insured is able to earn $2,000 per month during the trial year, his monthly DI benefits might be reduced by 50 percent of those earnings, or $1,000. If, during or following such a trial work period, the disabled employee is unable to continue working, the full long-term DI benefits will resume.

Transplant Donor Benefit

A ***transplant donor benefit*** specifies that if an insured undergoes surgery to donate a part of his body to another person, the insurer will treat that surgery as a sickness and will pay benefits for any resulting disability. Most insurers limit the transplant donor benefit by requiring that a transplant surgery occur at least 12 months after the policy's effective date. Among other facts, the claim analyst verifies that the required time period has passed since the policy issue date.

Future Increase Option Benefit

A ***future increase option benefit*** allows a DI policyowner-insured to buy additional DI protection without providing evidence of insurability. The increases are available only at scheduled intervals and only for certain maximum amounts. The waiting period and the maximum benefit period for each increase usually are the same as for the original policy. The premium for each increase is calculated using the rates in effect at the insured's attained age at the time the increase is purchased. If any extra premiums or riders are attached to the original policy because of an impairment, they also apply to future increases. When an insured exercises a future increase option, the insurer generally requires proof that the insured's earnings meet the insurer's financial underwriting requirements so that the insured does not attempt to purchase coverage that she cannot afford or that might provide an incentive to avoid work.

Terminating DI Insurance Benefits

DI benefits terminate in several circumstances: when the end of a policy's benefit period is reached; when a claimant is no longer disabled under the terms of the policy; and, for group coverage, when a group member or a group is no longer eligible for coverage.

End of Benefit Period

As we mentioned earlier, the length of the benefit period differs depending on whether the DI coverage is individual or group and short- or long-term. Individual DI coverage rarely is offered with a maximum benefit period of less than one year. Short-term individual DI coverage provides a maximum benefit period of one to five years. Long-term individual DI coverage provides a maximum benefit period of five years or more. The maximum benefit period provided by individual long-term coverage for sicknesses commonly extends until the insured reaches age 65; for injuries, benefits often are provided for the insured's lifetime.

Group DI coverage generally specifies shorter benefit periods than those found in individual policies. Short-term group DI coverage provides a maximum benefit period of one year or less; such coverage commonly specifies a maximum benefit period of 13, 26, or 52 weeks. Long-term group DI coverage provides a maximum benefit period of more than one year. Many policies extend the maximum benefit period to the insured's normal retirement age or to age 70.

When an insurer has paid benefits to the end of the maximum benefit period, the claimant is no longer eligible to receive DI payments. Under a policy with a two-part definition of disability, an insured may reach the maximum benefit period under the "own occupation" definition of disability and then may be eligible for benefits paid under the "any occupation" definition.

End of Disability

If an insured recovers from a disability and is no longer eligible to receive DI benefits, the insured—or, for group coverages, sometimes the employer—sends the insurer a notice of recovery from disability. After receiving such a notice, the claim analyst stops payment of DI benefits. Figure 15.5 shows a typical notice of recovery from disability.

A claim analyst can terminate DI benefits to a claimant at any time that the analyst concludes that the claimant is no longer disabled according to the policy requirements. Making such a decision requires the analyst to gather sufficient information to be certain that the claimant is no longer eligible for benefits.

End of Eligibility for a Group Member or a Group

Termination of a group insured's DI coverage typically results when

- The group insured is no longer a member of the group
- The group insured is no longer a member of an eligible class covered under a group policy

FIGURE 15.5 Notice of Recovery from Disability

NOTICE OF RECOVERY FROM DISABILITY

This form is to be sent to the Insurance Company by the Employer as soon as possible after the Employee recovers.

THIS IS TO INFORM YOU THAT ________________________ insured under
(Name of Employee)

Group Policy No. ______________ Certificate No. ________________ returned

to work on ____________________________ 20_____, having recovered from

his recent disability on __________________________ 20_____.
(Last Day of Actual Total Disability)

____
(Employer)

Date ______________________ 20 ________

By ___________________________________

- The group insured's class is no longer eligible for coverage under the policy
- The group policy lapses because of nonpayment of premium
- The group policy is canceled or not renewed

Most group policies contain a provision that if the policyholder fails to pay any premium within the grace period, the policy terminates at midnight on the last day of the grace period. A policyholder who does not wish to renew a group policy or who wishes to cancel the policy can do so, usually by giving advance written notice to the insurer. Similarly, a group will no longer be eligible for coverage and an insurer may terminate the policy by giving advance written notice to the policyholder on any premium due date if the group does not meet the participation rate specified in the policy or the policyholder fails to furnish information that the insurer reasonably requires. Even if a group retains its eligibility, when the group policy is up for renewal, an insurer may terminate the policy if it so chooses.

Settling DI Insurance Claims

Instead of paying claims throughout a benefit period, sometimes insurers pay a claimant a ***claim settlement***, which is a lump-sum payment of money from the insurer to the claimant in exchange for the claimant's agreement to release the insurer from further responsibility for coverage under the policy. In effect, a claim settlement cancels the coverage under the DI policy. When an insured accepts the terms of a settlement offer, the insured usually signs a full, final, and complete release of all liability.

Most insurers present the offer of claim settlement in writing to the insured. Typically a settlement offer is negotiable, and the claimant can make a counteroffer if the terms of the insurer's offer are not satisfactory. If the claimant rejects the settlement offer, the insurer has a continuing contractual obligation to pay DI benefits according to the provisions of the policy. A claim settlement can be offered whether a claim is disputed or undisputed.

Disputed Claims

Some claim settlements result from a disputed claim in which the insurer and the claimant cannot agree on all the terms of the claim. For instance, suppose a claimant reports that a disability is the result of a new sickness or an injury, but that information developed during the course of the claim investigation indicates strongly that the disability resulted from a pre-existing condition excluded by a policy provision. If the insurer cannot gather sufficient proof to support its contention that the disability is not covered under the policy, the insurer may offer to settle the claim by paying the insured a lump sum instead of paying a series of DI benefits. The advantages to an insurer of settling a disputed claim are that the insurer saves the costs of litigating the claim and does not have to commit its staff resources to the conflict over a lengthy period.

Some claim disputes are resolved through mediation. ***Mediation*** is a conflict resolution method in which an impartial third party facilitates negotiations between the parties in an effort to create a mutually agreeable resolution to the dispute. During such mediation, the claim analyst may be asked to provide specific information gathered during the investigation of a claim. In general, this information includes

- The reason for the dispute
- The provisions of the policy
- Medical information, including the results of independent medical examinations

Undisputed Claims

Sometimes the insurer and the claimant agree to the terms of the claim and mutually agree that a claim settlement is preferable to paying DI benefits over a period of time. Examples of when the claimant may prefer to receive a lump sum are when he needs a large sum of money to pay for unusual rehabilitation, to obtain education or training appropriate to another vocation, or to purchase a business that can be managed even with the disability. Offering a lump-sum settlement is to the insurer's advantage because the costs of administering the DI claim over a period of time are eliminated.

The insurer typically considers what approach—lump-sum payment or series of benefit payments—is in the best interest of the claimant. The degree to which the claimant is financially dependent on a monthly benefit and the ability of the claimant to use a lump-sum payout to provide for his own well-being are issues that the insurer weighs in reaching a decision about a settlement. In offering a lump-sum settlement, an insurer typically advises the claimant to seek professional advice on the legal, tax, accounting, and investment issues related to the settlement. In no case does the insurer provide such advice to a claimant because to do so would risk a possible charge of conflict of interest.

Key Terms

work site assessment
sickness
injury
income protection insurance
presumptive total disability
partial disability
recurring disability
offset
cost-of-living adjustment (COLA) benefit
rehabilitation
rehabilitation benefit
transplant donor benefit
future increase option benefit
claim settlement
mediation

Part 5:
Customer Service

chapter 16

Organization of Customer Service

Outline

Qualities of Effective Customer Service

Benefits of Providing Effective Customer Service

Customer Service Organization
Staffing
Levels of Authority
Organization

Customer Service Activities
Service for Individual Policyowners, Insureds, and Beneficiaries
Service for Group Policyholders and Group Insureds
Service for Producers

Legal Issues Affecting Customer Service

Delivering Effective Customer Service
Determining Strategies for Effective Customer Service
Automating and Simplifying Customer Service Delivery
Ensuring Excellent Telephone Communication
Documenting Customer Service Guidelines and Procedures

Customer Service and Conservation
Conservation Through Communication with Policyowners
Conservation of Orphan Policyowners
Conservation Through Superior Claim Service
Conservation Through Customer Feedback
Conservation Through Producers

Customer Service Quality Control
Quantitative Performance Measurement
Qualitative Performance Measurement

Learning Objectives

After studying this chapter, you should be able to…

- List the qualities of effective customer service
- Discuss the benefits to insurers of providing effective customer service
- Describe the typical ways that insurers organize customer service departments
- Discuss the legal issues affecting customer service
- Discuss the delivery of effective customer service and describe the tools that insurers use to automate and simplify customer service delivery
- Explain how providing excellent customer service helps conservation and discuss strategies for improving customer loyalty and retaining business
- Discuss the quality control methods insurers use to evaluate customer service and give examples of quantitative and qualitative performance measurement techniques

In earlier sections in this text, we covered the importance of underwriting, reinsurance, and claim administration. We also discussed the many ways in which underwriting, reinsurance, and claim personnel cooperate with one another, with other functional areas of the insurer, and with producers and insurance regulators. Now we turn our attention to customer service. Because effective service to clients is a cornerstone of successful organizations, customer service is an essential insurance administration function.

As we mentioned in Chapter 1, customer service refers to the broad range of activities that a company and its employees perform to keep customers satisfied so they will continue doing business with the company and speak positively about it to potential customers. More specifically, some insurers use the terms *policyowner service* and *member service* to refer to the types of customer service performed for policyowners and groups, respectively.

The term *customer service* refers not only to the activities performed by customer service staff, but also to the functional unit that performs these activities. To simplify the discussion, we use the term *customer service department* to refer to the organizational unit that provides customer service to individual insurance customers. We use the term *member services department* to refer to the organizational unit that provides customer service to group insureds. A customer service staff member typically is known as a ***customer service representative (CSR)***, who is a person whose primary job responsibility is to support external customers through face-to-face communications or through communication media.

Customer service helps maintain important contractual and business connections between the insurer and its customers. Effective customer service also enhances the insurer's reputation for taking good care of its customers and thereby helps increase sales and preserve existing business. Another function of customer service is to compile information for reports to insurance regulatory organizations regarding customer complaints.

In this chapter, we begin by explaining the qualities of effective customer service and discussing the benefits of providing effective customer service. We then examine the organization of a customer service department and the types of service that insurers deliver to various types of customers. We also discuss the legal issues affecting customer service and describe approaches insurers use to deliver effective customer service. After we examine the relationship between customer service and preserving an insurer's existing business, we conclude with a look at how insurers evaluate the effectiveness of the customer service they provide.

Qualities of Effective Customer Service

Generally speaking, effective customer service is prompt, courteous, complete, convenient, accurate, and confidential. An insurer that delivers customer service with these qualities keeps customers satisfied, thus enhancing its strength and competitive position.

Customer service is *prompt* if it is delivered in a timely manner. Ensuring that customers do not experience unnecessary service delays enhances customer service. By contrast, delays can often frustrate customers, leading to reductions in new business, lapses, surrenders, and even legal actions against the insurer. For example, a policyowner who has to wait an unreasonable period of time to obtain a policy loan may become irritated and choose to surrender his policy.

Customer service is *courteous* if the employee delivering the service is polite, tactful, and attentive to the customer's feelings and situations. Courteous CSRs strengthen the bond between an insurer and its customers. Considering the feelings of customers and making every effort to handle transactions politely and professionally can make transactions pleasant experiences for everyone involved and help maintain long-term customer relationships.

Customer service is *complete* when every aspect of the customer's problem or inquiry is resolved to the customer's satisfaction. Providing complete service is sometimes a challenge, especially when requests for service cover a variety of transactions or when transactions are complicated or unusual. Attending to the details of each transaction helps ensure that all parts of a transaction are completed and that the customer will be fully satisfied. Providing complete service saves time for customers and CSRs and reduces the insurer's expense in unnecessary follow-up correspondence and customer contacts.

Customer service is *convenient* if customers have relatively easy access to the services they need. Customers want to obtain service through the communication methods and at the times that work best for them. Virtually all insurance companies have toll-free customer service telephone numbers. Many insurers have customer service staff available from early in the morning until late at night. Also, many insurers have automated phone systems and Internet Web sites that allow customers to perform certain transactions at any time.

Customer service is *accurate* if the insurer provides the customer with correct information or processes transactions without errors. Most insurers enhance accuracy by creating checklists, worksheets, and procedures manuals that guide CSRs through the steps of transactions, particularly those that are complex or have various options. In addition, insurers provide either manual or electronic logs by which CSRs can record every customer transaction processed. Certain transactions also may be audited by a senior CSR.

Customer service is *confidential* when the customer's privacy has been protected by the insurer. Confidentiality is essential in customer service as in all other aspects of insurance administration. Confidentiality in customer service helps the insurer earn the customer's trust and strengthens the bond between the customer and the company. We discuss the legal aspects of confidentiality later in this chapter.

Benefits of Providing Effective Customer Service

The insurance industry is highly competitive, and customers may see little difference among insurers and their products. An insurer with a reputation for effective customer service can differentiate itself from its competitors and increase its ability to attract new customers. In addition, exceptional customer service often encourages customers to maintain their coverage with the insurer. Customers who are satisfied with an insurer's service are more likely to renew and increase their current coverage and to buy new products. They also may recommend the insurer to friends and family members.

Furthermore, retaining customers can greatly increase an insurer's profit margin, because the cost of keeping existing customers is much less than the cost of acquiring customers. Avoiding the time and resources required to replace customers lost due to poor service allows the insurer to direct those resources into building its business.

Not only does exceptional customer service help attract and retain customers and improve profitability, but it also enhances the insurer's work environment. Working for an organization that prides itself on delivering good customer service helps motivate CSRs to excel at their jobs. In contrast, poor customer service can cause the morale of CSRs to drop as they cope with the stressful effects of dealing with unhappy or angry customers. As the quality of a company's customer service improves, CSRs become more productive because they spend less time dealing with problems caused by poor customer service.

Customer Service Organization

As with other administrative areas of insurance companies, customer service areas come in many varieties. Staffing, levels of authority, and organization differ according to the types of services an insurer provides and the preferences of management.

Staffing

A customer service representative typically begins her career as a customer service associate, which is an entry-level position based on the candidate's computer skills, core competencies, and pre-employment test scores. Associates may receive training to handle customer requests for various company products and to conduct various service transactions.

An insurer typically promotes a customer service associate to the position of customer service representative after approximately 18 months of service. Considerations for promotion may include accuracy, communication skills, productivity, completion of continuing insurance education requirements, and attendance. Customer service associates also must demonstrate a proficiency in the company's insurance operations and products. A customer service representative may be promoted to a senior customer service representative after he has successfully completed training on all the duties performed by CSRs, including complicated service requests. In addition to performing CSR duties, senior CSRs may be responsible for contacting new customers to promote loyalty and answer questions. They also may train and serve as mentors for new CSRs.

Some insurers divide CSRs into separate ***work teams*** or *work groups*, which are two or more people who work together on a regular basis and coordinate their activities to accomplish common goals. These work groups report to a specified supervisor. The work group supervisor reports to the department manager, who generally reports to a member of senior management. The common types of work teams are listed in Figure 16.1. These types of work teams also may be found in other departments such as underwriting and claims.

In the past, the nature of their work frequently required CSRs to concentrate primarily on administrative tasks, such as processing paperwork. Because administrative services are part of what customers purchase when they buy insurance products, performing such tasks always will be an important part of what CSRs do. Over the years, however, information technology has streamlined many administrative tasks. The reduction in the CSR time needed to perform administrative tasks has led many insurance companies to ask their CSRs to go a step further—to think not only of the customer's specific request, but also to consider the array of customer needs that the company can fulfill. Customer service representatives are being trained to understand the full range of a company's products and activities and to recognize marketing opportunities. For example, some insurers encourage CSRs to go beyond the customer's current request and identify life events—such as birth, marriage, or retirement—that would suggest the need for an insurance program review. Typically, however, CSRs do not actually sell products unless they are licensed and trained to do so.

FIGURE 16.1 Common Types of Work Teams

A ***traditional team*** is a type of work team in which the manager or supervisor performs most or all of the management tasks, such as organizing, planning, monitoring, and controlling the work; other team members concentrate solely on doing the work—performing the business functions for which the team is responsible.

A ***semi-autonomous team*** is a type of team in which the manager or supervisor manages the team, while the other team members, in addition to doing their "regular" work, provide input into planning, organizing, and monitoring the work.

A ***self-directed team*** is a type of team in which the members handle many traditional management responsibilities, such as planning and monitoring work. Self-directed teams are sometimes called *self-managed teams*.

Source: Adapted from Mark Adel and Barbara Foxenberger Frown, *Foundations of Customer Service* [Atlanta: LOMA (Life Office Management Association, Inc.), © 2003], 281. Used with permission; all rights reserved.

Levels of Authority

Customer service representatives receive increasing amounts of decision-making authority as they gain experience and demonstrate enhanced ability and quality of judgment. Usually, a new customer service representative primarily handles routine inquiries and service requests, such as address changes, that present few difficulties or unusual circumstances. A senior customer service representative or a customer service supervisor normally reviews the new customer service representative's work. As the new customer service representative gains experience, he handles less routine, more challenging services and performs his work without the review of a more experienced person. Senior customer service representatives and customer service supervisors usually handle service requests that require extensive contract knowledge, investigation, or consideration.

Organization

Some insurers establish one department or area to deal with every kind of customer service activity, while other insurers divide customer service activities by product, territory, distribution system, customer, method of communication, or service request.

Organization by Product

In organizing customer service activities by product, an insurer usually trains CSRs to handle requests concerning one or two products—for example, an individual disability income product or a group life insurance product. A CSR who understands all the details of a product, especially a complex one, is able to provide top quality service to customers.

The biggest challenge to organization by product is making sure that customer interactions do not become fragmented. For example, if a customer has purchased health insurance and life insurance and each is supported by separate customer service units, then coordination of effort is important. Customers calling to make an address change may assume that the change has been made on all policies they own, only to discover the change was implemented for just one product. In Chapter 1, we discussed insurers' technology solutions to this problem.

Organization by Territory

Multinational insurance companies often establish separate customer contact centers in each country where they do business to more effectively address differences in language, culture, products, regulations, and time zones. A ***customer contact center*** is an organizational unit that provides customers with a variety of channels for communicating with a business entity. Companies that operate in a single country are more likely to establish centralized customer contact centers, often organized into separate units to support different territories. However, if a company supports a number of regions within a country, it may decide to place customer contact centers in several different locations. This geographical dispersion makes it easier to support customers in different time zones, develop expertise in unique regulatory requirements, and become familiar with specific types of customers and their needs, enabling the customer contact center to be "closer to the customer."

Organization by Distribution System

Insurance companies that use multiple methods of product distribution sometimes organize customer service according to the types of distribution systems. For example, an insurer may assign one group of CSRs to provide service on policies sold through insurance producers and another group of CSRs to provide service on policies sold through direct marketing.

Organization by Customer

Another way to organize customer service activities is according to clients served. For instance, some CSRs handle inquiries only from producers, while other CSRs respond to requests from large group clients. Particularly when an insurer provides coverage for a very large group, assigning certain

CSRs to handle the service for that group can prove efficient. The CSRs learn the needs and typical requests of the group and can develop response systems that provide prompt, accurate member service.

Organization by Method of Communication

Face-to-face communication with customers plays an important role in ensuring effective communication.[1] However, most customer service communication is provided through remote customer contacts, such as telephone, paper correspondence, e-mail, and Web sites. As mentioned earlier, a customer contact center is an organizational unit that provides customers with a variety of channels for communicating with a business entity.

Telephone. Despite the availability of new methods of communication, many customers continue to use the telephone to obtain customer service. Consequently, many companies operate ***call centers***, which are organizational units that receive and/or place telephone calls to customers.

Paper Correspondence. Like the telephone, paper correspondence is a traditional communication channel that still accounts for a substantial number of customer contacts in many companies. Mailed or faxed documents often are used to provide information, handle complaints, and process transactions, such as payments, withdrawals, changes of address, policy loans, and reinstatements. When paper correspondence is received, it is routed to the appropriate CSR for processing.

E-mail. Like mail and faxes, insurers route e-mail correspondence to the appropriate CSRs. Many companies use an automated response system that automatically replies to customers to acknowledge receipt of e-mails and to indicate an expected response time, which is often 24 to 48 hours. For basic, predictable requests, some firms utilize systems that generate automatic responses triggered by certain keywords in the customer's e-mail. Typically, to ensure that these responses are appropriate, automatic e-mails are closely monitored.

In some companies, e-mails are routed the same way telephone calls are routed. In other words, e-mail messages go into a queue and are quickly routed to available CSRs, keeping response times to a minimum and sometimes providing customers with a response while still logged into their e-mail systems.

Web Sites. Most insurers have Internet Web sites that give customers access to product information and frequently asked questions (FAQs). For example, some Web sites enable customers to check premiums due, change personal information, process transactions such as address changes, and perform other functions. Many Web sites allow customers to send an e-mail through a link on the Web site, request a live internet chat session with a CSR, or request a telephone callback.

Organization by Service Request

Some insurers assign certain CSRs to respond to certain types of service requests, such as address or beneficiary changes and policy loans. In dividing customer service activities by service request, insurers typically establish such divisions as premium billing, loans, and cancellations and surrenders.

Keep in mind that a company may change its method of customer organization over time, as illustrated in Insight 16.1.

Customer Service Activities

An insurer's CSRs provide essential services to customers. In this section, our discussion focuses on the primary activities of customer service; we discuss these activities in more detail in the next chapter.

INSIGHT 16.1 Organizing Customer Service Work Teams

In the past, Hypothetical Financial used a service request-based approach to organizing its customer service activities. Each work team specialized in providing a specific type of service for customers. However, if customers needed more than one type of service, they had to contact more than one work group. For instance, a customer who wanted to check account values and make deposits and withdrawals from different accounts had to place multiple telephone calls or ask to be transferred to several areas to obtain the desired services.

Recently, Hypothetical began using a region-based approach to organizing its customer service activities. Now, when customers call the centralized toll-free telephone number, their calls are automatically routed to the appropriate service team: East, Central, or West. The service providers on all three teams are trained to help customers with a variety of inquiries and transactions, such as:

- Requests for account values
- Fund transfers
- Disbursements
- Monthly bank deductions
- Name, address, and telephone number changes

Working on these region-based work teams, service providers are more familiar with their customers and are able to deliver more consistent customer service. Furthermore, the cross-trained team members seldom have to transfer customers to other work teams; they can provide one-stop customer service in most instances.

Source: Adapted from Mark Adel and Barbara Foxenberger Brown, *Foundations of Customer Service* [Atlanta: LOMA (Life Office Management Association, Inc.), © 2003], 287. Used with permission; all rights reserved.

Service for Individual Policyowners, Insureds, and Beneficiaries

Customer service for individual insurance often involves providing information and processing policy transactions for policyowners, insureds, beneficiaries, and payors. Typical individual insurance customer service activities are listed in Figure 16.2.

Service for Group Policyholders and Group Insureds

The member services department for group insurance provides member service for both the group policyholder and the group insureds. In addition to assisting the policyholder with policy installation and member enrollment, CSRs also provide information and process policy transactions for group insureds and beneficiaries.

FIGURE 16.2 Typical Individual Insurance Customer Service Activities

- Changing the owner and/or the beneficiary of a policy
- Changing addresses
- Processing coverage changes or adding riders
- Determining cash values, loans, and dividends
- Changing policy features such as how dividends are used and nonforfeiture options
- Sending premium due notices and handling premium payments
- Changing billing arrangements and methods of payment
- Answering questions on coverage amounts, policy provisions, and billings
- Providing information about claim submission, status, or settlement
- Processing policy disbursement requests such as loans, partial withdrawals, surrenders, and cancellations
- Changing fund allocations for variable life insurance policies
- Processing reinstatements of lapsed policies

Service for Producers

Establishing and maintaining productive relationships with producers are important to an insurer's competitive position. Providing exceptional customer service to producers attracts and retains successful producers. To help producers solicit, sell, and conserve business, CSRs may provide information about products and procedures if this function isn't handled by new business analysts, as we discussed in Chapter 1. For instance, CSRs indicate which forms the producer must complete and what additional information the producer must submit with an application. By helping producers submit complete applications, CSRs increase the probability that underwriters can promptly evaluate the application.

CSRs also provide information and service to help producers provide top-quality service directly to policyowners. Many policyowners consider the producer to be their link to the insurance company, and they communicate directly with the producer when they have questions or problems.

Promptly addressing customer concerns is vital to a continuing relationship between the policyowner, the producer, and the insurer. The producer typically bears the burden of a policyowner's irritation if the insurer makes errors in transactions, is unresponsive to requests for information, or otherwise fails to meet policyowner expectations.

Some CSRs also calculate and pay commissions to producers. If an insurer enables producers, at a policyowner's request, to make certain contractually permitted changes to policies and to submit the changes to the insurer, CSRs usually oversee and maintain records of the changes.

Legal Issues Affecting Customer Service

An insurance policy is a contract between the policyowner and the insurance company. First and foremost, customer service helps fulfill the insurer's contractual obligations by completing service requests that pertain to customers' rights under their policies. For example, a life insurance policy may give the policyowner the right to take policy loans, change the amount of the death benefit, or add or remove riders.

As we mentioned earlier, protecting the identities of customers is essential to customer service. A contract of insurance between an insurer and a policyowner requires that the insurer protect the customer's privacy. Governmental privacy regulations also determine what type of policy information can be released and to whom that information can be released.

In addition to privacy requirements, CSRs must be aware of the impact of many other types of laws and regulations. Because work practices often vary due to the regulatory requirements of various jurisdictions, CSRs must be knowledgeable of or have access to information about all applicable regulations. Among other things, failure to comply with laws and regulations can result in fines, lawsuits, and negative publicity for the company.

Also, an insurer's customer service function must comply with applicable insurance regulatory requirements by maintaining accurate, complete, and current records of oral and written complaints for annual submission to insurance regulatory organizations. State and provincial departments of insurance generally reconcile insurers' annual reports of complaints with records of complaints submitted directly to those departments. In jurisdictions that have established specific standards for handling complaints, state and provincial departments of insurance determine whether each insurer has met such standards and what, if any, actions the insurer has taken to resolve problems involving any standards that were not met. For example, if a jurisdiction has established a time limit within which complaints must be resolved, regulators examine an insurer's resolution time. If the standard is not being met on a consistent basis, the regulator will want to know what steps the insurer is taking to improve the timeliness of its complaint resolutions.

Complaints that could have legal implications usually are referred to the insurer's legal staff. Such complaints might involve customer demands for reinstatement beyond the period allowed, allegations that instructions to the insurer or its producers were not followed, or allegations that the insurer's CSRs or producers behaved in an incompetent, negligent, or dishonest manner.

Furthermore, CSRs must be knowledgeable of work practices designed to reduce the risk of costly errors, lawsuits, unintended liability, and fraud. For example, if a CSR suspects fraud, he may enter the incident into a company-wide tracking system. Then he gives all applicable information and documents to his supervisor, who reviews the file and decides whether or not to forward the incident to the company's law or compliance department for further investigation.

Delivering Effective Customer Service

Every insurer wants to deliver effective service so that all customers are satisfied. Determining specific strategies for providing effective customer service, automating and simplifying customer service delivery procedures, ensuring excellent telephone communication, and documenting customer service guidelines and procedures are some of the approaches insurers use to deliver effective customer service.

Determining Strategies for Effective Customer Service

Insurers implement various customer service strategies according to the types of coverage involved and the type, frequency, and complexity of the service transactions required. Each insurer adopts strategies that reflect its attitude toward customer service, and these strategies serve as a guide for CSRs in their interactions with customers.

Customer service strategies generally focus on all types of customer interactions, including written and spoken communications and face-to-face meetings. Figure 16.3 illustrates such strategies.

Automating and Simplifying Customer Service Delivery

Insurance companies have long used technology to make customer service more efficient and effective.[2] For example, replacing traditional paper document and file systems with computerized systems that provide instant access to a customer's records enables insurers to provide faster, more accurate customer service.

Computer Networks

CSRs may use internal networks, external networks, or a combination of both to route a customer's inquiry or request, access the records and information necessary to handle the inquiry or request, and document the actions taken. For example, an insurer with multiple service locations may

FIGURE 16.3 Examples of Customer Service Strategies

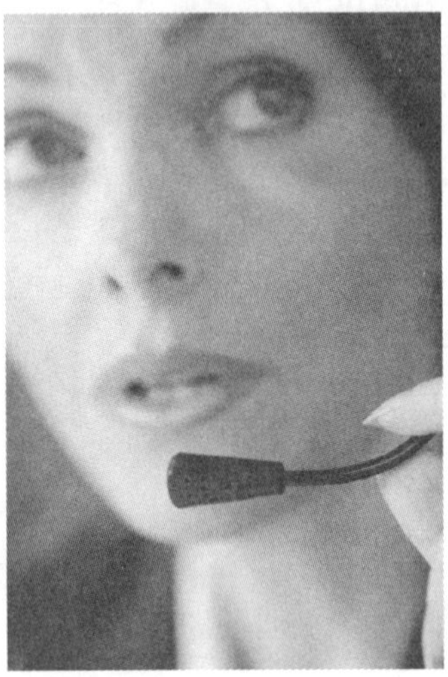

- Treat all customers as valuable individuals.
- Approach every customer contact with empathy for the customer's situation.
- Treat each customer contact as an opportunity to build a relationship, not just to process a transaction.
- Ensure that customers receive accurate and timely responses.
- Improve written communication by using personalized letters.
- Improve verbal communication by returning all telephone calls within a timely manner, asking permission before placing any customer on hold, and informing the customer first of the anticipated hold time.
- Implement technologies and processes to make conducting business easier for customers.

use an internal network to automatically route, complete, and document service requests. When a service request is received, it is input into the administrative system, where it can be accessed by a CSR in any service location. Networking allows customer service locations to share work, and it allows service requests to be handled by multiple personnel in multiple locations if necessary.

Knowledge Management Systems

CSRs rely upon certain technical resources, such as procedure manuals and internal memos, to provide the information needed to assist customers. In the past, such technical resources were available only in paper format, but today a growing number of insurers provide the information from these technical resources on desktop computers, giving CSRs quick and easy access to the information they need. Such information is part of an insurer's ***knowledge management system***, which represents the strategies, resources, and processes that organizations use to apply institutional knowledge to business activities. By using electronic knowledge management systems, an insurer can take information about products and procedures—which once may have been hard to find in volumes of paper manuals—and make this information easily and rapidly accessible throughout a department or an entire organization. Knowledge management systems facilitate the addition or modification of customer service procedures and the immediate distribution of such changes to all CSRs.

Databases

Much of the information found in knowledge management systems comes from databases. Some databases are separately maintained for specific functions. For example, a call center might maintain its own database requiring CSRs to input information into a customer contact system after each transaction. A ***customer contact system*** is a customer database and work tracking tool that combines a variety of features—such as data entry and retrieval, history of previous customer contacts, document management, scripted presentations, and follow-up tools—to provide a framework for handling and documenting customer contacts.

Document Management Systems and Automated Workflow Systems

Document management systems provide CSRs with computer access to a variety of company-specific forms, such as completed applications, explanations of benefits, account statements, and signature cards. In addition, these systems can provide computer access to correspondence and other documents—such as medical, financial, or other records—from outside the company.

Increasingly, document management systems play an important role in automated workflow systems. The automated workflow system shows the type of transaction, the person to whom it was assigned, when it was received, questions that arose, actions taken, documents created, completion dates and times, and so on. By storing this information electronically, CSRs have immediate access to the information, allowing them to provide a quicker, more complete response to customer requests or inquiries. Such immediate access can be invaluable in handling lengthy or complex transactions on which more than one CSR has worked or that have to be transferred temporarily to a manager for consideration and advice.

Self-Service Options

Advances in technology have led to a variety of self-service options for customers and their intermediaries. One of the most common self-service options is an ***interactive voice response (IVR) system***, which is a computer-based technology that answers telephone calls, greets callers with a recorded or digitized message, and prompts them to enter information or make requests by voice or telephone keypad. An IVR also may be called a *voice response unit*. Using an IVR system, customers may pay premiums, check on the status of applications and claims, and order forms.

Many insurers also allow customers to perform transactions through the Internet. For Web-enabled self-service options to be of value to users, the Web site must provide accurate information and reliable service in an easy-to-use format.

A few of the many self-service options available on insurers' Web sites allow customers to

- Complete and submit paperless applications and claim forms and to check on the status of these transactions
- Make policy changes
- Determine their financial needs and get assistance in implementing an appropriate strategy

Similarly, self-service options allow CSRs to obtain information and conduct transactions over the Internet. For example, some insurers' Web sites allow customers visiting the sites to click a button and immediately be connected to a CSR via real-time online chat. The CSR's computer automatically identifies the customer and provides the customer's records for the CSR. In addition, many insurers offer self-service options to producers, who can visit a Web site to obtain information about products; print copies of marketing materials; download interactive software that enables them to prepare sales presentations for customers; view information about sales commissions and the status of transactions they have submitted; view policyowner correspondence and information regarding claims and policy transactions processed on policies belonging to their customers; and obtain information, complete forms, and submit changes on behalf of their customers.

While some customers view self-service as a convenience, others prefer to interact with CSRs. Thus, most insurers offer customers a choice of self-service or human-assisted service.

Ensuring Excellent Telephone Communication

Although other technologies have become increasingly important, the telephone remains the essential link in maintaining communication between an insurer and its customers. CSRs use telephones extensively to explore customer needs and to gather information to fulfill those needs.

To ensure effective communication with customers, CSRs are taught to avoid using technical terms, but instead to use everyday language and to keep their responses simple and specific. Rather than saying, "Your EOB just arrived, and copayments and deductibles are being accounted for so that our comm center can cut a check," a CSR would be trained to say, "We now have everything we need to handle your claim, and we'll mail your check this afternoon."

Providing customer service by telephone over a long period can lead to employee frustration and burnout. Therefore, most insurers allow CSRs to rotate off this service for certain hours each day or to work in other customer service areas for weeks or months before returning to telephone duties.

Documenting Customer Service Guidelines and Procedures

To ensure consistency and accuracy in the service provided to all customers, insurers document the guidelines and procedures that CSRs are to use. Insurers use many means of documenting such guidelines and procedures, including—as we mentioned earlier—electronic manuals available on each CSR's computer and printed manuals.

One of the most important ways of ensuring consistent service is to inform every employee promptly about changes in guidelines and procedures. If an insurer uses an electronic procedures manual, such changes can be highlighted or presented in a bright color to capture employees' attention. Many companies also use a daily online bulletin board to inform the staff of changes and additions to procedures and regulations. If an insurer uses a printed manual, employees typically are required to update their manuals regularly and follow the most recent procedures and guidelines. Most insurance companies assign one employee or one team, depending on the size of the department, to be responsible for updating documentation and communicating the changes to all the staff.

Customer Service and Conservation

As we mentioned previously, an important goal of customer service is to preserve the insurer's existing business. ***Conservation*** is the process of ensuring that policies do not lapse but are retained on an insurer's books for as long as possible. Today, most conservation efforts are computer-generated. The main role of the CSR in these efforts is knowing what material was generated by the computer so the CSR can respond if the policyholder has questions, needs more information, or is looking for more options. Figure 16.4 lists many approaches an insurer may take to conserve policies, some of which we will elaborate upon in this section.

Providing exceptional customer service helps foster customer loyalty, and as customer loyalty increases, so does policy conservation. ***Customer loyalty*** represents a customer's feeling of attachment to or preference for a company's people, products, or services. A loyal customer is less likely to surrender her policy or allow it to lapse.

FIGURE 16.4 Approaches to Conserving Business

- Giving producers access to information about payments that policyowners make to flexible premium policies so that producers can take action if payments decline or fall below the required level
- Providing annual reports containing projections of values on flexible-premium policies to ensure products are meeting policyowners' current and future needs
- Providing multiple reminders of premiums due
- Sending notices of late premiums to both policyowners and producers
- Conferring with policyowners who make maximum loan requests to ensure that policy values are adequate to keep coverage in force
- Advising policyowners who request a policy surrender about alternatives, such as a policy loan
- Offering insureds who leave a group plan options for continuing their coverage on an individual basis
- Offering a toll-free number and a Web site or e-mail address for policyowners to contact the insurer
- Surveying policyowners about their satisfaction with producers and products to identify problems and devise solutions
- Providing extensive and ongoing training to CSRs
- Testing the effectiveness of notices, letters, and other communication with policyowners to determine the most effective and efficient approaches
- Tracking the relationship between conservation and persistency and publicizing the results to staff and management

An insurer typically earns customer loyalty by cultivating a strong relationship with the customer and being responsive to the customer's needs and wants. Providing customers with easy access to a CSR is important to customer satisfaction. In addition, by monitoring all customer complaints to identify trends, an insurer often can help policyowners who appear concerned about their coverage or who indicate dissatisfaction with the insurance company.

Providing basic satisfaction of a customer's needs does not automatically guarantee customer loyalty. Customers who claim to be satisfied with the service they have received may be willing to defect to another company if they are offered lower prices or more value for the money. To attain customer loyalty, a company must provide outstanding customer service as well as good products. Figure 16.5 provides examples of how exceptional service can turn a satisfied customer into a loyal customer.

In addition to conserving policies through providing exceptional customer service, CSRs help insurers achieve conservation through communication with policyowners, retention of orphan policyowners (which we describe later in this chapter), superior claim service, customer feedback, and producer efforts. Keep in mind that insurers' customer service functions typically are automated and that many of the activities we attribute to CSRs actually are performed by administration systems.

FIGURE 16.5 Examples of Providing Exceptional Customer Service to Create Customer Loyalty

- During the course of a telephone conversation with a CSR at Black Rock Insurance Company, an elderly customer, Albert Jameson, remarks that he is worried about his health during the coming snowstorm because he cannot afford to pay his heating bill. Recalling a local news report about reduced heating costs for those in need, the CSR, Jenna Trong, suggests that Mr. Jameson contact his local utility company to see if it offers a similar service. Now, whenever Mr. Jameson calls Black Rock with a question, he asks to speak to Ms. Trong because he feels this CSR cares about him as a person as well as a customer.
- A customer, Ruth Brown, calls her insurance company because her last premium payment was not credited to her account, although she mailed it several days ago. The CSR, Bryan Kelley, politely explains that the process can sometimes take several days. Hearing the concern in Ms. Brown's voice, Mr. Kelley promises to check her account each day and notify her as soon as the payment is posted. Ms. Brown is confident that Mr. Kelley will follow through on his commitment. Two days later, she receives confirmation from Mr. Kelley that her account has been credited, and because of the special attention she has received, she recommends the company to several friends.

Conservation Though Communication with Policyowners

Conservation requires communication with policyowners. For example, insurers conserve business by informing policyowners of upcoming changes in premiums or coverage. For policies that require higher premiums at certain ages, a CSR usually informs each policyowner of the change and asks whether the policyowner is interested in discussing other coverage options with a producer. If a certain type of coverage terminates on a specific birthday of the insured—for instance, the 60th or 70th—most insurers send policyowners a letter stating that the coverage will terminate on that date and asking whether they would like to have a producer explain how to continue coverage with the insurer.

Because customers can feel resentful if the only time they hear from an insurer is on the occasion of such a premium change or policy termination, many insurers maintain frequent contact with customers throughout the length of the business relationship. The insurer may mail an annual summary of benefits statement that explains all existing coverages and the benefits paid during the previous year. CSRs also may stay in touch with customers by asking about their satisfaction with the insurer's service, a topic we discuss later in this chapter.

CSRs also contact policyowners who have not paid premiums in a timely manner to indicate the insurer's interest in continuing the business relationship. CSRs may suggest that the policyowner simplify his premium payment method. Premiums that are paid on a monthly basis by check are the most likely to lapse and to experience problems with late payments. Therefore, many insurers encourage policyowners to pay premiums through ***electronic funds transfer (EFT)***, a method of transferring funds between financial intermediaries through an electronic computer network. In some cases, insurers accept credit cards for premium payments.

Insurers also acknowledge that customers' needs change and that insurance coverage may no longer be needed. Every insurer hopes that if customers do terminate their coverage, they will purchase other products from the insurer in the future. Surveying customers about the reasons for the termination of their coverage can help insurers determine if their products or procedures can be improved to conserve business and affect customers.

Conservation of Orphan Policyowners

An ***orphan policyowner*** is a policyowner whose original producer is no longer available to provide service. The producer may have moved from the area, stopped marketing the insurer's products, retired, or died; or the policyowner may have moved to another geographic area that his original producer does not serve. Without regular communication from the producer, a policyowner could cancel or surrender the policy and purchase coverage from another insurer whose producer can provide ongoing service.

To help conserve the business of orphan policyowners, CSRs attempt to recommend to them a producer who is in the same geographic area. Alternatively, a CSR might contact a nearby producer directly and ask the producer to contact the orphan policyowner. Insurers generally offer some financial incentive to producers to encourage them to "adopt" orphan policyowners and provide them with effective service.

Some insurers have established electronic tracking of producer activities to identify producers who are no longer active and may have left orphan policyowners. The sooner an insurer can identify an orphan policyowner, the more likely the insurer can conserve that person's business. In addition, some insurers establish a unit in the home office to work with orphan policyowners by phone or by mail to fulfill policyowner needs for additional insurance products. Some insurers have established a program to communicate regularly with every policyowner so that even if a policyowner becomes an orphan, she will still feel that she has strong ties to the insurer and can obtain answers to questions and solutions to problems.

Conservation Through Superior Claim Service

Customers who purchase insurance generally interact with an insurer or its producers when the coverage is sold and when a claim is submitted. For health insurance, for example, a customer may interact with the insurance company many times. Therefore, insurance companies that provide top-quality service usually encourage their claim analysts to provide rapid, accessible, customer-focused, and simplified claim handling. Customers want their claims processed as rapidly as possible; they want easy ways to get in touch with the insurer to submit a claim; and they want personal treatment and clear explanations while their claims are being handled. Insurers whose claim handling satisfies these customer desires enhance their relationship with customers.

Conservation Through Customer Feedback

Most insurers demonstrate their interest in providing excellent customer service by evaluating customers' needs through telephone surveys and printed questionnaires. Some insurers have established online feedback systems to gather information about customers' needs, preferences, and knowledge of insurance products and services.

In designing an online feedback system, an insurer must take into consideration the need to preserve a customer's privacy and confidentiality. Transmitting contract numbers, personal identification numbers, and other confidential information may inhibit a customer's willingness to use such a system, so most insurers do not require that kind of information from customers who complete an online survey.

Some insurers' online feedback systems permit customers to respond freely about any topic. Typically, such a system invites customers to send an e-mail, using a statement similar to the following:

> We welcome your questions and invite you to ask our experts questions about life and health insurance 24 hours a day, 7 days a week. We also welcome your thoughts about the way we have treated you as a customer and how we might serve you better. Please write your questions and comments in the space below, and then click on "SEND" to e-mail your questions and comments to us. We will immediately acknowledge receipt of your e-mail, and we will provide you with a prompt answer.

Other online feedback systems provide surveys to which customers can give responses. Figure 16.6 provides an example of an online feedback survey system.

Conservation Through Producers

Most insurers have found that a principal cause of lapse or transfer of business is lack of producer involvement with policyowners. Thus, insurance companies train producers to provide on-going, top-quality customer service. Insurers often encourage producers to contact their customers at least once a year to review customers' needs and to maintain relationships.

In addition, insurers (1) try to recruit producers who are concerned with selling only coverage that is appropriate for customers' needs; (2) educate producers about how to match coverage to customers' needs; (3) provide producers with information about the insurer's underwriting principles and requirements; and (4) maintain records of the persistency of each producer's business.

Some unethical producers attempt to generate commission income by engaging in twisting and churning when replacing policies, as we discussed in Chapter 3. To help prevent such activities, insurers who receive notice of surrenders and lapses not only contact the producer, but also send a letter to the policyowner with information comparing the coverage and the premiums of the original policy and the proposed new policy.

Some insurers also structure their commissions to reward producers whose business remains in force for an extended period. For instance, an insurer might pay a producer a ***persistency bonus***, a sum of money paid as compensation to an insurance producer when a policy continues in force beyond an initial period, usually five years.

FIGURE 16.6 Example of an Online Feedback Survey System

1. How often do you visit www.expresslife.com?

   ___ Daily ___ Weekly ___ Monthly ___ Rarely

2. What's the main reason for your visit to www.expresslife.com today?

   ___ Look up daily price information for mutual funds and/or annuities

   ___ Read the latest news about Express Life

   ___ Contact my area representative

   ___ Learn about products and services from Express Life

   ___ Follow-up on a topic I learned about elsewhere

   ___ Other:________________________________

3. What is the most important function or content you would like to see added to www.expresslife.com?

   ___ Access to all of my account information

   ___ More detailed information about products and services

   ___ Downloadable forms (which ones):

   ____

   ____

Thanks for responding to our survey. Now tell us a little about you.

First Name ________________________ MI _____

Last Name ________________________

Address 1 ______________________________

Address 2 ______________________________

City ____________________________ State _____

Zip ______________

E-mail ________________________________

I would like to receive more information about Express Life products, services and offers. ___ Yes ___ No

Customer Service Quality Control

Insurers evaluate their customer service function by using quantitative and qualitative performance measurements.

Quantitative Performance Measurements

Insurers use quantitative performance measurements to assess all administrative functions, but these types of measurements are particularly useful in evaluating customer service. Figure 16.7 lists various customer service quantitative performance measurements, some of which we discussed in Chapter 1.

Qualitative Performance Measurements

Most insurers use various methods to gather qualitative performance-related information about customer service. For example, randomly selected customers may receive mail surveys or telephone inquiries asking their views on the customer service they have received and inquiring about their level of satisfaction with it. Other methods include observation and monitoring, mystery shoppers, and complaint monitoring.

Customer Satisfaction Surveys

Customer satisfaction surveys are surveys designed to help a company determine whether its products, prices, and services are meeting customer expectations. Although surveys generally are not used to provide feedback on the performance of individual CSRs, customers may be asked to comment on the following elements concerning verbal and written customer service:

- Friendliness and professionalism of customer service staff
- Easily understood communication
- Timeliness of service
- Accuracy in completing a request
- Overall level of service

Observation and Monitoring

To gather information about the quality of service delivered by individual CSRs, many insurers require managers, senior staff, or trainers to observe or monitor a percentage of each employee's transactions. A manager or trainer might examine files of completed cases and those in progress and might listen to live or taped telephone calls between customers and the CSRs. Figure 16.8 illustrates a portion of a checklist used to evaluate the quality of telephone conversations between CSRs and customers.

FIGURE 16.7 Customer Service Quantitative Performance Measurements

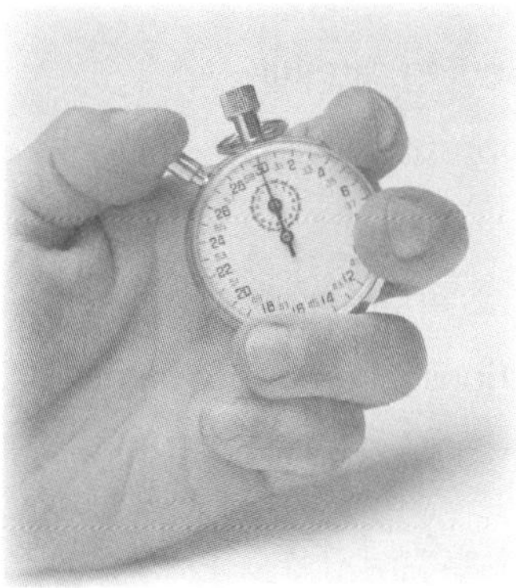

SERVICE LEVEL/ACCESSIBILITY TO THE CUSTOMER

- **Service level**. The percentage of inbound customer contacts answered within a specified time frame—for example, 80 percent within 20 seconds.
- ***Number of blocked calls***. The number of telephone calls that encounter a busy signal and cannot get through to the customer contract center.
- ***Average speed of answer***. The amount of time, on average, that telephone callers are on hold before being connected with a CSR.
- ***Abandonment rate***. The percentage of inbound telephone calls that are automatically placed on hold and then terminated by the caller before the call is answered by a CSR.
- ***Misdirected calls***. The number or percentage of inbound telephone calls that are transferred to the wrong department.

TIMELINESS

- **Turnaround time**, also known as *average handling time*. The amount of time necessary to complete a particular customer-initiated request or transaction.
- ***First contact resolution***. The percentage of inbound customer contacts that are successfully completed at the initial point of contact—that is, without being transferred and without the need for follow-up work.

QUALITY

- **Quality rate**. The accuracy of a particular type of transaction. Quality rate is often expressed as a percentage of the total number of transactions handled or processed, such as 99.5 percent of account transactions having no reported errors.
- ***Error rate***. The percentage of transactions that resulted in errors, such as 0.5 percent of account transactions reported errors.

PRODUCTIVITY

- **Processes completed**. The number of transactions that are handled within a specified period of time

Source: Adapted from Mark Adel and Barbara Foxenberger Brown, *Foundations of Customer Service* [Atlanta: LOMA (Life Office Management Association, Inc.), © 2003], 321. Used with permission; all rights reserved.

FIGURE 16.8 Checklist Used to Evaluate the Quality of Phone Conversations

- ✓ Identify self and offer assistance
- ✓ Determine the reason for the call by listening carefully
- ✓ Express help/regret/acknowledgment appropriately
- ✓ Request and verify caller information
- ✓ Use caller's name and "sir" or "ma'am" as appropriate
- ✓ Accept appropriate responsibility for actions taken or not taken
- ✓ Provide accurate, complete information in an organized fashion
- ✓ Inform caller of any risks involved
- ✓ Summarize action to be taken and verify customer's understanding, giving an expected timeline where appropriate
- ✓ Offer additional assistance
- ✓ Offer alternative solutions to problems
- ✓ Avoid insurance jargon
- ✓ Use appropriate presentation: pace, inflection, enunciation, courtesy, personalization
- ✓ Use "please" and "thank you"
- ✓ Use a proper approach to placing a customer on hold or transferring customer to another department
- ✓ Avoid short or curt answers
- ✓ Remain calm and avoid becoming defensive
- ✓ End call by saying "Thank you for calling" and "Have a nice day"
- ✓ Accurately record the call

Generally, a manager looks especially carefully at cases that are returned to a CSR for additional work as the result of an error in the initial transaction. Sometimes the manager makes follow-up telephone calls to customers to ask how well their transactions were handled and to solicit suggestions for improving service. Insurers also use peer review, by which CSRs monitor and evaluate one another's service delivery. Peer review requires careful training so that the assessments will be consistent.

Mystery Shoppers

Insurers also measure performance through mystery shoppers. A ***mystery shopper*** is a trained evaluator who approaches or calls CSRs and pretends to be a customer. Mystery shoppers may be company employees who are not known to the CSR, or they may be employed by an outside company. The mystery shopper conducts a transaction with the employee and then evaluates the employee's handling of the transaction. Mystery shoppers provide greater flexibility than monitoring "real" customer interactions because mystery shoppers can manipulate the circumstances to see how CSRs respond to various scenarios.

Complaint Monitoring

Studying complaint letters, e-mails, and telephone calls also can be a valuable method of gathering performance-related information. Typically, isolated complaints are not a reliable measure of a customer service system's overall performance, but a study of the source, number, frequency, and nature of complaints can indicate customer service problems or trends.

Key Terms

customer service representative (CSR)
work team
traditional team
semi-autonomous team
self-directed team
customer contact center
call center
knowledge management system
customer contact system
interactive voice response (IVR) system
conservation
customer loyalty
electronic funds transfer (EFT)
orphan policyowner
persistency bonus
number of blocked calls
average speed of answer
abandonment rate
misdirected calls
first contact resolution
error rate
mystery shopper

Endnotes

1. This section is adapted from Mark Adel and Barbara Foxenberger Brown, *Foundations of Customer Service* [Atlanta: LOMA (Life Office Management Association, Inc.), © 2003], 190–195. Used with permission; all rights reserved.

2. Ibid., 336–343.

chapter 17

Customer Service Practices

Outline

Basic Customer Service Practices for Life and Health Insurance
Providing Information and Answering Questions
Changing Names and Addresses
Administering Policy Changes
Handling Premium Payments
Handling Returned Mail
Handling Complaints
Fulfilling Other Customer Needs

Customer Service Practices Specific to Life Insurance
Changing a Beneficiary
Assigning Policy Ownership
Administering Loans and Dividends
Handling Variable Life Insurance Products

Learning Objectives

After studying this chapter, you should be able to…

- Discuss basic customer services practices for life and health insurance
- Describe insurance administration processes handled by customer service departments
- Describe the process for making changes to a policy
- Discuss customer service processes that are specific to life insurance

In Chapter 16, we reviewed general customer service principles and practices, including providing customer service for policyowners and producers and helping to conserve business. In this chapter, we discuss how an insurer's customer service representatives handle specific types of insurance service transactions.

Typically, only policyowners legally have the right to receive information about the policy. Most insurers accept telephone requests from policyowners for most services, including changing personal information and coverage and requesting policy loans. To ensure that the individual calling is the policyowner, a customer service representative (CSR) requests key personal information—such as the account number or identifier, date of birth, last four or five digits of her Social Security or social insurance number, or password—before providing information or processing requests.

Many insurers also offer policyowners the option to make changes and requests through the insurer's Web site. In addition to being personalized, this information is secure—only authorized individuals can view the information. To ensure this security, policyowners typically are assigned a login and password or personal identification number (PIN) that helps to confirm their identities before proceeding to a "Members Only" area of the Web site to request information or complete transactions. Many common customer service requests—such as changing contact information, changing beneficiaries, requesting coverage changes, and handling premium payments—can be completed through the insurer's Web site without policyowners having to speak to CSRs.

We begin this chapter by discussing some basic customer service practices performed for both life insurance and health insurance, such as providing information, processing requests, and handling complaints. We conclude the chapter by examining some additional practices that CSRs perform specifically for life insurance.

Basic Customer Service Practices for Life and Health Insurance

Many customer services provided by insurers are similar, regardless of the type of insurance the policyowner owns. CSRs handle requests for information and transactions, and they respond to concerns about various aspects of coverage and service. A complete list of the types of requests fielded by an insurer's customer service staff would fill many pages, but some of the most frequently encountered customer requests relate to

- Providing information and answering questions about the type, amount, and features of the coverage
- Changing names and addresses
- Changing coverage
- Handling premium payments
- Handling returned mail
- Handling complaints
- Fulfilling other policyowner needs, including providing duplicate policies and converting, reinstating, and terminating a policy

Insurers use technology and policy administration systems to complete transactions and generate customer correspondence whenever practical. CSRs can request frequently used forms and correspondence to be automatically generated and sent to policyholders.

In the following discussion, we first distinguish between the types of information generally requested for individual and for group insurance. In discussing other types of customer service activities, we do not distinguish between these types of coverage unless such a distinction is necessary because many of the customer service activities are basically the same whether the coverage is individual or group.

The administration of a group insurance plan is primarily a matter of recordkeeping. For example, some of the necessary records for a group life insurance plan include the name and amount of insurance on each group insured and dependent and the name of each beneficiary. Whether the coverage is an insurer-administered group plan or a self-administered group plan, the insurer receives monthly reports regarding the composition of the group and any changes in the group.

Installation is a series of activities involved in issuing a master contract and its individual certificates to an insured group. Whether the group plan is insurer-administered or self-administered, member service plays a part in ensuring that a group policy is installed correctly and completely. The role of member service in a group installation generally involves providing information and answering questions about the plan's eligibility requirements, benefits, and provisions, as well as the portion of the premium, if any, that each group insured must pay.

The policyholder typically informs the group insureds about the policy purchase. The insurer provides sample letters, brochures, enrollment forms, and other information that can be distributed to the group insureds. Member service might help prepare these materials.

While a self-administered group policy is in force, a group representative of the insurance company may provide member service by answering questions and assisting the group in administering the coverage effectively. This representative maintains close contact with the insurer's claim staff to identify and help resolve any problems. For instance, if a group insured is having difficulty in providing information required to process a claim, the insurer's group representative may advise the employee or the group plan administrator about the required information and ways to obtain it. To provide adequate assistance to group insureds, the insurer's group representative must be well informed about the coverage, the claim administration process, and the general administration of group products.

In addition to providing information as requested, the insurer's group representative also enhances communication by making periodic calls on each insured group. During these calls, the group representative checks the activities of the group plan administrator in administering the plan, informs the administrator of changes in laws and insurance practices that affect the group plan, and provides guidance if the plan administration fails to meet the insurer's standards.

The group representative also helps conserve the business by discussing the group's evolving needs for coverage and suggesting changes to the coverage. By evaluating the group's claim history, the group representative helps prepare the group for the next year's rates, which often depend on the level of claims made by the group during the preceding year.

Providing Information and Answering Questions

From the time a policy is sold until the relationship between the policyowner and the insurer comes to an end, a policyowner can have questions about any topic related to his coverage. For example, life changes such as marriage, the birth or adoption of a child, divorce, death of a spouse, or a debilitating illness or injury often cause policyowners to question the effect on their coverage.

CSRs provide valuable information and assistance by knowing the answers to the most commonly asked questions and being familiar with the information sources needed to readily answer the uncommon questions. CSRs often explain policy language and answer questions about policy benefits. For example, a group insured who has been diagnosed as morbidly obese and at risk for diabetes is considering having gastric bypass surgery but is unsure if the procedure is covered by her group health insurance policy. The group insured contacts her insurer, and a CSR informs her that the procedure is covered if she meets certain criteria.

Changing Names and Addresses

The name of a policyowner, beneficiary, or insured may need to be changed for several reasons. Sometimes a name has been misspelled, and correction is needed to ensure that the individual's records don't get confused with another person's. More commonly, a name change results from marriage, divorce, adoption, or court order. Most insurers require an individual to complete and sign a form requesting the name change, and many insurers also require a copy of a marriage license, divorce decree, or other legal documentation verifying the name change. When a name change is requested because of naturalization of citizenship, many insurers require as proof a notarized sworn ***affidavit***, which is a written statement made before an official who is authorized to administer oaths. After a name change has been made, a CSR sends the policyowner a copy of the face page of the policy or an endorsement to the policy to verify that the insurer has made the requested change.

Figure 17.1 illustrates a form that an insured, a policyowner, or a beneficiary uses to request a name change. Note that this form would be used only for name changes, not to change the policyowner or beneficiary of the policy; however, some companies may include several transactions on one form rather than using separate forms for each request.

Changing the name of a policyowner, a beneficiary, or an insured requires that the insurer modify many different insurance records. The master policy file, the billing file, the producer's file, and other records should all be in accord with one another. If an insurer's administration systems are integrated, a name is changed in all locations when it is changed in any location. Therefore, if a policyowner requests a change in his name, that change will be reflected throughout the insurer's records. As we mentioned in Chapter 1, some insurers' systems are not integrated, in which case the insurer may use middleware or a centralized data repository to effect a name change in all the insurer's records.

Another of the most common changes requested is a change of address for an individual policyowner, beneficiary, or insured. Because the insurer often sends premium notices, correspondence, and checks to the policyowner, beneficiary, or insured by mail, having correct addresses is imperative for continuing communication without delays due to returned or lost mail. Like changing a name, changing an address requires that all of an insurer's records reflect the change. To prevent fraudulent changes, some companies mail a letter to the policyowner's old and new addresses verifying the changes that were made.

For a self-administered group policy, the policyholder typically maintains records of names and addresses. The insurer needs to verify names and addresses only at the point of a claim submission.

FIGURE 17.1 Name Change Form

Current name of the ____ Insured ____________________
____ Owner ____________________
____ Beneficiary ____________________

Social Security Number ______________________

Change the name of the ____ Insured to ____________________
____ Owner to ____________________
____ Beneficiary to ____________________

Because of ____ Marriage
____ Divorce
____ Other

(If the name has been changed for any reason other than marriage, divorce or adoption, a certified copy of the legal document authorizing the change must be submitted.)

______________________________ ______________________________
Signature of Owner or Officer with Title Date Signature of Joint Owner (If any) Date

____
Signature of Witness (Disinterested Party), if required Date

Administering Policy Changes

Often, a policyowner's financial situation, insurability status, or insurance needs make it necessary or desirable for the policyowner to request a policy change. Policyowners may want to increase or decrease the amount of coverage, add or delete people from coverage, change the plan of insurance, add or delete riders, or reduce or remove a previously assigned rating or extra premium.

Policy changes to group insurance occur frequently as employees join or leave an organization. Member service handles the ongoing changes in group insurance coverage by enrolling new insureds and terminating coverage for those who leave the group. In self-administered group plans, the policyholder keeps these records.

Policy changes that involve an increased risk to the insurer often require CSRs to work with underwriting. The underwriter's primary concern is to evaluate the increased risk represented by the requested change in coverage. In considering requested policy changes, the underwriter considers (1) whether a proposed change increases a policy's net amount at risk and/or (2) whether the insured's original insurability status has changed. CSRs and underwriters work closely to ensure that each requested change is promptly evaluated and that those involved—principally the policyowner and, sometimes, the producer—are kept informed of progress on the case.

A policyowner who wants to make a policy change must complete a policy change form specifying the requested changes. Figure 17.2 illustrates part of a typical form used to request a change of coverage.

Increasing the Amount of Coverage

Policyowners often want to increase the amount of coverage provided by a policy. For example, a policyowner may want to increase the amount of her disability income coverage because her income is higher than when the policy was issued.

Depending on the type of coverage, increasing the amount of coverage can be accomplished by

- Increasing the dollar amount of insurance
- Increasing the period during which benefits will be paid
- Reducing the deductible amount or the waiting period
- Adding a new type of benefit or rider not included under the existing coverage

Such requests to increase the amount of coverage usually are handled in a routine manner by customer service, but, because increasing the amount of coverage may increase the risk for the insurer, granting a policyowner an increase in coverage may require additional underwriting. Each insurer establishes its own procedures to define those benefits and levels of coverage that do and do not require the involvement of underwriting.

Decreasing the Amount of Coverage

Just as policyowners may wish to increase the amount of coverage, they also may wish to decrease the amount of coverage provided by a policy.

Depending on the type of coverage, decreasing the amount of coverage can be accomplished by

- Reducing the dollar amount of insurance
- Reducing the period during which benefits will be paid
- Increasing the deductible amount or the waiting period
- Removing one or more benefits or riders offered by the existing coverage

FIGURE 17.2 Portion of a Typical Change of Coverage Request Form

For Contract/Policy Number____________________________

Subject to the terms of this policy, I hereby apply for change(s) checked below:

1. (a) Change: ___ Entire Policy ___ Continue Bal. ___ Term Rider
___ Rollover Cash Value ___ Refund Cash Value

Amount____________________________________
Policy Date_________________________________
Plan______________________________________
Premium/How Payable _______________________
Auto Premium Loan ___ yes ___ no

(b) Complete if changing existing Universal or Variable Life

___ Increase in Specified Amount of $____________________
___ Decrease in Specified Amount of $____________________
___ Change Death Benefit Option to
 ____ Increasing, as defined in the policy (check one)
  ____ Reduce the Specified Amount to equal the death benefit minus the cash value, as of the effective date of this change
  ____ Do not change the Specified Amount (satisfactory evidence of insurability may be required)
 ____ Level, as defined in the policy
___ Change my Premium to $______ effective on the
____________________________________ mode

(c) Additional Benefits (include benefits being continued)

Include	Cancel	
____	____	Disability Waiver Benefit on Insured
____	____	Waiver of Specified Premium $_______ on Insured
____	____	Guaranteed Insurability Rider $_______ Option Amount
____	____	Accelerated Benefit Rider

Because requests to decrease the amount of coverage entail reducing rather than increasing risk, CSRs can handle such requests without referring them to underwriting.

Adding or Deleting an Insured

An individual policyowner (if allowed by the policy) or a group insured under a group health insurance policy may wish to add a dependent to his coverage for many reasons, including the birth or adoption of a child or the loss of a job and insurance benefits by his spouse. In these cases, the policyowner or group insured must provide the insurer with the new dependent's full name, Social Security number, date of birth, and relationship to the policyowner or group insured. The CSR then adds the new insured to the policy and adjusts the premiums as necessary. The proposed insured may be required to complete an application and provide evidence of insurability, which must be reviewed and approved by underwriting. This requirement usually occurs when someone other than a newborn is being added to an individual policy, or when a dependent is a late enrollee under a group policy.

To remove a dependent, the policyowner or group insured simply requests, usually in writing, that the insurer remove the dependent. Generally no reason for the removal needs to be supplied, and the CSR makes the change and adjusts the policy and premiums.

Usually, when a dependent child reaches an age specified in the policy, the insurer will inform the policyowner or group insured that the dependent is no longer eligible to remain on the policy as a dependent unless she is disabled or a full-time student. Unless the policyowner or group insured provides information verifying the dependent's disability or enrollment, the dependent is automatically removed from the policy. However, under some group policies, the policyholder or the group insured has the responsibility to inform the insurer that a dependent child has reached the age limit under the policy and is no longer eligible for coverage.

Change in Type of Insurance

For a policyowner who wants to make a change in the type of insurance, the underwriter considers several factors, among them the reason for the requested change. A policyowner might want to change the insurance program into a higher-premium plan with a greater investment in the policy. This type of change usually poses no problem for the underwriter because the insurer's net amount at risk will decrease more rapidly under the higher-premium plan than under the original plan. An underwriting problem may result, however, if a waiver of premium benefit is included in the contract because the high premium for the new plan will increase the amount at risk for the waiver of premium benefit. Thus, a premium increase above a certain dollar amount may require additional evidence of insurability.

Some policyowner requests for a change to a lower-premium plan result in only a moderate increase in the insurer's net amount at risk. Underwriting for such a request may be more liberal than the original underwriting because the first-year acquisition costs, such as the producer's commission, probably already have been paid. In many insurance companies, therefore, policy changes involving only moderate increases in the amount at risk are approved by customer service without referral to an underwriter, but only under the following conditions:

- The insured has no history of impairment or rating
- The height and weight of the insured are within current standard limits
- All answers on the health declaration of the policy change form are acceptable

In addition to the previous conditions, some insurers allow customer service to approve such changes only if no MIB codes are listed for the insured.

Figure 17.3 shows a sample health declaration section of a policy change request form.

Adding or Deleting Riders

When a policyowner makes a request to add a rider, the CSR first evaluates if the product allows for the requested change and, if so, sends the customer the appropriate forms to sign. Because increasing the amount of coverage may increase the risk for the insurer, granting a policyowner an increase in coverage often requires additional underwriting and possibly an increase in premium.

Removing or canceling a rider requires no underwriting action because the risk to the insurer is decreased when the coverage is changed. Instead, the insurer calculates the new premium and, if necessary, sends a premium refund to the policyowner.

Rate Reduction

Another type of requested change is reduction or removal of a previously assigned rating or extra premium. Most rate reductions are made in situations in which an insured has received a substandard rating. In general, an

FIGURE 17.3 Sample Health Declaration Section

SUPPLEMENTAL APPLICATION

The undersigned hereby amends Contract/Policy Number ____________________ dated ___________ .

All the following questions apply to the proposed insured and any additional proposed insureds.

Since the date of the application, have you	Proposed Insured		Additional Insureds		If the answer of any of these questions is "YES", give complete details for each insured including date of last treatment and name/address of attending physicians.
	Yes	No	Yes	No	
a. Started racing of any kind; skin or scuba diving; parachuting, sky-diving, or hang gliding; mountain, rock, or technical climbing; or participating in private aviation?					
b. Applied for life or health insurance to any other insurance company or had any life or health insurance reinstated, declined, postponed, or modified?					
c. Been paid or made claim for any benefits for injuries or sickness?					
d. Had any surgical operation or been advised to have any surgical operation which has not been performed?					
e. Been admitted to a hospital or other medical facility or been treated at any hospital, clinic, or any other medical facility?					
f. Consulted or had an appointment to consult a doctor, surgeon, or other medical practitioner?					

I agree that this Supplemental Application will be considered an amendment and supplement to my original application. I have read the completed Supplemental Application before signing below. All statements and answers in this application are correctly recorded, and are full, complete and true. I understand that any false statements or material misrepresentations may result in the loss of coverage issued in reliance on this application.

_______________________________ Signature of Proposed Insured

_______________________________ Signature of Additional Insured, if applicable

_______________________________ Signature of Agent

_______________________________ Signature of Owner/Trustee (if other than Proposed Insured)

insurer will consider a rate reduction either (1) if the insured was originally rated incorrectly or (2) if the reason for the rating is no longer present—for instance, when a disease or condition is either cured or brought under an acceptable degree of improvement or control. An insured person who was rated for being overweight and who later loses the excess weight more than likely will receive a rate reduction if other medical factors remain the same. An underwriter, whose expertise is necessary to evaluate all pertinent medical indicators, typically makes such a decision.

Many insurance companies advise new policyowners that they can request removal of an extra premium rating at certain times, usually on the first or second policy anniversary date. When a CSR receives such a request, he typically forwards it to underwriting for evaluation.

Rate reduction is not a contractual right. A request for a rate reduction usually requires the insured to submit an application that is similar to the original application but not as detailed. Such a request also requires evidence of insurability to demonstrate that the insured's case warrants a reduction in the current substandard rating. CSRs generally are responsible for providing the necessary forms to the insured and for answering questions about the procedure followed in considering such a request.

Handling Premium Payments

In many insurance companies, customer service sends premium due notices and handles premium payments. Many insurers use automated systems to generate these notices, record the payments, and update the status of the policy. For fixed premium insurance, to continue a policy in force, a policyowner must send premium payments to the insurer according to an established schedule, which may be monthly, quarterly, semiannually, or annually. For flexible premium insurance, such as universal life coverage, the automated systems send reminder notices to encourage policyowners to pay premiums even if additional premiums are not necessary to keep the policy in force.

For group insurance, the policyholder pays premiums to the insurer whether the group plan is contributory or noncontributory. If the group plan is contributory, the policyholder collects the premium amount due from the group insureds, usually by payroll deduction, and submits them to the insurer.

If a premium payment is late, most insurance companies send the policyowner a ***policy grace notice***, also called a *lapse notice*, which is a written notification that the policy's grace period is about to expire. If a premium is paid during the grace period, the premium is considered to have been paid on time. Figure 17.4 shows one version of wording used in a policy grace notice.

FIGURE 17.4 Sample Policy Grace Notice

There is no longer sufficient surrender value in your policy to prevent termination or lapse of the policy. Accordingly, your policy has entered a grace period and will lapse if a sufficient premium payment to continue your policy is not received before the end of the grace period.

To continue your coverage in force, you must pay the minimum premium, which is $_________. This premium must be received on or before the grace period expiration date, which is _______________________.

We appreciate your business and hope that you will remit your premium promptly.

Some policyowners choose to increase or decrease the frequency of premium payments. For example, a policyowner who previously has paid monthly premiums for health insurance may decide to change to a semiannual or annual premium payment mode because the premium charged for less frequent payments is usually somewhat lower than for more frequent payments.

Generally, when a policyowner submits a request for a change of premium payment frequency, a CSR can approve the change if the request meets the insurer's premium payment requirements. However, insurers sometimes do not permit changes in premium payment frequency because of complications resulting from due dates that are inconsistent with a policy's anniversary. In addition, if a policy has a waiver of premium provision and the premiums currently are being waived, an insurer generally does not allow a change to a more frequent premium payment mode.

CSRs also assist policyowners who may wish to change the method of premium payment. For example, rather than using the direct billing method, where a policyowner would mail a check to pay for the premium, the policyowner may want to authorize *electronic funds transfer (EFT)* and have her bank automatically pay the premium on its due date. A group insured may authorize *payroll deduction*, which allows her employer to deduct the payment from her paycheck.

If insurance coverage provides for a change of premium when an insured reaches a specified age, customer service sends the policyowner a premium bill or a notice that reflects the new premium. In addition, customer service notifies the staff responsible for paying producers' commissions to modify the premium-based commission amount due to a producer, if applicable.

Customer service also handles various other age-related changes to certain coverages. For example, a health insurance policy might specify that an insured can continue to be covered if the insured is still employed past a certain age. Similarly, some types of coverage terminate when an insured reaches a specified age, and other types of coverage provide that an insured becomes eligible for alternative coverage at a stated age. For these and other types of changes, customer service is responsible for notifying policyowners of coverage changes and premium rates and arranging premium payment according to policy provisions.

To conserve business, most insurers send producers a list of policyowners whose premium payments have become 20 to 90 days overdue or send producers a copy of the payment notice. Thus, producers have an opportunity to contact policyowners who have not paid their premiums in a timely manner and encourage them to retain the coverage or to modify it so that the coverage and the premium amount more nearly match their current needs.

Handling Returned Mail

Many departments of insurance companies designate staff to handle mail that has been returned. Claims and underwriting, for example, carefully investigate returned mail and send it to its intended recipients, if possible. Customer service also is concerned with handling returned mail because of the need to communicate with the customer and ensure that requested changes and other transactions are completed promptly and accurately.

For most insurers, the first step in attempting to resend mail to its intended recipients involves checking whether a more current address has been received. An insurer's administration system may contain updated address information. If, after checking the system, a CSR discovers that no current address has been entered, a note or code is put into the system to show that mail was returned and that no further mail should be sent to that address.

Many insurance companies subscribe to a national database that allows CSRs to search for a more current address by entering a recipient's name, Social Security or social insurance number, date of birth, and last known address. Insurers usually pay only for successful searches—that is, searches that result in identification of a usable address.

For mail related to variable insurance and other regulated products, CSRs usually intensify the search by calling directory assistance in the city of the last known address and attempting to seek a new address. In many instances, CSRs call a producer to inquire about the location of the addressee.

At the completion of a search, if a CSR has been unable to find a viable address, another note or code is usually entered into the information system to indicate that the insurer not only received returned mail, but also could not locate a mailing address. Having made a good faith attempt to find the addressee, the CSR files the undelivered mail in the event that the client later contacts the insurer.

Handling Complaints

Handling complaints takes priority over many other customer service tasks.[1] The procedures for handling customer complaints are designed to comply with regulatory requirements, minimize the risk of lawsuits, and improve customer service. Customer complaints can be related to virtually any product or activity and can vary in intensity from minor irritation to extreme frustration and anger. Most insurers establish different policies and procedures for dealing with complaints based on the subject matter and the way the caller presents the complaint.

A complaint that pertains to the timeliness, accuracy, courtesy, or professionalism of the company's interactions with its customers is known as a ***service complaint***. Service complaints can be related to customer contacts as well as other types of customer service, such as record-keeping and billing. Upon the receipt of a service complaint, some firms institute ***service recovery***, which are the efforts an organization makes to fully resolve the problem that caused a customer's dissatisfaction and win back the customer's goodwill. In addition to service complaints, an insurer may receive complaints about its products, advertising, sales activities, and compliance with regulatory or legal requirements.

Most insurers establish ***escalation processes***, which are procedures that specify how an issue or complaint is to be handled in situations where the CSR is not able or authorized to address a particular request or demand. An escalation process can be as simple as transferring a call to a manager on duty or providing the customer with an address so he may mail in a letter of complaint.

Complaint handling involves many of the same issues associated with any other type of customer contact. Some of the strategies that insurers use to enable CSRs to successfully handle complaints include

- Empowering CSRs to work with dissatisfied customers and to resolve problems
- Empowering CSRs to provide first contact problem resolution
- Training CSRs to acknowledge the customer's feelings and concerns and provide empathy
- Training CSRs to interact with customers and not to take customer complaints personally
- Establishing documentation processes
- Establishing and encouraging CSRs to use escalation processes

By repeating and summarizing the customer's concerns, the CSR can validate those concerns and help the customer understand that the CSR is eager to help. Rather than indulge in blaming, denying fault, or making excuses, the CSR asks questions to help control the dialogue and obtain information needed to resolve problems.

Recognizing the importance and difficulty of complaint handling, some organizations establish work groups called ***complaint teams***, also known as *customer relationship teams* or *problem resolution teams*, dedicated solely to resolving customer complaints. When a complaint arrives anywhere in the company, it is forwarded immediately to the complaint team, where it is logged in and assigned for response. A critical role of the complaint team is to identify trends in complaints and determine what might be done to prevent similar problems from occurring in the future. The complaint team is usually comprised of experienced CSRs and/or staff from the law and compliance departments.

Fulfilling Other Customer Needs

In addition to performing the functions already discussed, customer service responds to other policyowner needs, including providing a duplicate copy of a policy and converting, terminating , or reinstating a policy.

Providing a Duplicate Policy

A policyowner may need to obtain a duplicate copy of a policy when the original policy has been lost or destroyed or is otherwise unavailable. Most insurers require a written statement signed by the policyowner stating that the policy has been lost or destroyed. A duplicate copy of a policy is stamped to indicate that it is a duplicate, and the insurer's file contains a record of the duplicate issuance.

Before issuing a duplicate copy of a policy, the CSR helps to avoid potential legal problems by verifying that the duplicate copy is needed and that the original copy is lost or destroyed. If a problem arises in verifying the loss of the original policy, the CSR usually issues a certificate of insurance rather than a duplicate policy. The ***certificate of insurance***, also known as a *certificate of coverage*, verifies that coverage exists, but does not contain all the provisions and riders that the original policy may have contained. Figure 17.5 illustrates a typical lost policy request form.

Converting a Policy

In Chapters 3 and 14, we discussed conversion provisions in group insurance policies. Some individual life policies also contain a conversion provision that permits a policyowner to change coverage from one type of policy to another—for instance, to change from an individual term insurance policy to an individual whole life insurance policy.

FIGURE 17.5 Typical Lost Policy Request Form

Insured ______________________________

Contract/Policy Number ______________________________

Choose one:

____Full Duplicate Policy ($30.00 Administrative Fee)

____Lost Policy Certificate (no charge)

____Life ____Health ____Annuity

The undersigned hereby represents that each policy, contract, and any attached amendment or endorsements specified on this form has been lost or destroyed, and requests a duplicate copy of each such policy, contract and amendment, or a lost policy certificate as evidence of the coverage. Each of the undersigned agrees that if the lost policy, contract and amendment is later found, the duplicate policy, contract and amendment or lost policy certificate will be surrendered to the insurance company for cancellation.

Each of the undersigned further attests that this policy is not now assigned, nor has it otherwise been transferred or encumbered in any manner.

Date	Signature of Owner, if other than Insured
Signature of Insured	Other Required Signature, if any

A CSR checks several items in handling a request for policy conversion. First, the CSR makes sure that the conversion occurs during the conversion period if one is specified in the policy. In addition, most insurers require that the first premium payment for the new, or converted, policy be remitted when the conversion request is made. After verifying that the conversion is valid and that any required paperwork and the correct premium have been submitted, the CSR instructs the policy issue department to prepare a new policy and updates the policyowner's records to reflect the converted coverage.

Terminating a Policy

If a policyowner does not renew a policy, or if premiums have not been paid on a policy and the policyowner does not respond to a series of premium due notices, then the policy is terminated in accordance with the insurer's established procedures. The insurer sends a letter or notice to the policyowner stating that the coverage has been lapsed. Most insurers also notify the producer when coverage has been terminated so that the producer can determine the cause for the termination.

A policyowner of most types of cash value life insurance, such as whole life and universal life, might decide to terminate—or *surrender*—a policy by requesting that coverage cease and that the insurer send the policyowner the net cash surrender value of the policy. The ***net cash surrender value*** is the actual cash value available to a policyowner upon policy surrender or lapse; it equals the cash value shown in the policy increased by any cash values of paid-up additions, policy dividend accumulations, and advance premium payments and decreased by outstanding policy loans and any charges imposed on the surrender.

When a CSR receives a surrender request, she first makes certain that the person who submitted the request is legally entitled to surrender the policy. If a policyowner has assigned some or all of the rights to the policy, then the policyowner is not allowed to surrender it without the assignee's authorization. Figure 17.6 illustrates a typical cash surrender request form.

Before processing a request to surrender a policy, the CSR usually attempts to conserve the business by contacting the policyowner to ask whether an alternative action might fulfill the policyowner's needs. For instance, the CSR might suggest that the policyowner use accumulated policy dividends to pay premiums, request a policy loan for the same purpose, or reduce the amount of coverage if the original amount is no longer needed or is too expensive.

Some insurers also require the policyowner to submit the policy to the insurer before the surrender is completed and the net cash surrender value is disbursed to the policyowner. Usually, the signature of the policyowner is required to surrender the contract.

Reinstating a Policy

Reinstatement—the process by which an insurer puts back in force a policy that lapsed because of nonpayment of renewal premiums—provides advantages for both the insurer and the insured. The insurer is able to keep business on its books without incurring the high first-year expenses normally associated with acquiring new business. The insured continues to have insurance protection that might no longer be offered to new applicants or for which the insured might not qualify because of advanced age. In addition, a reinstated policy usually maintains the original, usually lower premium and typically can be reinstated with more liberal underwriting standards than would apply to an application for new coverage. Figure 17.7 shows a typical application for reinstatement of coverage.

When a policyowner applies for reinstatement of a lapsed policy, the CSR determines whether the policy contains a ***reinstatement provision***, which is a provision that describes the conditions a policyowner must

FIGURE 17.6 Typical Cash Surrender Request Form

General Information

Policy/Certificate No ____________________

Owner's Name ____________________

Owner's Date of Birth ____________________

Owner's Social Security Number ____________________

Declaration of Lost Policy

We do not require the policy be returned to us. However, we do ask that the policy be destroyed once payment is received.

Income Tax Withholding Election

Federal law requires 10 percent tax to be withheld from the taxable portion of certain life insurance payments, unless you request not to have tax withheld. Even if you decide not to have federal tax withheld, you are still liable for payment of the income tax on the taxable portion of this payment. You may be subject to tax penalties under the Estimated Tax Payment Rules if your payment of estimated tax and withholding, if any, are not sufficient.

This section must be completed. If no selection is made and your surrender is considered taxable, taxes will be withheld.

I request payment of the cash surrender value in exchange for surrender of the attached policy.

Check ONE BOX:

____I do NOT want to have Federal Income Tax withheld.

____I DO want to have Federal Income Tax withheld.

____________________	____________________
Date	Signature of Owner, if other than Insured
____________________	____________________
Signature of Insured	Other Required Signature, if any

meet for an insurer to reinstate a policy within a specified time after lapse. The right to reinstate a policy is generally not available if the policyowner has surrendered the policy for its net cash surrender value, nor does the reinstatement provision obligate the insurer to reinstate the policy.

Most insurers require applicants for reinstatement to pay back premiums. Some insurers, however, allow policies that meet certain strict criteria to be reinstated without payment of back premiums in order to encourage

FIGURE 17.7 Typical Application for Reinstatement of Coverage

Policy # ______________________

Insured ______________________

Owner ______________________

APPLICATION FOR REINSTATEMENT OF POLICY DESCRIBED ABOVE

1. Your present occupation ______________________

2. Have you for any reason received medical attention or advice since the date you became covered by the policy in question? If so, give the nature of the illness, date, and name of the physician.

   ____

   ____

   ____

3. Do you declare that you are of sound constitution and that you are now in good health? ______________________

4. In the past 3 years, have you smoked a cigarette, cigar or pipe, chewed tobacco, or used tobacco or nicotine in any form? _______
   If yes, last used (form) ______________ on Month, Year __________

5. Name and address of family physician

   ____

   ____

   ____

I hereby certify that the above declarations are complete and true, and I agree that no reinstatement shall take effect until this application is approved by the insurer at its home office.

Date __________ Insured's Signature ______________________

Date __________ Owner's Signature ______________________

reinstatement of policies that may have lapsed because of temporary financial hardship, as explained in Insight 17.1.

If a policyowner applies for reinstatement, most insurers also require the insured to present evidence of insurability in the form of a completed medical questionnaire. If no significant changes in the insured's health have occurred since the original policy was issued, the CSR reinstates the policy without further investigation. However, if evidence shows the possibility of a significant change in health, the CSR usually refers the reinstatement

INSIGHT 17.1 Reinstatement by Redating

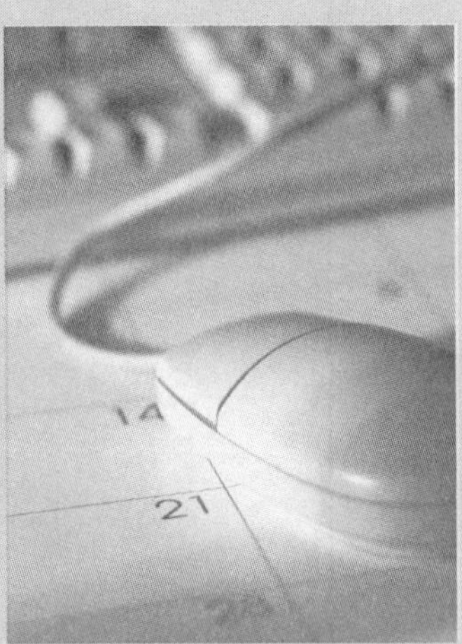

Some insurance companies attempt to conserve canceled business, especially small amount policies, by permitting lapsed policies to be reinstated without requiring the payment of back premiums. Policies that have lapsed but that meet certain criteria can be reinstated by *redating*—advancing the policy date and the paid-to date (the date to which premiums were paid up) by the number of months that the policy has been lapsed.

A policy reinstated in this manner generally must meet the following criteria:

- The policy must be less than two years old and have no cash surrender value.
- The policy must have been lapsed for more than 60 days, but not more than six months beyond the paid-to date.
- The face amount plus any supplementary term coverage cannot exceed a specified amount, usually $20,000 to $30,000.
- Redating can occur only once during the life of the policy.

request to the underwriting staff. After reviewing evidence of insurability, the underwriter can take one of the following three actions:

1. Grant reinstatement as requested
2. Decline reinstatement if the risk has increased so much that the underwriter cannot justify allowing the person to remain insured
3. Offer to reissue the policy at a higher premium rate

Customer Service Practices Specific to Life Insurance

Although most common customer service practices apply to both life and health insurance, CSRs provide certain specific services that are unique to life insurance policies. In this section, we examine these customer service practices.

Changing a Beneficiary

CSRs must be familiar with the numerous and often complex ways in which beneficiaries may be designated. Many different people and entities can be named as the beneficiary of a life insurance policy. These include the spouse and children of an insured person, other people who may be unrelated to the insured, trustees under trust agreements or wills, and the estate of the insured. Moreover, a policyowner can specify contingent, concurrent, or irrevocable beneficiaries and can further specify distribution of proceeds per stirpes or per capita. These beneficiary designation terms are defined in Figure 17.8.

Many insurers establish guidelines for submitting beneficiary changes. The guidelines are designed to prevent mistakes in recording a policyowner's beneficiary designation and avoid delays in the event of a claim.

FIGURE 17.8 Beneficiary Designation Terms

- **Contingent beneficiary.** The party designated to receive the proceeds of a life insurance policy following the insured's death if the primary beneficiary predeceases the insured.
- ***Concurrent beneficiaries.*** Two or more life insurance beneficiaries who share the policy proceeds on the death of the insured. The shares are distributed equally unless otherwise provided.
- **Irrevocable beneficiary.** A life insurance policy beneficiary who has a vested interest in the policy proceeds even during the insured's lifetime because the policyowner has the right to change the beneficiary designation only after obtaining the beneficiary's consent or upon the beneficiary's death.
- ***Class designation.*** A life insurance beneficiary designation that identifies a certain group of people rather than naming each person individually. Class designations can be either per stirpes designations or per capita designations.
- ***Per stirpes beneficiary designation.*** A type of life insurance policy beneficiary class designation in which the descendants of a deceased class member take the deceased class member's share of the policy proceeds by representation. For example, a policyowner-insured who has three children—Abraham, Benjamin, and Carol—might provide that each child would receive an equal share of the policy proceeds, per stirpes. If Benjamin died before the insured died, then at the insured's death Abraham and Carol would each receive one-third of the proceeds, and the heirs of Benjamin would receive equal shares of the remaining one-third of the proceeds. If Benjamin died without heirs, however, Abraham and Carol would each inherit one-half of the policy proceeds. Many insurers prohibit the use of some classes, such as "nieces and nephews of the insured" or "children of the insured's brother," in per stirpes beneficiary designations because such classes are not specific in naming the persons who are to be included in the division of the proceeds.
- ***Per capita beneficiary designation.*** A type of life insurance policy beneficiary class designation in which the class members all stand in the same relationship to the policyowner and the class members who survive the insured share the policy proceeds equally. For example, a policyowner-insured who has three children—Abraham, Benjamin, and Carol—might provide that each child would receive equal shares of the policy proceeds, per capita. If Benjamin died before the insured died, then at the insured's death Abraham and Carol would each receive one-half of the proceeds, whether or not Benjamin had heirs.

The following beneficiary change guidelines are the most common:

- The full name—given name and surname—of the beneficiary is required; initials are not acceptable. For example, while "John and Louise Jones" is acceptable, "Mr. and Mrs. John Jones" is not.
- The relationship of the beneficiary to the policyowner must be specified.
- Dates of birth for minors must be provided.
- Use of the words "or," "either/or," "and/or" makes the intent unclear; therefore, the use of these words in a designation is unacceptable.
- Names that are scratched out or marked over or that contain correction fluid marks are not acceptable.
- Information about the beneficiary that would allow the insurer to locate him at the time of a claim should be provided. Such information includes the beneficiary's social insurance or Social Security number, address, or date of birth.
- Dollar amounts cannot be specified for any or all beneficiaries because the final death benefit payable may vary if there are any outstanding loans on the policy or if the policy is in the grace period. In instances of an outstanding policy loan or a policy in the grace period, the loan amount or premium due will be deducted from the death benefit. Also, some policies provide a death benefit that varies with the cash value of the policy at the time of death. Fractions (such as one-fourth or two-thirds) and percentages (such as 30 percent or 70 percent) can be used to specify shares.
- The beneficiary form must be signed and dated by the policyowner.
- If a trust is designated, the exact date, legal name of the trust, and the trustee's name must be provided. Some insurers request a copy of the trust. Because some trust documents are difficult to interpret, some insurers attach a disclaimer noting that the insurer is not obligated to inquire into the terms of the trust agreement and will not be liable to other claimants after the policy proceeds have been paid.

Beneficiary changes can be made through the insurer's Web site because the policyowner's identity has been verified by the login and password or PIN. Beneficiary changes cannot be made by telephone, but a policyowner may request a change form by phone. CSRs then mail, e-mail, or fax a change of beneficiary form; when it is returned, the signature is compared to the policyowner's signature on file. No matter how the request was made, if the original beneficiary was designated as irrevocable, that person also is required to sign the change of beneficiary form before the change can be made.

Assigning Policy Ownership

As we noted in Chapter 13, assignment of a life insurance policy is a transfer of some or all of the policyowner's rights in the life insurance policy. The insurance company is not a party to the assignment, which involves only the assignor—the person or entity that transfers ownership rights—and the assignee—the person or entity that receives ownership rights. Ownership of some or all of the rights to a policy is most often transferred when a policyowner wishes to use the cash surrender value of a life insurance policy as collateral for a loan or when a divorce results in one party's assumption of full ownership of an insurance policy. As we mentioned in Chapter 13, the irrevocable transfer of all the ownership rights in a life insurance policy is known as an *absolute assignment*, whereas the transfer of some of the policyowner's rights in a life insurance policy to provide security for a debt is known as a *collateral assignment*. Figure 17.9 illustrates a portion of an absolute assignment form.

In an absolute assignment, the assignee, in effect, becomes the owner of the policy, and the assignor may no longer change the beneficiary or exercise any other policy rights. However, in a collateral assignment, the rights assigned revert to the assignor when specified requirements—such as repayment of a loan—have been satisfied. When such requirements have been fulfilled, the assignee notifies the insurer that the assigned rights of ownership are being returned to the assignor.

Because the insurer is not a party to the assignment, the insurer rarely asks the reason for the assignment. The role of a CSR in an assignment is to record the change of ownership so that rights of ownership are granted to the proper party and so that, in the event of a claim, benefits can be disbursed to the appropriate party.

Before recording an assignment, the CSR checks whether the policy has an irrevocable beneficiary. If so, that beneficiary must sign the request for assignment. If the irrevocable beneficiary does not sign the request, no assignment can be made. The CSR also reviews the policy provisions to determine whether any provisions exist that would prevent an assignment.

Administering Loans and Dividends

Policy loans made on individual cash value life insurance coverage are actually cash advances issued to policyowners. The policyowner is not legally obligated to repay the policy loan, but may do so at any time. If the loan is not fully repaid, the amount of the outstanding policy loan, plus interest, is deducted from the amount of death benefits paid under the policy at the time of a claim.

The requirements for policy loan requests vary among different insurers. Many insurers will accept telephone requests for loans under a certain

FIGURE 17.9 Portion of an Absolute Assignment Form

ABSOLUTE ASSIGNMENT

Policy # ____________________ Life of ______________________________

The undersigned hereby assigns and transfers without any exception, limitation, or reservation whatsoever to

____
[Name and address of each assignee]

all (his, her, its, their) assignable benefits, interest, property, and rights in the policy described above.

The nature and effect of this assignment shall be as indicated in the following expressions of intent and purpose, namely

- This assignment is ____ for a valuable consideration. ____ without a valuable consideration.
- If two or more assignees are named above, their interests under this assignment shall be as indicated in the line before which an "X" is inserted below.

  ___ Joint owners with right of survivorship between them

  ___ Common owners with no right of survivorship between them

  ___ Life interest, use, and enjoyment in ______________________________
  [Name of life owner]
  with absolute control and power of disposition in such assignee during his or her lifetime; remainder interest in other assignee(s). If there are two or more assignees entitled to receive remainder interests, such interests shall be of the nature indicated in the line before which an "X" is inserted below:

  ___ Joint owners with right of survivorship between them

  ___ Common owners with no right of survivorship between them

- This assignment cancels and rescinds any reversionary provision in favor of the assignor or his estate, whether contained in the policy or in any writing or provision pertaining to the policy.
- This assignment does not affect or change the beneficiary designation or settlement presently contained in the policy assigned. Proceeds payable on death will be paid in accordance with such designation or settlement unless same be hereafter changed by the assignee(s), when the right to make such change exists under the policy.

monetary amount and require written requests only for amounts over that limit. Other insurers require a written request for all policy loans. For written loan requests, some insurers require the policyowner to complete a policy loan request form and other insurers will accept a signed letter from the policyowner.

If the policy loan request is written, the CSR verifies that the person or people requesting the loan are entitled to do so by comparing the signatures on the loan form to the signatures on the insurer's records. If the signatures do not match, the CSR typically sends a letter with a loan form to the policyowner and instructs the policyowner to return a loan request form with a notarized signature.

Upon receiving a request for a policy loan, the CSR examines the policy record to ensure that the request has been made by an eligible person and that, if the policy has been assigned or has an irrevocable beneficiary, the necessary signatures of the assignee or beneficiary (or a spouse in a community property jurisdiction) are provided.

Although the policy loan does not have to be repaid, most insurers offer policyowners a choice of one of the following loan repayment plans:

- ***Dividend plan***. The insurer applies available dividends plus future dividends against the loan amount.
- ***Coupon plan***. The insurer supplies the policyowner with coupons to return with periodic payments against the loan amount.
- ***Automatic deduction plan***. The policyowner authorizes the insurer to automatically deduct a set amount from the policyowner's bank account each month until the loan is repaid.
- ***Lump sum plan***. The policyowner submits a check or money order for the entire loan plus the loan interest due.
- ***Partial loan repayment plan***. The policyowner submits a check or money order for a partial loan payment.

After calculating the cash value of the policy and verifying that it is adequate to fulfill the requested loan, the CSR then issues a check in that amount. If the cash value is inadequate to fulfill the requested loan, most insurers issue a check for the greatest amount available and notify the policyowner of the reason for not granting the full amount requested.

Most insurers offer individual policyowners the option of obtaining an automatic premium loan to cover unpaid premiums. An ***automatic premium loan (APL) provision*** in a policy allows an insurer to automatically pay an overdue premium for the policyowner by making a loan against the policy's cash value as long as the cash value equals or exceeds the amount of the premium due. In most jurisdictions, such an option is available only if the policyowner requests it. If a policyowner who has chosen an APL option fails to pay a premium on a timely basis, the insurer automatically grants a loan if the policy's loan value is sufficient to cover the amount of the premium plus interest. A policyowner's use of the automatic premium loan option can signal a potential lapse or surrender of the policy. The insurer, therefore, attempts to conserve the business by notifying the policyowner and the producer that the loan provision has taken effect.

Life insurance policies can be classified as either participating or nonparticipating. All mutual insurers and many stock insurers issue participating life insurance policies. A ***participating policy***, also known as a *par policy* or a *with profits policy*, is an insurance policy under which the policyowner shares in the insurance company's surplus. The portion of the insurance company's earnings that is available for distribution to policyowners is called the ***divisible surplus***. A policyowner's share of the divisible surplus is a ***policy dividend*** and is payable to owners of participating policies at the end of the policy year or on the policy anniversary. Policy dividends are considered a return of the part of the premiums that these policyowners paid to keep their policies in force for that year. Policy dividend amounts are not known in advance, and the policyowner is not guaranteed that policy dividends will be paid.

A person who owns a participating life insurance policy elects a dividend option at the time of policy application. The policyowner is usually free to change the selected option at any time while the policy is in force. The available options usually include

- Receiving cash payment of dividends on a periodic basis, usually quarterly or annually
- Applying dividends to pay some or all of the premiums on the policy
- Applying dividends to pay some or all of the loan on the policy, if any
- Allowing dividends to accumulate at interest, adding to the policy's cash value
- Using dividends to buy additional insurance

The customer service department is responsible for making appropriate changes to the insurer's records when a policyowner changes the dividend option. If the policyowner chooses to receive cash payment of dividends or to withdraw some or all of the dividends that have been left to accumulate with interest, the CSR enters this information into the policy administration system and makes appropriate disbursements to the policyowner.

Although dividend earnings are not taxable in the United States, any interest earned on accumulations is taxable. Typically, automated systems in customer service calculate any amount of taxes due.

If a policyowner chooses to apply existing dividends to buy additional insurance, the CSR verifies that the additional coverage is allowable without further evidence of insurability. Elements the insurer generally considers include the amount of insurance already in force, the amount of coverage that dividends would purchase, and the insured's risk classification. If additional evidence of insurability is necessary, the CSR usually notifies both the policyowner and the insurer's underwriters of the required evidence and turns the case over to the underwriters for further processing.

Handling Variable Life Insurance Products

Variable life insurance is a form of cash value life insurance in which premiums are fixed, but the death benefit and other values may vary, reflecting the performance of the investment subaccounts selected by the policyowner. Most variable life insurance products permit a policyowner to choose from several separate subaccounts and to change the selection at least annually and sometimes more often.

Most insurers allow policyowners to make reallocation choices by telephone or through the insurers' Web sites, although some insurers require written notification of the policyowner's desire to reallocate funds. Therefore, in addition to processing other customer service requests, CSRs help policyowners of variable life products (1) reallocate money from one investment subaccount to another—for example, from a money market or bond account to a growth and income stock account—and (2) designate the allocation of future premium payments by specifying the investment subaccounts into which future premiums will be placed. Depending on the jurisdiction, CSRs who assist policyowners with variable life products may be required to obtain special licenses.

Key Terms

affidavit
policy grace notice
service complaint
service recovery
escalation process
complaint team
certificate of insurance
net cash surrender value
reinstatement provision
concurrent beneficiary
class designation
per stirpes beneficiary designation
per capita beneficiary designation
dividend plan
coupon plan
automatic deduction plan
lump sum plan
partial loan repayment plan
automatic premium loan (APL) provision
participating policy
divisible surplus
policy dividend
variable life insurance

Endnotes

1. This section is adapted from Mark Adel and Barbara Foxenberger Brown, *Foundations of Customer Service* [Atlanta: LOMA (Life Office Management Association, Inc.), © 2003], 306–307. Used with permission; all rights reserved

Glossary

abandonment rate. A service level quantitative performance measurement that indicates the percentage of inbound telephone calls that are automatically placed on hold and then terminated by the caller before the call is answered by a customer service representative. [16]

absolute assignment. An irrevocable transfer of all of a policyowner's ownership rights in a life insurance policy to the assignee. [13]

accelerated death benefit. A supplemental benefit that gives a policyowner-insured the right to receive all or part of the policy's death benefit before her death if certain conditions are met. Also known as a *living benefit* in the United States. [6]

access to records provision. A reinsurance agreement provision that gives the reinsurance company the authority to examine the direct writer's records related to the business conducted between the companies. [11]

accidental death benefit (ADB). A supplemental benefit that provides a death benefit above the face amount of the policy if an insured's death occurs as the result of an accident. [6]

accounting. The functional area of an insurance company that collects, records, summarizes, analyzes, and reports data about a company's financial condition. [1]

accredited reinsurer. In the United States, a reinsurer that is not licensed by the insurance department in a given state, but that meets specified financial and reporting requirements of that state and is licensed to transact insurance or reinsurance in at least one other state. *Contrast with* **authorized reinsurer** and **unauthorized reinsurer**. [9]

acid-test ratio. *See* **quick ratio.**

acquisition expense. A cost a direct writer incurs in developing, marketing, and issuing new business. [9]

actively at work provision. A group insurance policy provision which states that, in order to be eligible for coverage, an employee must be actively at work—rather than ill or on leave—on the day the group coverage is to take effect. [8]

activities of daily living (ADLs). The activities of eating, bathing, dressing, continence, toileting, and transferring into or out of a bed, chair, or wheelchair. [7]

actuary. An expert in financial risk management and the mathematics and modeling of insurance, annuities, and financial instruments. [1]

ADA. *See* **American with Disabilities Act**.

ADB. *See* **accidental death benefit**.

ADEA. *See* **Age Discrimination in Employment Act**.

ADLs. *See* **activities of daily living**.

administration expense. *See* **maintenance expense**.

administration system. An information system that an insurer uses to manage information about insurance policies. [1]

admitted reinsurer. *See* **authorized reinsurer**.

adult day care. Care provided to adults in a group setting during hours when primary caregivers are working. [14]

adult day care center. A safe environment in which people in need of assistance with activities of daily living and instrumental activities of daily living can receive this help, associate with others in similar situations, and return home each day. [14]

adverse action. For insurance purposes, a denial or revocation of insurance coverage, a change in the terms of existing insurance coverage, or a refusal to grant insurance in substantially the amount or on substantially the terms requested. [3]

affidavit. A written statement made before an official who is authorized to administer oaths. [17]

affinity group. A type of association group consisting of people who share a common bond, background, or interest and who belong to an association or organization. [8]

age and amount requirements chart. A list that specifies the kinds of information an underwriter must obtain and review in assessing the insurability of a proposed insured. Also known as *table of underwriting requirements*. [2]

Age Discrimination in Employment Act (ADEA). A U.S. federal law that protects workers who are age 40 and older from being discriminated against because of their age. [3]

agent's statement. A section on most individual life and health applications in which the producer can comment on any factors relevant to the case and the risk it involves. [2]

agreement effective date. (1) The date on which the written agreement is signed by authorized representatives of the direct writer and the reinsurer and a copy of the agreement is delivered to each party, or (2) any agreed-upon date when the direct writer submits policies to the reinsurer for automatic reinsurance or the reinsurer approves policies for facultative or facultative-obligatory reinsurance. [10]

allowable expense. A usual, customary, and reasonable expense that a group insured incurred and that is covered under a group insured's medical expense insurance policy. [14]

allowance. An amount paid by the reinsurer to the direct writer and that is designed to recognize the direct writer's acquisition, maintenance, and other expenses. Also known as an *expense allowance*, a *reinsurance allowance*, a *ceding commission* or a *reinsurance commission*. [9]

alternate care. Plans of long-term care and services not otherwise covered under the long-term care insurance policy, developed cooperatively by a physician and an insurer to substitute for more expensive nursing home care. [14]

Alzheimer's disease. A cognitive impairment that causes deterioration of a person's intellectual and cognitive functions, including memory, orientation, intellect, and judgment, and can cause deterioration of a person's speech and motor functions. Also known as *primary degenerative dementia*. [7]

Americans with Disabilities Act (ADA). A U.S. federal law that protects disabled individuals against all types of discrimination, including employment discrimination. [3]

annual premium amount. The amount the insurer charges annually for the total amount of coverage provided. [2]

annual report. A financial document that a corporation issues to its stockholders to report the business's activities and financial status for a specified period, which is usually the preceding year. [5]

antiselection. The tendency of people who believe they have a greater-than-average likelihood of loss to seek insurance protection to a greater extent than do those who believe they have an average or a less-than-average likelihood of loss. [2]

antivirus software. A software application that detects viruses and prevents them from infecting a computer and/or helps an infected computer recover. [1]

APL provision. *See* **automatic premium loan provision.** [17]

applicant. The person or entity that submits an application for individual insurance and seeks to purchase the insurance coverage. [1]

application. *See* **application software.**

application software. The software used to perform specific tasks or solve particular types of problems. Also known as a *software application* or simply an *application*. [1]

approval premium receipt. A conditional premium receipt that provides temporary insurance coverage only when the insurer approves the proposed insured as a standard or better-than-average risk. [3]

APS. *See* **attending physician's statement.**

arbitration. A method of dispute resolution in which impartial third parties—known as arbitrators—evaluate the facts in dispute and render a decision that usually is binding on the parties to the dispute. [10]

arbitration provision. An indemnity reinsurance agreement provision that requires the reinsurance parties to submit disputes that they cannot resolve through negotiation to an arbitration panel rather than to a court of law and that describes the procedures the parties must use to select arbitrators and conduct the arbitration process. [10]

arbitrator. An impartial third party who evaluates the facts in dispute and renders a decision that usually is binding on the parties to the dispute. [10]

article. A relatively standard contract provision found in reinsurance agreements. [10]

assignment. An agreement under which a policyowner—the *assignor*—transfers some or all of her ownership rights in a particular policy to another party—the *assignee*. [13]

assignment of benefits. A statement that directs an insurer to pay benefits directly to a health care provider rather than to an insured. [14]

assisted living facility. An inpatient residential facility designed to meet long-term care needs for persons who are not in need of the level of care provided in a hospital or nursing home but who are in need of assistance with activities of daily living or are cognitively impaired. [14]

association group. An insured group that consists of the members of an association, which is an organization of employers or individuals formed for a purpose other than to obtain insurance. [8]

assuming company. *See* **reinsurer**.

assumption certificate. An insurance certificate issued to each of an insurer's existing policyowners to show that a reinsurer has taken responsibility for all risk under the policies. See also assumption reinsurance. [9]

assumption reinsurance. A reinsurance arrangement designed to permanently and entirely transfer blocks of existing insurance business from one company to another. Also known as *portfolio reinsurance. Contrast with* **indemnity reinsurance**. [9]

assured. *See* **insured**.

attachment point. In a nonproportional reinsurance arrangement, the specified monetary limit at which a reinsurer becomes obligated to reimburse the direct writer for claim payments. [10]

attending physician. A physician, whether he is a primary care physician or a specialist, who has provided medical care for a proposed insured. [4]

attending physician's statement (APS). A report by a physician who has treated or is currently treating the proposed insured. [4]

audit. An evaluation of a company's records and operations to ensure the accuracy of the records and the effectiveness of operational policies and procedures. [2]

audit log. A record of the work that has been completed on a case. [1]

audit report. A written report prepared by an audit team to document the findings of an external audit. [11]

authentication. A combination of technology and procedures designed to verify a user's identity before giving the user access to a system or database. [1]

authorized reinsurer. In the United States, a reinsurer that is licensed or otherwise recognized by the insurance department in a given state. Also known as an *admitted reinsurer. Contrast with* **accredited reinsurer** and **unauthorized reinsurer**. [9]

auto-adjudication. An electronic claim processing system. [12]

automated workflow system. A technology used to create computer-based records pertaining to the status and processing of specific transactions. Also called a *workflow application*. [1]

automatic binding limit. Under an automatic cession basis, the maximum monetary amount of risk the reinsurer will obligate itself to accept automatically on a given policy or case without making an independent underwriting assessment. [9]

automatic deduction plan. A policy loan repayment plan under which the policyowner authorizes the insurer to automatically deduct a set amount from the policyowner's bank account each month until the loan is repaid. [17]

automatic premium loan (APL) provision. A cash value life insurance policy provision that allows an insurer to automatically pay an overdue premium for a policyowner by making a loan against the policy's cash value as long as the cash value equals or exceeds the amount of the premium due. [17]

automatic reinsurance. A reinsurance cession basis in which the direct writer agrees in advance to cede and the reinsurer agrees in advance to assume all risks that meet the specifications in the reinsurance agreement. *Contrast with* **facultative reinsurance** and **facultative-obligatory (fac-ob) reinsurance**. [9]

average handling time. *See* **turnaround time**.

average speed of answer. A service level quantitative performance measurement that indicates the amount of time, on average, that telephone callers are on hold before being connected with a customer service representative. [16]

B2B e-commerce. *See* **business-to-business e-commerce**.

backward number sequence test. A type of cognitive screen that examines a person's ability to recall a series of numbers and name them in reverse sequence. [7]

balance sheet. A financial statement that shows a business's financial position on a certain date. [5]

benchmark. A performance standard, often based on a standard achieved by leading companies, that represent a company's goal for performance. [1]

beneficiary. The person or party the policyowner named to receive the policy benefit. [1]

benefit schedule. In group insurance, a table or schedule that specifies the types and amounts of coverage provided for each class that is insured. [8]

benefit trigger. A long-term care insurance policy requirement specifying the conditions that establish an insured's eligibility to receive long-term care benefits. [14]

billing statement. A reinsurance report that lists the amounts owed by and due to each party to the reinsurance agreement. [11]

binding premium receipt. A premium receipt that provides temporary insurance coverage that becomes effective from the time the applicant receives the receipt. [3]

biometric authentication. Technology that identifies users by "reading" a physical trait that is unique to each user, such as the user's fingerprints or retina. [1]

blended rating. A premium rating method for group insurance that uses a combination of manual rating and experience rating. [8]

blood chemistry profile. A group of laboratory tests that analyze a sample of blood to identify factors that point to possible chronic and acute disease. [4]

BPM. *See* **business process management.**

BRE. *See* **business rules engine.**

build. The shape or form of the body, including the relationships among height, weight, and distribution of the weight. [4]

build chart. A chart that indicates average weights for various heights, along with the mortality debits associated with increases in weight. [4]

bulk administration. A method of reinsurance record administration in which the direct writer periodically submits summarized reports—such as reinsurance premium and policy summaries—to the reinsurer, but does not provide detailed information about individual risks reinsured other than an annual detailed in-force listing. [10]

business continuation insurance plan. An insurance plan designed to enable a business to continue operations upon the death or disability of an owner or other person important to the business. [6]

business financial supplement. A specialized underwriting questionnaire that requests information about the type of business, the current financial condition of the business, and the purpose for which the insurance is being requested. [6]

business process management (BPM). A strategy for optimizing business processes or adapting them to meet changing needs. [1]

business rules engine (BRE). An application software that automates the decision-making process by creating and applying rules to all available information. [1]

business-to-business (B2B) e-commerce. The electronic transmission of data or information between organizations to perform or facilitate business transactions. [9]

buy-sell agreement. An agreement in which one party agrees to purchase a second party's financial interest in a business following the second party's death, and the second party agrees to direct his estate to sell his interest in the business to the purchasing party. [6]

call center. In customer service, an organizational unit that receives and/or places telephone calls to customers. [16]

Canada Health Act. A federal law that affirms the Canadian government's commitment to providing a universal, accessible, comprehensive, portable, and publicly administered health insurance system. [3]

Canada Pension Plan (CPP). A Canadian federal program that provides a pension for wage earners who have contributed money into the plan during their working years. The CPP covers workers in all provinces except Quebec. [3]

Canadian Council of Insurance Regulators (CCIR). A body formed by Canadian provincial regulators that recommends uniform insurance legislation to the provincial legislatures. [3]

Canadian Life and Health Insurance Association (CLHIA). A voluntary association with member companies that account for 99 percent of Canada's life and health insurance business that adopts guidelines with which member companies are expected to comply, although they are not law. [3]

Canadian Reinsurance Guidelines. A set of common reinsurance principles under the governance of the Canadian Life and Health Association that companies can use voluntarily as a basis for writing and interpreting reinsurance agreements. [9]

capital. An amount of money invested in a company by its owners, or a company's long-term financial resources. For insurers, may refer to capital and surplus together. *See also* **capital and surplus**. [9]

capital and surplus. For insurers, the amount remaining after liabilities are subtracted from assets; owners' equity in an insurance company. [9]

capital ratio. A ratio that expresses the relationship between an insurer's capital and surplus and its liabilities. [9]

captive reinsurer. A reinsurer that was formed by an insurer for the purpose of providing reinsurance and that is controlled by the insurance company that formed it. [9]

caregiver training benefit. A long-term care insurance policy benefit that covers the cost of training the informal, non-paid caregiver to help care for a covered person who is to receive care at home. [14]

case assignment system. A method of assigning cases to underwriters based on the characteristics of the case. [2]

cash value reimbursement. A monetary amount the reinsurer reimburses the direct writer under a coinsurance or modco reinsurance agreement when a life insurance policyowner surrenders a reinsured policy in exchange for the policy's cash value. [11]

catastrophe coverage. A type of nonproportional reinsurance designed to partially protect direct writers from (1) a single catastrophic event resulting in multiple claims or (2) an annual total of claims in a catastrophic amount. Also known as *cat cover*. [10]

cat cover. *See* **catastrophe coverage**.

CCIR. *See* **Canadian Council of Insurance Regulators**.

ceding allowance. *See* **coinsurance allowance**.

ceding commission. *See* **allowance**.

ceding company. *See* **direct writer**.

census. A document that lists demographic information about a group prospect as a unit and about individual members within the group. [8]

centralized data repository. A database that houses all the relevant data contained in the insurer's separate administration systems. [1]

certificate holder. *See* **group insured**.

certificate of coverage. *See* **certificate of insurance**.

certificate of insurance. (1) A document that describes (1) the coverage that the master group insurance contract provides and (2) the group insured's rights under the contract. [1] (2) A document issued instead of a duplicate policy when the original policy has been lost or destroyed or is otherwise unavailable that verifies that coverage exists, but does not contain all the provisions and riders that the original policy may have contained. Also known as a *certificate of coverage*. [17]

cession. (1) A unit of insurance risk that a direct writer transfers to a reinsurer. (2) The document used to record the transfer of risk from a direct writer to a reinsurer. [9]

change in health statement. A statement contained in most individual life insurance applications and premium receipts that requires a proposed insured to notify the insurer in writing if his health or any material information in the application changes before the policy is delivered. [13]

churning. A prohibited practice that occurs when a producer induces a customer to replace one policy after another so that the producer can earn a series of first-year commissions on the replacements. [3]

CI insurance. *See* **critical illness insurance**.

Civil Rights Act of 1964. A U.S. federal law that prohibits employment discrimination on the basis of race, color, sex, religion, or national origin. [3]

claim adjuster. *See* **claim analyst.**

claim administration. The process of evaluating each submitted claim, deciding whether or not the claim is eligible, informing the person who submitted the claim of the decision, and authorizing the payment of each eligible claim according to the terms of the policy. [1]

claim analyst. An insurance company employee who evaluates claims and determines the company's liability under each claim. Also known as a *claim examiner* or *claim adjuster*. [12]

claimant's statement. *See* **claim form**.

claim examiner. *See* **claim analyst**.

claim file. An organized collection of all the information relevant to a claim. [11]

claim form. A document containing information about a loss under an insurance policy that is submitted to an insurance company to begin the claim evaluation process. Also known as a *claimant's statement*. [12]

claim fraud. An action by which a person intentionally uses false information in an unfair or unlawful attempt to collect benefits under an insurance policy. [12]

claim philosophy. A statement of the insurer's objectives for administering claims. [12]

claim practices. Statements developed by the senior management of claim administration using the insurer's claim philosophy as a foundation that guide the day-to-day handling of claims. [12]

claim provision. An indemnity reinsurance agreement provision that states the terms and conditions of the reinsurer's liability for claims submitted under reinsured policies. [10]

claim settlement. A lump-sum payment of money from the insurer to the claimant in exchange for the claimant's agreement to release the insurer from further responsibility for coverage under a disability income policy. [15]

class. A group of group members categorized according to some nondiscriminatory characteristic for purposes of determining eligibility for coverage and benefit levels. [8]

class designation. A life insurance beneficiary designation that identifies a certain group of people rather than naming each person individually. [17]

CLHIA. *See* **Canadian Life and Health Insurance Association**.

CLHIA Guidelines. Guidelines adopted by the Canadian Life and Health Insurance Association with which member companies are expected to comply, although they are not law. [3]

close notice. *See* **drop notice**.

COB provision. *See* **coordination of benefits provision**.

COBRA. *See* **Consolidated Omnibus Budget Reconciliation Act of 1986**.

COBRA continuation coverage. Group medical expense insurance coverage that is continued under the provisions of the Consolidated Omnibus Budget Reconciliation Act of 1986. [3]

cognitive impairment. A reduction in a person's ability to think, reason, or remember. [7]

cognitive screen. A test designed to determine a person's powers of recollection or short-term memory. Also known as a *cognitive test*. [7]

cognitive test. *See* **cognitive screen**.

coinsurance. (1) The percentage of all eligible medical expenses in excess of the deductible the insured must pay. [7] (2) A plan of proportional reinsurance under which a direct writer and a reinsurer proportionately share monetary responsibility for almost every aspect of each policy covered under the arrangement. [10]

coinsurance allowance. In a coinsurance arrangement, an allowance that the reinsurer provides to the direct writer to proportionately share in the direct writer's expenses for commissions, administration, and sometimes premium taxes. Also known as a *ceding allowance*. [10]

COLA benefit. *See* **cost-of-living adjustment benefit**.

collateral assignment. A transfer of some of a policyowner's rights in a life insurance policy to provide security for a debt. [13]

committee underwriting. A work division system in which a committee of highly qualified people from inside and outside the underwriting function is called together for case assessment. [2]

community property laws. In the United States, state laws that provide that a spouse is entitled to receive an equal share of earned income and an equal share of property acquired by the other spouse during a marriage. [13]

comorbidity. The simultaneous appearance of two or more unrelated illnesses or conditions that may act in conjunction with one another. [2]

compensatory damages. Monetary awards intended to compensate an injured party for the amount of the monetary losses that resulted from the defendant's improper conduct. [12]

complaint team. A work group dedicated solely to resolving customer complaints. Also known as a *customer relationship team* or *problem resolution team*. [17]

compliance. The functional area of an insurance company that is responsible for ensuring that an insurer adheres to all applicable laws and regulations in each jurisdiction in which the company does business. [1]

compound inflation provision. A long-term care insurance policy inflation protection provision under which the coverage amount increases each year by a specified percentage of the compounded daily benefit amount. [14]

concurrent beneficiaries. Two or more life insurance beneficiaries who share the policy proceeds on the death of the insured. [17]

condition. *See* **schedule.**

conditional premium receipt. A premium receipt that specifies certain conditions that must be met before the temporary insurance coverage provided by the receipt becomes effective. [3]

conservation. The process of ensuring that policies do not lapse but are retained on an insurer's books for as long as possible. [16]

consideration. Whatever a promisor asks for and receives in exchange for making a contractual promise. [3]

Consolidated Omnibus Budget Reconciliation Act of 1986 (COBRA). A U.S. federal law that imposes requirements on group insurance plans that provide medical expense benefits and that are sponsored by employers with 20 or more employees. [3]

Consumer Price Index (CPI). A national measurement of the rate of inflation compiled monthly by the U. S. Bureau of Labor Statistics. [14]

consumer report. For purposes of the Fair Credit Reporting Act, any communication of information by a consumer reporting agency that (1) bears on a consumer's creditworthiness, credit standing, credit capacity, character, general reputation, personal characteristics, or mode of living and (2) is used or collected as a factor in establishing a consumer's eligibility for insurance or credit. [3]

consumer reporting agency. A private business that assembles or evaluates information on consumers and furnishes consumer reports to third parties in exchange for a fee. [3]

contest. In the context of insurance claim administration, a court action to determine the validity of a claim. [10]

contestable claim. A claim for life insurance policy proceeds following the death of an insured during the policy's contestable period. [11]

contestable period. The time period within which the insurer has the right to avoid a life insurance policy on the grounds of a material misrepresentation in the application. [3]

contingent beneficiary. The person or entity designated to receive the proceeds of a life insurance policy following the insured's death if the primary beneficiary dies before the insured. Also known as a *secondary beneficiary*. [13]

continuation. For an insurance policy, an event that occurs either when (1) the provisions of an in-force policy are significantly modified or (2) a policy replaces an existing policy from the same direct writer, but that differs from a new insurance policy in at least one of the following ways: the policy is not subject to the direct writer's new business underwriting requirements; the direct writer does not pay full first-year commissions to the insurance producer; the policy does not introduce a new suicide exclusion period; or the policy does not introduce a new contestable period. [10]

continuation provision. An indemnity reinsurance agreement provision that addresses which reinsurer(s) should provide the reinsurance, the amount of reinsurance, and the effective date of reinsurance for continued policies. [10]

contract. A legally enforceable agreement between two or more parties. [3]

contractual capacity. The legal capability to make a contract. [3]

contributory plan. A group insurance plan for which group insureds must pay some or all of the premiums for their coverage. [8]

conversion. A new policy that is issued on the basis of the policyowner's contractual right to change the policy form, as provided in the original policy. [10]

conversion provision. (1) A provision sometimes included in individual insurance policies or group insurance policies that allows the policyowner or insured group member to change from one type of insurance coverage to another in certain prescribed situations. [3] (2) An indemnity reinsurance agreement provision that typically states (1) that the direct writer must continue the reinsurance on converted policies with the original reinsurer unless the reinsurer releases its right to reinsure the policies and (2) any conditions under which the direct writer or the reinsurer can cancel the reinsurance on conversions. [10]

cookie. A file that a Web server places on a user's personal computer that enables the server to recognize the personal computer. [1]

coordination of benefits (COB) provision. A provision in a group medical expense policy designed to prevent a group insured who is insured under more than one group medical expense insurance policy from receiving benefit amounts that are greater than the amount of medical expenses the group insured actually incurred. [14]

copayment. A specified, fixed amount that an insured pays for a specified medical service at the time the service is rendered. [7]

cost basis. In terms of an insurance policy, the total premiums paid minus paid or credited policy dividends. [6]

cost-of-living adjustment (COLA) benefit. A disability income insurance policy supplemental benefit that provides for periodic increases in the disability income benefit amount that the insurer will pay to a disabled insured; these increases usually correspond to increases in the cost of living. [15]

coupon plan. A policy loan repayment plan under which the insurer supplies the policyowner with coupons to return with periodic payments against the loan amount. [17]

covered person. *See* **group insured**.

CPI. *See* **Consumer Price Index**.

CPP. *See* **Canada Pension Plan**.

CPT. *See* **Physician's Current Procedural Terminology**.

credibility factor. A percentage that represents the amount of weight given to a group's actual claim experience for premium rate calculation purposes. [8]

creditable coverage. For purposes of the Health Insurance Portability and Accountability Act, coverage under virtually any type of individual or group health care plan without a break in coverage of 63 days or more. [3]

Credit for Reinsurance Model Law. In the United States, a National Association of Insurance Commissioners model law that specifies requirements for taking reserve credits, including requirements that the reinsurer must meet. [9]

creditor insurance. Life insurance coverage designed to pay for the economic loss suffered by a creditor when a key person of a debtor business dies before the debt is paid. Also known as *loan coverage* or *debt coverage*. [6]

credits. A proposed insured's medical and personal risk factors that have a favorable effect on mortality or morbidity and are sometimes assigned "minus" values (such as -25) in a risk classification system. *Compare with* **debits**. [5]

critical illness benefit. *See* **dread disease benefit**.

critical illness (CI) insurance. A type of individual health insurance that pays a lump-sum benefit when the insured is diagnosed with a specified illness or condition. [7]

cross-purchase agreement. A type of buy-sell agreement under which each partner or stockholder agrees to purchase a portion of a deceased partner's or stockholder's interest in the partnership. *Contrast with* **entity agreement**. [6]

CSR. *See* **customer service representative**.

current asset. An item that a company presently has or owns that can be readily converted to cash at a close approximation of its true value. [6]

current liability. A company's debt or obligation that is due and payable within the next accounting period. [6]

current ratio. A ratio that measures liquidity by dividing a company's current assets by current liabilities. [6]

custodial care. The most basic level of nursing care, largely of a non-medical nature, provided by professionally trained nurses or other qualified people. Also known as *personal care*. [14]

customer contact center. In customer service, an organizational unit that provides customers with a variety of channels for communicating with a business entity. [16]

customer contact system. A customer database and work tracking tool that combines a variety of features—such as data entry and retrieval, history of previous customer contacts, document management, scripted presentations, and follow-up tools—to provide a framework for handling and documenting customer contacts. [16]

customer loyalty. A customer's feeling of attachment to or preference for a company's people, products, or services. [16]

customer relationship team. *See* **complaint team**. [17]

customer service. The broad range of activities that a company and its employees perform to keep customers satisfied so they will continue doing business with the company and speak positively about it to potential customers. [1]

customer service representative (CSR). A person whose primary job responsibility is to support external customers through face-to-face communications or through communication media. [16]

daily benefit amount. Under a long-term care policy, the amount the insurer will pay for each day of an insured's long-term care at a care facility or in the insured's home. [14]

data. Unprocessed facts. [1]

database. An organized collection of data and information. [1]

database management system (DBMS). A group of computer programs that organizes data in a database and allows users to obtain the information they need. [1]

data mining. The analysis of large amounts of data to discover previously unknown trends, patterns, and relationships. [1]

data warehouse. A type of database management system that collects data from the company's existing databases and possibly from sources outside the company, screens and edits the data, puts the data in a standard format, and then stores the data in the centralized data repository. [1]

date of expiry. The date on which a reinsurer will cancel the reservation of reinsurance capacity if the reinsurer does not receive a cession or other placement information from the direct writer. [11]

DBMS. *See* **database management system**.

DD benefit. *See* **dread disease benefit**.

death certificate. A document that attests to the death of a person and that bears the signature—and sometimes the seal—of an official authorized to issue such a certificate. [13]

debits. A proposed insured's medical and personal risk factors that have an unfavorable effect on mortality or morbidity and are sometimes assigned "plus" values (such as +25) in a risk classification system. *Compare with* **credits**. [5]

debt coverage. *See* **creditor insurance.**

debtor-creditor group. An insured group consisting of individuals who have borrowed money from a specific lender or lenders. [8]

debt ratio. *See* **debt-to-equity ratio.**

debt-to-equity ratio. A ratio that measures solvency by dividing a company's total debt by its owners' equity. Also known as a *debt ratio*. [6]

declined class. A risk class composed of proposed insureds whose anticipated mortality or morbidity rates are so great that the insurer cannot provide coverage at an affordable cost or whose mortality or morbidity risk cannot be predicted because of recent or unusual medical conditions or other risk factors. [2]

deductible. A flat monetary amount of eligible medical expenses that the insured must pay before the insurer will begin making any benefit payments under a medical expense insurance policy. [7]

defamation. A civil wrong that occurs when a person makes false statements that tend to damage the reputation of another. [12]

delayed word recall (DWR) test. A type of cognitive screen that examines the person's ability to remember a number of common words. [7]

dementia. A general term used to describe mental deterioration characterized by loss of essential intellectual abilities such as memory, judgment, and abstract thinking, of such a degree as to interfere with social functioning. [7]

dependent. A group member's (1) spouse, (2) unmarried child who is under age 19 and who relies on the group member for financial support and maintenance, (3) child older than 19—up to a stated maximum age, often 25—if she is a full-time student, and (4) a disabled child for as long as the disability exists, regardless of the child's age. [8]

desk audit. In reinsurance, a reinsurer's systematic review of the quality of the direct writer's reinsurance administration that is performed by the reinsurer's staff at the reinsurer's own offices. [11]

diagnostic code. Numbers and words that represent a specific medical diagnosis. [14]

DI insurance. *See* **disability income insurance**.

direct response distribution system. A type of distribution channel in which customers purchase products directly from a company by responding to advertisements, Internet Web sites, or telephone, e-mail, fax, or mail solicitations. [6]

direct response policy. A policy distributed through a direct response system. [6]

direct writer. An insurer that sells insurance coverage to the public. In a reinsurance arrangement, also known as a ceding company. [9]

disability income (DI) insurance. A type of health insurance that provides periodic benefits to replace income if the insured is unable to work as a result of sickness or injury. [7]

dividend plan. A policy loan repayment plan under which the insurer applies available dividends plus future dividends against the loan amount. [17]

divisible surplus. The portion of the insurance company's earnings that is available for distribution to policyowners. [17]

document imaging. A process of converting printed characters or graphics into digital images on a computer by inserting paper documents in a type of hardware called a scanner. Also known as *scanning*. [1]

document management system. A type of technology that stores, organizes, and retrieves documents that have been converted to digital images. [1]

dread disease (DD) benefit. An accelerated death benefit under which the insurer agrees to pay a portion of the policy's death benefit to a policyowner-insured if she suffers from one of a number of specified diseases. Also known as a *critical illness benefit*. [6]

drop notice. A written notification from a direct writer to a reinsurer stating that the direct writer no longer needs reinsurance that it previously requested and asking the reinsurer to cancel the reservation. Also known as a *close notice*. [11]

DWR test. *See* **delayed word recall test**.

ECG. *See* **electrocardiogram**.

e-commerce. *See* **electronic commerce**.

EDI. *See* **electronic data interchange**.

EFT. *See* **electronic funds transfer**. [16]

electrocardiogram (ECG). A graphic record of the electrical forces produced by the heart that is a diagnostic tool for detecting a disease or an abnormality of the heart. [4]

electronic application system. A technology that allows producers or applicants to enter application information into a computer, rather than on paper, and transmit the information to the insurer over a computer network. [2]

electronic commerce (e-commerce). The use of the Internet and other networks to deliver commercial information and to facilitate business transactions and the delivery of products and services. [1]

electronic data interchange (EDI). The computer-to-computer exchange of data between organizations using a data format agreed upon by the sending and receiving parties. [1]

electronic funds transfer (EFT). A method of transferring funds between financial intermediaries through an electronic computer network. [16]

electronic mail (e-mail). A form of telecommunication that allows a user to type a message into a computer and then send the message to other computers connected to a network. [1]

electronic signature. A unique personal identifier that makes a legally binding contract using electronic communications media like the Internet. [2]

Electronic Signatures in Global and National Commerce (E-SIGN) Act. A federal law in the United States that gives electronic signatures the same legal status as hard-copy signatures. [2]

eligibility period. The period of time—usually 31 days—during which eligible group members may enroll for contributory group insurance coverage without having to provide evidence of insurability. Also known as the *enrollment period*. [8]

elimination period. *See* **waiting period.**

e-mail. *See* **electronic mail.**

employee application. *See* **enrollment card.**

employee benefit plan. A program under which an employer provides its employees with various benefits in addition to their wages. [6]

Employee Retirement Income Security Act (ERISA). A U.S. federal law that regulates employee retirement plans and specifies minimum requirements that employee welfare benefit plans must meet. [3]

employer-employee group. *See* **single-employer group**.

encryption. Technology that encodes data so that only an authorized person, who possesses the required hardware and/or software that contains the decryption key, can decode the data. [1]

enrollment application. *See* **enrollment card**.

enrollment card. A document that must be completed and signed by a group member to enroll in a group insurance plan. Also known as a *group enrollment card*, an *enrollment application*, or an *employee application*. [8]

enrollment date. For purposes of the Health Insurance Portability and Accountability Act, the date a person becomes covered under a group medical expense insurance plan or the first day of the probationary period for enrollment, whichever occurs earlier. [3]

enrollment period. *See* **eligibility period**.

entire agreement provision. An indemnity reinsurance agreement provision stating that the written agreement articles, schedules, and any amendments represent the whole agreement between the parties, which have no further agreement than that stated in the written document. [10]

entity agreement. A type of buy-sell agreement under which the partnership or small corporation agrees to purchase the interest of any partner or stockholder who dies. Also known as a *stock redemption agreement* when the entity is a small corporation. *Contrast with* **cross-purchase agreement**. [6]

EOB. *See* **explanation of benefits**.

equity. In the context of valuing a business, the amount of a business that is owned—and not financed—by the owners. [5]

ERISA. *See* **Employee Retirement Income Security Act**.

error rate. A quality quantitative performance measurement that indicates the percentage of transactions that resulted in errors, such as 0.5 percent of account transactions reported errors. [16]

errors and omissions provision. An indemnity reinsurance agreement provision that states that if either party to the agreement fails to comply with the terms of the agreement through unintentional administrative mistake or clerical error, then both parties will be restored to the position they would have occupied if the mistake or error had not occurred. [10]

escalation process. A procedure that specifies how an issue or complaint is to be handled in situations where the customer service representative is not able or authorized to address a particular request or demand. [17]

E-SIGN Act. *See* **Electronic Signatures in Global and National Commerce Act**.

ethics. A system of accepted standards of conduct and moral judgment that combines the elements of honesty, integrity, and fair treatment. [1]

examining physician. A physician who performs an examination of a proposed insured at the request of an insurance company. [4]

excess-of-loss ratio reinsurance. *See* **stop-loss reinsurance**.

excess-of-loss reinsurance. A type of nonproportional reinsurance in which a reinsurer is responsible for paying a specified amount of a direct writer's claim benefits paid on a single loss, within a specified range of monetary amounts. [10]

excess of retention. In proportional reinsurance, the monetary amount of risk remaining after a direct writer's retention limit is subtracted from the net amount at risk on a case. [10]

excess-of-retention arrangement. A method for assigning risk in proportional reinsurance in which the direct writer establishes a monetary amount as a retention limit and the reinsurer agrees to assume monetary amounts greater than the direct writer's specified retention limit, up to the reinsurer's automatic binding limit. [10]

excess-of-time reinsurance. *See* **extended-time reinsurance**.

excess quota share arrangement. A method for assigning risk in proportional reinsurance in which the direct writer keeps its full retention limit and cedes the remaining risk to two or more reinsurers on a percentage basis. [10]

exclusion rider. A policy amendment that specifies that benefits will not be paid for any loss that results from the condition specified in the rider. Also known as an *impairment rider*. [2]

exculpatory statute. In the United States, a state law that permits an insurer to pay life insurance proceeds according to the terms of a policy without fear of double liability. [13]

exhibit. *See* **schedule.**

expected claim experience. The monetary amount of claims that the insurer estimates a group will submit during the upcoming policy year. [8]

expense allowance. *See* **allowance**.

experience rating. A method of establishing group insurance premium rates using a group's own claim experience. *Compare with* **manual rating**. [8]

experience refund. (1) The portion of a group insurance premium that is returned to a policyholder if the group's claim experience during the year was more favorable than expected when the premium was calculated. [8] (2) An amount the reinsurer credits the direct writer as compensation for favorable risk experience. [9]

explanation of benefits (EOB). A detailed statement showing each treatment or medication submitted as part of a claim; the insurer's decision concerning payment of benefits for each charge; any amount that is considered to be a deductible, copayment, or coinsurance; an explanation of any nonpayment of part or all of a charge; and the total amount paid to a health care provider or the insured. [14]

extended-time reinsurance. A type of nonproportional reinsurance in which the reinsurer reimburses the direct writer for all claims paid under reinsured policies after the direct writer has paid claims for a specified amount of time. Also called *excess-of-time reinsurance*. [10]

extension request. A request from a direct writer to a reinsurer to extend the direct writer's reservation of capacity for a specified period so that the direct writer can gather all information needed to move the case from *reserved* to *placed* status. [11]

external audit. An audit conducted by a third party who is not employed by the company being audited. [2]

external replacement. A policy replacement in which the new policy is purchased from an insurer other than the insurer that issued the original policy. *Contrast with* **internal replacement**. [6]

extranet. A portion of an organization's intranet that is accessible to people within the organization and to selected external parties. [1]

extra-percentage table. A document that lists all the tables used in the table rating method. [5]

face-to-face assessment. A meeting between a proposed insured and an interviewer who represents the insurance company and who observes and, to some extent, examines the proposed insured's physical and mental condition. [7]

fac-ob reinsurance. *See* **facultative-obligatory reinsurance**.

factor table. A chart that shows the maximum amount of life insurance—expressed in multiples of a person's salary or current gross earned income—that an insurer typically will approve in each of several age ranges. [5]

facultative application. *See* **request for coverage**.

facultative-obligatory (fac-ob) reinsurance. A reinsurance cession basis in which (1) the direct writer may choose to submit specific cases to the reinsurer and (2) the reinsurer must accept the risks based on the direct writer's underwriting, up to a stated maximum amount, if the reinsurer has available financial capacity. *Contrast with* **automatic reinsurance** and **facultative reinsurance**. [9]

facultative reinsurance. A reinsurance cession basis in which a direct writer chooses whether to cede a risk and the reinsurer chooses whether to accept that risk. *Contrast with* **automatic reinsurance** and **facultative-obligatory** (fac-ob) reinsurance. [9]

Fair Credit Reporting Act (FCRA). A U.S. federal law that regulates the reporting and use of consumer information and seeks to ensure that consumer reports contain only accurate, relevant, and recent information. [3]

family benefit. A supplemental benefit that insures the lives of the insured's spouse and children. [6]

FCRA. *See* **Fair Credit Reporting Act**.

FDQS arrangement. *See* **first-dollar quota share arrangement**.

field underwriting. The practice of gathering initial information about applicants and proposed insureds and screening proposed insureds to determine if they are likely to be approved for a specific type of coverage. [2]

field underwriting manual. A document that (1) presents specific guidance for a producer's assessment of the risk represented by a proposed insured and (2) guides the producer in assembling and submitting the application and any other information needed for the underwriter to evaluate the risk. [2]

financial capacity. The total monetary amount of risk a company can accept based on the investable funds it has available to write new business. *Contrast with* **underwriting capacity**. [9]

financial ratio analysis. A financial analysis that consists of calculating the relationships between various pairs of financial values for the purpose of assessing a company's financial condition. [6]

financial risk factor. Financial information that an underwriter considers to determine whether a person is applying for more insurance than he reasonably needs or can afford. [2]

financial status. A person's (1) current income expressed in terms of amount, sources, and permanency and (2) net worth. [5]

financial underwriting. The assessment of a proposed risk based on financial factors. [5]

financial worksheet. A document that enables an underwriter to organize financial information and develop a clear picture of a person's financial situation. [5]

firewall. A combination of hardware and software that creates an electronic barrier between the public and private areas of a company's systems. [1]

first contact resolution. A timeliness quantitative performance measurement that indicates the percentage of inbound customer contacts that are successfully completed at the initial point of contact—that is, without being transferred and without the need for follow-up work. [16]

first-dollar quota share (FDQS) arrangement. A method for assigning risk in proportional reinsurance in which the direct writer retains a stated percentage of the risk for each policy in a given block of business, up to its retention limit, and cedes the remaining risk to one or more reinsurers. [10]

first-to-die life insurance policy. A type of multi-life policy which provides that proceeds will be paid when the first of two (or more) insureds covered by the policy dies. Also known as a *joint life insurance policy*. [6]

fixed-amount option. A life insurance policy settlement option under which the insurance company pays the policy proceeds in equal installments of a stated amount until the proceeds, plus the interest earned, are exhausted. [13]

fixed-period option. A life insurance policy settlement option under which the insurance company agrees to pay policy proceeds in equal installments to the payee for a specified period of time. [13]

flat extra premium method. A method of charging for substandard risks in which the insurer adds to the standard premium a specified extra dollar amount. [5]

fraud. An act by which someone intentionally deceives another party and induces that other party to part with something of value. [10]

full portability option. A long-term care insurance policy provision that permits a group insured who leaves the group to take her coverage with her and continue to pay premiums. [14]

fully insured group plan. A group insurance plan for which an insurance company is financially responsible for incurred claims. *Contrast with* **self-insured group plan**. [8]

funds withheld coinsurance. A plan of proportional reinsurance and a variation on coinsurance under which the direct writer and reinsurer proportionately share responsibility for almost all aspects of a reinsured policy, but the direct writer retains the initial gross reinsurance premium and the reinsurer retains the initial coinsurance allowance. *See also* **coinsurance**. [10]

future increase option benefit. A disability income insurance policy supplemental benefit that allows a disability income policyowner-insured to buy additional disability income protection without providing evidence of insurability. [15]

genetic test. A test of human DNA used to indicate a person's predisposition to a certain illness or disease. [3]

geriatrics. The branch of medicine that deals with the diagnosis and treatment of diseases and problems specific to the aged. [7]

GI benefit. *See* **guaranteed insurability benefit**.

GLB Act. *See* **Gramm-Leach-Bliley Act**.

good faith. A party's honesty of intention and avoidance of attempts to deceive or take unfair advantage of another party to an agreement. [10]

Gramm-Leach-Bliley (GLB) Act. A U.S. federal law that removed many of the barriers to affiliations among institutions in the various segments of the financial services industry. [3]

group enrollment card. *See* **enrollment card**.

Group Health Insurance Definition and Group Health Insurance Standard Provisions Model Act (Group Health Insurance Model Act). In the United States, a National Association of Insurance Commissioners model law that defines the types of groups eligible for group health insurance, as well as sets forth provisions that such group policies must contain. [3]

Group Health Insurance Model Act. *See* **Group Health Insurance Definition and Group Health Insurance Standard Provisions Model Act**.

group insurance policy. *See* **master group insurance contract**.

group insured. An individual covered by a master group insurance policy. Also known as a *covered person* or *certificate holder*. [1]

Group Life Insurance Definition and Group Life Insurance Standard Provisions Model Act (Group Life Insurance Model Act). In the United States, a National Association of Insurance Commissioners model law that defines the types of groups eligible for group life insurance, as well as sets forth provisions that such group policies must contain. [3]

Group Life Insurance Model Act. *See* **Group Life Insurance Definition and Group Life Insurance Standard Provisions Model Act**.

group member. An individual who is part of a group but is not covered by insurance. [8]

group prospect. A group that has applied, but has not yet been approved, for group coverage from an insurance company. Also known as the *proposed group*. [1]

group representative. A salaried insurance company employee specifically trained in the techniques of marketing and servicing group products. [8]

guaranteed insurability (GI) benefit. A supplemental benefit that gives the policyowner the right to purchase additional insurance of the same type as the basic life insurance policy—for an additional premium amount—on specified option dates during the life of the policy without supplying evidence of the insured's insurability. [6]

guaranteed-issue basis. A means of offering insurance products in which no individual underwriting takes place; every eligible proposed insured who applies and meets specified conditions is automatically issued a policy. [6]

guaranteed purchase option. A long-term care policy inflation protection provision that allows an insured to add to the original daily benefit amount at intervals specified in the policy without having to provide evidence of insurability. [14]

hands-on assistance. The assistance provided when an individual is unable to perform an activity of daily living without the physical assistance of another person such as a personal aide. *Compare with* **standby assistance**. [14]

hardware. The types of computers the insurer uses. [1]

Health Insurance Portability and Accountability Act (HIPAA). A U.S. federal law that sets forth requirements that insurers, managed care organizations, and employer-sponsored group insurance plans must meet in providing individual and group medical expense insurance coverage. [3]

HIPAA. *See* **Health Insurance Portability and Accountability Act**.

home health care. Care a patient receives at home—whether medical care or custodial care—including physical therapy, the services of a registered nurse, and homemaker services. [14]

home service agent. A commissioned producer in the home distribution system who sells a range of products and provides specified policyowner services, including the collection of renewal premiums, within a specified geographical area. [6]

home service distribution system. A method of selling and servicing insurance policies through commissioned producers, known as home service agents. [6]

hospice. A facility that specializes in the treatment of terminally ill people. [14]

hospice care. Care provided to terminally ill people, either in a facility or the patient's home. [14]

human resources. The functional area of an insurance company that recruits and screens applicants; helps select qualified employees; plans and presents appropriate orientation, training, and development for each employee; administers employee benefit programs; and maintains employee records. [1]

IADLs. *See* **instrumental activities of daily living**.

ICD. *See* **International Classification of Diseases and Related Health Problems**.

impairment. A physical or psychological abnormality or loss of function. [2]

impairment guide. A list of common impairments and the probable underwriting decision for proposed insureds who have each type of impairment. [2]

impairment rider. *See* **exclusion rider**.

income protection insurance. A type of disability income insurance that defines total disability as the insured's loss of income as a result of disability. [15]

income replacement table. For purposes of disability income insurance underwriting, a table that states the limits on the amount of disability insurance—usually expressed as a monetary amount of monthly income benefit—the insurer will issue based on a proposed insured's net earned income. [7]

income statement. A financial statement that reports a business's revenues and expenses during a specified period and indicates whether the business experienced net income or a net loss during the period. Also known as a *profit and loss statement*. [5]

incontestability provision. (1) A group insurance policy provision that states that, after the policy has been in force two years, the insurer may not contest the validity of the group contract except for nonpayment of premium. The provision also limits the insurer's ability to contest the validity of a group insured's coverage under a group policy after that coverage has been in force for two years during the group insured's lifetime. [3] (2) An individual insurance policy provision that denies the insurer the right to rescind, or avoid, the contract on the grounds of a material misrepresentation in the application after the contract has been in force for a stated period, typically two years, during the life of the insured. [3]

indemnity benefit method. A method of determining the daily benefit amount under a long-term care insurance policy that pays a specified benefit regardless of the actual expenses for long-term care of the insured. [14]

independent underwriting. A work division system in which underwriters work alone to assess each risk. [2]

individual cession administration. A method of reinsurance record administration under which the reinsurer prepares its own cession records based on detailed information about individual cessions provided by the direct writer. [10]

industry experience. The collective data about insurance claim experience generated by industry-wide studies. [2]

inflation protection provision. A long-term care insurance policy provision that either automatically increases the benefit amount each year by a specific percentage or allows the insured to opt for a higher daily benefit at specified intervals during the lifetime of the policy without having to show evidence of insurability. [14]

in-force policy report. A reinsurance report that lists all in-force reinsured policies as of a given date and provides detailed information about each policy. [11]

information. A collection of data that has been converted into a form that is meaningful or useful for the accomplishment of some objective, such as performing a transaction, drawing a conclusion, or solving a problem. [1]

information management. The use of information systems to provide a company's information users with the information they need to carry out their job responsibilities. [1]

information system. An interactive combination of technology, people, and processes that collects, manipulates, and disseminates information. [1]

information technology (IT). The functional area of an insurance company that develops and maintains the company's information systems and oversees information management throughout the company. [1]

injury. An accidental harm resulting from an unforeseen external force that (1) causes trauma to a person's body and (2) occurs while the disability income policy is in force. [15]

insolvency. A condition in which an entity is consistently unable to meet its financial obligations on time. *Contrast with* **solvency**. [9]

insolvency provision. An indemnity reinsurance agreement provision that describes the rights and responsibilities of the direct writer and the reinsurer in the event that either party becomes insolvent. [10]

inspection report. A type of investigative consumer report that a consumer reporting agency prepares about a proposed insured. [4]

instant-issue underwriting. *See* **real-time underwriting**.

instrumental activities of daily living (IADLs). Activities that are usually less essential to daily life than activities of daily living (ALDs), including managing finances, cooking, doing laundry, shopping for food and clothing, transporting oneself in a car or on public transportation, using the telephone, and taking medications. [7]

insurability premium receipt. A conditional premium receipt that provides temporary insurance coverage on condition that the insurer finds that the proposed insured was insurable as a standard risk on a certain date specified in the premium receipt. [3]

insurable interest. In insurance, a person exhibits an insurable interest in a potential loss if that person is likely to suffer a genuine economic loss should the event insured against occur. [3]

insurance administration. Those insurance company activities specifically associated with administering insurance policies, such as underwriting, reinsurance, claims, and customer service. [1]

insurance fraud. Any fraud that involves an insurance company, whether committed by consumers, insurance company employees, producers, health care providers, or anyone else connected with an insurance transaction. [12]

Insurance Fraud Prevention Model Act. In the United States, a National Association of Insurance Commissioners model law that is designed to permit the state insurance departments to investigate and discover fraudulent insurance acts more effectively; halt fraudulent insurance acts; and receive assistance from state, local, and federal law enforcement and regulatory agencies in enforcing laws that prohibit fraudulent insurance acts. [12]

Insurance Information and Privacy Protection Model Act (Model Privacy Act). In the United States, a National Association of Insurance Commissioners model law that establishes standards for the collection, use, and disclosure of information gathered in connection with insurance transactions. [3]

insured. The person whose life, health, property, or income is covered by an individual insurance policy. Also known as the *assured* in some countries. [1]

insurer-administered group plan. A group insurance plan for which the insurer handles most of the administrative aspects of the plan. *Contrast with* **self-administered group plan**. [8]

interactive voice response (IVR) system. A computer-based technology that answers telephone calls, greets callers with a recorded or digitized message, and prompts them to enter information or make requests by voice or telephone keypad. Also known as a *voice response unit*. [16]

interest option. A life insurance policy settlement option under which the insurance company invests the policy proceeds and periodically pays interest on those proceeds to the payee. [13]

intermediate nursing care. Nursing care provided on less than a 24-hour basis that is usually rehabilitative in nature. [14]

internal audit. An audit conducted by a company's own staff. [2]

internal replacement. A policy replacement in which the new policy is purchased from the same insurer that issued the original policy. *Contrast with* **external replacement**. [6]

International Classification of Diseases and Related Health Problems (ICD). A common system of describing typical medical diagnoses. [14]

interpleader. A procedure by which the insurer pays the policy proceeds to a court, advises the court that the insurer cannot determine the correct recipient of the proceeds, and asks the court to determinc the proper recipient or recipients. [13]

intranet. An organization's internal computer network that uses Internet technology but is accessible only to people within the organization. [1]

intrusion detection software. Software that monitors system traffic and identifies sequences of commands that indicate an unauthorized user is attempting to access the organization's systems or databases. [1]

invasion of privacy. A civil wrong that occurs when a person (1) appropriates someone's name or personality, (2) publicizes someone's private affairs, (3) intrudes into someone's private affairs and the wrong causes mental suffering, shame, or humiliation, or (4) places someone in a false light in the public eye. [12]

investigative consumer report. A consumer report that contains information obtained through personal interviews with an individual's neighbors, friends, associates, or others who may have information about the individual. [3]

irrevocable beneficiary. A life insurance policy beneficiary who has a vested interest in the policy proceeds even during the insured's lifetime because the policyowner has the right to change the beneficiary designation only after obtaining the beneficiary's consent or upon the beneficiary's death. [13]

IT. *See* **information technology**.

IVR system. *See* **interactive voice response system**. [16]

jet issue electronic system. An information system that uses business rules engines to determine that certain criteria are met and an application is approved for issue; or the criteria are not met, and an application is either declined or sent to an underwriter.

jet unit underwriting. A work division system in which a separate group of employees is authorized to approve certain types of individual insurance applications for immediate policy issue. [2]

joint life insurance policy. *See* **first-to-die life insurance policy**.

jumbo limit. The maximum allowable monetary amount of total insurance—in force and yet-to-be-placed—with all companies on any one life that a reinsurer will accept for automatic cession. [9]

juvenile insurance policy. A policy issued on the life of a child but owned and paid for by an adult—usually the child's parent, grandparent, or legal guardian—who typically is also the beneficiary. [6]

key person. A person whose continued participation in a business is necessary to its success and whose death would cause substantial financial loss to the business. [6]

key-person life insurance. Individual life insurance that a business purchases on the life of a person whose continued participation in the business is necessary to its success and whose death would cause substantial financial loss to the business. [6]

knowledge management system. The overall strategies, resources, and processes that an organization uses to apply institutional knowledge to business activities. [16]

lapse notice. *See* **policy grace notice.** [17]

late enrollee. A group member or eligible dependent who is not enrolled when coverage is first offered and later decides to enroll in the plan. [8]

law department. *See* **legal**.

legal. The area of an insurance company that handles all legal matters for the company. Also know as the *law department*. [1]

life income option. A life insurance policy settlement option under which the insurance company agrees to pay the policy proceeds in periodic installments over the payee's lifetime. [13]

life settlement. The sale of a life insurance policy to a third party for a discount from the policy's face amount. [5]

lifetime maximum benefit. For a medical expense insurance policy, the maximum amount that the policy will pay for all eligible medical expenses an individual incurs while insured under the policy. [14]

liquidity. A company's ability to readily convert its assets to cash for an approximation of their true value. [6]

litigation. The process or act of resolving a dispute by means of a lawsuit. [10]

living benefits. A term used for health insurance in some countries, notably Canada, because insurance benefits are paid while an insured is living. *See* **accelerated death benefit**. [1]

loan coverage. *See* **creditor insurance**.

long-term care (LTC) insurance. A type of health insurance that pays benefits for medical or other health-related services needed by the insured who, because of his advanced age or the effects of a serious illness or injury, needs care in his own home or in a qualified facility. [7]

long-term care (LTC) insurance benefit. An accelerated death benefit under which the insurer agrees to pay periodic benefits to a policyowner-insured if he requires care in his own home or a qualified facility. [6]

LTC field underwriting manual. For purposes of underwriting long-term care insurance, a guidebook that lists a number of medical conditions associated with aging and provides general underwriting criteria for those conditions. [7]

LTC insurance. *See* **long-term care insurance**.

LTC insurance benefit. *See* **long-term care insurance benefit**.

lump sum plan. A policy loan repayment plan under which the policyowner submits a check or money order for the entire loan plus the loan interest due. [17]

maintenance expense. A direct writer's ongoing expense for administering and servicing a policy or a block of business after it has been placed in force. Also known as a *renewal expense* or an *administration expense.* [9]

manual rating. A method of establishing group insurance premium rates under which the insurer establishes rates for very broad classifications of group insureds using its own experience with the product and information collected by various governmental and trade associations. *Compare with* **experience rating**. [8]

market conduct examination. In the United States, a formal investigation of an insurer's nonfinancial operations that is carried out by one or more state insurance departments and is designed to determine whether the insurer's market conduct operations comply with applicable laws and regulations. [12]

marketing. The functional area of an insurer that has primary responsibility for identifying the insurer's prospective customers and what they want, as well as planning the promotion and distribution of the insurer's products. [1]

master application. An application for group insurance that contains the specific provisions of the requested plan of insurance and is signed by an authorized officer of the proposed policyholder. [8]

master group insurance contract. An insurance contract that insures a number of people. Also known as a *group insurance policy.* [1]

material misrepresentation. A misrepresentation that induces the other party to enter into a contract that it would not have entered into as written had it known the truth. [3]

MDO policy. *See* **monthly debit ordinary policy**.

mediation. A conflict resolution method in which an impartial third party facilitates negotiations between the parties in an effort to create a mutually agreeable resolution to the dispute. [15]

medical expense insurance. A type of health insurance that pays benefits for the treatment of sickness and injury. [7]

medically necessary. A service or supply that is needed and appropriate for the diagnosis or treatment of an injury or sickness based on generally accepted current medical practice. [14]

medical report. A type of Part II application for individual life insurance that contains the proposed insured's answers to medical history questions recorded by a physician and the results of a medical examination conducted by a physician. [4]

medical risk factor. A physical or psychological characteristic that may increase the likelihood of loss. [2]

member service. A specific type of customer service that includes all the service activities performed for group insureds. [1]

MIB. *See* **MIB Group, Inc.**

MIB Group, Inc. (MIB). A not-for-profit membership corporation established to provide coded information to insurers about impairments that applicants have disclosed or other insurance companies have detected in connection with previous applications for insurance. [4]

middleware. A type of software used to enable two or more systems to work together. [1]

minimum capital and surplus requirements. In the United States, solvency requirements that set a required minimum flat dollar amount of capital and surplus for a company as a whole and for each of the company's product lines. Also known as *statutory minimum capitalization requirements*. [9]

minimum cession. The smallest monetary amount of risk a reinsurer will accept or a direct writer will cede in an automatic cession. [9]

minor. A person who has not attained the age of majority, which is the age at which a person is given by law the rights and responsibilities of an adult. [3]

misdirected calls. A service level quantitative performance measurement that indicates the number or percentage of inbound telephone calls that are transferred to the wrong department. [16]

misrepresentation. An untrue statement of a fact. [3]

modco. *See* **modified coinsurance**.

model law. A sample law that legislatures are encouraged to enact. [3]

Model Privacy Act. *See* **Insurance Information and Privacy Protection Model Act**.

Model Privacy Regulation. *See* **Privacy of Consumer Financial and Health Information Regulation**.

model regulation. A sample regulation that state insurance departments are encouraged to adopt. [3]

modified coinsurance (modco). A plan of proportional reinsurance under which (1) the direct writer and reinsurer share proportionately in the policy reserve obligation, the direct writer's gross premiums, and the risks of loss from expenses for death, surrender, other benefits or from lapse and (2) the direct writer holds the entire reserve for each reinsured policy. [10]

money laundering. The practice of engaging in financial transactions to hide the identity, source, and/or destination of money associated with criminal activity. [3]

monthly debit ordinary (MDO) policy. An individual life insurance policy that is marketed under the home service distribution system and paid for by monthly premium payments. [6]

moral hazard. A characteristic that exists when the reputation, financial position, or criminal record of an applicant or proposed insured indicates that the person may act dishonestly in the insurance transaction. [2]

morbidity. The incidence of sickness and injury among a specified group of people. [2]

morbidity rate. The rate at which sickness and injury occur among a specified group of people during a specified period. [2]

mortality. The incidence of death among a specified group of people. [2]

mortality rate. The rate at which death occurs among a specified group of people during a specified period, typically one year. [2]

motor vehicle record (MVR). A report that contains information about a person's driving history, including information about traffic violations, arrests, and convictions. [4]

multi-life policy. A life insurance contract that is written on two or more lives. [6]

multiple-employer group. An insured group that consists of the employees of (1) two or more employers in the same industry, (2) two or more labor unions, or (3) one or more employers and one or more labor unions. [8]

MVR. *See* **motor vehicle record**.

mystery shopper. A trained evaluator who approaches or calls customer service customer service representatives and pretends to be a customer. [16]

NAIC. *See* **National Association of Insurance Commissioners**.

NAR. *See* **net amount at risk**.

National Association of Insurance Commissioners (NAIC). A private, nonprofit association of insurance commissioners from all 50 states and the District of Columbia that promotes uniformity of state insurance regulation within the United States. [3]

negative testing. In the context of reinsurance auditing, the process of ensuring that the direct writer ceded all of the policies that met the qualifications specified in the reinsurance agreement and no policies that were not covered by the agreement. [11]

net amount at risk (NAR). Generally, the difference between the face amount of a life insurance policy—other than a universal life policy—and the policy's reserve (or cash value) at the end of any given policy year. [10]

net cash surrender value. The actual cash value available to a policyowner upon policy surrender or lapse; it equals the cash value shown in the policy increased by any cash values of paid-up additions, policy dividend accumulations, and advance premium payment and decreased by outstanding policy loans and any charges imposed on the surrender. [17]

netting off. A process by which a direct writer subtracts the claim amount owed to it by a reinsurer from the amount that the direct writer owes the reinsurer for premiums. [11]

network. A group of interconnected computers and computer devices, including the telecommunications equipment and software that connect them. [1]

net worth. The difference between a person's assets and liabilities. [5]

new business. The activities an insurer undertakes in receiving applications, underwriting those applications, and issuing policies. [1]

new business strain. *See* **surplus strain**.

nonadmitted reinsurer. *See* **unauthorized reinsurer**.

noncontributory plan. A group insurance plan for which the group insureds are not required to pay any part of the premium for the coverage; the premiums are paid entirely by the policyholder and all eligible group members are provided with coverage automatically. [8]

nonduplication of benefits provision. A coordination of benefits provision that limits the amount payable by the secondary policy to the difference, if any, between the amount paid by the primary policy and the amount that would have been payable by the secondary policy had that policy been the primary policy. [14]

nonmedical basis. A method of applying for life insurance without providing medical proof of insurability. [4]

nonmedical limit. The total amount of insurance that the insurer will permit to be issued on a proposed insured without requiring the proposed insured to undergo a physical examination. [4]

nonmedical supplement. A type of Part II application for individual life insurance that contains the proposed insured's answers to medical history questions recorded by a producer or teleunderwriter but that does not require the proposed insured to undergo a physical examination. [4]

nonproportional reinsurance. A type of reinsurance in which neither the reinsurer nor the direct writer knows in advance what share of a risk the reinsurer will ultimately assume. [10]

nonpublic personal information. Under the Gramm-Leach-Bliley Act, personally identifiable information about a consumer that is not publicly available. [3]

nonqualified long-term care policy. In the United States, a long-term care policy issued before or after 1996 that does not meet HIPAA requirements and thus is not eligible for favorable tax treatment under federal law. *Compare with* **qualified long-term care policy**. [14]

notice of expiry. A document that a reinsurer uses to notify the direct writer that an offer to reinsure is due to expire and to request additional information, a cession, a drop notice, or an extension request from the direct writer. [11]

notification for automatic reinsurance provision. An indemnity reinsurance agreement provision that specifies (1) the details about each policy that a direct writer must send to a reinsurer to begin automatic reinsurance coverage and (2) how frequently the direct writer must notify the reinsurer of new automatic cessions. [10]

notification for fac-ob reinsurance provision. An indemnity reinsurance agreement provision that specifies the (1) information the direct writer must provide to notify the reinsurer of risks ceded on a facultative-obligatory basis and (2) maximum time periods allowed for the reinsurance parties to respond to each other concerning capacity available and the amount of risk ceded and accepted. [10]

notification for facultative reinsurance provision. An indemnity reinsurance agreement provision that specifies the (1) information the direct writer must provide to notify the reinsurer of a request for facultative reinsurance coverage, (2) procedures the reinsurer must follow to make an offer of reinsurance to the direct writer, and (3) procedures the direct writer must follow to accept the reinsurer's offer. [10]

number of blocked calls. A service level quantitative performance measurement that indicates the number of telephone calls that encounter a busy signal and cannot get through to the customer contract center. [16]

numerical rating system. A risk classification method in which an underwriter calculates a numerical value for the degree of risk a proposed insured presents to the insurer; the underwriter then places the proposed insured in a risk class according to the numerical value. [5]

nursing care. Basic nonmedical and medical care provided as necessary to patients. [14]

occasional reinsurer. An insurer that accepts some reinsurance business but is not a professional reinsurer. *Contrast with* **professional reinsurer**. [9]

occasional retrocessionaire. A reinsurer whose primary business is not retrocessions, but who accepts retrocessions. *Contrast with* **professional retrocessionaire**. [9]

occupational rating classes. For purposes of underwriting disability income coverage, groupings of occupations according to the relative degree of risk the occupations present. [7]

Office of the Superintendent of Financial Institutions (OSFI). The federal agency in Canada responsible for regulating the solvency of federally incorporated insurers, insurers incorporated in other countries, and specified provincially incorporated insurers in accordance with the federal Insurance Companies Act. [3]

offset. The use of the benefits paid under one type of insurance coverage to reduce the benefits paid under another type of coverage. [15]

open claimant. A group insured who is receiving short- or long-term disability income benefits. [8]

operating systems software. A type of software that controls the basic operations of a computer. [1]

oral specimen (saliva) test. A means of screening a proposed insured for habitual use of nicotine or cocaine and the presence of HIV antibodies by testing a specimen of the proposed insured's saliva. [4]

orphan policyowner. A policyowner whose original producer is no longer available to provide service. [16]

OSFI. *See* **Office of the Superintendent of Financial Institutions**.

outsourcing. A business practice in which a company hires a vendor to conduct a specific activity that the company would otherwise perform itself, such as billing administration or customer contacts. [1]

overinsurance. An amount of applied-for insurance that, together with in-force insurance, is excessive in relation to the need for which coverage is being purchased. [5]

overinsurance provision. A provision in individual health insurance policies, which specifies that, under certain circumstances, policy benefits will be reduced if an insured has more insurance than needed to cover medical expenses. [14]

par policy. *See* **participating policy**. [17]

paramedical report. A type of Part II application for individual life insurance that contains the proposed insured's answers to medical history questions recorded by a paramedical examiner and the results of a paramedical examination conducted by a paramedical examiner. [4]

partial disability. A disability that prevents the insured either from performing some of the duties of her usual occupation or from engaging in that occupation on a full-time basis. [15]

partial loan repayment plan. A policy loan repayment plan under which the policyowner submits a check or money order for a partial loan payment. [17]

participating policy. An insurance policy under which the policyowner shares in the insurance company's surplus. Also known as a *par policy* or a *with profits policy*. [17]

parties to the agreement provision. An indemnity reinsurance agreement provision stating that the reinsurance agreement exists solely between the direct writer and the reinsurer. [10]

payee. The person or entity who is to receive life insurance policy proceeds under a settlement option. [13]

PBM. *See* **pharmacy benefit manager**.

per capita beneficiary designation. A type of life insurance policy beneficiary class designation in which the class members all stand in the same relationship to the policyowner and the class members who survive the insured share the policy proceeds equally. [17]

percentage-of-income rule. A tool underwriters use to determine ability to pay premiums that stipulates the amount of money a proposed insured can afford to spend annually on insurance according to a specified percentage of the proposed insured's current gross earned and unearned annual income. [5]

percentage rating method. A method of establishing the health insurance premium rate to charge for substandard risks in which the insurer adds to the standard premium rate an extra percentage of that standard premium rate to reflect the additional risk. [7]

performance measurement. A process through which a company (1) decides what activities are key to the achievement of the company's goals and objectives, how to measure the performance of those activities, and what performance standards it hopes to achieve, (2) gathers the information, and (3) communicates the results. [1]

performance standard. An established level of performance against which a company or an individual compares actual performance.

permanent flat extra premium. An amount added to the premium for cases in which a personal risk factor is expected to remain constant throughout the life of the policy. [5]

persistency bonus. A sum of money paid as compensation to an insurance producer when a policy continues in force beyond an initial period, usually five years. [16]

persistency rate. The percentage of a specified group of contracts that remain in force during a specified period, such as a year. [5]

personal care. *See* **custodial care**.

personal history interview (PHI). A conversation between an underwriter or another insurance company employee and the proposed insured in which the underwriter verifies the accuracy of information already received about the proposed insured and obtains any additional information needed for underwriting. [4]

personal information. For purposes of the Model Privacy Act, information gathered about an individual in connection with an insurance transaction and from which judgments can be made about the individual's personal characteristics, such as character, habits, finances, credit, and health. [3]

Personal Information Protection and Electronics Document Act (PIPEDA). A Canadian federal law that governs the collection, use, and disclosure of personal information by organizations in the private sector. [3]

personal risk factor. A lifestyle choice that can significantly affect a person's health or longevity. [2]

per stirpes beneficiary designation. A type of life insurance policy beneficiary class designation in which the descendants of a deceased class member take the deceased class member's share of the policy proceeds by representation. [17]

pharmacy benefit manager (PBM). A clearinghouse that manages health care prescription benefit programs and maintains pharmaceutical databases that contain records of prescriptions filled by the persons enrolled in such benefit programs. [4]

PHI. *See* **personal history interview**.

Physicians' Current Procedural Terminology (CPT). A common system of describing medical treatments. [14]

physiological age. The relative age or youthfulness of a person's vital organs and their functioning. [7]

PIPEDA. *See* **Personal Information Protection and Electronics Document Act.**

placement. A process in which the direct writer and reinsurer activate reinsurance coverage for a new automatic, facultative, or fac-ob cession. [11]

plan administrator. The party responsible for handling the administrative aspects of a group plan. [8]

policy audit questionnaire. A document that allows a reinsurance audit team to examine the accuracy and timeliness of data about insureds, compliance with the reinsurance agreement, premium rates, and other elements by comparing the reinsurer's data with the direct writer's data. [11]

policy change report. A reinsurance report that shows details for all policies that, during the reporting period, have changed in a way that affects the amount of the reinsurance coverage, the reinsurance premium, or the allowance. Also known as a *transaction report.* [11]

policy dividend. A policyowner's share of the divisible surplus that is payable to owners of participating policies at the end of the policy year or on the policy anniversary. [17]

policy exhibit. A reinsurance report that summarizes and reconciles the changes that have occurred in reinsured policies during the reporting period. [11]

policy grace notice. A written notification that the policy's grace period is about to expire. Also known as a *lapse notice.* [17]

policyholder. The employer or other organization that decides what kind of coverage to purchase for a group and negotiates the terms of and enters into the master group insurance contract with the insurer. [1]

policy issue. The insurance company unit that prepares the insurance contract and facilitates the delivery of the policy to the customer. [2]

policyowner. The person or entity that owns an individual insurance policy. [1]

policyowner service. A specific type of customer service that includes all the service activities performed for people or entities that own individual insurance policies. [1]

policy reserves. A liability amount that, together with future premiums and investment income, the insurer estimates it will need to pay contractual benefits as they come due under in-force policies. [9]

pooling. A rating method by which the insurer combines several small groups into one large group, or pool. [8]

portfolio reinsurance. *See* **assumption reinsurance**.

precertification. A statement from an insurer approving certain nonemergency, inpatient and/or outpatient hospital services or treatments. [14]

predictive modeling. An automated technique for predicting future behavior or events. [1]

pre-existing condition. (1) According to the Health Insurance Portability and Accountability Act, a physical or mental condition for which medical advice, diagnosis, care, or treatment was recommended or received within the six-month period preceding an individual's enrollment date in a group medical expense insurance plan. Other group health insurance policies define pre-existing conditions in a variety of ways. [3] (2) As defined by an individual health insurance policy, an injury or illness that (1) occurred or manifested itself within a specified period before the policy was issued and (2) was not disclosed on the application. [14]

pre-existing conditions provision. An individual or group health insurance policy provision which states that benefits will not be paid for a pre-existing condition until the insured has been covered under the policy for a specified length of time. [3]

preferred beneficiaries. In Canada, certain family members named as the beneficiary in any life insurance policy issued prior to July 1, 1962, in common law jurisdictions whose written consent is required for the policyowner to change the beneficiary to anyone outside this group of family members, obtain a policy loan, surrender the policy for its cash surrender value, or assign the policy benefits if doing so would diminish the rights of the preferred beneficiary. [13]

preferred class. A risk class composed of proposed insureds whose anticipated mortality or morbidity rates are lower than average and who represent the lowest degree of mortality or morbidity risk. [2]

pre-funded inflation option. In a long-term care group insurance policy, a provision that typically provides that the policy's daily benefit amount will increase by a certain amount or percentage each year after the insured reaches age 65, the cost of which is built into the policy's premium structure. [14]

Pregnancy Discrimination Act. A U.S. federal law that is a part of the Civil Rights Act and that requires employers to treat pregnancy, childbirth, and related medical conditions the same as any other medical condition. [3]

premium-based reciprocity. A reciprocal arrangement that involves the exchange of blocks of reinsurance business representing approximately the same amount of gross premium on the reinsured risks. *Contrast with* **results-based reciprocity**. [9]

premium rate. A charge per unit of insurance coverage. [2]

premium receipt. A written acknowledgment that an insurer has received the initial premium submitted with an application for insurance. [3]

premium refund. *See* **experience refund**.

premium tax. An amount of tax that a government levies on a direct writer's premium income.

preplacement. The process by which a reinsurer (1) reviews a direct writer's request for coverage, (2) establishes appropriate records and reserves capacity for the case, and (3) as necessary, follows up on reservations for capacity that have been inactive for a specified period of time. [11]

presumptive death certificate. A court-issued document stating that a person is presumed to be dead. [13]

presumptive total disability. A stated condition that, if present, automatically causes the insured to be considered totally disabled. [15]

pretext interview. For purposes of the Model Privacy Act, an interview in which one person attempts to gain information from another person by (1) pretending to be someone he is not, (2) pretending to represent someone he does not represent, (3) refusing to identify himself, or (4) misrepresenting the purpose of the interview. [3]

primary degenerative dementia. *See* **Alzheimer's disease**.

Privacy of Consumer Financial and Health Information Regulation (Model Privacy Regulation). In the United States, a National Association of Insurance Commissioners model regulation that includes requirements similar to those contained in the Gramm-Leach-Bliley Act, including limits on an insurer's right to disclose nonpublic personal information about a consumer without the consumer's consent. [3]

privileged information. For purposes of the Model Privacy Act, information that relates to either an insurance claim or a court proceeding. [3]

probationary period. In group insurance, the length of time—typically from one to six months—that a new group member must wait before becoming eligible to enroll in a group insurance plan, as specified in the master group insurance contract. Also known as a *waiting period*. [8]

problem resolution team. *See* **complaint team**. [17]

Proceeds of Crime (Money Laundering) and Terrorist Financing Act. A Canadian federal law that requires companies, including life insurers, to report every financial transaction that occurs for which there are reasonable grounds to suspect that the transaction is related to money laundering or financing terrorists. [3]

process control. A procedure that allows an organization to monitor the accuracy of its processes on a regular, ongoing basis. [11]

processes completed. A quantitative measurement of how many transactions are handled within a specified period of time. [1]

producer. Any person or entity that (1) sells insurance, including agents, brokers, financial advisors, and bank personnel or (2) is involved in insurance sales made through direct marketing or the Internet. [1]

professional association group. A type of association group consisting of people who share the same type of occupation and who belong to the association. [8]

professional reinsurer. An insurance company whose sole or primary line of business is selling reinsurance to direct writers. *Contrast with* **occasional reinsurer**. [9]

professional retrocessionaire. A reinsurer whose sole or primary business is providing reinsurance to reinsurers. *Contrast with* **occasional retrocessionaire**. [9]

profitability. The degree to which a company is successful in consistently generating returns to its owners and a measure of the productivity of the company's assets and its return on the owners' investment in the company. [6]

profit and loss statement. *See* **income statement**.

proportional reinsurance. A type of reinsurance under which the direct writer and reinsurer agree to share premiums and claim obligations according to a specified amount or percentage. [10]

proposal for insurance. In group insurance, a document that details the specifications of a group insurance plan proposed by an insurer for a group prospect. [8]

proposed group. *See* **group prospect**.

proposed insured. The term used during the underwriting process to refer to the person whose life, health, property, or income is to be covered by an individual insurance policy. [1]

public curator. In Canada, a person authorized to handle the affairs of missing people. [13]

punitive damages. Damages awarded in addition to compensatory damages when a defendant's conduct meets the jurisdiction's standards for behavior that is so egregious as to warrant such damages. [12]

QPP. *See* **Quebec Pension Plan**.

qualified beneficiary. For purposes of the Consolidated Omnibus Budget Reconciliation Act, a covered individual who is eligible to continue group medical expense insurance coverage for a limited time following a qualifying event. [3]

qualified long-term care policy. In the United States, a long-term care policy that provides all the features HIPAA requires and consequently is eligible for favorable tax treatment under federal law. *Compare with* **nonqualified long-term care policy** [14]

qualifying event. For purposes of the Consolidated Omnibus Budget Reconciliation Act, a specified situation in which a covered employee and his covered spouse and dependent children whose group medical expense insurance would otherwise terminate are allowed to continue the group insurance coverage for a limited time. [3]

qualitative performance measurement. A type of performance measurement that focuses on behaviors, attitudes, or opinions to determine how efficiently and effectively processes and transactions are completed. [1]

quality control. The process of ensuring that an organization accomplishes its objectives and follows its standards. [1]

quality rate. A quantitative measurement of the accuracy of a particular type of transaction. [1]

quantitative performance measurement. A type of performance measurement that relies on numerical methods to track and report results to determine how quickly, how often, how accurately, and how profitably processes and transactions are completed. [1]

Quebec Pension Plan (QPP). A Quebec provincial program that provides a pension for wage earners in Quebec who have contributed money into the plan during their working years. [3]

quick liquidity ratio. *See* **quick ratio**.

quick ratio. A ratio used to measure a company's ability to liquidate debt immediately that is calculated by dividing a company's most liquid current assets by the company's current liabilities. Also known as a *quick liquidity ratio* or an *acid-test ratio*. [6]

quota share. (1) In general reinsurance terms, each insurance company's—direct writer's or reinsurer's—fixed percentage share of the total risk being divided between or among companies. (2) In the context of reinsurance pools, the amount each reinsurance pool member accepts as its liability under a specific reinsurance arrangement. Also known as a *subscription* for reinsurance pools. [9]

quota share arrangement. A method for assigning risk in proportional reinsurance in which the direct writer retains a specified monetary amount or percentage of the risk on a case and cedes the remaining risk to one or more reinsurers. [10]

rating. Approving a higher-than-average risk by charging a higher-than-usual premium rate for the coverage applied for. [2]

rating schedule. A table that lists the rating percentages that are to be assigned to proposed insureds based on the total debits assigned to them by the underwriter. [7]

ratio. A comparison of two numeric values that results in a measurement expressed as a percentage or fraction. [6]

RBC ratio. *See* **risk-based capital ratio**.

real-time underwriting. A straight through processing system that evaluates insurance applications quickly and almost instantly provides the applicant or producer with an underwriting decision. Also called *instant-issue underwriting*. [2]

reasonable and customary charge. *See* **usual, customary, and reasonable charge**.

recapture. The process by which a direct writer takes back some or all ceded business from a reinsurer. [10]

receiver. In an insurance context, an individual who is appointed by a court to hold and administer an insolvent insurer's assets and liabilities. [10]

reciprocal arrangement. A two-way reinsurance arrangement in which two insurance companies cede business to each other and assume risk from each other. Also known as *reciprocity*. [9]

reciprocity. *See* **reciprocal arrangement.**

records inspection provision. An indemnity reinsurance agreement provision that states the rights of each party to inspect the other party's records and documents relating to the reinsurance provided under the agreement. [10]

recurring disability. A disability that results from the same cause as a previous disability and that reappears after (1) the previous period of disability and (2) an intervening period of recovery. [15]

reduction of reinsurance. The process of reducing the amount of reinsurance covering an insurance policy. [10]

rehabilitation. The process of helping a disabled person return to work, either at her own occupation or at another occupation if she is unable to perform the duties of her own occupation. [15]

rehabilitation benefit. A disability income insurance policy benefit that provides that an insurer will reimburse the insured for the expenses associated with participation in a rehabilitation program during any period in which an insured is receiving total or partial disability benefits. [15]

reimbursement method. A method of determining the daily benefit amount under a long-term care insurance policy under which the insured receives reimbursement for approved long-term care expenses up to a maximum limit specified in the policy. [14]

reinstatement. The process by which an insurer puts back into force an insurance policy that has lapsed due to nonpayment of premiums. [10]

reinstatement provision. (1) An indemnity reinsurance agreement provision that typically specifies that when a reinsured policy lapses for nonpayment of premium, the reinsurance can be reinstated if certain conditions regarding the timing of the request for reinstatement and the payment of reinsurance premiums due are met. [10] (2) A provision that describes the conditions a policyowner must meet for an insurer to reinstate a policy within a specified time after lapse. [17]

reinsurance. Insurance that one insurance company obtains from another insurance company on risks associated with insurance policies issued by the first company. [1]

reinsurance account executive. *See* **reinsurance marketing officer**.

reinsurance administration. All of the day-to-day activities conducted by the direct writer and the reinsurer to process and manage each risk that the direct writer cedes automatically or submits for facultative or facultative-obligatory consideration. [9]

reinsurance allowance. *See* **allowance**.

reinsurance analyst. A direct writer or reinsurer employee—except the person holding top leadership responsibility—who is involved in any phase of reinsurance administration.

reinsurance certificate. A document that a reinsurer issues to notify the direct writer that reinsurance is officially in force. [11]

reinsurance commission. *See* **allowance**.

reinsurance company. *See* **reinsurer**.

reinsurance effective date. The date on which the reinsurance coverage for a specific risk takes effect. [10]

reinsurance intermediary. A third party who is not employed by a licensed insurer or reinsurer, but who acts on behalf of a direct writer or reinsurer to place reinsurance. [9]

reinsurance intermediary—broker. In the United States, under the National Association of Insurance Commissioners Reinsurance Intermediary Model Act, any person, firm, or corporation that solicits, negotiates, or places reinsurance cessions or retrocessions on behalf of a direct writer, but that is not authorized to enter into a binding reinsurance contract on behalf of the direct writer. *Contrast with* **reinsurance intermediary—manager**. [9]

reinsurance intermediary—manager. In the United States, under the National Association of Insurance Commissioners Reinsurance Intermediary Model Act, any third party that acts as an agent of a reinsurer and either has authority to bind the reinsurer to a reinsurance contract or manages all or part of the reinsurer's assumed business. *Contrast with* **reinsurance intermediary—broker**. [9]

Reinsurance Intermediary Model Act. In the United States, a National Association of Insurance Commissioners model law that regulates the activities of reinsurance intermediaries and the companies that use the services of reinsurance intermediaries. [9]

reinsurance marketing officer. A reinsurer's employee who sells reinsurance and coordinates the marketing process for the reinsurer. Also known as a *reinsurance account executive*. [9]

reinsurance pool. A group of two or more insurance companies who jointly reinsure ceded risks.

reinsurance premium. A periodic payment made by a direct writer to a reinsurer as compensation for indemnity reinsurance coverage. [9]

reinsurer. An insurer that provides reinsurance coverage by accepting, or assuming, insurance risk from a direct writer or another reinsurance company. Also known as a *reinsurance company* or an *assuming company*. [9]

renewal expense. *See* **maintenance expense**.

renewal underwriting. The process by which an underwriter assesses the risk presented by a group that has requested to renew its group insurance coverage. [8]

replacement. The purchase of one life insurance policy or annuity contract to take the place of another. [3]

Replacement of Life Insurance and Annuities Model Regulation. In the United States, a National Association of Insurance Commissioners model regulation that states that replacement of policies is generally permissible if the replacing insurer provides full and fair disclosure and no deceptive practices are involved. [3]

request for coverage. A document that a direct writer sends to a reinsurer to request facultative or fac-ob reinsurance coverage on a particular insured or group of insureds. Also known as a *facultative application*. [11]

request for proposal (RFP). In group insurance, a document that provides detailed information about the group and the requested coverage and solicits a bid from an insurer for providing that coverage. [8]

required reserves. In the United States, an insurer's reserves calculated according to regulatory requirements. Also called *statutory reserves*. [9]

rescission. A remedy provided by law to an insurer that discovers that it has issued a policy based on material misrepresentation. [3]

rescission provision. An indemnity reinsurance agreement provision that describes the notification and administrative procedures required when a direct writer rescinds a reinsured policy. [10]

reserve credit. In the United States, the accounting entry a direct writer uses to record an offset of its required reserves due to the use of reinsurance. [9]

reserved capacity. The portion of a reinsurer's financial capacity that the reinsurer sets aside to fund its financial obligations under anticipated new business. [11]

reserve listing. A reinsurance report that shows all policies reinsured and the reserve held for each policy. [11]

respite care. Care provided by a nursing home or other qualified long-term care facility or entity to allow a primary caregiver in the home a break from the day-to-day care of an insured receiving home health care. [14]

restoration of benefits provision. A long-term care insurance policy provision that allows an insured who has some benefits available under a long-term care insurance policy to regain a full benefit period after a stated period of recovery time has passed following delivery of long-term care services. [14]

results-based reciprocity. A reciprocal arrangement that involves the exchange of blocks of reinsurance business representing approximately the same projected monetary amount of claims experience on the reinsured risks. *Contrast with* **premium-based reciprocity**. [9]

retention limit. A specified maximum monetary amount of insurance that an insurer is willing to carry at its own risk without transferring some of the risk to a reinsurer. [9]

retention limit corridor. A monetary amount greater than the company's retention limit that a direct writer is willing to retain to avoid ceding small amounts of coverage. [9]

retrocession. (1) A unit of reinsurance that a reinsurer cedes to a retrocessionaire. (2) The document used to record the transfer of risk from a reinsurer to a retrocessionaire. [9]

retrocessionaire. An insurance company that accepts risks from—and provides reinsurance to—a reinsurer. [9]

retrocession claim file. A file prepared by a reinsurance analyst that contains all the information relevant to a claim, plus information about the retrocession to use when the reinsurer notifies its retrocessionaires of the claim. [11]

retrocession pool. A group of two or more professional retrocessionaires or reinsurers that jointly reinsure retroceded risks. Also known as a *retro pool.* [11]

retro pool. *See* **retrocession pool**.

return-on-equity (ROE) ratio. A ratio for evaluating profitability that is calculated by dividing net income by owners' equity. [6]

revocable beneficiary. A life insurance policy beneficiary who has no right to the policy proceeds during the insured's lifetime because the policyowner has the unrestricted right to change the beneficiary designation during the insured's lifetime. [13]

RFP. *See* **request for proposal**.

right of recommendation. The right of a reinsurer to review a claim and offer its opinion to the direct writer on whether to pay the claim. [11]

risk assessment. The process of determining the degree of risk represented by each proposed insured person or group using a number of factors established when the insurance product was designed and priced. [2]

risk-based capital (RBC) ratio. In the United States, a requirement for insurers to use a specified formula to demonstrate to state regulators the adequacy of an insurer's capital relative to the riskiness of the insurer's operations. [9]

risk class. A group of insureds who represent a similar level of risk to an insurance company. [2]

risk factor. Any aspect of a proposed insured's present health, medical history, family history, health habits (such as tobacco use), financial condition, reputation, driving record, criminal record, occupation, or activities that increases the likelihood that the person will suffer a covered loss. [2]

ROE ratio. *See* **return-on-equity ratio**.

saliva test. *See* **oral specimen test**.

scanning. *See* **document imaging**.

schedule. A part of a reinsurance agreement that covers one or more variable elements of the agreement. Also known as an *exhibit* or a *condition*. [10]

secondary beneficiary. *See* **contingent beneficiary**.

second-to-die life insurance policy. *See* **survivorship life insurance policy**.

Section 1035 exchange. In the United States, a tax-free replacement of a life insurance or annuity contract for another contract insuring the same person and meeting conditions specified in the tax code. [6]

security. The physical, technical, and procedural steps a company takes to prevent the loss, wrongful disclosure (accidental or intentional), or theft of data or information. [1]

self-administered group plan. A group insurance plan for which the group policyholder handles most of the administrative aspects. *Contrast with* **insurer-administered group plan**. [8]

self-administration. A method of reinsurance record administration in which the direct writer maintains detailed records for each ceded policy and sends the reinsurer periodic reports outlining the risk ceded and reinsurance premiums due for each policy. [10]

self-directed team. A type of work team in which the members handle many traditional management responsibilities, such as planning and monitoring work. Also known as a *self-managed team*. [16]

self-insured group plan. A group insurance plan for which the group sponsor rather than an insurance company is financially responsible for the claims incurred by group insureds. *Contrast with* **fully insured group plan**. [8]

self-managed team. *See* **self-directed team**. [16]

semi-autonomous team. A type of work team in which the manager or supervisor manages the team, while the other team members, in addition to doing their "regular" work, provide input into planning, organizing, and monitoring the work. [16]

service complaint. A complaint that pertains to the timeliness, accuracy, courtesy, or professionalism of a company's interactions with its customers. [17]

service level. A quantitative measurement of the percentage of inbound customer contacts answered within a specified time frame. [1]

service recovery. The efforts an organization makes to fully resolve the problem that caused a customer's dissatisfaction and win back the customer's goodwill. [17]

settlement option. An alternative method that the owner or beneficiary of a life insurance policy can elect for receiving payment of the life insurance policy proceeds. [13]

sickness. An illness or a disease that (1) includes pregnancy unless it is specifically excluded under the contract and (2) begins while a person is insured under the disability income policy. [15]

simple inflation provision. A long-term care insurance policy inflation protection provision under which the coverage amount increases each year by a specified percentage of the original daily benefit. [14]

simultaneous death act. In the United States, a state law that provides that if both the insured and the beneficiary die under circumstances which make it impossible to determine which of them died first, the insurer is to presume that the insured survived the beneficiary, unless the policy provides otherwise. [13]

single-employer group. An insured group that consists of the employees of one employer. Also known as an *employer-employee group*. [8]

SIU. *See* **special investigative unit**.

skilled nursing care. 24-hour treatment, rehabilitation, and care at a special facility that provides the services of a registered nurse (RN) or a licensed practical nurse (LPN) under the supervision of a physician. [14]

small employer. For purposes of the Health Insurance Portability and Accountability Act, an employer that had an average of at least 2 but not more than 50 employees during the preceding calendar year and had at least 2 employees on the first day of the group plan year. [3]

software. Computer programs that provide the sequences of instructions for a computer and that govern its operation. [1]

software application. *See* **application software**.

sole proprietorship. A business owned by one person (or, in some jurisdictions, by a husband and wife). [6]

solvency. An entity's ability to meet its financial obligations on time. [6]

solvency law. A law that is designed to ensure that insurance companies are financially able to meet their debts and to pay policy benefits when they come due. [9]

special class. *See* **substandard class**.

special investigative unit (SIU). A group of individuals who are employed by an insurance company and are responsible for detecting, investigating, and resolving cases involving insurance fraud. [12]

specialized medical questionnaire. A document that requests detailed information about a specific illness or condition from a proposed insured's attending physician or examining physician. [4]

speculation. The unethical purchase of insurance to make a profit on the proceeds rather than to protect against the risk of financial loss. [5]

split-dollar life insurance plan. "Any arrangement between an owner of a life insurance contract and a non-owner of the contract under which either party to the arrangement pays all or part of the premiums, and one of the parties paying the premiums is entitled to recover (either conditionally or unconditionally) all or any portion of those premiums and such recovery is to be made from, or is secured by, the proceeds of the contract."[1] [6]

spread-loss coverage. A nonproportional reinsurance arrangement—similar to a loan—under which the reinsurer pays on a specified block of business a specified amount of claims that exceed a stated monetary amount in a stated period, and the direct writer repays the reinsurer for the benefits the reinsurer has paid, plus interest. [10]

standard class. A risk class of proposed insureds whose anticipated mortality or morbidity rates are average. [2]

standby assistance. The assistance provided when an individual requires the presence of another person within arm's reach to prevent by physical intervention an injury to the individual while the individual is performing an activity of daily living. *Compare with* **hands-on assistance**. [14]

statement of cash flows. A financial statement that indicates the amounts of cash received and paid in the operating, investing, and financing activities associated with a business. [5]

statement of changes in owners' equity. *See* **statement of owners' equity**.

statement of owners' equity. A financial statement that shows the changes in owners' equity during a specified period. Also known as a *statement of changes in owners' equity*. [5]

statutory minimum capitalization requirements. *See* **minimum capital and surplus requirements**.

statutory reserves. *See* **required reserves**.

step rates. Group insurance premium rates that are based on an insurer's experience expressed in age-graded, and sometimes sex-specific, tables and that are used especially for insurance that provides a limited number of benefits and limited amounts of coverage. [8]

stock redemption agreement. *See* **entity agreement**.

stop-loss ratio reinsurance. *See* **stop-loss reinsurance**.

stop-loss reinsurance. A type of nonproportional reinsurance in which the reinsurer agrees to pay for a portion of total claims on a block of business in an amount between stated lower and upper limits for a specified operating period. Also known as *stop-loss ratio reinsurance* or *excess-of-loss ratio reinsurance*. [10]

STP. *See* **straight through processing**.

straight through processing (STP). The electronic processing of every step of a transaction without manual intervention. [1]

subrogation clause. An insurance policy provision that gives the insurer a contractual right to recover payments made to an insured for medical care if that insured receives payment for damages through a legal action. [14]

subscription. *See* **quota share**.

substandard class. A risk class of proposed insureds whose anticipated mortality or morbidity rates are higher than average, but who are still considered to be insurable. Also called a *special class*. [2]

supplemental benefit. A benefit added to the coverage specified in the basic insurance policy. [6]

surplus. For an insurer, the amount of assets a company has over and above its policy reserves and other financial obligations. In insurance, may refer to capital and surplus together. *See also* **capital** *and* **capital and surplus**. [9]

surplus relief. A decrease in potential surplus strain. [9]

surplus strain. A decrease in surplus caused by the high initial costs and reserve requirements associated with issuing new insurance policies. Also known as *new business strain*. [9]

survivorship clause. A clause that is included in some life insurance policies and that requires the beneficiary to survive the insured by a specified period, usually 30 or 60 days, to be entitled to receive the policy proceeds. [13]

survivorship life insurance policy. A type of multi-life policy which provides that proceeds will be paid when the second (or last) of two (or more) insureds covered by the policy dies. Also known as a *second-to-die life insurance policy*. [6]

table of underwriting requirements. *See* **age and amount requirements chart**.

table rating method. A method for adjusting individual life insurance premium rates to compensate for extra mortality that divides substandard risks into broad groups—or tables—according to their numerical ratings; the extra mortality for each substandard group is expressed as a percentage added to standard mortality as has been shown by the insurer's actual mortality experience. [5]

team underwriting. A work division system in which underwriters are divided into small groups. [2]

technology platform. The combination of hardware and operating systems software on which an administration system runs. [1]

telecommunications. The electronic transmission of communication signals. [1]

teleunderwriting. A method by which the insurer, rather than a producer, takes responsibility for gathering from the proposed insured most of the information needed for underwriting. [2]

temporary flat extra premium. An amount added to the premium for cases in which a risk factor is expected to decrease and eventually disappear over a limited time period. [5]

temporary insurance agreement (TIA). A contract between the insurer and the applicant that provides temporary coverage on the proposed insured before a policy is issued and delivered, although such coverage may be subject to certain conditions. [3]

terminal illness (TI) benefit. An accelerated death benefit under which the insurer pays a portion of the policy's death benefit to a policyowner-insured if he suffers from a terminal illness and has a physician-certified life expectancy of 12 months or less. [6]

termination. The complete cancellation of a reinsurance agreement for both new business and in-force business. [10]

termination for new business. An indemnity reinsurance agreement cancellation under which the parties to the agreement no longer cede or assume new business under that agreement, but reinsurance coverage continues on business already in place. [10]

termination of reinsurance. The process by which a direct writer cancels the reinsurance covering a policy issued by the company. [10]

third-party administrator (TPA). An organization that is not affiliated with an insurer and that provides various administrative services to insurers and group policyholders. [8]

third-party notification provision. A long-term care insurance policy provision under which the policyowner provides the name of another person that the policyowner authorizes the insurer to contact in the event of a missed premium payment. [14]

third-party policy. A policy in which one person purchases an individual insurance policy on the life of another person. [1]

TIA. *See* **temporary insurance agreement**.

TI benefit. *See* **terminal illness benefit**.

time limit on certain defenses provision. The incontestability provision included in some individual health insurance policies which states that after the policy has been in force for a specified period—usually two or three years—the insurer cannot use a material misrepresentation in the application to contest the policy or deny a claim unless the misrepresentation was fraudulent. [14]

TPA. *See* **third-party administrator**.

traditional indemnity reinsurance. A reinsurance arrangement that is used to transfer a portion of a direct writer's accepted risk on an ongoing basis and that is intended to be a permanent transfer. *Contrast with* **assumption reinsurance**. [9]

traditional team. A type of work team in which the manager or supervisor performs most or all of the management tasks, such as organizing, planning, monitoring, and controlling the work; other team members concentrate solely on doing the work—performing the business functions for which the team is responsible. [16]

transaction. Any business-related exchange. [1]

transaction processing system. An organized collection of procedures, software, databases, and devices used to perform high-volume, routine, and repetitive business transactions. [1]

transaction report. *See* **policy change report**.

transplant donor benefit. A disability income insurance policy supplemental benefit that specifies that if an insured undergoes surgery to donate a part of his body to another person, the insurer will treat that surgery as a sickness and will pay benefits for any resulting disability. [15]

treasury. The functional area of an insurance company that manages cash as it flows through the company. [1]

treatment code. Numbers and words that represent a specific medical treatment. [14]

turnaround time. A quantitative measurement of the time necessary to complete a customer-initiated request or transaction. Also know as *average handling time.* [1]

twisting. A prohibited practice that occurs when a producer misrepresents the features of a policy to induce a client to purchase a policy. [3]

UCR. *See* **usual, customary, and reasonable charge**.

unauthorized reinsurer. In the United States, a reinsurer that is not authorized or accredited in a given state. Also known as a *nonadmitted reinsurer. Contrast with* **authorized reinsurer** and **accredited reinsurer**. [9]

undeliverable. A policy which an applicant chooses not to accept when a producer attempts to deliver it. [2]

underwriter. An individual who (1) assesses and classifies the degree of risk represented by a proposed insured or group with respect to a specific insurance product and (2) makes a decision to accept or decline that risk. [1]

underwriting. The process of (1) assessing and classifying the degree of risk represented by a proposed insured or group with respect to a specific insurance product and (2) making a decision to accept or decline that risk. [1]

underwriting capacity. The highest monetary amount of risk that a company will accept on an individual insured so that unusual fluctuations in claims will not damage the ongoing solvency of the company. *Contrast with* **financial capacity**. [9]

underwriting guidelines. General standards that underwriters follow as they establish the level of risk presented by a proposed insured or group. [2]

underwriting manual. A document that contains the information an insurer uses to assign numerical values to life and health insurance medical and personal risks, provides descriptive information on impairments, and serves as a guide to underwriting action. [5]

underwriting objective. *See* **underwriting philosophy.**

underwriting philosophy. A set of objectives that guides all of an insurer's underwriting actions, generally reflects the insurer's strategic business goals, and includes its pricing assumptions for products. Also known as an *underwriting objective.* [2]

underwriting worksheet. A document that contains records of telephone calls, letters, and other communications; documentation of requests for reinsurance; lists of reports and other information requested; and other notations that will explain clearly the manner in which the underwriter has handled the case beginning with the submission of the application to the insurer. [3]

Unfair Claims Settlement Practices Act. In the United States, a National Association of Insurance Commissioners model law that lists a number of actions that are considered unfair claims practices if committed by an insurer (1) in conscious disregard of the law or (2) so frequently as to indicate a general business practice. [12]

Unfair Life, Accident and Health Claims Settlement Practices Model Regulation. In the United States, a National Association of Insurance Commissioners model regulation that establishes minimum standards that insurers must meet in handling life and health insurance claims. [12]

Uniform Accident and Sickness Insurance Act. A model law that governs both individual and group health insurance contracts upon which laws are based in all the provinces and territories of Canada except Quebec. [3]

Uniform Act. *See* **Uniform Life Insurance Act.**

Uniform Life Insurance Act (Uniform Act). A model law that governs both individual and group life insurance contracts upon which laws are based in all the provinces and territories of Canada except Quebec. [3]

unintentional lapse provision. A long-term care insurance policy provision that permits reinstatement of a lapsed policy if the reason for the lapse is that the policyowner has a cognitive impairment and that the reason for the missed premium payment was cognitive impairment, as defined in the policy. [14]

urinalysis. The analysis of a urine specimen. [4]

USA Patriot Act of 2001. A U.S. federal law designed to strengthen the federal government's ability to investigate, prosecute, and seize the assets of terrorists. [3]

usual and customary charge. *See* **usual, customary, and reasonable charge.**

usual and prevailing charge. *See* **usual, customary, and reasonable charge.**

usual, customary, and reasonable (UCR) charge. The amount that health care providers within a particular geographic region commonly charge for a particular medical service. Also known as *usual and customary charge, reasonable and customary charge,* and *usual and prevailing charge.* [14]

valid contract. A contract that satisfies all legal requirements and, thus, is enforceable at law. [3]

variable life insurance. A form of cash value life insurance in which premiums are fixed but the death benefit and other values may vary, reflecting the performance of the investment subaccounts selected by the policyowner. [17]

virtual private network (VPN). An organization's network that uses public telecommunications infrastructure such as the Internet to provide authorized individual users or remote offices with secure access. [1]

voice response unit. *See* **interactive voice response system**. [16]

voidable contract. A contract under which a party has the right to avoid his obligations under the contract without incurring legal liability. [3]

void contract. A contract that does not satisfy one or more of the legal requirements to create a valid contract and, thus, is never enforceable at law. [3]

VPN. *See* **virtual private network.**

wagering agreement. An agreement under which either party may gain or lose depending on the outcome of an uncertain event, such as the timing of an individual's death. [3]

waiting period. (1) Under a health insurance policy, a stated period of time that must pass before benefits are payable. Also known as the *elimination period* for certain types of coverage. [7] (2) *See* **probationary period**.

waiver of premium for disability (WP) benefit. A supplemental insurance benefit that provides that, in the event an insured is totally disabled as defined in the WP benefit, the insurance company will waive the payment of all premiums that become due during the period of disability. [6]

waiver of premium for payor benefit. A supplemental benefit sometimes found in a juvenile insurance policy that provides that an insurer will waive payment of the policy's premiums if the payor—the person paying the policy premium—becomes disabled or dies prior to the insured child's attainment of a specified age, usually 21. [6]

with profits policy. *See* **participating policy**. [17]

work division system. A method of assigning cases to underwriters that divides cases according to the person or group that underwrites them. [2]

workflow application. *See* **automated workflow system**.

work group. *See* **work team**. [16]

work site assessment. An activity performed by a claim analyst or an investigator who interviews an employer and reviews the claimant's actual job duties and level of success in performing those duties. [15]

work team. Two or more people who work together on a regular basis and coordinate their activities to accomplish common goals. Also known as a work group. [16]

WP benefit. *See* **waiver of premium for disability benefit.**

yearly renewable term (YRT) reinsurance. A plan of reinsurance that is used to reinsure only the mortality portion of a life insurance risk. [10]

YRT reinsurance. *See* **yearly renewable term insurance.**

Endnote

1. IRS Final Regulations, 17 September 2003.

Index

A

abandonment rate 441
absolute assignment 353
accelerated death benefit 168–169, 348, 358
access to records provision 313
accidental death benefit 166, 356, 357
accounting 9
accredited reinsurer 250–251
acid-test ratio. *See* quick ratio
acquired immune deficiency syndrome. *See* AIDS
acquisition expense 236
actively at work provision 216
activities of daily living 191, 381
actuary 9
ADA. *See* Americans with Disabilities Act
ADB. *See* accidental death benefit
adding or deleting an insured 452
adding or deleting riders 453
adequate financial resources 5–6
ADEA. *See* Age Discrimination in Employment Act
adequate financial resources 5–6
ADL. *See* activities of daily living
administer loans and dividends 467–471
administration expense 236
administration system 2, 12, 15, 16, 21, 446, 448, 457
admitted reinsurer *See* authorized reinsurers
adult day care 376
adult day care center 376
adverse action 66
adverse claimants 354
affidavit 448
affinity group 211
age
  misstatement of 77, 346–347
  underwriting factor 107, 175, 198
age and amount requirements chart 33
Age Discrimination in Employment Act 82
age distribution 212
agent's statement 31
age of insured 268
agreement effective date 273
AIDA Reinsurance and Insurance Arbitration Society 284
AIDS 71–72
alcohol abuse 177
alcohol markers 116
alcohol use, underwriting factor 116
allowable expense 372
allowance 236
alternate care 376
Alzheimer's disease 192–193
American Arbitration Association of New York City Rules of Arbitration 284
Americans with Disabilities Act 82
annual income 133, 136
annual premium amount 41
annual report 131
antiselection 42, 126, 170
  disability income coverage 185–186
  group insurance 210
  policy replacements 163
any occupation disability 403
antivirus software 23
APL. *See* automatic premium loan provision
applicant 3, 19
application. *See* application software
application for insurance 29–35
  individual health 172
  individual life 92, 95, 110–111, 128–129
application software 12, 14, 18
approval premium receipt 60
APS. *See* attending physician's statement
arbitration 271, 284
arbitration provision 284
arbitrators 284
article 271
assessing medical factors 106
asset-based approach 154
assigning policy ownership 467
assignment 75, 120, 353, 373, 386, 467
assignment of benefits 373, 386
assisted living facility 376–377
association group 211
assuming company. *See* reinsurer
assumption certificate 234
assumption reinsurance 234
assured. *See* insured
attachment point 258–259
attending physician 94, 100–101
attending physician's statement 101, 390
audit 38, 40
auditing reinsurance operations 312
audit log 21
audit report 315
authentication 23
authority levels 49–50, 323
authorized reinsurer 230, 250
auto-adjudication 333
automated workflow 17
automated workflow system 20, 431
automatic binding limit 241–242
automatic deduction plan 469
automatic premium loan provision 469
automatic reinsurance 240–241
average handling time. *See* turnaround time
average speed of answer 441
aviation exclusion 344
avocation
  exclusion 344
  underwriting factor 110, 115, 176

B

B2B. *See* business-to-business e-commerce
backward number sequence test 197
balance sheet 132
bankruptcy 134
benchmark 22
beneficiary 4
benefit level 216
benefit period 413
benefit schedule 202
benefit trigger 381–382
billing statement 288, 298, 302, 304, 310, 311
binding premium receipt 60
biometric authentication 23
birthday rule 373
blended rating 200, 220–221
block of business 229, 236
blood chemistry profile 103–104
BPM. *See* business process management
BRE. *See* business rules engine
build 108–109
build chart 108
bulk administration 279
business continuation insurance plan 150
business financial supplement 151
business insurance 149, 163, 166
business life insurance 149–150, 157
business process management 15
business rules engines 17–20
business-to-business e-commerce 248
business valuation 154
buy-sell agreement 144, 150, 157–160, 166

C

calculating policy benefits payable 370, 383, 405
calculating the amount of the policy proceeds and how they are payable 346
call center 425
Canada
  antidiscrimination statutes 71
  group insurance regulation 82–83
  insurance regulatory system 64–65
  privacy guidelines and laws 69–70
Canada Health Act 65
Canada Pension Plan 83
Canadian Council of Insurance Regulators 64
Canadian Life and Health Insurance Association 64, 249
  Guidelines 64
Canadian Reinsurance Guidelines 249
capital 250
  surplus 252
  ratio 252
captive reinsurer 231
caregiver training benefit 377
case assignment system 51–52, 54
cash value reimbursement 304–305
catastrophe coverage 259, 261
cat cover. *See* catastrophic coverage
CCIR. *See* Canadian Council of Insurance Regulators
ceding allowance. *See* coinsurance allowance
ceding commission. *See* allowance
ceding company. *See* direct writer
census 204–205
centralized data repository 16–18, 21–22
certificate holders. *See* group insured
certificate of coverage provision. *See* certificate of insurance
certificate of insurance 4, 77, 459
cession 229–230, 239–242
cession amount 261
cession arrangements 239
cession basis 239–240, 242
charitable contributions 132
changing a beneficiary 464–468
churning 74
CI. *See* critical illness insurance
civilian aviation 119
Civil Rights Act of 1964 82
claim adjuster 321
claim administration 6, 8
  activities 319
  authority levels 323–324
  calculating policy benefit amounts 346–349
  cooperation with underwriting 325–326
  critical illness coverage 374–375
  disability income insurance 388–416
  evaluation process 321
  financing terrorists 329
  fraud 330
  legal issues 326–327
  life policy claims 337–359
  long-term care insurance 359, 375–387
  medical expense insurance 361–374
  organization 324–325
  philosophy 319
  practices 319
  privacy 328–329
  quality control 333–334
  settlement options 348
  supplemental life insurance coverage 356
  staffing 323
  technology 333
  unfair practices 327–328
claim analyst 321–324, 329, 332, 333
claimant's statement. *See* claim form
claim examiner. *See* claim analyst

claim file 306–310
claim form 321
  critical illness 374
  disability 389–394
  life 337–340
  long-term care 379–380
  medical expense 361–367
claims experience 215
  group insurance 220
  smoothing fluctuations in 238
  underwriting factor 215
class 202, 204, 207, 209, 214–215, 217
class designation 465
CLHIA. *See* Canadian Life and Health Insurance Association
CLHIA Guidelines 64
close notice 296
COB provision. *See* coordination of benefits provision
COBRA. *See* Consolidated Omnibus Budget Reconcilation Act of 1986
COBRA continuation provision 80
cognitive impairment 191, 194, 196–198, 380, 382
cognitive screen 194, 196–197
cognitive test. *See* cognitive screen
coinsurance 182, 370, 372, 374
coinsurance allowance 265–266
COLA. *See* cost-of-living adjustment benefit
collateral assignment 353, 359, 467
combination system 54
commercial fraud 144, 153
committee underwriting 52, 54
communications technology 14
community property laws 354
commute 235
comorbidity 45
compensatory damages 326–327
complaint teams 459
compliance 10
compound inflation provision 385–386
computer network 430
concurrent beneficiaries 465
condition. *See* schedule
conditional premium receipts 60
conservation 434, 436–438
consideration 58
Consolidated Omnibus Budget Reconciliation Act of 1986 79–80, 363
Consumer Price Index 386–387
consumer report 65–67
consumer reporting agency 66
contest 283
contestable claim 310
contestable period 85, 402
contingent beneficiary 351, 356, 465
continuation 276, 280–281
continuation provision 280
contract 57–58
contractual capacity 59, 61
contributory plan 207, 214, 220, 222
conversion 276, 281
conversion provision 76–79, 281, 363, 459
converting a policy 459
cookie 23
coordination of benefits provision 371
copayment 182, 199, 370
cost basis 164
cost-of-living adjustment benefit 409
cotinine 104, 116
coupon plan 469
covered person. *See* group insured
covered services 367
CPI. *See* Consumer Price Index
CPP. *See* Canada Pension Plan
CPT. *See* Physician's Current Procedural Terminology
CRC. *See* Canadian Reinsurance Conference
credibility factor 220
creditable coverage 81
Credit for Reinsurance Model Law 253
creditor insurance 144, 150, 161, 163
credits 137–141
criminal history 118
critical illness benefit. *See* dread disease benefit
critical illness insurance 171, 190
  benefit 168
  claims 374
  underwriting 190–191
cross-purchase agreement 158
CSR. *See* customer service representative
current asset 156
current income 129, 133
current liability 156
current ratio 156
custodial care 376
customer contact center 424–425
customer contact system 431
customer feedback 437
customer information 5
customer loyalty 435
customer relationship teams. *See* complaint teams
customer satisfaction surveys 440
customer service 5–8, 11
  activities 426–428
  benefits of effectiveness of 421
  complaints 443, 458–459
  conservation and 434–439
  department 419, 471

documenting guidelines and procedures 433
effective delivery of 420–421, 429
legal issues 428
levels of authority 423
loans and dividends 471
organization 421, 423–426
policy changes 449–455
practices 445–471
premium payments 455–457
quality control 439–443
relationship to underwriting 450
returned mail 457
staffing 421
strategies 430
technology 430–433
telephone communication 438
variable insurance products 471
customer service representative 419, 445
levels of authority 423
training 422

D

daily benefit amount 383–386
data 14
entry and review 30
mining 17–18
warehouse 18
database 2, 14, 16–17, 21, 23, 26
database management system 17
date of expiry 296
DBMS. *See* database management system
DD. *See* dread disease benefit
death benefit 346–348
death certificate 341–343, 346
debits 137–141
debt-to-equity ratio 155–156
debt coverage 150
debtor-creditor group 211
debt ratio. *See* debt-to-equity ratio
declined class 44
decreasing the amount of coverage 450
deductible 182, 370
defamation 331
defining the reinsurance coverage 272
delayed word recall test 197
dementia 192–193
dependent 205, 216, 218, 222–223
desk audit 314
diagnostic codes 362, 364
DI Insurance. *See* disability insurance
direct response distribution system 148
direct response policy 144, 148
direct writer 230
DIRS. *See* Disability Insurance Records System
disability income insurance 171, 184, 389
claim administration 388
claim form 389–390
contestable 402
continuing claims 406–408
disputed claims 415
estimating length of disability 408
exclusions 405
information sources for claims 390–399
processing claims 396–406
questionable claims 400–401
rehabilitation 409–412
settling claims 414–416
supplemental benefits 409–412
terminating benefits 412–414
underwriting 184–190
Disability Insurance Records System 395
disappearance of the insured 342
disputed claim 415
dividend plan 469
divisible surplus 470
documentation of reinsurance arrangements 239
document imaging 19
documenting 85
document management system 19–20, 33, 431
dread disease benefit 168
driving history 115, 177
drop notice 296
drug abuse 117, 177
duration of the agreement provision 272–273
DWR. *See* delayed word recall test

E

e-commerce. *See* electronic commece
e-mail. *See* electronic mail
earlier birthday method 373
earned income 133
ECG. *See* electrocardiogram
EDI. *See* electronic data interchange
EFT. See electronic funds transfer
electrocardiogram 93, 104
electronic application system 34
electronic commerce 15
electronic data interchange 15
electronic funds transfer 436, 456
electronic mail 15
electronic signature 34–35
Electronic Signatures in Global and National Commerce Act 35
eligibility period 216, 222
eligibility requirements 216
elimination period. *See* waiting period

employee application 207
employee benefit plan 150
Employee Retirement Income
Security Act 79, 206
employee-employee group.
See single-employer group
encryption 23
enrollment application. *See* enrollment card
enrollment card 207, 222
enrollment date 80
enrollment period. *See* eligibility period
entire agreement provision 272–273
entire contract provision 77
entity agreement 158
EOB. *See* explanation of benefits
equitable claim handling 5
equity 132
equity in risk acceptance 4
ERISA. *See* Employee Retirement
Income Security Act of 1974
error rate 441
errors and omissions provision 283–284
escalation processes 458
estate settlement 132
ESign. See electronic signature
ethics 4
evidence of insurability 77, 92
examining physician 101, 103
excess-of-loss ratio reinsurance.
See stop-loss reinsurance
excess-of-loss reinsurance 258, 261
excess-of-retention 263
excess-of-retention arrangement 262–263
excess-of-time reinsurance
See extended-time reinsurance
excess coverage 208
excess of retention 261, 263–264, 270
excess quota share arrangement 263
exclusion rider 37, 49, 174, 179, 183–184, 186
exclusions 183, 344, 369, 382–383, 405
exculpatory statutes 355
exhibit. *See* schedule
existing health coverage 178
expected claim experience 210, 219–220
expected persistency 214
expense allowance. *See* allowance
expense participation requirements 182
experience rating 219
experience refund 220, 236
explanation of benefits 374
extended-time reinsurance 260–261
extension request 296–297
external audit 40, 313–314, 316
external replacement 163
extranet 15
extra-percentage table 140

F

face-to-face assessment 194, 196
fac-ob reinsurance. *See* facultative-obligatory
reinsurance
factor table 124, 135–136
facultative application. *See* request for coverage
facultative-obligatory reinsurance 242
facultative reinsurance 240
facultative reinsurance underwriting 293
Fair Credit Reporting Act 65
family benefit 144, 166–167, 356, 358
family history 176, 183
family income protection 131
FAQ. *See* frequently asked questions
FCRA. *See* Fair Credit Reporting Act
FDQS arrangement. *See* first-dollar quota share
arrangement
federal employment laws 82
field underwriter 7
field underwriting 29–30, 33, 173, 193–195
field underwriting manual 33
finanical aspects of
indemnity reinsurance 236
financial capacity 237, 242–243
financial questionnaire 130
financial ratio analysis 155
financial risk factor 43, 125
financial statements 131–132
financial status 128, 131, 133
financial underwriting 124–127, 129
financial worksheet 127
firewall 23
first contact resolution 441
first-dollar quota share arrangement 264
first-to-die life insurance policy 145
fixed-amount option 350
fixed-period option 350
flat extra premium method 141
FMLA. *See* Family and Medical Leave Act
foreign citizenship, underwriting factor 121, 178
fraud 283, 330–331
frequently asked questions 425
full portability option 378
fully insured group insurance plan 206
functional capacity 197
funds withheld coinsurance 266
future increase option benefit 412

G

genetic test 72–73
geriatrics 198
GI benefit. *See* guaranteed insurabilit benefit
GLB Act. *See* Gramm-Leach-Bliley Act

good faith 283
good order check 30, 35
grace period 77, 340, 348, 378, 396, 414, 455–456, 466
Gramm-Leach-Bliley Act 68
group enrollment card. *See* enrollment card
Group Guidelines. *See* Guideline G-3: Group Life and Group Health Insurance
Group Health Insurance Definition and Group Health Insurance Standard Provisions Model Act 76
Group Health Insurance Medical Act. *See* Grouop Health Insurance Definition and Group Health Insurance Standard Provisions Model Act
group insurance 3
  Canadian statutory requirements 82–83
  information sources for underwriting 204–207
  policy issue process 201–207
  post-issue underwriting 222–224
  rating methods 217–222
  risk assessment factors 207–215
  self-administered 217
  table of underwriting requirements 33
  terminating disability income coverage under 413–414
  U.S. statutory requirements 76–82
  underwriting for 201, 204
group insured 4, 202
Group Life Insurance Definition and Group Life Insurance Standard Provisions Model Act 76
Group Life Insurance Model Act. *See* Group Life Insurance Definition and Group Life Insurance Standard Provisions Model Act
group member 201
group prospect 202
group representative 201
guaranteed availability 81
guaranteed-issue basis 148
guaranteed insurability benefit 167
guaranteed purchase option 386
guaranteed renewability requirement 81
Guideline G-3: Group Life and Group Health Insurance 83

H

hands-on assistance 382
hardware 12, 19, 23
health history, underwriting factor 175, 186
Health Insurance Portability and Accountability Act 67, 80–81
HIPAA. *See* Health Insurance Portability and Accountability Act of 1996
HIV 71–72
home health care 376
home service agents 148
home service distribution system 147
hospice 376
hospice care 376–377
human immunodeficiency virus. *See* HIV
human resources 10

I

IADL. *See* instrumental activities of daily living
ICA. *See* International Claim Association
ICD. *See* International Classification of Diseases and Related Health Problems
impairment 33, 37, 106, 175, 181, 194
impairment guide 33
impairment rider. *See* exclusion rider
income-based approach 154
income protection insurance 403
income replacement table 187, 190
income statement 132
incontestability provision 77, 85, 402
indemnity benefit method 384
indemnity reinsurance 228–229, 233–237, 239
independent underwriting 52, 53
individual cession administration 279
individual health insurance
  claims 360–416
  underwriting for 170–199
individual life insurance
  claims 318–359
  underwriting 124–169
industry experience 44
inflation protection provision 385–386
in-force policy report 298–299
information 14
information management 10
information system 10, 12
information technology 10
injury 9
insolvency 249
insolvency provision 285
inspection report 93, 103, 105, 109, 112, 116, 118–119, 129
installation 446
instant-issue underwriting. *See* real-time underwriting
instrumental activities of daily living 192
insurability premium receipt 60
insurable interest 62–63
insurance administration 2–4, 6, 8, 11–12, 14, 21
insurance application 92, 110
Insurance Companies Act 65
insurance fraud 330
Insurance Fraud Prevention Model Act 330–331

insurance in force 134
Insurance Information and Privacy Protection Model Act 68
insurance regulatory systems 65–66
insured 3–4, 7, 18
insurer-administered group plan 217, 225
intangible assets 154
interactive voice response system 432
interest option 350
intermediate nursing care 376
internal audit 40, 312
internal replacement 163
internal trip report 315
International Claim Association 320
International Classification of Diseases and Related Health Problems 364
International residence and Travel 121
internet 15
interpleader 354
intranet 15
intrusion detection software 23
invasion of privacy 331
investigative consumer report 66
irrevocable beneficiary 352–353, 358, 465
IT. *See* information technology
IVR. *See* interactive voice response system

J

jet issue electronic system 19
jet unit underwriting 52–55
joint life insurance policy 145
jumbo limit 241, 242
juvenile insurance policy 146

K

key person 150, 153, 160–163
key-person life insurance 144, 150, 160–162
knowledge management system 431

L

laboratory tests 103–104, 116
labor union group 211
lapse 126, 128
lapse notice. *See* policy grace notice
late enrollees 200, 222–223, 402
late notice of claim 400
law department. *See* legal
lawful purpose 62
legal 2, 4–5, 7–10
legally adequate consideration 58
levels of authority 423
licensing requirements
  direct writers 250
  reinsurance intermediaries 251
  reinsurers 250
life income option 350
life settlement 127
lifetime maximum benefit 371, 384
liquidity 155–156
litigation 284
living benefits 3, 168, 171
loan coverage. *See* creditor insurance
long-term care insurance 148, 167–173
  administering claims for 375–377
  benefit 169, 376, 383
  benefit triggers 381
  exclusion 382–383
  paying benefits 383–386
  verifying loss 377–383
  underwriting 191–198
loss rate 41
LTC field underwriting manual 193–194
LTC insurance. *See* long-term care insurance
LTC insurance benefit. *See* long-term care insurance benefit
lump sum plan 469

M

maintenance expenses 236
manual rating 219, 221
market approach 154
market conduct examinations 334
marketing 8–9
master application 202, 204, 206–207
master group insurance contract 3–4, 202
material misrepresentation 84–85, 343, 366, 381, 402
MDO. *See* monthly debit ordinary policy
mediation 415
medical expense insurance 171
  administering claims 361
  benefits 4, 370
  determining coverage 366
  exclusions and limitations 369
  underwriting 171
medically necessary 367, 376
medical report 90, 92, 95–98
medical risk factors 43
  individual health insurance 173
  individual life insurance 91
medical tests 71–73, 103–104
member service 8, 419, 427
mental disorders 401
mental incapacity 61

MEWA. *See* multiple-employer welfare arrangement
MIB. *See* MIB Group, Inc.
MIB Group, Inc. 95
middleware 21
military aviation, underwriting factor 119–120
military status, underwriting factor 120
minimum capital and surplus requirements 252
minimum cession 241
minor 59, 61
misdirected calls 441
misrepresentation 84–85
misstatement of age provision 77
modco. *See* modified coinsurance
model law 64
Model Privacy Act. *See* Insurance Information and Privacy Protection Model Act
Model Privacy Regulation. *See* Privacy of Consumer Financial and Health Information Regulation
model regulation 64
modified coinsurance 256, 265–267
money laundering 75, 127–128
monthly debit ordinary policy 147
moral hazard 42
morbidity 41
morbidity rate 41
morbidity risk 171, 180, 182
mortality 41
mortality cost 268
mortality rate 41
mortality risk 171, 268
motor vehicle record 109, 112
multi-life policy 145–146
multiple-employer group 211
multiple-employer welfare arrangement 211
mutual assent 58
MVR. *See* motor vehicle record
mystery shopper 442–443

N

NAIC. *See* National Association of Insurance Commissioners
NAR. *See* net amount at risk
National Association of Insurance Commissioners 64, 249
  Credit for Reinsurance Model Law 253
  Group Health Insurance Definition and Group Health Insurance Standard Provisions Model Act 76
  Group Life Insurance Definition and Group Life Insurance Standard Provisions Model Act 76
  Insurance Information and Privacy Protection Model Act 68
  Reinsurance Intermediary Model Act 251
  Replacement of Life Insurance and Annuities Model Regulation 74
  Unfair Claims Settlement Practices Act 327
negative testing 313
net amount at risk 263, 268
net cash surrender value 461–462
netting off 311
network 14–15, 23, 26
net worth 128, 130, 133–134
new business 7, 16, 28–29, 33–38
new business case analyst 33–36
new business strain. *See* surplus strain
niche personal life insurance policies 145
nonadmitted reinsurer. *See* unauthorized reinsurer
noncontributory plan 207, 214
nondiscrimination 70–71, 80
nonduplication of benefits provision 372
nonmedical basis 92, 94
nonmedical limit 94
nonmedical supplement 90, 92, 94–95
nonproportional reinsurance 257
nonpublic personal information 68
nonqualified long-term care policy 375
notice of expiry 296–297
notice of recovery from disability 413–414
notification for automatic reinsurance provision 278
notification for fac-ob reinsurance provision 278
notification for facultative reinsurance provision 278
number of blocked calls 441
numerical rating system 124, 137
nursing care 376

O

observation and monitoring 440
occasional reinsurer 231
occasional retrocessionaire 231
occupation 110–111, 114, 170, 176, 186–188
occupational rating classes 187
OFAC. *See* Office of Foreign Assets Control
off-shore outsourcing 11
Office of Foreign Assets Control 75
Office of the Superintendent of Financial Institutions 64, 249
offset 83, 405–406
on-shore outsourcing 11
open claimants 203–204, 215
operating system software 12
oral specimen (saliva) test 103–104
organization 28, 48, 318, 323, 335, 421, 423–426
organizational systems 51, 324

orphan policyowner 436–437
OSFI. *See* Office of the Superintendent of Financial Institutions
outsourcing 11
overinsurance 134, 178
overinsurance provision 373

P

par policy. *See* participating policy
paramedical report 90, 92, 94–95
partial disability 403–404, 410
partial loan repayment plan 469
participating policy 470
participation level 204
parties to the agreement provision 272–273
partnership 152, 158–159
payee 349–350, 352
payment into court 354
payroll deduction 455–456
PBM. *See* pharmacy benefit managers
per capita beneficiary designation 465
percentage-of-income rule 124, 136
percentage rating method 180
performance measurement 22
performance standard 22
permanent flat extra premium 141
persistency bonus 438
persistency rate 126
personal care. *See* custodial care
personal risk factors
  individual health insurance 176–178
  individual life insurance 108–122
personal history interview 103, 194, 196
personal information 69–70
Personal Information Protection and Electronics Document Act 69–70
personal insurance 125, 134
personal questionnaires 112
personal risk factor 43, 108, 110
per stirpes beneficiary designation 465
pharmacy benefit managers 105
PHI. *See* personal history interview
Physicians' Current Procedural Terminology 364
physiological age 198
PIPEDA. *See* Personal Information Protection and Electronics Document Act
placement 297
placement stage 289, 290
plan administrator 203, 207, 217
policy audit questionnaire 314
policy benefits 370, 383, 405
policy cash value 268
policy change report 298, 300, 302
policy dividend 304–305, 461, 470
policy exhibit 298–299, 303
policy grace notice 455
policyholder 3–4
policy issue 30, 37
policy modifications 182
policyowner 3
  changing 467
  juvenile insurance underwriting factor 147
  service 8, 78, 419
policy reserve 236, 268
pooling 221
portfolio reinsurance. *See* assumption reinsurance
portability 378
post-issue underwriting 222
potential income 129, 133
precertification 368
predictive modeling 17–18
pre-existing condition 80–81, 382
pre-existing conditions provision 80, 370
pre-funded inflation option 386
preferred beneficiaries 352
preferred classes 42
Pregnancy Discrimination Act 82
premium-based reciprocity 231
premium rate 30, 37, 40–41, 46–47
premium rating methods 180
premium receipt 59–60
premium refund. *See* experience refund
premium tax 237
preplacement of reinsurance 290
prescription drug profiling services 105
presumptive death certificate 342–343
presumptive total disability 403–404
pretext interview 69
primary degenerative dementia. *See* Alzheimer's Disease
prior coverage 215
privacy 22
privacy and confidentiality of customer information 5
Privacy of Consumer Financial and Health Information Regulation 68
privacy protection 65–70
privileged information 69
probationary period 207, 213, 216
problematic diagnosis 400
problematic prognosis 401
problem resolution team. *See* complaint team
Proceeds of Crime (Money Laundering) and Terrorist Financing Act 76
process control 312–313
processes completed 24, 441
producer 3, 24, 129
  conservation and 438
  service for 428
  source of financial information 129
  underwriting contribution 31
producer's letter 205–206
productivity 441

professional association group 211
professional reinsurer 231
professional retrocessionaire 231
profitability 144, 155, 157
profit and loss statement. *See* income statement
prompt and equitable claim handling 5
proof of loss 321, 327–328
proportional reinsurance 257, 260–261
proposal for insurance 202
proposed group. *See* group prospect
proposed insured 3, 7, 18
providing a duplicate policy 459
public curator 352
punitive damages 318, 327

Q

QPP. *See* Quebec Pension Plan
qualified beneficiary 80
qualified long-term care policy 375
qualifying events 80
qualitative performance measurement 25, 440
quality control 22, 28–29, 38, 40, 333–334, 439–443
quality rate 24, 441
quantitative performance measurements 24, 440
Quebec Pension Plan 83
questionable claims 400
quick assets 156
quick liquidity ratio. *See* quick ratio
quick ratio 156–157
quota share 233
quota share arrangement 263–264, 275

R

rate reduction 453
rating 37
rating methods 217
rating schedule 180
ratio 155–157
RBC ratio. See risk-based capital ratio
real-time underwriting 54
reappearance of the insured 343
reasonable and customary charge 370
reason for existence 210
reasonable and customary charge. *See* usual, reasonable, and customary charge
recapture 235, 273
receiver 285–286
reciprocal arrangement 231–233
reciprocity. *See* reciprocal arrangement
records inspection provision 279
recurring disability 403–404
reduction of reinsurance 280
regulation of reinsurance 249
regulatory compliance issues affecting group insurance underwriting 76
regulatory compliance issues affecting individual insurance underwriting 63
rehabilitation 409–411
rehabilitation benefit 409
reimbursement method 384
reinstatement 281
reinstatement provision 281, 461–462
reinstating a policy 461
reinsurance 6–7
  administration activities 243, 277
  agreement 268–285
  allowance. *See* allowance
  arrangement 229
    documentation of 239
    reciprocal 231
  claims handling 306–311
  claim notice 307
  commission 236
  company 230
  effective date 245
  errors and omissions 271
  information systems 248
  licensing 249–250
  methods of administering 278–279
  parties to 229–230
  pool 233
  premium 236
  providers 230–231
  purposes of 237–239
  recapturing coverages 235, 273–274
  regulations 249–253
  staffing 244
  termination of 305
  treaty 239
reinsurance account executive. *See* reinsurer marketing officer
reinsurance analyst 244, 247
reinsurance intermediary 251–252
reinsurance intermediary—broker 251
reinsurance intermediary—manager 251
Reinsurance Intermediary Model Act 251
reinsurance marketing officer 245
reinsurer 230
remote underwriting 11
renewal expenses. *See* maintenance expense
renewal underwriting 223
replacement 73–75
Replacement of Life Insurance and Annuities Model Regulation 74
reporting on in-force business 298
reporting party 298, 302, 304
Report of Death of an American Citizen Abroad 342
request for coverage 290–291, 293

request for proposal 201, 203–205
required reserves 253
rescission 84–85
rescission provision 283
reserve credit 250–251, 253
reserved 292
reserved capacity 290
reserve listing 298, 302
respite care 377
restoration of benefits provision 383–384
results-based reciprocity 231
retention limit 237, 240–241
retention limit corridor 240
retrocedent 230
retrocession 230
retrocessionaire 230–231, 233
retrocession claim file 308
retrocession pool 294, 296
retro pool. *See* retrocession pool
return-on-equity ratio 157
reviewing applications 83
revocable beneficiary 352–353
RFP. *See* request for proposal
right of recommendation 309
risk 4–7, 18, 228–253
risk-based capital ratio 252
risk assessment 41–42
risk-based capital ratio 252
risk class 28, 41–42, 46
risk classification 42, 136
risk factor 42–43, 173
  financial 125
  medical 91
  personal 108
ROE. *See* return-on-equity ratio

S

saliva test. *See* oral specimen test
scanning. *See* document imaging
schedules (in reinsurance treaties) 271
secondary beneficiary. *See* contingent beneficiary
second-to-die insurance policy. *See* survivorship life insurance policy
Section 1035 exchange 164
security 22
self-administered group plan 217
self-administration 279
self-directed team 423
self-insured group plan 206
self-managed teams. *See* self-directed teams
self-service options 432
semi-autonomous team 423
service complaint 458
service level 24, 441
service recovery 458
settlement options 336, 348–349
settling DI insurance claims 414
sex 107
sickness 96, 367, 369, 371, 389, 390–391, 394–395, 401–402, 404, 408, 412, 415
simple inflation provision 385–386
simultaneous death act 355–356
single-employer group 211
SIU. *See* special investigative unit
skilled nursing care 376
small corporation 159–160
small employer 81
software 12–13, 23
software application. *See* application software
sole proprietorship 157–158
solvency 155
solvency law 249
special classes. *See* substandard class
special investigative unit 332
specialized medical questionnaire 101
speculation 125–128, 134
split-dollar life insurance plan 150, 161
spread-loss coverage 259, 261
staffing 11, 318, 323, 421–422
standard classes 43
standby assistance 382
statement of cash flows 132
statement of changes in owners' equity. *See* statement of owner's equity
statement of owners' equity 132
statutory minimum capitalization requirements. *See* minimum capital and surplus requirements
statutory reserves 253
step rates 221
stock redemption agreement. *See* entity agreement
stop-loss ratio reinsurance. *See* stop-loss reinsurance
stop-loss reinsurance 258, 261
STP. *See* straight through processing
straight through processing 16–17
subject of physical abuse 118
submission stage 289
subrogation clause 373
subscription. *See* quota share
substance abuse 102, 117, 401
substandard class 44
substandard risks 139
suicide exclusion 60, 344–345
suitability check 30, 36
supplemental benefit 145, 164–165
surplus 237–238, 250, 252–253
surplus relief 238
surplus strain 237–238, 253
survivorship clause 356
survivorship life insurance policy 145

T

table of underwriting requirements.
See age and amount requirements chart
table rating method 139–140
tangible assets 154
tax documents 130
team underwriting 52–53
technology components 12–13
technology platform 12
telecommunications 13–15, 23
telecommuting 11
teleunderwriting 30, 35, 172
temporary flat extra premium 141
temporary insurance agreement 60
terminal illness benefit 168
terminating a policy 460
terminating DI insurance benefits 412
termination 256, 268, 270, 272, 274, 281
termination for new business 274
termination of reinsurance 305
termination stage 289
terrorists 75
third-party administrator 217
third-party notification provision 378
third-party policy 3
TIA. *See* temporary insurance agreement
TI benefit. *See* terminal illness benefit
time limit on certain defenses provision 366
timeliness 24, 441
tobacco Use 116
tools to determine appropriate
amount of insurance 135
total disability 403–404, 414
TPA. *See* third-party administrator
trade association 211
trading partners 15
traditional indemnity reinsurance 234–235
traditional team 423
training and development 10
transaction 14
transaction processing system 14
transaction report. *See* policy change report
transplant donor benefit 409, 412
treasury 9
treatment codes 362, 364–365
turnaround time 24, 441
turnover of group membership 213
twisting 74
type of group 210

U

UCR. *See* usual, customary, and reasonable charge
unauthorized reinsurer 251
undeliverable 47
underwriter 7, 19
underwriting 7
authority levels 49
capacity 237
cooperation with claim administration
325–326
coverage changes or adding riders 449–455
critical illness coverage 190–191
death of proposed insured during 60
decision options 37
disability income insurance coverage 184–190
documenting 85–86
factors. *See* ability to pay, abuse (subject of), age, alcohol use, aviation, avocation, bankruptcy, build, civilian aviation, claim experience, criminal history, driving history, drug use, face amount, financial information, foreign citizenship, foreign residence, foreign travel, health, health history, health insurance, income, income stability, insurance in force, international residence, international travel, military aviation, military status, occupation, persistency, policy ownership, professional sports, proposed coverage, substance abuse, tobacco use
guidelines 44
information sources for
group 172–173
individual health 127–131
individual life 91–108
job positions 48–49
manual 139
niche policies 145
organization 48
philosophy 34
policy changes 449–455
policy replacements 163
post-issue for groups 222–224
principles 40–47
relationship to customer service 450
risk assessment 41–42
standards 83
worksheet 86
underwriting, group insurance
group prospect 209–215
process 201–207
proposed coverage 215–217
statutory requirements 76–83
underwriting, individual health insurance
critical illness insurance 190
disability income insurance 184
long-term care coverage 191
medical expense 172
substandard health risks 179

underwriting, individual life insurance
antidiscrimination statutes 70–71
application 29–35
business insurance 149, 157–163
guaranteed-issue products 148
juvenile insurance 146–147
multi-life products 145–146
policy replacements 163–164
premium receipts 59–60
privacy and confidentiality laws 65–70
replacement regulations 73–75
supplementary coverages 164
undisputed claims 415
unearned income 133
Unfair claims settlement practices 318, 327–328, 334
Unfair Claims Settlement Practices Act 318, 327–328, 334
Unfair Life, Accident and Health Claims Settlement Practices Model Regulation 318, 327, 334
Uniform Accident and Sickness Insurance Act 65, 83
Uniform Act. *See* Uniform Life Insurance Act
Uniform Life Insurance Act 64
unintentional lapse provision 377
urinalysis 104
U.S. Federal Fair and Accurate Credit Transactions Act 67
USA Patriot Act of 2001 75
usual and customary charge. *See* usual, customary, and reasonable charge
usual and prevailing charge. *See* usual, customary, and reasonable charge
usual, customary, and reasonable charge 370

V

valid contract 58
variable life insurance 471
virtual private network 23
voice response unit. *See* interactive voice response system
voice signatures 35
voidable contract 58
void contract 58
voluntary benefits 224
VPN. *See* virtual private network

W

wagering agreement 62
waiting period 179, 182–183, 192, 207, 218
waiver of premium for disability benefit 165, 356
waiver of premium for payor benefit 147
with profits policy. *See* participating policy
work division system 51–54
workflow application. *See* automated workflow system
work groups. *See* work team
work site assessment 401
work teams 422, 426
WP. *See* waiver of premium for disability benefit

X

Y

yearly renewable term reinsurance 257–275
YRT. *See* yearly renewable term insurance

Z